S0-BTD-798

The publisher gratefully acknowledges
the generous contributions to this book provided
by the General Endowment Fund of the University
of California Press Associates and the following
individuals and organizations:

Benjamin F. Biaggini
Joanne W. Blokker
The Candelaria Fund
Michael McCone
Denman McNear
Robert F. Miller
Thormund A. Miller

Sunset Limited

Sunset

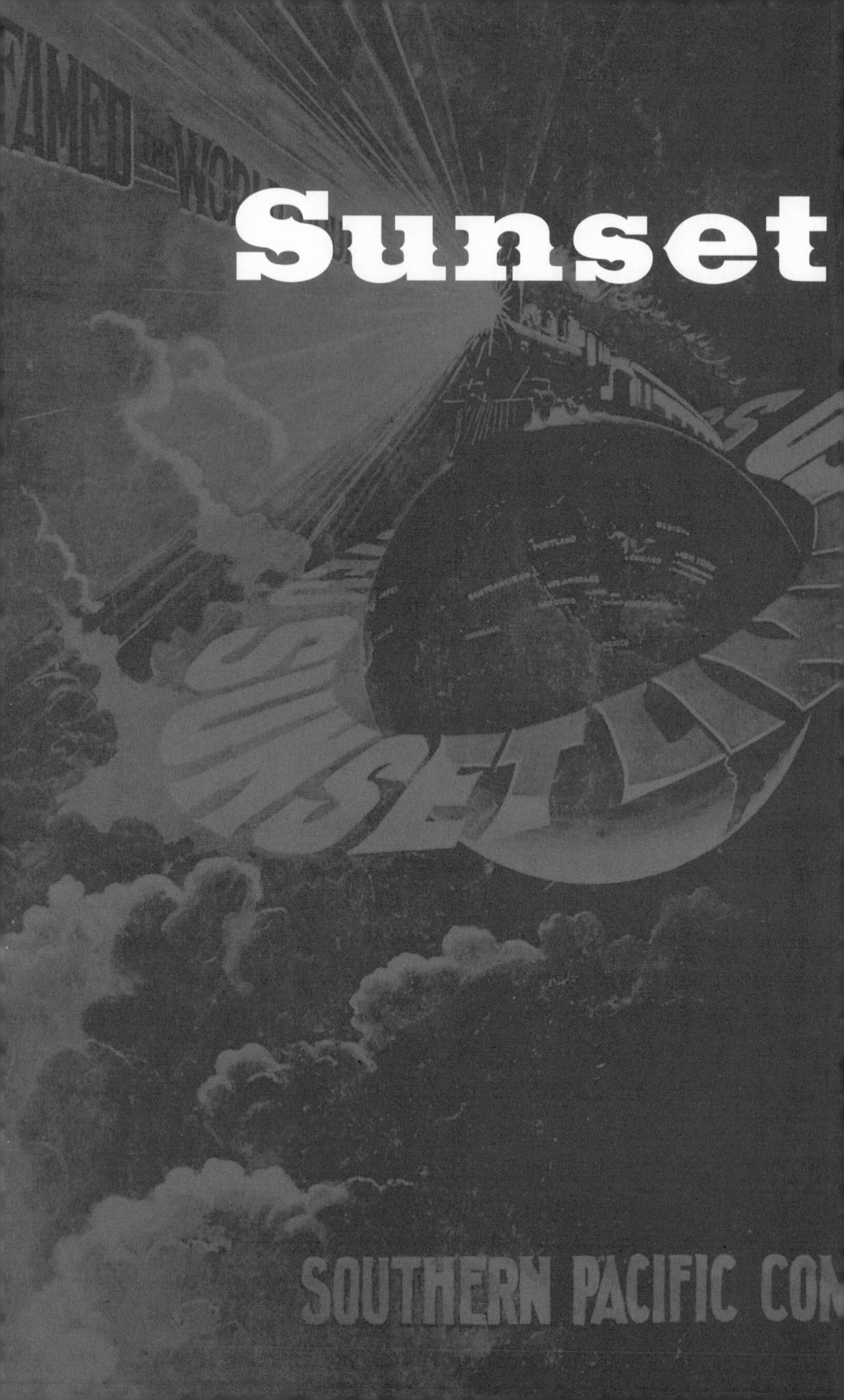

Limited

The Southern Pacific Railroad
and the Development of the American West

1850 – 1930

RICHARD J. ORSI

UNIVERSITY OF CALIFORNIA PRESS

Berkeley   Los Angeles   London

Title page image: detail from W. H. Bull's advertising poster for the Southern Pacific's "Sunset Limited" train, ca. 1900. Author's collection.

University of California Press
Berkeley and Los Angeles, California

University of California Press, Ltd.
London, England

© 2005 by the Regents of the University of California

Library of Congress Cataloging-in-Publication Data

Orsi, Richard J.
    Sunset limited : the Southern Pacific Railroad and the development of the American West, 1850–1930 / Richard J. Orsi.
        p.   cm.
    Includes bibliographical references and index.
    ISBN 0-520-20019-5 (cloth : alk. paper).
        1. Southern Pacific Railroad Company—History.   2. Southern Pacific Company—History.
    3. Railroads—California—History.   4. Water resources development—West (U.S.).   5. Land use—West (U.S.)—History.   6. West (U.S.)—Economic conditions—20th century.   7. West (U.S.)—Economic conditions—19th century.   I. Title.

    TF25.S68077   2005
    385'.0978—dc22   2004008782
                                                                           CIP

Manufactured in the United States of America

13   12   11   10   09   08   07   06   05
10   9   8   7   6   5   4   3   2   1

The paper used in this publication meets the minimum requirements of ANSI/NISO Z39.48–1992 (R 1997) (*Permanence of Paper*).

For Dolores, my dear wife, partner, and love

Contents

Illustrations

FIGURES

MAPS

Preface

This book derives its title in part from the famed passenger train *Sunset Limited,* which as railroaders and rail fans will quickly tell you, was the Southern Pacific Railroad's luxury passenger liner that plied the company's transcontinental Sunset Route between New Orleans and San Francisco. Inaugurated in 1894, the train captured the public's imagination and took its place alongside the other great named trains of the rail passenger era—the New York Central's *Twentieth Century Limited,* the Pennsylvania's *Broadway Limited,* the Union Pacific's *City of Los Angeles,* the Western Pacific's *California Zephyr,* and the Santa Fe's *Super Chief.* The book title's significance also extends onto another level: to say that something is "sunset-limited" is to say, in effect, that it really has no limits. For as one advances westward toward the horizon, the sunset simply recedes farther into the distance, visible yet never reached or fully comprehended, seemingly there forever. The Southern Pacific Railroad's creative influences on the development of its western territory were indeed sunset-limited—complex, manyfold, and far-reaching, their ramifications rebounding from place to place and from group to group with no culmination in sight. According to the traditional historiography, on the other hand, that creative influence is precisely what is *not* supposed to have happened.

My study of the Southern Pacific, from the 1850s founding of its first predecessor lines in Texas and California to the company's maturation in the 1920s, attempts a new approach to an important theme in the history of the American Far West: the complex impact of a large, powerful business corporation on the process of settlement, economic development, and environmental change in a frontier region. The Southern Pacific and its associated rail lines from Oregon and California east to Texas and Louisiana have traditionally been regarded by historians as atypical of western land-grant railroads. Allegedly, monopolistic control of transportation (and land) in much of its territory made it unnecessary for the Southern Pacific to spend much energy developing lands or promoting the welfare of farmers, businesses, and other groups. Indeed, historians have usually characterized the Southern Pacific as a diabolical organization—

the legendary "Octopus"—that used its dominance of freight tariffs, land grants, and political power to deprive farmers, workers, and shopkeepers of their just profits. Until the Progressives harnessed the railroad with their early-twentieth-century reforms, most historians have maintained, the Southern Pacific was a major deterrent to economic development and modern, honest public policy in its territory.

My research for this book, done mostly in rarely used primary source materials, demonstrates that, despite some contradictions and inconsistencies of policy and action, the Southern Pacific identified its corporate interests with the public welfare and promoted more organized, efficient settlement, economic development, and more enlightened resource policies in its service area. As a result, the company was a major force shaping agricultural, industrial, commercial, and urban growth and modernization. The railroad's importance in encouraging greater success for many residents in the newly settling regions was especially significant because, on these frontiers, the company was often the most powerful organizational presence, while other private groups and official government agencies typically were absent, just forming, poorly funded, and/or relatively weak. Indeed, many functions the railroad initially found itself called on to provide in thinly settled new regions were later transferred to other private and, especially, public agencies. This was the case, for example, with farm mortgaging, agricultural marketing, forest management and firefighting, urban water systems, and irrigation engineering and management.

To some extent, this book follows in the tradition of the railroad "colonization histories," such as those of the Northern Pacific (James Hedges), the Illinois Central (Paul Gates), the Burlington (Richard Overton), and the Santa Fe (William Greever), which have become classics of western historiography. Like these other western land-grant roads, the Southern Pacific subdivided and sold its lands quickly and at generally low prices, promoted small-farm settlement, and adopted many programs to assist farmers in its territory. The railroad also encouraged the development of modern agriculture in the West, particularly the founding of farm organizations, the spread of scientific farming, the expansion of agricultural colleges and experiment stations in California, Oregon, Nevada, Arizona, New Mexico, and Texas, and the general shift from frontier crops such as cereals and livestock to higher-value fruit and specialty crops.

Although I have been informed by these earlier historians of the railroads' impact on the settlement process, I seek to go beyond them. Influenced by the fresh perspectives of environmental historians, this study devotes more attention than its predecessors to the railroad's influence on the development of western resources and environmental policy. In the absence of vigorous government action on resource questions, the Southern Pacific took a major role in the emergence of modern management of water, wilderness parks, forests, and range-lands. This was particularly apparent in the area of water development for urban use and irrigation, a subject of emphasis in my study. Illustrative are accounts of the Southern Pacific's influences on the California local irrigation district movement (1880s–1920s), on Imperial Valley irrigation (1891–1920s), and on the Truckee-Carson Reclamation Project (the first, pioneering federal project under the National Reclamation Act) in western Nevada and eastern California (1902–1920s). Chapters 7 through 10 as well as chapters 13 and 14, which deal with resource policy, are in my opinion the most original contribution this study makes to railroad, business, and western American history. In fact, to my knowl-edge, there is no other major work that examines in detail the impact of railroads on American environmental policy, especially regarding water, in its formative stages during the late nineteenth and early twentieth centuries.

This book stands out from earlier histories of western railroads in its appli-cation of the thesis developed by Alfred D. Chandler, Jr., in *The Visible Hand: The Managerial Revolution in American Business* (Cambridge: Harvard Univer-sity Press, 1977). Chandler demonstrated that, in the late nineteenth century, American railroads, as the pathbreaking modern business enterprises, evolved complex, professionalized, centrally coordinated structures and management models that influenced other businesses as they modernized. My study of the Southern Pacific, at one time the largest of the great railways, certainly bears out Chandler's thesis. While Chandler has stressed the importance of the rail-roads in blazing management trails for other types of businesses, however, my research demonstrates also that the modern structures being developed and ap-plied in the West by the Southern Pacific (and other railroad companies) were emulated by the broader non-business community as well. With regard par-ticularly to the Southern Pacific, this broader impact was particularly true in the areas of land subdivision, agricultural marketing, forestry practices (in-cluding firefighting), rangeland management, parkland preservation, and, once again, water resource development.

This book also builds on and extends further the findings of other recent scholars who have analyzed the modernizing effects introduced by American railroads, including John R. Stilgoe, *Metropolitan Corridors: Railroads and the American Scene* (New Haven: Yale University Press, 1983); James A. Ward, *Rail-roads and the Character of America, 1820–1887* (Knoxville: University of Ten-nessee Press, 1986); William Cronon, *Nature's Metropolis: Chicago and the Great West* (New York: W.W. Norton, 1991); Albro Martin, *Railroads Triumphant: The Growth, Rejection & Rebirth of a Vital American Force* (New York: Oxford University Press, 1992); Carlos A. Schwantes, *Railroad Signatures across the Pacific Northwest* (Seattle: University of Washington Press, 1993); Robert F. Himmelberg, ed., *The Rise of Big Business and the Beginnings of Antitrust and Railroad Regulation, 1870–1900* (New York: Garland Publishing, 1994); Maury Klein, *Unfinished Business: The Railroad in American Life* (Hanover, N.H.: University Press of New England, 1994); and Sarah H. Gordon, *Passage to Union: How the Railroads Transformed American Life, 1829–1929* (Chicago: Ivan R. Dee, Publisher, 1997). Like Stilgoe's and Cronon's, my book particularly explores the influence of the railroads' revolutionary technology and organization on land-use and environment, but in this case I have focused on U.S. far-western regions.

My work also has greatly benefited from the publication of Don Hofsommer's *The Southern Pacific, 1901–1985* (College Station: Texas A & M Press, 1986), the first modern, scholarly work on Southern Pacific history. Our books share a common attempt to interpret the company's history as objectively as possible in a broad context, but they differ in chronology and emphasis. While Hofsommer's excellent work emphasizes internal corporate evolution in the twentieth century and is thus more in the tradition of classical railroad business histories, mine emphasizes early company origins in the 1850s through 1930 and particularly the railroad's interaction with other forces to shape life, economy, and resources in its broader territory during the settlement period.

Throughout, my study, unlike most other railroad histories, emphasizes the importance of middle-level leaders in shaping and executing Southern Pacific policy. Previous writers have focused almost exclusively on the spectacular careers of the owners and top executives, such as the Big Four (Collis P. Huntington, Leland Stanford, Charles Crocker, and Mark Hopkins), who built and operated the associated Southern Pacific companies from 1861 to 1900, and Edward H. Harriman, who after 1901 acquired the Southern Pacific lines and merged them with his own nation-wide rail empire. While I have not ignored the famous leaders, my research has convinced me that there is another story—hitherto untold but just as significant—to be found in the work of legions of middle-level executives and experts. They developed specialized skills, had considerable freedom to create and implement railroad programs, and took leadership roles in the company and the larger society in such fields as science and engineering, land settlement, agriculture, and environmental policy that had great influence in western settlement.

A word of disclaimer: the book does *not* include systematic analyses of the following dimensions of Southern Pacific history (although they are discussed briefly as they pertain to the main themes): politics, government regulation, labor, and freight and passenger tariffs. With the exception of politics, which has been ably analyzed by R. Hal Williams in *The Democratic Party and California Politics, 1880–1896* (Stanford: Stanford University Press, 1973) and more recently and thoroughly by William Deverell in his outstanding study, *Rail-*

road Crossing: Californians and the Railroad, 1850–1910 (Berkeley: University of California Press, 1994), historians have not examined those themes adequately. Those important subjects, of course, cry out for investigation, but my doing so comprehensively would have required a very different, and impossibly long, book.

It is not my purpose to "whitewash" the Southern Pacific's history. Both popular and scholarly commentators on the company have depicted the railroad as a negative, anti-social force in its territory. Historians, moreover, have generally interpreted political and economic conflict associated with the railroad within a dichotomous framework: on the one side stands the Southern Pacific as a malevolent monopoly representing selfish, greedy, corporate interests; on the other side are the "people," representing the inherently democratic, "public" interest. My revisionist view of the railroad's history does not try to convert the Southern Pacific from an all-evil into an all-public-spirited entity. It does not maintain that the company's interests never collided with those of other groups or with the "public interest" at large (difficult though that might be to define).

Instead, I seek to go beyond the dichotomous model, which, I have found, is not supported by the evidence. Throughout, wherever appropriate, I examine the Southern Pacific's conflicts with numerous groups (businesses, land settlers, farm groups, and others). Those conflicts, however, were not dichotomous alignments of two monolithic interests against each other (the monopoly versus the people). They were invariably complex and shifting, depending on the issue at stake, and usually pitted the company against only some specific groups who were, like the railroad, pursuing their own private interests. Often, as well, the company did indeed identify its corporate interest with what most people at the time would probably have agreed was the public welfare, particularly in areas of overall regional economic development, small-farm settlement, agricultural change, and environmental policy. And for that reason, various interest groups, including farmers, sometimes gained from and supported the Southern Pacific's policies and sided with the railroad in its conflicts with other interest groups. This book focuses on the intersections between corporate and public interest and the railroad's creative role in bringing about change in those areas.

The company's unique history and character led the Southern Pacific's leaders to identify strongly with broader regional interests. The Southern Pacific was the only major U.S. railroad to be organized and operated by westerners and to be built from west to east. Throughout its history, from its founding in the mid-nineteenth century to its absorption into the rival Union Pacific in the late 1990s, the company continued to be managed from a western locus of power, in California and particularly San Francisco. Pioneers in their region, or at least longtime residents, Southern Pacific managers also often had extremely long tenure in their company positions. Their western roots ran deep, and they had wide connections to outside movements and organizations as well as friendships and business relationships with other prominent business, civic, educational, artistic, and scientific leaders, with whom they shared values and hopes for their communities.

Moreover, like other large railroads, the Southern Pacific was simultaneously an intensely national, indeed eventually global, as well as an intensely local, entity. Its tracks and its business stretched from California north to Oregon and eastward through the Great Basin and Southwest to Texas, Louisiana, Atlantic tidewater, and beyond to Mexico and via its steamship lines to Asia, the Caribbean, Europe, and the east coast of the United States. In pursuing its business interests, the company tended to take the larger and long-term, as opposed to the local and short-term, view of its welfare. At the same time, however, the railroad was required to invest in expensive roadbed, tracks, bridges, yards, stations, maintenance facilities, fuel lines, and water plants. The Southern Pacific thus was literally and figuratively nailed to the earth, its immense, immobile infrastructure plus its large federal land grant and local labor force tying it and its destiny to the districts though which it operated. Especially in the wide, lightly populated, frontier regions it traversed to reach eastern markets, the company had a large stake in local development. If only to generate sufficient traffic to keep the railroad solvent, it had little choice but to become actively engaged and to pioneer in arenas of regional problem-solving, assuming responsibility for promoting population growth, social change, and economic development. In doing so, the Southern Pacific brought to bear outside capital, modern technologies and business organization, legal expertise, and political influence needed to solve the problems of isolated locales.

In the 1980s, the Southern Pacific Company provided a research grant to my university that gave me release time to allow me particularly to examine vast, company-held records. The company also granted me complete, unrestricted, and unobserved access to all documents and manuscripts. At no time, however, has any person associated with the Southern Pacific ever attempted to influence—or even to discuss with me—my choices of topics, the evidence I should examine or not examine, or the interpretations I might give to events. On the contrary, at all times, the company officials I have dealt with have indicated their unqualified commitment to opening the railroad's records, and its history, to independent scholarship resulting in objective conclusions based on the evidence.

Finally, I have attempted to organize and write this book so that it is accessible to a broad audience of historians and general readers. It is a work of scholarship, and thus is fully documented and placed firmly in the historiography of the American West. It is, however, written, to the best of my ability, in a narrative style so as to appeal to persons, scholars and non-scholars alike, interested in railroad history, business history, environmental history, and western regional history. I hope I have succeeded.

RICHARD J. ORSI
California State University, Hayward

Acknowledgments

In writing large works such as this, over so many years, authors build up long lists of personal debts. I am no different. Many people furnished information, directed me to where evidence might be hiding, talked over my ideas, and gave me much-needed encouragement when my spirits flagged. I must start by thanking brilliant and gracious graduate mentors from long ago, Merle Curti and J. Rogers Hollingsworth at the University of Wisconsin-Madison, who not only helped me develop basic approaches to some of the subjects in this book, as well as to regional history in general, but who also showed me how to be a historian and why history is important in the first place. Although some of them may be unaware of how important their help was, other scholars, archivists, and librarians, a few no longer with us, shared in the creation of this particular book, including Martin Ridge, Ray Billington, Rodman Paul, Andrew Rolle, Doyce Nunis, Donald Pisani, William Rowley, Albert Hurtado, Robert Kelley, Richard White, Elliott West, Kevin Starr, J. S. Holliday, Karen Lystra, Gordon Bakken, Morton Rothstein, William Reuter, Dan Gilliard, Alan Smith, Mark Van Aken, Tom Hall, Richard Rice, William Bullough, Theodore Goppert, Don Hofsommer, Carlos Schwantes, Keith Bryant, Judith Austin, Mark Fiege, Brit Storey, Toni Linenberger, Robert Chandler, Teena Stern, Walter Gray, Stephen Drew, Ellen Halteman, Blaine Lamb, Alan Jutzi, Jennifer Watts, Peter Blodgett, William Deverell, James Williams, Leo Lyman, Russell Martin, Anne Peterson, Andrea Boardman, Sherry Smith, Robert Righter, Susan Snyder, Bonnie Hardwick, Mary Morganti, George Abdill, and Ed Culp.

My two talented sons have been indispensable. Historian Jared Orsi, himself a specialist in the American West, read and evaluated much of the manuscript, made many suggestions for changes that I almost always followed, conceived the book's final structure, and proved why he is the most insightful critic I've ever encountered. Editor Peter Orsi, whom I have come to rely on in many of my projects, devoted his keen eye and mastery of the English language to helping me through the critical final editing and publication. Four friends of long standing, Anthony Kirk, Alfred Runte, Marlene Smith-Baranzini, and Mike

McCone, gave me exceptional assistance and encouragement and inspired me to keep going when finishing the book sometimes seemed impossible. My dear wife, Dolores Cottle Orsi, endured seemingly endless delays, disappointments, and sacrifices, cheerfully accompanied me in my treks to libraries literally across the country, and, despite "the book" that dominated our life, still kept her faith in me and made it possible for me to complete my work.

A number of Southern Pacific Company people, in their way historians all, contributed mightily to my work, while never attempting to shape my research and conclusions. Especially, my thanks goes to Jim Shea, vice president of Public Relations, who conceived of the company's policy to open up its records and its history to outside scholars and who personally helped immeasurably with his faith and patience. Southern Pacific chairman Benjamin Biaggini was a constant supporter, and others furnished information, served as guides to corporate records and the holdings of libraries and archives, and shared their broad knowledge of and commitment to the railroad's history. In particular, these people include Andrew Anderson, David Myrick, Lynn Farrar, George Kraus, Henry Ortiz, Joe Bart, Ken Jones, Robert Hoppe, and Larry Hoyt.

To the great people at the University of California Press, I owe special appreciation. First as associate director and then as director of the Press, Lynne Withey has believed in this book from the beginning. If she hadn't approached me, so long ago, gently persuaded me to come into the Press, provided constant encouragement and sound judgment, and above all exercised unbelievable patience, I think it's safe to say that there might not be any book at all. I can't thank her enough. Other editors, particularly Kathleen MacDougall, Suzanne Knott, Julie Brand, and Monica McCormick, have been of great collegial assistance as we have worked together over the years. To Kathleen MacDougall I am particularly indebted, once again, for her masterful, thorough editing of my entire book manuscript.

PART I

Foundations

1 · "These Mountains Look Too Ugly and I See Too Much Work Ahead"

BUILDING THE SOUTHERN PACIFIC COMPANY, 1850–1930

Origins

The railroad that by the early twentieth century would come to be called the Southern Pacific can be likened to a giant river system. Its broad, main corporate stream carried the outflow of many tributaries, predecessor companies that had risen in nearly every state and territory in the Far West and Southwest between the 1850s and the 1920s and had been acquired one by one by the parent line. Though by no means the oldest line associated with the Southern Pacific, the Central Pacific Railroad was the principal fork and the one into which all the other later-acquired railroad companies would ultimately merge. The Central Pacific originated during the turbulent times of the fading Gold Rush in California, the most populous and economically developing area of a vast territory acquired by the United States in 1848 as spoils of war with Mexico.

In the 1850s and 1860s, commerce in California labored under serious geographical burdens: immense distances separated the state from the outside world and its various parts from one other, the state's terrain was rugged and its waterways and roads were limited and poor. All these conditions made the movement of goods and passengers slow, expensive, and unreliable. As a result, much of the state remained isolated and sparsely populated, its resources other than gold barely tapped. The cost, duration, and hazards of ocean and overland travel by wagon or stagecoach also discouraged immigration, particularly by women and children. Transportation problems were a major reason why, after the initial gold-rush spurt in the late 1840s and early 1850s, California's population growth and economic development settled down to a sluggish pace. As mining waned after 1852 and promoters began exploring new enterprises, agitation for improved transportation increased, especially for railroads within the state and across mountains and deserts to the Middle West and East. The Central Pacific Railroad emerged from California's quest for a solution to its transportation and related, larger economic problems.[1]

Central Pacific Railroad locomotive in the Bloomer Cut, near Auburn, California, photographed in mid-1860s by the company's photographer, Alfred A. Hart. Building the railroad over the Sierra Nevada was one of the nineteenth century's greatest engineering achievements. Courtesy California State Railroad Museum, Sacramento.

While California was being settled, steam railroads were revolutionizing society and economy in the middle and eastern parts of the United States. Beginning as early as the 1820s, prophets of Manifest Destiny envisioned a transcontinental railroad to spread settlement and civilization across the empty plains, mountains, and deserts, secure American control of the Pacific Coast, channel the fabled Asian trade through the United States, and unify the divided nation. In the late 1840s and 1850s, conventions in eastern and western cities proposed routes and promoted transcontinental railway bills in Congress. Because laying tracks across 2,000 miles of rugged wilderness was immediately recognized as beyond the ability of private enterprise, almost all plans called for heavy government subsidies. Little resulted from these initial proposals. Despite wide agreement on the desirability of building such a line and the need for government subsidy, divergent interest groups clashed over precise routes and conditions of construction. In the East, local rivalries over the route and sectional conflict between North and South stalled the project. Even Californians, ostensibly the major beneficiaries of the railway, could not agree on its location. San Francisco, Benicia, Vallejo, Sacramento, Stockton, Los Angeles, and San Diego all claimed to be the best western terminus and attacked their rivals' proposals. Local and national politics thus doomed early Pacific railway bills.[2]

Unable to get the national government to subsidize the Pacific railway, Californians in the 1850s and early 1860s turned to replacing existing stage, wagon, and steamboat routes with short railroads, some of which would one day become parts of the Southern Pacific system. Speculative and plagued by delay, incompetent engineering, nonexistent or corrupt financing, and scarce machinery and labor, most of these "railways" failed to advance from paper and hot air to steel and steam, and were never built. One exception, the Sacramento Valley Railroad, pushed its tracks from Sacramento's inland port twenty-three miles east along the American River into the Sierra Nevada foothills to the new town of Folsom and became the state's first working railroad in 1856. Affording quicker transport to the gold mines than the wagon roads then in use, the railway was an immediate success.[3] Understandably, most other early railways emerged in the San Francisco Bay Area, the state's wealthiest and most populous region. Among these, the San Francisco & San Jose Railroad spanned the fifty miles between those major cities in 1864. Other short lines radiated south and east from the East Bay port towns of Oakland and Alameda. Although laboring under poor construction, crushing debts, and opposition from rival communities and transportation companies, these early railways sparked agricultural and urban booms and strengthened the Bay Area's hold on the state's economy.[4]

Above all others, engineer Theodore D. Judah kept alive the hope that a transcontinental railroad would one day bind California and the East. Hired in 1854 by the Sacramento Valley Railroad to design and build its line, the young Judah completed the task in less than two years, a remarkable feat in those days of shaky railway ventures. Typically, however, the speculative, debt-ridden railroad halted construction at Folsom, and Judah left the company in 1856. Though naive in business matters, Judah was ambitious and persistent. Intrigued by the idea of a transcontinental railway, he became convinced that a line could be built over the seemingly insurmountable Sierra Nevada. While he scoured the mountains for a route, Judah tried to organize a new company to secure the government subsidy vital to his scheme. He authored pamphlets, addressed public meetings, harried potential investors and political figures in California, and journeyed to New York and Washington in a fruitless quest for aid from the federal government and eastern capitalists. So passionately did the young engineer pursue his dream of a railroad over the central Sierra that leery investors mocked him as "Crazy Judah." Doubting his business acumen and the feasibility of the Sierra route, they dismissed him as an impractical pest. Although Judah did succeed in keeping the transcontinental railway in the public eye, after four frustrating years he had failed to win government or private funding for his project.[5]

The Central Pacific Railroad

By the time Judah returned from the East in 1860, the lucrative mining commerce between California and the just-discovered and booming Comstock Lode of western Nevada had increased interest in a railroad across the Sierra. Controlled by a consortium of San Francisco investors, the Sacramento Valley Railroad, hoping to monopolize the trade, rehired Judah to build another rail and wagon route from Folsom through the Sierra north of Lake Tahoe to the Nevada mines. It was while he was working for the Sacramento Valley Railroad in 1860 that Judah discovered a central Sierra rail route and secretly hatched a plan to found his own company to use that route to tap the Comstock mining trade and at the same time to build the western segment of the transcontinental railroad. He settled on a path that started at Sacramento, rose seventy miles northeastward through 7,000-foot-high Donner Pass, and plunged down the Truckee River canyon to the Nevada border. Although Judah's plan would require the railroad to scale unprecedented grades, combat huge snowfalls, and bore expensive tunnels, the Donner Pass, or Dutch Flat, route was shorter than its rivals and mounted only one summit to cross the Sierra. With a definite route now in hand, Judah and a few other Sacramento and foothill men formed the Central Pacific Railroad Company in October 1860. From their own limited resources, however, they could raise only a few thousand of the $115,000 in stock subscriptions required to incorporate the company under California law. Unwisely, Judah openly sought backing from wealthy San Francisco business-men. Not only was he rebuffed again, but the Sacramento Valley Railroad got wind of his plan. Outraged that one of its employees was promoting a rival company, the railroad fired Judah. Its bankers attacked his scheme as poorly planned and impossible to construct, thereby undermining investor confidence in the Central Pacific for years.

At this point, Theodore Judah's railroad resembled most others in Califor-nia: it existed only on paper and in the mind of its promoter, and was unlikely ever to be built. To salvage his plan, Judah turned to small investors in Sacra-mento and other towns along the Donner Pass route. After a string of disap-pointing public meetings, Judah finally interested Sacramento hardware mer-chant Collis P. Huntington in the venture. Huntington brought in his partner Mark Hopkins, along with other Sacramento businessmen including Charles Crocker and Leland Stanford. The group agreed to buy enough stock to incor-porate the company. In April 1861, at a momentous meeting at the Huntington-Hopkins store, the Central Pacific Railroad was reorganized to admit the new investors. Later, a committee that included Judah nominated and the board of directors elected Stanford president, Huntington vice president, Hopkins trea-surer, and Judah chief engineer. On June 27, 1861, the Central Pacific legally in-corporated and began the struggle to convert the dream into a reality.[6]

All former residents of the Northeast who had settled in California during the Gold Rush, Huntington, Stanford, Crocker, and Hopkins quickly emerged as the most powerful leaders of the new company. With their solid entrepre-neurial backgrounds, the "Big Four," or the "associates," as they came to be called, brought essential business strength to Judah's struggling enterprise. Though by no means wealthy, they were respected, successful merchants whose word and credit were as good as gold. Because he knew eastern suppliers and financiers, Huntington was a particularly valuable addition. Members of the tiny band of militantly anti-slavery men who had founded California's Re-publican Party in 1856, the Big Four also had political influence that proved crucial in starting up the company during the Civil War. As leaders of the new party, the associates had ridden to victory in November 1860 with their party's successful presidential candidate, Abraham Lincoln. With close ties to power-ful local and national Republicans, newly elected members of Congress, and officials of Lincoln's incoming administration, the Big Four wielded the polit-ical clout that Judah lacked.[7]

Ironically, the onset of the Civil War (prompted by the secession of south-ern states following Lincoln's inauguration as president in March 1861) improved the Central Pacific Railroad's prospects. Republican leaders controlling Congress and the White House already had favored federal aid for a transcontinental railway to encourage national economic development. Such a railroad became even more vital as part of the Union war effort. It would assure the allegiance of the frontier and strengthen military control of the Far West. At the same time, the secession of the Confederate states from the national government effectively ended southern obstruction of a northern route into California. Nevertheless, formidable obstacles still dimmed the Central Pacific's prospects in 1861. Practically every facet of the ambitious project—financing, engineering, construction, even administration and operation over such a vast territory—lacked precedent. Experts smugly predicted that the company would be unable to build a rail line over such a rough landscape, and if it could, locomotives would be too weak to haul cars over steep High Sierra grades. Even if it turned out that they could, critics predicted that the railroad would not operate reliably and profitably through the heavy snows and arctic winter temperatures of Donner Pass. Furthermore, most construction and operating equipment, including rails, cars, locomotives, and heavy machinery, would have to be shipped at great expense around Cape Horn. Wartime shortages of iron, railroad machinery, and shipping tonnage, along with the federal government's inflationary monetary policies, pushed prices high and caused wasteful delays. Finally, with construction workers scarce in California, the railroad would have labor shortages.[8]

Even using Judah's sanguine estimates, the cost of building the Central Pacific, especially the Sierra segment, would far exceed the likely federal subsidies. Their own private wealth limited, the Sacramento businessmen could expect no help from San Francisco financiers, who were already committed to steamship lines or rail competitors of the Central Pacific. Moreover, in the early 1860s, risky large-scale ventures like the Central Pacific and other would-be transcontinental railroads could raise little cash by selling stocks or bonds in the tight wartime market. Symptomatic of the Central Pacific's scant resources, the first stock subscription of 1861 brought in only $10,000 in cash, which the railroad devoted to a more detailed survey of the Donner Pass route. Funds quickly ran out, however, and Judah had to halt his work prematurely. In the summer of 1861 he returned from the mountains, bearing only the disheartening news that his original survey was seriously flawed. The rail distance through the Sierra would be 140 miles, not 115, and more than three miles of tunnels would have to be bored through hard granite. To build the line as far as Nevada would take at least $13 million, or $88,000 per mile, over 50 percent more than he had originally estimated and several times the predicted federal subsidy.[9]

To make matters worse, the Civil War's outbreak and the imminent passage of a Pacific railway subsidy act spawned a host of rival companies in California and the East vying for a share of the government's aid, including the San Francisco & San Jose and the Sacramento Valley railroads, both controlled by powerful San Francisco interests hostile to the Central Pacific. Encouraged and financed by corporate giants like the Pacific Mail Steamship, California Steam Navigation, and Wells Fargo companies, who feared losing business and federal mail subsidies to the Central Pacific, vested business interests and Sacramento's jealous rival cities joined forces to crush the city's paper railroad.[10]

Without much support outside Sacramento, the leaders of the Central Pacific, their private fortunes now committed, turned to securing crucial federal subsidies. To assure that the state would favor their company, the associates ran Stanford for governor on the Republican ticket. In September 1861 he triumphed, carrying with him a group of sympathetic Republican legislators and congressmen. Judah, Huntington, other Central Pacific investors, and congressional Republican allies sailed for the East in the fall of 1861. The Central Pacific's powerful Republican friends, along with eastern business associates of Huntington's, secured positions on the legislative committees writing the subsidy legislation and had Judah appointed clerk of both the House and Senate railway committees. Now responsible for administering the committees' business, Judah could guard Central Pacific interests while the transcontinental bill was being shaped. Through the winter and spring of 1862 Judah and Huntington lobbied furiously. To bribe legislators and leaders of other railroads, they lavishly dispensed Central Pacific stock, still worthless since the company possessed no assets. Central Pacific partisans overcame a major obstacle when they worked out a bargain with the rival San Francisco & San Jose Railroad, which agreed to drop its opposition in exchange for the Central Pacific's promise to assign it the right to build and collect the subsidy for the transcontinental segment between San Francisco Bay and Sacramento.

Judah and Huntington achieved an even more stunning victory in July 1862, when President Lincoln signed the historic Pacific Railway Act. This law empowered the Central Pacific to construct tracks from San Francisco Bay or the navigable waters of the Sacramento River to the eastern boundary of California, and the Union Pacific Railroad, a speculative eastern company, to complete the connection westward from the Missouri River. Both lines were awarded rights-of-way as well as the right to take timber and stone from the public domain for construction and grants of ten alternate sections of public land per mile constructed, in a checkerboard pattern within a swath ten miles on each side of the tracks. The act also authorized a loan to the companies of thirty-year government bonds at the rate of $16,000 per mile of track across low-elevation plains at each end of the line, $48,000 per mile in rugged mountains, and $32,000 per mile across the Great Basin. The railroads were to sell the land and bonds to raise capital for construction.[11]

Pathbreaking as it was, the 1862 act probably would never have by itself brought about a transcontinental railway. Not only was the subsidy much lower than the estimated cost of construction, but the law contained serious constraints. Each company was obligated to complete the entire line by 1876 if the other failed to build its portion, and the federal government would confiscate the assets of a company that did not meet its responsibilities. Because they were to be delivered gradually, after the railroads had already completed segments of track, bond subsidies, and especially the land grant, would not provide much start-up capital during the critical early construction years. Moreover, the government's loan of bonds was secured by a first mortgage against the railroads' property, thereby reducing the companies' own bonds to less valuable second mortgages. All of these provisions discouraged private investors from buying the railroads' stocks and bonds. As late as 1864 neither the Union Pacific nor the Central Pacific had been able to sell enough of its own securities to complete the mileage needed to qualify for the federal loans.

Aware that the Pacific Railway Act of 1862 would have to be amended, the Central Pacific sought for the moment to finance initial construction through local and state subsidies and loans secured by its personal assets. In the eighteenth and nineteenth centuries, colonial, state, and local governments, including in California, commonly subsidized new businesses, particularly transportation ventures.[12] Between 1862 and 1864 Governor Stanford and his allies pushed through many state laws favoring the Central Pacific, particularly bills that passed the legislature early in 1863 granting millions of dollars in state bonds and allowing local communities to assist the railroad by subscribing to its stock. After hotly fought local elections blemished on both sides by charges of bribery and ballot-box stuffing, the people of San Francisco, Sacramento, Placer, and other counties overwhelmingly approved the purchase of more than $1 million in Central Pacific stock. Tenacious in their opposition to the railroad, competing railway, steamship, and wagon companies and communities far from the Donner Pass route tried to get the legislature to revoke Central Pacific subsidies and extend them instead to rivals, filed lawsuits challenging the legality of state and local aid, and attempted to overturn local subsidy elections. In their abusive pamphlet and newspaper war, enemies charged that the Central Pacific's route was impractical, the speculative company would go bankrupt without completing the rail line, and its corrupt officers were interested only in absconding with the public subsidies.

As governor of the state as well as president of the railroad, Leland Stanford led the fight after 1862 to preserve the Central Pacific's privileged position. The company dispatched agents to help local supporters get subsidy referendums passed, compromised with communities lowering the amounts of their stock purchases, thwarted competing lobbyists in the legislature, and successfully defended most of the lawsuits. By 1865 the opposition had been quelled, at least for the moment, and the railroad began to receive the much-needed local money. The anti–Central Pacific campaign of the early 1860s, however, depleted the railroad's funds, reduced and delayed subsidies, and postponed the railroad's completion. Also, its own heavy-handed tactics, magnified by exaggerations and untruths hurled by partisan opponents, gave the Central Pacific a lingering reputation for corruption and ruthlessness. Many Californians thus were predisposed against the Central Pacific before it had laid even a mile of track. Born in the business and community rivalries inherent in early railway building, these suspicions laid the groundwork for later anti-railroad movements that became commonplace in the politics of California and other western states.[13]

While the battle against its rivals raged, the Central Pacific began construction in late 1862 and early 1863. Although the railroad still could not raise substantial funds, some tangible work, however symbolic, was essential to shore up public and investor confidence. The company scraped together a small amount of capital through new stock subscriptions and levies on its few stockholders, including contributions of $35,000 from each of the Big Four. In December, Crocker, in league with other railway investors, founded Charles Crocker & Co., which received the contract to build the first segment of rail line. Finally, on January 8, 1863, the first transcontinental railroad broke ground at the Sacramento riverfront, accompanied by prayers, speeches, parades, waving American flags, and the music of the Sacramento Brass Band.[14] After several months, though, work on the roadbed halted about eighteen miles into the countryside. Characteristically, grading crews became mired in the mucky Sacramento Valley earth, and the railroad again ran out of money. No tracks had been laid. In fact, the Central Pacific had no rails, cars, and locomotives— nor the cash to buy them.

In March 1863, Collis P. Huntington again went east in a desperate attempt to sell $1.5 million in nearly worthless Central Pacific bonds to purchase rolling stock and construction materials. Although the Union Pacific and other builders of eastern links to the transcontinental railroad had been able to raise virtually no capital in the stringent wartime market, Huntington, relying on old business friends and the excellent credit of his hardware firm, coaxed financiers into lending him several hundred thousand dollars, secured by some of the bonds and his personal guarantee of repayment. This was the first significant influx of outside funds into the Central Pacific. Huntington then bought rails, locomotives, and other equipment and shipped it around Cape Horn, with payment in cash, more discounted bonds, and Huntington's personal promissory notes. The Central Pacific Railroad was finally in business, though heavily in debt.

Huntington returned from the East in the summer of 1863 to find the Central Pacific in shambles. Enemies still tied up local subsidies, and some stock-holders were defaulting on payments due on their subscriptions. Unless it obtained more capital, and quickly, the company could not finish the fifty miles of track needed by the November 1864 legal deadline to qualify for the federal bonds and land grants. In that case, the railroad would probably go under, taking with it the personal businesses of its founders. Under mounting pressure, the Central Pacific's leaders fought bitterly over finance, engineering, and control of the railway. The Big Four, who owned most Central Pacific stock and had already mortgaged their personal assets to begin construction, insisted that delinquent stockholders pay their subscriptions and that all investors be further assessed. Less wealthy minority stockholders, led by Judah, who had received his stock free and had little of his own money in the railroad, were equally determined that the company raise funds by further mortgaging its equipment and uncompleted roadbed. The Huntington faction countered that this added debt would crush the shaky company.

Judah also demanded absolute control over engineering and construction. Fearing that Crocker's arrangement drained profits from the Central Pacific into a company in which Judah held no stock, he blocked the letting of more contracts to Crocker & Co. The Big Four countered that the outside construction firms did shoddy work, charged higher prices, and often defaulted on contracts. Already opposed to some of the Big Four's questionable methods, Judah was furious when Governor Stanford augmented early construction subsidies by getting the state geologist to declare that the Sierra Nevada began with the first low rises seven miles east of Sacramento, instead of at the steeper grades twenty-seven miles farther east. For their part, the Big Four had long been exasperated by Judah's unrealistic cost estimates, his damaging mistakes in designing and installing roadbed, bridges, and culverts that had already washed out in floods, and his insistence on building grandiose stations while the company flirted with bankruptcy. Judah, the associates were certain, was a careless engineer and an impractical obstructionist who would ruin the railway and their personal fortunes.

In July the Huntington faction won control of the board of directors and demanded that other board members pay their stock assessments or relinquish their seats. When Judah and his supporters refused, the Big Four insisted that Judah buy them out or consent to sell his stock. Eventually, they reached an agreement. Again unable to raise cash, Judah exchanged his stock for $100,000 in Central Pacific bonds and withdrew from the board. He retained his post as chief engineer at a salary of $5,000 per year, as well as an option to buy out the Big Four for $100,000 each. In early October, Judah left by steamer to try to borrow the money from eastern railroad financiers. He contracted yellow fever while in Panama, however, and died in New York City on November 2, 1863.[15]

Relying on hindsight and the worshipful writings of Judah's wife, Anna, some historians have converted Judah into a martyr to the Big Four's greed. Some have asserted that the railroad would have been less corrupt and more public-spirited, and California better off, if Judah had gained control.[16] The evidence, however, undermines such speculations. Judah's contributions to the Central Pacific had been undeniably important. An inveterate optimist, he popularized the transcontinental railway, located a feasible route, conceived the original plan for the Central Pacific, and with Huntington lobbied through the Pacific Railway Act of 1862. However, at the time he died, Judah was only one among many would-be railroad builders, the great majority of them unsuccessful, and everything in the historical record suggests that he would never have been able to build and manage the railroad by himself. When he left California in the autumn of 1863, the Central Pacific was still a speculative railroad, indistinguishable from many that failed to survive. It owned little equipment and had yet to lay a single rail, haul a passenger or a sack of flour, or earn one cent of profit. While Judah's modest engineering talent was adequate for preliminary work, he had made some costly design errors and had yet to prove he could solve the unprecedented technical problems looming ahead in the Sierra. However passionate his vision, Judah's business skills and political influence were minimal. Particularly, he had demonstrated no ability to raise capital on his own. The Central Pacific's victories to date, as they would be in the future, were primarily in finance, administration, and politics, areas in which the Big Four's contributions were consistently more important than his. Judah also shared fully the lax business ethics for which his generation was infamous.[17] If Judah had succeeded in wresting the Central Pacific from the Big Four, the railroad would probably have quickly failed. If it had survived, it would have been in the grip of carpetbagger eastern railroad tycoons, the likes of Jay Gould and Cornelius Vanderbilt, who at least as much as the Big Four used disreputable methods and disdained the public welfare.

On to Promontory

The Central Pacific's 1863 management crisis was the nadir in its history. Though the future remained bleak, the associates resumed work on the roadbed and bridges. The company set October 26 as the date for laying the first rails in Sacramento, but it avoided fanfare. "If you want to jubilate in driving the first spike go ahead and do it," Huntington complained to an associate. "I don't. These mountains look too ugly and I see too much work ahead."[18] Even in the gloomy fall of 1863, though, the tide was beginning to turn in favor of the Central Pacific. Crews finally were driving rails through the streets of Sacramento.

On November 9, the first locomotive, *Gov. Stanford,* began shuttling supplies, work gangs, and dignitaries back and forth between the river port and the construction front. The railroad's finances also improved dramatically. Starting in September, litigation blocking the state and local subsidies began to be resolved in the company's favor. County and municipal subsidy bonds started trickling into the Central Pacific's coffers. State grants soon followed.

With the company's position somewhat bolstered, Huntington again headed east to secure all-important amendments to the Pacific Railway Act. From that time forward, Huntington spent most of the rest of his life in the East, establishing an office for his railroad in New York City, from which he directed the challenging business of financing the Central Pacific and managing its relationships with the federal government. Fending off another campaign by rivals in Washington to repeal public subsidies to the Central Pacific, Huntington struck an alliance with the Union Pacific, which was having even greater trouble raising capital and had yet to break ground. Six months of lobbying by Huntington and Union Pacific's Thomas Durant produced the Pacific Railway Act of 1864, which modified most of the burdensome features of the 1862 law. The new act extended the deadline for completing the first fifty-mile portion to 1865 and doubled the land grant to twenty alternate sections per mile, within a twenty-mile checkerboard corridor on each side of the right-of-way. Also important, the 1864 law reduced the federal bond loan to a second mortgage and allowed the railways to sell their own first-mortgage bonds equal in amount to the government subsidy, thereby doubling the companies' potential construction capital. In 1866, to finish the job faster, Congress authorized each company to build as much of the transcontinental line as it could, thus setting the Central and Union Pacifics off in a race against each other.

The Pacific Railway Act of 1864 was an important turning point for the Central Pacific. Realizing the company's superior position, its California rivals either went out of business, reoriented their lines to feed into the Central Pacific, or sold out to the Big Four. With local and federal subsidies assured, investors grew more confident. For the first time, Huntington could sell the railroad's and government's bonds, though only at heavy discounts. The Central Pacific was lucky to receive one-half the face value of the securities, although it was of course obligated to repay the entire amount, with interest. Laboring under a heavy debt with staggering interest payments, in the next few years the railroad time and again stood days or hours away from financial disaster, especially when the high costs of building over the mountains drained its resources. But Huntington established close ties with American and European bankers and railroad equipment manufacturers. Somehow, often by pledging his own or his associates' businesses or by juggling funds in deceptive ways, he always managed to come up with the money to buy supplies and cover interest payments, as

An early Central Pacific Railroad locomotive heads out over newly laid tracks east of Sacramento and the American River, ca. mid-1860s. Author's collection.

well as to ship a steady stream of machinery and material from the East by sea around Cape Horn to the railroad's construction front on the west coast.[19] The Central Pacific's credit remained spotless, and Huntington came to be acknowledged as one of the business geniuses of his era.[20]

Fueled by new capital, construction on the Central Pacific gained momentum after 1863.[21] Locomotives first hauled passengers and freight the eighteen miles between Sacramento and Roseville in April 1864.[22] Traffic was light until June, when the company completed the track to Newcastle and its subsidiary Dutch Flat Toll Road the rest of the way across the Sierra to the Comstock Lode. The Central Pacific's combined rail and wagon service immediately proved faster and cheaper than competitors, and most Comstock trade shifted to the new route, seizing much of the traffic from other free and toll roads over the mountains.[23] Income exceeded operating expenses, making stocks and bonds easier to sell. The Central Pacific looked like it might yet turn a profit.

Nevertheless, when the company tried to push its line higher into the Sierra in the winter of 1865, it again bogged down, this time because of labor problems. Few men answered the company's call for thousands of construction workers, and they often deserted quickly to the Comstock mines soon after the railroad had transported them to the mountains, particularly after a taste of toiling in deep snows at $35 per month. Having employed Chinese immigrants on the Dutch Flat Road, Charles Crocker, over the objections of some company leaders, successfully transferred the Chinese to the heavier Central Pacific work. By May 1865 the Chinese composed two-thirds of the Central Pacific's labor force.[24] So efficient were the Chinese crews that the company, after the completion of the transcontinental line, transferred them to build its extensions northward into Oregon and eastward to Texas. The railroad's Chinese workers pioneered in establishing Chinatowns in cities across the West. Many Chinese continued as construction or operations workers with the railroad for decades, the last of the original Sierra Nevada construction crewmen retiring as late as the 1920s.[25] Other immigrant groups also furnished laborers, particularly the Irish and Portuguese. About one-fifth of the Central Pacific's employees were Portuguese, with many of them remaining for long periods with the railroad after the completion of the transcontinental line. Some, such as Frank Frates, rose to positions of responsibility.[26]

Beyond Auburn, Central Pacific crews combated some of the most forbidding terrain in the country. The railroad faced a climb of 6,000 feet in forty miles over the Sierra crest, culminating in the treacherous cliffs of Donner Pass. Below-zero temperatures and forty-foot-deep snow drifts halted work for weeks at a time in winter. Weakened by illnesses and bad food and water, the workers were in summer also harried by mosquitoes "as big as hornets" and swarms of rattlesnakes whose dens had been disturbed during construction. Cave-ins and misfired explosions killed and maimed scores of men.[27] Somehow, the Central Pacific inched upward. The railway developed new construction techniques, experimented with new, more powerful explosives, and worked its more than 14,000 men in round-the-clock shifts. While the Chinese bored away at tunnels a few inches a day from both ends, or carved out narrow ledges to carry the tracks around precipices, Crocker took advantage of the Dutch Flat Road to send materials and disassembled rolling stock ahead by wagon—by sled in winter—so that work could proceed simultaneously on different fronts. To shield its line from the crushing drifts at Donner Pass, the Central Pacific in 1868 began installing miles of long wooden snowsheds, to this day a distinctive feature of this rail line.[28] All this devoured capital. Some stretches, particularly the tunnels, cost between $150,000 and $1 million per mile, and the company always teetered on the brink of insolvency. Finally, after nearly three years of strenuous mountain construction, trains chugged over the summit in November 1867.[29] They reached Nevada in June 1868, more than five years after breaking ground, but still only 140 miles from Sacramento.

Once clear of the mountains, though, the Central Pacific raced across the more moderate Great Basin terrain to meet the Union Pacific, which was itself stalled in the mountains northeast of the Great Salt Lake.[30] Although troubled by water shortages and extreme heat and cold, Crocker's experienced Chinese and European immigrant crews worked quickly and efficiently. During the next year they laid 550 miles of track, including a then-record ten miles on one April 1869 day.

On May 10, 1869, hundreds of jubilant laborers and executives of both companies joined dignitaries and reporters for a legendary event at barren Promontory Summit, Utah, north of the Great Salt Lake. After the customary prayers and flowery speeches by seemingly scores of people, Central Pacific president Leland Stanford swung his silver hammer at a golden spike fastening the last rail. Nervous and awkward, the "Governor" missed, but telegraph keys tapped out the terse message: "It is done." Wild celebrations erupted in Sacramento, San Francisco, Chicago, New York, Philadelphia, indeed worldwide. Central and Union Pacific trains from west and east rolled through the Promontory junction immediately; the first through passenger train all the way from Omaha arrived in Sacramento carrying 500 pioneer tourists and reporters on May 26. A few months later, to facilitate rail operations, the junction of the two lines was moved eastward to the established city of Ogden.[31]

The day after driving the golden spike, Stanford telegraphed to Collis P. Huntington in New York City simply: "The rails connected with appropriate ceremonies." When he read detailed newspaper accounts of the gaudy show, and especially what he saw as Stanford's self-glorifying role in it, Huntington shot a contemptuous letter to friend and partner Mark Hopkins. Hopkins, however, objected: "I regret you should speak offensively of Stanford's connection with the driving the 'last spike'—for it dont appear to me quite right or politic." Even at the moment of the associates' greatest triumph, a rift was opening between Huntington and Stanford. Widening and becoming increasingly public, it would two decades later break up their partnership.[32]

Consolidation of California Railroads

The driving of the golden spike signaled more the beginning than it did the climax of the Central Pacific Railroad's development. In California, capitalizing on the transcontinental line's potential for stimulating economic growth, promoters organized dozens of railways in the late 1860s and 1870s. Some were even built. New railways usually fell quickly into the Big Four's grasp, however. Often outgrowths of real estate schemes or designed by their promoters for quick speculation, rather than long-term efficient operation, the new railways suffered from shoddy construction, insufficient traffic, and excessive debt. Their builders were all too eager to skim off their profits and unload the shaky companies.

Moreover, the Big Four had reasons of their own for acquiring other lines. The revenues of the Central Pacific were at first disappointing. The Suez Canal, also completed in 1869, siphoned off the Asian trade. Traffic from eastern states in goods, tourists, and immigrants also failed to match predictions, in part because of a serious depression that struck California beginning in 1869.[33] In the late 1860s and early 1870s the Big Four themselves were mired in debt and anxious to sell the Central Pacific. Because of the company's immensity, its troubled finances, its massive indebtedness to the government, and the recurrent depressions of the 1870s, the associates were unsuccessful in several attempts to dispose of the railroad.[34] The only way to avert disaster, Huntington convinced his sometimes reluctant partners, was to continue to build new lines, to defeat or absorb potential competitors for California's scant traffic, and to systematize the railroads and make them turn a profit. Borrowing heavily and reinvesting profits from constructing the Central Pacific, the associates purchased most other transportation companies operating or building in California. The more lines the Big Four acquired or built, the more deeply involved they became. By the end of the 1870s, they had transformed themselves from railroad promoters and builders into railroad operators.[35]

Most California railways came under the control of the Big Four in the 1860s and 1870s. The first to fall was their old nemesis, the Sacramento Valley Railroad, whose owners sold out in 1865. In 1868 the Big Four purchased the railroads around San Francisco Bay, including the San Francisco & San Jose (the only line into San Francisco), the Western Pacific (which had received a federal land grant to build the final link in the transcontinental railroad between Sacramento and the bay at San Jose), and strategic short railways stretching southward from the East Bay ports of Alameda and Oakland. Using these lines, Central Pacific trains from the East arrived at San Francisco Bay a few months after the driving of the golden spike. In the autumn of 1869, the Central Pacific moved its rail terminal from Sacramento to Oakland, instantly transforming that sleepy village into a boomtown. Freight and passenger ferries connected the terminal to San Francisco across the bay.[36] In 1873, the Central Pacific's corporate offices and the Big Four themselves vacated Sacramento for San Francisco.

From the late 1860s into the 1880s, the Big Four continued to expand their California transportation holdings. To seize the gateway to the Northwest, the associates in 1867 acquired the California & Oregon Railroad, which was building under a federal land-grant subsidy from present-day Roseville, on the Central Pacific transcontinental line, northward to Marysville and up the Sacramento Valley toward Oregon. To reduce water competition, they reached a rate and traffic agreement with the Pacific Mail Steamship Company in 1871, and in 1874 they formed their own trans-Pacific firm, the Occidental and Oriental Steamship Company.[37] The Big Four also absorbed inland riverboat enterprises, San Francisco Bay ferries, and urban streetcar lines. They integrated some of these newly acquired rail and other transportation facilities as important main links in the Central Pacific system. Others became branch lines or closed down altogether.[38]

The Big Four's prize acquisition was the Southern Pacific Railroad. Because of severe winter weather and high elevations along the Central Pacific–Union Pacific route, a southern, low-elevation railroad just north of the Mexican border was likely one day to carry much cross-country traffic. The original owners of the San Francisco & San Jose had founded the Southern Pacific Railroad in 1865 and secured a state charter and a federal franchise and land grant to build the western end of such a southern transcontinental line, between San Jose and the Colorado River. When they purchased the unbuilt Southern Pacific in 1868, the Big Four gained control of a proposed western link in the southern transcontinental route, thus defeating their most threatening potential competition.[39]

Immediately upon acquiring the Southern Pacific Railroad, the Big Four set off to forge that link and capture the strategic crossing of the Colorado River at Yuma. Starting in 1869, they extended the Central Pacific Railroad from its current transcontinental line at Lathrop south into the San Joaquin Valley through Fresno to Goshen (reached in 1872). They also opened construction on the Southern Pacific Railroad line from San Jose southeast to Tres Piños (reached in 1873), where a precipitous ridge in the Coast Range blocked access to the railroad's federally approved route down the San Joaquin Valley. To make haste toward the Colorado River while they raised capital and solved engineering problems for a crossing of the Coast Range, the Big Four resumed construction of the Southern Pacific Railroad on its planned route south down the valley from the end of the Central Pacific's line at Goshen. Trains arrived in Bakersfield at the head of the valley in 1874.[40]

Pushing the Southern Pacific Railroad's main line from Bakersfield south over the rugged Tehachapi Mountains into southern California took two more years and required stunning engineering feats rivaling the crossing of the Sierra. To enable a leap over a four-thousand-foot pass in only sixteen air miles, engineer William F. Hood designed the famous Tehachapi Loop. The track tunneled up through a ridge and ascended sharply in a tight circle back onto the ridge and over itself. Meanwhile, to the south, three thousand Chinese workers dug the seven-thousand-foot-long San Fernando Tunnel, at the time the second longest railroad bore in the United States.[41] In exchange for a subsidy from Los Angeles, the railroad had in 1872 agreed to build through the city. With customary fanfare, Charles Crocker connected Los Angeles to the state's northern railway system and the Central Pacific's route to the east when he drove the last golden spike near present-day Palmdale in the Antelope Valley on September 5, 1876.[42]

While the Southern Pacific Railroad was approaching the city, the associates had acquired most other Los Angeles railways, including the strategic Los Angeles & San Pedro from the city's downtown to its harbor at Wilmington, more than twenty miles to the south. Shortly later, they added the Los Angeles & Independence, which ran from the ocean at Santa Monica eastward to downtown, heading eventually toward the Owens Valley silver mines several hundred miles northeastward.[43] By the time Southern Pacific trains arrived from the north in Los Angeles, the associates had already begun extending the railroad eastward from the city across the cattle ranches in the valleys of San Gabriel and San Bernardino (reached in 1874) and the parched Colorado Desert and below-sea-level Salton Sink (reached in 1876), founding new towns and water stations as they went. Determined to beat other railroads to the critical river crossing, the Southern Pacific bridged the Colorado before the federal government had given its approval, and in the autumn of 1877 steamed into Yuma, Arizona Territory. Eager to become a rail terminal, the desert village had granted the company land for right-of-way and station.[44]

·Originally, the Big Four had intended eventually to complete the challenging and expensive Southern Pacific Railroad segment from Tres Piños across the Coast Range to Goshen in the San Joaquin Valley. Once in operation, however, the combined Central–Southern Pacific line south from Sacramento and Lathrop to Bakersfield and Los Angeles proved sufficient to carry north-south traffic through central interior California, and the gap was never closed. Instead, without federal bond or land subsidies, the associates concentrated on building the even more difficult route south from San Jose through the Salinas Valley and coastal cities to Los Angeles. The Southern Pacific Railroad's famed "Coast Route" through the Salinas Valley opened in sections beginning in the 1870s, reached San Luis Obispo from the north and Santa Barbara from the south in the late 1880s, and was finished in 1901.[45]

Already by the end of the 1870s the Big Four effectively monopolized California transportation. Capitalized at $225 million, their California railroads in 1877 had 2,340 miles of track, including 85 percent of the rail lines in the state and all the important ones in the San Francisco Bay Area, Los Angeles, and the Sacramento and San Joaquin valleys. In addition to their main lines, the Big Four had extended many branches into almost all settled areas of the state.[46] The Central Pacific Railroad's leaders also controlled two transcontinental rail connections in California, one completed, the other in progress. Their successful enterprises had brought the associates great fortunes. From modest beginnings as Sacramento shopkeepers, the Big Four now ranked among America's richest and most powerful business leaders. In the 1880s, the Big Four built or acquired large railroad properties in Oregon, Arizona, New Mexico, Texas, and Louisiana, although they were never able to dominate markets in those states as completely as they did in their home state.

Its California origins left a lasting mark on the Big Four's rail system. Conflicts during the 1860s and 1870s between the Central Pacific and rivals over the control of routes, terminals, government subsidies, rail services and rates, and influence over public policies left a legacy of animosity toward the company. Sometimes justified, sometimes sour grapes, the sense of disaffection and grievance against the Central Pacific among some regions and economic interests fueled anti-railroad political movements and spread from state to state as the company expanded. Also complicating the Central Pacific's political situation were its financial subsidies and especially its numerous land grants, which, as will become clear in subsequent chapters of this book, entangled the company with the government to an extent unusual for a private enterprise in the nineteenth century.[47] Henceforth, federal, and to a lesser extent state, policies greatly affected the railroad's fortunes, drawing the company deeply into lobbying and partisan politics and keeping it vulnerable to criticism and opposition. Finally, the Central/Southern Pacific was the only major American railroad that built from west to east. It introduced and consolidated its business practices initially in California, its most populous and advanced region, before expanding outward. The railroad's founders and most of its later top executives and, importantly, its middle-level managers were Californians, often long-time residents. With remarkable tenure in their positions, these men identified their company's interests with those of their home state, its economic, social, and cultural development, and secondarily with the larger West. Thus, the railroad's character as a Californian, and to a lesser extent western, enterprise was stamped from its beginning. In many ways, although the Central/Southern Pacific extended operations into the Southwest, the Pacific Northwest, and internationally, and despite its longtime corporate office in New York, and even during the period when it was controlled from outside by the Harriman Lines from 1901 to 1913, it remained a California-based company.

Expansion beyond California

"A rail line that should stretch straight way across the continent," Huntington had long believed, would be the "natural" culmination of railroad development. After years of Huntington's haranguing, his debt-phobic partners finally relented and agreed to make the Southern Pacific Railroad into that single national transportation system.[48] In 1879, to the consternation of eastern railroad moguls such as Tom Scott and Jay Gould, who coveted the southern transcontinental route for themselves, the Southern Pacific Railroad began building eastward across southern Arizona and New Mexico without a federal subsidy or land grant.[49] Overcoming grievous shortages of water for crews, passengers, and locomotives, it advanced to Tucson in March 1880 and the following December to Deming, New Mexico. There, in early 1881, the oncoming Atchison, Topeka & Santa Fe Railroad connected to the Southern Pacific, completing the second transcontinental route; the first through-trains over the line from the Middle West arrived in California in March.[50] In May 1881 the Southern Pacific's Chinese track-laying crews arrived at El Paso, Texas, a major rail crossroads, with access to direct routes connecting to the Gulf Coast and Atlantic tidewater.[51]

For several years Huntington had been moving toward control of a network of Texas and Louisiana railroads from El Paso eastward. Anticipating the day when his company would possess its own transcontinental route, starting as early as 1878, he quietly began investing in the Galveston, Harrisburg, & San Antonio Railroad, which was slowly building westward from the Galveston-Houston harbor toward El Paso through San Antonio, which it had reached in 1877. Huntington increased his holdings in that and other railroads as opportunity arose, until in the early 1880s his interests allowed him to take over these lines one by one and begin their consolidation into a system. Having just gained control of the line, the Southern Pacific's associates in 1881 set about completing the Galveston, Harrisburg, & San Antonio's long segment between San Antonio and El Paso. They quickly laid tracks eastward from El Paso to take the only pass into the city from the east. On the basis of that strategic move, Huntington in November 1881 could impose a momentous and favorable truce agreement on rival Jay Gould's Texas & Pacific Railroad that conceded to the Southern Pacific a large rail empire in central and southern Texas. After more than a year of grueling construction over hundreds of miles of rugged country, highlighted by the erection of a spectacular bridge over the three-hundred-foot-deep Pecos River gorge, the last spike on the El Paso–San Antonio line was driven on January 12, 1883.[52] In early 1883, Southern Pacific locomotives entered Galveston-Houston and New Orleans on the Galveston, Harrisburg, & San Antonio and associated lines, completing the first coast-to-coast railway under one management. The first through passenger trains between San Francisco and New Orleans left those two cities to traverse the Southern Pacific's famed "Sunset Route" on February 5, 1883.[53]

Ultimately, by 1883, the associates controlled not only the Galveston, Harrisburg, & San Antonio, but the Houston & Texas Central and the pivotal Texas & New Orleans between Houston and Lake Charles, Louisiana, which connected Galveston-Houston to the Mississippi River and the major Gulf port at New Orleans. Continuing to extend these and to acquire other lines, by the early 1900s the Southern Pacific's Atlantic System, resembling what had happened earlier in California, combined dozens of railroads in Texas and Louisiana, with more than 3,000 miles of track.[54] Crucial was Huntington's 1883 acquisi-

In west Texas, the Southern Pacific's famous new Pecos River High Bridge (shown ca. 1900) replaced the strategic original structure in 1892. Author's collection.

tion of the New Orleans-based transportation empire assembled by Charles Morgan, including his Louisiana & Texas Railroad and the Morgan Line steamship company. The Morgan company provided the Southern Pacific Railroad's trains direct passenger and especially freight connections from New Orleans and Texas harbors to the Caribbean, New York, other east coast ports, and Europe. When consolidated with their California-based and other Texas holdings, the Morgan Line gave the associates' transport system global reach, including not only extensive regional trackage throughout the west coast and Southwest, but multiple rail and rail/sea transcontinental connections, several of which were under their sole management and free from winter snow blockades such as frequently shut down northern railroads. The reach of their railroads extended beyond the American shoreline, via trans-Pacific steam-shipping lines to Latin America and Asia and trans-Atlantic lines to the Caribbean and Europe.[55] The Central/Southern Pacific associates' acquisition,[56] beginning in 1884 and completed in 1887, of the Oregon & California Railroad,[57] connecting their California & Oregon Railroad in the northern Sacramento Valley to Portland and the Columbia River, and the subsequent absorption of other Oregon lines, rounded out their unrivaled western railroad empire.

The Southern Pacific Company

The Southern Pacific's mushrooming business empire caused acute management problems for the Big Four. They generally did not fully merge new lines into the Central Pacific, but owned them in partnership and controlled them by varied, complicated leases to the Central Pacific Railroad or stock-holding arrangements that proved unwieldy, particularly after the addition of the Texas and Louisiana railroads. Confusion was compounded because some states and territories prohibited out-of-state companies from operating railroads within their jurisdictions. Thus, just to build their southern transcontinental line, the associates had to create separate Southern Pacific Railroad companies in California, Arizona, New Mexico, and Texas. Also, large construction and acquisition outlays sapped the railroad's financial resources, as did declining traffic caused by the collapse of Nevada silver mining and competition from the newly completed Atchison, Topeka & Santa Fe and Northern Pacific roads. Revenue per mile of the associates' rapidly expanding railroads fell steeply from 1881 to 1884, driving their enterprise close to insolvency.[58]

To improve management, increase earnings, and provide a better mechanism for distributing traffic, expenses, investment capital, and profits among their far-flung lines, Huntington convinced his partners in 1884 to set up a holding company, the Southern Pacific Company. To broaden the holding company's powers and insulate it from legal and political attack in the West, it was incorporated under the benevolent laws of Kentucky. In early 1885 the associates transferred railway stock and leases to the new Southern Pacific Company.[59] The venerable, but financially vulnerable, Central Pacific Railroad, now an isolated entity and no longer leasing and operating the Southern Pacific Railroad companies and the other affiliated lines, was also leased to the holding company. The new arrangement had the added advantage of affording a better shield for the associates' other railroads from a threatened congressional takeover of the Central Pacific to collect on its still-unpaid debt to the federal government. Quickly, the Southern Pacific Company's corporate name and identity came to subsume those of its controlled lines. The Southern Pacific Company operated from headquarters in San Francisco. Initially, Leland Stanford served as president, but, to Huntington's mounting disgust, he was becoming increasingly absorbed in his Washington, D.C., duties as a newly elected U.S. senator from California. As company vice president, Huntington directed the finance and lobbying office in New York City, with long visits to San Francisco and other Southern Pacific centers once or more each year.[60]

In 1890, years of simmering bad blood between the two surviving members of the Big Four finally boiled over. Huntington had long been exasperated by Stanford's public posturing, by his lavish displays of wealth, and especially by his laxity, indeed laziness, in attending to business matters, which had frequently hurt the company financially and politically. The last straw fell in early January 1890. Huntington was livid when Stanford started campaigning in the California legislature for reelection to the U.S. Senate. Not only did he think that Stanford's electoral antics exposed the company to reprisals, Huntington had already promised the Southern Pacific's support to A. A. Sargent, the company's longtime political friend.[61] At the early 1890 meetings of the board of directors of the Southern Pacific Company, Huntington, after securing the acquiescence of the Crocker and Hopkins interests, forced his own election as president by threatening to release damaging political documents regarding Stanford's first senatorial election. Then, although all parties to the deal had agreed to refrain from public calumny of each other, in his April 1890 presidential acceptance speech in San Francisco, Huntington openly attacked Stanford for having neglected his business duties and for jeopardizing the Southern Pacific's interests by his dallies in politics. Although the legislature did return him to the U.S. Senate, the embittered Stanford withdrew from active management of the Southern Pacific. He died three years later.[62] Combined with the deaths of Hopkins in 1878 and Charles Crocker in 1888, Huntington's ouster of Stanford gave him dominant control of one of the nation's and the world's largest business enterprises. He remained as president until his own death in August 1900.

In the decade and a half following its founding in 1884, the Southern Pacific Company modernized and integrated the Big Four's holdings for more efficient and profitable operation. Much of the new company's organizational success resulted from a transfusion of new executive blood. Increasingly under Huntington's sway even before his ascension to the presidency, the Southern Pacific Company selected and groomed an elite corps of middle-level executives, most of them handpicked by Huntington, and then delegated them authority to run company affairs in their departments.[63] Young men at their initial appointment, the Southern Pacific's middle-level leaders attained great longevity with the company, moved up in responsibility, and lent remarkable effectiveness and continuity to corporate policy into the early twentieth century. First, to improve day-to-day operation of the Southern Pacific's some five thousand miles of railroads in dozens of companies, as well as extensive steam-shipping lines, and to make them run as one rail/sea network, management in 1885 was centralized into two massive systems. Assuming charge of lines west of El Paso, the Pacific System was headquartered in San Francisco and directed by the Central Pacific's capable longtime general manager, Alban N. Towne, a respected and popular confidante of Huntington.[64] An Atlantic System took control east of El Paso, from an office in New Orleans under A. C. Hutchinson, a former Morgan Lines executive whom Huntington had brought into top management.[65]

Other changes systematized operations and extended policies over the entire company. From his office in San Francisco, the Southern Pacific Company's traffic manager, J. C. Stubbs, undertook to rationalize traffic movement among the transportation lines. Especially, Stubbs faced a bewildering diversity of freight and passenger tariffs and policies of the many subsidiaries, each with varied capitalization, debts, and operating costs derived from different terrains and traffic densities. The rate-setting problem, which business historian Alfred D. Chandler has maintained was at the time "much more complex than physically linking the roads," proved especially formidable for the country's first truly nationwide and international transportation system.[66] Stubbs had to reconcile divergent internal corporate needs, as well as contradictory outside business and political pressures. Nevertheless, he installed improved schedules of local, transcontinental, and international rates to better recoup costs and assure profits for the company's affiliated lines, while still encouraging business and agricultural development in the Southern Pacific's hinterland. He moved to shorten east-west transit times and increase business volume and profits, while overcoming the obstructionism of the Union Pacific and other eastern lines that gave low priority to and delayed west-coast freight bound for the Central Pacific. Stubbs took advantage of the company's new acquisitions and developed rates and routings for west-bound transcontinental traffic originating in the Atlantic Coast or the Middle West that diverted it southward to the Southern Pacific's wholly owned rail/sea routes via New Orleans and Texas. Also, through the 1880s and 1890s, Stubbs lowered overall Southern Pacific rates, in part to encourage more traffic, in part because of the company's increased efficiency and competition from other railroads. The Southern Pacific Company's traffic and profits improved dramatically after 1885, and Stubbs became renowned in his profession. In 1904, E. H. Harriman, after he had taken over the Southern Pacific, elevated Stubbs to traffic director of the entire Harriman Lines system.[67]

First appointed chief agent of the company's federal land grants in 1883, William H. Mills took charge of promoting colonization and subdividing, developing, and selling the public land grants of newly added railroads, as well as private properties purchased by the associates. One of his first activities after the formation of the Southern Pacific Company was to travel to Texas, evaluate the unsold state lands there granted to predecessor railroads, and make recommendations to Huntington regarding their development and sale. In the 1880s and 1890s, Mills emerged as one of Huntington's most trusted executives, influential in establishing the Southern Pacific's land, water, agricultural, promotional, and resource-conservation policies that prevailed into the mid-twentieth century. From 1883 through 1900, Mills also served as Huntington's principal political and press-relations adviser.[68]

Also indicative of the Southern Pacific Company's early expansion and sys-
tematization was its employee health-care and hospital program. As it was building the transcontinental line in the mid-1860s, to further company loyalty, reduce employee turnover, cope with the severe injuries common in railroad work,
and compensate for the lack of medical services over much of its territory, the
Central Pacific Railroad began contracting with leading physicians in settlements along its tracks to form a network of "railroad surgeons" to treat injured
and ill workers. At some especially important, though remote, rail towns, such
as Truckee, a major operations center in the High Sierra, the company itself
hired a physician and opened a railroad medical office and pharmacy. Often,
the railroad's physicians also provided the first professional services to other residents in fledgling frontier towns.[69] As early as 1867, to supplement this "on-
the-road" care, the Central Pacific founded a hospital for employees at Sacramento, temporarily housed in a former orphanage at Thirteenth and D streets.
Meanwhile, the railroad constructed a four-story permanent building, a quarter of a city block in size, that would become one of the largest, most up-to-
date hospitals in the American West. When it opened in early 1870, with its six
wards and eight private rooms, the new Central Pacific Hospital could accommodate 125 patients. The railroad recruited well-educated, research-oriented physicians from across the country to staff its hospital, and in the late nineteenth
century it became an important innovator, responsible for introducing into
the West new medical theories and procedures, including antiseptic surgery.
The Central Pacific's was one of the first comprehensive industrial hospitalization and compulsory health-care insurance programs in the United States,
and the first in the world for a railroad. Beginning in 1867, all employees were
eligible for free medical attention and hospitalization, either on the road or
in Sacramento. All, including top executives, paid premiums of fifty cents per
month, automatically deducted from their pay.[70] The company also transported employees free by rail to the road surgeons' offices or the Sacramento
hospital.[71]

When new railroads joined the Central Pacific system, their employees entered the medical care program, as did the company's retirees. In 1883, the Sacramento facility treated 3,313 railroad employees and retirees, thirty of whom died
at the hospital.[72] After the holding firm's founding in 1884, the Southern Pacific
Company extended the health-care insurance and hospitalization program to
the Atlantic System and created a hospital department, administered directly
under the president. In 1887, the Sacramento facility was renamed the Southern Pacific Railroad Hospital. As the company's workforce increased and its
territory expanded beyond the reach of Sacramento, the Southern Pacific negotiated agreements with private hospitals to treat its employees in other cities,
including by the early 1890s San Francisco, Oakland, Los Angeles, Tucson, and

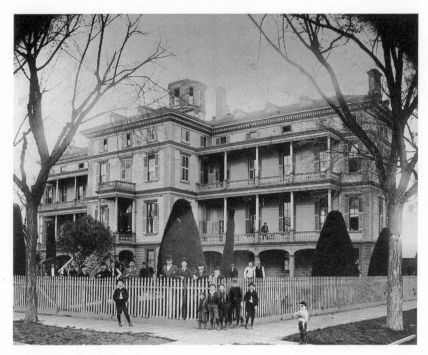

The Central Pacific Railroad Hospital, Sacramento, ca. 1892. Author's collection.

Portland. In 1899, the Sacramento facility now considered cramped, outmoded, and remote from the company's headquarters, the Southern Pacific Hospital moved into a new, larger building near the railroad terminal in downtown San Francisco. Three additional structures on the site housed doctors, interns, nurses, and hospital employees.[73] By the end of the nineteenth century, mobile medical cars were supplementing the work of the main and satellite private hospitals at especially remote construction or operations sites. In 1911, the company opened a general hospital in Houston, and another at Tucson in 1924. Employees' monthly insurance payments remained at fifty cents until raised to seventy-five cents in 1922 and one dollar in 1927.[74]

Over the early decades of the twentieth century, the railroad expanded its employee health-care program into a region-wide network of company-owned general hospitals and smaller emergency hospitals, hospitals the railroad managed for other agencies, and private hospitals under contract to care for railroad employees. Overall by 1950, the Southern Pacific owned, managed, or contracted for service at more than fifty hospitals, annually providing company workers with 195,000 patient-days of care and 520,000 out-patient visits.[75] In the 1960s and 1970s, after more than a century as one of the nation's largest medical providers, the railroad gradually closed down the hospitals or spun them off as independent institutions and shifted employees onto company-financed private insurance plans. By then, however, the Southern Pacific's insurance and hospital program had not only cared for hundreds of thousands of workers, but had also served as the model for the industry. Following the company's example, other railroads built hospitals and adopted universal health care for employees and retirees.[76]

Most instrumental, save Huntington, in the Southern Pacific Company's early organization was William Mahl. Although, like many of the company's powerful middle-level executives, he has been all but ignored by historians, contemporaries recognized Mahl's importance. "His was the analytical mind which permitted the carrying out of the dreams of Mr. Huntington in an economical and scientific way," *Railway Age* concluded about Mahl's career upon his death in 1918. Having emigrated as a child from Germany to Texas, Mahl rose quickly from a teenage shop's apprentice to become auditor, purchasing agent, and later general superintendent of several Texas and Kentucky railroads. Huntington got wind of his growing reputation and in 1882 brought the thirty-nine-year-old protégé to Huntington's New York City office. Until Huntington's death in 1900, Mahl served in various capacities as general agent, comptroller, or special assistant to the president in all the magnate's railroads.[77]

When the Big Four founded the Southern Pacific Company in 1885, Huntington set Mahl to introduce order into the chaotic books of the many subsidiary railroads. Mahl spent up to half of each year in residence in California, Texas, and Louisiana, systematizing the finances of the Southern Pacific's lines to assure that short- and long-term costs and profits could be accurately identified, measured, predicted, and distributed efficiently among the various units. Regularizing the books also generated additional capital for expansion and modernization.[78] Insisting, in *Railway Age*'s words, on "utmost precision" and "absolutely uncompromising honesty" in his and others' work, Mahl set up coherent and comparable accounting procedures for the companies, converted all their annual reports into accurate financial summaries that could be relied on in management planning, and raised the credit ratings and stock and bond values of the Southern Pacific Company and subsidiaries.[79] To improve Southern Pacific fiscal management, Mahl also conducted elaborate studies of other railroads so that his firm could emulate their successful procedures, and avoid their mistakes.[80]

It was Mahl who in the late 1880s and early 1890s transformed the Pacific Improvement Company into an important instrument of finance and stability for the rail lines. A private firm created by the Big Four in 1878 to take over railroad construction and property management from the earlier Charles Crocker and Contract and Finance companies, the Pacific Improvement Company has, like Mahl, been largely ignored by historians. Yet, it was an integral ingredient in the Southern Pacific's success. Under Mahl's tutelage, the Pacific Improvement Company continued to own, manage, and develop the various mining, streetcar, utility, town-site and rural real-estate subdivisions, and resort holdings of the Southern Pacific and its owners. In addition, the company began actively to furnish capital and insulate the railroad end of the business from the vagaries of money markets. The company advanced the railroads funds for construction and expansion, receiving in return stocks and bonds in the railroads and leaving those companies with low outstanding debt and high creditworthiness. The Pacific Improvement Company then held the securities, waiving dividends and interest payments while rail profits were low, and sold only when the price was high, usually much later, when the railroads' earnings had increased. The money was then redistributed to the rail lines and the owners as profit and additional construction capital. It was this arrangement, according to Mahl, that made the Southern Pacific Company and its affiliated railroads financially stable and especially kept them out of receivership during the great depression in the rail industry following the Panic of 1893, although the Pacific Improvement Company itself was hard pressed to meet its obligations. As it turned out, building and financing the rail lines turned extremely low profits to the Pacific Improvement Company, according to Mahl, and the company performed those functions as a service to the railroads, with the company's sizable earnings continuing to come from its real estate developments. Mahl managed the assets of the Pacific Improvement Company from 1889 until Huntington's death in 1900.[81]

In 1897 and 1898, as had become commonplace for him, Mahl accomplished something the Big Four interests had tried many times and failed to do, a much-needed full accounting of the Pacific Improvement Company and a separation of its assets and liabilities from the Southern Pacific Company's.[82] In 1899, Mahl's assistance was also important in helping Huntington reorganize the precarious finances of the Central Pacific and fund its nearly $59 million construction debt owed the federal government and due that year. The Southern Pacific Company assumed the obligation, receiving Central Pacific stock in return, reached an agreement with the government to make semi-annual payments, and retired the debt in full in 1909. The settlement averted receivership for the Central Pacific and paved the way for long-term stability and modernization for the entire Southern Pacific system.[83]

William Mahl became perhaps the only person who understood the Southern Pacific in its entirety, as well as in its minute complexities. No fiscal detail escaped his scrutiny. For instance, he devised a scheme for classifying all disbursements systemwide, so that even minor costs could be identified and controlled. Perhaps most ingenious were the procedures he developed for systemwide inventory, purchase, deployment, and rotation of heavy equipment so that, in his words, "greatest good would be derived by the property as a whole."[84] When, for example, new locomotives were needed by companies operating over gentle terrain, with easy grades, as in east and south Texas, Louisiana, and California's Central Valley, he transferred there the older locomotives from lines with steeper grades, such as over the Sierra Nevada or Tehachapi Range. Those locomotives he then replaced with the latest, most-powerful models. Similarly, Mahl rotated older cars to roads with less traffic and purchased new, modern cars for the busier lines. Rolling stock lasted longer, immense maintenance and purchase costs were saved. Particularly, Mahl, as he put it, lavished "time and attention to the development of the weaker properties," shifting to them concessions in rates and terminal charges from the prosperous lines, "thereby improving their showing and making them an asset and future basis of credit."[85]

Mahl was, indeed, the principal fiscal and organizational architect of the Southern Pacific Company's success—its modernization, its continued expansion, and most of all its welding of one transportation network out of a series of separate, contiguous rail lines. His work was instrumental to making the Southern Pacific the most financially stable of all major nineteenth-century railroads, and the only one to avoid bankruptcy and receivership. With unusual insight, for Mahl operated mostly beyond public scrutiny, the anti–Southern Pacific *San Francisco Examiner* in 1895 noted about this "expert accountant" and "shrewd judge of men" that "no one is closer than he is to Huntington. He knows more of Huntington's business than any other man living, and his authority to examine into all railroad matters is absolute."[86] Even Huntington, who was not given to effusive personal praise, acknowledged to Mahl that "as you know, I depend almost entirely upon you in such [financial] matters."[87] After E. H. Harriman took over the Southern Pacific in 1901, William Mahl became vice president and comptroller of the Union Pacific and Southern Pacific systems and, in the eyes of many contemporaries, his era's most celebrated railroad financial officer. He retired because of illness in 1913, also the year the Southern Pacific separated from the Harriman Lines.

Other important future leaders of the Southern Pacific emerging to prominence between 1885 and 1900 under Huntington's management included William F. Herrin, who was named Mills's successor as political coordinator in the late 1890s and then vice president and general counsel from the early 1900s until his death in the 1920s.[88] James Horsburgh, Jr., joined the Passenger Department and became passenger agent and director of promotion after 1900, remaining in that position until 1915.[89] Sent by Huntington from the Atlantic System, Julius Kruttschnitt was Towne's replacement at the head of the Pacific System upon his death in 1895. Ultimately, Kruttschnitt became one of the most important executives of the Harriman Lines after 1900 and chairman of the Southern Pacific after its separation from the Harriman Lines in 1913.[90] William R. Sproule, longtime Pacific System president after 1911, also first joined the executive corps in the 1880s and 1890s.[91] Henry E. Huntington, appointed by his uncle in 1892 as special representative of the president in San Francisco and later in the 1890s as vice-president, went on to become a key figure after 1900 in the development of the Pacific Electric interurban railway, ultimately a Southern Pacific subsidiary in southern California.[92] Epes Randolph, whom Huntington dispatched in the mid-1890s from his personally owned Kentucky railroads to take charge of the Southern Pacific Company's division headquartered in Tucson, in the early 1900s became also the president of the Southern Pacific de Mexico and the Pacific Electric.[93] Indicative of the significance of these men in the Southern Pacific, they all sat near Collis P. Huntington at the president's annual sumptuous banquets for executives and California dignitaries in the 1890s at San Francisco's Palace Hotel or Huntington's mansion atop Nob Hill.[94]

From the mid-1880s through the early 1900s, the Southern Pacific Company continued to expand by extending local branches of its rail lines into new territories, building new major throughways, and adding other railroads to its empire. In addition to the Oregon & California Railroad, acquired and finished between 1884 and 1887, the company in 1887 gained control of the South Pacific Coast Railroad, a narrow-gauge connecting east San Francisco Bay communities through San Jose and Los Gatos and over the redwood-rich Santa Cruz Mountains to tap fishing, logging, and recreational traffic on Monterey Bay at the city of Santa Cruz.[95] Also in California, new branches of the Central Pacific and California & Oregon were added in the Sacramento Valley, including one in 1887 into the emerging fruit-growing region in the Capay Valley, west of Sacramento. The Southern Pacific Railroad built a second north-south line in the San Joaquin Valley, down its west side, along with other branches in the valley, and continued to open new segments of its Coast Route between San Francisco Bay and Los Angeles, completed in 1901. In 1903–1904, the railroad extended a spur south from its mainline in the Colorado Desert to the Mexican border town of Calexico to tap the rich agricultural potential of the Imperial Valley.[96] During the 1880s and 1890s, the Southern Pacific expanded into Mexico, buying and then extending the Mexican International Railroad Company south from Piedras Negras (Eagle Pass, Texas) to Durango and leasing the Sonora Railroad from Nogales, at the Arizona border, south to the Gulf of California port at Guaymas.[97] Other railroads also continued to be added to the Southern Pacific's system in Oregon and Texas, until the company dominated large shares of the transportation markets in those states.[98]

Harriman Lines Interlude

When Collis P. Huntington died suddenly on August 13, 1900, the Southern Pacific Company, with nearly ten thousand miles of rail line and more than sixteen thousand miles of steam-shipping routes, was the world's largest transportation corporation.[99] In the power vacuum left in Huntington's wake, management was confused and drifted under new board chairman Charles H. Tweed and president Charles M. Hayes. Banking interests, particularly Speyer & Company of New York, which now held the former Stanford shares, grew in power within the company, pressing for a change in leadership and ownership. Desirous of liquidating their immense holdings when Henry E. Huntington failed in his quest for the Southern Pacific's presidency, Collis's heirs soon put much of their stock up for sale through Kuhn Loeb & Company in New York. By the spring of 1901, after complicated financial maneuvers with Kuhn Loeb, railroad empire-builder Edward H. Harriman, who already controlled the Union Pacific and the Illinois Central, owned nearly 50 percent of the Southern Pacific's stock, purchased through the Union Pacific, enough to secure firm power over the line's affairs. He soon had himself elected president. Harriman's motives were varied—increasing his influence in the Southwest, preventing rivals from acquiring the Southern Pacific, his passion for building the largest rail combination around the Southern Pacific and the companies he already controlled, and the simple challenge of improving the management and physical plant of railroads. Undoubtedly also important was fulfilling the Union Pacific's long-cherished ambition to possess for itself the Central Pacific's old connection from Ogden west to San Francisco Bay, thus gaining sole control of the entire transcontinental route.[100]

The interlude from 1901 to 1913, during which the Southern Pacific was controlled by the Union Pacific and the new Harriman Lines combination, has been fully analyzed by able railroad business historians Don Hofsommer, Lloyd Mercer, and Maury Klein, and it is not necessary to go into detail here.[101] The standard interpretation of the Harriman Lines' impact on the long-term development of the Southern Pacific is that E. H. Harriman's more modern business methods and huge capital resources produced a sort of coming of age of the Southern Pacific, a period of growth, standardization, and modernization of physical plant and management. Harriman had taken over the Union Pacific only in 1898, Klein observed, yet in a few years had "rebuilt the line, reorganized its management, reacquired its lost subsidiaries, and turned it into one of the most profitable properties in the nation. He did the same with the Southern Pacific . . . and worked the same formula on it." His "bold management" blazed the trail for "railroad success in the twentieth century."[102]

And so it was. Harriman insisted on more systemwide management, standardization of procedures and equipment, pooling of rolling stock, and efficiency in moving traffic and handling business matters through the Union–Southern Pacific. Most important, he quickly infused an unprecedented amount of capital into the Southern Pacific, particularly into its aged Central Pacific. Central Pacific routes and portions of other lines were double-tracked, curves straightened, grades reduced, and cutoffs built to shorten tracks and haul times. The famed Lucin Cutoff replaced the original rugged loop in northern Utah by crossing wide and deep salt flats, which railroads had never built on before, and by extending a long causeway-trestle across the Great Salt Lake. The Bay Shore Cutoff eased traffic into San Francisco from its peninsula to the south, and the Montalvo Cutoff shortened the Southern Pacific's Coast Route between San Francisco Bay and Los Angeles.[103] The Southern Pacific, particularly its Central Pacific portion, could now, like its Union Pacific connection to the east, carry more traffic, faster, at lower cost, and more profitably. Altogether, according to Harriman's early biographer, George Kennan, Harriman spent more than $240 million on the Southern Pacific system, including track improvements, additional lines, upgraded locomotives, cars, and steam vessels, and new buildings and real estate.[104] An important example of the cooperative ventures resulting from combining the resources of the Union and Southern Pacifics was the founding of their joint refrigerator-car subsidiary, Pacific Fruit Express. The largest refrigerator-car company, Pacific Fruit Express revolutionized, indeed made possible, the mass shipment of perishable fruits and vegetables and opened the door to new agricultural expansion in California and other western regions served by the Harriman Lines. Operated essentially as a subsidiary of the Southern Pacific, Pacific Fruit Express was headquartered at San Francisco and carried mostly the produce of the Southern Pacific's territories.[105] The period from 1901 to 1913 was certainly a time of consolidation, modernization, and upgrading of the Southern Pacific system, as Hofsommer and Klein have emphasized.

On the other hand, the partnership, if such it could be called, between the Southern Pacific and the Union Pacific was often a troubled one, and certainly more complicated than appears at first glance. In the first place, the Southern Pacific system was not in bad shape when Huntington departed. It had already made great strides in improving facilities, service, and management and was sounder financially than any western railroad, as attested to by rail leaders of the time such as Cornelius Vanderbilt, Chancey M. Depew, William Hood, and William Mahl.[106] Even the vaunted modernization program was not solely, or even particularly, a product of the Union Pacific/Harriman Lines' superior management. Track and service modernization on the Southern Pacific had proceeded apace in the late 1890s, as it had since the 1880s. The post-1901 improvements had been planned and engineered before 1901 by Huntington and chief engineer William Hood and awaited only the raising of capital and res-

Southern Pacific president E. H. Harriman brought west an entourage of sixty company executives and eastern railroad leaders riding in fifteen private rail cars to celebrate the opening of the famed Lucin Cutoff in November 1903. Cheyenne, Wyoming, photographer J. E. Stimson photographed the group. Straddling the right rail is Henry E. Huntington; left of him is the cutoff's planner and builder, head engineer William Hood; to his immediate left is operations chief Julius Kruttschnitt; and second to his left, carrying the coat, is Southern Pacific/Harriman Lines traffic manager J. C. Stubbs. Harriman shepherds his flock from the far right. Courtesy Huntington Library.

olution of the Central Pacific's complicated debt to the federal government. Huntington, indeed, took care of the Central Pacific's debt in 1899, the year before he died. Money for the rail line upgrades had been allocated and equipment purchased, and work on the improvements had already commenced between 1898 and 1900 but was suspended during the period of drift after Huntington's death. What Harriman did do in 1901, after Southern Pacific executives convinced him that the projects were important, was to make the decision to proceed and to provide the funds quickly to restart and speed to completion the Huntington management's already existing modernization plans. It was Hood, then, who directed the construction of improvements. Not only that, in the early 1900s, the Southern Pacific's more modern and efficient engineering specifications were transferred to the entire Harriman Lines system, and the Union Pacific's physical plant was also improved accordingly.[107]

As this suggests, old Southern Pacific executives were themselves important in establishing the new Harriman Lines management. Like Huntington before him, Harriman appreciated the talent of many Southern Pacific men, and in assembling a systemwide management for his rail enterprises, he immediately brought them into top leadership. Among the most important of these was J. C. Stubbs, who took over traffic management of the entire Union Pacific–Southern Pacific system. William Hood, who had started with the Central Pacific during the conquest of the High Sierra, was given charge of engineering and carried out the Southern Pacific track improvements and other Harriman Lines construction projects. William Mahl became comptroller, and eventually vice president, of the Harriman Lines. Julius Kruttschnitt, previously general manager of the Southern Pacific, became special assistant to Harriman and in 1904 chief operating officer of the entire Harriman system. William Sproule, another old Southern Pacific executive, assumed the presidency of the Southern Pacific Company in 1911, replacing Harriman, who had died in 1909. And there were others.[108] The leadership of Southern Pacific people in the formation of the Harriman Lines was true at lower levels as well. For example, the Southern Pacific's Passenger Department, with its flagship promotional monthly magazine, *Sunset,* and staff of editors and writers, provided the talent for the Harriman Lines' aggressive program to increase tourism and economic development in its entire western region.[109]

In most interpretations of Southern Pacific history, the Harriman Lines interlude usually emerges as a time when, under E. H. Harriman's business genius, a vibrant, modern, well-heeled Union Pacific breathed new life into a backward, bankrupt, moribund Southern Pacific. A more apt metaphor would be cross-fertilization. No matter how decrepit its tracks might have appeared to some, the Southern Pacific was not without important human and physical resources of its own. And not just the Southern Pacific benefited from the relationship. The Harriman Lines also gained greatly, and was itself transformed, from an infusion of Southern Pacific people, ideas, and traffic.

Nor did all the Harriman Lines' actions benefit the Southern Pacific. While the lavishing of money on Southern Pacific track and equipment modernization, around which all railroad men and community leaders were likely to rally, was easy for Harriman to facilitate, more substantial policies of business or political import and subtlety were another thing. As could be expected from two bitter corporate rivals of long standing, conflicts of corporate culture, philosophy, personality, and even region erupted when Harriman undertook to impose some Union Pacific/Harriman Lines policies and people on the Southern Pacific. With the exception of executives elevated to Harriman Lines management, the Southern Pacific's middle-level leadership, composed mostly of westerners, remained largely intact after 1901, with the company running much of its own day-to-day internal affairs from San Francisco. In a few cases, to take over some Southern Pacific departments and bring their policies into conformity with Union Pacific's, Harriman dispatched his own eastern people, who often lacked understanding of regional conditions and were condescending if not haughty toward business colleagues and local leaders they dismissed as provincial. Friction was heated, leading old Southern Pacific executives to close ranks to isolate the interlopers, thwart their efforts, and delay, if not defeat, policies that ran counter to Southern Pacific tradition. Sometimes this devolved merely into comic-opera office intrigues, but at other times it could make for corporate disaster.

Such was the case with land-grant policy. Almost immediately after taking over, influenced by his associate in the Union Pacific, William D. Cornish, Harriman sent Charles W. Eberlein from New York to San Francisco to assume charge of Southern Pacific land-grant administration and impose the Union Pacific's approach. Contrary to the Southern Pacific's policy since the founding of the Central Pacific, henceforth, land received from the federal government would no longer be quickly subdivided and sold to small-scale farmers, miners, and loggers to encourage long-term settlement, economic growth, and rail traffic. Instead, the company was instructed to hold its lands so the railroad itself could extract, process, and use or sell its natural resources, especially ores, oil, and lumber, or speculate on higher future prices and profits. Old-time Southern Pacific leaders, including land agent William H. Mills, corporate counsel William F. Herrin, and eventually even Harriman's now-close assistant Julius Kruttschnitt, warned that such a change ran counter to the long-term development needs of the lightly populated western hinterland, violated in some cases the legal requirements of the original congressional land-grant legislation, and would call down the wrath of press, farm, business, and governmental leaders in the West. Ignoring opposition from within and without the company, Eberlein persisted in his ham-handed efforts, causing Southern Pacific people to combine forces and ally themselves secretly to outside interests. They sabotaged Eberlein's authority, eventually sending him packing, and undid or at least ameliorated some of the new Harriman Lines land policies. The basic no-sale rule, however, continued in effect throughout the Harriman interlude, infuriating economic and political groups in California, Nevada, and especially Oregon. In 1907, the state of Oregon got the U.S. Department of the Interior and the attorney general to sue the Southern Pacific in federal court for violating the original 1860s act granting land to its predecessor Oregon & California Railroad. The law required that the land be sold to settlers. In the next decade, the courts and Congress confiscated the remaining portion of the land grant, more than two million acres. The Harriman Lines' loss of the Oregon & California land grant was the largest such defeat by a railroad in United States history.[110]

Finally, unfortunately for his vision of railroad consolidation, Harriman had chosen to assemble his empire during the early 1900s, when anti-monopoly public sentiment was intensifying nationwide. It was also one of those rare times when, under presidents Theodore Roosevelt, William Howard Taft, and Woodrow Wilson, the federal government took seriously its responsibility to enforce anti-trust laws and break up anti-consumer monopolies. In 1908, the U.S. Department of Justice filed suit to dismember the Harriman Lines under the Sherman Anti-Trust Act, passed by Congress in 1890. In 1912, the U.S. Supreme Court declared the Union Pacific's ownership of Southern Pacific stock to be an illegal restraint of trade and, in the middle of the next year, effected the separation of the hitherto competing Southern Pacific and Union Pacific systems. The Union Pacific was forced to sell its Southern Pacific stock.[111]

During the messy corporate divorce, the rivalry and distrust between the old Southern Pacific and Union Pacific managements bore its bitterest fruit. In the breakup, virtually all the old-time Southern Pacific men in Harriman Lines management were pressured, or themselves elected, to return to their former company. While the Southern Pacific was being spun off, the Union Pacific, as it had tried for decades, did its best to detach the Central Pacific and retain that strategic line for itself. As the corporate separation unfolded and Southern Pacific people discovered what the Union Pacific had in mind, despite their continuing positions of responsibility with their parent company, they became determined to keep the Central Pacific. This became especially vital when the U.S. Attorney General insisted as part of the settlement of the court case that the Southern Pacific sell its stock and give up its lease of the Central Pacific. Harriman Lines bosses initially forced the old-time Southern Pacific men to acquiesce in the loss of the Central Pacific, maintain public silence, and sign a damaging agreement relinquishing the lease, granting to the Union Pacific the right to buy the Central Pacific's stock, and conceding trackage rights for the Union/Central Pacific over Southern Pacific lines.[112]

Privately, the Southern Pacific men seethed. Severing the Central Pacific would cut out their railroad's traditional heartland in central and northern California, exclude it from most of San Francisco Bay, strand its Oregon system, and put it at a severe traffic disadvantage vis-à-vis the Union Pacific. The weakened, truncated railroad might not survive on its own.[113] First, in late 1912 and January and February 1913, they worked quietly within the Harriman Lines to get the Union Pacific to drop its proposal, or at least to modify the terms of its takeover of the Central Pacific along more favorable lines. When that failed, they became more aggressive. After privately debating among themselves how to proceed, Southern Pacific leaders concluded that the likelihood of keeping the Central Pacific was greater if they defeated the Union Pacific immediately, during the breakup. They could then take their chances later in the federal courts, while defending against the Justice Department's expected lawsuit.[114]

To stop the "mutilation" of their company, Southern Pacific men secretly encouraged and fed inside information to allied outside parties. They helped western newspapers, shippers' groups, and the state of California mount an effective campaign against the Union Pacific's scheme. Particularly, they enlisted the aid of the California State Railroad Commission, which had to approve several elements of the agreement. Convinced the transfer of the Central Pacific would hand the Union Pacific monopoly power over the state's transportation, the commission opposed and delayed the transfer of the Central Pacific until after the formal dissolution of the Harriman Lines.[115] After the Southern Pacific finally was freed from Union Pacific control in February 1913, and more especially after the Supreme Court's final order in the late spring, President William Sproule broke the silence and announced to the press that his company had agreed to give up the Central Pacific only "under duress" and that it would now resist the Union Pacific's threatened takeover. The Central Pacific, he announced, was "not for sale at any price." Moreover, he told an Oregon newspaper in September, the Southern Pacific had been "an unwilling partner" to the Harriman Lines merger in the first place and had always resented being controlled by Union Pacific outsiders.[116]

After the formal separation of the Union and Southern Pacific companies, the U.S. Attorney General retaliated by filing suit in early 1914 to force the Southern Pacific to sell its stock in the Central Pacific. The case dragged on through the early 1920s, with the company retaining control of the Central Pacific and the Union Pacific working behind the scenes to seize the line. Finally, in 1922, the Supreme Court ordered the lower court to strip the Southern Pacific Company of its subsidiary. Before the decision could be carried out, however, the Southern Pacific, under the Transportation Act of 1920, which in this instance superseded the Sherman Anti-Trust Act, applied to the Interstate Commerce Commission for permission to continue controlling the Central Pacific through stock ownership and lease. Chambers of Commerce, shippers' groups, and government agencies throughout Southern Pacific territory supported the petition. Despite the Union Pacific's campaign to block it, the ICC approved the application as "in the public interest," and federal courts accepted the decision.[117]

The Southern Pacific Reborn

Made whole, the Southern Pacific Company regrouped during the "unmerger" crisis and reestablished itself as a major, independent carrier in the Far West and Southwest. Initially in 1913, corporate headquarters remained in New York City, where it had moved during the Huntington presidency. Operations continued to be conducted from another office in San Francisco. In 1917, upon completion of a spacious building prominently placed at the gateway to downtown, across from the Ferry Building at the foot of Market Street, the Southern Pacific's headquarters returned to San Francisco, where it remained into the late 1990s.

Major additions to the Southern Pacific system continued to be made in the early twentieth century, during and after the period of Harriman Lines domination. The company first subsidized the San Diego & Arizona, then acquired the line in 1916 and completed it from San Diego east through rugged country to meet the Southern Pacific Railroad in the Imperial Valley, finally giving the company access to the port city of San Diego.[118] In 1907, the Southern Pacific jointly with the Santa Fe formed the Northwestern Pacific Railroad and by 1915 had pushed it from the Marin County ferry terminals across the Golden Gate from San Francisco, northward to California's northwest redwood coast ports.[119] In 1924, the Southern Pacific bought the strategic El Paso & Southwestern Railroad, which brought with it an important regional water system. The El Paso & Southwestern also connected the extreme southern Arizona and New Mexico mining districts to the Southern Pacific mainline at Deming and El Paso and on to Chicago via a Rock Island Railroad hookup at Santa Rosa in northern New Mexico.[120] The company also expanded its Mexican holdings. In 1909, it reincorporated the Sonora Railway, which ran south of Arizona, into the Southern Pacific de Mexico, and began extending its mainline south from Guaymas along the Gulf of California coast, and simultaneously northward from Guadalajara. Suspended for more than a decade during the Mexican Revolution, construction was finished in 1927.[121]

In the spring of 1915, a great world's fair, the Panama-Pacific Exposition, debuted in San Francisco. As part of its support for the city's rebuilding after the 1906 devastation by earthquake and fire, the Southern Pacific Company had made the largest private business financial and administrative contribution to the fair. The imposing Southern Pacific building, seventy feet in height, with soaring galleries, symbolized the company near its pinnacle of early twentieth-century reach, power, and diversity. Visitors entered through a tunneled section of a California redwood tree and filed past scenes depicting the best-known places within reach of the company's lines through eight states—Yosemite Valley, Lake Tahoe, Crater Lake, Mount Shasta, Santa Clara Valley orchards, the Monterey Peninsula, the Santa Barbara Mission, Catalina Island, Riverside County orange groves, Nevada's Truckee-Carson Reclamation Project, Arizona's Roosevelt Dam and cliff dwellings, San Antonio's Alamo, and a Louisiana plantation on Bayou Teche. Inside the galleries, to re-create the atmospheres of its many hinterlands, the railroad mounted displays of cities, landscapes, soils, trees,

Southern Pacific Company building at the Panama-Pacific Exposition, San Francisco, 1915. Author's collection.

and the produce of farms, mines, factories, and lumber mills. The Sunset The-
ater, seating 350, featured round-the-clock slide lectures on the resources of California, Oregon, Nevada, Utah, Arizona, New Mexico, Texas, and Louisiana.
On opening day, at least, all appeared forgiven. Eight thousand Southern Pacific
employees attending the building's dedication on March 10 cheered welcom-
ing speeches thanking the railroad for its support by anti–Southern Pacific mayor
James D. Phelan and a representative of anti–Southern Pacific governor Hiram
Johnson. The Big Four, as well as E. H. Harriman, were honored for their roles
in building the West, and executives of the Southern Pacific and the Union
Pacific sat together on the stage.[122]

Only a few years free from its Harriman Lines bondage, the Southern Pacific
Company's transportation network remained the largest in the world. Its Pacific
System alone consolidated an astounding 160 separate predecessor companies
under one management by 1916, with dozens more in the Atlantic System.[123]
Upwards of fifteen thousand miles of steam railways crisscrossing eight states
and Mexico, in addition to untold numbers of ferries, streetcar and electric interurban lines, buses, international steamship routes, and more, traversed landscapes that ranged from cities to farms, from rain forest to desert, from below-
sea-level sinks to many-thousand-foot mountain passes, from the Pacific to
the Atlantic. Much Southern Pacific trackage had opened up thinly settled,

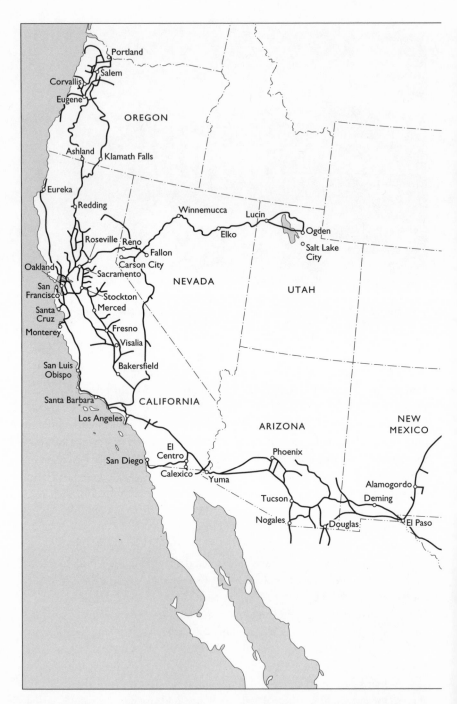

The Southern Pacific Company's rail system, 1924. Adapted from Southern Pacific Company, *Forty-First Annual Report of the Southern Pacific Company and Proprietary Companies . . . , 1924* (1924). Courtesy California State Railroad Museum, Sacramento.

undeveloped land, some of it virtually unpopulated. The trains brought people, farms, towns, factories, resorts, parks, and universities. Not just the incidental fact of its construction, but also the railroad's purposeful actions shaped land use and tenure, agriculture, irrigation, produce-marketing, resource conservation, and the preservation of natural landscapes. Nary a square mile escaped the railroad's influence. The transformation wrought by the Southern Pacific over its territory is one of the great untold stories in the history of the American West.

2 Men of Vision

SOUTHERN PACIFIC LEADERS, LAND, AGRICULTURE, AND THE DEVELOPMENT OF CALIFORNIA AND THE WEST

From Euphoria to Disillusionment

As the Central Pacific approached completion of the first transcontinental line to the East in the 1860s, most westerners celebrated the railroad as their link with destiny. "Over slumbering California is stealing the dawn of a radiant future," exulted Mark Twain in his farewell lecture in the state in 1866. "The Pacific Railroad is creeping across the continent, the commerce of the world is about to be revolutionized. California is the crown princess of the new dispensation. . . . This sparsely populated land shall become a crowded hive of busy men: your waste places shall blossom like a rose, and your deserted hills and valleys shall yield bread and wine for unnumbered thousands."[1]

The driving of the golden spike in 1869 punctured such naive hopes. Instead of bringing new immigration, markets, and prosperity, the iron rails at first ushered in an era of new eastern competition, inter-regional rivalry, unemployment, and depression, especially in already settled places like California. Instead of social, cultural, and political maturity, the railroad appeared to many people to create only transportation monopoly, industrial strife, uncertain regional fortunes, and political corruption.[2] By 1868, the Big Four had also gained control of the Southern Pacific Railroad. Quickly, they built it into a second, southern, transcontinental line from California to Atlantic tidewater and absorbed most other rail and water competitors within their territories from Oregon south and east to New Orleans. In 1884, the associates created the powerful Southern Pacific Company to consolidate their far-flung rail properties. As elsewhere in the nation, many Californians heaped their troubles, particularly the slowness with which agriculture developed, on the railroad giant. For the rest of the century, that state's and other western regions' political leaders, journalists, and pamphleteers used the growing anti-railroad sentiment to build popular support until by 1900 opposition to the Southern Pacific had become the stock-in-trade of politicians of every stripe, from Socialist to Populist to Republican.[3]

One particularly strident theme of anti–Southern Pacific rhetoric was the charge that monopoly control in its territory freed the company to engage in practices that deterred land development and agricultural growth. The railroad, its critics complained, speculated in its congressional land grant by refusing to sell fertile land to await higher prices, charged outrageously high prices on what the company did sell, and favored sales to large speculators rather than actual farmers. Indeed, it was charged, the Southern Pacific adopted many policies that discouraged small-farm settlement, especially ruinously high freight rates on agricultural produce, thus furthering the trend in the West toward large-scale corporate agriculture. Throughout its territory, denunciation of the railroad's land and agricultural policies was rife in pamphlets, editorials, and campaign speeches and even became enshrined in literature, notably novels, plays, and poems attacking the railroad's treatment of San Joaquin Valley settlers in the 1880 Mussel Slough tragedy, an incident that for many came to symbolize the irreconcilable conflict between the Southern Pacific's policies and the public interest. In the most famous of these works, Frank Norris's classic novel *The Octopus* (1901), the leading character captured the widespread antipathy toward the Southern Pacific felt by many turn-of-the-century westerners when he envisioned the railroad as a

> galloping monster, the terror of steel and steam, with its single eye, Cyclopean, red, shooting from horizon to horizon . . . the symbol of a vast power, huge, terrible, flinging the echo of its thunder over all the reaches of the valley, leaving blood and destruction in its path; the leviathan, with tentacles of steel clutching into the soil, the soulless Force, the iron-hearted Power, the monster, the Colossus, the Octopus.[4]

Historians have generally sided with the Southern Pacific's nineteenth-century critics. Sympathizing with the West's troubled citizens, even some recent scholarly works continue to maintain that the Southern Pacific's land and agricultural policies were a major, if not *the* major, deterrent to small-farm settlement in California and other regions.[5] By deliberately appropriating the profits of farms and businesses and thus discouraging settlement, the railroad was also the principal retarding force in its territory's economic development before 1900, a diabolical force arrayed against the agricultural and commercial interests, the major sponsor of graft, and the primary obstacle to governmental adaptation and reform, notably in California. Only after "the people" of California mounted a series of anti-railroad political campaigns, so the story goes, did the Progressives capture control of state government in 1910, enact effective railroad regulatory laws, and finally free the state to follow its destined course toward social and economic greatness. Similar movements in Nevada and Texas, historians have maintained, attacked railroad abuses in those states.[6]

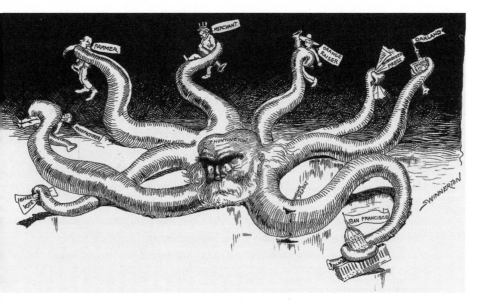

A typical cartoon by Swinnerton in the *San Francisco Examiner,* 1896, depicted Southern Pacific Company president Collis P. Huntington as an octopus, squeezing the life out of California interests. The railroad and Huntington were favorite targets of discontented groups from the 1860s through the early 1900s. Courtesy California State Library, Sacramento.

Unfortunately, however, although the company did on occasion abuse its economic and political power, the traditional framework for interpreting the Southern Pacific has focused on questions that no longer yield new insight. By dutifully, and often accurately, reciting the depredations of the Big Four, historians have oversimplified, de-emphasized, or completely ignored the complex role played by the Southern Pacific, for generations its territory's largest economic institution, in the process of growth and change that revolutionized California and the West from the 1860s into the early twentieth century.[7] The multifold agricultural and land promotional activities of the Southern Pacific and its officials demonstrate that, contrary to the traditional interpretation, the railroad linked its own interest with the welfare of its territory. In response to expansion and change within itself and the national industry, the corporation was evolving an extensive, specialized organization, whose middle-level managers—generally overlooked by historians who have emphasized the more spectacular careers of the Big Four, E. H. Harriman, and other visible top executives—were developing expertise and responsibility for fostering development. As a result, the company often used its power consciously to strengthen and diversify its region's economy, to organize and stabilize its chaotic society, and to further the welfare of its residents, particularly farmers.

The Corporate and the Public Interest

Despite the irreconcilable conflict traditionally assumed to have existed between the railroad and the public good, many lines of self-interest bound the Southern Pacific to the welfare of its region. As corporate leaders clearly understood, successful railroad operations hinged on general social and economic progress. Freight and passenger traffic, by far the major source of the railroad's income, was of course directly related to regional population and productivity, as was the sale value of railroad lands. In addition, the railroad's extensive land grant, scattered throughout California's Central Valley and Sierra Nevada foothills, Oregon's valleys and forested mountains, and Great Basin and Southwest deserts, could only be converted into capital if there were farmers willing to buy and cultivate the lands and investors willing to advance funds to the company on faith in the railroad's ability to dispose of lands profitably. Financing the building and expansion of the Central and Southern Pacific lines, a constant concern to Collis P. Huntington and other associates, also depended, the railroad's leaders knew, on traffic revenues, land-grant sales, and general economic development in the company's territory, which would derive primarily from agricultural development.[8]

Because its profitability relied on the progress of its region, the railroad, just as other businesses and economic interests in the late nineteenth century, was profoundly affected by the arrested development of its territory. The prime example was California, where the most valuable company interests were located. Caught in the breach between a rapidly declining mining industry and slowly emerging agriculture and other enterprises, California in the period from 1869 into the early 1900s suffered chronic depression, broken up by sudden speculative flurries and collapses in mining stocks or real estate prices. Despite many real gains, the state's instability signified an unbalanced, immature economy, booming or busting according to the market at a given time for a few commodities: mining stocks, land, or grain. Although more diversified agriculture had been developing sporadically since the 1850s, peculiar conditions in California continued to retard growth: land and water monopoly, the large capital requirements for beginning and operating farms, confusing and contradictory water laws, a lag in the development of irrigation technology and agencies, damaging crop pests and weather disasters, a continuing overdependence on mining and livestock and cereal agriculture, an imbalance in political power favoring the mining regions and San Francisco, and the formidable market disadvantages of distance and poor organization.

These economic problems, along with the state's tenacious reputation for violence and shortage of opportunity, reinforced the natural preference of migrating Americans and Europeans for readily accessible and more easily farmed states in the Middle West and Great Plains and stifled California's population growth. After an initial gold-rush spurt through 1852, population grew slowly by western standards, from 390,000 in 1860 to 560,000 in 1870 and to only 1,485,000 in 1900, with high outmigration rates during most of those years and with much new population resulting from natural increase. Overall, from the mid-1850s to 1900, California was one of the slowest-growing regions in the West. As a result, in 1900, California remained about twentieth in rank of state population, just as it had been in 1860, at the same time that other areas of the Middle and Far West were making spectacular gains. Similar problems stunted the population growth of other Southern Pacific regions. Central and western Texas, Nevada, and southern Arizona and New Mexico, which like California had gotten their starts as mining or open-range cattle-producing regions, remained lightly inhabited into the early twentieth century, some areas actually losing population.[9]

California's economic retardation, like that of the rest of Southern Pacific territory, impinged directly on the company's business. Frequent depressions, crop failures, and slowdowns in migration were a constant vexation to railway officials. The prolonged depression from the mid-1870s to the early 1880s, for example, shrank land-sales revenues for the Central Pacific Railroad from $1,203,870 in 1877 to $201,716 in 1879 and for the Southern Pacific Railroad from $365,811 to $68,153 during the same period. Meanwhile, through-passenger traffic on the Central Pacific's transcontinental line between California and the East tumbled from 105,341 travelers in 1875 to 62,056 in 1879 and failed to regain pre-depression form until 1883. The depression also bred unemployment, social disorder, and anti–Southern Pacific sentiment, which culminated in a new, decidedly anti-railroad California constitution and the establishment of a state railroad regulatory commission in 1879.[10] Similarly, another long depression in California during the 1890s decreased company traffic revenues and land sales and increased the rate of default on land-grant purchase contracts. During the decade preceding 1898, the amount of acreage its time-payment buyers annually abandoned and relinquished to the railroad soared from 1,351 to 207,927 for the Central Pacific and from 4,869 to 118,682 for the Southern Pacific, greatly complicating the already difficult task of disposing of the land grant. In the same period, depressed conditions in agriculture and industry strengthened Californians' tendency to make the Southern Pacific the scapegoat for the state's problems and spawned more anti-corporate and anti-railroad outbreaks among farmers, laborers, and businessmen, setting the stage for the Progressive movement of the early 1900s.[11]

Impulses from within the railroad industry also led the Southern Pacific to identify with development in its territory. Historians James Hedges, Paul Gates, Richard Overton, and others have shown that during the last half of the nineteenth century western land-grant railroads, out of self-interest, evolved many programs to advertise their territories, promote compact settlement by small farmers, and encourage agricultural diversity and stability. By the 1880s, railway land, advertising, and agricultural departments, through extensive interchange of personnel and wide reporting of effective policies in publications such as *Poor's Manual,* had become largely professionalized and standardized. The Southern Pacific, then, in sponsoring growth in its territory, was applying welltested principles of railroading. Rivalry among the land-grant roads likewise spurred the Southern Pacific to greater promotional efforts. Especially in the decade of the 1880s, western railroads raced to expand and consolidate their domains by redoubling efforts to settle land with small-scale farmers and to attract domestic and foreign immigrants to their regions. Well aware that success would swell profits while failure meant possible receivership, Southern Pacific executives increasingly devoted the resources of the railroad to developing its territory's potential, especially for agricultural growth.[12]

These officials were not strangers to regional development activities. To design and manage the advertising and farm-improvement programs of their lines, the Big Four chose longtime residents of the company's territories. The careers of these officials before, during, and after their work for the railroad, in government, journalism, agriculture, science, and general civic improvement, demonstrate that they were people who identified with social and economic progress in their communities and regions and who viewed railroad employment as another dimension of that larger task. Before his appointment as the company's first chief land agent in the mid-1860s, for example, Benjamin B. Redding had dabbled in mining, journalism, and law and had been elected California's secretary of state. While land agent, Redding also became a leading authority and writer on climate, agriculture, and natural science, a state fisheries commissioner, a regent of the University of California, and an organizer and patron of the California Academy of Sciences in San Francisco.[13] William H. Mills, who directed Southern Pacific land and advertising programs from Redding's death in 1882 until his own demise in 1907, edited the *Sacramento Record* through 1875 and its successor, the *Sacramento Record-Union,* beginning in 1875, co-owning those newspapers with the railroad. After his appointment as land agent, Mills continued to manage and write editorials for the *Record-Union* until 1903.[14] Mills was also a leader of prison reform and temperance organizations and the movement to end the scourge of hydraulic mining debris. Before and after becoming the railroad's land agent, Mills was also an active member of the California state Yosemite park commission and an organizer of various conservation, irrigation, and agricultural reform movements.[15] Similar career patterns characterized other officials,[16] such as Jerome Madden, longtime land agent of the Southern Pacific Railroad, Isaac N. Hoag, immigration commissioner in the 1880s, Charles B. Turrill, exposition manager in the 1880s and 1890s, James Horsburgh, Jr., director of advertising and settlement-promotion programs for the Passenger Department in the 1890s and early 1900s, and B. A. McAllaster, who replaced Mills as chief land agent in 1908 and served until 1933.

Promoting Agriculture

Realizing that its region's prosperity was in the company's self-interest, Southern Pacific officials from the 1860s to the 1920s aimed a broad range of activities at quickening development, particularly in agriculture. Indeed, their promotional "philosophy" was indistinguishable from that of other business, agricultural, and governmental leaders, who in states like California were formulating programs to solve social and economic problems by encouraging the subdivision of large estates into small farms, advocating modernization and specialization in farming, modifying laws to favor agricultural growth, pressuring for public development of irrigation facilities, and advertising regional resources in order to stimulate migration and farm settlement. While these leaders were institutionalizing their programs in government agencies, trade organizations, chambers of commerce, agricultural and horticultural societies, and more specialized immigration and irrigation promotion groups, Southern Pacific officials worked primarily within the company's own organizational structure to achieve the same goals.[17]

Convinced that the railroad's future depended on the replacement of mining and open-range livestock raising with diversified farming as the basis for economic development, Southern Pacific officials particularly focused their promotion and development programs on agricultural change. As early as 1863, California governor Leland Stanford, also president of the newborn Central Pacific Railroad, opened the campaign by addressing the State Agricultural Society with a proposal that Californians remedy their state's slack population growth by fostering easier transportation, developing agricultural resources, and spreading "out before the farming communities of the other states authentic information, in the shape of reliable statistics, as to the productions of our soil, and the noble field that is here offered for the industrious and energetic farmer."[18] Other executives, including Huntington and especially those in charge of the railroad's promotion programs, amplified Stanford's early support of agriculture. Land agent Benjamin B. Redding also contributed many writings on agricultural topics, including irrigation, citrus and olive culture, wheat production, and climate. Isaac N. Hoag, a longtime booster of agriculture as secretary of the California State Agricultural Society, early pioneer of silk culture, and agricultural editor of several San Francisco and Sacramento newspapers in the 1860s and 1870s, continued to publicize the need to revolutionize California farming after his appointment as immigration commissioner for the Central Pacific and associated lines in 1883 by traveling throughout the state, addressing local business and agricultural organizations, and writing articles for local newspapers. The railroad's development officials in other regions also aggressively promoted agriculture. Headquartered in Reno, Robert L. Fulton, land agent for Nevada and Utah, sponsored numerous private and public farming, land subdivision, and irrigation projects from the 1870s through the early 1900s. The *Reno Gazette,* owned and edited by Fulton during some of the time he served the railroad, took the lead in efforts to convert Nevada from a mining into an agricultural state. Daniel K. Zumwalt, the railroad's land agent for the San Joaquin Valley between 1869 and 1893, was an agricultural and irrigation promoter and civic leader in Visalia and Tulare County. Beginning in the 1890s, Epes Randolph and other Southern Pacific managers in Arizona also worked for agricultural and irrigation improvement, particularly by developing cooperative research programs between the railroad and the University of Arizona's College of Agriculture. Company leaders in Oregon and Texas followed suit.[19]

Undoubtedly the most influential expositor of the pro-agricultural ideas of the Southern Pacific was William H. Mills, chief land agent from 1883 to 1907, the time when the railroad's major agriculture, land, and resources policies took shape. In widely reported speeches and writings, Mills attacked mining—the earliest industry in California, Nevada, and southern Arizona—for causing economic instability, social disorder, and sluggish population growth. He appealed instead for efforts to expand farming in California and other far western and southwestern regions. "The pioneer population of any country gives direction, color, and character to its growth," he told the California State Agricultural Society in 1890. "We are by no means emancipated from the influences of our earliest environment. The speculative is at war with methodical and plodding industry." Two years later, Mills warned that mining was an industry whose production was not capable of renewal from year to year. "The very prosecution of the industry is itself a process of impoverishment," he noted, and since "countries prolific of precious metals are proverbially poor," true progress could ultimately be built only on an agricultural base. In the "fertility of our soils, and the expanded possibilities of our own climate," the region would find "hopeful direction of permanent greatness."[20]

Like other railroad leaders, Mills was unsatisfied with general farming or the growing of cereal crops, since these approaches did not take full advantage of rare agricultural potentials, particularly in semi-tropical California. California's diverse climates, which duplicated those of many different agricultural regions of the world, made the state ideal for high-value specialty crops. The im-

Two important Land Department executives guided Southern Pacific land, agriculture, water, and resource policy from the 1860s into the early 1900s. Benjamin B. Redding served from 1865 to 1882, and William H. Mills from 1883 to 1907. Redding portrait, author's collection; Mills portrait from *San Francisco: Its Builders Past and Present* (Chicago: S.J. Clarke, 1913). Courtesy California Historical Society, San Francisco.

provement of railroad lines enhanced this potential by connecting producing districts to distant urban markets. Mills repeatedly pointed out that, as railroad building caused freight rates to decline between California and the population centers of eastern America, distinct agricultural subregions, with their markets rapidly expanding, would be free to specialize even more in the crops for which they were suited. The great variety among the state's local growing regions would ensure a diversity of specialty crops and a corresponding economic stability. Fruit production, then in its infancy, would provide the most important specialization. Such a system, Mills predicted, would produce higher farm profits, more developed rural areas, increased land values, and greater population density, as well as multiplier benefits to towns and cities servicing agriculture. From the 1870s until his death in 1907, Mills welcomed the evolution of horticulture and specialty-crop agriculture in southern California and urged the northern and central sections of the state and other parts of the railroad's territory to adopt this farming model. In the late nineteenth and early twentieth centuries, Mills and other Southern Pacific leaders promoted fruit production and other specialty-crop industries in California, as well as Oregon, western Nevada, southern Arizona, and the Gulf Coast of Texas.[21]

Reflecting the conclusions of other land-grant railroads, Mills, along with other Southern Pacific officials, understood that commercialized specialty-crop agriculture would enrich the corporation as well as its territory's citizens. Even Collis P. Huntington, target then as now of some of the most vehement attacks by critics of the Southern Pacific, agreed that one of the surest ways to increase rail traffic was to refine agricultural techniques. Frequently, as in a detailed letter to Mills in 1894, Huntington called attention to foreign crops that might be introduced with profit into California.[22] His annual reports in the 1890s, after he had replaced Stanford as president of the Southern Pacific Company, also reflected Huntington's awareness that the railroad's destiny was linked directly to the success of farmers. The reports of 1891 through 1896, for instance, analyzed the impact of low wheat prices and other California economic troubles on the declining profits of the company but rejoiced that progress in irrigation, the subdivision of large tracts into small farms, and the development of horticulture foretold better days to come. "The many advantages of climate and soil which the State of California offers to settlers are becoming better known each year," he observed in 1892, "and as the large tracts of land are cut up and new sections are opened up by the railroads, there will be a steady increase in the population and material wealth of that State, and in which this company will receive its share in the improvement of its earnings."[23] After the Big Four and their families lost control of the Southern Pacific in 1901, the company's new leaders continued to relate the railroad's well-being to agricultural development. In 1911, passenger agent James Horsburgh, Jr., who had succeeded Mills as the railroad's chief booster, told the Counties Convention of the California Development Board, ancestor of the California State Chamber of Commerce, that "California's broad and fertile acres represent her most important and inexhaustible resource." The building of a legion of "well-tilled little farms" would bring "better markets for our products, more products for our markets, and greater prosperity for all."[24]

The agricultural ideas of Southern Pacific leaders were not mere public relations ploys to silence the railroad's critics. Public statements became embodied in company actions to aid farmers, first in California where those programs emerged, and then in the railroad's other regions. In addition to speaking and writing on behalf of agricultural change, the company's promoters also worked to solve internal regional problems inhibiting change. The railroad, for example, began in the 1870s to assist movements to organize California's farmers and rural regions. The Southern Pacific provided powerful and possibly decisive support in the 1870s and early 1880s for the movement in the Sacramento Valley to halt hydraulic mining, which for more than two decades had been dumping millions of cubic yards of debris (gravel, sand, and silt) into the valley's river system, filling streambeds, unleashing catastrophic floods, and destroying farmland and towns. William H. Mills used the railroad's *Sacramento Record-Union* to rally support for the valley's farmers, and he took the lead in calling for the founding of a statewide Anti-Debris Association. I. N. Hoag, agricultural editor of the newspaper, served as secretary of the Anti-Debris Association until his appointment in 1883 as the railroad's immigration commissioner. It was the organizing of the valley's farmers and townspeople and the instituting of lawsuits against the miners that resulted in a revolutionary 1884 federal court decision prohibiting further dumping of hydraulic mining wastes, a landmark in the early American conservation movement.[25]

As did other Southern Pacific leaders, Mills, through the *Record-Union* and later as company land agent, also supported the founding of local granges and other farm organizations to solve problems of overproduction and marketing. When farm marketing cooperatives finally emerged in the 1880s and 1890s, the railroad assisted them by encouraging growers to join and helping them attend meetings, improving refrigeration technology, devising icing and fruit express systems, and sponsoring advertising campaigns in conjunction with crop cooperatives to expand and manage markets for California and western fruit.[26]

In addition to creating potentials for specialty-crop agriculture, environmental differences between arid western regions and the settled areas of the East raised obstacles to agricultural development. Since previous experience with eastern conditions proved to be a poor model for cultivating the West, farm success required new, reliable knowledge of the region's peculiar climates, soils, pests, and crop possibilities.[27] With the structure, capital, and will to accomplish such a task, the Southern Pacific collected and disseminated vital agricultural information. In the absence of alternatives, the railroad itself established some of the earliest systems for gathering data, such as about prevailing temperatures, wind, precipitation, topography and geology, water resources, soil characteristics, and farm commodity prices. The company tabulated the information, used it in rail operations, and furnished it at no charge to private producers, government research agencies, and newspapers and farm journals. In that way and others, the Southern Pacific became one of the leading patrons of scientific farming in the West, as well as of advanced agricultural research and education. In California, Arizona, Nevada, Oregon, and Texas, the railroad played major roles in the founding and operation of public agricultural colleges, contributing critical financial and political assistance to these fledgling, often beleaguered institutions. As new information and techniques accumulated, the railroad publicized them through promotional pamphlets and other publications, including the Passenger Department's monthly magazine, *Sunset*.[28] Beginning with a demonstration train the railroad helped organize in Texas during the early 1900s to teach cotton farmers how to cope with the boll weevil, the Southern Pacific supported the extension education efforts of agricultural colleges in its states and territories.[29]

Land Settlement

Perhaps the most influential part of the Southern Pacific's development program was converting the railroad's land grant into productive farms and attracting more people to cultivate and consume their crops. Southern Pacific leaders' ideas about land and its social and economic importance reflected their commitment to agricultural development and illustrated the congruence between the railroad's business interests and those of other groups promoting western development. The company's granted land with agricultural potential was concentrated in California, primarily its Central Valley and southeastern deserts. There was also arable railroad land in Oregon's Willamette River Valley and in eastern Nevada near the Truckee and Carson rivers. Because of unique state railroad land-grant policies, lands the Southern Pacific inherited from its predecessor lines in Texas were dispersed throughout central and western parts of the state, often remote from the company's own lines. Contrary to the common charge made by the railroad's contemporary and scholarly critics that the company was a deliberate land monopolist, refusing to sell in expectation of increased future values, the Southern Pacific, as did other land-grant roads, disposed of its lands as quickly as possible to buyers of small farms, a task that required heroic expenditures of energy and money. As was true of its agricultural promotion, the railroad's efforts to boost land sales and immigration, formulated in California and spread from there to other parts of Southern Pacific territory, were rooted in enlightened self-interest. Land pamphlets and the reports of land officials repeatedly announced that the policy of the company

> is and has always been, to sell its lands at low prices, and upon easy terms of payment. Its Directors believe its best interests are promoted by selling its lands near the line of the road to men who will personally cultivate the soil, and who will own the land they cultivate. By this means an industrious, agricultural population is invited, whose improvements and the product of whose labor, tend to enhance the value of the unsold lands.

As Collis P. Huntington put it somewhat differently in a private letter in 1892, "What we get by the sale of the lands is not the object; but it is that we may have a title to convey to others, so that they can put on the necessary improvements and cultivate the same so as to give the railroad something to transport, which is of course what it wants."[30]

To some extent, rapid sale of the land grant also grew logically from the railroad's sponsorship of agricultural change. The most direct way for the Southern Pacific to stimulate the spread of agriculture through its territory, delivering many benefits to the railroad, was to convert its own acres into productive farms. Political considerations also shaped land policy. By the mid-1870s, agitation by squatters on railroad lands and a nationwide revulsion against the lavishness of the original grants to all the land-grant lines caused bills to be introduced into Congress to confiscate unsold western railroad lands. Accommodation of settlers desiring land and the rapid and orderly disposal of the land grant, company officials believed, would also mollify the growing adverse public opinion toward the Southern Pacific and its land grant and protect the company's ability to profit from the lands. Periodically, railway officials, in thwarting attempts to rescind the grant, pointed to voluminous land sales as visible proof that the road was providing a valuable public service by subdividing its lands.[31] Such arguments proved successful. In 1884, for instance, a bill in Congress to force the Central Pacific to forfeit the land of the California & Oregon Railroad, now one of its subsidiaries, was widely opposed by California newspapers. For all its faults, many editors grudgingly admitted, the Central Pacific would probably develop the lands more rapidly than other owners, particularly the federal government.[32] Thus, out of many considerations, the company instituted an aggressive land-development and sales program under the Big Four's management in California during the 1860s, and it continued, with an interruption during the Harriman era, into the 1930s.[33]

In addition to having their own economic and political reasons for promoting rapid settlement of railroad lands, Southern Pacific officials also operated within the context of Jeffersonian "agrarian" social ideas popular in the late nineteenth century among boosters of California and the West, and with many other Americans as well. Railroad promoters viewed land and its intensive cultivation by small-scale farmers as the basis of both wealth and social order. Not only would the expansion of farms cure the West's economic ills and fatten railroad coffers but it would also stabilize society, a development from which the company also stood to gain. Land agent Redding, in an 1881 address on the necessity of promoting agricultural immigration to California, observed that the way to enhance social progress in the state was to

fasten men, by ownership, to the land they cultivated. This ownership converts the "tramp" into an industrious citizen; the agrarian and communist into conservative and law abiding members of our society; and the indifferent and thriftless into habits of prudence and economy. Every man who goes on the public land to make a home, not only adds to the wealth of the nation, and to the permanence and security of civilized society, but he becomes an additional surety for the enactment of just laws, for honesty and economy in public expenditures and for perpetuity of good government.[34]

Though they were urban businessmen, Southern Pacific executives and promoters in the Land and Passenger departments echoed Redding's agrarian sentiments into the early decades of the twentieth century. In 1911, for example, the Passenger Department's James Horsburgh, Jr., challenged a convention of the California Development Board with a call for greater cooperation between booster groups and the railroad in order to double the state's rural "yeoman" population by subdividing the remaining large, mechanized farms. Large-scale farm operations brought relatively small returns per acre and contributed little to social and cultural development, Horsburgh warned: "While the introduction of improved mechanical appliances has beneficently resulted in an extension of activities and a multiplication of opportunities, no one but the builders of machinery would regret to see every combined harvester and steam gang-plow superseded by a hundred well-tilled little farms."[35]

The Southern Pacific's commitment to solving social and economic problems in its region led some railroad officials to more radical positions about land than might be expected from Gilded Age business leaders. In the 1850s, the Big Four had emerged as public figures in Sacramento as founders of the California Republican Party, and they shared the Republican adherence to the "Homestead Principle," which posited that public lands in the West should be used to encourage small-farm settlement. When he ran unsuccessfully for governor in 1859, and again when he was elected in 1861, Leland Stanford campaigned on a platform calling for a national homestead law, which would grant free small farms to actual settlers, and in general for a public-land distribution system that would keep land away from speculators and get it into the hands of small-scale farmers. As governor, while also in his early years as president of the Central Pacific Railroad, Stanford agitated on behalf of settlers' rights to public lands. As one of its first orders of business, despite being absorbed in the Civil War emergency, the 1862 Republican Congress, with support from newly elected California Republicans, did pass the famous Homestead Act, granting free 160-acre tracts to actual settlers. Later, Stanford, after reading *Progress and Poverty* in 1880, reputedly declared himself to be a "disciple" of Henry George's "single tax" method of breaking down land monopolies. As U.S. senator from California from 1884 to his death in 1893, Stanford pushed other populist public land reform measures in Congress, including his 1890 bill, supported enthusiastically by California newspapers and mass public meetings, for low-interest federal mortgage loans to small farmers. Other early Southern Pacific leaders, such as Collis P. Huntington and land agent B. B. Redding, also advanced proposals to withhold public land from speculation and to reserve it, at least the arable portions, for distribution only in parcels under 160 acres.[36]

William H. Mills, who designed and managed the Southern Pacific's land and agricultural programs for a quarter-century, was foremost among Southern Pacific leaders in working for public land reform. In essays and public addresses from the 1870s into the early 1900s, he denounced land monopoly as California and the West's most debilitating social illness and advocated cures that echoed Henry George and other reformers. In 1873, as editor of the railroad-owned *Sacramento Record*, he compiled and published a statistical attack on land monopoly in the state that, building on Henry George's publication of his 1871 pamphlet, *Our Land and Land Policy*, ignited a vigorous public debate.[37] Beginning in 1875 and through the 1890s, Mills's *Sacramento Record-Union* led California newspapers in condemning monopoly land ownership and championing voluntary and forced subdivision of large estates.[38]

Mills's most vigorous and comprehensive statement was a speech before San Francisco's Chit-Chat Club in December 1891, ultimately published as the pamphlet *California Land Holdings* (1892) and widely reprinted and applauded by California newspapers. Mills drew on the census returns from four Sacramento Valley counties where growing concentration of land ownership in a few huge "bonanza" wheat ranches during the 1880s had stagnated or decreased the population. Large landholdings, he charged, retarded economic growth, kept rural areas thinly settled and undeveloped, degraded common people, drove young people from the farms, increased growers' reliance on unskilled "tramp" and Chinese labor, exacerbated class divisions and social disorder, crowded cities with unemployed people, and in other ways jeopardized a free society and government. In proposing methods to control land monopoly, Mills advanced beyond the views of other California promoters, who generally were satisfied with exhorting landowners to subdivide their property. When society was endangered, Mills held, it had the right to defend itself by governmental action to protect the public welfare, which was in his view superior to the rights of private property. Mills called on the California legislature to prohibit the mortgaging of land as security for loans, to make illegal the accumulation of land by mortgage foreclosure, and to restrict land ownership to the amount that could be cultivated by one family. This could be accomplished, he believed, by prohibiting the conveyance of more than 1,000 acres to any individual in a will. Excess lands should be sold for the estate at an auction supervised by the courts to ensure subdivision into small parcels.[39] Ironically, the most vigorous objection to Mills's anti-monopoly crusade was raised by the small-farm-dominated California State Grange, which was dead set against any legal limits on farmers' ability to engross acreage. In 1879, for example, the organization's state weekly, *The California Patron*, condemned a recent

Artist W. H. Bull's advertising poster for the Southern Pacific's "Sunset Limited" train, ca. 1900. Author's collection.

Record-Union call for laws limiting farm holdings to 160 acres. The *Patron* accused Mills's newspaper of being an "agrarian howler" working in the service of "communism."[40]

Enlightened self-interest, the railroad's identification with its hinterland's advancement, and acceptance by company leaders of conventional social theory,

all prompted the Southern Pacific in its land, agricultural, and promotional activities to encourage the development of densely settled rural communities of
small farmers. Booster literature sponsored by the railroad, ranging from subsidized writings such as Charles Nordhoff's popular works to official company
pamphlets and magazines, stressed the value of cooperative colonies in overcoming social and economic impediments to agricultural advancement and
called attention to successful examples at Anaheim southeast of Los Angeles
and Fresno in the San Joaquin Valley. The *Sacramento Record-Union,* both before and after editor Mills became the company's land agent in early 1883, advocated agricultural colonies in the valleys of northern California, arguing that
only by following the lead of pioneers to the south could the northerners keep
in step with agricultural change. Other Southern Pacific officials, especially Redding, Hoag, and colonization agent Bernhard Marks, as well as the railroad's
land-grant advertising publications, repeatedly exhorted farm settlers to pool
their resources to form colonies. Increasingly, the Southern Pacific's own land-
development agencies and its subsidiary, the Pacific Improvement Company,
rejected haphazard land disposal in favor of founding organized agricultural
settlements as stimulants to land sales and freight and passenger traffic.[41]

Water Development

In addition to land monopoly, also stunting agricultural growth was the primitive and disorganized water management that prevailed in California and other
arid and semi-arid portions of the Southern Pacific's domain.[42] Company
officials at an early stage perceived that more intensive, diversified, small-farm
agriculture, and thus the future health of the railroad, could never be built on
natural rainfall alone. Beginning in the 1860s, railroad leaders promoted irrigation in speeches and writings, introduced irrigation works on railroad lands,
and supported private and public water projects. Along with other water-development advocates in state and local governments, business groups, and farm
organizations, the Southern Pacific worked for laws and programs expanding
and systematizing irrigation, as well as increasing governmental control over
orderly development and distribution of water resources. Land agents such as
Mills, but also other officials at all levels of management, were deeply involved
in water development well into the twentieth century.[43] After taking over from
Mills as land agent in 1908, for example, B. A. McAllaster and his immediate
superior, chief counsel William F. Herrin, also adhered to a general policy of,
wherever feasible, using irrigation to foster the subdivision of railroad, government, and privately owned lands into small farms.[44] Growing from its perceived interest in western expansion, the Southern Pacific became one of the

most important sponsors of western irrigation, as well as other forms of re-source conservation.[45]

The land and water ideas of Southern Pacific officials were closely related. In Mills's view, for example, family farms could also be fostered by government ownership and development of water resources and by restricting the amount of publicly subsidized irrigation water allowed each user to that needed for a small tract. Mills pushed the concept of legal limits on public water in many forums. As a leading organizer of the International Irrigation Congress movement in the 1890s and early 1900s, Mills, as eminent social scientist Paul Taylor has noted, was one of the originators of the important "160-acre principle," the provision Congress eventually incorporated into the 1902 National Reclamation Act in order to restrict public water subsidies to small, family-owned farms. After 1902, Mills and the railroad assisted the newly founded U.S. Reclamation Service in its first implementation of the provision on the pioneer federal irrigation project, the Truckee-Carson (later Newlands) Project, in the Southern Pacific's land-grant area in western Nevada. Established by Mills and supported by Collis P. Huntington and other executives in the late nineteenth century, the acreage-limitation principle for publicly subsidized water remained a cornerstone of Southern Pacific policy into the 1960s.[46]

PART II

Land
Settlement

3 "Stand on the Rights of the Company and Make a Square Fight of It"

LAND-GRANT MYTHS, CONFLICTS WITH THE GOVERNMENT, AND SQUATTERISM

Railroad Land-Grant Myths

More than a half-century ago, Robert S. Henry demonstrated that general histories of the United States perpetuated numerous "legends" exaggerating the extent and misinterpreting the significance of railway land grants in the American West. Statistics commonly cited in such texts, Henry pointed out, greatly overstated both the acreage and the percentage of land area Congress actually granted western railroads to encourage and aid construction from the 1850s to the 1870s. Naively borrowed by historians from inaccurate and misleading government documents, maps republished in the standard texts displayed alarmingly wide swaths of valuable public lands supposedly doled out to the companies along east-west corridors hundreds, in some cases more than a thousand, miles long. The maps, Henry demonstrated, visually magnified the relative land area actually granted to railroads at least fourfold everywhere, and in places much more than that. Some states, such as Iowa and Minnesota, appeared to have been consumed nearly in toto by the voracious railroads. In others, such as North Dakota, Montana, Washington, Oregon, Arizona, and California, settlers were supposedly blocked from access to half or more of their region's territory. Less systematically, Henry also took historians to task for having been too critical in assessing the impact of the grants. The public gained as much or more than it gave, he maintained, especially in terms of the stimulus the grants gave to constructing valuable new transportation routes through unsettled and largely worthless lands. Henry's article came to be seen as a "pivotal interpretation" of American history. Although disagreements continue down to the present day over the wisdom of the railroad grants as public policy, Henry's work eventually led many general historians to be more careful in portraying railroad land grants.[1] On the other hand, with regard to the land grants of the Southern Pacific Company and its numerous subsidiaries, especially in California, Henry need not have bothered to write.

In both popular and scholarly accounts of Southern Pacific land grants, myths

Map distributed by California's People's Independent ("Dolly Varden") Party for its 1875 anti-railroad ticket for state and congressional offices. An early political "dirty trick," the map indicates huge swaths of land granted to the railroad. Originally shown in color, the purported swaths appear here in gray screen outlined by either solid black or a hatched line. Within the alleged railroad grants is about half the state's land area, including the entire coast from San Francisco Bay south, the Los Angeles–San Bernardino area, and the border region north of Mexico. Virtually no continue to abound, some reminiscent of those Robert Henry was attacking, some peculiar to that particular company. From the late nineteenth century down to the present day, oversimplifications, half-truths, distortions, honest errors, and outright fabrications have dominated the discourse. Rarely consulting primary sources, historians, other scholars, social reformers, and journalists have almost always uncritically incorporated the hearsay of earlier writers. In the retelling, what should have been treated as hypothesis, subject to research and testing, became transformed into axiom. Even recently, some common assertions about Southern Pacific land-grant policy and history, including those by otherwise respected social scientists such as Paul Taylor,[2] Ellen Liebman,[3] and William Preston,[4] are so contrary to any possible factual evidence that they are, to put it directly, ludicrous.

Expunged of absurdities and boiled down to essentials, Southern Pacific land-grant myths contain several major, interrelated elements:[5]

- The Southern Pacific's land grant, as with other western land-grant roads, is always conceptualized geographically as a vast, uninterrupted "checkerboard pattern," in which 640-acre odd-numbered railroad sections (squares, one mile on a side) stretch interspersed with the even-numbered public land sections for ten to twenty miles on either side of the tracks.

- As did the historians that Robert Henry studied, land-grant critics grossly exaggerate, through inaccurate maps, language, and/or statistics, the acreage and relative percentage of land area granted along its rail lines to the Southern Pacific, even sometimes to the extent of depicting grants that never existed.

- Critics routinely characterize the Southern Pacific as a land monopolist and speculator by alleging that the company refused to sell its land, withholding it from the market for long periods in order to await higher prices and sales profits and to use the land and its resources for the company's own enrichment. They also charge that the railroad cooperated with and sold its land primarily to other monopolists and speculators and thus played a major role in consolidating landholdings into

land whatsoever was conveyed to railroads in those areas, and the actual grants in other areas were not nearly as large as the map portrays. Overall, the map is about a 500-percent exaggeration of the land granted the railroad. An egregious example of the railroad land-grant myth, the map has nevertheless been republished recently by some historians, geographers, and social critics as an accurate depiction of land grants to the Southern Pacific Company. Courtesy Huntington Library.

the immense tracts that persist in its territory to the present, particularly in California.

- Critics claim that the Southern Pacific delayed the course of settlement and economic development in its territory by purposely dragging its feet in selecting its lands to be received from the federal government, thus preventing distribution to other parties, again so that the railroad could await higher land values as well as avoid having to pay property taxes to county governments.

- Critics charge that the company especially discouraged small-farm settlers by choosing and acquiring its lands from the government deliberately in order to steal the most valuable land away from already established, legitimate homesteaders and other settlers and, when it did deign to sell land, by charging buyers prohibitory high prices.

- More broadly, critics charge that, by stalling the public land-distribution process, holding land off the market, demanding high prices, and ejecting or at least discouraging small-farm settlers, Southern Pacific land policies in general retarded settlement and economic development and worsened land monopoly, again especially in California.

Some Southern Pacific land-grant myths can be rebutted simply. One, for example, is its "checkerboard" geography, which everyone assumes but no one has ever examined closely. Certainly, no western land-grant railroad traversed such different natural landscapes, dramatically varied in geology, elevation, growing season, rainfall, water availability, vegetation, soil fertility, mineral resources, and accessibility to concentrated urban populations and markets. Acquired at different times through numerous predecessor and subsidiary rail companies, Southern Pacific land-grant areas included some of the most well-watered lands in the western United States (particularly in western Oregon and northern California valleys and forests), with 30 to 80 inches annual rainfall. Some land (in the Sacramento and northern San Joaquin valleys), however, had annual rainfall theoretically adequate for farming but so highly concentrated in winter that irrigation was actually required for most of the valuable crops. Other Southern Pacific areas (the central and southern San Joaquin Valley and interior valleys east of Los Angeles) were basically arid but could nevertheless be irrigated relatively easily from rivers or wells. The extremely arid land (Nevada and Utah's Great Basin, and the southern California Mojave and Colorado deserts), lacked water for farming or urban concentrations without monumental water projects, which were possible only later and in a few places, such as in western Nevada and southeastern California's Imperial Valley. Some of this desert land would support large-scale livestock grazing; some would not. Some high-elevation land was lush with forest or brush cover; some was grassy plain or foothill; some was barren, indeed moonscape-like. Much of the grant, especially in low-elevation valleys or lying along rivers rapidly descending from steep mountain ranges, was prone to severe periodic flooding; some, especially in the near-sea-level Sacramento and northern San Joaquin valleys, was in fact "swamp and overflowed" land. Some land, particularly in the Sierra Nevada and the state of Nevada, contained rich mineral deposits, particularly already identified gold and silver, and on some, particularly in the eastern central and southern San Joaquin Valley, petroleum and natural gas would later be discovered. The Southern Pacific's numerous Texas state land grants encompassed representatives of several of the above landscape types, but most were located in the more arid western part of the state.

Because of geographical variability, once the railroad received the land in its varied grants and began to sell it, some Southern Pacific low-lying valley land was immediately perceived as potentially very valuable and sold almost as soon as acquired by the railway, typically within a few weeks or months. Other more arid or outlying land, however, was of only modest value and sold gradually, and often only after extensive regional improvements in water facilities and agricultural modernization that could take decades. Almost all Southern Pacific desert, Great Basin, and west San Joaquin Valley land, at least in the late nineteenth century, was considered worthless, or nearly so, and remained unwanted and not salable for decades, generations, and indeed in some regions to the very present.[6] Because of geographical variability, the fact that the railway received its land along completed stretches of track only gradually and intermittently from the U.S. Department of the Interior and the Texas state General Land Office, and the different rates at which the land sold, the Southern Pacific's pattern of land tenure within its granted lands was always irregular. Except for some arid, isolated regions that are described below, the company never at any one time owned a consistent checkerboard of land over large areas, particularly of more valuable, arable, low-elevation territory near its tracks.

In addition to varying topography and climate, many of the Southern Pacific's land-grant areas, unlike those of other western land-grant roads that built through mostly unoccupied territory, had already been settled, sometimes decades before the awarding of rail land grants. Such was true in most of Oregon's Willamette Valley, the gold mining areas of California's Sierra and its foothills, the entire Sacramento Valley and its foothills, the northern San Joaquin Valley, the San Francisco Bay, Monterey Bay, and Salinas Valley regions, southern California's Los Angeles Basin and the San Gabriel, Pomona, and San Bernardino valleys to the east, the Mormon settlements east of the Great Salt Lake, and much of Texas. By the dates the railroad's grants took effect, much, in some cases all or nearly all, land in those districts was already privately held in Spanish and Mexican land grants, mining claims, town sites, state or municipal government reserves, and prior private sales, preemption, and homestead entries from the public domain. Naturally, Congress and the Texas state legislature excluded from rail grants all of these privately held lands, as well as mineral, swamp and overflowed, state public school, Morrill land-grant college, and Indian reservation lands still in public control.

Thus, the numerous regions within the Southern Pacific's land grant actually had dramatically different geographies. In some areas, but generally only the most remote and extremely arid, where little or no prior settlement existed, the classic checkerboard pattern pertained from the rail right-of-way outward ten or twenty miles in each direction. Such was the case in the southern Oregon and northern California forested mountains, the higher pine forests and granite cliffs of the Sierra Nevada, all the Nevada and Utah Great Basin except for its far western and eastern fringes, the central and southern San Joaquin Valley, and the deserts of extreme southeastern California. Elsewhere, the Southern Pacific received no, very few, or at least not all, odd-numbered sections within land-grant areas near its line. In the Willamette Valley, the Sacramento Valley, the Sierra Nevada foothills, much of the northern San Joaquin Valley, and all of the Pomona and San Bernardino valleys farther south, the railroad had virtually no land along the right-of-way. To the extent that the company had any land grant at all, it consisted only of scattered small, irregular, low-value section-fractions of hitherto unclaimed lowlands within a few miles of the tracks, and intermittent, narrow checkerboard fringes of higher, drier, more rugged, even lower-value, mostly foothill and mountain land ten, twenty, or more miles distant. In the San Francisco Bay, Monterey Bay, Salinas Valley, Los Angeles Basin, and San Gabriel Valley, for all intents and purposes, the Southern Pacific had no land grant whatsoever because of contiguous prior settlement. The company's Texas lands had no discernible regular pattern. Seeking to block railroads from monopolizing lands along their tracks, and since most railways after the 1850s were often building through already settled territory, the state furnished the railroads land certificates, which companies could locate in batches scattered willy-nilly on the open portions of the Texas public domain, usually in far western and Panhandle regions, with little or no relationship to, and sometimes hundreds of miles away from, their rights-of-way.[7] As far as the Southern Pacific was concerned the checkerboard land-grant pattern is a myth.

Similarly, the grossly exaggerated statements of the size of the Southern Pacific's landholdings, though nearly universal, are easily disproven. Regarding popular and scholarly views of the size of the Southern Pacific's landholdings, hyperbole seemingly knows no limits. Not only are maps greatly magnifying the grant's actual land area commonly used,[8] but statistics and verbal imagery as well. Much contemporary exaggeration traces back to a 1913 report by Luther

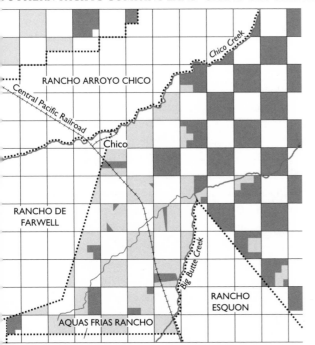

Railroad land grant in a previously settled region in the vicinity of Chico, Sacramento Valley, California

Land granted to railroad on odd-numbered sections

Land railroad lost from odd-numbered sections:

Due to prior settlement

Due to Mexican rancho grants

••••• Rancho boundaries

┣━━━┫ Railroad lines

Because of prior entries and other exclusions and revocations, the federal land grants of Southern Pacific companies in California had sharply varying geographies. The plat map (top) of a portion of the Central Pacific Railroad's land grant in the vicinity of Chico, illustrates a general pattern in the Sacramento Valley, where, when the railroad's land grant took effect, most of the potential grant was already owned in prior purchases, homesteads, or Mexican rancho grants. In such places, the railroad received little or no land, except in outer fringes and foothills. The plat map (bottom) of a portion of the Southern Pacific Railroad's land grant in the Salton Sink region of southeastern California's Colorado Desert, where little settlement had occurred prior to the railroad's grant, illustrates the classic checkerboard pattern common in western railroad grants. Both maps adapted from Central Pacific Railroad and Southern Pacific Railroad, "Land-Grant Map Books" (mss., 1907 and subsequent years). Courtesy California State Railroad Museum, Sacramento.

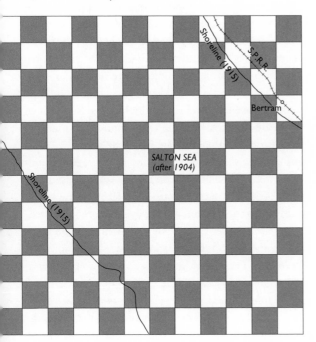

Railroad land grant in a previously unsettled region, Salton Sink, California

Conant, Jr., commissioner of the U.S. Department of Commerce and Labor, Bureau of Corporations, attacking monopoly of timberlands, particularly by Northwest railroads. As his most vivid example, Conant cited the Southern Pacific's landholding, which he described as still intact and so vast as to be incomprehensible. The grant, Conant charged, stretched "practically all the way from Portland, Ore., to Sacramento, Cal." During the thirty-one hours it took the fastest train to traverse that path, "the traveler is passing through lands a large portion of which for 30 miles on each side of him belongs to the corporation over whose tracks he is riding, and in almost the entire strip, 60 miles wide and 682 miles long, the corporation is the dominating owner of both timber and land."[9] Picked up immediately by newspapers, who often sensationalized it further, Conant's outrageous falsehood echoes to the present.[10] In an early 1970s book condemning the Southern Pacific's Oregon & California Railroad grant, Robert Bradley Jones cited the same Bureau of Corporations report. Jones, however, now extended the grant all along the tracks as far as San Francisco, and his hypothetical traveler was "never out of sight of the Oregon and California grant lands, which stretched as far as the eye could reach to the east and west."[11] Not to be outdone, journalistic muckrakers attacking corporate monopoly picked up the theme. Joel Kotkin and Paul Grabowicz, in their 1982 book *California, Inc.,* described the Southern Pacific's land grant as a "massive feudal kingdom," which they treated as if it existed at one time and exaggerated as consisting of 11.5 million acres in California alone, constituting one-fifth of all privately owned land in the state.[12] A year later, journalists John Ross and Tim Redmond, in their attack on the power and policies of the company, went even farther, claiming that the Southern Pacific was "the largest private landowner in the West," whose current holdings in the region, "if consolidated, would equal the total land size of the Golden State."[13] Even scholarly authors commonly measure the Southern Pacific's landholdings in California in figures between 11 and 12 million acres, with the clear implication that the railroad at one time actually owned a domain in the state that large.[14]

Exaggerations as extreme as those of Conant, Jones, and Ross and Redmond raise the possibility that they were deliberate falsehoods. By 1913, along more than half its mainline from Portland to Sacramento, specifically through the Willamette and Sacramento valleys, as anyone who was seriously interested could readily have found out, the Southern Pacific possessed virtually no land whatsoever, except a little here and there at far distances, and it had absolutely none between Sacramento and San Francisco. At no time, and in no place, was the land "as far as the eye could reach, to east and west," in railroad ownership. Indeed, the vast extent of land inherent in Conant's and Jones's imagery would likely have approached all the land Congress ever granted to all the railroads in the entire nation. Ross and Redmond's wild claims were even worse, particularly since they were made about the Southern Pacific's current holdings in the early 1980s. At that time, the company in truth owned only about 3.8 million remaining land-grant acres in all states, with a good chunk of it, about half, actually in Nevada and Utah. The current holding, even in all states, was nowhere near the equivalent of California's land area, approximately 101.5 million acres.[15]

Even the overall figure used by reputable historians, 11 to 12 million acres, as the upper limits on land patented from the federal government in California, seriously overstates the amount of land ever actually possessed by the Southern Pacific. Because the railroad only received its grants in small batches upon completion of segments of its lines from the mid-1860s onward, because the Department of the Interior delayed for years and decades in furnishing some of the patents, and because as quickly as it could the railroad immediately sold the great majority of the land it did receive, especially near the tracks, the Southern Pacific at no time owned any more than a small fraction of the theoretical upper limit of its grant in California. Already by internal Southern Pacific accountings made in 1903, for example, the railroad had sold a total of 8.1 million acres, the great majority of it in California, and patents to much of the remaining land had not been received yet, some not until the World War II era.[16] By the time of an internal company inventory of its remaining California land-grant holdings in 1907, the Southern Pacific had sold all of its agricultural land that was arable at that time, and all it had left was forest land in the far north and higher, extremely arid tracts in the western San Joaquin Valley and far southern deserts, the latter of which the company considered practically worthless.[17] Until the early 1940s, the railroad continued to sell, as well as to receive, additional land.

The Southern Pacific's holding in California, and to a lesser extent in other states, was thus an abstraction, with the actual possessed acreage constantly fluctuating, shuffling around in location, no parcel larger than one section (640 acres), with new tracts periodically being added when the federal government issued new patents even while other tracts were being sold or lost when the government revoked the patents. The overall sum that the railroad actually possessed remained relatively small, probably peaking at any one time between three and five million acres near the close of the nineteenth century and altering little, though declining slowly in the twentieth century. At any given time, because the railroad sold its good land immediately, most of what the company did have in its possession was low in value and had little or no market. In Nevada and Utah, and to some extent in Oregon, isolation and ruggedness resulted in the land's remaining even longer in company ownership. In Texas, most of the state land grant had already been taken up and sold by predecessor lines before the Southern Pacific acquired them in the 1880s, and the company had liquidated virtually all the rest except a few town lots by the early 1900s.[18]

None of this is to suggest, on the other hand, that the Southern Pacific's grant of public lands and its effects on the history and settlement of the Far West were inconsequential. The theoretical aggregate of acres in the federal land grants in California, Oregon, Nevada, and Utah was by all measures large— upwards of 18 million—and although the company never received all of that, some of what it did receive was valuable and profitable to sell.[19] The geography of the Southern Pacific's land grant, however, has almost universally been misconstrued and the extent, particularly the amount and value, of land the company owned at any one time seriously exaggerated. Other, more complex issues pertaining to railroad land grants in Southern Pacific territory, particularly those related to effects on patterns of settlement, require detailed historical analysis of the company's land policies and practices, and their results.

Land Department Organization

The Southern Pacific from the mid-1860s to the mid-1880s established specialized corporate agencies that would ultimately carry the major responsibility for promoting the Far West. Since its most immediate problem was how best to exploit the land grant in the company's interest, the railroad at first focused on establishing a land development and sales program. The Big Four organized a Land Department for the Central Pacific Railroad, the first of their railway interests to acquire a land grant, and opened their first land office in Sacramento in September 1865.[20] To design and manage the new organization, the Big Four chose Benjamin B. Redding, former assemblyman from Yuba City and mayor of Sacramento, currently California's secretary of state, and an amateur scientist of some repute. Redding was a wise choice. Widely respected, Redding lent legitimacy to the railroad's land-development and promotional programs and applied his broad knowledge, especially of agriculture, to the important task of instituting procedures for surveying, classifying, improving, selling, and settling Central Pacific lands.[21]

At first, the work of the Central Pacific Land Department proceeded slowly. The federal government did not begin issuing land patents to the company until 1867, and even then most of the early lands the Central Pacific could offer for sale were Sierra Nevada foothill or mountain lands, isolated and of little value except for grazing or lumbering. By late 1867, the railroad had sold only 33,567 acres for a total of $65,983, a little less than $2 per acre.[22] The Big Four's other California-based land-grant railways, the Western Pacific, the California & Oregon, and the Southern Pacific, experienced similar delays in patenting, surveying, and sales. Limited business in the early years did not warrant the establishment of separate land departments for all subsidiary roads. Indeed, the

Central Pacific's granted land in extremely arid and isolated northern Nevada and Utah had virtually no market, even as late as the early 1900s, except for limited leasing for livestock grazing, and the company expended little effort or expense to sell it until the twentieth century. Finally, in the early 1870s, with patents beginning to accumulate for the fertile lands along the Southern Pacific Railroad's San Joaquin Valley route and later in southern California, a separate land agency for the Southern Pacific Railroad opened in San Francisco in 1875. Jerome Madden, a pioneer of 1849 and former Sacramento County recorder and state librarian, became the land agent of the Southern Pacific Railroad in 1876. He had been Redding's assistant in the Central Pacific Railroad Land Department for six years at the time of his appointment. Serving for nearly thirty years as the land agent of the Southern Pacific Railroad, Madden became a leading writer of railroad promotional literature. Redding and his successor as chief land agent of the Big Four's rail interests overall, William H. Mills, continued to have ultimate responsibility for all company land programs, despite the later establishment of specialized departments for some of the subsidiaries.[23] In the autumn of 1873, along with the rest of the Southern Pacific's executive operations, the Land Department office moved from Sacramento to the new, large corporate headquarters at 4th and Townsend streets, San Francisco.[24]

In the late 1860s and early 1870s, as the railroad received and put more land on the market, the company appointed local agents, usually also attorneys practicing near district federal land offices. The local agents represented the Southern Pacific in land matters before the land offices, handled the railroad's property-tax business at county seats, recruited land-grant buyers and took their applications for purchases, and investigated, negotiated, and if necessary contested rival claims to the company's lands. Among the more significant local railroad land agents was Daniel K. Zumwalt of Visalia, employed in 1870 to manage Southern Pacific Railroad land-grant business in much of the San Joaquin Valley. W. C. Belcher was appointed about the same time in Marysville to administer Central Pacific and California & Oregon Railroad lands in the Sacramento Valley and foothills. Robert L. Fulton, from the mid-1870s to the early 1900s, oversaw Central Pacific holdings in the eastern Sierra, Nevada, and Utah from his office in Reno. For several decades after 1900 C. E. Wantland of Los Angeles managed Southern Pacific Railroad lands from Los Angeles across interior valleys and deserts into a fringe of southern Arizona. After the Big Four acquired their Texas lines in the 1880s, a succession of Southern Pacific agents, particularly longtime official C. C. Gibbs, operated a railroad land office at the headquarters of the Galveston, Harrisburg, & San Antonio Railroad in San Antonio and Houston.[25]

Under Redding's direction, with Madden's assistance, the associated railroads' land-development programs began to take shape in the late 1860s and 1870s as

Railroad line and land surveyors struggled against rugged conditions. This Central Pacific crew is depicted working in Humboldt Canyon, Nevada, in the late 1860s. From *Harper's Monthly*, May 30, 1868. Courtesy California State Railroad Museum, Sacramento.

granted lands in California and Nevada went on the market. Generally, the Southern Pacific followed paths already blazed by earlier land-grant railways. Initially, surveying, selecting, patenting, "grading" (classifying), and subdividing the land grant absorbed the company's energies. Southern Pacific surveyors and Land Department field representatives, some regular employees, some local residents under contract to the railroad, were the first on the scene. In the late nineteenth and early twentieth centuries, parties of railroad land surveyors and graders, traveling by saddle horses and mule-drawn wagons and outfitted with tents, preserved foods, water barrels, and feed for their animals, roamed remote desert regions for weeks or months on end, locating, marking, mapping, and evaluating the railroad's lands, along with local wood supplies, gravel and building stone, water sources, nearby developments, and even flora and fauna. The travails of a later party of four men whose records survive suggest brutal conditions that probably were even worse in earlier decades. Led by

Land Department field agent F. L. Mary, the men investigated the railroad's Mojave Desert land near Victorville and Barstow, California, between January and April 1911. Constantly battling the effects of nearly total isolation, they often ran out of food and water, endured seemingly endless delays in being re-supplied, and were rendered yet more miserable by bitter cold nights in win-ter and searing daytime heat after April 1. Relentless gales were so severe, Mary reported, that the party "experienced much difficulty in holding our camp to mother earth." Winds ripped apart maps and scattered papers, supplies, and equipment, and more seriously, drove nagging sandstorms down on the crew. Unable to see, to cook and eat, even sometimes to breathe or stand, the men had to burrow in for up to a week at a time. But sand drifts buried and invaded their tents and bedding, with fine dust penetrating even into "sealed" telescopes, ruining them along with other instruments, and the water and foodstuffs as well. The horses, dust irritating their eyes and lungs, sickened and became lame and useless. Nevertheless, the assignment completed, the men packed up their gear and headed out to repeat the ordeal on another stretch of Southern Pacific land in Nevada.[26] The maps, drawings, and land descriptions such parties recorded in field notebooks proved essential to Land Department officials in selecting tracts for patenting from the Department of the Interior, and later in subdividing, pricing, advertising, and marketing the land.

Problems Getting Patents

After railroad land agents had examined and entered potential grant tracts onto lists according to township, range, section, and fraction numbers on standard federal rectilinear survey maps, the Southern Pacific's next task was to get patents for the land on the alternating odd-numbered sections from the federal gov-ernment's real estate arm, the General Land Office of the Department of the Interior. The company was eligible to submit lists for patents as it completed segments of track, generally in twenty- to fifty-mile-long increments. When the government had approved the selection lists and issued the patents, they could be taken to local county seats, recorded, and exchanged for deeds, which the railroad could begin selling to settlers. The common charge by historians, that the Southern Pacific deliberately delayed securing patents and thus retarded settlement in order to withhold land from the market, raise prices, and evade property taxes, is completely without basis.[27] To the contrary, as countless doc-uments in company manuscript collections and the National Archives show, from the inception of its land-grant program, the Southern Pacific's clear ob-jective, consistently and vigorously pursued over the seven decades from the 1860s to 1930, was to submit land selection lists as soon as the law allowed and to press the Department of the Interior aggressively until it furnished the patents. The railroad executives' principal motive was simple: to sell the land as soon as possible in order to pay off construction debts and speed settlement and economic development, and thus traffic revenues. Additionally, delays in patenting and selling land exacerbated the company's already serious difficulties with squatters and poachers. Finally, particularly through the first few decades, the Southern Pacific's period of expansion and heavy indebtedness, leaders also believed, correctly, that securing land patents increased the company's assets and standing with investors and creditors.[28]

Unfortunately for the Southern Pacific and would-be settlers, however, acquiring and then defending reliable patents proved to be the most problematical step in the railroad land-grant process. Great delays there would indeed be, caused by the Department of the Interior, and more broadly by the monumental, unprecedented, and contradiction-riddled problem that railroad land-grant patenting turned out to be. The federal General Land Office was a confused, cramped, understaffed, and underfunded agency run by less-than-competent persons, typically patronage appointees turning over at breakneck speed. It was overwhelmed by the task of arranging to survey much of the land, maintaining maps and information nationwide, developing administrative policy, and servicing the flood of new railroad land grants, containing tens of millions of acres, suddenly demanding action beginning in the mid-1860s. Then periodically, individual new commissioners or secretaries of the interior, committed to revoking the railroad grants, took charge and deliberately slowed down the process or suspended action on patents altogether. Often influencing new commissioners or secretaries, large-scale land speculators like William S. Chapman, San Joaquin Valley land king who reputedly controlled as much as two million acres of former state and federal lands in California, constantly lobbied to slow down or block transfer of land to the railroads, meanwhile seeking to engross as much public land close to the lines as they could.[29]

Like other rail lines, immediately upon the first patent conflicts in the mid-1860s, Southern Pacific leaders retained the services of several Washington attorneys with expertise in railroad grant law and politics, most notably Henry Beard and John Boyd, to counter opponents and represent the company's interests at the Department of the Interior.[30] Nevertheless, to secure their land patents, railroads at best had to wait many months, but often years, occasionally generations, and sometimes forever.[31] The companies, moreover, had to fight for the patents. For example, the first lands applied for by the Central Pacific, finally received in 1867, had required more than two years for Department of Interior approval. After five years of submitting lists for 1.7 million acres in California alone, the Central Pacific, despite innumerable protests over years by railroad officers, had by 1870 received patents for only 144,600 acres, less than one-tenth of what it had applied for. As late as 1873, though its line had been completed and the land patents requested in 1869, the Central Pacific had received not one acre in Nevada and Utah. And the situation never got much better.[32]

Selling Land to Promote Settlement and Rail Traffic

Gradually, however, in the late 1860s, as more patents began to arrive in fits and spurts from the government and the market for railroad lands quickened in the wake of completion of its lines, the Southern Pacific's policies and techniques for subdivision, advertising, sales, and settlement evolved. Like other land-grant roads, which typically operated long, expensive lines across vast, unpopulated distances, the Southern Pacific conceived of itself not as a speculator, but as a land distributor and colonizer.[33] The company's goal was to manage and sell its land grant in a businesslike fashion designed, of course, to turn a profit in sales in order to repay construction loans. More important, though, the railroad sought to promote rapid, long-term population and community growth and economic development in its territories, hence even more lucrative traffic revenues and corporate profits. "The company, of course, is very anxious to settle the land in such a way that there would be a large amount of money to the transportation side of the account," land agent William H. Mills testified before the United States Pacific Railway Commission in 1887. "Here is an instance where the owner of the land is interested in the progress of settlement. The land pays the company, perhaps, much better after it is settled than it does by the price of it."[34] At all times after the 1860s, for the Southern Pacific, income from the land grant contributed only slightly to the company's overall profits, most of which derived from hauling freight and passengers. Into the twentieth century, company leaders viewed land sales primarily as a stimulus to that vital traffic. "The unsold lands of the grant are an expensive asset to carry," land agent B. A. McAllaster wrote in reviewing the railroad's policy for his superior, vice president William F. Herrin, in 1923. "Consequently, it behooves the company to sell the lands as rapidly as buyers can be found; when sold they become a revenue producing asset, both from sales revenue and from traffic resulting from the improvement and development of the lands."[35]

As a result, the railway developed a land-management and sales program aimed primarily at building traffic for its lines, and from the start adopted a supportive and conciliatory stance toward small-farm settlers.[36] As was true of other dimensions of its business, in its land-grant administration the Southern Pacific especially strove to systematize its policies. Like other emerging modern businesses of the era, the railroad had to grapple with the ever-changing and growing complexities of large-scale operations: maintaining records for a constantly fluctuating landholding eventually of millions of acres scattered over tens of thousands of square miles in six states; entering into and servicing sale or lease contracts with tens of thousands of individuals; and keeping up with the bewildering tax, legal, political, administrative, financial, and, increasingly, environmental problems of the grant, for which there were often few precedents. With land-grant matters always on the verge of chaos, Southern Pacific land officials and higher executives were constantly attempting to impose the order of modern business methods on the company's land programs. Land was to be selected, mapped, evaluated, subdivided, and priced according to uniform criteria. Sales and general relations with settlers were to be regularized around consistent, publicly announced policies. Company activities also had to be conducted so they could withstand legal challenge and the glare of publicity. To do otherwise, the railroad recognized, would retard settlement and render the land grant less profitable, as well as invite public outrage, political reprisals, and perhaps even confiscation of the land itself, which indeed happened to a few western railroads.

It was the Southern Pacific's policy to apply for land-grant patents from the federal government as soon as it became eligible by completing a segment of line. Also, as it did so, the company wanted clear land titles. Seeking to prevent conflicts with settlers, the railroad carefully avoided selecting public land tracts already occupied by homesteaders, preemptors, or earlier grantees or buyers with legitimate rights. The company's land agents and attorneys in Sacramento, San Francisco, local federal land-office towns, and in Washington, D.C., were instructed to comb federal, state, and county land records in order to delete all legal earlier land entries from the railroad's selections. Indeed, since the government would compensate the company for its lands lost to prior settlers by substituting equivalent grants in the indemnity strip farther out from the rail line, the Southern Pacific had little incentive to force prior settlers from their holdings, and every incentive to avoid doing so.[37]

After receiving patents from the General Land Office, the Southern Pacific "graded" (classified) the land according to terrain, resources, accessibility, soil fertility, and water availability. Land officials then subdivided potentially arable land into viable small farms of varying size and shape, taking care to distribute fertile acres, pasturage, water, trees, and proximity to roads as evenly as possible, so that all the tracts could be productive and would sell readily. In contrast to the federal government, which sold or granted land on a first-come, first-served basis, in standard-sized section-fraction tracts, the Southern Pacific's policy was to refrain from selling small plots monopolizing valuable soil, stone, timber, and water. Instead, the railroad divided up and maximized access to those essential resources in order to assure a higher value and productivity for all of the land grant, as well as a more evenly distributed, contiguous population in rural areas.[38]

From the beginning, the Southern Pacific designed its land policies to favor actual small-farm settlers, even if that meant sacrificing short-term sales profits or the company's claims to specific tracts of disputed land. "We want the country settled because it does not pay to run Railroads to places where there are no people," wrote B. B. Redding, head of the Southern Pacific's Land Department, in instructing company San Joaquin Valley agent D. K. Zumwalt on how to manage land sales in his district in 1875:

> The settlement of the country, the transportation of tea, coffee, grind-stones, mowers, looking-glasses and reapers, etc., etc., for all time to come, is a very much more important thing to the company than the sale of a piece of land at from $3 to $6 per acre. The company wants the land settled, and it desires to hold out the strongest inducements to actual settlers to go upon unencumbered land, to use it and occupy it, and to give such persons who do so, the preference over all others, under all circumstances. I do not know how to vary the language so that I can convey the idea to you.[39]

Southern Pacific executives and land agents reiterated that philosophy for decades, and it provided the basis for the railroad's general land policies and for specific decisions into the mid-twentieth century.

To stimulate immediate cultivation of its lands, the company particularly emphasized sales to buyers of small tracts who would quickly occupy and put their lands under the plow. "The policy of the company is to give preference and sell to the actual [small-scale] settler," chief land agent Redding wrote his San Joaquin Valley district agent in 1872. "The Company wish to settle up the Country and the smaller the tracts are that they sell to actual settlers the better it is for the Company and for the State. . . . The Company invites them to go on and make it [the land grant] their homes, cultivate the soil, enrich the State and thus create business for the Railroad."[40] The Southern Pacific thus strongly discouraged speculators from purchasing its lands and instructed its agents to avoid sales to buyers who intended to hold large tracts and then later subdivide and sell farms at higher prices.[41]

So that the land would sell as speedily as possible, the railroad then purposely priced its land somewhat below—usually about 10 percent under—prevailing local market values on unimproved land. To facilitate small-scale farming, the company charged especially low prices for good agricultural land (generally $2.50 to $7.00 per acre, sometimes higher, sometimes lower, for specific times and places). Such low prices prevailed on Southern Pacific Company land grants from the 1860s well into the twentieth century.[42] Meticulous internal audits of Land Department business conducted by the Harriman Lines' accountants after their company's acquisition of the Southern Pacific in 1901 disclosed that the Central Pacific Railroad between 1865 and 1903 sold a total of 4.2 million acres, at an average price of $2.85 per acre; the Southern Pacific Railroad sold 3.96 million acres, at an average of $3.14 per acre.[43] Actually, Southern Pacific land on the odd-numbered sections in the arable and accessible portions of the railroad's grant area was priced as low as, or even lower than, land available on the even-numbered, so-called "public," sections. Within railway land-grant areas, Congress had prohibited further homestead and preemption claims and had raised the minimum price the government charged from $1.25 to $2.50 per acre. Before the railroad built its lines and received patents to its land sections, however, speculators using cash or scrip had already taken up much of the remaining unimproved government land on the public sections in regions such as the San Joaquin Valley, and they sold it for much more than $2.50.[44]

Credit and Leasing Programs

In addition to offering low prices, the Southern Pacific, like other land-grant roads, tried to attract settlers, speed sales, and increase the likelihood that farms would be successful and rail traffic generated by developing a credit system in the late 1860s. Railroad-held mortgages enabled small farmers of modest means to acquire agricultural lands with minimum start-up capital. Initially, the plan required 20 percent down, a yearly interest payment of 10 percent on the balance, and the rest of the principal due in five years. To revive lagging sales during the depression of the late 1870s, the railroad lowered interest rates in 1880 to 7 percent, but otherwise the credit system remained the same on all of the associated lines until it was further liberalized in 1906.[45] The credit system of the Southern Pacific was an important service to farm builders and contributed mightily to speedy settlement and cultivation of land along the railroad's lines. Typically of newly developing agricultural areas, California and other Southern Pacific states suffered from a capital shortage and high interest rates for farm development in the late nineteenth century. By extending credit at extremely low interest rates to tens of thousands of its land customers, the railroad helped to finance many agricultural enterprises, both large and small.

Surviving Land Department records for the Southern and Central Pacific lines held by the Southern Pacific Company's San Francisco archives and by the California State Railroad Museum in Sacramento indicate that from the 1860s through the early 1900s, the great majority of Southern Pacific land sales were on credit. For extended periods, indeed, virtually all sales were on time-payment contracts. Land buyers made small down payments, were responsible only for an interest payment each year after harvest time, and deferred most principal until the conclusion of the contract, when the fields were producing, the farms presumably profitable, and the land worth much more. In effect, the Southern Pacific was capitalizing initial farmsteads in its territory. Under the early 10-percent-interest plan, for example, to purchase an eighty-acre tract (a typical size for a railroad land sale in this period) at a value per acre of $5 (a somewhat higher than average price), farmers would pay the sale price of $400, with $80 down and interest payments of $32 per year for five years, after which the principal balance of $320 would be due. Later time-payment plans were more generous, with lower interest rates and up to ten years or more to repay. In California and other western regions, characterized in the nineteenth century by extremely high interest rates on borrowed capital, the 10-percent rate was very low, lower than charged by private land-mortgage firms, and the 7-percent rate even lower.[46] Since free private entries on remaining public lands in the railway grant areas were prohibited, and the minimum price on purchased government land raised to $2.50 per acre, cash due on purchase, settlers actually needed *much less* initial capital in hand to buy from the railroad than to acquire public land or to buy from speculators in the critical new transportation corridors. That helps explain why almost all rail land sales were on time, and almost all fertile railroad land near the tracks sold quickly.[47]

In addition, in practice, if railroad land buyers ran into financial trouble due to drought, crop pests, or other difficulties, the company routinely granted persons actually cultivating the land time-extensions on interest and final principal payments, and sometimes forgave interest payments altogether and even provided free seed to help farmers recover. In a sense, by doing so, the Southern Pacific furnished a sort of crop insurance to pioneer farmers along its lines. If after the five-year period, farmers were still having difficulties on their lands, the company often refinanced their contracts and extended the time for final payment of principal for additional years. As a result, some farmers did not pay off their contracts for a decade or more, while continuing to use the land for small annual interest payments. The company's policy of flexibility and lenience regarding land buyers in distress was amplified by the sympathies of the railroad's district land agents. San Joaquin Valley agent Zumwalt, for example, pitied poor settlers whose hard labors were regularly undermined by drought, crop pests, and market gluts. Time and again, he pleaded his neighbors' cases to higher Land Department officials, almost always getting his superiors to forgive interest payments and grant extensions on mortgages and leases.[48] On the other hand, the company gained considerable income from its collection of interest; for the Central Pacific alone, this amounted to nearly $2 million between 1882 and 1919.[49]

Although the company preferred to sell land to permanent users, the Southern Pacific also encouraged persons lacking start-up capital to put its unsold land into production by developing a flexible, low-cost leasing program.[50] Instituted in the mid-1870s and systematized in the 1880s, the leasing program also served to discourage the widespread poaching on vacant railroad land, especially by itinerant sheepmen. Applicants could lease railroad land for cultivation, hay-cutting, or pasturage, including the unusual grazing of hogs on acorns in San Joaquin Valley foothill oak woodlands. Annual fees were uniformly lower than on other private lands, varying from 50 cents to $1 per acre for farmland to as little as 10 cents per acre for grazing land. To protect the renters and their crops from having the land sold to others, leases also included either an option or first right of refusal to buy the land. If they refused to take up their options, the railroad allowed lessees time to remove crops and improvements before turning the land over to buyers. In practice, however, most customers leased on credit, with fees due after crops or livestock were sold, and payable either in cash or in crop shares, typically one-fifth of grain or one-fourth of hay, sacked or baled and delivered to the nearest railhead. The company used its crop shares of grain and hay, the most common types, to feed the great herds of horses, mules, and oxen that it used in building and operating its lines, including its subsidiary urban streetcar lines. As was the case with land-purchase contracts, the railroad typically postponed, lowered, or forgave rental fees altogether if farmers ran into financial, market, weather, or crop-pest difficulties.[51] Lessees, thus, needed no initial capital whatsoever to use land, with the railroad in effect financing farm-building and providing several forms of crop insurance.

The Southern Pacific's leasing rules, like those governing land purchases, aimed at spreading valuable resources and discouraging speculation. Leaseholders had to take entire subdivided parcels and could not lease only small tracts with water supplies. Sheep grazers, particularly, attempted to lease small portions of land controlling water, thereby keeping others out, while they poached on surrounding government and railroad grazing land.[52] To encourage the highest possible land-use, the company required persons leasing farmland to cultivate the land. Parcels under grazing leases were sold and the leases not renewed when purchasers who intended to farm appeared, if, that is, the renters refused their options to buy.[53] Contracts prohibited lessees from removing soil, stone, trees, and water from the land or damaging it in any other way. The great majority of leases were for the same small-farm units that dominated land sales, but a few extremely large tracts of arid grazing land were also leased, including in the 1870s and 1880s to the Lloyd Tevis–James Ben Ali Haggin agricultural enterprise in the southern and western San Joaquin Valley, and to some large-scale cattle and sheep raisers in the Great Basin.[54]

Land Conflicts

Despite the Southern Pacific's accommodation of actual small-farm settlers and its great volume of what appear to have been mutually satisfying land transactions, some disagreements invariably arose. Conflicts especially resulted from confused government processing of land patents: tardy or faulty land surveys, inaccurate maps and records, breakdowns in communication between the General Land Office in Washington and district offices, delays in issuing patents to the railroad and others that sometimes stretched over years, vacillating policies, insufficient staffing, and a high rate of turnover among politically appointed local and Washington land officials.[55] These problems were compounded by the railroad's own incomplete records, inadequate staffing, and the crush of business transactions. Numerous disputes over land titles erupted between the railroad and legitimate prior homesteaders, preemptors, and buyers who in good faith thought they held claims to government land but were residing on what the railroad viewed as its property. Typically of the mad scramble for frontier land everywhere, two or more settlers often also contested each other for title to land that the railroad also claimed as part of its grant. Whether the fault lay with railway blunders, decrepit government machinery, or the settlers themselves, such conflicts soured relations between the company and pioneers in some areas of the land grant. The Southern Pacific, many concluded, was a "land-grabber."

The railway worked constantly to minimize and resolve those conflicts. At no time did the Southern Pacific deliberately seek to "float" its grant onto the legitimate prior holdings of others but instead took great pains to avoid doing so. Seeking clear titles and to avoid conflicts with settlers, before filing lists of lands to receive patents from the General Land Office, the company had its local land agents check and recheck the lists against the records of government land offices to delete all prior claims, a procedure company attorneys in Washington often repeated.[56] Some conflicts occurred anyway, and since the official process of contests and appeals from the local land offices through the Department of Interior bureaucracy and the courts was long, cumbersome, and expensive for all parties, the Southern Pacific preferred private methods of conflict resolution. Railroad land agents in Washington, Sacramento, San Francisco, or in local districts conducted investigations of their own, and if, as often happened, they found the settler's prior rights to be legitimate and in good faith, even if faulty because of technicalities, the company invariably withdrew its claim and applied to the Department of the Interior for compensatory acreage in the indemnity strip farther from the rail line.[57] The company's policy against challenging rival good-faith settlers, even if their claims contained technical flaws, was instituted with the inception of the railroad's land program in the 1860s and was consistently followed into the twentieth century. "I would not advise opposition to . . . [that kind of ordinary small homestead or preemption entry] unless a case of fraud can be well-established," the Southern Pacific's longtime Washington, D.C., land attorney, Henry Beard, early explained, enunciating the company's policy. To press frivolous claims on flimsy pretexts, he warned, would be time-consuming and costly in comparison to the low value of the land, would probably be unsuccessful since Department of the Interior officials in Washington rarely overturned decisions of local land officials against railroads, and would jeopardize the credibility of the company, causing it to lose later, more important cases.[58]

In those conflicts where the Southern Pacific did not withdraw its claim, the railroad tried, often successfully, to reach private settlements with rival claimants. In hundreds of cases in the San Joaquin Valley alone, settlers gave the company quit-claim deeds to the disputed lands or formally withdrew their claims at government land offices in exchange for contracts to buy the parcels from the railroad on favorable terms.[59] In particularly tangled cases, local Southern Pacific land agents such as Zumwalt toured the countryside by horseback, buckboard, or train, holding hearings, with all the trappings of trials, including formal presentation of documents and testimony by witnesses, to sort out privately the conflicts between the railroad and rival claimants, several of whom often claimed the same piece of land. In all cases, local land agents were instructed, the equities of actual settlers residing on and cultivating the lands in question were to prevail.[60] During some periods of heavy land business from the late 1860s through the 1890s, Zumwalt and other agents were on the road for weeks on end, holding dozens of hearings per week.

Squatterism

Not all those contesting Southern Pacific land titles were legitimate settlers, however. Some tried to exploit title uncertainties, government delays and confusion in issuing patents, vague land laws, venal public officials and local railway agents, and social and economic turmoil to appropriate railroad property free or at low cost. Squatting on public or private lands had been common on all frontiers since the colonial period, but especially in late-nineteenth-century California it became a more or less respected way of life. Moreover, widespread antipathy toward the Southern Pacific there made invading railroad land seem particularly legitimate, even to otherwise law-abiding citizens. To many, the "Octopus" was fair game.[61]

From the late 1860s onward, Southern Pacific lands were beset by hordes of squatters and resource thieves, many if not most of them petty speculators, whose ingenuity rivaled their lack of scruples.[62] Squatters on railroad land forged documents, moved surveyors' markers, extended fences to enclose railroad property, plowed and planted crops on company land, filed multiple homestead and preemption claims to railroad land under their own or assumed names or on behalf of persons who were actually dead, and perjured themselves or got relatives or paid witnesses to lie about dates of settlement. They transported cabins from tract to tract to establish residence and homestead or preemption rights in more than one place, moved houses and buildings to straddle property lines in order to claim adjacent parcels at the same time, or simply moved onto railroad land without even a pretext of legality. By the mid-1860s, nearly as soon as the Southern Pacific received its first patents, law and real estate firms specializing in organizing and representing squatter and speculator claims against the railroad's lands had emerged in various localities, in Washington, D.C, and in towns with district government land offices. Often themselves in the land speculation business, such firms organized mass challenges to the railroad's titles, often involving hundreds of clients and thousands of disputed acres. Frequently, outside parties came to the support of one or both sides in a contest. Sometimes one of the railroad's rivals turned out to be the state of California, Nevada, or Oregon, or Utah Territory, attempting to acquire railroad land for themselves or powerful speculators under one of the laws granting federal lands to states for schools, universities, or swamp drainage. Clearly, squatterism on Southern Pacific lands was big business.[63]

Meanwhile, others uninterested in possessing the land merely stole its resources. Poachers illegally cut hay, logged forests, quarried for sand, gravel, and stone, diverted water, and, most commonly, grazed cattle, sheep, and hogs on railroad property. By the early 1880s, illicit grazing, particularly by sheepmen, had stripped the grass and started severe soil erosion on large areas of steeper railroad foothill land in the San Joaquin Valley and the Great Basin.[64] Some enterprising souls even bribed Southern Pacific land surveyors, graders, and land agents, who were often local residents, to get them to alter maps, reduce sale prices on railroad tracts, or ignore squatter use of railroad land or resources. This became such a serious problem that the company had to fire several agents, conduct careful investigations of their replacements, and field a staff of detectives to go undercover to put local surveyors, graders, and land agents under surveillance.[65] The clandestine nature of their activities makes it difficult to estimate their numbers, but at all times into the early twentieth century, squatters and poachers on Southern Pacific land undoubtedly numbered in the many hundreds, if not thousands. Squatterism also troubled the railroad's rural and town lands in Texas.[66]

Taken aback, the Southern Pacific at first in the 1860s and early 1870s dealt leniently with squatters, not immediately interfering with their use of the land but trying to get them to buy or lease legitimately. Essentially, the railroad treated

Jerome Madden, land agent specifically for the Southern Pacific Railroad's grants in California from the 1870s until the early 1900s, and Daniel K. Zumwalt, Southern Pacific Railroad district land agent for the San Joaquin Valley from 1869 to 1893. An important part of Madden and Zumwalt's job was to deal with squatters and poachers on the railroad's lands. Madden portrait, courtesy California Historical Society, San Francisco; Zumwalt portrait, courtesy California State Library, Sacramento.

squatters as potential customers, which some of them indeed became once confronted by the company's agents. As squatters grew bolder, more numerous, and increasingly organized, however, company officials became first discouraged, then cynical, about the supposed virtues of American "yeomen." "We are accustomed to having handles made on all possible occasions," Land Department head Redding complained to Zumwalt in 1875 when apprised of new methods San Joaquin squatters were using to swindle the company. "It is one perpetual attempt to get land at less than the regular price for all conceivable kinds of reasons."[67] As time passed, the Southern Pacific more and more distinguished between legitimate settlers who happened to be contesting the railroad's rights to particular parcels, and squatters. Becoming more aggressive in defending its property rights, the company by the mid-1870s directed its local land agents like Zumwalt to check all new land claims made at the district federal land offices and new deeds filed at county courthouses against maps of railroad lands. After painstaking investigations, they filed protests against those they thought to be illegal. Attending government hearings at which rival claimants sought to "prove" their settlement on the land prior to the railroad's grant, railroad agents presented evidence and witnesses to trip up perjurers. The tactic was partially successful. Many exposed squatters, caught in the act, withdrew claims, bought the land from the company, or vanished from the neighborhood.[68]

When it lost contests against fraudulent claims at local land offices, as it often did, the Southern Pacific took appeals to the Department of the Interior in Washington, and if that failed, to the federal courts. Although the company generally refrained from pressing its legal rights against legitimate settlers, it spared no effort or expense to defeat the challenges of squatters, often spending far more than the land was worth, out of fear that seemingly innocuous cases could establish damaging precedents later involving thousands of acres. Because it held that the company's failure to appeal legal questions constituted tacit agreement to the principles involved, and hence established precedent for future disputes, the Department of the Interior guaranteed that the Southern Pacific would have to fight many cases tenaciously.

Contemporary opponents, as well as some historians, charged that the railroad, through bribery and power politics, "owned" federal and local agencies and thus was able to dictate land and other policies. Clearly, this was not the case. The railway lost a great many contests, including important ones, and even the victories were hard won in the teeth of obstructionism or outright opposition by the land bureaucracy. Particularly, the company tended to lose title conflicts caused by tardy federal verification and survey of pre-1846 Mexican land grants in California and the government's floating of them onto land to which the railroad had already gotten patents.[69] The Department of the Interior then revoked the railroad's patents to the land, much of which the company had already sold. Even if the Mexican grant was later located somewhere else, the land did not revert to the railroad but was returned for public entry. When the Department of the Interior revoked Southern Pacific patents to lands within and in the vicinity of later-approved Mexican ranchos, as happened numerous times from the late 1860s into the 1880s, masses of innocent buyers of railroad land lost titles and improvements on their lands, although the Southern Pacific refunded their land-purchase prices. Widespread confusion and discontent resulted. Some law firms specialized in representing clients with squatter claims against the railroad's land in areas around Mexican grants. Ultimately, the bulk of land taken from the railroad because of confused Mexican rancho grants appears to have gone quickly to groups of speculators, frequently organized by the same law firms, who simultaneously challenged the railroad's patents and filed mass rival claims to the land on behalf of themselves or speculators.[70] Although the company vigorously protested the General Land Office's actions, district federal land officials, many of whom were themselves speculating in public lands, steadfastly refused to cooperate. They accepted rival claims to railroad land on virtually any pretext, failed to take any action against squatters or poachers on unpatented railroad lands, and even routinely refused to notify the company when adverse claims were filed against its lands.

The General Land Office's delays in issuing land patents to the Southern Pacific, already a serious problem for the company and would-be settlers by the mid-1870s, grew much longer and more common in the 1880s. Delay became almost the permanent condition by the end of that decade, as the Department of the Interior periodically suspended action on all new railroad land patents while actively pressuring Congress to revoke the railroad grants. By 1887 in California's San Francisco, Stockton, Visalia, and Los Angeles land districts alone, for example, the General Land Office was sitting on thirty-five Southern Pacific "lists" (applications) for patents, involving hundreds of thousands of acres, some of which had been pending for longer than a decade. Government land agents were spreading word across the state that authorities would soon revoke the company's entire grant. In each of those districts during the late 1880s, responding to the government's inducements, hundreds of squatters, many of them speculators recruited and organized by a few law firms, invaded the railroad's unpatented land, to which the railroad still held legal title. The General Land Office began routinely accepting the squatters' multiple land applications to railroad land under various homestead, preemption, timber and stone, desert land, and cash-purchase laws. Some individuals were claiming thousands of acres of railroad land. From 1886 through at least 1891, when the logjam of withheld patents was partially and temporarily broken, the Southern Pacific was forced on numerous occasions to file mass protests against hundreds of squatter claims and then to prosecute the cases through the land bureaucracy.[71] By the early 1890s, the Department of the Interior still owed the Southern Pacific Company more than 3 million acres in patents, for which the railroad had submitted lists and paid surveying fees as long as a decade before, 1.6 million acres on the Central Pacific's grant alone.[72] The problem continued into the early 1900s. By 1896, a full two-thirds of the Central Pacific's grant remained unpatented because of Department of Interior delays. Some would never be patented.[73]

In Washington, the Department of the Interior, at least from the company's viewpoint, applied the laws capriciously or illegally in open defiance of U.S. Supreme Court decisions that had mandated that only congressional or federal judicial actions could void railroad land-grant titles.[74] The department also frequently reversed itself, overturning earlier decisions favorable to the railroad and inventing new principles to enlarge the loopholes through which rival claimants were able to detach company property. If anything, because of conflicts over rival claimants and squatters, in addition to ongoing disputes over the government's delays in issuing patents, relations between the Southern Pacific and the Department of the Interior worsened greatly during the 1870s and 1880s. The Department of the Interior's Washington and local land officials continued to encourage rival claims to the railroad's unpatented land-grant sections well into the twentieth century.[75]

Local government officials—judges, sheriffs, county recorders, and tax collectors—were apathetic to the railroad's protests or openly sympathized with and abetted the squatters. On the one hand, county recorders encouraged the squatters, even going so far as to quickly record squatter "deeds" to land for which the railway actually held patents. On the other hand, county tax collectors continued to levy against the railway the land and school taxes on those very same lands, usually at higher assessment rates than for non-railway land. By the 1880s, counties, holding for this purpose that the railroad's titles were perfect, also began levying taxes even against the railroad's unpatented land, which the company could not legally sell or lease yet and which was often occupied by squatters. Apparently intentionally, counties in the San Joaquin Valley and elsewhere also frequently failed to notify the railway of its land taxes, and when of course the taxes went unpaid, quickly auctioned off the land cheaply and issued "deeds" to squatters or speculators, thereby clouding titles to thousands of acres for years to come.[76] Local citizenry and organizations also encouraged, and in some cases actively directed, large-scale squatting enterprises. In northern Utah during the late 1880s, for example, the Mormon church assisted a large group of squatters to fake claims to railroad sections that supposedly predated the Department of the Interior's withdrawal of the land for patenting to the company. When the railroad's investigator alerted them, General Land Office officials dispatched an investigator of their own. The federal agent submitted a report with affidavits showing that the local church hierarchy had conspired with the claimants to acquire patents to the land by fraud, and in a rare instance of siding with the railroad, the General Land Office filed suit to recover the illegal patents.[77] In some areas, mass local support for encroachment on railroad lands continued unabated into the twentieth century. "From what I am able to learn," a Southern Pacific forest fire warden reported from northern California in 1911, "about two thirds of the inhabitants of Yreka are stealing [land and timber] from the Company and the other third are helping them."[78] Already by the late 1870s, the Southern Pacific was forced to conclude that it was pointless to pursue eviction cases in local courts because juries there rarely delivered and sheriffs rarely enforced verdicts in favor of the company. The railroad began instead to institute its litigation in federal courts, where the judgments stood a chance of being more favorable and eviction orders were more reliably executed by U.S. marshals.[79]

4 The Mussel Slough Affair

The "Octopus" Myth

The most notorious conflict between the Southern Pacific and rival claimants to its lands, the so-called "Battle of Mussel Slough" of 1880, can only be properly understood within the context of the company's long-term vexations with squatterism. That context, however, rarely appears in the innumerable published accounts of the event. In the century and a quarter since the actual dispute in the Tulare Basin of California's San Joaquin Valley, the railroad's nineteenth-century opponents, along with commemorators of the battle at local anniversary pageants, journalists, historians, and even cartoonists, novelists, dramatists, poets, and folksingers have all recounted the incident so many times that the battle at Mussel Slough has assumed mythic proportions. It has evolved into the archetypal story of the conflict between pioneer settlers and monopoly corporate greed on the American frontier.

Unfortunately, in their retelling, historians generally have consulted earlier, flawed, secondhand sources. For their basic structure of the story's issues and details, many historians have relied on Frank Norris's muckraking, anti–Southern Pacific novel, *The Octopus* (1901), a fanciful, fictional account that bears virtually no resemblance to the actual event.[1] Thus, hearsay, rather than evidence, has dominated the historical discussion. Historical accounts vary considerably, and nearly all have passed along from generation to generation errors of fact and substance, ranging from relatively minor mistakes in spelling the names of combatants and tabulating the body count to important errors of chronology and sequence of settlement, the legal issues involved, the character, motivation, and behavior of the actors in the drama, and the influence of the conflict on landholding patterns.[2] The mythic story, complete with exaggerations of the Southern Pacific's landholdings and errors of chronology, legal issues, and the goals of the railroad and the Mussel Slough settlers, even dominates a leading California state-approved history textbook for fourth-grade public school classrooms.[3] Some published accounts, including those by James L. Brown, Richard M.

"Impending Retribution," a cartoon by Edward Keller appearing in California's satirical magazine, *The Wasp*, October 7, 1882, attacked the Southern Pacific monopoly. Mussel Slough victims are depicted at upper left, and the villains—railroad executives Stanford, Crocker, and Huntington— at lower right. To the present day, the railroad's opponents and critics have evoked the Mussel Slough incident of 1880 to support their case against the Southern Pacific. Courtesy Bancroft Library.

Brown, William Deverell, and George L. Henderson, as well as some unpublished theses, do stand out for their greater reliance on primary evidence and hence more valuable contributions to the understanding of that complex event.[4]

Ignoring the dissonance of wildly different versions of the story, the traditional account of the Battle at Mussel Slough boils down to several core elements:

- The Southern Pacific deliberately delayed getting patents to its land grant in order to avoid taxes and force buyers to pay the higher prices brought by development. Even though it could or would not convey titles to them, the railroad lured settlers onto its lands in Mussel Slough country, publishing pamphlets promising settlers they would later be able to buy the land at low prices, normally about $2.50 per acre, without any charges for improvements they made to the land before they could buy it.

- After getting honest farmers to settle, improve, irrigate, and greatly increase the value of its lands, the railroad reneged on its agreements (some historians call them "written contracts"). When it belatedly took title from the federal government, the company raised the price on the land to ruinously high levels (variously stated by historians as $20 to $40 or even $80 per acre) that sought to charge farmers for their own improvements to the land. The poor settlers could not afford such high prices. Moreover, the railroad immediately put the land on the open market for sale to the highest bidder, thus threatening to dispossess those already cultivating the land.

- Faced with the railroad's deceit and their own ruin, the duped settlers appealed to federal land officials and the courts, who, bribed and controlled by the railroad, sided with the corporation. The settlers' test cases were decided against them in federal court, to which the railroad had moved the cases because it had more illicit influence over federal judges.

- When the railroad came to eject the settlers, on May 11, 1880, the settlers resisted the illegal evictions. The company's minions (described variously by different historians as company employees, dummy land purchasers, or hired gunfighters) opened fire and murdered seven innocent settlers. (Some accounts go so far as to describe the event as a "massacre.")[5]

- The Mussel Slough settlers thus lost their lands to an unscrupulous, cheating, all-powerful, monopoly railroad. The incident typified the Southern Pacific's land-grant policy and illustrated the experiences of settlers elsewhere in the company's territory.

- Universally, the railroad's contestants are portrayed as simple, innocent, impoverished frontier yeoman settlers, interested only in building and protecting their homes, but lured onto the land, lied to, cheated, and some of them even murdered by a greedy corporation.[6]

The actual story of conflict over railroad land in the Mussel Slough country is exceedingly complicated, and space limitations do not allow a retelling in full detail here. Elsewhere, I have published a more complete account, but even the simplified version of the basic story that follows demonstrates that the settlers were essentially squatters and that the issues, events, and outcomes of the battle differed dramatically from the traditional myth.[7]

Legal Origins of the Dispute

Careful attention to the detailed chronology of events is essential. Still under control of its original founders, a group of San Francisco investors led by Lloyd Tevis, and not yet the Big Four, the Southern Pacific Railroad in 1867 filed a map with the Department of the Interior calling for a change in its route between San Jose and southern California, from the original one following the coast to one through the San Joaquin Valley. At first, the department accepted the new route and, following its procedure, closed further public land sales or homesteads in the odd-numbered sections along the proposed new route and placed the land in a reserve for eventual granting to the railroad. The department entered the reserve on federal land maps in Washington and at the local government land office in Visalia, so that potential settlers on public land in the area would know what land was and was not already granted to the railroad. Within a few months, however, Secretary of the Interior Orville Browning, under intense lobbying pressure from a ring of California speculators and congressional allies led by the notorious William S. Chapman, who sought to engross the lands themselves, reversed himself, rejecting the route as in violation of the company's original state incorporation charter. Although without any legal authority to do so, Browning announced his intention to revoke the congressional land grant. However, he never did actually restore the railroad's land-grant reserve to the public domain or open it up to general settlement. Under the control of different secretaries over the next few years, the department reversed itself several more times but all the while the land remained reserved for the railroad and legally closed to other entries. The Big Four purchased the Southern Pacific Railroad in 1868 and continued to press for reconfirmation of the company's route and land grant.[8]

By 1870, through lobbying in Washington by Collis P. Huntington and the company's attorneys, Congress, the Department of the Interior, and the state legislature had all confirmed the Southern Pacific Railroad's altered route and its right to its land grant. At that time, the company had not yet built any track through the central and southern San Joaquin Valley, and only a few true settlers with valid homestead or other entries predating the railroad's 1867 map were occupying the odd-numbered sections within the railroad's grant in the Mussel Slough district. The region remained largely an unsettled frontier. Though of scant population and meager rainfall, the land had rich potential because its fertile alluvial soils could be easily irrigated by gravity from the nearby Mussel Slough branch of the Kings River. Importantly, the Department of the Interior had since 1867 closed all further rival settlement on the mostly vacant odd-numbered public land sections along the revised railroad route pending the company's building the line and the government's issuing land-grant patents to the company. Valid prior holdings, as always, were excluded from the railroad reservation, and original settlers retained secure rights to those lands.[9]

Squatters Move In

Contrary to their later claims that they were innocent pioneers lured by the Southern Pacific Railroad to its land grant by its advertising pamphlets promising them low prices, the company's Mussel Slough opponents, from the beginning, took up their claims with the intention of defeating the railroad's title and acquiring the land free of charge. The Southern Pacific Railroad did not even start publishing its land pamphlets until 1876.[10] Mass movement onto the railroad's land, on the other hand, began about 1870 with John J. Doyle. Later to become the principal squatter leader, Doyle was at that time a typical frontier drifter who, after migrating to California from Indiana in the mid-1860s, had mined, taught school, and farmed in several locales. In 1870, he read a San Francisco newspaper's prediction that, because the company had years earlier changed its route, the Southern Pacific Railroad's land grant along that line would one day be declared invalid and thrown open again to homesteading. Fired with the vision of fertile land, free of purchase price or rent, he sold his farm, and in 1871, believing that, as he later stated, "the railroad had no right to a title to these lands," Doyle moved onto a Southern Pacific section of land near the hamlet of Grangeville, a few miles north of the railroad's by-then-approved route through the Mussel Slough country. He discovered that a sprinkling of other contestants had already beaten him to railroad land in the area, also in anticipation that the company would lose its title.[11] A squatter by his own admission, Doyle advertised the alleged legal loophole and ignited a land rush into the area.[12]

Hundreds of squatters, most of them recent arrivals in the district, including numerous refugees from war-torn Confederate states in the upper South, had invaded Southern Pacific land by 1875 and more continued to arrive into the early 1880s. Some people already residing in the area sold their legitimate holdings on even-numbered sections and moved onto railroad land. Now declaring himself a lawyer, Doyle established a land business predicated on challenging the railroad's right to its grant. He entered into secret contracts with hundreds of his neighbors to secure title for them for a fee of 25 cents per acre plus, if they wound up paying less than $2.50 per acre, one-half the difference between their cost and $2.50 per acre, all payable in gold coin.[13] Doyle orchestrated repeated mass filings of rival homestead, preemption, and cash-purchase claims to the odd-numbered railroad sections at the nearby federal land office in Visalia. The land office rejected all of these, which the law required since the land was reserved for future granting to the railroad and closed to further rival settlement. Doyle, alleging that the railroad's revised route was illegal, took several rounds of appeals to hundreds of claims to the Department of the Interior in Washington. Although critical of the railroad grants and prone to decide against the Southern Pacific in other cases, Interior officials reluctantly rejected the appeals, ruling that in this particular instance, the legality of the railroad's route and land titles had long since been clearly established and tested in the courts. When appeals failed, Doyle and other leaders gathered signa-

Thomas Jefferson McQuiddy, Mussel Slough squatter vigilante chief. With other family members, the former Confederate officer and spy joined the migration of southerners to the Mussel Slough region in the early 1870s. Like others, he speculated in private and public land and also squatted on the railroad's grant. Experienced in politics and soldiering, McQuiddy soon gravitated to a position of leadership as head of militia for the Settlers' Grand League, formed in 1878 to intimidate railroad employees, public officials, and prospective buyers of railroad land. Courtesy California State Library, Sacramento.

tures on numerous petitions to Congress, the California state legislature, and other government bodies calling for a revocation of the Southern Pacific's land grant.[14]

Despite the squatters' repeated failures to secure titles, throughout the 1870s and early 1880s, speculative contesting claims against the railroad's land circulated as a form of local currency, bought and sold on an open market and advertised in newspapers, with ownership of the claims turning over rapidly and prices fluctuating wildly according to latest developments in the squatters' challenge to the railroad's title. Few of the squatters, despite their rhetorical defenses of their actions, were defending their "homes."[15] It was common for individual squatters also to occupy legal holdings on the even-numbered sections, while pursuing challenges against the railroad's title on adjacent or distant odd-numbered sections. Little of the contested railroad land was actually inhabited. Much remained undeveloped and uncropped, and little was being irrigated. Some was being plowed and sown in crops, but almost always grain or hay, typically raised in the district without irrigation.[16] The cooperative irrigation systems that squatters claimed to have built were actually mostly constructed and owned by old-time settlers belonging to the anti-squatter faction. The squatters' own irrigation works, such as they existed, were small, hand-dug trenches that were not permanent and had to be renewed each year on most tracts.[17] Similarly, squatters generally sheltered their buildings, wells, fences, major irrigation facilities, and other improvements on their secure legal properties.[18] Some squatters were merchants living in local towns. Some asserted multiple claims engrossing hundreds, in a few cases even thousands, of acres of railroad land, while simultaneously owning and buying and selling large legal tracts on the public, even-numbered sections. After the railroad started selling the land in 1877, a few Mussel Slough people went as far as to buy or lease some tracts legally from the Southern Pacific, while at the same time pushing other squatter claims against the company's title. Clearly, many of the railroad's Mussel Slough contestants were not just squatters but petty land speculators.[19]

The Railroad Seeks Compromise

With its line through the area still unbuilt, the Southern Pacific had no patents to Mussel Slough land and could not sell it. However, the railroad followed its policy of allowing actual settlers to use unpatented lands if they submitted applications to buy the land when it was eventually put on the market. Reluctant to inflame the explosive situation further and still seeking, as was its practice, to convert the squatters into customers, the company during the early and middle 1870s took no action to interrupt the squatters' use of its land. Several times, it instructed local land agent Daniel K. Zumwalt to send rounds of letters to the Mussel Slough people asking them to file standard applications to purchase with the railroad, which would have guaranteed the claimants first rights to their lands. Engaged in challenging the legality of the company's entire land grant, however, squatter leaders warned that completing such applications would amount to tacit acknowledgment of the railroad's title. Although some squatters made their peace with the company along the way, most rebuffed the Southern Pacific's overtures. From 1870 until the few weeks just before the battle in May 1880, contrary to their public defense of themselves as innocent, law-abiding land buyers, the Mussel Slough claimants actually refused to purchase the railroad's land at any price.

In 1877, the company built the rail line through the area, began to receive patents to its lands, and set its advertising and sales campaign in motion. It published its first land advertisements specifically for the area and, following its standard procedures, graded, subdivided, and put the land on the market for the first time. Viewing the fertile, alluvial, irrigable land as the most valuable and immediately salable in its entire grant, the Southern Pacific attached relatively high prices to its parcels, from about $8 to slightly more than $20 per acre. Though significantly higher than the railroad charged elsewhere, the railroad's prices were in keeping with those common for unimproved farmland in the Mussel Slough district and much lower than the $30- to nearly $100-per-acre figures squatters and, later, historians claimed.[20] Several more times from 1877 through 1879, the railroad sent out rounds of letters offering the land first to the squatters.[21] Again, although some legitimized their holdings, most categorically refused to buy, at any price, or to deal with the company in any way. Late in 1877, with its land development program in the region stymied, the company began, though reluctantly and selectively, to sell a few of the contested parcels to other buyers, generally longtime local residents who were willing to pay the railroad's prices. Still wanting to avoid trouble and to reach a compromise with the squatters, the company decided not to recruit new purchasers and to sell tracts claimed by squatters *only* when other buyers applied for the land of their own accord. Also, when it did propose to sell a contested tract to another party, the railroad instructed land agent Zumwalt to give the squatter yet one more chance to buy the claim first.

The Grand League and Squatter Violence

Faced with the possibility that the railroad would sell claims from under them, squatters, led by Doyle and the fiery Thomas Jefferson McQuiddy and other former Confederate soldiers, in the spring of 1878 formed an armed extralegal militia, the Settlers' Grand League, to resist "the occupation of so-called railroad lands in the Mussel Slough District by the Southern Pacific Railroad Company." In the age-old tradition of American frontier regulators and squatter claim clubs, the Grand League assessed members to pay for court appeals, published pamphlets to build public support, pressured local governments to refrain from interfering with squatters' use of railroad lands, and boycotted persons who were willing to come to terms with the railroad. Most threatening to the railroad, the League sent off new petitions to the state and national governments calling for revocation of the railroad's land grant and dispatched emissaries across the San Joaquin Valley to foment additional squatter movements. The League also forged alliances with other anti–Southern Pacific political groups, particularly the statewide Workingmen's Party, an anti-corporation and anti-Chinese group powerful in San Francisco and other major cities.[22]

Enrolling, according to John Doyle, about six hundred members, the Grand League assumed the trappings of a secret society—secret membership, closed meetings, and costumes of masks, hoods, and long red robes—reminiscent of the Ku Klux Klan and other white-supremacy groups then terrorizing freed slaves in the southern states from which many of the squatters had come. Like the Klan, the League announced that it would resist with force any attempt by the Southern Pacific to oust squatters from their claims. To emphasize its power, the group's mounted militiamen, rifles at the shoulder, paraded down the main streets of Mussel Slough towns. Public banishments, threats of violence, and even death sentences were proclaimed against railroad officials and those willing to cooperate with the company, especially to buy its lands. A night-riding "cavalry" of armed, masked men—in what the *San Francisco Chronicle* facetiously applauded as "domiciliary visits in disguise"—"arrested" and deported railroad employees, terrorized local supporters of the company, and evicted railroad land buyers, tore down their fences, and burned their crops, buildings, and possessions.[23] D. K. Zumwalt, the Southern Pacific's Visalia land agent, a gentle church elder, philanthropist, and temperance and wilderness-preservation advocate, after his office was broken into, his records rifled, and his life threatened, bought a stronger safe and his first pistol to defend himself.[24] With tension and violence mounting, many Mussel Slough residents, particularly old-time settlers who had long clashed with the newcomers over political influence and access to land and water, openly criticized the squatters and the Grand League's tactics. The region divided sharply between pro- and anti-squatter factions, with people on both sides arming themselves, threatening their enemies, and backing it up with fisticuffs and potshots from ambush. Some local officials, however, lent their support to the Grand League.[25] By early 1879, squatter intimidation and violence had severely reduced legitimate railroad land sales in the district and some other parts of the San Joaquin Valley.[26]

The Railroad Decides on Eviction

Also by early 1879, try as it did to avert a confrontation with occupants on its land, the company now realized that it was up against its most organized and dangerous squatter threat, with the fate of the entire Southern Pacific Railroad land grant hanging in the balance. Complicating matters and increasing the pressure on the company, Tulare and Fresno counties had begun to charge the company property taxes on the land grant, even though the railroad did not have actual possession of much of the land and was having trouble selling it to others.[27] Yet, the associates controlling the railroad, though appalled at the violence, disagreed over how to proceed. Central Pacific Railroad president Leland Stanford and vice president Collis P. Huntington, sensitive to unfavorable public opinion, fearful of possible political reprisals, and believing that the squatters were being exploited by unscrupulous leaders, favored compromise with the claimants by selling them the land cheaply if they would acknowledge the company's title to its land grant. On the other hand, Charles Crocker, president specifically of the Southern Pacific Railroad and the one legally responsible for its land grant,

insisted on holding fast to the current prices and, if necessary, aggressively evicting squatters who refused to abandon their claims.[28] Nevertheless, between 1877
and 1879, the railroad reduced its land prices several times and liberalized its
sales procedures in order to mollify contestants and lure them to acquire their
claims legally. Some squatters chose to accept the company's terms, but most
continued to attack the Southern Pacific's right to the land.

Though still uncertain how to resolve the conflict, the associates were emphatic that their title to the land was legal and had to be defended. Indeed, the
more the squatters attacked the Southern Pacific's land titles and the more intense their violent resistance, the more immovable the railroad's position became on the legality of its land grant. In early 1879 the Southern Pacific Railroad began to institute a few trespass lawsuits against squatter leaders in federal
court, test cases to pressure squatters to purchase their lands legally and to discourage squatterism elsewhere. However, when its undercover detectives informed the company that the squatters had signed a pact to ignore test cases,
to defend against all lawsuits one by one, and to resist each eviction with armed
force, company attorneys filed lawsuits against all contestants, until hundreds
of cases were before Judge Lorenzo Sawyer of the San Francisco federal court.[29]

Beginning in December 1879, Sawyer handed down orders of eviction and
financial judgments against all of the squatters. The judge ruled that the railroad's altered route had been legal; its title to the land had been perfected with
the 1867 filing of its revised route; settlers arriving on the land after that date
had no standing to attack the railroad's title; and a succession of lower federal
and U.S. Supreme Court decisions regarding the land-grant rights of other railways provided solid precedent for the legality of the Southern Pacific Railroad's
title.[30] The company, however, still hoping for a peaceful settlement, delayed
asking the judge to send marshals to enforce the orders and actually evict the
squatters.[31] Until this point, the squatters, insisting that the Southern Pacific's
land titles were flawed, refused to pay any price for the land. However, squatter leaders, faced with losing the land altogether, made a last-minute attempt
in March 1880 to work out a deal with Stanford to buy the land at a discount.
The compromise fell through, however, when squatters, thinking they had defeated the railroad, insisted on a reduction of at least 50 percent from the railroad's asking price, and, it appears, Crocker refused to lower prices more than
a few dollars per acre.[32] Finally, in early May 1880, with several of its legitimate
land buyers threatening lawsuits against the company if it did not place them
in possession of their holdings, the Southern Pacific asked the court for a few
evictions, but only in selected test cases where the disputed tracts had been sold
to other parties who were demanding possession. Beyond that, the railroad remained determined not to provoke the majority of squatters and to continue
to seek an agreement with them.[33]

The Battle of Mussel Slough

On May 11, 1880, U.S. marshal Alonzo W. Poole and Southern Pacific land-grader William H. Clark, on orders from Judge Sawyer, tried to put railroad-land purchasers Mills Hartt and Walter Crow in possession of their holdings near Grangeville, northwest of the rail center of Hanford. When the marshal attempted to serve the first order on squatter Henry Brewer, a mounted force of fifty armed men blocked the party's way. The militia "arrested" and tried to disarm the marshal and the other three, all of whom refused to give up their guns. In the shouting and shoving, a shot was fired, igniting a brief but explosive gun battle between the rival land claimants.[34] Five squatters and the two railroad land-buyers lay dead or mortally wounded in the hot sun. Marshal Poole and land-grader Clark, however, had not drawn or discharged their weapons and emerged unhurt.[35]

Local law enforcement officials at first refused to arrest anyone, but after the Southern Pacific pressed the U.S. Attorney General to prosecute, the San Francisco federal court indicted, tried, and in late 1880 convicted John Doyle and four other squatter leaders of obstructing a federal marshal. They served a bizarre, eight-month sentence at the San Jose jail, coming and going as they pleased from their unlocked cells. During his incarceration, one prisoner even wooed and married the sheriff's daughter. A wave of public sympathy swept the state and nation, transforming the squatters into innocent pioneers, duped by the railroad into settling its lands and then defrauded and murdered by the monopoly. They had become martyrs in the anti-corporate—in California, the anti–Southern Pacific—political crusade. Novelist Frank Norris later secured the squatters' national literary fame and historical influence with his 1901 novel, *The Octopus.* Local memorial ceremonials, at first annually and then periodically, featuring speeches and letters from surviving squatters and their descendants, have kept the legend alive in Mussel Slough country for more than a century. To this day, tour guides still point out the manicured graves of the fallen martyrs at the Grangeville cemetery.[36]

Local myth and traditional historical accounts agree regarding the fate of the Mussel Slough pioneers: they lost their farms and homes to the greedy railroad. Actually, in late May 1880, a delegation of anti-League community leaders, while still also critical of the railroad's actions, in the interest of civil peace and economic development, arranged a compromise with Charles Crocker. The railroad lowered its land prices 12.5 percent in addition to the earlier reductions, made retroactive for those who had already purchased their holdings. The railroad also started deducting the federal court's trespass damage fines from the prices of tracts that squatters agreed to buy. The great majority of the railroad's remaining Mussel Slough contestants, hundreds of persons, rushed to take advantage of the offer and bought or leased their lands over the next few months.[37] Only a few, the most militant, held out, refusing to bargain with the railroad, obey eviction orders, or abandon their claims. Again, local sheriffs and even federal marshals delayed serving papers on them for months, sometimes years, with remaining squatters continuing to claim and use the land.[38] Most of them had left the area by the late 1880s, however. The Grand League, its membership depleted and openly denounced by community leaders for having brought violence and ruin to the district, limped along for about a decade, unsuccessfully trying to raise money for more legal challenges and to intimidate land buyers from dealing with the railroad.[39] John J. Doyle served his prison term, paid his trespass judgment of $1,214, and bought his land legally from the railroad. He farmed it and served two terms as justice of the peace of Lemoore. In 1885, he sold out, left the district, and invested the profits in land in the eastern San Joaquin Valley and Sierra farther east. Doyle went on to become a large-scale farmer, land developer, and timberland speculator, at one time cultivating more than one thousand acres in the east valley. Later in the 1880s, he became reconciled with Collis P. Huntington, and the two former combatants over land were friends until the latter's death in 1900. Doyle died, moderately wealthy, in 1915.[40]

Aftermath

To the end of the century, age-old divisions continued to trouble Mussel Slough country. Railroad employees, though threatened, were never again attacked, but shootings and destruction of property persisted among persons competing for Southern Pacific land. On the American frontier, squatting and land speculation, like hope, sprang eternal. Even the 1880 battle and the furor that followed did not end the invasion onto the Southern Pacific's Mussel Slough lands. Yet more interlopers kept moving onto the railroad's property, refusing to buy or lease the land, plowing, planting crops, filing contesting claims, and buying and selling the claims. Some squatters who had lost their eviction cases, with large financial fines hanging over them, sold their illegal claims to other squatters before fleeing the area.[41]

As is clear from its Mussel Slough troubles, although its vigilance yielded results in specific cases, the Southern Pacific was never able to resolve the general problem of squatterism and poaching satisfactorily. The company pressed its claims vigorously and defeated many contestants, only to have squatters, sometimes the same individuals, invade other areas of the land grant. Under the best of circumstances, it could, and frequently did, take years, sometimes a decade or more, to eject determined squatters or poachers, and by that time, they had often stripped the land of much of its value.[42] Southern Pacific people came to accept combating squatters as an ordinary, if disagreeable, part of the land business. Trusting little to public officials, the railroad seized the initiative. It had its agents review county and federal land records to keep track of its interests and filed protests or lawsuits to prevent illegal claims or deeds from being issued against the company's title. The company hired detectives and roving guards, particularly to keep poaching stock-raisers away from railroad grass and water. At various times, the railroad reduced sales and lease prices in the hope of enticing squatters to legitimize their use of the land. All to little avail. Into the early twentieth century, squatterism and poaching plagued the Southern Pacific, and the company's actions against interlopers, as happened at Mussel Slough, tarnished its public image and soured relationships with some settlers and local communities.

5   A Land of "Well-tilled Little Farms"

LAND-GRANT DEVELOPMENT

Early Land Sales

At first, in the 1860s and early 1870s, with its land patents accumulating slowly and the company's attentions absorbed in constructing or buying new lines, the Southern Pacific advertised its lands only sporadically. When a new section of land grant opened up for sale, the company would broadcast advertisements to lure buyers. Early railroad promoters used a variety of familiar techniques, but without any evident long-term planning or organization, at least before the early 1880s. Land agent Benjamin B. Redding and his staff ran ads in newspapers and magazines in California, other western regions, and eastern states and answered letters from prospective buyers from as far away as Europe. The major focus of the advertising program, however, was the issuing of land pamphlets. Beginning with short and simple flyers in the late 1860s, Central and Southern Pacific land brochures by the mid-1870s had grown into lengthier and more elaborate summaries of regional resources, not just the virtues of the company's own lands. Those authored by Jerome Madden for the Southern Pacific Railroad after 1876 contained detailed maps and descriptions not only of railroad lands but also of their regions' agricultural and commercial activity and future potential.[1]

Despite increasing advertising in the 1870s, however, limited land sales, the serious depression in California and the West during the middle and end of the decade, and competition from other land-grant roads on the Great Plains did not warrant enormous expenditures of funds or energy in attracting settlers to the company's lands. No specialized immigration agent network had grown up as it had for the other land-grant railways. The job of selling railroad land, promoting settlement, and advertising California remained mostly an unspecialized one, involving land executives, including Redding and Madden, a few district land agents such as Daniel K. Zumwalt operating in the San Joaquin Valley and Robert L. Fulton in eastern California and Nevada and Utah, higher rail officials, and even, on occasion, the Big Four themselves. Huntington,

The H. P. Gray residence and farm, adjacent to the Southern Pacific Railroad's line in San Joaquin Valley, Tulare County, California, in the early 1880s. From its inception in the 1860s, Southern Pacific land-grant and settlement policies aimed at fostering small-scale family farms. Courtesy California State Library.

Hopkins, and Isaac Gates, an assistant of Huntington in New York, negotiated one land deal in 1873 with a group of farmers who wanted to settle in Kern County.[2]

In addition to using its own internal facilities for advertising and selling land, the Southern Pacific sought assistance from other agencies. In the 1870s, the California Immigrant Union, one of the state's first promotional organizations, subdivided and publicized several railroad tracts, one of which was near Colton, a new railroad town near San Bernardino.[3] After the demise of the Immigrant Union in the late 1870s, the Southern Pacific formed a working alliance with the Pacific Coast Land Bureau, a privately owned real-estate firm founded in 1881 by Wendell Easton, a skillful promoter who, through massive advertising, ultimately built his business into one of the largest and most successful land-development companies in nineteenth-century California. Billing itself as the "General Agent" for Central and Southern Pacific lands, the Land Bureau, from its headquarters in San Francisco, forty-six local offices throughout the state, and branches in Omaha, New York, New Orleans, London, and Hamburg, turned out promotional literature, sponsored traveling lecturers, including Easton himself, and in other ways tried to lure settlers onto railroad lands. Reflecting Easton's earlier success in the 1870s as the organizer of irrigated agricultural colonies near Fresno, the Land Bureau specialized in settling groups of small-scale farmers in cooperative and semi-cooperative communities on railroad lands.[4]

In this early period, the Southern Pacific inaugurated several successful land-selling techniques that would later become cornerstones of company policy. In addition, a sizable quantity of land was surveyed, patented, graded, and sold. By 1880, more than 700,000 acres of Central Pacific and 300,000 acres of Southern Pacific lands had been disposed of.[5] Despite progress in establishing an effective land-sales system, the railroad nevertheless suffered many setbacks as well, especially in relation to the goals of company development policies: selling land as soon as possible, expanding population along its lines, especially the number of small farmers, and increasing freight and passenger revenues. The agricultural future and the market for rural real estate in California, still the most developed Southern Pacific region, remained uncertain, and immigration to the state was relatively light. The depression of the 1870s lasted into the early 1880s, taking a heavy toll from company revenues and land sales. The Central Pacific, which had sold 92,000 acres in 1877, could only dispose of 43,000 in 1879, a small fraction of the annual total a few years later. By the early 1880s, although aggregate land sales were large, since they were mostly on credit, actual income barely exceeded the expenses of the Land Department. As of 1877, for instance, the accumulated revenue of the Central Pacific's Land Department was $407,000, but because expenses incurred for surveying and selling reached $420,000, the department actually operated at a $13,000 loss during its first decade. As time-payment contracts matured and became due, the company's income from land sales improved, but actual profits in these early years remained less than officials hoped and critics of the railroad charged.[6]

In addition to the region's depressed economy, the company had at first only partially succeeded in building effective advertising programs and agencies. In the early 1880s, despite the railroaders' founding of land departments, hiring of promotional writers, experimenting with sponsoring eastern exhibits of California products, and building closer ties to booster organizations like the California Immigrant Union, officials readily admitted that the Southern Pacific had not yet devised a systematic plan to attract settlers to California or other parts of its territory.[7] The advertising expenditures of the California railways were still small, especially when compared to future outlays. Exclusive of Land Department expenses, the Central Pacific's annual advertising budget in the 1870s and early 1880s fluctuated between $12,000 and $15,000, and the Southern Pacific's remained between $1,600 and $7,000.[8] The lavish advertising for which the railroad would later be famous was clearly not yet a part of the company's operations.

Promoting Small Farms

Initially, the Southern Pacific's intention of settling its lands primarily with small farmers was being realized but not without discontinuities. As early as 1867, promotional literature, as well as internal correspondence and policy statements of the Land Department, reiterated that the company desired to sell "in limited quantities to those who will cultivate the soil, and who will own the land they cultivate."[9] Land agents Redding and Madden, as William H. Mills would later do, repeatedly instructed regional agents like Daniel K. Zumwalt in the San Joaquin Valley that they should conduct the company's local business so that lands stayed out of the hands of speculators and went instead to small-scale working farmers who resided on the land. Nonetheless, the railroad did not uniformly achieve its goal of maximum density settlement in these early years. By inspecting deed and patent books for counties containing railroad lands, historian Walter A. McAllister concluded in his 1939 dissertation that the California railways appeared at first to sell land to anyone who offered to buy it, regardless of the size of the parcel. According to McAllister, the Central Pacific particularly followed this practice. In Sacramento County, for example, Charles McLaughlin of San Francisco in 1881 and 1882 made twenty-three purchases totaling nearly 65,000 acres. In Stanislaus County, from 1870 to 1881, McLaughlin made nineteen acquisitions totaling 51,506 acres; for that period, only 7,000 acres of Central Pacific land in this county were sold to others. Including purchases of 133,000 acres in San Joaquin and 79,000 in Alameda counties, McLaughlin by 1881, with 330,000 acres, almost half the company's total sales, was clearly the largest recipient of Central Pacific lands. Although it did not duplicate the performance of its sister road, the Southern Pacific Railroad in this period transferred parcels of thousands and tens of thousands of acres to a few large operators in the San Joaquin Valley counties, particularly huge sales to the agribusiness partners Lloyd Tevis and James Ben Ali Haggin.[10]

The railroad's anti-monopoly critics have traditionally focused on the failure of the company to convert all its grant immediately into small producing farms and its apparent complicity with some buyers engrossing huge landed estates. Critics at the time as well as more recent scholars, some of whom cite McAllister's old study, have generally overlooked some straightforward explanations for these early railroad practices, however. The land grant in California was concentrated mostly in the Central Valley, foothill, and southern desert regions, most of which lacked sufficient rainfall for intensive farming. Aridity was also severe in the Great Basin. Such conditions, in view of the primitive level of irrigation technology in the 1860s and 1870s, virtually dictated that much railroad land was initially of little value except for large-scale grazing or cereal agriculture.[11] Also, the railroad felt some pressure to dispose of lands quickly in order to acquire additional capital for expansion, a chronic concern of Huntington and others in the 1860s and 1870s. Temptations were apparently occasionally too great in the early years of land sales to sacrifice long-term development goals, which would have required unavailable capital and energy, for short-term income. Once again, however, this reflected, more than it diverged from, the initial practices of the other land-grant roads, particularly the trans-Missouri railways, which were also short of funds and whose lands were often too arid for immediate subdivision into small-scale farms.[12]

Moreover, speculator Charles McLaughlin's specific acquisition of immense holdings from the Central Pacific had an entirely different meaning from surface appearances, illustrating once again that comprehensive documentary research is essential to untangling the Southern Pacific's complicated history. Almost all of McLaughlin's acquisitions were actually from the grant area of the Central Pacific's subsidiary, the Western Pacific Railroad, between San Jose and Sacramento. In the late 1860s, the Central Pacific had acquired the line from a group of investors led by McLaughlin, but as part of the transaction, the group retained the Western Pacific's right to its land grant as partial payment from the cash-strapped Big Four. After the Western Pacific had been constructed and when the patents to its subsidiary's lands began to be received from the General Land Office, however, the Central Pacific discovered that the government would not issue the patents directly to the Western Pacific's original owners. Under the circumstances, the simplest way to fulfill the contract with McLaughlin and partners, as well as the government's regulations, was for the Central Pacific to take title itself and then to "sell" the land to McLaughlin for a token payment. Similarly, when they completed their purchase of the San Francisco & San Jose Railroad in 1870, the Big Four, unable to finance the deal, were forced, over Collis P. Huntington's objections, to pay Lloyd Tevis, president of the San Francisco & San Jose, an undivided one-twentieth interest in the land grant of the Southern Pacific Railroad, another subsidiary. In the 1870s, Tevis and his partner Haggin cashed in the debt in exchange for 320,000 acres, mostly in the southern San Joaquin Valley. In that manner, the majority of the Southern Pacific's initial large-tract land sales were residues of the politics and finance of railroad consolidation and thus bore no relationship to the company's actual land-settlement policy or its practices after the early years.[13]

Failure to convert all lands into small holdings did not mean that the Southern Pacific had relinquished the goal of dense settlement of its granted lands. The railroad's early subdivision programs succeeded in large part, particularly in more arable regions nearer to rail lines. As the Southern Pacific Railroad in the 1870s extended its line southward down the San Joaquin Valley to Los Angeles and westward to Yuma, it built towns, some of which, such as Modesto, Turlock, Tulare, Hanford, Delano, and Colton, quickly became bustling

HO! FOR CALIFORNIA!!

THE LABORER'S PARADISE!!

Salubrious Climate, Fertile Soil, Large Labor Returns.

NO SEVERE WINTERS, NO LOST TIME, NO BLIGHT OR INSECT PESTS.

Daily Trains from Boston, New York, Philadelphia, Baltimore, Chicago, St. Louis, Omaha and Intermediate Points, for San Francisco.

EMIGRANT TICKETS AT LOW RATES.

Choice from nearly every Variety of Farming, Fruit, Grazing and Timber Lands.

The Central Pacific Railroad Co.

now offer, in sections, adjacent to their Railroad lines in **CALIFORNIA, NEVADA** and **UTAH,** a large body of Land, most of which is well adapted to cultivation, and offer unequaled advantages for settlement or investment.

IN CALIFORNIA the lands lying on each side of the main line of the Central Pacific Railroad extend from the navigable waters of the Sacramento, above the Bay of San Francisco, across the broadest and most populous portion of the Sacramento Valley and both slopes of the Sierra Nevada Mountains. They are diversified in soil, climate and conditions—embracing the semi-tropical productions in the lower valleys—corresponding with those of Spain, Italy, and the shores of the Mediterranean—the vine, orchard and grain lands of the foot-hills corresponding with those of France, Germany and Austria—and the timber lands of the mountain slopes—corresponding with those of Maine, Sweden, Norway, etc. This central portion of California is already noted for the excellence of its wheat, grapes, pears, cherries, strawberries, small fruits and garden vegetables generally, *and for the ease with which they can be grown to dimensions and perfection unattainable elsewhere.* The lands in this belt, purchased of the Company, have resulted in gratifying success to the settlers. Wheat can safely lie in the field till threshed and shipped, and the fruit trees are not troubled by insects or blight.

Along the CALIFORNIA and OREGON BRANCH, in the renowned Valley of the Sacramento, extending from the centre to the northern boundary of the State, the Company also offer a choice selection, with the same general characteristics. This valley is at present the seat of the most successful culture of small grains (wheat, barley, oats, etc.), in the country, and also offers unrivaled facilities for extensive and profitable sheep and stock grazing. The whole comprises *some of the Best Land in California.*

IN NEVADA the main line of the Central Pacific Railroad occupies the Truckee and Humboldt Valleys, the largest and best settled in the State, at a short distance from numerous and important mining regions, whose yield of the precious metals is estimated at from fifteen to twenty million dollars annually. The lands of the Company are so situated as to command these markets for their produce. Wherever the proper cultivation has been applied, these lands have yielded good crops of cereals and esculents.

IN UTAH, in the great Salt Lake and contiguous valleys, where the Mormons have so successfully demonstrated the fertility of the soil and the healthfulness of the climate, the Company have also good land.

TITLE, PATENT DIRECT FROM THE UNITED STATES GOVERNMENT.

These lands will be sold in quantities and on terms to suit. Immigrants, colonists and capitalists, who desire to acquire indestructible real property, certain to advance in value, will be benefited by an examination. Pamphlets, maps, etc., will be furnished by application to

B. B. REDDING, Land Commissioner Central Pacific Railroad Co,
SAN FRANCISCO, CAL.

ALONG THE ROUTE OF THE SOUTHERN PACIFIC RAILROAD.

The undersigned has been authorized by the Southern Pacific Railroad Company of California, to offer, in conjunction with the above, a vast extent of land, among the best in the southern half of the State, situated on both sides of the line of their road, now building, extending from the Bay of San Francisco to San Jose, southwardly to the Colorado River (700 miles). This grant covers some of the best lands in the coast and valley counties, of the southern half of California, including the far-famed wheat lands of the Contra Costa, San Joaquin, Tulare, Kern River and other valleys. Wine-making, orcharding, tobacco, cotton and fibrous plant-raising, and sheep and cattle husbandry, are extensively and successfully carried on there.

Parties desiring information relative to large tracts can apply at the Offices of the Southern Pacific Railroad Company,

No. 9 Nassau Street, New York, and **C. P. HUNTINGTON.**
Cor. Fourth and Townsend Sts., San Francisco, California.

Central Pacific and Southern Pacific land-sales poster from the mid-1870s. Author's collection.

agricultural and commercial centers. The railroad endowed these towns with hotels, hospitals, churches, schools, and parks and promoted settlement aggressively.[14] Countless small farms were also established on railroad land in the period. Land agent Redding reported that in 1877 alone five hundred families, many of them driven north by drought in southern California, had settled on Central Pacific land in Colusa and Tehama counties in the Sacramento Valley.[15] Moreover, both the California Immigrant Union and the Pacific Coast Land Bureau, who handled consignments of much railroad land, specialized in planting colonies of small-scale farms, several of which were founded on railroad lands in San Bernardino and Siskiyou counties.

Analysis of data about all Southern Pacific Railroad land-grant sales in the 1870s and early 1880s, covering much of the San Joaquin Valley from Fresno south, shows that, despite occasional transfers of a few large tracts to the Tevis-Haggin interests to fulfill obligations over which it had no control, the railroad strongly favored sales to small purchasers. By far the majority of sales contracts—nearly all in some periods and regions—were for small tracts between 40 and 160 acres, particularly near the rail lines.[16] Although the railroad did sell some large, mostly remote tracts to a few buyers, promoting compact settlement by small-scale farmers was the principal Southern Pacific land-development strategy in the early period of sales from 1865 to the early 1880s.

Land-Grant Development
during and after the Boom of the Eighties

Despite its official policy of favoring land sales to small-scale, resident farmers, the company still faced the threat that, since the land could simply be purchased by persons who would hold it for speculation, the railroad's new policies might not have the desired effect on social or economic development in rural areas. Undoubtedly, some Southern Pacific land, even small-scale purchases, was acquired by speculators; however, this was also often the case with public lands, particularly in California.[17] To minimize this possibility, the railroad after 1883 coupled its expanded advertising with more effort to colonize lands, promote higher-density settlement, and modernize agriculture on the lands it sold. In response to widespread complaints that some of its buyers were slow to improve or subdivide their lands, the company in 1884 adopted new sales policies to encourage even more the rapid settlement and cultivation by actual farmers. Those willing to occupy and improve agricultural lands immediately qualified for a discount of 33 to 40 percent off sale prices. In these contracts, however, the railroad retained control of the land until the occupant fulfilled the agreement to improve the land within three months. If the new owner failed to do so, the lands reverted to the company and no future applications for land from that individual would be accepted. Even grazing land had to be fenced or occupied, or it too would revert. Subsequent land contracts negotiated by the Southern Pacific and its subsidiary agencies contained these provisions.[18]

By the mid-1880s, the railroad was in a position to devote more energy and funds to land-grant development, not just rapid sales. The company's financial affairs were more settled. With the trackage expansion program slowing to a manageable pace, the pressure to find quick capital and dispose of the land grant as quickly as possible subsided.[19] California's and the West's economies were reviving somewhat from the doldrums of the 1870s, largely because of an influx of middle-class land-seekers who demanded and could afford developed farms. The railroad matched its new advertising and land promotion operation with additional programs to carve the land grant into small parcels and to settle organized colonies of farmers on them.[20]

In addition to relying on the experience of its own land agents, the railroad in the 1880s and 1890s sought the assistance of outside experts in planning its land colonization programs. In the late 1880s, the Southern Pacific commissioned William Hammond Hall, former California state engineer and a respected authority on irrigation, to conduct a detailed study of the land grant, particularly the ways irrigation might be employed to enhance its value and productivity. Hall's report encouraged railway officials to rethink land policies and to shift their focus from rapid disposal to building irrigation systems and developing lands before selling them.[21]

In 1889, these concerns were embodied into a new corporate department, the Southern Pacific Colonization Agency, to establish settlements of small-scale farmers on railroad lands, particularly in California. Led by Bernhard Marks, who had planned the pioneer agricultural colonies of the Fresno area in the mid-1870s, the bureau dispatched agents to Europe and states east of the Rocky Mountains and unleashed a barrage of promotional materials, much of which stressed the cooperative colony as the best technique for overcoming California's farming difficulties, which included the large amount of capital needed for successful farming, the requirement for specialized knowledge, and the social disadvantages of isolated life on a new frontier. Within a few months, the agency's agents were directing farm families from the Middle West onto railroad and other lands. By early January 1890, Dutch, French, and Spanish groups of up to fifty families each had arrived in California bound for railroad land, some of which the company had already improved with houses, roads, and other facilities. In its annual review edition of 1890, the *Alta California* praised the agency as "one of the most important matters relating to the settlement of the State."[22]

Actually, beyond the formal work of the railroad's specialized Colonization Agency, Southern Pacific lines in California, and in Texas as well, from the 1870s into the early twentieth century worked with organized groups of farmers or would-be farmers to found colonies on the company's granted lands, sometimes consolidated with adjacent public or private tracts. In 1884 and 1885, for example, a group of five hundred Lutheran families from St. Louis colonized 7,700 acres of Central Pacific land, subdivided along with intervening public land sections, west of Redding in the far northern Sacramento Valley. The colony's leaders anticipated expanding the community to twenty thousand acres.[23] A year later, Collis P. Huntington, from his New York office, cooperated with philanthropists from the Danish island of Iceland to colonize impoverished countrymen in California.[24] In 1882 and again in 1891, Huntington and other Southern Pacific officials worked with Pacific Coast Jewish colonization societies to place recently arrived Russian Jewish refugees on lands in California.[25]

Perhaps the most unusual Southern Pacific colonization scheme, and one with significant potential for social and cultural impact on California, was the attempt in 1899 and 1900 by Henry E. Huntington, Collis P. Huntington, and William H. Mills to bring the controversial Russian sect, the Doukhobors, to the state. Anarchistic secessionists from the Russian Orthodox Church, the Doukhobors rejected the formal authority of church and government. Resorting to both passive and aggressive tactics of resistance against paying taxes, serving in the military, and eventually even taking baths and wearing clothes, the group developed a reputation for trouble-making. Persecuted ruthlessly by the church, civil authorities, and the general citizenry, the Doukhobors were hounded from place to place in Russia in the eighteenth and nineteenth centuries. Leo Tolstoy and other Russian and English philanthropists arranged in early 1899 for more than 7,000 of them to resettle on public lands in southern Saskatchewan, Canada, just above the border with Montana; thousands more were set to follow as soon as a new homeland was secured. Bitterly discontented with the harsh Canadian climate and their bleak, primitive lands and misled into thinking they were to be granted autonomy from governmental control, the impoverished Doukhobors refused to swear allegiance to the government and resorted again to their flamboyant resistance tactics. Many Canadians opposed them as crude, religiously subversive, and unassimilable.[26]

Leaders scouting out another refuge in the United States in late 1899 came to the attention of Henry E. Huntington in San Francisco. Henry enlisted the enthusiastic support of his uncle in New York. A vehement opponent of ethnic and religious prejudice, Collis P. Huntington praised the Doukhobors as "excellent people," of whom "we could [not] have too many in California."[27] The railroad resolved to find a tract of fertile, but inexpensive, company or private land on which to colonize about 12,000 Doukhobors on small farms, as well as to find work for them in the state to help finance their migration and resettlement. In addition to the immigrants' value as farm builders, the Huntingtons especially looked to the sect as a potential temporary workforce to ease the Southern Pacific's critical labor shortage on the construction front then completing the Coast Line at Point Conception north of Santa Barbara.[28] William H. Mills ushered the sect's agents around California, examining railroad and private lands in the Sacramento Valley and a privately owned ranch in the Cholame Valley near San Luis Obispo. The Doukhobors' agents appeared to have decided on the Cholame Valley site, and the group's immigration to California appeared assured. By early 1900, the railroad had already brought several hundred Doukhobors from Canada to work in California factories and lumber mills and especially on the Coast Line project; by mid-summer five more of the workers were arriving at the construction front each day.[29]

The Doukhobors' notoriety had preceded them to the Golden State, however, and newspapers predictably raised a furor over the group's resettlement. Some papers, notably the *Los Angeles Herald,* after some initial trepidation, welcomed the Doukhobors, but editors, particularly of San Francisco's *Call* and *Examiner,* attacked the group and denounced the railroad for foisting such inferior troublemakers off on the state. William Randolph Hearst's ultra-racist *Examiner* condemned the Doukhobors as "a slavic horde.... generally ignorant, generally dirty."[30] Labor unions also opposed the immigration of these foreign workers, and the Canadian government, despite its aggravations with the group, protested against losing thousands of settlers from its western prairies. Ultimately, holding that their arrival would violate the law prohibiting the importation of contract laborers, the United States government in early 1900 started blocking the entry of Doukhobors at the border. Already under fire from unions and newspapers in California for employing Mexican and Japanese immigrants and American Indians on its construction and maintenance projects, and hesitant to bring down the wrath of the federal government, the Southern Pacific let the matter drop in the late summer of 1900.[31] Several hundred Doukhobors remained working at lumber mills and on the Southern Pacific for a few months before returning to Canada. In 1908, their lands seized by the Canadian government because they still refused to take the required loyalty oaths, the Doukhobor colony began a move to British Columbia, where for the rest of the century they gained international fame for their periodic tangles with government officials and their sit-ins and parades in the nude to protest having to pay taxes or meet other obligations of citizenship.[32]

The Pacific Improvement Company and Land Development

Not only did the Southern Pacific promote the settlement of its own lands, which was predictable, but self-interest also encouraged the Big Four to acquire and develop additional land beyond the limits of their companies' original grants. Like other builders of nineteenth-century land-grant railroads, the associates founded auxiliary corporations to handle construction and other kinds of business that were either expressly forbidden by railroad charters or more easily and profitably accomplished without glaring public scrutiny. The Contract and Finance Company, which initially undertook these tasks, was succeeded by the Western Development Company in the early 1870s, and in November 1878 by the Pacific Improvement Company. Into the early twentieth century, the company managed and developed the far-flung business empire accumulated by Huntington, Stanford, Hopkins, Crocker, and their families.[33] Although the holding companies have been justly criticized as covert devices to extract extra profits from railroad construction and operations, these concerns, particularly the Pacific Improvement Company, also had a more profound meaning for the history of California, and indeed the entire Far West and Southwest.[34]

By the 1880s, the Pacific Improvement Company was a gigantic holding company, certainly one of the largest corporations in the American West. In addition to owning the stocks and bonds of many of the Southern Pacific Company's rail lines, the Pacific Improvement Company controlled dozens of subsidiary companies conducting diverse activities in shipping, mining, publishing, urban and rural land development, resort hotels, electric streetcars, and water systems and other public utilities throughout the railroad's territory.[35] In immensity and scope, the Pacific Improvement Company, now largely overlooked by historians, dwarfed all other western enterprises, save only the giant railroads such as the Union Pacific and the Southern Pacific themselves. Its assets by the mid-1890s totaled an astounding $64 million.[36] Although technically separate, the Pacific Improvement Company and the Southern Pacific Company were owned by the same people and operated as one in practice, at least until the Harriman interests gained control of the railroad in the early 1900s. Even Collis P. Huntington chronically complained that it was impossible to discern where one company left off and the other began, or which assets controlled by the improvement company belonged to which family. Huntington's periodic attempts to force an accounting and separation of interests proved unsuccessful until late in his lifetime. The Big Four, members of their families, and executives of the Southern Pacific served also as officials of the Pacific Improvement Company and its subsidiaries. William H. Mills, for instance, not only supervised the land departments of the Southern Pacific Company's many rail lines, but, beginning in the late 1880s also managed land development and sales activities for the improvement company and its many real estate firms. Lands owned by one were often developed or marketed by the other, or were consolidated into larger subdivisions. The decisions and activities of the two corporations so closely paralleled and supplemented each other, particularly in land development and promotion matters, that, as historian Earl Pomeroy has observed, the Pacific Improvement Company served as the railroad's "versatile alter ego."[37]

One important function of the Contract and Finance Company and especially the Pacific Improvement Company was to create towns along the newly constructed tracks of the Southern Pacific lines. In the 1870s and early 1880s, the holding companies founded and fostered the early growth of such rail centers in the San Joaquin Valley as Lathrop, Turlock, Modesto, Merced, Tulare, Delano, Tipton, Goshen, Hanford, Sumner, and Fresno. By planting towns, the railroad and its associated firms were organizing and shaping local settlement. The Southern Pacific usually established yards, shops, and local railroad offices, while the holding company surveyed, laid out the streets and lots, constructed buildings, and made other improvements, particularly installing a water supply. To attract attention and lot-buyers to the new towns and to establish them as the commercial centers of their regions, the railroad staged elaborate advertising campaigns, including widely dispersed pamphlets, excursion trains of Pullman Palace cars from San Francisco and other cities, and auctions of town lots with free lunches and brass-band music.[38] The Southern Pacific's holding companies also developed town sites in the San Francisco Bay area, around Los Angeles, and throughout the railroad's territory, including Oregon, Nevada, Arizona, and Texas. Where its own land grant was insufficient for viable town sites, as was usually the case, the railroad secured the necessary land from others. Once established, the railroad's towns, especially because of their transportation and marketing facilities, raised land values in their vicinities, encouraging subdivisions of tracts and concentration of small-farm populations. Sometimes, decades after the Southern Pacific had built a rail line, the Pacific Improvement Company was still selling town lots, developing parks, and fostering business and community development in the market towns.[39]

From the 1880s into the early 1900s, the building of the Southern Pacific's Coast Route between the San Francisco Bay area and Los Angeles occasioned more town and farm community development by the Pacific Improvement Company. Since the line along the coast mostly traversed Mexican-era ranches that were already privately owned, the railroad, with no land grant in the area, had to purchase its right-of-way. In order to increase traffic along the line and to convert this relatively isolated and low-value land into profitable investments, the improvement company undertook projects that left a lasting imprint on California's seacoast. In Monterey, the company in the early 1880s built Hotel Del Monte, first and perhaps most famous of the great western resort hotels, for decades a major watering place for the world's elite as they toured California.[40] Near the hotel, the company bought 7,000 acres of ranch land from

The first trains enter Merced, California, on the Southern Pacific's new line down the San Joaquin Valley, on January 25, 1872. Characteristically, by the time the trains arrived, the company had already platted the town and built the large El Capitan Hotel to serve as a local business and social center. Author's collection.

David Jacks for $35,000 in 1880 and founded the town of Pacific Grove. After building reservoirs and bringing water to the town and spending hundreds of thousands of dollars in improvements, the company advertised, sold lots, and fostered the community's development over several decades into a peaceful, modest village, a center of Methodist Chautauqua activities.[41]

To secure a right-of-way a few miles west of Santa Barbara, the company in 1887 purchased land from John Hope on a magnificent oceanside highland. By the early 1900s, the company had also acquired land and water rights in the nearby mountains, had conveyed the water overland to a reservoir constructed on the ranch, and had begun to irrigate and plant the surrounding lands. Subdivided into "villa sites" from two to fifty acres in size, Hope Ranch was lavishly advertised as a ranching subdivision for the rich, with a country club, lake, polo field, and race track. Within a few years, sumptuous estates had been erected and the ranch had become one of California's most attractive rustic residential areas.[42] The Pacific Improvement Company promoted similar developments in the 1890s and 1900s on former David Jacks–owned land at Pebble Beach near Monterey, and in Sonoma County, where a subsidiary company, the El Verano Improvement Association, subdivided ranch property into resort hotels, town lots, and estate-size tracts selling for $300 per acre.[43]

The Pacific Improvement Company also purchased, improved, and subdivided agricultural property in the vicinity of railroad lines, including new branches built specifically for that purpose. The activities of the Southern Pacific and its associated corporations in the Capay Valley after the 1880s represent an excellent example of the complex influences the railroad had on social and economic change in California and other parts of its territory. Although the valley, extending twenty miles into the eastern foothills of the coastal range about thirty miles west of Sacramento, possessed rich agricultural resources of climate, soil, and water, before the railroad entered in the late 1880s the region's potential remained unrealized. Land usage had changed little since the Mexican period. Most land was still vacant or devoted to livestock raising, with some conversion to wheat farming after the 1860s. The absence of transportation facilities and long-term declines in the cattle and wheat markets delayed intensive economic development of the region, however. During the 1880s, despite the boom that transformed some other areas of California, the valley and indeed all of Yolo County languished in depression. By the end of the decade, Capay Valley was dotted with ghost ranches and villages, monuments to its unfulfilled natural promise.[44] Beginning with the initial planning of the Southern Pacific's branch line from Sacramento to Clear Lake through the Capay Valley, however, the impact of the railroad was profound. The mere planning of the line was used effectively by local promoters as evidence of impending prosperity. The new economic potential that came with the rail connection immediately stimulated increased land sales, the founding of farms, and the conversion of acreage to higher-profit cultivation.[45]

Capitalizing on this potential, Southern Pacific leaders actively shaped a social and economic revolution in order to expand traffic along its new route and to profit from land subdivision. In June 1887, they incorporated the Capay Valley Land Company as a subsidiary of the Pacific Improvement Company, with William H. Mills as general agent. For $408,689, the new real-estate firm purchased 8,700 acres in the valley that had previously been planted in grains and began the long-term process of carving it into more valuable small farms and orchards. In subsequent years, the Capay Valley Land Company spent large sums building roads, bridging rivers, and subdividing the parcel into twenty-acre farms. By October 1887, work had progressed enough to begin advertising. For more than a decade, the company ran ads in newspapers throughout California and the rest of the country.[46]

Within only a few years the economic change stimulated by the railroad and the Capay Valley Land Company was visible. By 1891, an especially successful year, several agricultural colonies had been founded by the company and 3,556 acres of the original ranch had been sold to 156 different purchasers, in parcels varying from seven to eighty acres, with almost all falling in the ten- to thirty-acre range and the average sale at twenty-two and one-half acres. The land sold for $50 to $150 per acre, but most buyers took advantage of the company's liberal credit plan of 20 percent down, an interest payment of 7 percent each year, and the remainder of the principal after five years. By 1898, the Capay Valley Land Company had sold 7,090 acres for a profit of $490,000 and had created over a hundred more small farms. The company also had begun purchasing additional land to subdivide. The total value of sales, outstanding time-payment contracts, and remaining land was $653,490.[47]

Not only was a large tract of land subdivided into smaller farms, but land use was also revolutionized. In order to call attention to the fruit-growing potential of the valley, the land company in the late 1880s began to plant orchards and vineyards on its lands. Buyers of the land were also required to raise fruit as a condition of purchase. The company also encouraged and aided purchasers of other lands in the valley to do the same by offering prizes to farmers for planting trees and achieving high productivity. By 1891, almost 1,700 acres of land belonging to the company and its customers had been planted with nearly 168,000 fruit trees. Others in the valley had set out 32,000 more. That year, Southern Pacific Company president Collis P. Huntington boasted in his annual report that "the effects of this subdivision of land and substitution in the product of the soil upon the material prosperity of that section, and in fact upon the entire State, is beyond estimate, and already there has been a considerable increase in the acreage planted in fruit in other parts of the central and northwestern sections of the State."[48]

While Huntington undoubtedly overestimated the impact of this single development on California as a whole, certainly the future of the Capay Valley was greatly altered. As late as 1889, when the area remained committed to livestock and wheat, it still suffered from "hard times." By 1890, however, a vigorous debate was in process over the advantages of fruit versus wheat production. By 1891, the debate was forgotten, and the valley was in midst of an orchard-planting boom. In its annual review for 1891, the *Woodland Mail* observed that since 1889 wheat production in Yolo County had fallen by one fifth while fruit and raisin production had doubled. By the twentieth century, Capay Valley was a leading fruit-growing region, specializing in such high-value crops as figs, oranges, raisins, apricots, and other deciduous fruit. In 1913, the Capay Valley Land Company, still buying and selling land in the area but no longer affiliated with the Southern Pacific since the separation of the railroad from the Pacific Improvement Company brought about by the Harriman Lines merger in 1901, had disposed of more than two-thirds of its holdings. In addition to profits gained from selling and financing hundreds of small farms, the company had also benefited from increasing property values. In 1913, its remaining 2,680 acres had a market value of $200,000.[49]

In the process of altering the valley's economy, the Capay Valley Land Company, in keeping with the goals of its parent Southern Pacific to promote dense settlement, sponsored social change as well. Instead of selling land indiscriminately, the land company founded concentrated agricultural colonies and disposed of lands in the vicinity of these centers first. By the early 1890s the land company had founded the towns of Esparto, Cadanassa, Guinda, and Rumsey at intervals of a few miles along the Southern Pacific branch line. Farther up the valley, the cooperative colony of Tancred was built on company land. In these communities, the land company erected parks, hotels, business buildings, railway stations, and warehouses. Businesses, including a newspaper, were lured from Woodland, the county seat, nearby Madison, and other towns. Railroad excursions from northern California cities were organized, with town lots sold at festive auctions. Within a few months, the valley was taking on a settled appearance, with schools in each community, numerous fraternal lodges, three Farmers' Alliances, two churches, and even a gas company. In 1891, Esparto alone boasted of $125,000 worth of buildings. The Tancred Colony soon demonstrated its march toward civilization by petitioning the county to designate its roads as county highways and by attaching restrictive covenants to all deeds barring the sale of intoxicating liquors. Reflecting his abhorrence of alcohol, land agent Mills got Collis P. Huntington to donate money toward the building of a temperance reading room at Rumsey.[50] Mills also worked out an arrangement with the Yolo County Board of Supervisors whereby the land company and the county shared the expense of bridging Cache Creek at Rumsey and building five miles of wagon road connecting the railhead at Rumsey with a hitherto isolated district, opening up yet more land to subdivision.[51]

The Southern Pacific and its allied companies from the 1880s well into the twentieth century were clearly engaged in the Capay Valley in the active subdivision of large tracts of low-value real estate into small farms, the introduction of new specialty crops, and the sponsorship of compact settlement. In other localities, the railroad instituted similar programs to promote social and economic development. Another subsidiary of the Pacific Improvement Company, the Sonoma Valley Improvement Company, purchased a ranch north of San Francisco Bay in 1888, carved it into small parcels, cleared away stones, set out vineyards and other new crops, and sold these farms at a profit. Also in the late 1880s and early 1890s, the Pacific Improvement Company itself acquired 12,000 acres in Tehama County, improved the land, and offered it for sale in

40- to 320-acre farms at $10 to $20 per acre, with the same time-payment plan as that used by the Capay Valley Land Company.[52]

Through the Pacific Improvement Company, other subsidiary companies, or on their own as individuals, the Big Four in the 1880s and 1890s bought or attempted to buy and subdivide numerous other large ranch properties. In the late 1880s, the Southern Pacific, again through the Pacific Improvement Company, made an abortive try to acquire and subdivide the famous Irvine Ranch in Orange County, southeast of Los Angeles.[53] Other, successful, purchases and subdivision projects included the Wilson Ranch in Butte County, a 140,000-acre tract of Miller-Lux property in the San Joaquin Valley, the Ione Ranch at the edge of the Sierra foothills in the lower Sacramento Valley, and many thousands of acres in the Crocker-Huffman Land and Water Company around Merced in the San Joaquin Valley, co-founded in partnership in the early 1880s and then bought out entirely by Charles Crocker in the late 1880s. Typically, either from their inception or at least eventually, these subdivisions came under the management of the railroad's land expert, William H. Mills. Into the early twentieth century, sometimes decades after it had severed its official ties to the Southern Pacific and its founders, the Pacific Improvement Company was operating utilities and developing urban and agricultural property near the railroad's lines not only in California but also in Oregon, Nevada, Arizona, and Texas.[54] In the early 1900s, after it had severed its ties to the Pacific Improvement Company, the Southern Pacific Company, operating through a newly formed Southern Pacific Land and Immigration Association, itself purchased, or helped other investors purchase, private land for subdivision into several successful small-farm colonies in Texas.[55] In 1904, the railroad went so far as to obtain options on more than one million acres in Cuba for a massive, but never completed, subdivision project to colonize farmers who would have been recruited in the United States and elsewhere and transported to the island by Southern Pacific steamships.[56]

The Pacific Improvement Company left a powerful influence on the development of farms and urban properties, as well as associated industries, particularly in California. Its work, however, was not without contradictions and conflicts. Particularly after Collis P. Huntington's ouster of Leland Stanford as president of the Southern Pacific Company in 1890 and Stanford's embittered death in 1893, long-simmering tensions and feuds among the Big Four families flared up, often becoming embodied in the complex affairs of the Pacific Improvement Company. As was also the case with the railroad, some of the subsidiary's many properties were co-owned in undivided equal shares by the Big Four or their heirs; others were owned privately by one or more of the four interests and just managed by the improvement company. Squabbles were frequent over costs, profits, accounting, management, and even who owned how much of which property. Generally, by the early 1890s, two factions emerged within the company, and within the railroad as well: the Crocker-Stanford heirs, led by Charles F. Crocker, deceased builder Charles's son, and Jane Stanford, Leland's widow; and the Huntington-Hopkins interest, still headed by Collis P. Huntington. Increasingly, the Crocker-Stanford faction pressed Huntington, who still held the most powerful position in both companies, for dissolution of the Pacific Improvement Company and division of its properties. Aggravating the situation was the depression after 1893, cash-flow problems that prevented the company from making payments on its loans, bonds, and stock dividends, and Mrs. Stanford's pressure to cash in her shares of both the Pacific Improvement Company and the Southern Pacific to support Stanford University.[57] Huntington, contemptuous as always of what he saw as the Stanfords' penchant for self-glorification, dismissed Jane Stanford as "a disagreeable, pestiferous, old woman."[58]

Unable to budge Huntington and too weak to attack him directly, the Crocker-Stanford faction instead struck out at Collis's associates in the West, especially his nephew Henry E. Huntington, the president's official representative in San Francisco, and William H. Mills, a well-known protégé and friend of Collis who often served as a "mole," spying on the California associates for the company president in New York.[59] In late 1897, unbeknownst to Collis, the Crocker-Stanford faction maneuvered themselves into control of the board of directors of the Pacific Improvement Company and immediately replaced some managers of the company with men loyal to themselves. The company then dismissed Mills as land agent of the non-railroad properties and attempted to press charges against him for selling land at below-market value to Collis's associates, including Henry E. Huntington, losing money on land subdivisions, and generally violating his financial responsibilities. Fortunately for Mills, the company had never empowered him to buy and sell property on his own, and he had always been required to have property independently appraised and to have all transactions approved by the president of the Pacific Improvement Company. Moreover, an exhaustive audit of his accounts by company officials more than eager to find proof against him actually exonerated Mills completely. Indeed, the audit disclosed he had never lost money in any land transaction and in almost all instances had earned large profits for the company. Mills was still out as land agent of the Pacific Improvement Company, but with Huntington's strong support, he remained as an effective chief land agent of the Southern Pacific Company, a position he held until his death in 1907.[60]

In 1898, Collis P. Huntington, with the assistance of the Southern Pacific's leading fiscal officer, William Mahl, finally was able to accomplish an audit of the complicated financial relationships of the Pacific Improvement Company and the Southern Pacific Company, and a formal separation of the two companies was agreed to at a conference among Huntington, George Crocker of the improvement company, and Thomas Hubbard, an associate of Huntington in New York who represented the Hopkins family interests.[61] In 1899, Huntington formally bought out the Crocker and Stanford one-fourth interests in both the Southern Pacific and Pacific Improvement companies, consolidating three-quarters of the former enterprises of the Big Four into his own hands.[62]

The Harriman Lines Debacle

The decade of the 1880s proved to be the zenith of Southern Pacific Land Department advertising, promotion, subdivision, and sales. The department continued to perform valuable services, particularly the leadership that William H. Mills and his successor, Birdsall A. McAllaster, provided for promotional activities and environmental and resource developments inside and outside the Southern Pacific's structure. Land disposal itself, however, was no longer as important in the company's total operations. By the late 1880s, the best of the granted lands—in arable portions of California's Central Valley, some areas of the southern part of the state, lower elevation valleys in Oregon, and in Texas—had been sold. The rest, generally arid, isolated, mountainous, or infertile, particularly in the Great Basin, generated little enthusiasm from potential farmers.[63] Moreover, the collapse of California's real estate boom in 1888 and shortly afterwards in other western regions and the long national depression from 1893 to 1900 further reduced the demand for railroad land. Despite occasional decent sales years, annual sales on the Central Pacific plummeted from 232,000 acres in 1887 to 71,000 in 1888 and 39,000 in 1893; Southern Pacific Railroad sales fell from 777,000 in 1887 to 174,000 in 1888 and 6,000 in 1894, and had only revived to 32,000 by 1899. During some years, the amount of land relinquished to the company by buyers unable or unwilling to make payments due on credit contracts exceeded the amount sold by several times.[64]

When E. H. Harriman of the Union Pacific seized control of the Southern Pacific Company in 1901, he extended the land policy of the Harriman Lines to his new Pacific roads. Harriman ordered almost all land sales halted on the Central Pacific, the Southern Pacific, and the Oregon & California railroads so that the benefits from minerals, timber, and rising land values might accrue to the company. In the occasional sales that would take place, moreover, the company henceforth was to raise its prices greatly and reduce the number of time-payment sales, while also reserving all mineral rights on the land to itself for future development. The vice president and counsel of the Harriman Lines,

William D. Cornish, assumed jurisdiction over Southern Pacific lands. In 1902, to institute the new procedures, he dispatched to San Francisco an "acting land agent," subordinate Charles W. Eberlein, who appears to have been the most ardent proponent of the new non-sales policy. By 1905 annual land sales on all Southern Pacific roads had fallen to virtually nothing. Eberlein also sought to discredit William H. Mills and Jerome Madden and to replace them himself as land agent of both the Central and Southern Pacific lines. He accused Madden of being short a small amount in his sales ledgers and got him fired in August 1903. The Central Pacific's books turned out to be perfect, however, and try as he might to find a pretext for getting rid of Mills, Eberlein failed. Harriman Lines officials reluctantly concluded that, because Mills knew so much about the company's political activities and land business and was well connected to powerful outside interests, especially the press and potential enemies of the railroad, he was too dangerous to discharge, and they retained him as head of the Central Pacific's Land Department.[65] In 1903, Harriman, through his assistant and former Southern Pacific executive Julius Kruttschnitt, also formally severed all connections between the railroad and the Pacific Improvement Company, which had remained under the control of the Big Four family interests.[66]

In this and other aspects of the company's business, however, the Harriman-arranged shotgun wedding of the Southern and Union Pacifics produced at best a troubled marriage. Land agent Mills and other west-coast railroaders, including Madden until he was fired, Southern Pacific vice president and general counsel William F. Herrin, and others, objected vigorously to the new land policy. Mills and supporters argued that prohibiting land sales and reserving mineral rights ran against the historic land-colonization tradition of the railroad and would retard population growth, economic development, and rail traffic in the company's territory. Moreover, angered farmers, miners, loggers, and business leaders would demand political retaliation against the railroad, Mills warned, and probably pressure Congress to confiscate the land grant. From 1902 through 1908, Southern Pacific leaders repeatedly urged the Harriman Lines to relent. When that failed, they closed ranks in order to stall and then sabotage the new policies. West-coast executives defied some of Eberlein's orders, persisting in selling some land anyway and refusing to insert mineral-rights reservations in deeds. To embarrass their Harriman Lines bosses and mobilize support from old-time Southern Pacific employees, allies, and even enemies, they secretly leaked to the press and vocal outside groups confidential information about the Harriman Lines' land-policy reorganization and the western executives' opposition to it.[67] On a more personal level, they intercepted and delayed Eberlein's mail, withheld vital information from him, failed to cooperate with his audits and land evaluations, reassigned programs he was seeking to change to other departments over which he had no jurisdiction, encouraged railroaders, outside interests, and political leaders to write to Harriman Lines leaders objecting to his actions and the new policies, lost his pay records, refused to compensate him for large business travel expenses, and forced him and his assistants to come back to San Francisco in person to receive their bimonthly pay in cash, rather than having it mailed by check as other executives enjoyed. Eberlein was reduced to begging Cornish for advances on his pay from New York.[68] These tactics surprised and confused Harriman Lines officials and led them to openly charge old-time Southern Pacific leaders with disloyalty, thus hardening the opposition and increasing their ranks and further delaying the new policies' adoption. Responding to the furor from constituents, the California, Nevada, and Oregon legislatures all passed bills or resolutions seeking to force the Southern Pacific to sell its lands. In the early 1900s, public outcry in the Far West against the Harriman Lines' apparent monopolizing of land and resources reinvigorated the anti-railroad sentiment of earlier decades and helped pave the way for progressive political victories and the passage of tougher railroad regulatory laws in those states.[69]

Finally, shortly before he died in 1907, after years of pressing Harriman Lines officials in New York, Mills, over Eberlein's objections, was able to convince vice president William Cornish at least to abandon the mineral-rights reservations in deeds for lands that were sold. Cornish also ordered Eberlein to defer to Mills and Herrin regarding new forms for land-sales contracts and deeds and other land matters.[70] Opposition to Eberlein continued to grow within the company. Ultimately, discredited, ignored, and feeling isolated, Eberlein was forced to resign in 1908, but the general no-sale policy remained in effect.[71] For the brief interlude of the Harriman Lines merger, from 1901 until at least 1909 or 1910, the Southern Pacific became in fact what some uninformed critics had always accused it of being—a land monopolist and speculator.

Repercussions to the Harriman Lines' reversal of the Southern Pacific's traditional developmental approach to its land grant were quick and catastrophic. The original 1869 congressional act awarding the Oregon & California Railroad its land grant had included an unusual "homestead clause" requiring that the land be sold, and only to actual settlers, in holdings no larger than 160 acres, and for prices no higher than $2.50 per acre. After the Southern Pacific acquired control of the Oregon & California in 1887, Mills, staunch enemy of land monopoly and advocate of small-scale farming, took charge of the line's land grant. Over the next decade of his management, the company continued to sell its grant, presumably mostly agricultural land, briskly in small parcels, usually forty to eighty acres, at low prices averaging between two and three dollars per acre.[72] Beginning in 1898, however, apparently because most of its arable land had been sold and there was little market for small pieces of forested land, the Oregon &

California, now in apparent violation of the congressional act, also began to dispose of a few large tracts of timber land of up to ten thousand acres to lumber companies at four to five dollars or higher per acre. After the Harriman Lines acquired the Southern Pacific in 1901, however, extremely large sales at yet higher prices became the rule for two years. Indeed, Eberlein in 1902 ordered Mills to halt completely the selling of small pieces of timberland on the Oregon & California as well as the Central Pacific. Furthermore, ten-year time-payment contracts, which small-scale farmers and lumbermen had relied on to afford purchases, were to be "abolished, and . . . not used again."[73] Then, beginning in January 1903, Eberlein took complete charge of the Oregon & California Land Department and announced that almost all forest lands were being withdrawn from sale in keeping with the Harriman Lines' new policy of retaining and managing its lands for profit. Henceforth, only some logging rights would be sold, with the land remaining in reserve for the railroad's own future uses for track ties and construction materials, as well as to take advantage of increased land values. The Southern Pacific would also reserve all mineral rights to itself.[74]

As Mills and other old Southern Pacific people had warned, Northwest logging companies were outraged at being closed off from buying the railroad's timberlands.[75] In league with commercial organizations, regional newspapers such as the *Portland Oregonian,* the state of Oregon, and some of its congressmen, particularly Rep. Willis C. Hawley, they successfully pressed the U.S. Departments of Interior and Justice in 1907 to sue to recover the unsold land-grant on the grounds that the Southern Pacific had violated the original congressional mandate that the land be sold to others. Lower courts found for the government. In 1915, however, after eight years of litigation, the U.S. Supreme Court overturned lower-court decisions, reconfirmed its earlier rulings in similar cases that the 1869 congressional act had passed perfect land titles to the railroad, and rejected the suit. Nevertheless, Congress responded in 1916 by passing a bill confiscating the Oregon & California's more than two million acres of unsold Oregon land, the largest single revocation of a railroad land grant. To satisfy the Supreme Court decision, Congress also provided for the railroad to be compensated for its equity in the land up to the maximum sale price of $2.50 per acre allowed in the original land-grant law, which a 1926 settlement established at slightly more than $4 million.[76] Ironically, although during their tenure as rulers of the Southern Pacific, the Big Four and subordinates exerted great efforts, in general successfully, to subdivide, improve, sell, and colonize land with small-scale farmers, they were, and still generally are, widely denounced as "land monopolists." On the other hand, the Harriman interests, who have sometimes been credited with introducing more enlightened and service-oriented management to the company, actually terminated temporarily most of the railroad's land-development programs.

The Land Department after 1906

The great San Francisco earthquake and fire of 1906 destroyed much of the Land Department's archives, including maps, correspondence, subdivision plats, deeds, land evaluations, and sales and lease records. Railroad land-development business was delayed or halted for several years while the company laboriously reconstructed the information from county, federal, and corporate documents in New York and major Southern Pacific terminal cities.[77] William H. Mills's death and the loss of yet more institutional memory in May 1907 deepened the confusion that beset railroad land policy in the mid-1900s. After more than a year of drift and less-than-competent land management under several successors to Mills, Harriman Lines bosses in September 1908 finally transferred Birdsall A. McAllaster, agriculture and irrigation expert and accomplished head of the Union Pacific Land Department in Omaha, to take over the demanding Southern Pacific post in San Francisco.[78] Beginning in 1908, McAllaster, with a solid reputation within the Harriman Lines, was able to secure some further liberalization of the no-sale policy, starting with the placing of mineral lands back on the market. The emerging controversy over Oregon & California Railroad lands had much to do with the reevaluation, as did the death of William D. Cornish in late 1908. By that time, New York company officials had begun to realize the folly of trying to dictate policy from afar in matters so sensitive to western economic and political interests.[79]

With the "unmerger" of the Harriman Lines by federal anti-monopoly lawsuit in 1913, the old western executives of the Southern Pacific recaptured control of the company. Land policy reverted to what it had been prior to 1901, and general land-grant sales and colonization resumed. Committed to the agrarian and development ideals of his predecessors, B. A. McAllaster stabilized the railroad's land management and steered it back onto paths originally blazed by Redding and Mills. There was remarkable consistency between policies that had emerged by the 1870s and 1880s and those followed after 1908 and through the first half of the twentieth century: a preference for promoting land sales to stimulate economic development and rail traffic; low land prices and inexpensive, liberal time-payment sales contracts; small-scale sales to actual settlers; and accommodation and support for farmers on the company's lands. In 1911, the railroad formed a closely controlled subsidiary, the Southern Pacific Land Company, managed by McAllaster, to take over title to and responsibility for settling the land-grant properties of all the company's predecessor lines in all its western states. McAllaster retired in January 1933, closing a seven-decade period during which corporate land policy was guided principally by only three likeminded men.[80]

The finale to historic Southern Pacific land-grant development programs

Birdsall A. McAllaster, shown in the early 1900s, when he was the Union Pacific Railroad's land commissioner in Omaha. In 1908, the Harriman Lines transferred McAllaster to San Francisco, where he succeeded William H. Mills as head of the Southern Pacific's Land Department and Land Company. Like predecessors Mills and B. B. Redding, McAllaster championed small-scale farming, public water development, scientific forestry, and resource conservation and influenced the railroad's policies in those directions. Courtesy Charles Ray McAllaster and the McAllaster family.

was written in the 1940s. With American railways in financial disarray from the Great Depression of the 1930s and many long-term problems in the industry crying for reform, Congress passed the comprehensive Transportation Act of 1940. Among its provisions, the law enacted a compromise the federal government had reached with the western land-grant roads. The companies waived their rights to lands still unpatented in exchange for the government's abrogation of the so-called "land-grant rates," by which the roads were losing tens of millions of dollars of annual income because they were required to carry federal passengers and freight free of charge as partial repayment for the original nineteenth-century construction subsidies. The Southern Pacific relinquished 136,000 unpatented acres, thus sounding the closing bell to the company's three-quarter-century-long wrestling match over land grants with the Department of the Interior.[81]

The Southern Pacific also halted most land sales and colonization programs after World War II. With the post-war boom, particularly in California, causing land values to soar, speculators and real estate development firms rushed to buy up large tracts of cheaply priced railroad land, even in remote arid regions. In late 1948, fearing it was losing potential profits from the lands, the company temporarily suspended such sales while Land Company officials and higher executives debated the railroad's future policy toward its remaining granted lands. At that time, the property amounted to about 2.3 million acres in California, 2.6 million in Nevada, and 250,000 in Utah, or a total of about 5 million acres, almost all of it then considered too arid or rugged for agriculture. Ultimately, in mid-1949, although some executives strongly defended the railroad's historic colonization policy, Southern Pacific president A. T. Mercier, on the recommendation of his trusted assistant, and future company president, Donald J. Russell, ordered sales discontinued. Henceforth, in order to take advantage itself of future mineral discoveries and development on its properties, the Southern Pacific would only provide leases to forest, farm, grazing, and mining lands under strict controls to protect their productivity and value. No longer viewed as an instrument for promoting regional development and rail traffic, the former land grant had now become a permanent, revenue-producing asset. In the words of the official company history written in 1956, "the general policy is to hold the outlying lands and to manage them for continuing income."[82]

6 Promoting the Far West

Early Programs

Despite Southern Pacific officials' commitment to develop and sell the company's land grants, as well as to encourage general agricultural growth and land subdivision in its hinterland, organized promotional programs for the railroad's territories evolved only slowly from 1865, when sales on the Central Pacific's land grant began, until 1883, when the first comprehensive colonization plan was inaugurated. In these early years, critics accused the railroad of deliberate delay. Regarding California, for example, one reporter for the *San Francisco Post* charged in 1878 that, in contrast to the farsightedness of other land-grant roads, the Southern Pacific's owners were withholding its lands from sale while awaiting higher prices in the future and had not adopted any promotional programs to develop the state. In failing to do so, the railroad displayed "a spirit that breathes of monopoly and smacks of retrogression."[1] Contrary to such accusations, these initial delays in land sales and colonization reflected, more than they differed from, the practices of other land-grant railroads. Invariably, the acquisition of land patents by a company resulted in a period of hesitant experimentation, while officials created the complex policy and machinery and solved the many problems preliminary to massive land-sales and regional advertising campaigns. Often, local citizens interpreted this groping as a conscious attempt by railway officials to retard the growth of their areas.[2]

These general, industry-wide problems were compounded for the Southern Pacific by conditions peculiar to that company in the 1860s and 1870s. Other, more pressing tasks than land promotion and regional advertising consumed the energies of railway officials in the early years. Securing patents to government land was a time-consuming process, dragging into and beyond the 1880s, in some regions well into the twentieth century.[3] Surveying, evaluating, and pricing the lands, scattered throughout inaccessible desert plains, foothills, and mountains of California, Nevada, and Utah and the forests of Oregon likewise delayed sales. These tasks were even more formidable and time-consuming in

Texas, where small parcels of state-granted land were flung willy-nilly across a vast landscape, often isolated even from the company's rail lines. Also complicated was the job, at least in some areas, of extinguishing squatters' claims, sometimes only after long court battles or occasional quasi-military encounters such as at the San Joaquin Valley's Mussel Slough district in 1880. The chronic financial troubles of the Big Four's railroads, particularly during the 1870s, and the devotion of scarce capital to expansion led Huntington to plead continually for economy in his letters from the East. The tenuousness of the railroad business and their struggles with Tom Scott and other rivals for hegemony over the available routes in Texas and across the Southwest periodically caused the associates to contemplate selling out. This created additional uncertainty in many company policies in the 1860s and 1870s.[4] Moreover, in these early years before completion of its Southern Pacific Railroad line to Texas in the early 1880s, the railroad did not possess a transcontinental connection of its own, and its major road, the Central Pacific, was forced to rely on other lines for access to the centers of potential immigration in the East and in Europe. Roads such as the Union Pacific, competing themselves for potential settlers on their lands, refused to cooperate with their California outlet. The Union Pacific, for example, ignoring the congressional mandate in the original charter that the transcontinental railroad had to be operated as one through-line, declined to honor the Central Pacific's reduced-fare tickets for California-bound land-seekers. Union Pacific salesmen also boarded overland trains in Chicago and Omaha in the attempt to divert California immigrants onto Union Pacific lands in Nebraska. Fearful, then, that their advertising would chiefly populate the lands of their competitors, Southern Pacific officials hesitated to commit badly needed company resources to what appeared, for at least the present, to be a hopeless task. When approached in 1881 by William L. Merry, an emissary seeking the railroad's assistance for the fledgling Immigration Association of California, Superintendent Alban N. Towne admitted that the company's promotional work had not as yet been extensive, due largely to the unwillingness of the Union Pacific to share traffic and revenues over the original transcontinental route, and that the railroad's systematic advertising program would not be activated until the imminent completion of the Southern Pacific Railroad's independent line to New Orleans.[5]

Despite vicissitudes in company affairs in the years before 1883, the Southern Pacific did initiate some promotional activities that would later evolve into important features of the railroad's development plan for its western territory. Once again, the Southern Pacific's colonization of the West began in California, where the bulk of its business and land was initially located. Models developed in California were later transferred to other portions of the company's hinterland, particularly Oregon and Texas, where the railroad eventually built up comprehensive development programs after the 1880s.[6]

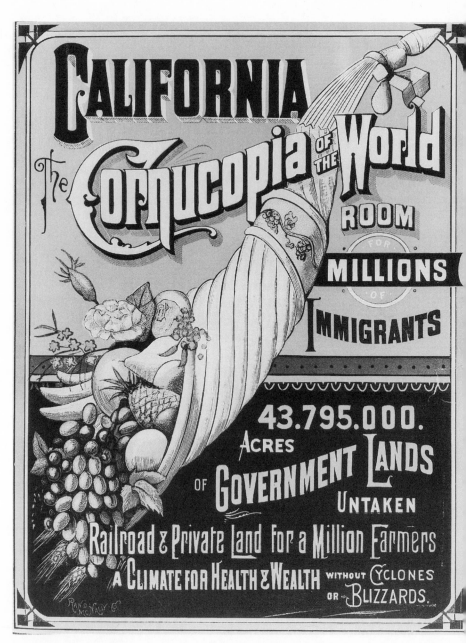

Cover of *California, Cornucopia of the World,* one of the major nineteenth-century western promotional books, written and published in several editions by the Southern Pacific's immigration commissioner in Chicago between 1883 and 1886. Courtesy Bancroft Library.

Lacking a staff of company writers, the railroad in the early 1870s began to subsidize the production of promotional materials by independent authors. The company regularly encouraged newspapers throughout California to publish special booster issues for distribution through railroad agents in the East and in Europe. Often, the company paid substantial amounts, in the form of advertising contracts and outright subsidies, for this service. Marcus Boruck, editor of the San Francisco weekly, *California Spirit of the Times,* testified that in 1884 and 1885 the Southern Pacific purchased $12,000 worth of his newspaper's promotional issues.[7]

The railroad also enlisted famous writers in its campaign to sell its lands and attract tourists and settlers to California. In 1872, Collis P. Huntington commissioned Charles Nordhoff, a widely known and respected author and editor, to present the lure of California to eastern audiences. After touring California by rail and stage, Nordhoff wrote a series of articles for *Harper's,* shortly afterwards collected and published as *California: For Health, Pleasure, and Residence* (1872), a book that went through numerous editions and revisions and quickly became a best-selling travel account. Focusing on the many attractions of California for tourism, health-seeking, and economic opportunity, Nordhoff assured visitors and would-be homeseekers that their previous conception of California as a rip-snorting mining camp was inaccurate. Violence was declining; travelers were safe from harm; and, despite its early ill-repute among easterners, the state's agricultural future was assured now that farmers had begun to break tradition and to adapt agriculture to California's special conditions. A devout communitarian, Nordhoff stressed that the best way to settle in California was in agricultural colonies of at least four families.[8] Although the impact of Nordhoff's writings on migration to California is difficult to assess precisely, evidence suggests that it was considerable. Travelers and settlers frequently attested to having read his book or articles. The Indiana-based founders of at least one important agricultural colony, the San Gabriel Orange Association, which later became the city of Pasadena, traced their initial interest in the project to their reading of Nordhoff. In the words of literary historian Franklin Walker, Nordhoff's writings were "certainly the most influential" by any visitor to the state in that period, especially since they attracted attention for the first time to southern California.[9]

The success of its initial venture encouraged the Southern Pacific to trust other established authors to generate interest in California. In 1874, Benjamin C. Truman, once a famous emissary of President Andrew Johnson, now a newspaperman and recent settler in Los Angeles, was commissioned to write *Semi-Tropical California,* a book concerning southern California timed for release just before the opening of the Southern Pacific Railroad's line from the Central Pacific down the San Joaquin Valley to Los Angeles in 1876. Truman's connection with the railroad eventually developed into a long and productive one. In the early 1880s, Truman became the director of the Southern Pacific's "literary bureau," a position he held for nearly a decade. Truman organized the writing talents of his staff, hired more outside talent (Nordhoff contributed another piece in 1883, *A Guide to California, the Golden State*) and founded *Wave*, a booster periodical published at the Big Four's new Monterey spa, Hotel Del Monte. Truman authored more promotional literature himself, including *Homes and Happiness in the Golden State of California* (1883) and a series of articles on California agriculture that appeared in the *New York Times* in 1887. He was certainly one of the most ubiquitous of California's promoters before, during, and after his employment with the Southern Pacific. The *Chicago Tribune* observed in 1887 that, while promoting California, "Truman flops around between the Atlantic and the Pacific like a railway postal clerk."[10]

Emigrant Cars

Like other western roads, as soon as it built through-lines, the Southern Pacific encouraged travel and settlement by attaching low-fare emigrant cars to its trains. The first such cars for the Central Pacific arrived in Sacramento in June 1869, only a few weeks after the driving of the golden spike. Although the *Sacramento Union* judged them to be "neat, internally and externally, and . . . quite comfortable," the contraptions became generally despised as instruments of torture by those condemned to ride on them. In his classic description, Robert Louis Stevenson, who took one across the plains to California in 1879, described the car as a "long, narrow wooden box, like a flat-roofed Noah's ark, with a stove and a convenience, one at either end, a passage down the middle, and transverse benches upon either end" and remarkable only for its "extreme plainness."[11] Unfortunately, emigrant cars were remarkable for other things. Creeping along at the ends of freight trains, they were notoriously slow. One old-time company employee, William R. Stockton, arrived himself from Illinois on such a car in 1872. The trip took nine days, he recalled, and "the mere statement gives us 'heart failure.'"[12] At first, the small, high windows, mere peepholes, would not open. The cars were jammed from stem to stern with poor, unbathed travelers, many of them European immigrants going west and Chinese immigrants going east. Light was dim, the heat often sweltering, and the stench sickening, even for onlookers in stations along the way. Improvements were made. By the end of the 1870s, more comfortable sleeping cars with berths of bare boards had been added, and roofs of the standard cars raised and windows enlarged and made to open and close so that, in the words of the *Reno Evening Gazette*, "the perfume is very different from the familiar

Central Pacific Railroad emigrant train with passengers stopped at Mill City, Nevada, in 1883. Aboard the train were westward-bound settlers of many nationalities. Author's collection.

one of former days."[13] Also by the late 1870s, special trains composed entirely of emigrant cars ran the lines during popular travel seasons, at speeds somewhat faster than freight trains.[14] Despite the spartan inconvenience and discomfort, many poor and middle-class settlers took advantage of the low fares to settle Southern Pacific territory. During the winter of 1875, for example, the *Carson Appeal* counted between three and five emigrant cars per day, carrying about 120 to 200 persons, moving west through Nevada at the rear of Central Pacific trains.[15]

Typically of the West at the time, and the nation at large for that matter, not everyone thanked the railroad for the influx of poor settlers, particularly those aboard the emigrant cars, many of whom arrived dirty and disheveled, dressed in shabby, strange clothes, and speaking unintelligible languages. To some early comers in the West, these outsiders, particularly foreign immigrants, appeared alien, suspicious, and threatening to community harmony. The *Nevada State Journal* scorned the newcomers the Central Pacific brought to town in 1873: "If there is any place on this wide earth, excepting in the vicinities of hospitals and . . . [leper] houses, where uglier and more repulsive looking people may be

seen than at the depot in this town, when the trains arrive, we do not know it."
In 1876, the *Reno Gazette* complained again when "this afternoon the western-
bound emigrant train disgorged the shabbiest lot of mortals it has been our mis-
fortune to see for some time. The bell rang, all got aboard and went off. Reno . . .
[was] relieved, but we could not help feeling for California."[16]

The Southern Pacific at the Fair

In its early, tentative years, the Southern Pacific also learned to take advantage
of promotional opportunities presented by the international exposition movement. Other western railroads did likewise, but no company developed as extensive or influential an exhibition program. The railroad's early efforts, however, were hesitant and poorly organized. When the American Geographical
Society asked Huntington in New York for photographs from California for
display at the Vienna Exposition of 1873, Huntington passed the request
enthusiastically along to his California associates. Views of San Francisco,
Yosemite, Big Trees, Lake Tahoe, and operations along the Central Pacific's line,
Huntington commented, "may be well as an advertisement." Apparently, the
western officials did not perceive the display's potential value. They sent photographs that were too small to be shown, and, after receiving a complaint from
the Geographical Society, told the exhibitors that they themselves should pay
to have larger prints made. Having been informed of the fiasco and of the lavish support the Geographical Society was receiving from other land-grant railroads, Huntington dispatched an angry letter to Mark Hopkins stressing that
the company had to exploit such promotional opportunities. "I have no doubt
that a few hundred dollars expended in this thing, in getting up such things as
are called for, and in such shape as to [be] a credit to our company may in the
end benefit us—or at least be no loss."[17]

As the Southern Pacific's commitment to promotion grew in the 1870s, however, sending displays of California products to eastern and European fairs
emerged as a permanent and productive feature of company policy. In fact, from
the mid-1870s until the Columbian Exposition of 1893, in the absence of much
official state support, the railroad constituted the major agency organizing displays of California's resources. The Centennial Exposition, America's first great
world's fair, held in Philadelphia in 1876, provided the opportunity for the dispatch of the first extensive Southern Pacific exhibit. Although other western
local governments were racing one another to ensure that the virtues of their
locales were adequately set before the fairgoers, attempts by promoters throughout California failed to move the stingy, mining-dominated legislature into
funding an official state display. When a statewide campaign collected enough

voluntary funds for the hasty construction of a small California building, the builders of the structure, lacking sufficient organization, gathered individual displays haphazardly. Opening day arrived with California's building essentially empty, useful principally to host receptions for visiting state dignitaries, and it remained so for the duration of the exposition. The sole exception was the display of the forest, mineral, and agricultural resources of California, collected and managed by J. R. Scupham of the Central Pacific. The Big Four also hired J. A. Johnson, longtime booster of Santa Barbara, at $250 per month to lecture at Philadelphia about California.[18]

Whatever positive impact California made at the exposition was likely due to the railroad. Generally, the state's efforts at Philadelphia were scorned by the few Californians who journeyed to see them. One state Grange leader, for instance, denounced the shabby building, meager displays, and apparent mismanagement of the general state display but praised the Southern Pacific for making "the most creditable and the only extensive exhibit from California." Although an adamant foe of the railroad, this Patron of Husbandry conceded that "the company is entitled to much credit for the extent and variety of California products exhibited, consisting of woods, wines, cereals, cones, mosses, minerals, manufactured articles, raw materials, together with many relics of natural history." At the exposition's close, both the American Museum of Natural History in New York and the Smithsonian Institution requested that the Southern Pacific's display be donated for permanent exhibition.[19]

After 1883, when the company's interest in advertising increased, largely due to completion of its Sunset Route from Los Angeles to New Orleans and the beginning of California's real estate boom, much of the railroad's new promotional energy at first went into expositions. In late 1883, one of the first activities of the railroad's newly appointed immigration commissioner in Chicago was to organize such an exhibition of California agricultural products at the Illinois State Fair. The railroad's immigration agent in Europe, W. G. Kingsbury, staged a similar exhibition in Birmingham, England.[20] These small-scale efforts were dwarfed, however, by the World's Industrial and Cotton Exposition, held in New Orleans in the winter of 1884–1885, an event that provided the Southern Pacific an opportunity in its own eastern terminal city to mount its most lavish attempt thus far to advertise California.

The railroad placed Charles B. Turrill of the Passenger Department in charge of the collection and management of the exhibit. He was assisted by J. R. Scupham, who had organized the railroad's efforts at Philadelphia, and Ben Truman, who handled press releases concerning the exhibit. Like other Southern Pacific promotional officials, Turrill was also involved in many other aspects of California civic life, including scientific inquiry and agriculture. At various points in his career he worked with the State Board of Viticultural Commissioners, the California Academy of Sciences in San Francisco, and the San Diego Chamber of Commerce. Although only in his early twenties, Turrill, who had also become a skilled photographer, had written a minor promotional book, *Californian Notes,* in 1876. By the time of his employment by the Passenger Department in the early 1880s, he had earned a reputation as a man of diverse advertising skills. On meeting him in 1884, W. G. Kingsbury observed that Turrill "knew every town, valley, and hilltop and most of the people, and could photograph, write and lecture, and is an enthusiastic lover of California."[21] Turrill presided over the display activities of the Southern Pacific during the 1880s and 1890s and helped make the railroad one of the most effective and famous creators of expositions of western products.

In the summer of 1884, Turrill began preparing the railroad's exhibit. He corresponded with leading citizens and organizations and traveled repeatedly throughout California, soliciting displays and supervising the collection and packing of the New Orleans exhibit. In some regions, he organized groups especially to build local support. In others, he contacted and attracted the support of already existing commercial or agricultural agencies. Working with Turrill, the Los Angeles Board of Trade organized an extensive display of southern California products, especially citrus fruit, while such organizations as the Immigration Association of Sacramento County provided similar services for northern and central California. Farm organizations, such as the Santa Rosa Grange, which furnished the largest individual display the railroad collected, also contributed. Railway agents gathered, crated, and shipped the exhibits to San Francisco. By late November 1884, the Southern Pacific had collected twelve railroad cars of displays for shipment at no charge to New Orleans.[22] Turrill subsequently moved the exhibit at no cost to contributors or the state to the American Exposition in Louisville from August to October 1885 and then back to the North, Central, and South American Exposition in New Orleans from November 1885 until March 1886. By the end of the last fair, the Southern Pacific's exhibit had grown to more than 30,000 square feet of displays; the railroad had moved hundreds of cars of specimens free of charge; and the company was supplementing the exhibition by running special excursion trains from the fairs to Los Angeles and San Francisco at greatly reduced fares.[23]

The Southern Pacific's displays at the expositions of the mid-1880s were important promotional events for California, in fact turning points in the formation of a new image for the state as an agricultural Eden. The first extensive, well-publicized California displays in the East, they attracted much attention, especially from correspondents who regularly commented on the fair in the columns of eastern newspapers. In keeping with the Southern Pacific's goal of fostering particularly the development of farming communities in Cali-

Morgan's Louisiana & Texas Railroad locomotive number 47, the last engine the company bought before being acquired by the Southern Pacific, photographed at Algiers, Louisiana, shortly after being featured in its new owner's famed exhibit at the New Orleans Exposition of 1884–1885. Courtesy DeGolyer Library, Southern Methodist University.

fornia, the railroad's display stressed agricultural resources and productivity, although it did include some representative samples from mining, manufacturing, and lumbering as well. The winning of several major citrus prizes by growers near Los Angeles and San Diego likewise attracted much favorable publicity. The rows of tables displaying citrus fruit, vegetables, and grains, freshly harvested and expressed daily by the railroad to the fairs even in the midst of the eastern winter, provided visual proof for the agricultural claims that boosters had been making about the state for decades. As a result, the traditional eastern reputation of the state as a mining-camp society was substantially altered. Many observers, both in and out of California, traced the real estate boom of the mid-1880s and the expansion of orange-planting, especially in southern California, to the promotional successes at the 1884–1886 exhibitions.[24]

California's propaganda victory depended on the organizing, financing, and transporting services of the Southern Pacific Company. Although the state appointed a commissioner, A. Andrews, to collect and manage an official display for the first New Orleans exposition of 1884 to 1885, it provided no funding, with the exception of a $10,000 appropriation in February 1885, two months after the beginning of the fair. Typically of California's haphazard state-sponsored promotional projects, the official exhibit, and especially Andrews's role in it, was severely criticized. Apparently viewing his position as a sinecure, Andrews spent little time collecting exhibits, left the state's display in Turrill's hands and returned home on private business for several months during the exposition, alienated many exhibitors, and spent most of the public's money to furnish and maintain a lavish reception room for wealthy Californians at the fair.[25] Turrill contributed the expertise and management that made the display a success. He particularly fostered cooperation among California's conflicting groups, regions, and communities, something that officially appointed California fair commissioners rarely succeeded in doing. In contrast to the legislature's $10,000 appropriation to support California's exhibit, the railroad by January 31, 1885, had contributed nearly $38,000 for transportation, lumber, and equipment for the displays, and salaries and lodging for Turrill and other employees who worked full- or part-time on the exhibit. By the end of the first New Orleans exposition, the Southern Pacific had spent about $75,000. The company also financed taking the display to Louisville and back to New Orleans in the next year.[26]

Californians of diverse groups and regions responded with gratitude for the Southern Pacific's efforts. Commercial bodies and newspapers, including many that opposed the railroad on other issues, praised Turrill and the company for acting in the public interest. In San Francisco, the *Post,* expressing a view typical of that city's newspapers, noted that the state's gold medal for citrus at New Orleans was due to "the liberality and public spirit of the Southern Pacific Railroad Company, which not only carried exhibits free of charge, but made special efforts to excite the interest of our fruit growers in the contest." In Bakersfield, the *Kern County Gazette* editorialized that "the Railroad Company is certainly entitled to credit for the part it has taken in putting our products before the world. Whatever may be said against that corporation on general principles, there is no doubt but what the managers have taken great pains to make our resources known." The *Los Angeles Herald* printed with approval the report of J. E. Pleasants, a southern California exhibitor, that while the official state participation was disappointing, especially in the light of the free transportation offered by the railroad, California still had a creditable exhibit because of the interest shown by the Southern Pacific "in having the Pacific Coast well represented at the fair." The Los Angeles Board of Trade likewise commended the railroad for making the exhibit.[27]

Spokesmen for farm organizations, which had never been particularly friendly toward the Southern Pacific, also admitted that the railroad had executed a public relations coup for their state at the fairs. W. H. Jessup, the widely known representative of the State Horticultural Society who had managed California's fruit exhibit at the World's Industrial and Cotton Exposition, noted in his report that the forty-two prizes the state garnered for fruit displays at that event would have been impossible without the efforts of the Southern Pacific.[28]

Even such avowedly anti-railroad agencies as the state Grange reprinted in its state journal an editorial from the New Orleans *Daily Picayune* praising the railroad for "exerting all the energies of its numerous departments . . . in exhibiting to the world the beauties, attractions and resources of a State." When one Granger wrote to the journal objecting to the dissemination of such pro-railroad material, the *California Patron* retorted that Turrill had performed valuable services for the community and that such railroad activities to build up the state were in the public interest:

> Although the PATRON is given to severe censure of many of the acts of the railroad company in its dealing with the people of the State, it would be entitled to very narrow influence if it therefore declined to publish an article from a distinguished journal near the exhibit . . . simply because it reflected great credit on the railroad company, through the skill and diligence of the present State Commissioner [Turrill].[29]

The great success of the Southern Pacific's displays at the expositions of 1884 through 1886 encouraged the railroad to continue using this method to advertise California and the company's other regions at eastern state and county fairs, at conventions of major national organizations, such as the Grand Army of the Republic and the National Education Association, and especially at other national and international expositions. Such exhibits went out at the direction of William H. Mills, chief land agent, to the Paris Exposition (1900) and the Pan-American Exposition in Buffalo (1901), and under other Southern Pacific exhibit managers to the United States Land and Irrigation Exposition in Chicago (1910), to cite only a few examples.[30] As in the case of the Centennial and the New Orleans expositions, railway displays often made the difference between California's having, or not having, adequate representation. When U.S. commissioners to the Paris Exposition decided to disassemble state exhibits and to regroup individual displays according to types of production, thus threatening California with anonymity, the Southern Pacific quickly mounted and sent a separate display of its own that preserved the identity of the state, its subregions, and its towns and cities.[31] In addition, the Southern Pacific assisted many booster organizations in making eastern displays by providing free executive time, transportation, and collection services. The California State Board of Trade, after its founding in the late 1880s, benefited particularly from massive railroad aid. The board and the Southern Pacific cooperated to stage shows at the Atlanta Exposition of 1895 and many others.[32]

By the 1890s and early 1900s, when organizing official displays of California products had become a function of state government, the Southern Pacific made its financial power, transportation resources, and accumulated experience available to state government as well. California's official exhibits were commonly collected and transferred east at no cost to the state or contributors, a service that was also provided by other western land-grant railroads for their tributary regions. More important, perhaps, was the assistance that the Southern Pacific's promotional experts gave to public officials and the state's commercial and agricultural organizations, who were just getting involved in this work. During the period when California's lavish display at Chicago's Columbian Exposition of 1893 was being organized, for example, the railroad lent the services of Charles Turrill to support the state's efforts. Released from his ordinary duties, Turrill was detailed by the railroad to work for the California World's Fair Commission. Throughout 1892 and early 1893, he took charge of the creation of the exhibit. Relying on his experience with the New Orleans events, Turrill contacted leaders and organizations in many communities, attempted to whip up local enthusiasm, solicited countless displays, smoothed over local rivalries and conflicts, and managed a successful preliminary exhibition in San Francisco.[33] William H. Mills was invited on several occasions to advise the World's Fair Commission on how it might best organize the state's $200,000 effort. Mills's assistance was also sought by subsequent state administrations charged with planning California's participation in promotional events.[34] In addition, the railroad worked with public and private exhibition managers to solicit displays and to transport the exhibits and exhibitors free of charge to and from the fair sites.[35] By creating its own displays, aiding booster groups, and helping state government to shape exhibition policies and methods, the Southern Pacific Company was the major force in California stimulating and organizing the exposition movement and helping the state to make it a successful technique for fashioning a more favorable image for the state, expanding markets for products, and attracting visitors and settlers.

The Southern Pacific also supported exhibition movements in other states in its territory, particularly Oregon and Texas. In the early 1900s, William D. Fenton, the company's attorney in Portland, was the initiator and leader of the campaign to hold the Lewis and Clark Exposition in Portland in 1904. Fenton drafted the bill and led the lobbying resulting in the Oregon legislature's passing and the governor's signing a $500,000 appropriation for the fair. The Southern Pacific, along with other Harriman Lines in the Northwest, then subscribed to shares in the private company launched to manage the exposition. As an influential member of the board of directors, Fenton served as a major fundraiser and organizer of the fair.[36] Throughout its territory and over the late nineteenth and early twentieth centuries, the Southern Pacific was in all likelihood the most important source of support for western expositions, meetings, and conventions, providing direct financial aid, management talent, transportation services for organizers and exhibitors, and low-price excursion tickets for fairgoers and attendees at meetings. From 1897 to 1916 alone, the railroad assisted no fewer than 455 organizations, conventions, and expositions involving just California and Oregon, an average of between seven and twenty each year, and carried 1.5 million passengers on reduced-fare tickets to these events.[37]

Partnerships with Booster Groups

Another significant promotional device the Southern Pacific developed in the 1870s was the use of existing booster organizations to achieve the company's goals of stimulating population and economic growth and thereby the railroad's own land sales and freight and passenger traffic. Southern Pacific aid to promotional associations in California began with the state's first important booster group, the California Immigrant Union, founded in 1869 in the wake of the driving of the golden spike on the Central Pacific–Union Pacific transcontinental line. Although at first the company's support of booster groups was mostly rhetorical, as the commitment to development policies grew in the 1870s and 1880s, railroad involvement in the state's commercial organizations became extensive. By the early 1900s, most local, regional, or state-wide booster groups in California, including the Grangers' Immigration Bureau, the Immigration Association of California, the Los Angeles Chamber of Commerce, the Immigration Association of Northern California, the State Board of Trade, the California Promotion Committee, and the California Development Board, had sought and received assistance from the railroad.

In traditional historical myth, the Southern Pacific is portrayed as engaging in constant, mortal combat with the agricultural and business interests of California. While booster organizations and the railroad disagreed about many specific issues, in the area of advertising California and its localities, their mutual interests led to much cooperation. The boosters were essential to the Southern Pacific's evolving promotional plans. In the 1870s and early 1880s, they substituted for a formal company promotional agency, which had not yet taken shape. Then and later, they were also valuable "fronts" for railroad programs. In the late nineteenth century, as the Southern Pacific's reputation sank before waves of anti-railroad criticism, propaganda emanating from the commercial organizations was thought to have more credibility with some segments of the public. Conversely, the booster groups needed the railroad. Governmental and voluntary support for these organizations in California was at first scant and unreliable.[38] Southern Pacific aid, however, was large and relatively dependable, thereby making large-scale and long-range projects feasible and successful. Often, such as in the case of the Immigration Association of California and the California State Board of Trade, railroad assistance was crucial to the very existence of the group. By consistently providing such sponsorship, the railroad in yet another way functioned as the major organizing and stabilizing force behind boosterism in California and in some other Southern Pacific regions.

Railroad support of California's promotional bodies came in several forms. The Southern Pacific itself, through its executives, helped to found some organizations. Such was the case with the Immigration Association of California in 1881 and especially the State Board of Trade, ancestor of the California State Chamber of Commerce, which was created in 1887 largely due to the efforts of William H. Mills.[39] The company also lent its financial prestige to struggling groups. The appearance of railroad executives among the ranks of officers of the booster organizations, which was common, increased their legitimacy in the eyes of business contributors. Charles Crocker, Mark Hopkins, and Leland Stanford served as directors of the California Immigrant Union in the 1870s, a precedent followed by other railroad officials.[40] Often, the membership of Southern Pacific officials was of specific importance in financing organizations. In 1875, for instance, Stanford, Crocker, chief land agent Benjamin B. Redding, and David D. Colton, an assistant to the Big Four, attended and actively participated in meetings of influential San Francisco businessmen called to reorganize and refinance the nearly defunct Grangers' Immigration Bureau. Through their efforts the bureau lasted for several more years.[41]

The business skills and connections of Southern Pacific leaders were likewise important resources of organization and innovation to booster groups. Often, effective or pioneering promotional methods did not originate in the organizations themselves but instead came from the railroad or its officials. Although other leaders contributed, William H. Mills best personifies the important role the company performed. As a founder, vice president, chairman of displays and publications, and head of numerous committees of the State Board of Trade, Mills more than any other individual made the board function as a powerful force for advertising California over nearly two decades. Drawing on expertise and relationships acquired during years as editor of the *Sacramento Record-Union* and land agent of the Southern Pacific, Mills initiated, organized, and accompanied the board's displays to eastern and European fairs, edited and wrote many of its major promotional and reformist materials, led its campaigns to encourage economic development, and defended the organization against its critics. In these and other ways, Mills served as a conduit through which the Board of Trade was able to draw support and cooperation not only from the railroad but also from other business, agricultural, and public groups. Mills also made the board influential in the modernization of California public policy in agriculture, irrigation, forestry, and wilderness preservation. President Norton B. Chipman hailed Mills in 1896 as "the life and

Sunset magazine's booth in the Southern Pacific/Harriman Lines exhibit at the London Exposition, 1909. On display were lavish *Sunset* covers and artworks by distinguished artists such as photographer Carleton E. Watkins and painter Maynard Dixon, both of whom worked at one time or another for the Southern Pacific. The railroad through its magazine and other publications used literature and works of art to promote the economic and scenic potentials of the Far West and Southwest. Author's collection.

inspiration of this Board," while the committee appointed to memorialize Mills after his death in 1907 noted that the State Board of Trade had become "the instrument of his ideas and activities in behalf of our great industries."[42]

Importantly, the Southern Pacific also financed California's booster organizations. Many groups received regular contributions that often provided a large share of the money for day-to-day operations and larger projects. To launch the Immigration Association of California in 1881, Alban N. Towne, general superintendent of the Central Pacific, pledged that the company would donate $25 to match each $75 collected from other sources. The reports of the Immigration Association disclose that during its existence from 1881 to 1887 the railroad's annual contribution of several thousand dollars provided about one-fourth of its support. After 1887, the State Board of Trade received a monthly subsidy of $250 from the Southern Pacific.[43] Financial assistance went to the booster groups in other forms as well: special grants for major publications,

free or low-cost transportation for displays and promotional leaders, and subsidies for large-scale projects beyond the means of the organizations. The State
Board of Trade, for instance, sent its many displays to the East in the 1880s and
1890s at no cost. The board's exhibit at the 1895 Cotton States and International Exposition in Atlanta cost the railroad almost $7,000 in transportation,
in addition to the executive time expended organizing the display. These services were also extended to southern California organizations such as the
Southern California Immigration Association and the Los Angeles Chamber
of Commerce.[44]

Many booster organizations' special publicity efforts depended on the
Southern Pacific's support. In late 1888, Mills and T. H. Goodman, general passenger and ticket agent, proposed that the State Board of Trade dispatch a traveling exhibit of California products to the eastern states. Railroad and Board
of Trade officials organized the display; the Southern Pacific provided cars and
transportation and arranged for the free use of the tracks of other lines. Surely
one of the most successful undertakings in the history of the state's advertising, "California on Wheels" toured the midwestern, eastern, southern, and
Rocky Mountain regions for the winters of 1889 and 1890. It stopped at most
major rural and urban communities and was inspected by an estimated two
million persons. Collecting just the second year's displays cost the Southern
Pacific more than ten thousand dollars.[45] Assistance for such projects, when
added to the corporation's regular contributions, totaled considerable sums.
From 1887 to 1896, support for the Board of Trade alone amounted to more
than $50,000.[46] During that period, the railroad was financing other booster
organizations and their special projects around California, including the emerging giant of the southern district, the Los Angeles Chamber of Commerce.[47]

The Southern Pacific also encouraged booster organizations to produce written California propaganda, the mainstay of nineteenth-century promotion. As
its corporate resources grew and matured, the railroad developed information
and publication facilities. As early as the 1870s, land and passenger agents assisted
local promoters in compiling exact data regarding the climates, soils, crops, and
available lands in their localities. The Southern Pacific's ticket outlets in the
United States and Europe disseminated the resulting pamphlets, newspapers,
and handbills free of charge. In the case of the Immigration Association of Northern California, one of the smaller Sacramento Valley regional organizations in
the 1880s, the railroad's system distributed 40,000 booster items per month.[48]

Later, when it had become a major publishing company in its own right,
the railroad directly published booster-group literature. After 1899, *Sunset,* the
newly founded Southern Pacific monthly magazine, regularly carried articles
written by local promoters to advertise agricultural and urban regions of California and the company's other states. The railroad's own writers also con-

tributed articles proclaiming the potential for establishing small farms or sub-
urban homes in California, and later in other parts of Southern Pacific territory, especially Oregon.[49] To encourage and subsidize county boards of supervisors, chambers of commerce, boards of trade, and development associations
in the production of promotional literature concerning their areas, the Southern Pacific created the Sunset Homeseekers' Bureau in the early 1900s.[50]

Ironically, the assistance of the Southern Pacific, upon which booster groups
relied so much, sometimes hindered their operations. If the presence of railroad officials and dollars among the organizations increased their prestige among
some potential supporters, it also alienated other groups who equated the involvement of the Southern Pacific with control by "the monopoly." From the
1870s to the 1900s, many of the company's enemies also attacked promotional
organizations for being the railroad's puppets, often undermining public
confidence and reducing voluntary or official state support. Critics used the
presence of the Big Four among the directors of the California Immigrant Union
in 1869 and 1870 to thwart its move to become an official state agency. Similarly, labor unions attacked the Immigration Association of California in the
1880s for its ties to the Southern Pacific.[51] The State Board of Trade drew opposition on the same grounds in the 1890s and 1900s. Promoters repeatedly
had to disclaim undue railroad manipulation of their organizations.[52]

Undeniably, booster organizations aided the Southern Pacific to achieve its
goals of attracting settlers to its territories and creating a favorable economic
and social environment for railroad expansion, land sales, and increased traffic.
The railroad subsidies, however, did not mean that the Southern Pacific "owned"
the booster groups or used them as fronts for direct land sales. In the 1870s, the
California Immigrant Union and the Southern Pacific did cooperate to found
agricultural colonies in San Bernardino and Siskiyou counties. This was a normal service that the Immigrant Union, as a land development agency, provided
for many landowners in California.[53] When by the 1880s the Southern Pacific
had developed its own land marketing system and it no longer needed the
booster organizations to sell land, this connection between land sales and the
organizations disappeared.

The promotional groups succeeded, moreover, in maintaining their independence, often against the railroad, on other questions. The Immigrant Union
attacked the Southern Pacific's practice of using Chinese laborers in the 1870s.
Its founder and early president, Caspar T. Hopkins, was one of the leaders of
the San Francisco business community's fight against the railroad's monopoly
over transportation serving their city. As a member of a "committee of one hundred," Hopkins also campaigned for the building of the Atlantic and Pacific
Railroad to California to break the Southern Pacific's grip on transportation.
When that failed, Hopkins in the early 1870s wrote and secured the passage of

the state's first railroad regulation law.[54] The Grangers in the 1870s were, of course, also loud critics of railroad policies. Both the Immigration Association of California and the State Board of Trade agitated for the building of a Nicaraguan canal to undermine the Southern Pacific's control over freight rates in the 1880s and 1890s.[55]

Later, the state's chambers of commerce were important forces behind municipal reform and Progressivism, often intensely anti–Southern Pacific movements. The Los Angeles Chamber of Commerce, at the same time as it received transportation subsidies for its eastern displays, was laboring to save the city's harbor from Southern Pacific domination and to oust the railroad from local and state politics.[56] After 1900, the California Promotion Committee, a statewide consortium of local booster groups that eventually absorbed the State Board of Trade and evolved into the California Development Board and then the California State Chamber of Commerce, also engaged in Progressive and anti-railroad activities. The 1907 convention of the Promotion Committee in Fresno, for example, overwhelmingly passed resolutions calling for rigid enforcement of current railroad regulatory laws, ejection of the railroad from politics, and increased federal control of railway abuses. One newspaper reporter called the Promotion Committee's document "probably the first trumpet call to arms in the beginning of the war of shippers of California on the Southern Pacific."[57]

Immigration Plan of 1883

As the increased Southern Pacific support for booster groups and displays of western products at expositions suggests, in the early and mid-1880s, new conditions revived railroad interest in more aggressive land subdivision and advertising and promotion through its own departments. Recovery from the depression of the 1870s, both in California and the nation at large, and the state's early successes with fruit and specialty crops were stimulating a greater demand for California land. Similar stirrings awakened other Southern Pacific states. Rosier prospects for the future, in turn, spawned a wave of boosterism, in which the Southern Pacific took an active part. In addition to altered circumstances in California and other southwestern and far-western states, the railroad also had its own reasons for expanding the scale of its propaganda. By the formation of the Southern Pacific Company in the mid-1880s, the railroad had become much larger, profitable, and geographically encompassing. Most important was the completion of the Southern Pacific Railroad's independent line from Los Angeles to Atlantic tidewater, first with a connection to the Texas and Pacific near El Paso in 1881, and then, using the tracks of various purchased

Texas and Louisiana lines, the opening of its own "Sunset Route" to Houston-Galveston and New Orleans in 1883. Thus in 1882 and 1883, the Southern Pacific and related lines accessed three additional Atlantic port cities, Houston-Galveston and New Orleans via the Southern Pacific and Newport News, Virginia, via the Huntington-controlled Chesapeake and Ohio, and the company reached agreements with steamship lines for through-transport of passengers and cargo directly between Europe and the far-western states.[58] The annoying interference of the Union Pacific in land, traffic, and immigration matters was lessened. Also in the 1880s, the Southern Pacific extended tracks north from the Sacramento Valley into Oregon to harbors at Portland, Coos Bay, and other northwest Pacific points and purchased or constructed other lines to consolidate its transportation hold on parts of Oregon, particularly the fertile Willamette Valley. Meanwhile, because of the issuance of some land patents by the federal government, the railroad was again accumulating a sufficient supply of land to sell, including some within the federal land grants of its recently acquired Oregon & California Railroad in Oregon, as well as the remaining Texas state grants to the Galveston, Harrisburg, & San Antonio and other roads in that state. To Southern Pacific promoters who had hesitated before, the 1880s appeared ripe for expanded land development and settlement efforts.[59]

Jerome Madden's annual Southern Pacific Railroad Land Department reports of the early 1880s repeatedly alluded to a systematic plan to promote immigration that the railroad was preparing for the day its independent transcontinental connections were completed. Benjamin B. Redding's death in August 1882 and the subsequent shift in land management probably interrupted the inauguration of the plan.[60] After some delay, William H. Mills was appointed in January 1883 to the position of land agent of the Central Pacific Railroad, with the auxiliary duty of also overseeing the land programs of the other associated lines, including the Southern Pacific Railroad. Mills brought to the railroad great journalistic, organizational, and political ability, acquired during a decade of experience as the editor of the *Sacramento Record* and the *Record-Union*, by the 1880s the leading booster newspaper of the Sacramento Valley, and a commitment to a complex of goals shared by many western promoters.[61]

As in the past, the new immigration program introduced by Mills in the spring of 1883 emphasized promoting land sales and thus centered in the company's land departments. Successful old programs were continued and expanded, including advertising in newspapers, issuing pamphlets, mounting displays, and aiding promotional organizations. In addition, more aggressive means of reaching prospective settlers, reminiscent of other land-grant roads, were also developed. The company appointed a California immigration commissioner, with headquarters in Chicago, to direct a world-wide network of immigration agents in most large American cities, as well as London, Bordeaux,

Berlin, and Gottenburg.[62] As the first commissioner, Mills chose Isaac N. Hoag, his associate as agricultural editor of the *Sacramento Record-Union*. Like Mills, Hoag brought to his position with the railroad a fund of experience with development activities stretching back to the 1860s.[63]

When Hoag took office in the spring of 1883, the railroad's new immigration machinery started to move. In order to gather complete and exact information about California, the company blanketed the state with circulars requesting that experts contribute materials concerning soil, crops, climate, irrigation, marketing, labor demand, timber resources, manufacturing, and town growth. The circular also pleaded with owners of rural real estate to curb their ambitions for larger tracts, bumper grain harvests, and immense herds of cattle, and to focus more attention on developing a dense farm population. Promising not to favor its own lands, the Southern Pacific invited private landowners to consign their holdings to the railroad for subdivision and sale. The railroad reported shortly that over 100,000 acres of private land had been turned over in Butte and Colusa counties, including 60,000 acres owned by land barons Henry Miller and Charles Lux.[64] To speed the flow of information into its new promotional network, the railroad also contacted specialists, such as George Davidson of the U.S. Coast Survey, for statistics on climate, health, elevations, and irrigation.[65] Meanwhile, from April to June 1883, Hoag traveled through central and northern California communities gathering information on local resources, writing articles on his findings for the *Record-Union,* and attempting to whip up grassroots enthusiasm for promotion. Local committees to collect information and displays for the railroad's immigration agency sprouted in response to Hoag's call in several counties. Railroad promoters combined their information with material from government agencies and issued a report on agriculture in California, a document that became the basis of the railroad's promotional literature for the next decade.[66]

In June 1883, Hoag moved to Chicago to open his immigration office. During more than two years of intense activity, Hoag established a permanent display of California products in downtown Chicago, the transportation hub of European immigrants and American settlers heading west, arranged for eastern journalists and authors to travel to California and write about the state, distributed literature emanating from the railroad or booster groups, particularly to passengers aboard westbound trains, addressed meetings of farmers and prospective emigrants throughout the Middle West on the glories of life and profit in the Golden State, and corresponded with and furnished information to thousands of others. He also wrote articles on California for newspapers and journals, including a series for *The Prairie Farmer* in the summer of 1883. His promotional writings culminated in the production of *California: The Cornucopia of the World,* one of the major nineteenth-century booster works about the American West. Hoag also organized one of the first specialized displays of California fruit to be seen in the East, at the 1883 Illinois State Fair. Other displays followed at fairs and horticultural societies all over the middle and eastern states. From his office in Chicago, Hoag managed a network of agents in American and foreign cities, who distributed California promotional materials, recruited buyers for railroad and private land in the state, and referred serious inquiries to Hoag. He organized several colonies of farmers and sent them west to settle tracts of railroad and private land in California.[67]

The scope of railroad publicity generated by the Immigration Commissioner's office increased rapidly. Before a year had passed, Hoag reported to the Sacramento Board of Trade that the Southern Pacific had already spent $6,000 on publications, while his monthly postage bill alone averaged more than $100. The Immigration Commissioner's monthly expenses, including rent, displays, and salaries for himself and an assistant and fees for field agents, exceeded $1,100. During periodic return trips to California, Hoag toured the state, collecting more displays and written materials and reinvigorating local interest in promotional activities. Often, he exploited community and regional jealousies to arouse enthusiasm. On one such occasion in 1884, he complained to a meeting of Sacramento businessmen that he was forced to distribute mostly southern California booster literature and displays since that region was most vigorous in its support of his office. Unless northerners organized themselves and promoted the virtues of their region, he warned, southern California would continue to attract more attention and settlers.[68] By spreading California propaganda in the mid-1880s and fostering community booster activities, the Southern Pacific's Immigration Commissioner's office in Chicago contributed to the boom in California from 1885 to 1888. When Hoag left his job in August 1885 to lead and settle in one of his own agricultural communities, the Chicago Colony (Redlands), east of Los Angeles, his place was taken by H. M. Van Arman, a Southern Pacific passenger official. For several more years, Van Arman continued to manage the railroad's California promotional activities from Chicago in the manner pioneered by his predecessor.[69]

Although the Southern Pacific's promotional plan aimed primarily at diverting some of the westward migration from the Middle West toward California, other agents in Europe and America penetrated their areas with information on California, as well as other Southern Pacific regions. Heading the European branch from headquarters in London, W. G. Kingsbury, a former Texan and promoter for the Southern Pacific's recently acquired subsidiary, the Galveston, Harrisburg, & San Antonio Railroad, managed an operation similar to Hoag's in Chicago. From 1883 to 1886 he maintained a permanent company display of California products in London, sponsored exhibitions at English country and city fairs, established a network of Southern Pacific agents throughout the British Isles and the Continent, distributed literature, delivered lectures on California, Texas, and other states, and sold emigrant tickets to land-seekers. After a fashion, Kingsbury and other foreign agents also sold specific Southern Pacific land-grant tracts to would-be emigrants. Even though they were not empowered to sign sales contracts, they identified the lands to be pur-chased overseas and then accepted some payments on the purchases, to be de-livered later to the company, minus their agents' commissions. In 1884, Kings-bury led a tour from England to inspect the railroad's lands in California and Texas. Subsequently published in London, his report on the tour circulated widely in Europe and the United States, calling attention to the agricultural and urban revolution taking place in California, as well as opportunities for settlement along the Southern Pacific's lines in Texas. In the mid-1880s, Kings-bury sent a colony of Englishmen to found the agricultural community of Lan-caster, one of the early settlements of the Antelope Valley, in the Mojave Desert north of Los Angeles.[70]

After 1883, the Southern Pacific's expanded promotion plan began to have immediate effects. Although the reception of the program was mixed, the rail-road, at the very least, was able to polish its image somewhat. Some traditional enemies remained unmollified. Ambrose Bierce, one of the most acerbic of the railroad's critics, declared in his satirical weekly, *The Wasp,* that while he wel-comed honest, self-interested plans to settle families on California's empty lands, the railroaders were not honest men: "They lie and they cheat. Their dealings with settlers have been characterized by a multitude of rapacities. They skin their clients and sell them back the skins at an advance. They will settle the im-migrants along their lines and take the entire profit of their industry for car-rying their crops to market." Bierce predicted that "in three years the people that they have tumbled from the frying pan into the fire will be fighting them on a crust of bread and a cold potato." San Francisco's *Chronicle,* in the midst of one of its periodic assaults against the "Octopus," barely noticed the railroad's announcement, except to denounce the Southern Pacific's "schemes of immi-gration" for being directed solely at foisting off its worthless real estate on un-suspecting newcomers.[71] Later, other newspapers and groups continued to crit-icize facets of the program. Responding to Hoag's urgings that the Central Valley counties organize themselves to develop promotional materials for the railroad to distribute, the *Solano Republican* claimed that the company was conspiring to "get the people of this section of the State to advertise, thereby inducing travel and consequently turning ticket money into the railroad's till." Contra-dicting the *Chronicle*'s more common reasoning, the *Republican,* repeating the myth that the Southern Pacific was a land speculator, charged that, even while it was stimulating immigration, the railroad intended to withhold its own lands from sale. "Land will advance in price, farms will be subdivided and sold, while the company will hold on to all it has until the land has reached a price commensurate with the company's avarice."[72]

Newspapers that approved of the Southern Pacific's plan denied these allegations. Understandably, Mills's *Sacramento Record-Union* repeatedly pointed out that the railroad, despite public criticism, was the best agency to further booster activities. "It has the ability, the facilities, and the self-interest so necessary to the work," the newspaper noted, and the railroad's activities were not confined to selling its own land grant. Rather, the company's agents also distributed information concerning government and privately owned lands, even in counties such as San Diego, where the railroad had no real estate.[73] Other papers in the Central Valley, the San Francisco Bay area, and southern California, including some that fought the railroad on other issues, likewise stressed that in this case the interests of the corporation and the public intersected in promotional matters. The *Oakland Times* admitted that, although it opposed in principle the practice of granting public lands to railroads, this was now a moot issue because the land had already been transferred. Since little desirable government land remained in California and owners of large private estates refused to sell, "the only hope for getting small tracts for settlement lies in the subdivision of the railroad land grants." The *San Francisco Call* concluded that "the complete and systematic plan of the Southern Pacific Company will doubtless bring thousands of the best kind of immigrants to this state each year, to the great benefit of the community at large, as well as to the immigrants themselves."[74]

The Southern Pacific's promotion of California and its other western territories expanded under the immigration plan begun in 1883. The Central Pacific, with William H. Mills in charge of the program, increased its advertising budget from $31,000 in 1882 to $67,000 in 1883. Meanwhile, the Central Pacific's annual land-department expenses grew from $24,000 in 1882 to $70,000 by 1884 and remained near that figure until 1888, the final year of California's nearly decade-long "boom." By 1887, the Central Pacific's land department had spent a total of $1,030,000 surveying, subdividing, and advertising its land grant.[75] Due to increased expenditures, more and larger pamphlets, and more systematic operations, the Southern Pacific in this decade became the most important agency organizing and spreading California propaganda and contributing to the sensational influx of settlers and capital into the state that has come to be called the "Boom of the Eighties." Both the public at large and the railroad benefited from this period of economic growth. Annual land sales for the Central Pacific expanded from 43,000 acres in 1879 to a crest of 398,000 in 1884, while disposal of Southern Pacific Railroad land increased from a mere 84,000 in 1883 to 777,000 in 1887. Although sales generally declined after 1888, reflecting the liquidation of the railroad's best land and an overall shrinkage in the market for California and other western lands after the boom ended, the middle years of the 1880s marked the apex in the history of land-grant disposal on both roads.[76]

Scoundrels and Scandals

The Southern Pacific's promotional programs of the mid-1880s did increase railroad traffic and land sales and delivered population growth and economic development to its western states, particularly California and Texas. But problems resulted from entrusting the company's funds, lands, and reputation to distant, lightly supervised agents, some of whom were themselves operating private, sometimes shady, land businesses on the side. Immigration agents Hoag and Kingsbury, to begin with, piled up large, often unexpected expenses maintaining branch offices in high-priced downtown neighborhoods, paying for mass printings and mailings, and dispatching displays. Railroad superiors constantly complained, pressed them to economize, and finally cut back the funding for both offices.[77] Several scandals also rocked the European program, particularly Kingsbury's London immigration agency, eventually leading to a public outcry against the Southern Pacific that reverberated from California to Great Britain. It started in late 1885, when some colonists that Kingsbury had sent from Britain to southern California's Antelope Valley complained to the railroad and publicly to the press that the London agent had misrepresented the company's land. The prime orchard property they assumed they were buying turned out to be desert wastes, and they filed a claim at the Southern Pacific headquarters in San Francisco demanding a refund.[78]

Far more serious was the bizarre "Fresno Farm Pupil" scandal of 1885–1886, to which the Antelope Valley land controversy was remotely linked. In the nineteenth century, well-to-do English families commonly sent unmanageable, delinquent, retarded, or simply surplus teenage sons to the United States, as well as to Canada and Australia, to be taught discipline and the value of hard work on farms or in so-called "farm schools."[79] After a stint on the land, some of the youths chose to stay in the "colonies," while some returned home, presumably "reformed" by the experience. By the 1880s, a flourishing trade in boys had grown up. Advertising for clients in newspapers of London and other cities, agents recruited groups of "farm pupils" and for a fee took them to America and placed them on farms or in farm schools. Predictably, abuses abounded. In the case that ensnared the Southern Pacific, one F. W. Green of London, in partnership with Kingsbury, specialized in supplying boys to San Joaquin Valley farmers. Kingsbury also employed Green to assist in organizing groups of English farm-buyers to colonize Southern Pacific lands. Green, Kingsbury, and some recipients of the pupils divided the placement fees, along with expense and pocket money parents provided for their sons, which commonly totaled about one hundred pounds each. Working with them, an enterprising Fresno-area couple named Newman founded "Newman's School of Fruit Farming" to enroll English boys for "instruction." The scheme unraveled in the summer and fall of 1885, when some of the boys wrote home complaining that there was no school, or farm either, at the Newmans' place. The couple also whipped them, locked them up in a shed at night, rented them out to work on nearby farms, and kept all their wages. When the Newmans savagely beat the youngest boy, only thirteen years old, he escaped, and sympathetic neighbors called in local authorities. Arrested, tried, convicted, and fined by a Fresno police judge, the Newmans promptly vanished, abandoning the boys to fend for themselves. When word leaked out about the outrage and railroad immigration agents' complicity in it, California newspapers, as could be expected, had a field day attacking the Southern Pacific for yet another example of its malevolence.[80]

In September and October 1885, Green and Kingsbury, unaware that the scandal was breaking in California, were leading fourteen more farm pupils bound for Newman's School in Fresno, along with another group of more than a hundred land buyers intending to join the railroad's English Antelope Valley colony at Lancaster, north of Los Angeles. The two cronies had a falling-out aboard ship, however. Apparently, Kingsbury discovered that Green, in exchange for a free farm, had secretly made a side deal with a land developer to divert the colony onto his land in the Fresno area, and Kingsbury left the party when they landed in the United States. On arriving in the Antelope Valley, Green found the local newspapers and law-enforcement authorities there already clamoring that the colonists had been defrauded, which indeed appears to have been the case for at least some of them. He was also alerted that the Fresno authorities were after him. Green quickly dumped some of the colonists in Lancaster, without land, their land-purchase money, and some of their baggage, and took most of the party on to Fresno. He lingered there only long enough to unload the rest of the colonists and the pupils at the train depot. Pocketing nearly ten thousand pounds of the boys' and land buyers' money, Green continued on the same train to San Francisco, whence he sailed for England. In early January 1886, Kingsbury, who had been roundly condemned in the press, surfaced briefly in San Francisco, denying to newspapers that he had known about abuses by the Newmans or that he had been a party to the swindles of the land buyers and the boys. He adamantly defended the farm-pupil system, however, as an important service to the boys and a source of immigration for the country.[81]

Southern Pacific officials in San Francisco and New York were incensed. Although they disavowed any responsibility for Kingsbury's actions, saying that the company had not given him authority to import farm pupils or to sign contracts for land sales on the railroad's behalf, they attempted to ameliorate losses of the injured persons. Huntington, general superintendent Alban N. Towne, and chief passenger agent T. H. Goodman provided the swindled land buyers with free transportation for them to go to San Francisco to discuss their claims in person and perhaps, if warranted, to get replacement railroad lands. The Englishmen also received free travel to inspect lands anywhere else in California, to return home, or to journey on to British Columbia or Australia.[82] In early 1886, the railroad dispatched investigators and a clergyman to Fresno to see to the needs of the stranded farm pupils. By that time, Fresno citizens had mounted volunteer efforts. Benefit concerts had raised funds for the children, temporary homes had been found, and some boys were now working, as originally intended, on local farms. Most wanted to stay in California, but the Southern Pacific, working with local residents, provided those who did not with free transportation home or to go to friends or family members in the United States. Some of the children, however, continued to suffer. A few became ill, one severely, and along with one retarded boy could not work or travel and were being cared for by Fresno families. Another became "deranged" and took to roaming the streets of Fresno with a shotgun.[83]

Despite his protestations of innocence, the Southern Pacific fired Kingsbury, closed his London office, and moved the company's British agency to Liverpool, the debarkation point for most British emigrants heading for the United States. This being only one of a number of nasty episodes the railroad had been through with dishonest, overly aggressive, or uncontrollable immigration agents, the company drastically reduced its foreign immigration operations, and soon discontinued all direct sales of land in Europe.[84] From then on, the railroad would advertise land and recruit settlers overseas and provide transportation for them, but potential buyers would have to purchase and pay for their land at one of the company's land offices in San Francisco, San Antonio, or Portland, or a regional office near their destination. When two years later the cheeky Kingsbury applied to Southern Pacific officials in California seeking once more to serve as their agent leading groups of railroad land buyers from Europe, they referred the inquiry immediately to Huntington in New York. "The Company. . . has no intention of resorting to the sale of lands in Europe, as the policy is too prolific of controversies and disappointments," Huntington explained with some understatement in refusing Kingsbury's request; "neither are we at liberty to issue to you the free pass you solicit."[85]

The Passenger Department Takes Over

From the late 1880s into the early 1900s, as land sales constituted less and less of the railroad's total business, the responsibility for initiating and organizing

Southern Pacific activities promoting California and the company's other western regions shifted toward the Passenger Department. Besides the decline of the land business, several other factors helped reorient railroad advertising. The Boom of the Eighties and the loud propaganda of the railroads and booster organizations were beginning to awaken American consciousness of California's climate, scenery, health, and investment opportunities, particularly among the increasingly mobile, affluent middle and upper classes. Meanwhile, the improvement of transcontinental railway service, the introduction of Pullman cars, and the sharp reduction of fares due to competition between the Southern Pacific and the Santa Fe after 1886 were making it easier, faster, cheaper, and more pleasant to reach California from the eastern states. When by the 1880s resort hotels and excursion companies were emerging to house and organize it, the "tourist rush" to California was in full swing.[86] As railroad leaders perceived that tourism was an increasingly important source of revenue, as well as a way of attracting potential settlers to the company's territory, the Passenger Department became an important promotional force. This agency had the added advantage of a ready-made network of passenger and ticket agents throughout the West and the rest of the nation who could funnel information into and serve as outlets for the Southern Pacific's propaganda machine. At first limiting itself to occasional forays, the department gradually increased the volume of its promotional activities until by the early 1900s it was clearly the railroad's major advertising unit. The completeness of this transfer within the structure of the corporation was apparent in 1901, when William H. Mills stepped down as the manager of Southern Pacific press relations and promotional and advertising programs, although he retained control of the Land Department until his death in 1907. Subsequently, James Horsburgh, Jr., assistant general passenger agent, directed the company's booster programs.[87]

One of the major results of the enlarged role of the Passenger Department was an expanded publications program by the railroad, particularly the issuing of pamphlets, magazines, and books aimed at tourists, as well as those seeking new homes and farms. The Southern Pacific had always sought to increase passenger traffic in that manner.[88] As the tourist market grew after the mid-1880s, however, the promotional literature of the Passenger Department increased and became more specialized. Booklets and maps describing the attractions of most of California's important communities and regions were issued, at first in modest numbers, and similar works promoted the resources of the rest of Southern Pacific territory, particularly Oregon, Arizona, and Texas. By 1900 editions numbering hundreds of thousands of copies were common.[89] The Southern Pacific's Passenger Department produced some of the most attractive and extensive western promotional pieces. In the late 1880s, many pamphlets on local areas were collected into the *Southern Pacific Sketch Book,* a volume of several

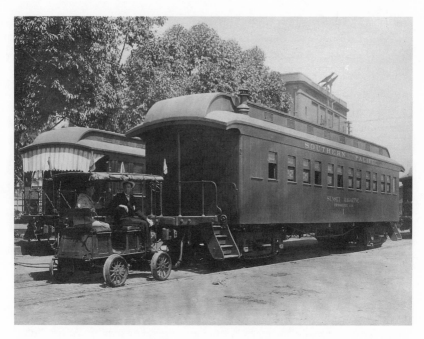

Sunset magazine's special photography car (shown ca. 1910) toured Southern Pacific lines capturing images of economic and social development and scenic wonders to promote the West. Courtesy Huntington Library.

hundred pages promoting the resources of California and other western states. To coincide with the Mid-Winter Exposition held in San Francisco in 1894, the railroad published *California for Health, Pleasure and Profit: Why You Should Go There*. By the early 1900s, the Southern Pacific was issuing heroic quantities of pamphlets and other materials advertising opportunities for travel, farming, and home-building in California, Oregon, Arizona, Nevada, and Texas. During one three-year period, the railroad distributed 10,000,000 pieces of promotional literature.[90]

The Southern Pacific also founded new periodicals to attract tourists and settlers to California and the larger West. In the 1880s, Ben Truman of the railroad's literary bureau, a branch of the Passenger Department, founded *Wave*, a journal designated particularly to publicize the new resort established by the Pacific Improvement Company at Hotel Del Monte, in Monterey.[91] As the passenger business grew and spread from California into other Southern Pacific regions and the Passenger Department developed into the leading railroad promotional agency, its publishing energies likewise expanded. In 1898, the department launched *Sunset*, a San Francisco monthly aimed initially at stimulating tourism throughout Southern Pacific territory. Early issues publicized the attractions of Yosemite, Hotel Del Monte, Paso Robles hot springs, Coronado, Santa Monica, and other attractions in California, especially focusing on the theme of the state as a health resort. By the end of 1899, *Sunset* had a circulation of 15,000, including schools, libraries, newspapers, and private subscribers in every state, and it was developing into a promoter of the entire Southwest.[92] In 1899 and 1900, the magazine expanded greatly in size, added new departments and services, and adopted a more attractive format, including lavish photographs and lithographs, covers and drawings by artists such as Maynard Dixon, and stories and poems by Mary Austin and other regional writers. By the early 1900s, *Sunset*, edited now by Charles S. Aiken, had become California and the West's leading promotional journal, emphasizing not only the opportunities for tourism and recreation, but also agricultural development, small-scale farming and cooperative colonies, irrigation, forestry and resource conservation, urban and industrial investment, and the preservation of the region's Indian cultures, historical heritage, and wilderness. *Sunset* also helped to popularize the Spanish colonial revival, a movement after the 1890s to romanticize the mission period and to create a distinctive regional architecture and artistic style for the California and Southwest borderlands.[93] By the end of 1904, *Sunset's* monthly issues had expanded in size from thirty-two to 208 pages and its circulation from 15,000 to 58,000. A study conducted in 1904 showed that newspapers throughout the country regularly reprinted *Sunset's* articles on California and the West. By 1911, the journal averaged more than 100,000 copies and 500,000 readers per month.[94]

As *Sunset* grew and diversified in the early 1900s, it became not only an important railroad advertising vehicle but also a supporter of booster efforts by local governments and business groups. Perhaps *Sunset's* most visible contribution to community development was the campaign the magazine led to support the reconstruction of San Francisco after its devastating earthquake and fire in April 1906.[95] But, the magazine's ongoing services for community development also stimulated an explosion of local promotional activities in Southern Pacific territory after 1900. Beginning in 1907, the magazine ran a "Development Section" devoted to publicizing local communities and providing a publishing outlet for grassroots boosters. That magazine feature supplemented the Sunset Homeseekers' Bureau, which had been inaugurated in the early 1900s. Using the writers and publishing facilities of the magazine, the bureau collected information for, wrote, and financed the publication of hundreds of local promotional pamphlets for county and town governments and local chambers of commerce, at first throughout California, but eventually also in Nevada, Oregon, and Arizona. During only one year of the California-based program, 1910, thirty-one counties issued 525,000 copies of booklets, at a cost to the Southern Pacific of nearly $20,000. Of special value to newly developing, sparsely

The cover of *Hood River, Oregon* (1910), published by *Sunset* magazine's Northwest Homeseekers' Bureau, illustrated the blend of traditional and modernistic design of Southern Pacific promotional materials in the early twentieth century. On his copy, William Bittle Wells, the bureau's founder and manager, wrote an inscription identifying the pamphlet as "the 'high water' mark of publication by the Bureau." Author's collection.

populated regions, usually short of capital, publishing facilities, and talented writers, the Homeseekers' Bureau increased the volume of California's booster materials and made them more sophisticated and attractive.[96]

So successful was the Homeseekers' Bureau that the Southern Pacific established a Portland branch serving the Harriman Lines' territory in the Pacific Northwest. The Northwest program, known as the Sunset Magazine Homeseekers' Bureau Cooperative Community Advertising Plan, was the handiwork of Portland's William Bittle Wells, one of the West's most brilliant and prolific publicists. Among the first graduates of Stanford University, Wells later founded and owned *Sunset*'s Northwest competitor, *The Pacific Monthly*. When Wells sold the magazine in 1906, the railroad's Passenger Department approached him with a proposal to start a Pacific Northwest regional Homeseekers' Bureau. After traveling to the San Francisco area for discussions with the department and with David Starr Jordan, Stanford's president, Wells agreed to go to work for *Sunset*, and the Cooperative Community Advertising Program started operating in early 1907. The Northwest bureau made possible the publishing of countless pamphlets for local governments and business groups. At token cost to them, many more than one hundred communities participated in the plan, whereby the railroad produced promotional booklets, using information provided by town and county governments and chambers of commerce. Wells conceived, organized, and administered the program, recruited the local booster agencies, hired and managed a network of agents, and wrote, designed, and distributed the colorful, lavishly illustrated pamphlets. The Northwest Homeseekers' Bureau was especially active in promoting Wells's home state of Oregon, producing more than one hundred pamphlets just on Oregon's communities, but it also worked in the larger country of the Harriman Lines in Washington and Idaho, and even British Columbia and Alaska. If anything, Wells's regional program was more productive than its California counterpart. By 1911, he had issued nearly twenty million copies of pamphlets advertising the Pacific Northwest, at a cost, according to a report by Wells, of at least $2 million, most of it paid by the Southern Pacific. That year, in a financial retrenchment related to the pending breakup of the Harriman Lines, the Southern Pacific discontinued the Northwest Cooperative Community Advertising Plan, and Wells went into private business.[97] In 1914, after the unmerger, however, *Sunset* founded a "Service Bureau," headed by Walter V. Woehlke, to spread information about the Southern Pacific's own territory—California, Oregon, and the Southwest—by facilitating the creation of local booster organizations and the interchange of ideas and methods among them.[98]

Sunset proved so successful as a Southern Pacific publicity organ that the railroad established a European counterpart and also *The Southwest Magazine,* based in San Antonio and promoting the company's Atlantic System territories, Texas and Louisiana. In 1912, the railroad also purchased the *Pacific Monthly,* located in Portland and specializing in the Pacific Northwest. The magazine was merged into *Sunset,* which took on the new title, *Sunset—The Pacific Monthly,* and the combined, enlarged magazine embraced an even grander vision of becoming a national journal expressing the interests of the entire western region. Partly to facilitate that, partly to free itself of its huge subsidy to the money-losing periodical, the Southern Pacific decided to sever its formal ties in 1914 and sold *Sunset* to a newly formed private company owned mostly by its staff and contributors. During six subsequent decades of management by the Lane family and today's ownership by Time-Warner, *Sunset* has remained the West's oldest magazine, by a long ways its most popular, and still devoted to some of the same goals that inspired the Southern Pacific to create it more than a century ago: travel, lifestyles, and conservation of nature and cultural heritage in the Far West.[99]

In addition to magazine publication programs, the railroad continued to expand its promotional activity in other ways after 1900 under the direction of James Horsburgh, Jr., and the Passenger Department. Horsburgh or his agents attended meetings of national organizations, sought to have California or other Southern Pacific states chosen as sites for conventions, and interceded with the states' governors to secure official invitations and assistance.[100] The railroad sent more displays of California products and attractions, as well as those of the company's other western states and territories, to eastern and European fairs. Lecturers sponsored by the railroad, often in conjunction with promotional

Early 1900s Southern Pacific's western advertising included such activities as cooperating
with the Portland Transportation Club in a saturation "Transportation Day" campaign to
promote Oregon. The railroad organized and
paid for a letter-writing project that dispatched
10,000 missives in one month alone. This publicity photo was used in the campaign. Courtesy Oregon Historical Society, Portland.

organizations, accompanied the displays or toured the country giving slide shows
on fun, profit, and homes in the West. In 1899 and 1900, for example, Helen
Kellehur presented illustrated lectures in more than one hundred eastern cities
before crowds as large as 1,500.[101] Perhaps the champion, though, was James
W. Erwin, veteran Southern Pacific lecturer, who by 1917 had delivered his presentation, "Wonders of the Western Country," 3,357 times to more than 1.5 million people.[102]

Keeping pace with changing media technology, the railroad had by the early
1920s produced and was sending around the country a promotional film, *Progress Follows the Rails,* to be shown to civic and business groups, sometimes accompanied by one of the company's traveling orchestras or bands.[103] The Southern Pacific saw to it that the new motion picture industry featured the
company's territory in cinema. In the early 1920s, with Los Angeles, an important Southern Pacific operations center, emerging as the movie capital and
moviemakers increasingly seeking more realistic settings, the railroad opened
a movie location bureau in the city to gather information and inform studios
about scenic, climatic, architectural, and historic locations along Southern
Pacific lines. One of those, the High Sierra town of Truckee, on the old Central Pacific route just east of Donner Pass, served as the setting for a growing
number of feature films about Wild West, mountain, and "frozen north" places.

Wilbur Maynard, manager of the Southern Pacific Hotel in Truckee, supplemented his company's general services. Movie directors routinely consulted with Maynard on where to shoot scenes, and he often made all arrangements needed by film companies before their arrival. Maynard provided vehicles, hired extras, carpenters, and transport workers, issued daily weather bulletins to aid in planning filming schedules, and at his hotel furnished room and board for actors and crew as well as offices, darkrooms for film processing, and cutting rooms for editing. Assistance from Maynard and his assistants was central to the successful filming of many movies, including Charlie Chaplin's 1925 masterpiece, *The Gold Rush.*[104]

To make it easier and cheaper for interested parties to reach the west coast, the Passenger Department in 1900 instituted a system of "colonist" rates, off-season, one-way fares designed especially for people moving to California. Heavily advertised, the reduced tickets of $30 from points in the Middle West attracted 140,000 passengers by 1903, 625,000 by 1910, and 795,000 by 1916, when the company discontinued colonist rates. Occasional "Homeseeker's Excursions" offered equally low round-trip fares to persons scouting out farms, homes, and jobs. The railroad established a separate homeseekers' fares program for Texas.[105]

The Southern Pacific's growing involvement in the movement to publicize the West in the 1890s and early 1900s was reflected also in expanded advertising budgets. The advertising and printing expenditures of the company increased from $150,000 in 1888 to $200,000 in 1892, $400,000 in 1900, $850,000 in 1907, and $1,800,000 in 1911.[106] As the railroad's separate Advertising Department emerged as an identifiable agency, it too placed materials on the West in the nation's newspapers and journals, including *Scribner's, McClure's, Everybody's, Harper's,* and *Collier's.* In December 1904 alone, for example, the Southern Pacific inserted forty pages of promotional copy into American magazines at an expense of $15,000.[107] The railroad, most often through its Passenger Department, continued to publish countless of its own pamphlets and other materials promoting its territories, increasingly illustrated with excellent photographs and full-color graphics by leading western artists such as Maynard Dixon and Maurice Logan. Some, such as the venerable *California for the Settler,* were regularly issued in revised, enlarged editions for several decades into the twentieth century, in print runs of hundreds of thousands of copies. From about 1900 and into the 1920s, the railroad, for the first time, began to feature Arizona in more, and increasingly lavish, pamphlets about healthful climate, recreation, agriculture, and city growth. Expanded advertising of the region by the Southern Pacific was an important impetus to the early twentieth-century movement to promote tourism, development, and settlement in the desert Southwest.[108]

The railroad also continued assisting regional booster groups. For the California State Board of Trade, the California Promotion Committee, the Los Angeles Chamber of Commerce, and other large and small organizations in the Southern Pacific's states and territories, the railroad provided general subsidies, exhibition services, and aid in writing, paying for, and distributing their publications. In 1921, the company reported that in that year it had distributed more than 6.2 million copies of folders, maps, pamphlets, and other forms of literature produced by itself and other agencies to advertise scenic, industrial, and agricultural resources along its lines, and more than 80 million in the last decade at a cost to the railroad of $5.5 million. The volume of its promotional activities expanded through the decade until by 1928 the railroad was spending several million dollars each year promoting the attractions of its territory, and it could boast that "it is safe to say that no other agency has been more effective than the Southern Pacific in the development of the West."[109]

As the major entity organizing and financing the promotion of California and the rest of its territory, the Southern Pacific played an important role in attracting the many tourists and settlers who came west from the 1860s to 1930. Nevertheless, as late as 1911, many westerners, particularly Californians, remained suspicious of the railroad's participation in booster activities. That year, with Governor Hiram Johnson and other Progressives whipping anti–Southern Pacific sentiment to a fever pitch, at a meeting of the Counties Committee of the California Development Board, after the reading of a paper by James Horsburgh, Jr., reviewing the advertising efforts of his company on behalf of California, Robert Lynch, the manager of the Development Board, which was dependent on a hefty subsidy from the Southern Pacific, made a point of disassociating his group from the company. In the words of the board's *Bulletin,* "Mr. Lynch took occasion to explain that the California Development Board is not a railroad organization as some people seem to think. He said that the Board works with all the railroads and does not accept a courtesy from one which is not accepted from all, and that the same facilities are afforded all the railroads by the Board."[110]

The Southern Pacific and the Development of the West

The traditional interpretation of the place of the Southern Pacific in the history of California and the West during the late nineteenth and early twentieth centuries has stressed the discontinuities and conflicting interests between the railroad and other groups. At a time when farmers, businessmen, laborers, professionals, and intellectuals were grappling with the issues of economic and social development, critics charged, the railroad blocked political reform and business progress. An analysis of the agricultural, land development, and regional promotional activities of the Southern Pacific exposes the inadequacy of that view. In its policies and actions the Southern Pacific resembled other land-grant railways. Although the railroad did occasionally use its considerable political and economic power against other specific groups, many Southern Pacific goals coincided with those of other western leaders who worked through the press, state and local governments, or farmers' and businessmen's organizations to stimulate economic diversification, agricultural growth and modernization, land subdivision, immigration, and community development. Following the logic of self-interest, the Southern Pacific and its executives supported this movement not only verbally but also with programs to improve farming practices, to subdivide its land grant and tracts owned by other parties, to foster settled rural communities, and to encourage population growth and general economic development.

The railroad also made a great impression on the movement to attract settlers to California, Oregon, Texas, and other parts of its territory. In an era when state and local governments provided only tenuous assistance for this task, the company was in all likelihood the most important agency organizing and expanding promotional activities in its region. Many attributes fitted the railroad for this function. In addition to powerful motives of self-interest, the Southern Pacific possessed a growing organizational structure, including promotional experts such as Benjamin B. Redding, Jerome Madden, William H. Mills, Isaac N. Hoag, Benjamin C. Truman, Charles B. Turrill, James Horsburgh, Jr., and William Bittle Wells, and a wide network of land, immigration, passenger, and freight agents to distribute promotional materials and translate company policies into local activities. The railroad, as its region's largest corporation, with an annual income exceeding the tax revenues of the individual states through which it passed, also had important financial and transportation resources, which were used not only for company projects but also to sustain booster activities by private groups and state and local governments. With these resources, the Southern Pacific was able to cut through sectional and economic rivalries in order to mount the earliest successful large-scale promotional efforts, to introduce new techniques, and in other ways to expand and give continuity to the advertising of the American West.

PART III
Water

7 "The Satisfactory Supply Is Yet Undiscovered"

THE SOUTHERN PACIFIC AS A PIONEER WATER DEVELOPER

Railroads and Western Water History

Nearly forgotten about the history of the nineteenth-century American West is the fact that, before private and public water agencies could take the field, railroads pioneered in water development on the arid frontier. Faced with the practical problem of constructing and operating across a vast, waterless, largely unpopulated landscape, railroads built extensive waterworks to supply themselves and early settlers, thus making initial transportation and economic development possible and establishing models of water use for urban and agricultural progress. Of the western lines, the Southern Pacific, which laid down its tracks a decade or more earlier than most other companies and was forced to cope with a generally drier territory, was the prototype of the water-pioneering railroad and thus warrants particular attention.

As it cast its net of lines across a harsh landscape after the Central Pacific's founding in 1861, the company, like other western roads, became immediately embroiled in environmental issues, particularly concerning water. The railroad's domain was arid or semi-arid. The entire region west of San Antonio lacked sufficient normal rainfall from spring through autumn to support traditional agriculture or urban-industrial concentrations. In some places, Southern Pacific tracks crossed or paralleled sizable perennial streams—the Rio Grande, the Gila, the Colorado, the Sacramento and San Joaquin and tributaries, the Truckee, and the Willamette. But over long desert stretches, there was little or no surface water, groundwater could be tapped only at great depths, and much available water was contaminated with alkali. Especially parched were southern New Mexico and Arizona, the 500-mile expanse of Great Basin between the California border and the Great Salt Lake, the central and southern San Joaquin Valley, and the fierce deserts of southeastern California, which included some of the driest areas in the Western Hemisphere. Moreover, the Far West was vulnerable to periodic, acute, multi-year droughts, making water supplies not only scarce but unpredictable. Southern Pacific country abounded in soil, forest, and mineral resources, but population growth and economic development, and hence railroad profits, hinged on water diversion, storage, and redistribution projects of unprecedented magnitude.[1]

That these improvements would be made, however, was anything but certain. Though richly endowed by nature, the far-western frontier initially was short on the human resources needed for speedy water development. Most of the region was sparsely populated or, excepting Indians, unsettled altogether. Its highly mobile people were attracted to short-term speculative enterprises, while large water projects required considerable start-up capital, took a long time to become productive, and were notoriously unprofitable. Thus, sufficient private or public funds were rarely available to develop isolated, rural areas and their water resources. With immature private organizations and weak local, state, territorial, and federal government agencies, the Southern Pacific's region also lacked the institutional structure necessary to plan, build, and manage complex water systems. Moreover, intense conflicts among rival interest groups over water rights and the direction of water development, pervasive inter-community jealousies, political factionalism, turnover among officeholders, and jurisdictional disputes among local, state, and federal authorities crippled governmental efforts to develop long-term policy. As a result, stalemate and confusion reigned in water questions, particularly because of contradictory laws governing water rights. Thus, bitter controversies among conflicting water interests spilled over into the courts, litigation expanded throughout the late nineteenth and early twentieth century, and few large-scale projects were completed. The dominant theme of western water history in this period, concluded Donald J. Pisani, one of the subject's leading interpreters, was the "persistent mismanagement and ineffectiveness of both private enterprise and government in regulating the use of water. The process of allocating this precious resource was seldom guided by wisdom or equity."[2]

In the absence of effective private or public leadership in its arid, thinly populated territory, the Southern Pacific was forced to take an active part in all stages of water development. In addition to the personal commitment of many of the company's leaders to promoting regional welfare, short- and long-range corporate interests convinced executives from the beginning that successful rail operations hinged on water improvements. First and most pressing, the railroad required a large, reliable supply of high-quality water for its own use in construction, maintenance, and operations, as well as to slake the thirsts of crews and passengers. Particularly critical was securing pure water, free of suspended debris and dissolved minerals, to prevent steam locomotive boilers, pipes, and valves from clogging and requiring costly repairs or replacement. In areas lacking established waterworks, the initial needs of farmers and town-dwellers also

Alfred A. Hart photographed the Central Pacific Railroad water station at Winnemucca, Nevada, during construction of the transcontinental line, 1868. Visible are large trackside storage tanks and a first-generation tanker car used for shuttling water to the construction front and remote, dry stations. Essential to rail operations, this installation and later, even more elaborate, water facilities were common along Southern Pacific lines. Author's collection.

had to be met for settlement to begin and rail traffic to become profitable. Also vital were new water supplies to support the profitable sale of the railroad's federal land grant of millions of acres and the many railhead towns founded by the company's real estate subsidiaries. Finally, company officials realized that long-range progress in agriculture and industry, essential to future freight and passenger revenues, could be assured only by fostering large, dependable regional water systems. In the area of water policy, enlightened corporate self-interest led the Southern Pacific to identify with "the public welfare" and to work vigorously to solve water problems.[3]

The Southern Pacific was well suited to playing a creative role in water development. The railroad's modern, centralized business structure, like its tracks, bridged the gaps between sections and rival interest groups and provided a measure of coordination. One of the few entities with a broad interest in water that transcended local parochialism, the company was also frequently the largest, most active organizational presence on the raw frontier. The railroad commanded the labor and capital essential for expensive water improvements as well as access to modern technology and the expertise of its own civil engineers and land agents or outside consultants. Since complex and contradictory laws often lay at the root of water problems, the railroad's staff of talented attorneys also proved valuable. In addition, while not as monolithic as its critics charged, the company's political power was useful in securing action on water issues and influencing policies adopted by private organizations and local, state, and national agencies. In his important book *The Visible Hand,* Alfred Chandler has demonstrated that in the late nineteenth century the American railroads, as the pioneer modern business enterprises, evolved complex, professionalized, centrally coordinated structures, based on the gathering of reliable information and capable of developing and managing powerful technologies and an unprecedented volume of transactions. While Chandler has stressed the importance of the rail industry in creating management models for other businesses, a study of the Southern Pacific's activities in water development suggests that the modern structures being developed by railroads had a profound influence on the broader community as well.[4]

Beginning with narrow, tentative efforts in the 1860s and early 1870s, the Southern Pacific's activities in water development grew ever more assertive and broader in scope after 1880, when the frenzied construction of new rail lines slowed down and the company attained its corporate maturity and turned more toward developing its territory. By working within its own structure and interacting with other groups, the railroad became a major, creative influence on evolving water facilities and modern water policy in the West into the 1920s. The railroad's service was particularly valuable in certain areas: its discovery and exploitation of new water sources for its lines and nearby farms and towns; its establishment of models for modern, efficient water systems, which were borrowed by other developers; its introduction of more order, stability, and centralized planning in water use and policy; and finally its support for the movement toward public, as opposed to private, ownership and management of water supplies. While it was serving as a principal water developer in its hinterland, the Southern Pacific was required to assume many functions that would later be assigned to specialized private or governmental water agencies. When those agencies did emerge, the railroad often promoted their founding, provided financing, and helped shape their early policies. The Southern Pacific's diverse contribution to water development is important not only to the understanding of this particular company and its impact on its region, but also constitutes a dimension of general western water history and railroad history that has yet to be examined adequately.

Early Southern Pacific Waterworks

As it built lines east across northern Nevada and Utah in the late 1860s, south through the San Joaquin Valley in the early 1870s, and east across the deserts of California, Arizona, and New Mexico in the late 1870s and early 1880s, the Southern Pacific was at first forced to import water by tank car, sometimes more than 100 miles, for construction and maintenance crews, passengers, locomotives, and stations. From the beginning, the railroad carried additional water to sell to residents of the new villages sprouting around desert stations, as well as to scattered ranchers and miners. During severe drought, the Southern Pacific hauled emergency supplies that saved even communities blessed with their own water source.[5] In the early years, the railroad's water problems and incentives to import water were intensified by speculators, who moved along the proposed route ahead of desert construction, acquired monopoly control of readily available water supplies, even on the public domain, and demanded high prices from the company as well as from pioneer settlers. "We are entirely at the mercy of a set of water speculators—real water sharks—familiarly known as ditch companies," Mark Hopkins complained to Collis P. Huntington in 1867. Their business was "to go in advance of our construction and take up and appropriate all the available springs and brooks, for the purpose of making the Rail Road, the Agriculturist, the Miner or anybody who must have water pay them largely for it." The advance guard of water entrepreneurs also dug ditches that deliberately crisscrossed the projected rail line, and then charged the company handsomely for right-of-way over the ditches.[6]

Extremely costly and limited in volume, the company's early makeshift delivery systems were usually temporary, but where local water sources could not be located, they became permanent, railroad-operated utilities.[7] In 1880, for example, the Southern Pacific moved to block the Santa Fe from invading its California empire by building a branch line across the waterless and largely uninhabited waste between Mojave and Needles. For its own use and to open up the territory to development, the company started running regular water cars, and eventually whole tanker trains, over the 200-mile-long section. Local rail agents took orders, especially from prospectors, and ordered water to be delivered at any point for two cents per gallon. The Southern Pacific's water service paved the way for miners and livestock raisers to invade the high desert country and contributed to the founding of boomtowns at Calico, Ivanpah, and Providence. After a corporate truce in the late 1880s, the Santa Fe acquired the Mojave-Needles line, but the new proprietor continued to serve as the region's water lifeline into the 1960s.[8] Into the mid-twentieth century, the Southern Pacific continued to haul water to serve railroad needs along a few dry portions of its line, occasionally even to serve outsiders. For example, in California's far northeastern Tule Lake Basin, where wellwater was tainted with toxic minerals, as late as the 1930s the company was still regularly spotting water tank cars at sidings, at which ranchers and farmers filled buckets and barrels for household use.[9]

Wherever possible, however, the Southern Pacific preferred developing local supplies to relying on the expensive and laborious hauling of water by rail. In charge of construction and operation of early Southern Pacific lines, Charles Crocker ordered immediate searches for water in arid districts. At countless points on the rail network, construction departments and local station agents prospected for water, bored ordinary and artesian wells, installed windmills or steam or kerosene pumps to move the water, built filtration and purification systems, constructed tanks, sumps, and reservoirs, and laid out canals and pipelines, often many miles long. As could be expected, some projects produced only costly dry holes, but at many places the railroad developed an adequate water supply that greatly expanded the scope of rail services. Often, the Southern Pacific sold surpluses to town-dwellers and nearby farmers and ranchers. Occasionally, the company laid mains down the streets of fledgling desert towns and, for a fee that only covered costs, allowed residents to hook up directly to the railroad's pipes. The Southern Pacific, in effect, served as the first water utility for many of its station towns and rural hinterlands, making settlement and economic development possible.

While building the first transcontinental line in the late 1860s, the Southern Pacific built its earliest extensive water utilities at Sierra Nevada towns like Truckee and especially on the high Nevada desert, at such way stations as Carlin and Wells, where small settlements soon formed around the railroad's depots. At Elko, however, although the company founded a county seat town and began promoting lot sales as early as 1869, the absence of local water restricted railroad facilities to a freight depot, passenger station, and hotel. Firefighting was limited; no suitable yard or repair and maintenance facility was possible; and a switching locomotive could not be headquartered there. For the first few years, a small switching engine made periodic trips over the twenty-mile track from Carlin to handle Elko switching and to haul water to fill the station's small emergency tanks. After years of prospecting, the company struck a well nearby in 1874 and installed a steam pump to lift water into a 62,500-gallon tank. At long last, the railroad could expand its operating facilities, and Elko began its emergence as a local freight distribution center.[10] Within ten years, as a result of constant prospecting for water, well-drilling, and reservoir and pipeline construction, the company developed water stations at many points along the hundreds of miles of its arid Great Basin line from the Sierra Nevada to the Great Salt Lake; often, the company provided water to outside parties for domestic, business, or agricultural use. The railroad's water system there was not only vital to its own operations, but also made possible settlement and economic development by others in an especially isolated and harsh landscape.[11]

The Southern Pacific also built extensive new water projects in the early 1870s as the company pushed the mainline of its second transcontinental road south through the San Joaquin Valley and eastward across the southern California desert. By the mid-1870s, the railroad had successfully discovered local supplies throughout the valley and had drilled wells or tapped streams and had installed steam pumps or gravity-flow systems. At more than fifty stations in the valley, large railroad tanks served operational needs, and in a few particularly dry districts, those of settlers. One project of far-reaching significance was south of the railroad-founded town of Tulare, where in 1875 the company brought in a field of artesian wells at a depth of 300 feet, providing water to irrigate the railroad's experimental tree ranch. The railroad's example encouraged others to successfully bore for artesian wells, thus sparking the first agricultural boom in the central San Joaquin Valley.[12]

Through and beyond Tehachapi Pass, southeast of the San Joaquin Valley, the Southern Pacific in the 1870s and early 1880s also developed major waterworks. At Mojave, the railroad installed an especially large facility to meet local rail needs, to fill locomotives and tanker cars for the long, hard runs westward over the Tehachapi Mountains and eastward across the Mojave-Needles branch line, and increasingly to provide a supply for the town that sprang up around the station. To satisfy the railroad's rapidly increasing water needs in the district, the Mojave water facility grew in extent and significance, until by the early twentieth century it had evolved into a widespread 12-inch pipeline system, bringing water into the town from numerous outlying springs and wells, particularly near Cameron, eight miles northwest and several hundred feet higher in elevation. Into the 1920s, the railroad's facility continued to serve as the town's water utility.[13]

In the late 1870s, the Southern Pacific faced even more arid country as it extended its mainline from Los Angeles east, through San Gorgonio Pass toward the Colorado River, across the below-sea-level sand dunes and alkali flats of the Salton Sink. Within a year of reaching Indio in 1876, construction crews there had drilled a ten-inch well and installed a steam pump. From Indio eastward, trains hauled water cars to the construction front. But the demand along the desert line was enormous; after the line was finished to Yuma in 1877, for example, a single steam locomotive pulling an average train required four to six cars of water, some 30,000 gallons, just to make the 131-mile trip. Facing a desperate shortage, Crocker's men tried, and at first failed, to find water elsewhere along the way. Finally, one good artesian well was struck; but although the water was adequate for men and livestock, Crocker reported to Huntington in 1877, it was too brackish for locomotives. "We shall continue boring wells at different points along the line of that road hoping to get water as will answer for railroad purposes," Crocker vowed.[14]

Between the late 1870s and the early 1890s, the Southern Pacific, seeking to lower its water costs and develop a water source for itself and settlers, persistently surveyed and drilled throughout the San Gorgonio Pass–Salton Sink region. Ultimately, wells were brought in at numerous sites, sometimes miles from the tracks. Steam pumps or windmills were installed to raise water from ordinary wells and distribute it more efficiently; pipelines carried the precious liquid to stations and watering stops; and tanker cars served the portions of the rail line remote from the wells. In some places, the railroad's water system produced a surplus that was sold to settlers.

When Southern Pacific locomotives steamed into the military and riverboat center of Yuma in the autumn of 1877, finding water became yet more urgent, complicated, and challenging. The company needed a supply sufficient for the extensive operations center it envisioned in Yuma, for the expected expansion of the town, which lacked an organized waterworks, and for hauling back across the desert into California, as well as forward to the even drier future construction front the railroad hoped to open across Arizona. An abundant, permanent water supply, of course, flowed by in the Colorado River, but the town sat on a bluff on the east bank, and more important, the silt-laden river water was unusable for any purpose other than agriculture. Moreover, if it were left to settle in tanks in the broiling desert sun, the water would become too hot to use. With no wells in town, residents had hitherto acquired small amounts of water by hiring Indians at ten cents per day to fill barrels with river water and haul them up the bluff for settling and eventual use.

Upon entering Yuma, the Southern Pacific immediately set about developing a water system, built on land granted by the city. A powerful, coal-burning steam pump was installed to lift water from the river to a series of large storage and settling tanks, located uphill from town and shaded by frame structures. Gravity lines drew the water down to trackside tanks, into railroad shops, and through a six-inch wooden main under Madison Avenue. For a fee of $2 per month, residents along the street were permitted to hook up. When the pumps started chugging in April 1878, the residents of Yuma rejoiced in their first waterworks. At first, the new redwood-slat reservoirs leaked, but delighted desert-town children turned out in droves to frolic through the sprinkles and make mud pies under the wooden tanks. Soon, property owners served by the Madison Avenue main boasted the most beautiful gardens in town; residents of more remote neighborhoods continued to haul water barrels up from the river.[15]

As the Southern Pacific resumed construction in late 1878 on its Midwest-bound line through southern Arizona and New Mexico, it encountered yet

Southern Pacific Railroad photographer Carleton E. Watkins took this image of the company's coal-fired, steam-powered pumping station, ca. 1880, shortly after its installation at the bank of the Colorado River in Yuma. Courtesy Huntington Library.

harsher land, where surface water was more likely to be tainted with alkali, potable groundwater lay at greater depths, and the distances between water sources were longer. Since the handiest source, the Gila River, which paralleled a portion of the railroad's route, was stagnant and salty for much of the year, there was virtually no large reliable supply for hundreds of miles. The increased demand caused by the building of the Arizona line thus strained railroad water resources as far back west as Indio. To serve the construction front, Southern Pacific engineers designed, and the company's shops manufactured, eight higher-capacity tankers, which were dispatched daily east from Yuma. Short even for its own use, the railroad initially had no surplus, and settlers at Gila Bend and other Arizona towns on the line at first had to import their water from great distances by mule train.

The acute water scarcity east of Yuma impelled the Southern Pacific to re-double its efforts to develop a regional water system after 1879. First, the com-pany expanded the capacity of its Yuma works by operating the pumping en-gine through the night hours and installing larger tanks and a second barrel from the settling basins to the town. Actually, this was only the beginning of a continual series of improvements the company had to make over the next decades on its Yuma project. Also in 1879, a second major water facility was developed at Texas Hill, a way station sixty-three miles east of Yuma. During wet months, a pump lifted water from the Gila River to a large settling reser-voir high on a hill, from which it flowed by gravity-pipeline five miles down to the town, relieving shortages during some seasons for railroaders and set-tlers as far away as Yuma. Back on the California desert, where the limits of its own engineers and equipment had been long since been reached, the South-ern Pacific hired a specialized Chicago firm that sent in expert crews and the latest in machinery. By drilling from eighty-foot-high derricks, the contrac-tor had brought in a series of new artesian wells by April 1879. Into the early 1900s, the Southern Pacific continued to bring in new artesian wells through-out the Colorado Desert of California, and even across the border in Mexico, thereby serving, as in the San Joaquin Valley and elsewhere, as a model of arte-sian water development that others followed to start their successful water facilities.[16]

After 1879, the Southern Pacific also instituted a systematic program of water-surveying, well-drilling, and waterworks improvement by its own crews or out-side contractors all along the 550-mile line between Yuma and El Paso. By 1881, the company had managed to construct local water systems at 22 of the 45 sta-tions on the 467-mile segment from Yuma to Deming, New Mexico, alone. Particularly along the Gila River, some wells had to be bored to unprecedented depths of 1,500 to 2,000 feet to descend below the brine and reach good water. In southern New Mexico, especially around Deming, the railroad in the early

1880s discovered and developed the first artesian fields in the district, stimulating considerable town and farm expansion there.[17]

At the same time as they denounced national, territorial, and local governments for doing nothing to meet the region's critical water needs, some citizens of the Southwest praised the railroad, not only for having made the first systematic attempt to develop water but also for having proven to others that, although scarce on the surface, copious water supplies lay waiting under the desert. While some of the Southern Pacific's critics might persist in seeing the company as an "evil genius," editorialized Tucson's *Arizona Star* in 1881, its water development work had demonstrated that the railroad was "a progressive power," vital to the future of the region's mines, farms, and ranches.[18]

When it expanded into Oregon and Texas after 1880, the Southern Pacific built additional facilities, until by the early twentieth century, the railroad had water stations at hundreds of points in all states along its lines. The numerous water stations between El Paso and San Antonio alone testify to the wide extent, as well as the diversity, of the railroad's water supplies, problems, and solutions. At El Paso, water from a large network of wells on a mesa high above the city was collected and piped six miles west to yards and shops. At Tesnus, at first, the water system relied on a spring, but the railroad's later effort to increase production went awry. When excavation failed to increase yield and the company exploded dynamite in the hole, the spring went dry permanently. At Dahlberg, wells descended nearly one thousand feet before striking water, but it was so hot that it had to be cooled before use. Lasca's facility got water from a deep, abandoned mine shaft flooding from underground seepage.[19]

Some projects in the Southwest, Great Basin, and Pacific Coast regions had grown into large complexes, encompassing many square miles of town and surrounding farm, ranch, and mining property. The railroad's Tehachapi Springs facility, near the desert mountain town of Tehachapi, east of Bakersfield, California, impounded the flow of several springs and fed it into a system of dozens of miles of pipelines that supplied the water needs of three stations, at Marcel, Woodford, and Bealville.[20] The water project at the major far-northern California railroad town of Dunsmuir was judged by a consulting engineer to be "the most important on the Shasta Division, and one of the most important on the Southern Pacific system." It delivered 400,000 gallons per day to serve the railroad's locomotives being watered for the long, high mountain grades to the north, as well as the company's shops, engine house, station grounds, division offices, and fifteen families of employees who were hooked up free.[21] Begun in 1874 and continually expanded into the 1920s, the gigantic Lemay-Strongknob project, near Utah's Great Salt Lake, channeled several groups of springs into a pipeline system that took the water in three directions, 28 miles to Lemay and 50 miles to Strongknob, both on the post-1902 mainline, and 14 miles to Watercress on the old Promontory mainline. It also supplied the needs of section gangs at a half-dozen other places, and its water was hauled in cars to supplement water stations over all of northern Utah. The Lemay-Stongknob facility produced more than one million gallons per day in 1923, and its water right alone was worth more than $100,000.[22]

By the early 1900s, what was perhaps the most impressive, elaborate Southern Pacific water facility was at Ogden, Utah, where the company had extensive yard, maintenance, station, and other facilities. A huge water system extended over dozens of acres, knit together by perhaps hundreds of miles of 4-inch or 10-inch mains that distributed water from two sources. Water purchased from the city flowed to the railroad's terminal, offices, and hospital, while the Southern Pacific's own pumphouse and purification plant on the Weber River supplied the water for trackside tanks, yards, and a large Pacific Fruit Express ice plant with an insatiable thirst.[23] Other major Southern Pacific terminals, such as those at Roseville, Sacramento, Oakland, Fresno, Los Angeles, San Diego, Yuma, Tucson, and El Paso, most of which also had large railroad ice-making facilities, had similar complex water systems.[24]

In the search for water in this harsh land to save itself huge expenses in hauling supplies, the railroad imported the latest in drilling, pumping, purification, and distribution equipment. What technology it could not purchase from others, the company invented and built itself. At its Shops and Mechanical Department at Sacramento, for example, engineers designed and workers manufactured a succession of complex, specially adapted devices to solve the Southern Pacific's unique water problems at diverse locations. More than 200 surviving drawings at the California State Railroad Museum Archives in Sacramento bear testimony to the wide variety of the railroad's water finding, distributing, and purifying needs, as well as the ingenious machines the company invented and produced, including pipes, motors, pumps, pneumatic pressure systems, valves, chemical containers, settling tanks, water softeners, mixing vats, testing apparatus, fully automated water-purifying plants, and ever larger, more cost-effective tanker cars.[25] The Southern Pacific's technological innovation resulted in achievements in water production—well depth, volume, and purity—beyond the reach of most other private and public agencies. Well into the twentieth century, the Southern Pacific Company was a pioneer in water technology and organization in the Far West, crucial to economic development and important in establishing models of water improvement within its territory.

Although fragmented surviving documents allow only for approximations of the railroad's service to outside parties, it is clear that, particularly in isolated, especially arid districts such as Nevada and Utah, the southeastern California desert, and southern Arizona, the company provided water supplies that allowed some towns, farms, ranches, and mines to exist. In those regions, about

Late nineteenth-century Southern Pacific Railroad pumphouse, water tower, and storage tank, Marathon, Texas, photographed in 1954. Courtesy DeGolyer Library, Southern Methodist University.

one-quarter to one-half of Southern Pacific water stations served the broader public. As of 1916 in Nevada, for example, the company furnished 37,000 gallons per day to outsiders at Wells, 10,000 at Montello, 10,000 at Imlay, and unknown but probably larger amounts at Carlin, Elko, and other population centers. Nevertheless, the Southern Pacific's steadfast policy was to avoid selling to outsiders, except when the company had a surplus and no alternative existed for settlers, and then at a charge that only recovered costs. An engineering consultant simply reiterated long-established company policy when he reported that, as of 1916, the business of selling water to outsiders "is so small and entails so much extra work for a trifling compensation that the Carrier avoids rendering service to other than its employees whenever it can do so."[26] In the early twentieth century, the only time for which reliable data is available, monthly water charges on railroad-operated water utilities ranged from 75 cents (the most common figure) for households, to $5 to $6 for businesses. On the other hand, at Tehachapi, California, the company furnished 39,000 gallons per day to settlers at no charge.[27] At Truckee, California, as in Yuma, Arizona, and some other towns, the railroad sold—in effect, wholesaled—its water to private companies, which in turn used their own systems to reach customers at fees, by the way, several times higher than what the railroad charged consumers at other points where it sold directly to the public.[28] Although most railroad water flowed to households, probably more important were the hookups to businesses such as stores, hotels, restaurants, stockyards and livestock shipping pens, mines, and other establishments that provided the basic commercial structure upon which local development and population growth depended.

Exchange of water involved the railroad in complicated arrangements with outside parties. The railroad did not only furnish others with water; it also purchased from others whenever a large, reliable, economical, pure source existed. At Ogden, San Jose, Sacramento, Los Angeles, San Diego, and other sizable communities, the railroad tapped into existing city water companies or departments. At Napa Junction, in California, the Southern Pacific built an elaborate connection to the pipeline of the California and Hawaii Sugar Company, complete with a meter to monitor the railroad's use.[29] At several locations by the early twentieth century, the railroad bought water from the federal government. Certainly the most ironic arrangement was at Hazen, Nevada, where through a mutually beneficial trade of water rights and distribution facilities, the Southern Pacific received 200,000 gallons per day from the Truckee-Carson Reclamation Project's canal in exchange for furnishing a purer water supply for the U.S. Reclamation Service's headquarters. The railroad wound up, in effect, as the water company to the federal government's water "company."[30]

Modernizing Southern Pacific Waterworks

The largest of the Southern Pacific's southwestern water systems was actually begun by a predecessor company. Building north from El Paso through eastern New Mexico in the late 1890s, the El Paso & Northeastern Railroad was plagued by alkali- and gypsum-saturated groundwater, which was unusable at stations, clogged locomotive boiler tubes, and raised operating and maintenance costs to ruinous levels. The company spent $1 million drilling deeper wells and installing a chemical treatment plant, to no avail. To meet operational needs, as well as those of the 3,000 residents in the railroad-developed town of Alamogordo, the company founded the Alamogordo Water Works in 1903 and built a small pipeline to bring purer water from nearby mountains into the town. Partially because of persistent, severe water problems, however, the railway sold out in 1905 to the El Paso & Southwestern Railroad, owned by the Phelps Dodge Mining Corporation.[31]

With the greater capital resources of Phelps Dodge, the El Paso & Southwestern, under the direction of William Ashton Hawkins, built an ambitious, coordinated railway water system serving a large area of eastern New Mexico.

In the Sacramento Mountains east of its line, the railway purchased land with water rights along the Bonito River. After complex negotiation and litigation over water rights and right-of-way with private landowners and territorial and federal agencies, the company in 1907 finished the Nogal Reservoir and the Bonito Pipeline to transport impounded surface water to Carrizozo in a 170-mile conduit, 107 miles of which paralleled the rail tracks. By 1914, the El Paso & Southwestern had built three major pipelines to bring runoff or springwater to major station towns on its route, including Carrizozo, Three Rivers, Tularosa, La Luz, and Alamogordo, and farmers in their vicinities. The railway's water project had stimulated town and agricultural growth in a region hitherto restricted to open-range livestock grazing. When the Southern Pacific bought the El Paso & Southwestern from Phelps Dodge in 1924, it inherited a large regional water system with more than 200 miles of major pipelines serving operations over the entire rail line from El Paso north to Santa Rosa, New Mexico, as well as farmers, ranchers, and town-dwellers in much of Lincoln County. The Southern Pacific continued to own, manage, and extend the system for the next three decades.[32]

The best-documented example of the Southern Pacific's continuing water-pioneering in the early twentieth century was the building of the San Diego & Arizona Railroad from San Diego eastward to the Imperial Valley. Although the San Diego & Arizona was technically founded as a separate company by the Spreckels interests, the Southern Pacific invested heavily in, eventually managed, and quickly absorbed the road.[33] During the early, agonizing years after starting construction in 1907, the railroad was only able to build a few miles into the rugged, dry mountains south and east of San Diego. The severe water shortage was one of the principal obstacles. The company's primitive water facilities proved inadequate, and Mexican teamsters had to drive ponderous wagons pulled by fourteen mules to haul some of the 15,000 gallons needed each day at the construction front. In 1916, the Southern Pacific acquired the railroad, infused more capital into the foundering venture, and assumed control of construction and operation. Under the general management of D. W. Pontius, who was also the traffic manager of the Pacific Electric Railway at Los Angeles, and with construction being directed by William Hood, longtime chief engineer of the Southern Pacific, the San Diego & Arizona picked up the building pace and completed its connection to the Southern Pacific at El Centro in 1919.[34]

Essential to invigorating the road was an aggressive water-development program using the equipment and specifications of the parent line. As had been done earlier during the building of lines across Nevada, Utah, and southern California and Arizona, railroad men drilled wells, tapped and improved springs, built reservoirs, installed pumps and windmills, and developed complex distribution systems of pipelines, flumes, purification plants, and giant trackside tanks. Between 1916 and the curtailing of water development after 1929, the San Diego & Arizona continually improved its water system with new sources and larger pipes and storage facilities, ultimately spending hundreds of thousands of dollars, probably much more than $1 million. Some water facilities were located along the Mexican portion of the tracks.[35] Nevertheless, despite the strenuous efforts of railroaders to increase production and conserve water, insatiable demand always outstripped the constantly expanding supply. The completion of the line to El Centro, and the subsequent running of regular trains across the mountains and desert, drastically increased the railroad's need for water. Water shortages plagued managers and engineers and periodically, as in 1920, stopped trains from operating.[36] The problem, ironically, was alleviated only when the Great Depression sharply reduced the railroad's business.

Like the El Paso & Southwestern and the San Diego & Arizona, other branches of the Southern Pacific Company continually had to expand and modernize their numerous water systems in the decades from the 1880s through the 1920s. Wells ran dry, and new ones had to be drilled. New water rights to groundwater, springs, and streamflow were purchased, traded for, and filed under various state and federal laws. The original wooden pipes and tanks deteriorated rapidly, leaked profusely, and what was often worse, sent streams of splinters along with the water to clog locomotive valves. Decaying wooden pipes were replaced with more durable and sanitary metal varieties. Wooden tanks gave way to larger metal tanks and brick and concrete reservoirs, which in turn had to be dredged regularly. New generations of kerosene, oil, and electrical pumps and pneumatic systems provided more power, and sophisticated filtration and purification plants delivered a purer product. Complicated systems for regular chemical testing and treatment of water supplies were introduced at a quarter of the railroad's water stations by 1922. The volume of water production rose in the attempt to keep pace with additional rail lines, booming traffic, larger locomotives and yards, growing towns, and multiplying farms and ranches. By 1916, although some Southern Pacific water stations delivered only a few thousand gallons per day, many delivered between 100,000 and 1 million gallons daily. New railroad-building technology, however, actually increased the need for water at the construction front and accelerated innovations. After 1880, the Southern Pacific began to use powerful water cannons (monitors) adapted from hydraulic mining to blast roadbed ledges and do other excavation tasks during the building of new lines in northern California and Oregon. Mobile water plants developed as a result: several parked locomotives working in tandem generated steam to operate riverside pumps, while portable pipes delivered the pressurized water to the monitors at the head of construction. By the

turn of the century, steam shovels became standard for construction, again increasing water needs.[37] By 1900, the company had organized a specialized internal department, known as "the water service," to plan, construct, and maintain
water projects. Until the Great Depression after 1929 reduced traffic and the
demand for water, the railroad was still building waterworks to serve itself and
new town sites and farm districts sprouting along its routes. Throughout this
period, the Southern Pacific also granted money, free transportation, and organizational assistance to agricultural colleges, such as Oregon State University
and the University of Arizona, to sponsor water developments.[38]

Into the 1920s, the Southern Pacific continued to be one of the largest and
most organized water utilities in the West, providing a supply for itself and
many others, while continuing to set standards of efficient water development.
All of this, of course, required large outlays of labor and capital. In only one
partial measure of the great cost involved, the railroad was spending nearly
$50,000 per year by 1915 just to maintain its Arizona water lines.[39] By another
measure, H. G. Butler, a consulting engineer who surveyed only sixty of the
Southern Pacific's water facilities, valued just their water rights at more than
$600,000 as of 1916; and his report ignored many of the railroad's largest fa-
cilities, such as those at Indio, Yuma, and indeed all of those from the Colorado River east through Texas. The overall size of the railroad's far-flung water
operations was stunning. By 1922, according to the U.S. Interstate Commerce
Commission's nationwide survey of the entire company—with its immense
holdings of urban property, trackage, rights-of-way, buildings, locomotives,
rolling stock, machinery, yards, factories, streetcars, ferries, steamships, non-
transportation subsidiaries, and millions of acres of granted land—the Southern Pacific's water facilities constituted 5 percent of the company's value.[40]

The scope and complexity of the Southern Pacific's early twentieth-century
water activities were evident in its modernization of the El Paso & Southwestern's water system after 1924. The Southern Pacific retained the services of
William Ashton Hawkins, the El Paso & Southwestern's water manager, and
embarked on extensive renovation and expansion of its inherited Lincoln
County project. At great expense, the railroad replaced deteriorating wooden
pipelines with metal and built a number of small supplemental collection and
storage reservoirs. To make the system more reliable, the railroad in the late
1920s purchased additional land and mining claims from the federal government and private parties in the upper Bonito Canyon watershed, for the purpose of constructing a major reservoir capable of serving the entire region. However, remaining landowners in the area, particularly downstream settlers fearing
that water diversion would reduce the flow in their artesian wells, opposed the
project. When they sued in Chavez County, the railroad countersued in Lincoln County to establish its water rights. Ultimately, railroad attorneys prevailed

in the lawsuits, and in the early 1930s Southern Pacific engineers completed the Bonito Reservoir at a cost exceeding $1 million, not counting thousands spent in litigation.[41]

Exiting the Water Business

The Southern Pacific's western water improvement program continued to grow for decades into the twentieth century, and the company remained one of the region's pioneers in technology and organization. But keeping up with burgeoning demand generated by growing rail operations, agriculture, and town populations proved to be a losing battle. In the absence of outside suppliers, the railroad could justify providing itself with the water necessary for operations, but running utilities for the public required large capital outlays and maintenance costs. As had proven true for other private and public agencies, selling water seldom turned a profit for the company. Yet, though they had to be heavily subsidized from operating revenues, the company's ever-expanding water projects could rarely provide enough water to meet soaring needs. After investing decades of time and countless thousands of dollars prospecting for water along the line between Indio and Yuma, for example, the company conceded defeat in 1920. "The hauling of water over this piece of desert track," the editor of the *Southern Pacific Bulletin* admitted to employees and customers, "runs into an enormous expense and notwithstanding many attempts to locate water and establish water stations, the satisfactory supply is yet undiscovered."[42] Henceforth, the company decided, it would shift its attention to developing locomotives that used less water.

Moreover, its control over such a scarce, yet vital, resource as water in an arid country, though it was often by default, involved the Southern Pacific in clashes with many economic and political groups. As in the instance of the Bonito Reservoir, disputes over the railroad's water rights erupted throughout its territory, often spilling over into the courts. At Wells, Nevada, where the railroad supplied the water needs of the entire town, for example, another party seeking to irrigate land filed a claim with the state to some unused water flowing from a spring on the railroad's property, with the justification that the company was not putting the water to "beneficial use." At a 1915 state hearing, the Southern Pacific, supported by the town, fought the adverse filing and secured a decision from the state engineer that the railroad was entitled to the spring's full flow. In California's Sierra, also in 1915, the railroad engaged the Pacific Gas and Electric Company over rights to streamflow, leading in 1920 to a truce and private agreement to share the water.[43]

Also, there never seemed to be enough water to go around, and conflicts with customers broke out over water charges and services, particularly in time of shortage. No sooner had water begun to surge through the mains at Yuma in 1878, for example, than the Southern Pacific became embroiled in a dispute with one of its customers, the county government. When local officials insisted on paying their bill quarterly, instead of monthly as the railroad required, the company shut off water to the courthouse. This prompted the local newspaper to complain that the government was "a good debtor," and since it had extended the railroad many privileges, the company's action seemed "narrow and contemptible."[44] Indeed, so much conflict with customers had occurred by 1918 that the Southern Pacific official in charge of water projects concluded in a report on the subject that trouble inevitably resulted when the company sold water to others. "There is continuous controversy with them," engineer W. Q. Barlow warned vice president E. O. McCormick. "At the present time [we] have difficulty with the water situation at Wells, also at Mojave, brought about entirely by the practice [begun] years ago of selling water to outsiders." Barlow advised against any more water sales, even for the purpose of protecting railroad land-grant values.[45]

Even as it was forced to expand service in some areas, the Southern Pacific Company gradually withdrew from the water business in the early twentieth century. Although it continued to furnish, and indeed to expand, water facilities for its own operations, the railroad shut down connections to the outside as soon as private or public agencies emerged to take over. Frequently, the railway gave—or sold at far below value—its water rights, wells, pumps, purification plants, pipelines, and mains to new water companies, municipal water departments, or irrigation districts. Thus, some Southern Pacific waterworks served as the foundation for the modern systems that were essential to later western development.

At the growing town of Yuma, for example, residents off the railroad's Madison Avenue main were still hauling water as late as the 1890s. In 1892, Hiram W. Blaisdell, with eastern financial backing, founded the Yuma Electric and Water Company, which received a town franchise to go into the water business. At first the water company purchased its water from the railroad and extended branches from the Madison Avenue main to reach customers in other neighborhoods. Blaisdell eventually installed his own pump at the river, but the product was so murky that citizens began mocking the company as the "Muddy Water System," and into the early 1900s, the Southern Pacific continued to sell water to the town. In 1906, twenty-eight years after the railroad first pumped water from the Colorado River, the water company was able to acquire the Southern Pacific's distribution system and built a large, modern water plant. Yuma finally had its own waterworks.[46]

In this manner, it took decades to liquidate all the railway's water service to outside parties. The largest, the old El Paso & Southwestern system, was also the last major railroad system to go. By the 1950s, diesel-electrics, using far less water, were replacing steam locomotives, while the growing city of Alamogordo and nearby Holloman Air Force Base needed far more water. Obviously eager to be relieved of its responsibility, the railroad in 1957 sold the entire multi-million-dollar project, including water rights and the Bonito Reservoir, to the city for $25,000 and made a $60,000 grant to the town of Corona, which was to be left out of the new municipal system. As had happened in the Imperial Valley, Yuma, Mojave, and elsewhere along Southern Pacific lines, the new public water system was a legacy of an earlier era, when the railroad was also the water company.[47] Into the 1960s, and even later, however, the Southern Pacific continued to operate extensive, sophisticated water systems for its own use.[48]

Although it decided that it would no longer operate water utilities for outside parties, the Southern Pacific did not lose its interest in broader, western water issues. If anything, finding reliable water sources became ever more crucial for the rapidly developing region after the 1880s. To resolve the problem in a more permanent way, however, the Southern Pacific, like other groups in its territory, increasingly worked to transfer control over water to governments and to foster public agencies to finance, build, and manage large-scale regional systems, particularly for agriculture. While pursuing these goals, the Southern Pacific became a major influence on local, regional, and national irrigation movements after 1880.

8 "A Great Encouragement for Others"

PRIVATE IRRIGATION

Railroads, Irrigation, and the Historians

An important, though little known, event in western water history occurred on June 22, 1916, in southeastern California's parched, below-sea-level Imperial Valley. After ten years managing the immense irrigation works of the defunct California Development Company, the Southern Pacific Company transferred control over the valley's water supply to a newly created public body. With a few pen strokes, the Imperial Irrigation District became the largest irrigation agency then operating in the United States. Between 1905 and 1907, the Southern Pacific had stemmed the disastrous Colorado River flood caused by the California Development Company's inept installation of its headgate on the river. As the irrigation company's largest creditor, the railroad had assumed principal management of the ailing company's properties. Over the next decade, the railroad's civil engineers had improved the water facility and expanded its delivery capacity severalfold, to more than 500,000 acres of farmland. Committed to the principle of public water management, the Southern Pacific then helped to promote the creation of the Imperial Irrigation District in 1911 and nurtured the agency through its early turbulent years. Finally, the railroad had bought the California Development Company at a receiver's auction and had purchased the $3 million in the irrigation district's bonds that made possible the Imperial Irrigation District's 1916 acquisition of the company's properties. All told, over its decade and a half of activity in Imperial Valley water development, the Southern Pacific had rescued, modernized, expanded, lobbied for, and financed the first truly successful large public irrigation system in the history of the United States.[1]

How had a transportation company—particularly this one—become so deeply involved in such a tangential, controversial, and unprofitable activity as furnishing water to farmers in an arid region? This apparently public-spirited behavior in the interest of economic and community development seems at first glance to be totally out of character for a company that opponents and, later, historians contemptuously branded as the "Octopus," the major obstacle to economic prosperity, as well as the principal instigator of political corruption, within its territory.[2]

In step with other western historians, most historians of irrigation have ignored or minimized the positive influence of the Southern Pacific and other western railroads. One writer expressed it succinctly: "Few railroads sponsored irrigation, preferring to leave the financing to other parties."[3] Even such recent comprehensive works as Norris Hundley's *The Great Thirst: Californians and Water, 1770s–1990s* do not mention the Southern Pacific's notable influence on that state's water history, including its role in the development of Imperial Valley irrigation.[4] Writers who have acknowledged that railroads played any part in water history have often cast railroads as villains, narrowly self-interested spoilers of popular movements for economic and social progress through water development. In accounting for the paucity of irrigation in late nineteenth-century Nevada, for example, one historian charged that it was the monopolistic Central Pacific, a Southern Pacific subsidiary, that, in league with large mining and stock-raising enterprises, had persistently blocked irrigation legislation. Miserly "Central Pacific Railroad officials opposed state-funded reclamation projects because they feared that increased property taxes would result," he explained.[5] Such views, of course, dovetail neatly into the Populist-Progressive, anti-corporate and anti-railroad consensus that has dominated western American historiography. They do not, however, account for the many contributions the railroads made to western water development, only one example of which was the Southern Pacific's work in the Imperial Valley.

The leading exception to this consensus on irrigation history is the work of Donald J. Pisani. In his important 1984 study, *From the Family Farm to Agribusiness: The Irrigation Crusade in California and the West, 1850–1931*, and even more in his 1992 work, *To Reclaim a Divided West: Water, Law, and Public Policy, 1848–1902*, Pisani acknowledged the work of some of the great western railroads, including the Southern Pacific, as lobbyists and financial supporters for irrigation crusaders in the late 1890s and early 1900s. Railroads, as Pisani demonstrated, most notably backed George Maxwell and the National Irrigation Association, whose agitation of the irrigation question was partially responsible for congressional passage of the monumental National Reclamation Act (1902), which committed the engineering and financial resources of the federal government to building large-scale public irrigation projects in the West.[6]

On the other hand, Pisani concluded in *To Reclaim a Divided West* that only "on rare occasions" did the railroads build water systems of their own. Indeed, he noted only one, a largely abortive land and irrigation development project launched in the early 1890s by the Northern Pacific through a subsidiary in Washington's Yakima Valley. Even while railway leaders mouthed platitudes about the glorious results expected from watering the arid West, according to

Pisani, they actually feared that irrigation would reduce railroad land sales in wetter areas, raise taxes on railroad property, and encourage agricultural development that would undercut their profitable traffic in livestock and mining cargoes. Additionally, Pisani reasoned that the geography of western railways' checkerboard land grants prevented the companies from consolidating the large tracts necessary for systematic irrigation. Most important, rail leaders knew water projects would not turn a profit; hence, he claimed, the railroads invested next to no capital in water development and even fought against some publicly and privately financed projects. Specifically, Pisani echoed the charge of earlier historians that the Southern Pacific had led the opposition blocking Nevada public irrigation between the 1860s and the 1890s. Overall, Pisani's books portrayed railroads, including the Southern Pacific, as being at best timid, fair-weather friends of western irrigation.[7]

The works of Pisani and a few others, because they are by nature general studies covering a multitude of water projects across a vast expanse of time and territory, cannot tell the full story of the railroads' intimate involvement in irrigation development. What are needed are detailed examinations of individual companies' long-term activities in irrigation. Such studies would disclose that at least some western railroads went beyond merely publicizing the need to create new projects; they also could be major contributors to the success or failure of private, local, state, and federal irrigation systems, as well as shapers of the fundamental policies that came to characterize modern American irrigation. The Southern Pacific Company, whose arid or semi-arid hinterland depended on massive irrigation improvements, was a prime example.

The Southern Pacific and Irrigation

Even more so than resulted from the building of its own water systems for rail construction and operation, the Southern Pacific's varied activities on behalf of irrigation affected the broader community over more than six decades between the 1860s and 1930. Most obviously, the railroad encouraged large-scale water developments throughout its territory, and to some extent in other western regions, in effect serving as a midwife at the birth of innumerable private water companies, public local irrigation districts, and federal reclamation projects.

Simple planning, or even the completion and operation, of a water facility, however, proved to be no panacea for arid lands' agricultural progress. The Southern Pacific's advocacy of irrigation emerged at a time when fragmentation reigned over western water policy, when almost all local, state, and federal governmental agencies abdicated responsibility for guiding development and distribution, other than to generate overlapping jurisdictions and conflicting water laws and court decrees.[8] As a result, water projects often fell prey to flawed engineering, environmental problems, financial difficulties, and expensive litigation. Typically, for a long time, water deliveries were inadequate and erratic, water charges were prohibitive, farmers were frequently driven to abandon their lands, and railroad, private, and government land watered by the projects failed to sell, in part because of the high prices necessitated by irrigation improvements. Compounding the woes of many water projects, as could be expected during a period of experimentation, government policy toward water projects was usually tentative, contradictory, and vacillating.

Nevertheless, because it viewed water development as fundamental to its business and because complex corporate interests inevitably became entangled in any significant project hatching in its hinterland, the Southern Pacific repeatedly found itself required to interpose a measure of order, if for no other reason than to protect itself. For water projects of all sorts, many of which, like the Imperial Irrigation District, were experimental and tenuous, the company furnished direction, administrative structure, scientific and economic information, engineering and legal expertise, political intercession, and subsidy or direct financing. Indeed, in Southern Pacific country, it was often the railroad that provided the level of community organization needed to bring into being successful irrigation systems. This sometimes required the company to mediate among warring factions of citizenry competing for control over land and water: small and large landowners, riparians and appropriators, would-be irrigators and anti-irrigators, upstream and downstream users, feuding government agencies, and contending farming, livestock, mining, urban/industrial, navigation, and even fishing interests.[9] In the void of public regulation, as was the case with its own transportation water facilities, the railroad was repeatedly forced to provide for irrigators what would later become governmental functions. In numerous cases in Southern Pacific territory, it was railroad support, or lack thereof, that spelled success or doom for incipient water projects.

Also, although more efficient development of water resources for economic growth and company profits drove Southern Pacific policy, the railroad came to understand as early as the 1870s that exploitation and conservation had to proceed hand in hand. This led the company to become an advocate for water conservation, including water-quality protection, flood control, streambed restoration, and watershed preservation. Its deep involvement in water-supply issues thus integrated and gave continuity over decades to diverse Southern Pacific Company resource policies affecting not only water, but also land use, forestry, wildland fires, and parks and wilderness preservation. Finally, as private enterprise's failure to meet western demands became apparent, the company advanced the gradual shift toward public ownership and management of water supplies, which became the hallmark of twentieth-century public policy.

It is in the complex area of its major contributions to the development of western irrigation systems and water policies that the Southern Pacific most clearly validated Alfred D. Chandler's thesis that the great nineteenth-century railways were the vanguard of economic modernization.[10]

If their long residence in California had failed to convince early Southern Pacific leaders of the importance of large-scale water systems, their experience building and operating railroads in arid regions did. Beginning in the late 1860s, the company's officials became avid promoters of irrigation as essential to agriculture and the broader economic development of the Pacific and Southwest regions, and hence to the profits of their expanding businesses. Southern Pacific founders Collis P. Huntington, Charles Crocker, and Leland Stanford, as well as E. H. Harriman, who took over the company after Huntington's death in 1900, invested their private capital in irrigation and land subdivision projects, directed the spending of corporate funds and energy on building or promoting water projects, and placed their prestige and political influence behind community efforts to build large water systems. Over the years, numerous official and private statements from company leaders announced and elaborated on the railroad's commitment to promoting water development in the broader community.[11] Company publications, including Land and Passenger Department pamphlets, articles and editorials in company-controlled newspapers and magazines, and other promotional materials, all proclaimed the benefits of irrigation.[12] After 1900, the Southern Pacific's booster monthly, *Sunset,* became one of the most important forums for scientists, government officials, and community boosters writing on the social and economic progress that would flow from expanded irrigation.[13]

Although between the 1860s and the 1920s the railroad remained committed to the concept of irrigation and was nearly always involved in major projects in some way, the intensity and nature of its interest varied. Like many other western leaders, Southern Pacific people shared the widespread faith that irrigation was the key to the re-creation of a new Jeffersonian rural society in the arid West. The railroad's irrigation work, however, was undertaken primarily out of carefully defined corporate self-interest—to increase land-grant values and sales and to promote general economic regional development and hence rail traffic receipts. Its calculation of complex and sometimes contradictory short- and long-term corporate interests in a given situation, in turn, led the company to respond differently to the irrigation issue, avidly supporting some water projects, while opposing or taking no action on them in other times and places. Thus, for example, during the very years that the Southern Pacific was supporting the new Wright Act local irrigation districts in California in the late 1880s and early 1890s, its caution led it to distance itself from a similar Nevada movement that the railroad judged likely to fail for lack of water supplies, arable land, and community support. Assessment of the Southern Pacific's role in western irrigation, therefore, requires not just intensive examination of a few dramatic events, but an overall study of the railroad's activities in many regions over the late nineteenth and early twentieth centuries.

Most active of the company's leaders in working on specific water projects were its chief land agents, Benjamin B. Redding (1865–1882), William H. Mills (1883–1907), and B. A. McAllaster (1908–1933), three men whose long tenure lent remarkable continuity to railroad natural resources policy during the most creative years of western irrigation history. Sharing the emerging conservationist and preservationist values of the age, these men became recognized experts on soil, climate, forestry, and agriculture, as well as irrigation, flood control, and watershed preservation. They not only guided the Southern Pacific's own work in promoting water development, but wrote and lectured on the subject and helped to organize and advise private and public agencies. Though operating in smaller jurisdictions, the company's regional land agents during various times, particularly Robert L. Fulton (eastern California, Nevada, and Utah), Daniel K. Zumwalt (San Joaquin Valley), and C. E. Wantland (Los Angeles and southern California), along with a legion of station agents, immigration agents, and civil engineers, also furthered local water improvements and occasionally regional and national projects.[14]

Particularly significant and indicative of the Southern Pacific's extensive involvement in western water history was the work of William H. Mills, who is little known today but in his time was one of the most important pioneer conservationists in the American West, one who in many ways prefigured modern thinking on water development. During four decades of association with the Southern Pacific, beginning in the early 1870s as prolific writer and editor and co-owner of the Big Four's newspaper, the *Sacramento Record-Union,* and continuing through a quarter century as manager of the railroad's land business during the critical decades after 1883, Mills more than any other company leader was responsible for establishing the Southern Pacific Company as an aggressive participant in western water development. He used his access to Huntington to convince corporate owners to promote water development within and outside of the company, wielded much influence over the setting of corporate water policy in its formative period, and served as the railroad's principal liaison with outside groups sharing the company's interests. Through his powerful railroad position and connections to other influential interests, Mills left a lasting mark on a host of important events associated with western water development. Having been introduced to the dangers of uncontrolled water use by the periodic flooding of the Sacramento River and his leadership of the successful campaign in the Sacramento Valley against hydraulic mining in the 1870s and 1880s, Mills realized early that complex water problems in California and the West generally could only be solved by a comprehensive, scientific, and long-range management program aimed at balancing the often conflicting requirements of flood-control, irrigation, wetlands drainage, water-quality protection, urbanization, and inland navigation. In editorials, speeches, promotional activities, and work as the railroad's chief land agent, Mills campaigned over more than three decades for such a complete water program on the grounds that it was essential to economic development, agricultural and city growth, and increased population density.[15] As the leading founder and director of the California State Board of Trade, Mills also converted that influential state-wide commercial organization into one of the major pressure groups for irrigation development and comprehensive water management.[16]

A perennial representative of the Board of Trade, the Southern Pacific Company, or the state's governors to the International Irrigation Congresses of the 1890s and 1900s, Mills helped to popularize the concept that long-range planning and equitable distribution required government ownership of water supplies. To prevent corporate interests from monopolizing publicly subsidized irrigation water and to ensure that the West would become the home of small farms, Mills, long before the 1902 National Reclamation Act, was one of the originators of the famous "160-acre rule"—the provision limiting the water that one landowner could receive from public supplies to the amount needed to irrigate one family farm—a principle for which Mills fought until his death in 1907.[17] His and the Southern Pacific's extensive involvement after 1902 in the creation of the new Truckee-Carson Reclamation Project in western Nevada, one of the first under the National Reclamation Act, was guided by Mills's deep commitment to irrigation as an instrument for democratizing western agriculture.

Linked to Mills's advocacy of irrigation and comprehensive water management were his other conservation causes. Believing that protection of watersheds, as well as the development of recreation areas for a growing population, required careful forest management, Mills, first as editor of the *Sacramento Record-Union* and later as railway land agent, became one of the early campaigners for scientific forestry in the West. He also had a distinguished record of leadership in early park and wilderness preservation projects, including California's state Yosemite Valley preserve, the establishment and expansion of Yosemite National Park, the creation of the Tahoe National Forest, and the founding of Big Basin Redwoods as California's first modern state park.[18]

Early Private Irrigation

As is clear from a brief survey of William H. Mills's activities, Southern Pacific activity on behalf of western irrigation was diverse, complex, and long lasting.

Although the railroad's officials had advocated irrigation earlier, the company did not become deeply involved in promoting irrigation until the 1880s, when the pace of constructing and acquiring new lines subsided, when Mills became head land agent and rose to a position of greater corporate influence, and when the company embarked upon aggressive programs to develop its lands and wider territory. One of its first attempts to encourage irrigation after moving into an unoccupied arid region was to build or subsidize water prospecting and irrigation demonstration projects. The earliest Southern Pacific demonstration project was south of the railroad-founded town of Tulare, where in 1875 company water-seekers brought in a field of artesian wells at a depth of 300 feet. The wells allowed the railroad to irrigate a forty-acre experimental tree ranch on one of its land-grant sections, where it bred shade trees for stations and rights-of-way in this mostly treeless region. Once the railroad had demonstrated the presence of artesian water and the fertility of the alkali-plagued district, other landowners bored wells and began irrigating crops, thus touching off an important farm settlement boom along the Southern Pacific's mainline in the southern San Joaquin Valley. Contemporaries widely credited the railroad with having discovered and proven the usefulness of the new water supply in the area. In his 1883 published review of artesian wells in California, C. E. Grunsky, assistant state engineer and a noted authority on water, concluded that the Southern Pacific's wells and tree farm were "a great encouragement for others," and that largely because of the company's pioneering, "the artesian water supply has been developed more energetically in Tulare County than elsewhere in the San Joaquin Valley."[19]

Even more than had been true in the San Joaquin Valley, the Southern Pacific's water prospecting and irrigation experiments shaped the future of the southeastern California desert, which was largely uninhabited except for Indians and where virtually no modern agriculture had been practiced. The railroad's most abundant water source in the area was at Indio, southeast of San Bernardino, where during line construction in the late 1870s the railroad had built one of its most productive wellwater stations. During the 1880s, local agents at Indio, at the direction of the company's general manager Alban N. Towne, who had taken a personal interest in the project, transformed the sandy waste around the station into a lush demonstration garden, to the astonishment of local "desert rats" and overland passengers. In this most forbidding of landscapes, railway people experimented with plants suitable for desert farming and demonstrated that irrigation could be used to raise figs, grapes, melons, date palms, alfalfa, and winter fruits and vegetables, all of which soon became paying crops in the district.

In the 1880s and 1890s, the Southern Pacific's Indio experimental garden was visited regularly by farm and water experts, including delegates to the 1893 Irrigation Congress, who proclaimed it to be, in the words of the *Los Angeles Times,* "a practical demonstration of desert reclamation." The railroad's successful Indio project was valuable not only as evidence to justify the gathering national reclamation movement. On the strength of these experiments, the railroad, after a decade of failure, was finally able to begin selling some of its granted land in the desert. Following the railroad's example, other private parties in the area bored wells, subdivided and advertised land, and began small irrigated farms. The railroad planted a similar, though smaller, demonstration garden around its station at Yuma, where the company maintained a water station on the Arizona bank of the Colorado River. By the early twentieth century, the Southern Pacific had helped to create models of desert agriculture that in the twentieth century would become the mainstay of development in California's Coachella and Imperial valleys, the Colorado River region, and the Salt and Gila valleys of Arizona.[20] Also in the 1880s and 1890s, the railroad's local artesian-well prospecting, agricultural experimentation, and land promotion produced the first settlement boom in the arid Antelope Valley north of Los Angeles. As late as the 1920s, the Southern Pacific was still a leading developer of artesian wells in the valley. Similar results flowed from the railroad's pioneering discovery of artesian wells near Deming, New Mexico, in the early 1880s.[21]

During and for a short time after the railroad's entry into arid regions, while the areas were initially being settled, most efforts to create large, regional irrigation facilities were private enterprises. In California's San Joaquin Valley, the first Southern Pacific region to experience widespread irrigation development, some of the early large-scale water firms, such as San Francisco financier William Ralston's San Joaquin and Kings River Canal Company, proposed in the 1870s to dig large canals capable of being navigated. They hoped thereby to help finance their ventures through traffic revenues and to attract wider support by claiming that canal boats would break the railway's monopoly over local transportation.[22] The Southern Pacific naturally shied away from such avowedly anti-railroad projects, but the company did encourage many of the budding private ventures, particularly on or adjacent to its granted lands. Railroad representatives frequently attended private and public meetings called to promote investment in irrigation, advised would-be founders of water companies, and occasionally lent their public support in order to enhance the entrepreneurs' credibility. During the 1870s, for example, the construction of the initial Central and Southern Pacific lines southward down the mostly unoccupied valley opened up new marketing potentials for farm products, raised land values, encouraged rapid population growth and more compact settlement in towns and rural districts, prompted the railroad to start aggressive sales programs on its granted lands, and ignited a boom in private land and water developments, particularly in the vicinity of Modesto, Merced, Fresno, the Tulare Basin, and Kern County.[23] The railroad kept itself informed about and contributed to the creation of many private irrigation enterprises in the region, such as those of

James B. A. Haggin along the Kern River and various irrigated agricultural colonies in the Fresno area. For the Fresno colonies, the railroad was of particular assistance by working with founder William S. Chapman to locate the Fresno town site, acquiring the site from Chapman's syndicate, platting and developing the town, and advertising the irrigated colonies' land sales.[24]

As large-scale private water projects emerged, the Southern Pacific Land Department developed procedures to accommodate them. For example, one of the most serious barriers to early private irrigation companies in regions like the San Joaquin Valley, where there was sometimes bitter opposition to water and land monopoly and skepticism regarding the effects of irrigation, was difficulty in securing canal rights-of-way across private and public property. As the Southern Pacific Railroad built through the San Joaquin Valley in the early 1870s, it negotiated agreements with existing and would-be irrigation companies to provide free easements across the railroad's granted lands and its own track rights-of-way for canals, reservoirs, headgates, and other water facilities. In one typical instance, on December 8, 1875, the railroad contracted with James P. Dixon to provide at no cost such an easement across sections of its lands, as well as the right of access to build and repair his canal from the Kern River. When the railroad finally sold the land to James B. A. Haggin on June 12, 1882, the irrigation project was functioning, and the railroad's deed to Haggin reserved the right-of-way to Dixon, as well as the right to build and repair dams, reservoirs, and canals, and to use materials on the land for such work.[25] By the time of that sale, however, such easements and reservations for irrigation improvements had become commonplace in Southern Pacific lines land contracts and deeds, eventually from California to Texas. In 1879, the company even granted such an easement to the ostensibly anti-railroad San Joaquin and Kings River Canal and Irrigation Company.[26]

Railroad Leaders as Irrigators

In addition to cooperating with private irrigation companies, railroad people invested earnings from their transportation activities directly into their own personal irrigation enterprises. In this era of blurred boundaries between official business employment and private fortunes, railroad leaders' success in these private projects often depended on their ability to secure favors from the corporation for which they worked. The Southern Pacific's founders, of course, accumulated huge stores of capital from their railroad business, some of which they used to create water systems. Owner of numerous expansive lands and water rights, Leland Stanford, for example, installed several large reservoir and irrigation systems, including those at his vast "farm" in the foothills and bayshore plains of Palo Alto down the peninsula from San Francisco and at his huge ranch near Vina, in the northern Sacramento Valley. Irrigation allowed Stanford to attain high production in cereals, feed, livestock, orchard crops, and grapes; for much of the late nineteenth century, Stanford's Vina ranch led the nation in brandy production.[27]

Lesser company officials, particularly those connected with land departments of various associated Southern Pacific lines, frequently invested salaries in, or worked as agents for, private land and irrigation developments. For example, Robert L. Fulton of Reno, the Southern Pacific land and political agent for Nevada and the Great Basin, managed or invested in many private irrigation projects between the 1870s and the early 1900s. Most notably, Fulton in 1889 became associated with wealthy Francis G. Newlands, newly arrived from California and eager to increase his fortune and make a political name for himself by developing land and water in eastern California and western Nevada. With Fulton working as his principal agent at $150 per month, Newlands into the early 1890s purchased and developed land and water rights in the hope that they would one day become part of a great, publicly run water system to transform Nevada from a mining into an agricultural state. Although public apathy, the opposing power of the mining and livestock interests, the Southern Pacific's own skepticism, and the national financial collapse of the 1890s prevented Newlands and Fulton from ushering in the "New Nevada," the several resulting private waterworks, particularly the dam at Donner Lake near Truckee, thirty miles west and up into the Sierra Nevada from Reno, were later incorporated either into federal reclamation projects or the Reno city water or electricity supply. It was for his longtime service to private, as well as to public, water development that one Reno newspaper eulogized Fulton at his death as the "father of the irrigation movement in Nevada."[28]

The most important private water venture by a Southern Pacific leader, however, was undoubtedly founder Charles Crocker's enterprise, which strongly influenced the direction of irrigation, agriculture, and urban growth in the Merced River region of California's San Joaquin Valley. In the 1870s, during what historian Donald Pisani has described as the "takeoff" period for large-scale private irrigation and agricultural-land development projects, the Southern Pacific became particularly interested in the potential for irrigating its own and other lands that lay downslope from the Merced River.[29] In 1873, regional landowners incorporated the cooperative Farmers' Canal Company, purchased the assets of some defunct earlier irrigation firms, and began digging a canal from the river to reach irrigable land. As often happened, after completing a small diversion dam, a six-mile-long canal, some branch ditches, and part of a tunnel, the company ran out of money and halted construction.[30]

Other landowners whose properties would have benefited, including the

Southern Pacific, sought to reorganize the canal company, broaden its owner-ship, and convert it into a regional water system by extending its potential cov-erage to several hundred thousand acres lying between the railroad's mainline towns of Merced and Chowchilla (twenty miles southeast) and the Sierra Nevada, some thirty miles east. Foreshadowing the later public irrigation dis-trict model, the group proposed to refinance the ambitious venture by getting affected landowners to place voluntary liens on their properties in order to sell twenty-year bonds to finish construction and operate the water system. Toward that end, the new investors hired George Davidson, respected University of California and U.S. Coast Survey scientist, to evaluate the project. When David-son had completed his study, landowners and prominent potential investors, including powerful capitalist William Sharon, who owned 10,000 acres in the area, gathered in San Francisco in early May 1877. Central Pacific general man-ager Alban N. Towne represented the railroad and its land-grant acres. Despite Davidson's lengthy, glowing report on the project's technical and financial fea-sibility, even some of the project's supporters expressed concerns that David-son's estimate of ten dollars per acre in irrigation costs was prohibitively ex-pensive, that few property owners would agree to thus mortgage their lands, and that the bonds could not be sold during the current national depression. Ultimately, although the assembled investors appointed a committee includ-ing Towne and Sharon to organize the new company, this Merced River irri-gation project also failed to materialize.[31]

Nevertheless, the idea of tapping the Merced was kept alive by Charles H. Huffman, a longtime associate of the Southern Pacific who in the early 1870s had acted as the railroad's chief representative in the location and development of Fresno and the company's other platted towns in the San Joaquin Valley. Now a Merced resident and large-scale land investor and grain farmer who had suffered steep, drought-related losses to his wheat crop, Huffman had been a member of the 1877 committee that had unsuccessfully attempted to reorga-nize the Farmers' Canal Company. In the early 1880s, Huffman acquired the defunct company himself, reorganized it into the Merced Canal & Irrigation Company, and approached the Southern Pacific's Charles Crocker proposing a private partnership to expand the project. The new venture would install a large diversion gate in the river where it exited the Sierra Nevada foothills, build a widespread network of dams, reservoirs, canals, and ditches, and purchase and subdivide largely unused tracts to go into the land and water business on a grand scale. Huffman would contribute his land, if Crocker would invest one million dollars to pay for the irrigation facilities. "Go on with the work," Crocker reportedly replied, and on March 1, 1883, construction began on the main ditch. Entry into the venture by the experienced railroad construction boss, who took an avid personal interest, quickened the pace, and by late 1885, with hundreds of men at work and reservoirs, tunnels, and sixty miles of canal in operation, the project neared completion. Already land was being sold, much of it in large tracts for fruit and raisin production. Just before water began flowing in the system, Crocker drove a team of horses through what was soon to become the largest irrigation canal tunnel in the world and declared to assembled dignitaries and newspaper reporters that one day this would be considered a more important accomplishment than building his railroad.[32]

When finished over the next few years, the irrigation system contained 100 miles of main distributing canals and 150 miles of smaller laterals. The principal waterway, more than fifty feet wide and eight feet deep, traveled twenty-two miles from the Merced River headgate to the main reservoir, Lake Yosemite, which fed more subsidiary canals, as well as a sixteen-inch pipeline to furnish a water supply to the city of Merced, five miles distant. Land in the development, which lay in both Merced and Fresno counties, was sold with a perpetual right to water from the irrigation system, and although the company sold water to parties who had not purchased its land, annual water charges to holders of the perpetual water rights were a small fraction of those paid by outsiders. The Merced Canal & Irrigation Company pioneered in the region in offering comprehensive services to promote settlement and conversion of hitherto unused or open-range land to intensive agriculture: subdividing, improving, and advertising the land; providing the water rights and irrigation supply; organizing colonies of farmers for compact settlement; introducing superior new crop varieties and breeds of livestock and dairy cattle; founding a bank— First National Bank in Merced, with Charles H. Huffman as president—to finance the mortgages; giving its land buyers added income by hiring them to work the company's properties; and purchasing some of the farms' produce. The Southern Pacific also assisted in founding and advertising the Merced Company's colonies through the railroad's Colonization Bureau.[33]

Although it had originated as Charles Crocker's personal investment, as so often occurred with the private ventures of the Big Four and their families, the Merced Canal & Irrigation Company's affairs soon became entwined with the railroad's. The company and the railroad, for example, jointly owned some new town and rural land projects in the area.[34] Then, after Crocker's death in 1888, Crocker's estate, managed by his son, Charles Frederick Crocker, purchased Huffman's interest, changed the company's name to the Crocker-Huffman Land and Water Company, and embarked on an aggressive program to subdivide and sell the company's land, which by 1893 had grown to 40,000 acres. In the early 1890s, C. F. Crocker applied to Southern Pacific Company president Collis P. Huntington to have the Crocker-Huffman land managed by the Pacific Improvement Company, the gigantic construction and land-development firm the Big Four had created in the late 1870s to administer railroad properties and the

Portal on one of the longest irrigation canal tunnels in the world, built in the 1880s to tap the
Merced River for the main water supply of the Crocker-Huffman Land and Water Company's
large irrigation development in the San Joaquin Valley, ca. 1900. From Crocker-Huffman Land
and Water Co., *Merced County, California* (1902), courtesy Bancroft Library.

families' private investments, both joint and separate. With Huntington's approval, the Crocker-Huffman Company became one of the Pacific Improvement Company's numerous land-development ventures, all managed by chief
Southern Pacific Company land agent William H. Mills.

In keeping with their oft-stated views, Huntington and Mills directed that
Crocker-Huffman lands, which hitherto had mostly been marketed to large purchasers, now be sold in a manner to encourage small farms, immigration and
population growth in the area, and presumably higher traffic revenues for the
railway. Given virtually complete control over the project, Mills merged the dispersed Crocker-Huffman tracts with 2,000 acres of Pacific Improvement Company land into what was called the "Merced Tract," prohibited sales to speculators by requiring that purchasers inhabit and farm the land, reduced the price
of land (which included perpetual water rights) 25 to 40 percent, and offered
buyers low-interest, long-term purchase contracts that postponed repayment of
principal in the first years in order to encourage settlers to invest capital in improvements. Throughout the 1890s, Crocker-Huffman continued to expand its
irrigation system, to supply water widely to land purchasers and non-purchasers
alike, and to acquire additional land for production and subdivision. The company's three hundred employees farmed land that was awaiting sale.[35]

Collis P. Huntington's death in 1900 prompted the Big Four's families to divest themselves of most of their holdings in both the Southern Pacific and Pacific Improvement companies, but the Crocker-Huffman Land and Water Company, once again under control of the Crocker family, continued to operate well into the twentieth century. By then, lands irrigated by the Crocker-Huffman project specialized in raising nuts, fruits such as raisins, citrus, peaches, pears, prunes, and figs, and increasingly alfalfa and corn for dairy-herd feed. The company further encouraged the inception of the rising dairy industry in the region when it organized the Fountain City Creamery to buy and market the milk and by-products of its land and water customers.[36]

Typical of the fate of Southern Pacific-connected water developments, the expansive Crocker-Huffman system evolved into successor public agencies of even wider import. With much of its land sold and its water system no longer delivering profits, the company, in league with other local leaders, campaigned for the creation of a regional public irrigation district. Formed in 1919, the Merced Irrigation District in 1922 purchased the company's water rights and irrigation facilities at a discount and used them to form the core of a public system that has become one of the most successful in the state. Ultimately, the city of Merced acquired the company's urban waterworks. At the time of its conversion into a public facility, the Crocker-Huffman system was irrigating 50,000 acres and had a value between two and three million dollars.[37]

The story of the Crocker-Huffman Land and Water Company illustrates again the important role the Pacific Improvement Company played in overall Southern Pacific Railroad land and water development activities. The Crocker-Huffman was but one of numerous water projects between the late 1870s and the early 1900s to result from the joint efforts of the Southern Pacific and its construction and land-development subsidiary. The Pacific Improvement Company built and/or operated many water projects for various Southern Pacific lines and, as in the case of the Crocker-Huffman Company, for private businesses of the Big Four families. As the subdivider and developer for the railroad's town sites, the Pacific Improvement Company also managed some of the urban water facilities that spun off from water systems the railroad constructed for its own operations. As the major instrument of the rail leaders' private land developments, particularly between the 1880s and the early 1900s, when its connection with the railroad was severed, the company also founded several notable water projects, including a reservoir and irrigation pipeline system for its agricultural and country-estate subdivision at Hope Ranch, along the Pacific Coast west of Santa Barbara, and town site systems for its subdivisions at Pebble Beach and Pacific Grove that eventually grew into the widespread regional Monterey County Water Works, which brought Carmel River water to Monterey Peninsula towns and resorts. Like the Crocker-Huffman water system, some of the Pacific Improvement Company's projects were major undertakings. The company, for example, employed seven hundred Chinese laborers to build the San Clemente Dam on the Carmel River and the twelve-inch pipeline that carried water across trestles to Monterey communities ten or more miles distant.[38]

9 "This Splendid Country Is to Be Reclaimed"

PUBLIC IRRIGATION

The Southern Pacific and Public Water

During the 1870s and 1880s, especially in states such as California, which had experienced extensive private irrigation development, support mounted for public financing and operation of larger-scale regional irrigation systems. Often adjuncts of land speculation schemes, private irrigation projects had typically suffered from high initial and operating costs, undercapitalization, scant and unreliable profits, poor engineering, misjudgment of land and water markets, deeply rooted public fears of land and water monopoly, and legal difficulties—not the least of which was the often tangled, acrimonious litigation between parties holding riparian and appropriation rights to the same water source. Depressions, particularly the severe one beginning in 1893, threw private irrigation markets and securities in California and across the Far West into disarray, resulting in widespread company failures and interruptions in the flow of water onto farm fields. By the mid-1890s, concluded historian Donald Pisani, "most large private irrigation companies had collapsed and the rest teetered on the edge of bankruptcy."[1] Clearly, if the West were ever to be transformed into an irrigated Eden, something besides private enterprise would have to do it. In this judgment, the major western railroads, including the Southern Pacific, concurred.[2]

In Southern Pacific country, the movement for public irrigation began in California in the early 1870s and reached an initial climax in 1887. Varying interests and coalitions introduced a succession of bills into the legislature after 1872 to create local or state public water agencies. In an explosive era of economic depression, political tension, and regional jealousies, however, bitter factionalism thwarted the nascent drive for public water. A few parties pushed for state control over water, while most groups—particularly in southern California—fearing that the state, as it was prone to do, would favor some regions or economic interests over others, fervently opposed centralized management and insisted instead on autonomous local agencies. Proposals for public irrigation water also ran afoul of the still-unsettled conflict between riparian and appropriation water rights, which persisted even after the state Supreme Court, in *Lux v. Haggin* (1884), judged riparianism to be supreme. Water issues of all sorts, moreover, were invariably caught up in the uproar over the flooding and drainage problems caused by the dumping of foothill hydraulic-mining debris into Central Valley streams. Many irrigation-bill opponents attacked even the concept of large-scale public water systems. California's strapped governments, they charged, could not raise the unprecedented capital required to aid a few state residents without inequitable burdens on other taxpayers. Caught in the cross fire between California's warring water factions, virtually all public irrigation bills, most of which would have created local districts, failed to pass one or both houses of the legislature.[3]

As California debated the public water question during the 1870s and 1880s, the Southern Pacific at first played an ambivalent, tangential role. One of California's first major interests to realize the advantages of public control of water, the company, still consumed by the burdens of expanding its transportation network and as yet uncertain about the direction of land and development policy, produced no detailed plan of its own for delivering public water to farmers. Some early public-irrigation proposals, the railroad found to be clearly unacceptable. Many early public-irrigation advocates, for example, appealed to widespread anti-monopoly sentiment by incorporating into their bills provisions for large Central Valley canals to be used not only for irrigation but also for commercial navigation to break the Southern Pacific's hold on local transportation. Naturally, the company fought against such patently anti-railroad measures, openly through editorials in the *Sacramento Record-Union* and other sympathetic newspapers and privately through its legislative allies.[4]

Although the company did not aggressively pursue a single public-water strategy before 1887, it appears on occasion to have made modest attempts to initiate policy. Legislators with known Southern Pacific ties, for instance, authored or prominently supported a few of the early irrigation bills, probably with some railroad instigation. Failed bills that would have created a state irrigation-canal system to furnish local districts with water, for example, were introduced during the 1875–1876 and 1877–1878 legislatures by state senator Creed Haymond, the chairman of the Senate's irrigation committee, who was also a well-known Southern Pacific attorney.[5] With the state's interests at odds with one another, and lacking a clear direction of its own beyond a general preference for state control, however, the Southern Pacific, at least as a corporation, usually steered clear of specific proposals, especially those to create local districts.

William H. Mills and the Fight against Hydraulic Mining

William H. Mills, who would become the leading architect of Southern Pacific water policy, did not advance from editor and manager of the *Sacramento Record-Union* to the more powerful position of chief land agent for the Southern Pacific until 1883. While the Southern Pacific provided little visible early leadership as a company, Mills, both before and after his elevation to land agent, was one of California's, indeed the West's, earliest and most important pioneers of public irrigation, scientific water management, and centralized state control. Mills's positions on these hotly debated questions, as well as on California's specific water legislation of the 1870s and 1880s and even later, stemmed directly from his residence in Sacramento since the 1850s and his experience with the Sacramento River Valley's complex, long-term, and region-wide water problems. With its near-sea-level elevation, flat terrain, and torrential runoff from high surrounding mountains, the valley was naturally flood-prone. These conditions were greatly aggravated in the 1870s and 1880s, when hydraulic-mining debris descending from the Sierra foothills filled in streambeds and produced massive, nearly annual floods that threatened to destroy the valley's agricultural potential. Localized (usually private) irrigation, swamplands reclamation, and flood-control projects, which proliferated after the early 1850s, proved ineffective and wasteful in dealing with the valley's water problems, often actually worsening the overall flooding. In reaction, business, political, and press leaders in the region, including Mills, increasingly stressed the need for comprehensive, region-wide, public control of water policy in order to balance the sometimes antithetical requirements of irrigation, flood control, reclamation, mining-debris removal, and navigation.[6]

When in early 1875 Mills and the Southern Pacific merged their *Sacramento Record* with the powerful, anti-railroad *Sacramento Union,* Mills assumed leadership in the fight against hydraulic mining. With nearly his first issue of the *Record-Union,* Mills launched a relentless editorial attack on hydraulic mining and mining in general. The newspaper charged that mining was a dying industry, benefiting only a few while injuring the well-being of the many, particularly Central Valley farmers, and indeed jeopardizing the future of the entire state. In issue after issue, the *Record-Union* described in detail how for years the hydraulic mining companies had been dumping into the tributaries of valley streams millions of cubic yards of debris that worked its way to the valley floor, where it filled in riverbeds and caused massive flood damage to farms, irrigation facilities, and riverside towns. Even worse, the receding floods left behind infertile debris deposits as deep as several yards, permanently destroying farmland and town property. Going beyond the mere economic threat to his region's farmers and town-dwellers, Mills attacked hydraulic mining on environmental grounds that were surprisingly broad for the time. The ruin caused by mining debris could not be contained, he warned, and if not halted immediately, would destroy not only valley streams and riverside lands but the Sacramento–San Joaquin river delta and even distant San Francisco Bay. Annual valley floods spreading over the state's most fertile farmland would be inevitable; protective levee systems would be futile; and inland rivers and the San Francisco Bay would cease to be navigable. The future potential of agriculture, the state's only hope for permanent prosperity, would be gone. Meanwhile, according to Mills, hydraulic mining was reducing even its own foothill region to a permanent "howling desert," with forests cut down or washed away, soil excavated down to bedrock, watersheds and wells depleted, and weather rendered drier and hotter. Yet, although the state faced a bleak future and despite popular opposition and declining profits and workforce, the hydraulic companies, aided especially by mining towns and the San Francisco business community, remained entrenched in the legislature and state courts, and almost all attempts to end, or even control, the debris went for naught. "Our descendants," Mills predicted, would condemn the current generation for having tolerated "an industry which is desolating immense areas of country and rendering them forever sterile, at the same time it is preparing climatic and meteorological changes fraught with anything but good to the future of California and the agricultural interest."[7]

Mills accompanied his unrelenting editorial assault on hydraulic mining with a call to action. Repeatedly in the 1870s and early 1880s, the *Record-Union* designed or supported a variety of state legislation to halt or control the debris. When bills failed or were defeated in court by mining companies, the newspaper sponsored protest meetings throughout the Sacramento Valley in the late 1870s that resulted in the formation of local anti-debris committees and ultimately the California Anti-Debris Association, the state's first nonlocal water-policy pressure group. Traveling around the valley to rally local support and assuming management of the association was Isaac N. Hoag, former executive secretary of the California Agricultural Society, the long-standing agricultural editor of the *Record-Union,* and a frequent associate of Mills and the Southern Pacific in various development programs, including a stint as the railroad's immigration agent during the mid-1880s. The Anti-Debris Association, with the support of the *Record-Union* and other regional papers and local governments, backed lawsuits against the hydraulic mining companies, and when these failed to achieve redress in local courts, moved litigation into the U.S. circuit court in San Francisco with the justification that the Sacramento and other large valley rivers were navigable waterways and therefore under federal jurisdiction.[8] The Southern Pacific itself openly assisted the growing coalition against hydraulic mining. In early 1878, Benjamin B. Redding, head of the railroad's land department and also a member of the state Fisheries Commission, appeared before the state Assembly committee on mining debris, offering data the railroad had collected on the extent to which in the last two decades debris had filled in valley rivers, damaging salmon fisheries, permanently swamping hitherto fertile farmland, requiring the building of ever-higher levees, and perpetually forcing the railroad, at great expense, to raise or relocate flooded bridges and roadbeds.[9]

For the trouble, Mills and his newspaper drew the ire of mining's allies. Pro-mining papers, particularly San Francisco's *Alta California,* denounced the *Record-Union* as the leader of a dangerous crusade to destroy the state's most important industry and organized boycotts of the newspaper's subscribers and advertisers. The *San Francisco Bulletin* and a growing cohort of valley and coastal newspapers, however, supported Mills's efforts. On one occasion, a delegation of Sacramento businessmen, frightened at the threat of a miner-led boycott of the city's supply firms, called on Mills and pleaded with him to cease his attack on the industry.[10] The battle against hydraulic companies was ultimately victorious in 1884, however, when U.S. Circuit Court judge Lorenzo Sawyer, who a few years earlier had handed down the famous decisions against the Mussel Slough squatters on Southern Pacific land, issued a perpetual injunction against dumping mining debris into Sierra streams.[11] Mills and the *Record-Union* had been instrumental in more than saving valley agriculture. Cited nationwide, Judge Sawyer's decision became an important early precedent in the assertion of governmental responsibility to protect the public from environmental damage.

State Control of Water

His leadership in the battle against hydraulic mining and a career as an ardent booster of modern agriculture, small-scale farming, land subdivision, and his Sacramento Valley region shaped William H. Mills into one of California's earliest and most influential advocates of centralized water planning. As early as 1873, when he had just become editor of the railroad-owned *Sacramento Record,* Mills predicted that public irrigation would usher in "the third great epoch in the history of California." He became perhaps the first to suggest a comprehensive approach to irrigation development and, since such large systems would be beyond private or local means, to advocate for the necessity of central state regulation of water policies and state ownership of water rights and major irrigation facilities. For the next three decades, Mills vigorously spoke, wrote, and lobbied organizations, political leaders, and governing bodies on behalf of comprehensive state water management to balance the needs of irrigation,

Ironically, the Southern Pacific, which had been instrumental earlier in the outlawing of hydraulic mining in California, itself used the technology in the late 1880s to speed and reduce the cost of constructing its Siskyou line connecting the state to Oregon. Steam from four locomotives rigged to work in tandem pumped and pressurized water from the Sacramento River, and movable pipes carried it to a hydraulic monitor at the rear of the train, which blasted a right-of-way and tunnels through a soft cliff. Author's collection.

flood control, watershed preservation, and navigation. In 1904, Mills summed up the commitment of a career of activism on behalf of that view in a series of articles in the *San Francisco Call,* reprinted in his pamphlet, *The Hydrography of the Sacramento Valley,* but his position had remained consistent since the early 1870s. Mills also accepted the utility of local irrigation districts to deliver the water to farmers, but only after state-wide water regulations had been instituted and a centralized reservoir, canal, and management system built. Since the federal government could not be trusted to guard California's interests, only the state could provide effective oversight of water resources.[12] Mills's stand was much more radical than most other advocates of state control. To prevent private water monopoly and speculation in water rights, Mills went as far as advocating legislation that would transfer all water rights—claimed and un-claimed, riparian and appropriation—from private to state ownership.[13]

Although the more numerous partisans of local control over irrigation blocked attempts to institute comprehensive, centralized, state-controlled water management, Mills and other members of the "state party" were able to get the legislature to establish two precedent-setting, though ephemeral and unsuccessful, experiments in state water planning, the first by a state government in the American West. In 1878, the legislature created the office of State Engineer to conduct scientific study of the mining-debris problem and to survey the state's irrigation facilities, remaining water resources, and potential for further irrigation development. Then, in 1880, the legislature established the California Drainage and Debris Commission to work in conjunction with the state engineer to create local drainage districts to implement flood-control measures. The irrigation studies, reports, and maps compiled by the first state engineer, William Hammond Hall, were particularly important as the initial systematic scientific examination of California's irrigation potential, which provided a basis on which further work could be built. The *Sacramento Record-Union* was one of the strongest proponents of both agencies. Unpopular with some regions and interests, however, both proved to be short-lived. The State Engineer's office endured constant criticism, legislative interference, and dramatic budget reductions, and struggled until its ultimate abolishment in 1893. From the beginning, the Debris Commission provoked intense opposition to its raising of taxes and was declared unconstitutional on a technicality by the state Supreme Court in 1881. Although Mills had helped to make a start in state water control and continued to campaign for it until his death in 1907, his vision was decades ahead of its time. State water management in California would not become a reality until well into the twentieth century, when decades of confusion caused by localism had finally convinced enough people of its necessity.[14]

Unsurprisingly in the light of his staunch support for state water management, during California's legislative debate over public irrigation in the 1870s and 1880s, Mills and his *Record-Union* fought nearly all of the numerous bills providing for local irrigation districts, not because he opposed irrigation but because he believed that a haphazard, piecemeal local approach was fraught with danger.[15] In combating a bill in 1875 to create local districts, the newspaper introduced reasoning that it would follow in years ahead. The *Record-Union* editorialized that without the prior existence of central state control over water, "all efforts to supply the needs of farmers [by means of the local districts] will result in failure and confusion." Local districts might one day be useful "but only on condition that each conforms to a State system of irrigation, which system shall be laid down by competent engineers." Without state-wide regulations and central management, nothing would prevent "usurpation on the part of individuals or districts" and "it would be worse than useless to attempt any measure of irrigation." The *Record-Union* condemned the local-district idea as "mischievous and against public policy."[16]

Many local-district bills, which were often promoted by advocates of the appropriation (diversion) principle of water rights, included language limiting or even suspending riparian rights, which protected the rights of downstream landowners to water flow and quality. Deeply involved in the Sacramento Valley's struggle to halt the deluge of hydraulic-mining debris from the foothills, which hinged on the valley's assertion of the riparian rights of downstream landowners, Mills opposed many local irrigation bills because they also threatened riparian rights. In 1885 particularly, the *Sacramento Record-Union* led the attack on the so-called "Fresno bills." The complex body of legislation, introduced as a result of the wave of popular reaction against the Supreme Court's 1884 *Lux v. Haggin* decision, proposed to create a local-district system while sharply curtailing riparian rights. "Better that the deserts remain unreclaimed and the parched lands go unwatered," the paper warned, "than that the law be blotted out, which is to-day the safeguard of the people against the unnatural descent of mining debris and slickens, and which, if unchecked, would render the fertile regions along the Sacramento river uninhabitable and utterly destroy the navigability of the chief free highway of the State." Popular around the state and supported by most major newspapers, the Fresno bills passed the Assembly overwhelmingly. They were killed in the Senate, however, by an unlikely coalition of Sacramento Valley and foothill county interests, the mining industry, and, in a rare instance of direct involvement in irrigation politics, the Southern Pacific, which instructed its legislative allies to fight the bills. The *Record-Union* was widely known to represent the Southern Pacific's point of view, especially on political matters. Mills's support of a comprehensive state approach to public irrigation and his opposition to the 1875 and subsequent local-district legislation, including the 1885 Fresno bills, probably carried weight with the railroad's legislative allies, and, as leading water historian Donald Pisani has acknowledged, was an important reason for the bills' defeat and the delay in the creation of local public irrigation in California.[17]

The Southern Pacific undoubtedly was aware of and granted at least tacit approval to Mills's highly visible, public campaign for a comprehensive state-owned and -managed irrigation system and against the local-district approach. Mills was the railroad's newspaper partner, its major press spokesman, its chief land agent after 1883, and all the while a confidante of Collis P. Huntington. That Mills must have reflected general company policy on these questions is further evidenced by the fact that many of the *Record-Union*'s editorials and articles on the subject were clipped and filed in the Southern Pacific's official scrapbooks, which were kept in the office of general manager Alban N. Towne and made available to other executives. Particularly from 1883 to the early 1900s, while railroad executive Mills continued to co-own and control the editorial stance of the *Record-Union,* the newspaper's viewpoint on irrigation should be read as a direct indicator of the railroad's company policies.[18]

California's Wright Law and Early Irrigation Districts

When the California legislature reconvened in 1887, pressures to resolve the riparian-appropriation dispute and to provide a mechanism for developing public irrigation works were irresistible. A bill reflecting the strong localism that had come to dominate the public irrigation movement—the Wright Act—overwhelmingly passed the Assembly and the Senate and was signed into law in March. Regarded in its time to be conservative and well-drafted, the Wright Act permitted landowners in a region, after a referendum, to form a public irrigation district governed by an elected board. Importantly, the law granted the local irrigation district the power to purchase or condemn land and water rights (riparian and appropriation), to issue bonds to build water facilities, and to tax all property (urban and rural) in the district according to valuation in order to repay bonds and subsidize water deliveries. For the most part, the irrigation districts were to be free from control by the state. Under the auspices of the Wright Act, a host of local irrigation districts sprouted up in the late 1880s and early 1890s, particularly in southern California and the San Joaquin Valley, and the state's irrigated acreage expanded greatly. By 1895, forty-nine districts, incorporating about two million acres (2 percent of the state's land area), had been formed.[19]

Unfortunately, William H. Mills's predictions about the dangers of an uncoordinated local approach to irrigation development were quickly borne out. The many districts that sprang up in the wake of the Wright Law's enactment were immediately beset by difficulties not unlike those of the private water companies. Unluckily, the late 1880s and 1890s were also a bleak period for experimentation in ambitious public-water development in California. The collapse in 1888 of the land boom in both southern and other counties devastated the state's banking institutions, halted immigration, and ushered in nearly a decade and a half of depression, which was only worsened by the serious national panic beginning in 1893. Simultaneously, a succession of drought years, killing freezes, bouts with crop pests, and erratic production, markets, and prices darkened the future of the citrus and other emerging orchard industries. Despite long-term economic uncertainty, however, the boomer mentality remained vigorous. Many of the would-be irrigation districts, particularly in southern California, were overtly speculative, concocted by land developers and local booster groups anxious to raise land values and sales with little regard to actual water resources, agricultural potential, or demand for irrigated farmland. Ruinous lawsuits brought by opposing large-scale landowners, excessive bonded indebtedness (an astounding $33-per-acre average among the southern districts founded between 1887 and 1890, for example), incompetent engineering, vicious local and inter-regional conflict, and more than a little fraud also burdened the districts, frequently driving them into bankruptcy and failure. Clouding the entire situation for nearly a decade were questions regarding the very legality of the districts, until the U.S. Supreme Court finally declared the Wright Act constitutional in 1896. By the early 1890s, the local irrigation districts' bad reputation had rendered further bond sales almost impossible.[20]

Although it had generally favored centralized, state-managed public irrigation, after the Wright Act passed in 1887, the Southern Pacific tried to make the local-district plan work. As it turned out, the railroad had little choice. Committed to irrigation and farm development as a way to increase its traffic and land-grant sales, the Southern Pacific thought it stood to gain greatly and initially supported the new irrigation districts, at least in principle. Even had that not been the case, the company was inexorably drawn into the districts' affairs. A major landowner in many districts, the railroad by the early 1890s was paying large irrigation tax bills, some to districts that delivered little water or failed outright. In fact, some districts in remote regions, with light population and few farms, attempted to finance themselves primarily by taxing the railroad's lands and operating property, leading the company to object that it was paying a disproportionate share of costs. As the districts built their facilities, plans often impinged on Southern Pacific interests, even in irrigation districts in which the railroad had no granted lands. Districts typically sought rights-of-way and easements for canals as well as reservoir sites on the railroad's granted lands or operating property. The districts' purchase or assertion of water rights also sometimes clashed with the railroad's own water rights. Occasionally, irrigation districts and other public water agencies such as flood-control districts inadvertently appropriated railroad lands or water without the company's knowledge or agreement; in at least several instances, they did so deliberately, on the chance they could forgo compensating the railroad.[21]

Moreover, as was true with all property within the districts, irrigation bonds and unpaid irrigation taxes constituted liens on tens of thousands of acres of the railroad's granted land, as well as even more valuable operating property, especially in the San Joaquin Valley and southern California. This situation caused particular difficulty for the company. Faced with high irrigation taxes, many of its land buyers, the great majority of whom had signed time-payment contracts and did not yet have deeds to the land, abandoned their farms or town lots within irrigation districts without paying the taxes, leaving the railroad stuck with the bills. Often failing to notify the company of its buyers' defaulted taxes, counties auctioned off land the railroad still owned.[22] When districts failed, irrigation-bond liens caused further expense to the company and complicated its land sales. By 1909, the company's Land Department had determined that the status of railroad property was at issue in sixty-seven court cases involving thirty-four irrigation districts.[23] By 1915, to free its lands from encumbrances caused by failed irrigation districts, the Southern Pacific had been forced repeatedly to reach expensive settlements with bondholders, with the litigation dragging out over years, sometimes decades, while its lands were unsalable.[24]

Riverside County's Alessandro Irrigation District, for example, was founded in 1891 and quickly issued $700,000 in bonds. Immediately challenged in court by opposing landowners, it was declared by the state Supreme Court to have been formed illegally and was promptly disbanded. Seeking repayment, bondholders sued, lost, and then won on appeal. Meanwhile, until 1913, there was a lien on *all* land within the boundaries of the district, including 800 acres of the railroad's land that the company valued at $60 to $75 per acre. Finally, after negotiations in which the Southern Pacific played a major role, the bondholders, whose legal position was weak, agreed to settle for a mere $5,500. Upon petition from landowners in the area, the railroad, which had concluded that its valuable lands were being tied up and that the entire district's development was in limbo, paid much of the settlement, and the bonds were repurchased and destroyed in 1913. In other cases, the railroad's costs were much greater. The Perris Irrigation District, also in Riverside County, was founded in 1887, and controversy over its bonds began almost immediately. Litigation was instituted in 1897, and nearly two decades later, after legal costs had bankrupted the district and shut down its waterworks, the courts finally ruled that the bonds were legal and binding liens and ordered all landowners in the inoperative district to pay an exorbitant 44 percent of their property's valuation, for a total of $229,000, to the Swiss bondholders. The Southern Pacific owned 700 of the 13,000 acres within the district, plus additional land the railroad had sold under time-payment contracts but still legally owned. When the Southern Pacific's land purchasers refused to pay and abandoned their lands en masse, the railroad was forced to make a whopping payment in 1915 to save its lands.[25]

The Southern Pacific and the Irrigation Districts

Chaotic conditions among California irrigation districts thus impinged directly on many areas of the railroad's business from the Wright Act's passage through the 1920s. To further the cause of irrigation, as well as to protect its own threat-

ened interests, the Southern Pacific found itself required to interject itself repeatedly into the affairs of local irrigation districts to furnish some of the overall coordination that was missing from the Wright Act and that state government would later provide. As local irrigation districts began to falter by the
early 1890s, Southern Pacific leaders first tried to shore up public confidence.
In 1891 and 1892, land agent William H. Mills enlisted the California State Board
of Trade in a campaign to support the Wright Act districts. In April 1891, the
board appointed a committee, led by Mills, to review the irrigation district
bonds. After consulting with the San Francisco Chamber of Commerce and
San Francisco financial houses, the committee issued a report two months later
that declared the bonds to be an "ample and valid security" more than backed
up by the increased value of the irrigated lands in the districts and the resultant higher taxes that would be used to retire the bonds. At Mills's recommendation, the Board of Trade adopted the report and had it circulated in financial centers around the world, especially New York City.[26]

Collis P. Huntington, by then president of the Southern Pacific Company,
added his own personal endorsement to the Board of Trade's campaign to encourage bond sales. In a public letter to the *San Francisco Chronicle* dated April
22, 1891, Huntington expressed strong support for the Wright Act and the new
irrigation districts. The bonds constituted a valid mortgage on the districts' lands,
and the agencies would be solvent if the value of the bonds did not exceed the
value of the lands, Huntington advised. According to his survey, the irrigation
works and bonds in California were only a small fraction of the lands' value, between 3 and 7 percent in most cases. The irrigation district plan for developing
public water, Huntington declared, was "wise, judicious and effective."[27] With
Mills's assistance, Huntington continued to support the irrigation districts. He
and Mills conferred with and encouraged leaders of solvent districts, and in early
1892, Huntington developed a plan to bolster sales of irrigation bonds. Huntington recommended that the solid districts consolidate their bonds and issue
one common bond, which would sell more readily, with the separate district
bonds deposited as collateral in a trust company in New York. The trust company would send experts to verify the districts' water resources and land values,
separate the legitimate from the fraudulent districts, and assure that money from
bond sales went into actual irrigation projects. If this were done, Huntington
promised to do all he could to market the consolidated bonds at the highest possible rates, just as he would any other "first-class security."[28]

Little came of the Southern Pacific leaders' efforts. Huntington's plan was
not adopted, and new districts continued to be founded willy-nilly, thirteen in
1891 alone. The outlook for the irrigation districts continued to deteriorate,
particularly after a nation-wide depression struck in 1893. By the mid-1890s,
most of the approximately fifty fledging agencies had failed, and few new ones

were being created. By 1910, only twelve of the initial districts survived, and they irrigated only 174,000 acres, about 5 percent of the state's total irrigated land. Reforms of the Wright Act were finally enacted by the state legislature in 1897, and again in 1911, 1913, and 1917, particularly requiring more state oversight of irrigation-district formation and bond issues. Although many new districts were founded after 1900 under closer state scrutiny, the early troubles continued.[29]

From the late 1880s into the 1920s, the Southern Pacific became entangled in the creation, operation, and politics of dozens of California irrigation districts.[30] Because the railroad's land was typically involved, relations with the districts were usually handled by the Land Department, under the direction of its supervisors in the Legal Department. Sometimes it was the railroad that intervened to preserve its own interests; usually, the districts' leaders themselves approached the company for assistance in forming or financing districts, in buying land or waterwork sites, or in combating opponents. Initially, as Huntington's and Mills's attempts to market district bonds in the early 1890s suggest, company leaders began their work in the districts with the optimism, if not altruism, typical of the early public-irrigation crusade. Irrigation would not only develop the West and further corporate interests, railroad officials expected, it would help fashion the Jeffersonian, small-farm democracy that had thus far eluded places like California. The railroad readily agreed to allow districts to form and its lands to be taxed. Repeatedly stung in its dealings with the districts, however, particularly after 1892, the company became more skeptical, and hardheaded business sense and corporate self-interest replaced idealism as the driving force of Southern Pacific support for public irrigation. The railroad grew especially wary of utopian schemes to combine irrigation projects with colonization of poor urban families on small farms.[31]

In the chaos of the 1890s, the Southern Pacific developed a cautious, flexible, pragmatic policy toward the irrigation districts, approaching each project separately, offering or withholding assistance on the basis of the district's technical, economic, and legal feasibility and the specific benefit to the railroad in greater traffic and land-grant sales and values. Carefully, the Southern Pacific measured the costs and risks of participation, weighed them against potential gains, and only then made its decision. If it chose to assist, the Southern Pacific was often an all-important ally to a blossoming local irrigation movement. But when the railroad was convinced that a project was unworkable or that corporate interests would be jeopardized, the company proved to be a formidable foe to those districts it avoided or actively opposed. Failure to secure the railroad's assistance doomed some would-be public, and private, irrigation projects.[32] The Southern Pacific not only developed ways to further its corporate well-being, but in implementing its policy toward the irrigation districts during and after the 1890s, the company pioneered in performing quasi-public, oversight services to the districts—often against their will—that anticipated and provided models for what state government would later do after Progressive-era reforms of the Wright Act. To the confusion of early public irrigation, the railroad offered a measure of stability, and in the process affected the future of water development in the arid West.

First, the railroad insisted that science, not wishful thinking, be the basis of public irrigation. The tradition of information-gathering that chief land agent Benjamin B. Redding had begun in the 1860s was continued by William H. Mills after 1883 and B. A. McAllaster after 1908, and by the early twentieth century, the Southern Pacific had assembled in the Land Department a staff of experts on water, soils, agriculture, and land development and had gathered masses of information about climate, water resources, land markets, and agricultural production in localities throughout its territory. If anything, dealing with irrigation districts intensified the railroad's reliance on science. So complicated had the railway's relations with the districts become, particularly after the 1906 San Francisco earthquake and fire destroyed many company land records, that in 1909 land agent McAllaster ordered comprehensive surveys of the burgeoning districts, their boundaries, water resources, potential crops, irrigation facilities, financial conditions, affected Southern Pacific properties, and the railroad's relationships with the agencies. The company collected data even about districts in which the railroad had no granted land.[33] When water questions proved to be beyond the ken of its own experts, the Southern Pacific by the early 1900s began routinely to hire consultants, many of them from the agricultural or water-resources faculty at the University of California as well as other universities in the company's territory.[34] Its commissioned studies and detailed files on irrigation districts, continually expanded and updated, guided the Southern Pacific's relations with the agencies and remain today an important resource for studying western agricultural and water history.

In deciding questions of irrigation district policy, particularly which agencies to support, the company came to engage in painstaking study of scientific reports, legal and economic analyses, and thorough discussion by all affected departments—particularly the Land, Legal, and Tax departments—of benefits and costs to the company, the irrigation district involved, and the region's development. When approached repeatedly after 1910 by Antelope Valley leaders for assistance in forming the Little Rock Creek and Palmdale irrigation districts, for example, the Land Department commissioned several studies of development, land sales, water supplies, and alkali soil problems in the valley. On the basis of the studies, land agent McAllaster, after consultation with the Tax and Legal departments and other executives, decided that, although it owned much land in the valley, the railroad would not participate, and he advised the promoters against going ahead with the new districts.[35]

A similar, intensive study in 1911 of the potential for a proposed irrigation district for the Coachella Valley convinced the company that, although it owned much land in the region that might benefit from irrigation, scant water resources made the current plan "not feasible" and the project speculative, designed to sell land to unsuspecting settlers rather than to deliver water.[36] In the years before World War I, even more thorough study demonstrated to the Southern Pacific the feasibility and value of forming a large umbrella irrigation district to build the Pine Flat Dam in the Sierra Nevada, supplemented by a network of smaller feeder districts to deliver water to a part of western Fresno, Kings, and Tulare counties that contained nearly 20,000 acres of company land. Although the project would have cost the company more than $36 per acre in irrigation taxes, the railroad concluded it would raise land values between $50 and $80 per acre and also help overcome the land's severe alkali pollution. The company agreed to sign petitions for the districts and worked aggressively with local promoters to build local support. An exhaustive analysis of the proposal by the Tax and Law departments, however, revealed serious legal flaws in the petitions, and when McAllaster informed the districts' promoters, they redrafted the petitions several times to satisfy the railroad's objections. Although all company leaders favored supporting the proposal, the war's onset, particularly the federal government's takeover of the nation's railways, postponed the railroad's participation until after the war.[37] When irrigation districts such as these sought the railroad's assistance, the company often required as a condition that the agencies also conduct intensive analyses. As they planned districts, the agencies' promoters and early managers, lacking their own reliable data, typically sought access to Southern Pacific soil, streamflow, and groundwater surveys, engineering studies, climate and rainfall statistics, and land-value and crop-price analyses, which the railroad usually provided, even to districts the company did not favor.

When the Southern Pacific decided to assist irrigation agencies, the company by various means furnished critical support, particularly financial. It allowed its property to be mortgaged and contributed irrigation taxes—often a high percentage of the districts' overall revenues—to build water facilities and to acquire rights-of-way, reservoir sites, and water rights. Sometimes, as it had been doing since the 1870s with private irrigation companies, the railroad granted districts rights-of-way or sold them easements at less than market value. The railroad also made direct monetary contributions or loans to some districts, reimbursed them for scientific studies and litigation, publicly lent its official approbation (and hence its reputation for prudent financial management) to back bond issues, and in a few instances even purchased the irrigation bonds to put the agencies into business. In addition to financial assistance, the Southern Pacific often mediated disputes and arranged compromises among rival groups of would-be local irrigators vying for control of scarce water resources, and the railroad helped some districts defend themselves against outside challengers—sometimes imperialistic cities—trying to expropriate and export local water supplies.[38]

Finally, despite the Wright Act's affirmation of the local approach, the Southern Pacific continued to serve as one of the most powerful pressure groups for more centralized state control of the irrigation districts. In the 1890s and early 1900s, for example, land agent Mills continued to work for state supervision in the interest of stability and long-term expansion of irrigation, through his many writings and public addresses, his lobbying of California governors, his continued control of the editorial policy of the *Sacramento Record-Union,* and his influence as founder and leader of the influential California State Board of Trade, the California State Association for the Storage of Water, and the California Water and Forest Association. Historian Donald Pisani has identified Mills as an important member of "an alliance of civic and business leaders, reform-minded politicians, economic boosters, and water resource specialists" who eventually brought about reforms of the Wright Act from 1897 into the Progressive era.[39]

Frustrated Railroad Intervention: Mojave District

The fates of two California public irrigation agencies—the Mojave River and the Imperial districts—best illustrate the Southern Pacific's complex, often decades-long involvement in California's irrigation districts and the railroad's general influence on the development of public irrigation. Between the 1900s and the 1940s, as residents and landowners along the Mojave River near the high-desert hamlet of Victorville struggled to build a public irrigation system, the Southern Pacific performed the wide range of the services it had been providing variously to further the work of many irrigation districts: inspiration, organization, continuity, scientific and legal expertise, mediation, protection from opponents, and finance. In this case, so pervasive and long lasting was the company's role that it is safe to say that without the Southern Pacific, a water system of any sort would never have come into being in the area. Although the railroad had sold its line through the region to the Santa Fe in the 1880s, it still had about 10,000 acres of granted lands within reach of the Mojave River, which originated in the San Bernardino Mountains and flowed intermittently above and below ground northward into a sink east of Barstow. Although the lands were within the indemnity limits of the original Southern Pacific Railroad grant and the government had yet to patent them to the company, the railroad's Land Department was aware of the land's fertility, the availability of water, and the potential for irrigation to raise the land's value, and by 1900, company agents were keeping a close watch on water developments in the valley.

In 1908, local residents mounted their first serious attempt to form a local irrigation district. The going was not easy, however. Even more than was true in most other areas in the state, the Mojave River region was plagued by a bewildering array of impediments to easy public irrigation. Local land ownership patterns necessitated complicated applications for water rights from both federal and state governments. Not only that, but two rival groups of would-be irrigators eventually formed opposing agencies competing for the desert river's meager flow: the Mojave Valley Irrigation District, organized by residents east of the river, and the Victor Valley Irrigation District, created by those west of the river. Blocking the path of both groups was the Arrowhead Reservoir and Power Company, which owned essential water rights in the mountain watershed of the upper Mojave River, was developing the luxurious vacation resort at Lake Arrowhead, and repeatedly made moves to impound the mountains' waters and transfer them via tunnel to sell to cities in the San Bernardino Valley to the south.[40] Periodically in league with the Arrowhead Company was the city of Pasadena, which though 50 miles to the west, was taking a cue from Los Angeles's conquest of a distant water supply in the Owens Valley. Beginning in 1911, Pasadena tried several times to combine forces with San Bernardino and Pomona-area cities to acquire rights to bring mountain water to foster urban development in the San Gabriel Valley.[41] Aggravating the situation were problems that by then had become routine for incipient irrigation districts: lack of local expertise in water development, scant population and local capital, opposition by some landowners to irrigation of any sort, the low prestige of California irrigation districts in general, and an extremely tight market for irrigation bonds.

In 1917, after delays and acrimonious hearings, the San Bernardino County Board of Supervisors finally accepted the eastsiders' petition, approved the formation of the Mojave River Irrigation District, which was to encompass 30,000 acres, and authorized the sale of irrigation bonds and the building of a mountain reservoir to impound the East Fork of the Mojave River. The Mojave River Irrigation District promptly announced plans to sell bonds and instituted proceedings to acquire the water rights of the Arrowhead Reservoir and Power Company. Despite being rebuffed, the westsiders continued pressing their plan for a rival 70,000-acre district. The future of water development along the Mojave River seemed bleak indeed.[42]

Beginning with the first attempt to organize an irrigation district after 1908, the railroad was one of the prime instigators and certainly the principal organizer of the movement. Land Department agents repeatedly went to the valley or corresponded with local leaders to build support for a public district. In 1911, the railroad hired Sam B. Rice, a water engineer, to conduct a comprehensive study of "the feasibility of an irrigation project in the vicinity of Victorville," which confirmed the company's earlier optimism about the region and which became one of the leading scientific justifications for the proposed irrigation project. From the start, the company formed ongoing alliances with irrigation promoters and provided them with maps, water surveys, and other bodies of data, and it would continue to do so for three decades.[43] As soon as the railroad got wind of Pasadena's plans to export almost all the water in the Mojave, the company ordered a study of the proposal in 1911. The company's Barstow field agent predicted "enormous damage" to the railroad's land grant in that area of the Mojave Desert. Pasadena's proposed reservoir site near Victorville would flood the most valuable several thousand acres in the river's bottomland— worth between $100 and $500 per acre with irrigation—and also prevent forever the irrigation of thousands of acres of upland. The agent recommended that the company resort "to every lawful method known" to thwart the city and reserve the water for local use.[44] Into the 1920s, the Southern Pacific was Pasadena's most vigorous antagonist, working publicly and behind the scenes with the desert communities to defeat Pasadena's invasion, and partly because of the railroad's opposition, the city lost its first two attempts to acquire the water in 1911 and 1913.

Intra-regional conflict not only complicated local water development, it also caused the Southern Pacific to move cautiously, even when, as was true in this case, the company strongly favored irrigation. Owning land in both the Mojave River and the Victor Valley districts, convinced by its detailed analysis that the river's flow was insufficient to irrigate even one of the ambitious projects, knowing from experience that litigation costs were likely to destroy both projects, and having been repeatedly embroiled in water districts that failed because of similar local rivalries, the Southern Pacific initially sued to get its lands excluded from both districts and refused to pay assessments to both districts. Instead, even though its analysis showed that less of its land was likely to be irrigated, the railroad shared its water survey with leaders of both districts and over and over again tried to get them to combine into one, smaller, more realistic district, which would be more likely to acquire water rights from the state and federal government, to defeat the designs of the Arrowhead Company and the city of Pasadena, and to sell bonds to actually build the system.[45]

When the company's efforts at mediation proved fruitless, the Southern Pacific privately came to favor the Mojave River Irrigation District, which it viewed as the sounder of the two and in which it owned more land. The Mojave River Irrigation District's organizers avidly cultivated the Southern Pacific's support, and the company responded. Land agent B. A. McAllaster was in constant communication by letter; he sent representatives to confer and exchange information with the district's leaders on the scene and in Los Angeles; and he frequently brought the leaders to San Francisco to plot strategy. The railroad's chief southern California land agent, C. E. Wantland, also made dozens of visits to the valley and met innumerable times with local leaders in his office in Los Angeles. Over more than a decade and a half in the 1910s and 1920s, in fact, Wantland was probably the most important individual behind the irrigation project, keeping the idea alive in discouraging times, providing information and advice to Mojave Valley people, bringing factions together, and working with his superiors McAllaster and William F. Herrin in San Francisco to keep the company committed to irrigation in the area. Nevertheless, to preserve its legal position and protect its lands from encumbrances, the company still officially refused to acknowledge that its lands were included or to pay irrigation taxes until local forces united behind one project.[46] In January 1918, after nearly twenty years of delaying, the federal government finally issued patents to the Southern Pacific for 9,160 acres in the proposed districts, clearing away at least one of the railroad's uncertainties.[47]

Nevertheless, despite constant attention from local leaders and the railroad, organization of the irrigation district languished. Into the early 1920s, the Mojave River District had failed to secure the state's approval of its bond issue, to reach a settlement with the Arrowhead Company, or to win water rights from the state and federal government. Then, in late 1920, Pasadena mounted yet another attempt to appropriate the water in the Mojave River watershed and export it to the city. Pasadena threatened not only the incipient irrigation district but also the supplies of several towns and many farmers who took water from the river through gravity diversion or pumping. The city's invasion intensified efforts by irrigators and the railroad to gain local control of the valley's water resources. Irrigation organizers formed the Mojave River Riparian Owners Association and appealed to the Southern Pacific to provide the leadership to seek a permanent injunction prohibiting Pasadena and other cities from diverting the river's water.[48] Vehemently opposed to Pasadena's siphoning of the valley's water, McAllaster gathered information about the city's plans, contacted the railroad's associates around the state to get their backing against the city, provided Mojave Valley leaders with the engineering data they needed for their battle, and used the threat to try once again to bring the opposing irrigation factions together behind one district.[49] Pasadena would win and prevent future development of agriculture in the area, McAllaster predicted to one irrigation district promoter, unless settlers "accept the situation with the best grace possible" and combine to lay immediate claim to the river's unused flow.[50]

Most importantly, the railroad moved decisively to block Pasadena. With the approval of McAllaster and other executives in San Francisco, in the summer and fall of 1921 land agent C. E. Wantland privately contacted the Cincinnati owners of the Arrowhead Reservoir and Power Company and arranged for them to sell out to "a local syndicate of strong men" with whom Wantland was "in close touch." When the Los Angeles investors at first also flirted with the idea of cooperating with Pasadena and other cities to pipe the water out of the Mojave watershed, Wantland got them to agree to transfer the water rights to the Mojave River Irrigation District.[51] At the same time, Wantland brought together the valley's scattered landowners and irrigation district leaders, some of whom lived as far away as Los Angeles and Fresno, encouraged them to put their organization in order and to revive their stalled condemnation lawsuit against the Arrowhead Company, and started them negotiating with the company's new owners.[52]

Unable to sell bonds or to convince local landowners to pay virtually any irrigation taxes, the Mojave River Irrigation District had no funds to buy out the Arrowhead Company or even to proceed further with its lawsuit, and the district once again appealed to the Southern Pacific for critical financial assistance. Not only were its negotiations with the Arrowhead Company progressing, but in the fall of 1921 the State Bond Certification Commission approved an issue of $500,000 in Mojave Irrigation District bonds, and the knowledgeable, if controversial, Joseph B. Lippincott, who had helped organize and build Los Angeles's Owens Valley project, became the district's chief consulting engineer. To put it in business, the district asked the railroad to pay back-taxes of $20,000, which would allow the district to bring its condemnation suit to a close, print bonds, and pay for further engineering studies.[53] In order to preserve for the time being the Southern Pacific's legal position that its lands were not a part of the irrigation district, McAllaster arranged a compromise with the district, and he and chief counsel William F. Herrin convinced company president William Sproule in New York and Paul Shoup, Southern Pacific general manager in San Francisco, who had initially opposed the arrangement for fear of angering Pasadena leaders. The railroad agreed to suspend its exclusion lawsuit against the district, and instead of paying back-taxes, the company lent the district $7,000 to proceed with its condemnation suit of Arrowhead Company interests. The railroad promised additional funds in the future, "from time to time as the District's necessities may require." If the district's condemnation were successful, the railroad agreed to concede its lands to be a part of the district, and the loan would become a partial payment of the company's back-taxes.[54]

Over the next decade, as the Mojave River Valley promoters struggled to get their water project off the ground, it was the Southern Pacific that furnished momentum and continuity. To reduce delay and save the irrigation district litigation costs, McAllaster, despite general manager Paul Shoup's lingering doubts, brought Arrowhead Company and district officials together for a series of meetings stretching over more than two years that in August 1923 produced an agreement preserving the company's interests in Lake Arrowhead, the lakeshore property, and enough water to maintain the lake, while transferring water rights below 5,000 feet elevation to the irrigation district for $250,000, nearly a 50-percent savings over what it had expected to pay.[55] The settlement, along with the overwhelming opposition of Mojave Valley residents and the Southern Pacific, forced Pasadena to withdraw its application for the river's water before the state had had time to call a hearing.[56]

Still, the Mojave River Irrigation District, unable to sell bonds, lacked funds to make the purchase or to begin any construction. The railroad continued to lend the district money—$2,500 for an engineering study of a reservoir site and $2,500 to print its bonds—which, together with a small irrigation tax revenue, kept the district in business.[57] To encourage bond sales by using the railroad's granted lands as backing, the company worked out an arrangement whereby the district would attempt to find a single buyer for all the bonds. The railroad agreed to sell all its lands in the district to the same investor at a discount. The company also agreed to undertake a vigorous advertising and colonization program for the area, despite having no tracks in the region.[58] Throughout the 1920s, the Southern Pacific's attorneys in Washington, D.C., and in northern California also aided the district in pressing its water-rights claims before numerous federal and state government agencies, filling out arcane applications, appearing on behalf of the irrigation district at hearings, and time and again securing extensions of deadlines.[59]

Nevertheless, success eluded the Mojave River Valley irrigators. Repeatedly sued by owners of riparian rights along the river, some of whom had ties to the old, now defunct, Victor Valley District, suffering several purges of its leaders caused by revolts of disgruntled members, and unable to sell any bonds or to buy the Arrowhead Company's upstream water rights, particularly after the 1929 New York stock market crash, the Mojave River Irrigation District barely clung to life through the 1930s and 1940s, able to start construction only on modest water facilities based on an appropriation right it was able to get from the river's flow.[60] Finally in 1944, with the railroad's suit against the irrigation district to exclude its lands still on hold and still refusing to pay irrigation taxes, the Southern Pacific sold all 6,285 of its acres within the district to Newton T. Bass and his wife. Simultaneously, the company reached agreement with the irrigation district to drop the company's lawsuit in exchange for the district's releasing the railroad from back-taxes.[61] After nearly four decades, railroad and irrigation district parted ways. As World War II drew to a close, water development along the Mojave River had hardly been spectacular, and the Southern Pacific had no remaining local tracks or lands. Although the irrigation district finally did expire at war's end, the railroad's effect on the valley had been profound. Without the continuity of leadership, scientific and legal expertise, political intercession, and financing provided by the railroad, there would have been little chance of locally controlled public irrigation. If nothing else, the Southern Pacific had played the decisive role in defeating raids by outsiders and in preserving the Mojave River's water for local use in the valley's post-war agricultural and urban boom.

Railroad Midwife to Public Irrigation: The Imperial Valley

If the story of the Southern Pacific in the Mojave River Valley illustrates frustrating, largely abortive, efforts to exploit water supplies, the railroad's work during the same period in the Imperial Valley exemplifies the fulfilled opportunities and revolutionary social and economic effects of public irrigation development, as well as the full array of services the Southern Pacific provided to the movement. By the 1890s, with the bulk of its original lands in the San Joaquin Valley sold, the most potentially valuable remainder of the railroad's grant lay in the desiccated, below-sea-level Salton Sink of southeastern California. In the 1890s, the Southern Pacific began a period of four decades of involvement in the birth of public irrigation in the region, during a portion of which the railroad served literally as the "irrigation district." Some of the story—notably the Southern Pacific's combat of the disastrous 1905–1907 Colorado River flood—is well known, but the railroad's important actions before and after the flood are nearly unremembered today.

Since building its mainline between Los Angeles and Yuma in the mid-1870s, the Southern Pacific had furthered water development in the southeastern California desert in a number of ways: by prospecting for supplies for its water stations, which demonstrated that groundwater lay beneath the sand; by creating its irrigated demonstration plot at Indio, which introduced models of desert farming; and by providing incentives for others to irrigate and colonize the land. In 1893, for example, through the agency of W. H. H. Hart, then California attorney general, the railroad, anxious to develop its land and traffic interests around the Salton Sink, sold one-half million acres of land in the area, at $2.50 per acre, to the Colorado River Irrigation Company, a syndicate of New York, Chicago, and Denver investors who proposed to subdivide and settle the land by building a 150-square-mile reservoir and a canal from the Colorado River through northern Mexico into the sink. In keeping with William H. Mills's and Collis P. Huntington's often-stated support of small-scale farming, the railroad's sale contract bound the irrigation company to bring the land to market as soon as possible, in small tracts, and with water rights attached to the land.

The agreement also assured the railroad an unlimited water supply for train operations, something that had eluded the company in nearly twenty years of well-drilling in the desert. At the time, the land transaction was considered to be the state's largest to date. After approving the contract in New York, Collis P. Huntington expressed his regret that he was not fifteen years younger so he could abandon railroading to take part in the enterprise. "I am glad," Huntington said, "to have lived long enough to realize that this splendid country is to be reclaimed by the irrigation plan." Typically of private water ventures, however, the ambitious Colorado River Irrigation Company, after starting to build a headgate and canal, failed in the late 1890s, victim of its lack of capital, the depression following 1893, Mexico's refusal to allow the water to be exported into the United States, and lawsuits among the investors themselves. The land reverted to the railroad.[62]

In the late 1890s, Charles Robinson Rockwood, a former Southern Pacific civil engineer working in Yuma and one of the organizers of the defunct irrigation company, formed a new firm, the California Development Company, to carry on the work. Bringing famed water engineer and colony-planter George Chaffey into the project, Rockwood and associates shrewdly renamed the unsavory-sounding sink the "Imperial Valley." Prehistorically, and even as recently as 1891, natural floods had periodically broken through the Colorado River's bank near the Mexican border and switched the stream's outlet from the Gulf of California to the sink, at times inundating much of the region for a century or more. The California Development Company audaciously asserted an unauthorized water right to the navigable, federally controlled stream and without permission made a cut into the bank just above the Mexican border. In 1901, the company brought the first irrigation water into the valley via one of the abandoned, prehistoric riverbeds. The company's leaders subdivided public land they had acquired under various federal laws, four hundred miles of canals and laterals were laid out, settlers and speculators flocked to the valley, and the towns of El Centro, Imperial, Brawley, Holtville, and Calexico sprouted. The Southern Pacific extended a branch line transecting the region south from Niland to Calexico, fostering easier travel and communication and connecting the area to outside markets, and in the early 1900s the Imperial Valley underwent an agricultural boom, especially in alfalfa and cantaloupe production.[63]

Speculative to the core, dependent on short-term profits from selling land, water, and "water stock" (a type of water right) to new settlers, and unable to increase water deliveries fast enough to fulfill all the contracts it had made to the farmers it was luring into the valley, the California Development Company was under great pressure to maximize the flow of water through the old river channels and its hastily dug, poorly maintained canals, most of which were unlined and leaked profusely. Ignorant of the region's unusual geology and hydrography, the company's engineers had installed an opening in the riverbank that silted shut, and repeated dredging failed to keep it open. In the summer of 1904, with four miles of its main canal solid with silt near the river, crops withering in the fields, and its water customers near rebellion, the company desperately made another, large, ungated cut in the west bank of the Colorado and dug a new, large channel directly between the river and the canal system heading for the valley.[64] When annual floods coursed downstream the next spring, the Colorado predictably broke through the new, poorly designed cut, and the entire river started storming down its old channels and the company's irrigation works through the Imperial Valley and into the Salton Sink, which quickly became an expanding Salton Sea.

What followed was one of the epic struggles between humans and nature in the American West. By 1906, the Colorado River had flooded about 400 square miles around the Salton Sea, destroying not only irrigation works but the farms and homes of thousands, including entire towns. Most threatening to the region was the river's "cutting back"—a massive, explosive form of erosion by which the Colorado began carving new, below-sea-level channels for itself back through the Imperial Valley toward the original streambed at the rate of hundreds of yards per day. The unharnessed river imperiled the future of settlement not only in the Imperial Valley but also in the entire Colorado River valley as far upstream as Nevada. If the flood continued unchecked, it would probably be impossible to force the river back into its old outlet to the Gulf, the federal Yuma Project dam under construction on the river would be wiped out, and irrigating the valleys from the river—its bed now in a canyon one hundred feet below its past level—would no longer be economically feasible. Later, a Southern Pacific Company analysis concluded that a total of $103 million of river valley property was on the verge of annihilation.[65]

By late 1905, the Southern Pacific was well aware that vital railroad interests were at stake in the Imperial Valley. Dozens of miles of mainline from Indio and branchline from Niland to Calexico had been inundated and had to be moved repeatedly, six times in 1906 alone. Stations, shops, employee housing, yards, loading platforms, and expensive, in some cases irreplaceable, railroad water stations had been lost. A half-million acres of granted land was jeopardized, 60,000 acres already under the still expanding Salton Sea. The higher value that irrigation promised to bring to the lands of the railroad and other owners was also threatened, as was future rail traffic from the valley. The railroad had long known the environmental dangers inherent in irrigating the Imperial Valley via the Colorado's prehistoric streambeds into the Salton Sink. Since the railroad's arrival in the region in the 1870s, tracks had often suffered expensive damages when the river broke through its low banks.[66] The chronic flooding problem was one reason why the railroad maintained a staff of engineers at

Photograph, early 1900s, of the nine-foot drop in the California Development Company's main canal just after its diversion point on the Colorado River bank. A flimsy, wooden structure was all that shielded the below-sea-level Imperial Valley from the Colorado's periodic rampages. At the height of a flood in late 1904, the jerry-rigged "gate" collapsed, and over the next several years the gap widened and much of the Colorado's flow inundated the valley, wiping out towns, farms, and railroad facilities and forming the giant Salton Sea. Courtesy California Historical Society, San Francisco.

Yuma. In fact, it had been teams of Southern Pacific scientists, engineers, and surveyors who during the brief natural flood of 1891—an eerie precursor of the 1905 event—had located the break, traced the river's flow through the un-inhabited desert into the sink, and compiled the maps and reports analyzing the causes and extent of flooding for the U.S. Department of the Interior.[67]

Long before the 1905 disaster, the railroad had become disenchanted with the California Development Company. In 1903 and 1904, detailed studies and confidential internal discussions within the railroad's Land and Law departments had concluded that the company was highly speculative, underfinanced, prone to sloppy engineering and construction, wasted water, was "dissipating its resources in building electrical lines," and had contracted to irrigate 300 percent more land than its actual water supply would allow. The company also had located much of its main canal in Mexico, which made the entire region's water supply vulnerable to the vagaries of another nation's politics. The railroad had made concessions to the company, had given it options on its lands, and had agreed to build the branchline, acting land agent Charles W. Eberlein concluded, but if the California Development Company failed, as looked likely, "our people in southern California would simply burn up, the land go back to desert, and the money expended by the Railroad Company, building lines, be lost." Vital interests were exposed, Eberlein warned corporate executives in early 1904, and to save them the company would probably need to intervene and commit more of its resources in the future.[68] That is exactly what the railroad had to do.

When the California Development Company quickly exhausted its funds in a futile attempt to stem the rapidly worsening flood, it appealed for assistance to the Southern Pacific. Some executives, aware of the development company's weaknesses, advised against extending aid, but President E. H. Harriman, who was intrigued with the idea of large-scale irrigation although he knew little about this specific case, overruled them. In the spring of 1905, to protect its interests and the Imperial Valley's future, the railroad, which had already advanced funds to the development company and was unwilling to further trust a group it viewed as corrupt and incompetent, lent the California Development Company an additional $200,000 but only on condition that its capital stock be turned over to a trustee and the railroad be allowed to appoint its own officers and engineers to take charge of the company until the loan was repaid.[69] Epes Randolph, head of the railroad's southwest division headquartered in Tucson, assumed control of the company, while Southern Pacific engineer Harry T. Cory soon replaced the fired C. R. Rockwood as chief engineer in charge of closing the break.[70]

The saga of the Southern Pacific's combat against the Colorado—"that great chocolate dragon," as *Los Angeles Times* reporter E. H. Howe described it—is well known and need not be recounted in detail here.[71] For nearly two years the railroad put dam after dam in place across the breach, only to have yet another vicious flood wash it away and further widen the errant river's new channel. By late 1906, the opening had swollen to nearly a quarter of a mile wide and the entire 360-million-cubic-foot-per-hour flow of the river was emptying into the Imperial Valley. When yet another massive break and flood occurred in November 1906, the region stood on the brink of permanent ecological disaster. Lacking expertise, capital, access to technology, and personnel in the area, the federal government was helpless to act, particularly since much of the work had to be done in Mexico. President Theodore Roosevelt appealed personally to E. H. Harriman to continue the railroad's efforts and promised that the federal government would reimburse the company.[72]

For the better part of three months, the Southern Pacific's immense resources were focused in a feverish, around-the-clock assault on the river. The strategy was the brainchild of the railroad's civil engineer, Harry T. Cory. One of the

For fifty-two days in late 1906 and early 1907, thousands of Southern Pacific workers and hundreds of side-dump cars called battleships carried rock from across the West and closed the gap in the flooding Colorado River's bank, which by then had swollen to more than one thousand feet wide and forty feet deep, allowing 160 million cubic feet of water per hour to descend into the Imperial Valley. In February, the railroad finally stemmed the great flood that had threatened the valley for two years. Author's collection.

greatest earth-moving feats in human history, the battle mobilized an ethnically mixed army of thousands of Indian, Mexican, and European immigrant workers, fleets of river dredges, herds of mules pulling scrapers and wagons, and mile-long trains of 60-ton side-dump cars called battle ships, filling the breach with jagged boulders carved from new quarries the railroad opened up across the West. Before it was finished, the railroad moved four times more earth and rock than was done in the building of the Panama Canal, in one-sixtieth of the time. As the climax approached, all other traffic on Southern Pacific lines in the Southwest and southern California was stopped to make way for special trains carrying the fill. Personally supervising the work, the exhausted Epes Randolph suffered repeated tubercular hemorrhages that forced him to take refuge in his private car. Finally, after the railroad had spent about $2 million, the last boulders tumbled down the levee to seal the Colorado River break on February 10, 1907. This time, it was "for good, I hope," Harriman confided to his friend John Muir.[73] The region had been rescued by the railroad's supreme effort, but the Imperial Valley and its irrigation system were a shambles.[74]

The California Development Company was defunct, to the utter relief of almost everyone except some of its creditors and former owners. As the company's largest creditor—to a total of more than $1.3 million—and legally manager of its operations, the Southern Pacific reluctantly found itself in the water business, in fact running perhaps the largest and potentially most valuable, but unlikely to be profitable, irrigation project in the world. In the decade between 1905 and 1916, the railroad served as the de facto water agency, protecting its own land and traffic interests, as well as those of the more than 10,000 farmers and town-dwellers in the Imperial Valley. The company stabilized water-flow, rebuilt banks and levees, installed new, stronger gates, reduced siltation, restored and lined washed-out canals, and extended irrigation to new lands. In 1910 and 1911, and again in 1915 and 1916, the company, in repeat performances, fought other, though milder, Colorado River floods. Perhaps most important for the valley's future water development, the railroad, through its complicated 1905 contract with the California Development Company, had acquired even firmer control of that company's vital subsidiary Mexican counterpart company, which operated the California Development Company's main canal from the Colorado and supplied all the water to the Imperial Valley across the border to the north. The powerful railroad, which was also incorporated in Mexico, was able to keep landowners and the government in Mexico from seizing the canal, shutting the tap to the United States, and diverting the water to irrigate lands below the border. Thus, the Southern Pacific preserved the integrity of the Imperial Valley's irrigation system during the time of its greatest vulnerability, while it awaited long-term public ownership.[75] Under the railroad's water management, irrigated acreage in the valley expanded from 104,600 in 1906 to 225,000 in 1911 and 500,000 acres in 1915. By 1913, production of alfalfa had increased to 101,000 acres, barley to 79,000 acres, and cotton to 22,000 acres, and cantaloupes were also emerging as one of Imperial Valley's most valuable crops.[76]

A few contemporaries, and some later scholars following in the tradition of anti–Southern Pacific historiography, have read a conspiracy into the railroad's control of the Imperial Valley's water system between 1905 and 1916. Once again, the "Octopus," eager for profits and power in water monopoly, was seeking a permanent stranglehold on the valley.[77] The voluminous corporate manuscripts of the Southern Pacific and the records of the Imperial Irrigation District contain no evidence to support that theory, and indeed abundant evidence to refute it. From the moment it assumed management of the California Development Company in 1905, the railroad understood that the arrangement would be temporary, that it would lose money, and that, as soon as possible, control over the Imperial Valley's water supply had to be transferred to a public agency. As problematical as had been its dealings with irrigation districts, experience had long since convinced the company that, in large regions, private enterprise could not be counted on to provide stable, long-term management and expansion of irrigation or to resolve conflicts over water resources. The California Development Company was certainly the prime example. When approached in 1910 by local leaders promoting formation of an irrigation district to take over the development company's water system and work toward long-range order in regional water development, the railroad's officials readily agreed, despite land executive McAllaster's prediction that the railroad itself would have to finance the transfer.[78] Supported by the railroad and most residents and organizations in the valley but opposed by some owners of water stock and the California Development Company's lesser creditors, led by the company's bankruptcy receiver W. H. Holabird, the referendum to create the Imperial Irrigation District passed overwhelmingly in July 1911 by a vote of 1,304 to 306.[79]

Like other irrigation districts of the era, legalization was a long way from operation. Opposition to the district continued, with challenges to its legality, the constitutionality of the law under which it was formed, and its irrigation taxes. Most important, opponents tried to block its acquisition of the development company's water system, which after 1909 was technically under the oversight of Holabird as receiver but actually was being managed by the Southern Pacific. As soon as the Imperial Irrigation District was formed, the railroad entered into negotiations and indicated its desire to transfer its interests in the California Development Company. The Southern Pacific, with the superior financial interest as by far the largest creditor of the irrigation company, brought about a favorable resolution of complex conflicts among the valley's contending factions. In effect, the railroad acted as the irrigation district's agent, holding the defunct company's water rights, canals, and other properties intact while forcing creditors and even the Mexican government to accede to a transfer of the water company to the Imperial District. It pressured other creditors, such as the New Liverpool Salt Company, whose salt works the expanding Salton Sea had washed out, either to sell out their interests to the railroad or to agree to a sale of the California Development Company to the irrigation district. Railroad attorneys, land agents, and executives advised the irrigation district on contracts, bond issues, and political strategy, and the irrigation taxes the company paid on more than 100,000 acres of land in the district constituted the agency's principal income. To the end, Holabird maneuvered, unsuccessfully, to preserve the development company as a private enterprise and to keep the Imperial Irrigation District from gaining control of the valley's water supply.

After years of wrangling in the courts and the press, contending Imperial Valley interests finally conceded a resolution of their differences, at least temporarily. Prompted by the railroad's petition, in early 1916, a court ordered California Development Company properties to be auctioned. As had been prearranged between the irrigation district and the Southern Pacific, the railroad, the sole bidder, bought the defunct company for $3,875,000 and immediately resold the property, minus the company's Mexican lands, to the Imperial Irrigation District for $3,000,000 in the agency's problematical bonds. The railroad turned over $600,000 of the bonds to the New Liverpool Salt Company to satisfy its claims against the California Development Company and on September 8, 1916, discounted the remaining $2.4 million in bonds to the Anglo-California Trust Company for 84.5 cents on the dollar, or $2,028,000. An internal Southern Pacific Company audit in 1925 of its transactions regarding the California Development Company and the Imperial Irrigation District fixed the company's loss, even taking into account the value of the Mexican lands, at more than $1,600,000.[80]

During the turbulent decade and a half between the Imperial Irrigation District's acquisition of the California Development Company's water system in 1916 and 1930, when the onset of the Great Depression sharply curtailed the Southern Pacific's land sales and development work, the railroad continued to support the irrigation district's struggle to protect, manage, and expand the Imperial Valley's water supply. As ever, the erratic Colorado River delivered canal-busting floods in rainy years and water shortages and ditch-clogging silt during droughts. Though most of the Southern Pacific's grant in the region was still vacant and unproductive, water taxes on the railroad's lands provided the district a major means of support. As it had done when it had operated the development company, the railroad company frequently lent its equipment, civil engineers, and other employees to the irrigation district to assist in repairing, modernizing, and expanding the water distribution system. When the district extended the canals to encompass more lands, it benefited from rights-of-way and easements the railroad provided free of charge. By the late 1930s, the Southern Pacific had deeded to the district irrigation or drainage ditch rights-of-way across seventy sections of railroad land, in addition to one ten-mile-long, 150-foot-wide pathway for a major canal.[81] At the district's inception in 1916, the company eased the district's immediate legal difficulties by also granting it an easement allowing the flooding of railroad land-grant sections under and adjacent to the Salton Sea, which even after the great Colorado River flood continued to expand from surplus irrigation water and field drainage.[82] When former California Development Company parties, including receiver W. H. Holabird, persisted in their attempts to discredit the new irrigation district and regain control of the waterworks, the Southern Pacific supported the district's management with public statements, private advice, and behind-the-scenes political leverage.[83] Disputes between the district and railroad, particularly over continued submerging of Southern Pacific lands around the Salton Sea, generally were resolved privately by meetings of irrigation district officials and railroad land agents and attorneys in San Francisco or the Imperial Valley.[84]

Most important, the Southern Pacific used its influence in the irrigation district to assure long-term, stable water and land development in the Imperial Valley. Upon acquiring the canals of the California Development Company, the irrigation district inherited the development company's temptation to raise revenue by expanding water service to new lands beyond available, reliable water

supplies. As the major benefactor of the district, as well as its major landowner
and taxpayer, with representation on the district's governing board, the railroad
was a power in the valley. Although in the short run the railroad stood to gain
enormously from higher values for land-grant sections that came under irrigation ditches, the Southern Pacific, from the inception of its involvement with
irrigation in the valley, took the long-term view, identifying higher company
interests with cautious expansion of irrigation through reliable water supplies
and facilities and the resultant solid agricultural development. Railroad officials
such as land agent B. A. McAllaster were also aware that, because of uncertain
water supplies and profits for local crops, there was also only a limited market
for new irrigated land. The railroad's view was that it, and the region, had nothing to gain from rapid expansion and much to gain from the long-range, stable building of an efficient water and agricultural system. Thus, the Southern
Pacific resisted repeated attempts coming from within and outside the irrigation district to raise much-needed revenue by quickly putting more land under the ditches without augmenting water supplies. The railroad also resisted
the district's creation of new irrigated subdivisions, even though the tracts included thousands of acres of company land.[85] Instead, the railroad preferred
raising Imperial Irrigation District revenues by assessing higher water tax rates
on lands in the district, including its own. Accordingly, the railroad, as the largest
landowner in the region, gave its required approval for the irrigation district to
issue new $2.5-million bond issues for improvement of water facilities in 1917
and again in 1919, although they would mean sharply increased tax assessments
on railroad lands. In doing so, railroad officials reviewed and reaffirmed their
long-held policy in the Imperial Valley. According to McAllaster in a private
letter to his superior, corporate counsel William F. Herrin, the railroad's decision was guided by "the interest which the S.P. Company has in the proper conduct of affairs in the Imperial Valley, regardless of the amount of taxes it may
have to bear." The company, McAllaster continued, benefited especially from
"permanent betterments [in water facilities], which in the first place, will probably cost more money, but will result in less expenditure in the end."[86]

From 1923 to 1925, the Southern Pacific also supported the Imperial Irrigation District's attempts to encourage more profitable farming, first in 1923 by
lowering water charges and doubling water taxes, and then in 1925 by eliminating water charges altogether and raising water taxes still further. Simultaneously, the district increased the valuation of unsold Southern Pacific–granted
lands in the district between 400 and 500 percent, accentuating the dramatic
burden on the railroad of the district's new financing system. Nevertheless, the
Southern Pacific continued to favor the plan in the belief that the costs were
more than compensated by benefits accruing from an enhanced water supply.
The railroad stood to gain higher values for its granted land, which a 1916 com-

pany survey disclosed was selling at prices between $50 and $85 per acre. A solid Imperial Irrigation District also provided shelter from flood damage to the Southern Pacific's tracks and other operating property, as well as increased traffic revenues from the more valuable crops, such as cantaloupes, the company was promoting in the valley. According to a comprehensive company survey of traffic in the area during 1923, the railroad was annually shipping more than 50,000 carloads to and from Imperial Valley points.[87] Over the rest of the decade, the valley's traffic greatly increased. In the 1920s, the railroad initiated an aggressive campaign to advertise and sell its remaining lands in the region, including the introduction of a new and much more generous nineteen-year, low-interest loan contract to make it easier for farmers to do, in McAllaster's words, the difficult "pioneer work on undeveloped land in outlying districts."[88]

The Southern Pacific also worked to retain control of the Imperial Valley's water system in local hands. When some problems that had plagued the California Development Company continued after the Imperial Irrigation District's acquisition of the water system, Ellwood Mead, then head of the California Settlement Commission, some landowners in the valley, and the U.S. Reclamation Service launched a campaign between 1916 and 1919 to transfer management of the irrigation system from the local district to the federal Reclamation Service. Not only did the Southern Pacific, as the major landowner, adamantly refuse to sign the petition, it fought the scheme politically on the grounds that federal operation of the water facility was illegal, since part of it was in Mexico, that federal enforcement retroactively of the 160-acre limitation on irrigation water would wreak havoc among already operating farmers with larger holdings, and that the federal water would almost certainly cost farmers much more. Undoubtedly, the decade and a half of experience the railroad already had with what it considered incompetent management by the Reclamation Service of western Nevada's Truckee-Carson Project was also a factor in the railroad's opposition. The petition drive failed.[89] On the other hand, the Southern Pacific did favor and furnish important political force, engineering consultation, and transportation services to the Imperial Irrigation District, the Reclamation Service, and other parties for the Laguna Dam, All-American Canal, and Boulder Canyon projects, all large Colorado River improvement facilities completed by the Reclamation Service from the 1910s through the early 1930s to regulate the river, avert future disastrous floods, relocate canals to the Imperial Valley from the river onto American soil, and assure more reliable water supplies to the valley and the larger region.[90]

As for the Mexican lands of the defunct California Development Company, some 83,000 acres that had fallen to the railroad as part of its 1916 purchase of the development company, the Southern Pacific placed the property in the hands of its Land Department, which gradually sold the land. By 1956, eighteen thousand acres remained in railroad ownership, two thousand acres had been expropriated by the Mexican government, and another nine thousand acres were under contract to be sold. With much unsold and contracted land actually in the control of squatters, who could not be ousted because of the foreign ownership of the company, the railroad sold its entire interest in the remaining property to Aurora Burgos Smith, an American who also held Mexican citizenship and thus could legally own real estate in Baja California.[91]

The Southern Pacific's involvement in the early development of the Imperial Valley, its land, its water, and its agriculture, illustrates the important part the company, and railroads in general, played in early public irrigation in the West. Committed to public control of water, the railroad fought the 1905–1907 flood, kept the valley's water system intact during the turbulent times that followed, and capitalized the Imperial Irrigation District's acquisition of the failed California Development Company. It then furnished ongoing financial support to the infant agency after 1916 through payment of taxes and grants of easements and also supplied critical scientific, legal, and managerial expertise, technology, organization, mediation among contending parties, and political influence—in both the United States and Mexico—necessary to the building of one of history's largest and most successful irrigation systems and the subsequent transformation of the Colorado Desert. Particularly in the case of the Imperial Irrigation District but also in numerous other local districts in California between the 1880s and the 1920s, the Southern Pacific was truly a "midwife" at the birth of public irrigation.

10 "The Government Is Hard to Deal With"

FEDERAL RECLAMATION

Genesis of the Truckee-Carson Project

In order to provide the unprecedented financial and organizational resources to irrigate and develop vast stretches of the arid West, much of which was still in public ownership, diverse interests mounted a campaign in the late nineteenth century to create a federal reclamation program. Meeting for more than ten years in a series of irrigation congresses, western reclamationists, who rarely agreed with one another except on the single objective of obtaining federal assistance, were finally able to forge enough consensus and support to overcome the objections of eastern farm competitors and their political allies. In 1902, with the sponsorship of Representative Francis G. Newlands of Nevada, Congress passed the National Reclamation Act, one of the landmark pieces of federal legislation, especially as it came to affect the landscapes and waters of western states. The first project selected to be built under the new law, and also the first to actually start construction, in 1903, was the Truckee-Carson Reclamation Project. Nevada promoters, including Newlands and such close associates as Reno-based Southern Pacific Company land agent Robert L. Fulton, had been advocating such a project for years. In adopting the proposal as its pioneer project, the newly created U.S. Reclamation Service anticipated impounding the waters of the Truckee and Carson rivers, which flowed into Nevada out of the High Sierra to the west, in order to subdivide and irrigate some 450,000 acres of hitherto uncropped public and private land in the Great Basin desert about sixty miles east of Reno.[1] The Truckee-Carson Project immediately became important to the Southern Pacific Company's plans to expand its Nevada traffic and land business.

In many ways, the railroad's interests paralleled the visions of federal reclamationists. In the late nineteenth century, the railroad had come to strongly favor large, public water projects to transform land use, intensify agriculture, raise land values, and build rail traffic. Particularly, since its inception the company had promoted subdivision of unused or lightly used lands into small, owner-operated farms to encourage dense settlement, economic development, institutional and town growth, and hence, again, rail traffic. The Southern Pacific had operated its own land-grant settlement programs to foster that sort of society and resulting profitable railroad business across the Far West and Southwest.[2] Specifically, in this part of Nevada, the old Central Pacific mainline eastward from California toward the Union Pacific connection in Utah passed through the northern edge of the huge Truckee-Carson Project, and the railroad stood to gain new freight and passenger traffic from the farms and towns planned for the area. Also, vast tracts of unsold, indeed mostly arid and unusable, company land grant stretched in a nearly perfect checkerboard pattern east of Reno. Tens of thousands of acres of railroad land would be within the Truckee-Carson Project, interspersed in one-mile-square, odd-numbered sections with the government's even-numbered sections. Sharing the landscape and the potential gains from harnessed irrigation water, the railroad and the new federal agency, in the decades after 1902, were drawn into cooperating in the building of the first reclamation project.

But, the high hopes of irrigation planners and railroad leaders for rapid transformation of deserts into irrigated small-farm Jeffersonian Edens were quickly dashed in the Truckee-Carson Project. Typically of the Reclamation Service in its early history, social reform zeal and Progressive-era anti-business biases overcame sound science, economics, and public policy. Reclamationists were also too eager for quick results in large-scale projects in order to quiet criticisms— particularly in eastern agricultural, business, and political circles—that the controversial program was a boondoggle, a tremendous waste of public resources providing subsidies to a few rich western landowners. Early reclamation projects also suffered from a lack of precedent, or even simple scientific understanding, regarding the land, water, people, and economic realities they would have to work with. Moreover, federal engineers and bureaucrats—typified by Reclamation Service engineer and second director Frederick H. Newell—were emerging professionals from the East. Many harbored condescending attitudes toward westerners and "country" people generally and sometimes conducted themselves with a self-righteousness bordering on arrogance. Newell, who had much to do with the founding of the Truckee-Carson Project, according to historian Donald J. Pisani, treated many of his western critics with "thinly veiled contempt."

Reclamation officials ignored the repeated warnings of Southern Pacific land agent William H. Mills, his successor B. A. McAllaster, and other experts on land, geology, water, and engineering in the railroad's Land Department, who had accumulated decades of experience and data dealing with desert irrigation in the Truckee and Carson river valleys. Newell and other newly arrived, self-assured but often naive, federal irrigationists vastly overestimated the flow of

A Central Pacific work train building the main transcontinental line along the Truckee River, east of Truckee, photographed by Alfred A. Hart in 1867. In the early 1900s, the Reclamation Service's campaign to send immense floods of water down the river to relieve its drought-ridden Nevada irrigation project threatened the line and was one of several points of contention between the railroad and the federal agency. Author's collection.

both rivers and neglected to account for evaporation, canal siltation, known periodic drought cycles, and legal water rights held by prior agricultural, urban, and industrial users. They also located some water facilities on ground that leaked and selected poor, alkali-laden lands on which to start the subdivision. In a few years the Truckee-Carson Project, like some other early federal projects, ran out of water to meet the needs of farmers to whom it had sold land and water rights and was forced to halt subdivision and sales of thousands of remaining acres in the project, a practice it would have to repeat. Moreover, reclamationists misjudged the types, markets, and prices of crops that could be grown in the isolated region and, as a result, the profitability of the farms it was hoping to create as well as the ability of growers to repay the crushing debts the Reclamation Service imposed for land and water charges. Unsurprisingly, when there turned out to be insufficient water for the land that was being farmed, particularly during droughts, conflicts erupted with disappointed local interests, especially over prior water rights other users owned along the Truckee and Carson rivers. Crop choices and growing techniques also remained problematical, and irrigation blighted much land and groundwater with alkali and other pollutants. Many farmers thus failed and deserted the land, and most acreage in the project remained unsettled. In the face of defeat, in 1926, the scope of the project had to be scaled back to 87,500 acres, one-fifth the original plan. Some of these problems on the Truckee-Carson and other federal projects, however, persisted for decades after subdivision, and indeed to the present.[3] Renamed in 1919 the Newlands Project after the political father of the 1902 act, the project turned into an embarrassment not only to the Reclamation Service but to the entire cause of federally sponsored western irrigation.

In 1923, two decades after the inception of the Truckee-Carson Project, *Engineering News-Record* carried an article by Frederick H. Newell, career government engineer, prime architect and author of the 1902 Reclamation Act, second director of the U.S. Reclamation Service, and principal initial planner of the star-crossed western Nevada project. In rationalizing the project's disasters, Newell attempted to push a large share of the blame onto the Southern Pacific Company. Because public distrust of the Southern Pacific ran so deep and its leaders "at that time were not inclined to make . . . [the company's lands] available for reclamation and settlement, excepting under terms which were practically prohibitory," Newell claimed in the article, the government had not reclaimed lands within the limits of the railroad's land grant; "therefore it was necessary to go outside of the railroad land grant limits and take lands which in some ways were less favorably situated." Newell's scapegoating of the railroad infuriated Southern Pacific chief land agent B. A. McAllaster. Since his appointment in 1908, he had been working closely with Newell and the Reclamation Service to develop water and sell land in the Truckee-Carson Project, and his records contained extensive correspondence showing that his predecessors, particularly chief agent William H. Mills, had done likewise. Much of the Truckee-Carson Project, McAllaster knew, did indeed lie within the railroad's land grant area. Moreover, as McAllaster also noted in his letter of objection written to Newell shortly after the publication of the article, to his "certain knowledge" the railroad had cooperated with the Reclamation Service by offering its lands for sale at prices and terms approved by the project's managers and Department of Interior officials and by conveying to the federal government huge tracts of land for reservoir sites and canals "at nominal prices."[4]

McAllaster might well have added that over the project's initial two decades the expertise of the Southern Pacific's engineers, surveyors, and land and agricultural agents had also been integral to the forging of land and water policies of the Truckee-Carson Project that served as models for the Reclamation Service's other western projects. Also, McAllaster knew, many of the project's problems stemmed from the agency's own refusal to take the advice of knowledgeable railroaders and other local critics of early federal practices. Moreover, Newell himself had been directly involved in the negotiations, contracts, and correspondence that had combined the efforts of the government and the railroad in the pioneering federal reclamation project. Just why Newell had forgotten about—or had lied about—the railroad-government partnership at the birth of federal reclamation remains unknown, but the subject is also ignored by virtually all historians of western irrigation.[5]

The Railroad and the Reclamation Service

To the emerging Truckee-Carson Project and the larger federal reclamation movement in the early 1900s, the Southern Pacific provided valuable services paralleling its contributions at the same time to local irrigation districts, especially in California: capital, technology, transportation, organization, tracts of land on which to locate irrigation facilities, and a fund of experience, often localized, concerning water resources, settlement patterns, soil quality, land values, crop potentials, farming techniques, and marketing. There were important differences on the federal project, however. Unlike with the fledgling local water districts, struggling to establish themselves or to survive, the Southern Pacific had long done business with the federal government, particularly the Department of the Interior, the supervising agency of the Reclamation Service. That relationship had often, perhaps usually, been antagonistic, particularly in disputes over the department's transfer of, or failure to transfer, land-grant titles to the company. Also unlike the local districts, the Reclamation Service's mandate was not just to control and distribute water, but also to settle vacant public lands within the project, thrusting the government and the railroad into the unusual, and often tense, competitive relationship of being co-landlords and real estate developers. Federal reclamationists also possessed the added stability and power of congressional establishment, relatively immense and more secure funding, the ability to control land in addition to water, access to legal and engineering talent in the national agencies, and external loci of bureaucratic influence in Denver, national headquarters of the Reclamation Service, and Washington, D.C., site of the parent agency. As a result, on the Truckee-Carson Project, the Southern Pacific's role and control over events was relatively smaller, vis-à-vis the public's, than it was in the local irrigation districts. Nevertheless, the railroad's partnership was important, as well as precedent setting.

The Southern Pacific Company was a longtime supporter of large-scale, publicly managed irrigation systems to transform deserts into productive farms and cities. At first, as in California from the 1870s through the early 1900s, the railroad, influenced especially by head land agent William H. Mills, preferred state-managed projects. Eventually, the company came to appreciate the advantages of federal involvement, which could mobilize larger capital resources, vast tracts of vacant public lands to subdivide and settle, and access to water rights on the public domain. Federal involvement seemed as well to provide more reliability and potential for expanding water supplies quickly than did the chaotic local irrigation districts. Also, some potentially irrigable lands and their waters, such as in western Nevada and the Colorado River area, transcended state boundaries. Thus, beginning in the late 1880s, the Southern Pacific supported the national irrigation movement by organizing and paying for rail excursions by irrigationists and public officials to visit working projects. One early example was the 1889 national tour of the U.S. Senate Committee on Irrigation sponsored by the company's close political ally William Stewart, senator from Nevada. The Southern Pacific also provided reduced-fare tickets to attendees and assisted in organizing and publicizing annual International Irrigation Congresses, which began meeting in 1891.[6] As the pressure to secure federal aid intensified in the late 1890s and early 1900s, Southern Pacific president Collis P. Huntington joined Great Northern leader James J. Hill in committing his influence and the Southern Pacific's substantial financial contributions to the lobbying effort. Railroad support was important to the passage of the National Reclamation Act in 1902.[7]

Western Southern Pacific officials, however, disagreed on the wisdom of the specifics of the new law. Land agent Mills, the executive most responsible for dealings with the Department of the Interior, was at first leery of direct federal building and operation of irrigation facilities. His objections stemmed from his long schooling in California water politics and his commitment to small-scale farming and public management to assure equitable and efficient use of water supplies. Mills charged that the federal projects, especially because specific proposals called for the projects to recoup high construction costs by charging them back to the landholders, would be too expensive for actual small farmers and would thus delay settlement and increase farm failures. He also opposed centralization of power over western water in the hands of the federal government and predicted that, once in control, officials of the distant federal government would be insensitive to diverse western regional interests. Especially, federal authority would threaten riparian rights, the doctrine Mills had long believed provided his Sacramento Valley with essential protections of its water supply and quality and its capacity to control flooding. (On all these scores, as it turned out, Mills was prophetic.)[8]

A perennial delegate of the railroad or California's governors to the International Irrigation Congress, Mills was in the late 1890s and early 1900s one of the most important region-wide leaders of what historian Donald J. Pisani has called the "state party" of irrigationists, who continued to support the original goal of the reclamation movement, securing federal grants of capital, public land, and water to the states for the development of state-run water and land-settlement projects that would adopt balanced, comprehensive irrigation, flood control, and hydroelectric generation programs. By 1899, however, the state party had been overtaken by the nationalist faction led by George Maxwell and the National Irrigation Association, and the irrigation movement veered strongly toward federally operated projects, resulting in the final form of the 1902 congressional act. Still committed to state systems, Mills continued to agitate against the federal approach, opposed the Reclamation Act as it was being formulated and passed, and afterwards sharply criticized its weaknesses. He denounced the act as "a menace to the vested rights relating in any way to the irrigation systems of California."[9] Mills's concerns were shared by some other western Southern Pacific officials, including Charles W. Eberlein, an executive E. H. Harriman dispatched to California after his takeover of the company in the early 1900s to assure that land-grant policies came into step with those of the Union Pacific and other Harriman properties.

On the other hand, Mills's subordinate in the Land Department and the Southern Pacific's Great Basin regional land agent, Robert L. Fulton, strongly favored the National Reclamation Act and the Truckee-Carson Project. Fulton had for decades been one of Nevada's most outspoken proponents of irrigation and farm development as an antidote for the decline of the state's mines. Since the 1880s, he had worked closely with Francis Newlands in promoting various private and public plans to irrigate western Nevada with Sierra Nevada water that were eventually subsumed within the Truckee-Carson Project. "Under the wise statesmanship of a benign government," he wrote about the project in 1905, "the idle men and idle money of the country will be used to carry the idle water to the idle land."[10] Some Harriman Lines executives, including apparently Harriman himself, agreed with Fulton's more sanguine view of the Reclamation Act's potential to benefit the company. In fact, shortly after the passage of the 1902 law, the Southern Pacific, through Fulton, had informed Newlands and the Reclamation Service that the railroad favored the Truckee-Carson proposal as the pioneer project. At a planning meeting of Department of Interior officials in Reno, including Frederick H. Newell, Fulton assured them of Harriman's support and the railroad's intention to cooperate with the government and to sell its land in the project at low prices. The railroad's promises were important considerations of the Department of the Interior when it chose the Truckee-Carson to be the first project.[11]

Despite some difference of opinion among its leaders toward federal irrigation and specifically the pioneer Truckee-Carson Project, the Southern Pacific entered into a partnership with the Reclamation Service that at the critical inception of federal reclamation programs helped to shape their potentials and directions.[12] The partnership was a reluctant one, however. It might be characterized as a "love-hate," or perhaps an "approach-avoidance," relationship, with each party needing the cooperation of the other, but with each, because of past experiences, preconceived prejudices, and divergent interests, remaining wary of dominance by the other, while constantly searching for ways to modify the other's policies.[13] Working out a system of cooperation between the federal government and a huge railroad company, particularly during a time of supercharged anti-monopoly politics, was, after all, a complicated, unprecedented affair. Also, within each camp, neither of which was monolithic, varieties of opinion and style among individual leaders and at different levels of authority needed to be resolved, but sometimes were not. Both parties on occasion moved slowly and in a manner that appeared to the other as devious, aimless, self-interested, or contradictory. Because of the inability of the Southern Pacific and the Reclamation Service to reconcile their differences, the railroad's participation in the Truckee-Carson Project created conflict, and that conflict helped to establish limits to federal reclamation, especially on the reclamationists' initial assertion of complete control over regional water supplies.[14]

Cooperation in Early Planning and Construction

Despite the qualms of some executives, in the early decades of the Truckee-Carson Project, the Southern Pacific strongly supported the goals and most of the policies of the Reclamation Service and sought to help the project succeed, even though doing so compromised some railroad interests and caused short-term losses to the company. Cooperation worked most smoothly in the transfer of information and property from the railroad to the Reclamation Service for use in planning, construction, and operation of irrigation facilities. As it was doing for the local California irrigation districts, as well as for federal officials in the newly established national forests, the railroad's land and engineering departments routinely furnished the project's planners with maps, soil and water surveys, and other data. Between 1903 and 1906, the company and the agency easily reached agreements providing for free easements on the railroad's rights-of-way for irrigation facilities and other reclamation improvements.[15] The railroad extended a new spur line from the Central Pacific's overland route thirty miles southeast through the project to its major town, Fallon, to facilitate transportation into the isolated district, construction of farms, towns, waterworks, and later marketing of products. As the line was built, railroad engineers worked with project engineer L. H. Taylor to plan and then to install, at company expense, all the bridges, culverts, conduits, and other improvements associated with the spur line that the Reclamation Service would need for future canals and other facilities.[16]

Despite some initial reluctance from their western people, top Southern

On June 17, 1905, at the Derby Dam in western Nevada, the congressional Committee on Irrigation and Reclamation and an entourage of dignitaries turned water into the just-finished diversion canal to christen the Truckee-Carson Reclamation Project. The Southern Pacific Company paid for the festivities and dispatched the special train, steaming in the distance, that had carried the legislators from Washington, D.C. to witness this and other irrigation developments in the West. Courtesy Nevada Historical Society, Reno.

Pacific management in the Harriman Lines negotiated a 1905 agreement with the Department of Interior to lower the price on all Southern Pacific granted land the Reclamation Service needed for reservoirs, canals, and other structures to a nominal $1.25 per acre, less than one-third what the company considered the land to be worth even before water became available. Reclamation's first such purchase, in 1905, was for 11,500 acres in Churchill and Lyon counties. Once established, the agreement became precedent for additional purchases by the Reclamation Service over the next two decades, totaling many tens of thousands of acres in the Truckee-Carson and other western projects.[17] In fact, the Service bought so many parcels so quickly and its record-keeping was in such "considerable confusion" that it periodically had to contact the railroad's Land Department for exact lists and locales of previously purchased lands.[18] In one unusual case in 1912, the Reclamation Service requested quick title to a tract next to a large project construction camp. Enterprising souls had erected several houses of prostitution on railroad land adjacent to the camp, and the Service wanted immediate authority to shut the squatter settlement down. Eager to cooperate in rooting out immorality, perhaps even more relieved not to have to deal with the sinners himself, land agent B. A. McAllaster dispatched the agreement within days and the offending establishments were summarily removed.[19]

Disagreements over Land, Water, and Prices

Issues related to land sales, farm settlement, and water delivery proved more difficult to resolve. The Southern Pacific and the federal agency immediately became embroiled in a decades-long series of intermittent clashes, concluding in reluctant compromises of differences. Repeatedly, though, broken "treaties" revived disagreements and brought about yet more haggling. While important cooperative government-railroad programs emerged to further the work of the Truckee-Carson Project, some of them establishing pioneering models that the Reclamation Service extended to its other western projects, many potentials for economic and social development in the region went unfulfilled.

Cases in point were policies and procedures that needed to be developed for selling and pricing both public and railroad land within the Truckee-Carson Project. Despite his uncertainties with the concept of federal irrigation, William H. Mills, as he had earlier done with California's local irrigation district law, accepted the reality of federal involvement and committed himself to make the Truckee-Carson Project work. The company delegated Mills to spearhead its negotiations with reclamation officials on the Nevada project's site from its inception in 1903 until his death in May 1907. In effect, Mills acted as an intermediary, working with sometimes skeptical government and company officials to forge compromises and a measure of cooperation embodied in some of the project's most important early policies. Deeply committed to small-scale, intensive farming and an originator of the acreage-limitation principle on publicly supported irrigation projects, Mills readily secured the railroad's agreement to the Reclamation Act's rule requiring that government-subsidized water go only to tracts smaller than 160 acres and owned by local residents. The railroad itself, since the inception of its own land-grant development programs in the 1860s, had strongly favored sales to small-scale resident landholders and sold the great majority of its better agricultural lands in parcels between 40 and 160 acres.[20] Actually, as it turned out in practice on the Truckee-Carson Project, reclamation managers ultimately adopted an 80-acre limitation, at least for irrigable land, which the railroad also favored. The railroad's major pamphlet promoting farming in the project praised the 80-acre policy as a "wise limitation, based upon experience . . . [which] will rule in general farm practice in Nevada."[21]

However, at the instigation of Mills and his successor McAllaster, who had before coming to the Southern Pacific Land Department also been active in the campaign to secure federal support for western irrigation, the railroad did press for and get the Reclamation Service to extend the residency limits in the extremely isolated, unsettled region from the initial twenty miles to fifty miles. This was to allow cash-strapped buyers starting farms to also continue working at jobs in other communities in the first few years in order to pay off steep land, water-rights, and start-up costs. As that instance suggests, Southern Pacific objections to early Reclamation Service land and water policies in the project sometimes stemmed not only from the railroad's conflicting goals but also from the company's strong interest in making small farming more reliable and profitable in the problematical Truckee-Carson Project. The railroad criticized what it saw as the government's unrealistic, haphazard, contradictory, and inflexible bureaucratic policies—such as charging land buyers ruinously high water prices—that were actually undermining the larger objectives of encouraging small, resident farmers to benefit from federal land and water.[22]

While the initial irrigation facilities were being planned and constructed, disagreements and conflicts of interest between government and Southern Pacific officials regarding how railroad land within the project would be sold and watered required years of frustrating negotiation before agreements could be reached. Shortly after the inception of the Truckee-Carson Project, in May 1903, chief engineer Newell of the Reclamation Service met with Mills and pressed him to get the Southern Pacific to voluntarily cede title to its lands within the project back to the Department of the Interior. Newell favored consolidating and subdividing railroad lands with public lands and opening them up together to entry by settlers, at nominal cost and subject to the acreage and residence requirements of the Homestead Act of 1862 and the ten-year water-facility repayment period of the Reclamation Act of 1902.[23] Although Mills, a strong proponent of the homestead principle, at first did not appear to object to the proposal, higher Harriman Lines executives quickly rejected the plan, which would have stripped the company of control of the land and any profits from sales. Moreover, such a give-away of land was illegal, prohibited by the terms of land bonds the railroad had sold as part of mortgages on its various land grants.

In late 1903, Morris Bien of the Reclamation Service contacted Harriman Lines land official Charles W. Eberlein with a counteroffer. The railroad would retain technical ownership of granted land while allowing the government to distribute it on the same terms as homesteaded land. The Southern Pacific also refused Bien's proposal. Such a "scheme," as railroad officials called it, not only shared the defects of the first proposal, it was from the railroad's viewpoint worse, since while the settler was waiting out the ten-year period of residence and water-charge repayment it took to get clear land title from the government, the railroad would still be responsible for annual property taxes due local governments. Experienced Land Department officials also believed that distributing land only through homesteading would actually retard development of the project. Over decades of land-grant management, the company had found that settlers generally preferred buying from the railroad to homesteading government land. The company's low prices and its long-term low-interest mortgage plans appealed to farm-builders, while the absence of a waiting period to receive title allowed them to mortgage the land to raise start-up capital. Moreover, long involvement with the Department of the Interior had made railroad leaders skeptical that the government could ever successfully complete the Truckee-Carson Project as planned, settle the land and foster solid agricultural development in the region, or, once placed in control of the property, be trusted to protect the railroad's interests in its land grant. "We ought to know by this time that the Government is hard to deal with in land matters," Land Department executive Eberlein put it succinctly in advising New York Harriman Lines executives against the Reclamation Service's proposals. "A partnership with it would, in my opinion, be most undesirable."[24] Nevertheless, because more was at stake than just the Truckee-Carson Project, Eberlein recommended in another letter to Harriman's assistant, Julius Kruttschnitt, that the company had to come to terms with the government, however cautiously, and develop a set procedure for selling land belonging to Harriman companies in the Nevada and other federal reclamation ventures. "It is important that the policy of our land departments toward Government irrigation projects be fixed at the present time," he wrote, "as whatever concession is made by the Southern Pacific in this case will be insisted upon by the Government as a precedent in all future transactions."[25]

During the next several years of negotiation, it was primarily William H. Mills who worked out that land-sales agreement. The arrangement ultimately not only governed Southern Pacific relationships with the Department of the Interior on the Truckee-Carson and other reclamation projects but became a model for sales and irrigation of privately held lands generally within the projects. Mills's efforts, clearly aimed at furthering the social and economic ideals of the 1902 reclamation law, brought the Southern Pacific into alignment with virtually all of the initial demands made of it in 1903 by Morris Bien of the Department of the Interior and helped to get national reclamation off to a more productive, secure start.[26]

In a series of meetings and correspondence, Mills and L. H. Taylor, supervising engineer of the Truckee-Carson Project in Nevada, arrived in 1906 at a draft agreement for what Mills termed sale by the railroad of its lands in a manner not subordinate, but "analogous," to the public's lands. The plan provided for efficient cooperation between government and company in the shared goal of encouraging dense, small-farm settlement while carefully preserving the autonomy and divergent interests of each party. The railroad would retain title and control of its land, advertise and sell the land, and keep any profits. But the company agreed to subdivide and sell land in conjunction with, and subject to the policies of, the government, in order to promote compact settlement and efficient distribution of irrigation water to one tract at a time. The Southern Pacific would also enforce in its land-sales contracts all the Reclamation Service's rules limiting acreage, prohibiting speculation in the land, and requiring buyers to reside on or near the land, to apply and pay for water rights from the government, to pay all taxes, and to use at least one-half the land for irrigated farming. The government would also retain rights-of-way in all railroad land-sales contracts for irrigation canals and other waterworks. At first, Reclamation Service engineer Taylor favored a complex form for the railroad's land-sales contract, which would have required all railroad-land buyers to join a special water users association that would have to acquire water rights collectively from the project. Mills, however, worked with the company's legal department and produced a simplified form that eliminated the unnecessary and expensive intermediary organization so that railroad-land buyers, like settlers on public land, would apply directly to the government for water rights. Pleased with the agreement and Mills's revised form for the land-sales contract, Taylor, advising Mills that he judged them acceptable to the secretary of the interior, signed the agreement and the proposed sales contract on August 25, 1906.[27]

Mills, working again with Taylor and other Reclamation Service leaders, secured the approval of hesitant Harriman Lines executives and the secretary of the interior. When, as a condition of approval, the secretary required that the railroad adopt a resolution assenting to the social and economic goals of the National Reclamation Act and committing its lands to be included for irrigation within the Truckee-Carson Project, Mills wrote the resolution and sent it to higher executives. The board of directors of the Central Pacific Railroad, meeting in Salt Lake City a few days later on September 8, 1906, approved Mills's agreement, sales contract, and resolution. Among its provisions, the resolution declared that the company's object was to "secure the settlement, occupation and cultivation of such lands, to secure and perpetuate density of population by subdivision of the land in accordance with the system of subdivision adopted by the Government for the disposition of public lands, and all to the end that population and wealth may be conferred upon the locality and that traffic upon the lines of the Central Pacific Railway Company may thereby be created."[28] Through its attorney in Washington, D.C., the Southern Pacific then submitted the documents to the U.S. Geological Survey and the secretary of the interior.[29] C. A. Hitchcock gave his final approval of the railroad's resolutions and the land-sales agreement and contract on November 3, 1906. In his letter to the Reclamation Service and the Geological Survey, Secretary of the Interior Hitchcock praised the railroad's proposal to "dispose of its lands . . . in a manner analogous to that in which the public lands are disposed of." Separately to the Southern Pacific Company, he extended "the full appreciation of the Department" for its "cooperative action" to carry out the reclamation law of 1902.[30]

For his part, Mills reviewed his actions to Harriman Lines executives in New York and pointed out the advantages to the company of cooperation with the federal government to distribute land in the irrigation projects. "We have," he told them, "discovered a simple comprehensive method of selling the land and of having no-one between ourselves and the purchaser . . . and of acting in perfect accord with the Government and protecting every interest of the Company."[31] The Southern Pacific's land-sales procedure and contract with buyers, developed to adjust railroad and government interests in the Truckee-Carson Project, became a model for federal cooperative administration of land sales by private parties within the Truckee-Carson and other western projects, which was important to those programs' success and to the general cause of irrigation development. Bringing the Southern Pacific and the Reclamation Service to work together in the Truckee-Carson and other reclamation works was a fitting climax to the decades-long labor of William H. Mills to link land subdivision and public water management in the promotion of economic development and democratic, small-scale farming in the American West. The editor, conservationist, and railroad land agent would die six months later.

The 1906 land-sales partnership in the Truckee-Carson Project proved to be close, but also tempestuous. The accord turned out to mark not the end, but only the beginning, of conflict between railroad and government. Perhaps intentionally, in the interest of securing quick approval, mention of the prices the railroad would charge for its lands had been left out of the agreement. When the plan was applied in late 1906 and early 1907, as some of the project's first subdivisions containing railroad land were beginning to receive water, controversy immediately broke out over the prices, requiring Mills to do more mediation. At first, in December 1906, Department of Interior officials in Washington insisted that, for all its thousands of acres in the project, the railroad establish a standard, fixed price, not to exceed $2.50 per acre, the approximate figure being charged for government land. Moreover, Washington reclamation officials issued an unrealistic ultimatum: if the company did not put its first 4,000 acres up for sale at $2.50 per acre or less and guarantee that the tracts would be sold and settlers in place by the spring of 1907, the project would cut off water to railroad land and divert it to other lands. Advertising and selling that much land within only a few months would have been impossible, of course, especially since the Reclamation Service had completed few subdivisions including railroad land, nor would it guarantee to buyers that it would ever deliver water to railroad land. Despite repeated appeals from the Southern Pacific over several years, local reclamation officials had also refused even to divulge which of the railroad's more than 20,000 acres of irrigable land in the project would be eligible first to receive water for irrigation, or when, thus blocking the company from preparing and selling any of the land.[32]

Mills attempted to convince Southern Pacific officials to agree to the $2.50 price. Assuming all along that the company would be able to charge an average of about $4 per acre, higher executives balked, however. Eventually, in early 1907, Mills was able to work out a compromise calling for "fair" but low prices, which at first appeared to be to everyone's satisfaction. As he had been trying to do for some time, Mills convinced local reclamation officials—by personally leading them on examination tours of the Nevada countryside—that much of the railroad's property was worth more than $2.50, while some isolated, infertile, or elevated and rugged land was worth less. The best way to value the land and to assure that all would be taken and used for irrigation without excessive empty tracts, he demonstrated, was to price each individual parcel according to its fertility and potential productivity, as the railroad had always done in its land grant. Project engineer Taylor also agreed to Mills's suggestion that the project immediately survey and grade the quality of the railroad's and the public's intervening land and subdivide it, not according to the government's prior rectilinear survey grid as was being done outside the railroad's land-grant area, but into parcels of varying size and shape oriented with respect to irrigation ditches and land contours. In that way, each parcel would contain about eighty acres of good irrigable land, along with a share of the additional marginal land. Railroad land would then be offered for sale according to soil quality and irrigability, at various prices from $1.25 to $15 per acre, to be approved by the Department of the Interior, with the average about $4 to $10, much less than irrigated land was worth in the project.

Although the Reclamation Service delayed another several months, which Taylor attributed to short funds and personnel on the project, the surveys were eventually finished and price lists drawn up and agreed to by Mills and local reclamation officials by late April 1907. To facilitate and complete the deal, Mills made a final visit to Nevada, a grueling two-week-long trek across the desert with project officials and Southern Pacific land experts to mutually inspect, grade, and price, on the spot, 11,000 acres of railroad lands. Exhausted, in fact fatally ill, Mills returned to San Francisco in late April and was confined to his house. He continued to conduct some Truckee-Carson land business from home for the next month, but he would never return to his office. He died in late

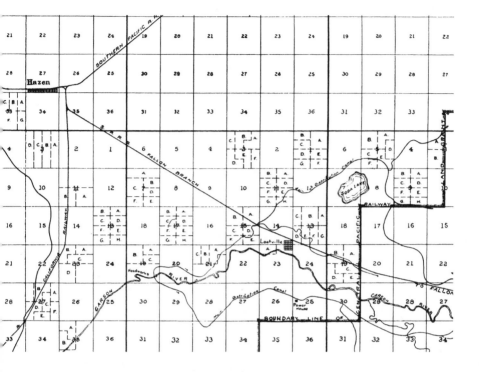

Plat of a portion of the Southern Pacific Land Department's original subdivision of its land grant on the odd-numbered sections in the Truckee-Carson Reclamation Project. Developed by land agent William H. Mills and approved by the U.S. Department of the Interior, the railroad's plat carved out many small parcels (section subdivisions are designated on this map by capital letters A through H), of irregular shapes and sizes, to account for variations in soil fertility, terrain, and access to irrigation ditches. Most farms were about eighty acres; some were slightly larger. From *Railroad Land for Sale: Irrigable Lands within the Truckee-Carson Project for sale by the Central Pacific Railway Company* (August 1908), author's collection.

May. That spring, Harriman Lines executives readily assented to Mills's plan and reconfirmed Mills's authority to speak for the company.

For reasons never made clear, Department of Interior officials in Washington dragged out the government's approval of the plan, the price lists, and the issuing of water rights for railroad land for more than a year. This was despite Harriman Lines vice president William D. Cornish's attempts to speed a decision by traveling from New York to the nation's capital for confidential but inconclusive discussions with Interior leaders. During the delay, various Department of Interior officials gave the Southern Pacific contradictory information. Some, particularly local project managers, assured the company that variable, low prices would be acceptable; some, particularly bureaucrats in Washington, continued to insist on a fixed price, $2.50, in the interest of uniformity across all of the government and railroad land in the project. On the other hand, even Newell, chief engineer of the Reclamation Service, maintained, at least in 1905, that as long as the railroad disposed of the lands to actual settlers and enforced the project's acreage and residence limits, the land sales should be "without any limitation as to price the railroad may put upon them."[33] In the interim, contrary to the railroad's intentions and despite its frequent entreaties for approval of its price lists, Southern Pacific lands in the Truckee-Carson Project remained without water and off the market. As the delay stretched into many months, some Department of Interior and Reclamation Service officials in Washington, including particularly Newell, lost track of progress of the negotiations, and apparently of the railroad's correspondence and the fact that it was their own failure to approve the railroad price lists that was stalling railroad land sales, and began spreading a story that it was the railroad's slowness to act and lack of cooperation that were retarding land sales and development of the project.[34]

As he chafed at the delays in early 1907, Mills, who was as knowledgeable as anyone about western land, agriculture, and irrigation, investigated in detail actual conditions on the Truckee-Carson Project. He studied water resources available for irrigation, land and water prices being charged by the Reclamation Service, current practices of the few farmers who had taken up land, and marketing potentials for likely crops. Mills despaired of success. He calculated minimal land costs, the Service's steep, mandatory water charges ($26 per acre), and typical farm start-up expenses, including the costly land leveling and preparation of ditches and pipes necessary for irrigation. Mills's investigation led him to the conclusion that settlers would require more than $3,200 in capital each just to survive the first year, even if they received the land at $2.50 per acre, figures that Nevada reclamation people agreed were accurate. Practically no settlers, the Reclamation Service reluctantly admitted to Mills, had such backing, or creditworthiness, and it was clear to him that few were likely to survive long enough to pay off land and water charges, let alone make a profit. He found that very few settlers were starting farms in the project, and even fewer were working the land seriously, efficiently, and profitably. Instead, they grew crops that harmed the land or were too low in value to recoup water and land charges, and they cultivated and watered in ways that destroyed soil fertility and hastened alkali pollution. Many never attempted any improvements other than to meet minimum project requirements while apparently holding the land on the chance of future speculative sales. Mills sent discouraging reports to superiors at Harriman Lines offices in New York, asking them to use the company's influence to get the Department of the Interior to alter policies and laws so that small-scale farming could succeed, particularly to lower water charges or at least to amortize repayment over a much longer period.[35] "The Government's scheme is utterly wanting in enterprise and wisdom," he wrote. Only two hundred persons, few of whom were "the better class of settler," had taken up government land in the project, and little guidance was given to new farmers, many of whom lacked experience in irrigated desert agriculture. Most "were merely subsisting on the ground," and "there is no evidence of great improvements, of growth of the enterprise, or energy."[36]

Mills himself repeatedly called the fundamental social and economic contradictions inherent in Truckee-Carson policies to the attention of local reclamation managers and higher government officials. Particularly, he pressed them—unsuccessfully—to increase the possibility for successful farm-breaking by lowering water charges drastically, doubling the time settlers were allowed to repay them to twenty years, and forgiving settlers all land and water charges in their first two years. If the government acceded, in return he offered to defer all land payments for purchasers of railroad land for their first two years; and he would do his best to get higher company executives to offer some land free to settlers.[37]

As his faith in the foundering Truckee-Carson Project dimmed, Mills placed his hopes on a demonstration farm, which he called "a key to the whole situation." He developed the idea and secured the quick and enthusiastic support of local project officials and the president of the University of Nevada, in Reno. Harriman Lines executives were reluctant at first, but once convinced by Mills of its benefit to the railroad, they committed to the plan and lobbied strongly in Washington for immediate implementation. The Southern Pacific would build, operate, and finance the farm, on a donated eighty-acre tract of fertile railroad land near Fernly, straddling and visible from both sides of the branch rail line into the project. In conjunction with the Reclamation Service and the university's college of agriculture, with whom the railroad had maintained close relationships since the institution's founding in 1874, experiments would be conducted in new crops and cultivation techniques suitable for the region. Also, settlers and prospective land buyers would be trained in local farm methods,

New farm and irrigation ditch on the Truckee-Carson Project, ca. 1905. Courtesy Nevada Historical Society, Reno.

and the lush growing fields would serve as a powerful advertisement of irrigation's potential. Once again, though, higher Department of Interior and Reclamation Service leaders in Washington stymied the plan, at first refusing to deliver any water to the proposed farm on the technicality that, since the railroad owned more than 160 acres in the Truckee-Carson area, the delivery would violate the congressional act of 1902. Deaf to the pleas of the railroad, local agricultural scientists, and even Reclamation Service officials at the site that such a prohibition was clearly not the law's intention, Department of Interior officials sat on the plan for months. By the time they reversed themselves and approved the railroad's use of the water, Mills had died and no one was left to push the demonstration farm aggressively within the company. The Southern Pacific's Land Department entered a brief period of confusion and drift under Mills's ineffectual replacement, F. C. Radcliffe, and the national Panic of 1907–1908 temporarily sapped company resources.[38]

In a way, it mattered not. Only a few months later, the Interior Department reversed itself yet again, this time rejecting the railroad's demonstration farm plan completely, although Southern Pacific leaders still wanted to go ahead. Apparently leery of relying on the railroad and other local people at the university, the Reclamation Service instead established a demonstration farm of its own, in league with the U.S. Department of Agriculture. The farm proved unsuccessful; the Service located the farm on poor, alkali-tainted land, and all the first crops failed. Effective experimentation and instruction in suitable growing techniques on federal irrigation projects would not become a reality for several more decades.[39]

Finally, in May 1908, Frederick H. Newell, now director of the Reclamation Service, wrote to the Harriman Lines' vice president William D. Cornish about the stalled railroad price lists and sales, admitting that "we seem to be going about in a circle." The matter, Newell explained, "has been discussed so often by so many different men that I appreciate the confusion that may arise through taking the matter up again with others." Newell directed that all correspondence henceforth would go through his office "so that we may avoid confusion in this matter."[40] In the late spring and summer of 1908, with Mills no longer guiding company negotiations, Cornish and Department of Interior officials in Washington finally hammered out a formal agreement on prices. The subdivision, variable pricing, sale, and watering of railroad land in the Truckee-Carson Project would go forth in a manner "analogous" to government land, essentially following the lines Mills had worked out in 1906 and early 1907. As sections of the Truckee-Carson Project were opened up for sale and water deliveries, local reclamation managers would survey, subdivide, and grade the railroad's land; the railroad would price the land parcels according to mutually agreed-upon criteria and then submit the price lists to the Department of the Interior for approval. Upon approval of the lists, the railroad's land department would sell the land using the contract form Mills had worked out in 1906, with buyers subject to the requirements of the 1902 law and the project's procedures. Periodically, the railroad would inform the project's managers of specific land sales and buyers, so that the Reclamation Service could ensure that they did in fact apply for water contracts. The railroad would deliver land contracts to buyers and complete the sales only after the Reclamation Service had certified that buyers had received water rights. Once this process was completed, the Department of the Interior agreed, purchasers of railroad land would be furnished water on an equal basis with holders of public land.[41]

In the summer of 1908, the Southern Pacific began an aggressive advertising and sales campaign. Ads in newspapers and magazines, as well as several widely distributed pamphlets, praised the opportunities available for irrigated farms on the Truckee-Carson Project, and promoted the settlement of railroad, as well as government, lands. Initially, because of lingering effects of the nationwide financial panic and especially public awareness of the severe problems on the Truckee-Carson Project, particularly the water shortage, railroad land sales were slow. The first sale was not made until September 10.[42] The crop year of 1908 turned out to be more successful on the project, however, and, testifying to residual public optimism that the project's prospects would brighten in the future, sales surprisingly picked up quickly. By September 1910, the Southern Pacific had sold 2,140 acres, all in tracts smaller than 160 acres, with most about 80 acres or less. The railroad enforced all Reclamation Service requirements, including the prohibition against the sale of more than one tract in the project to any one person. The partnership between company and government appeared to be working efficiently to start irrigated farms on railroad land in keeping with the socioeconomic goals of federal reclamation. From mid-1908 through the early autumn of 1910, routine and generally amicable cooperative give-and-take business was conducted by the two parties.[43] So optimistic about the future of the partnership was the Southern Pacific that as late as 1911, the Land Department began to work with Francis G. Newlands, now U.S. senator from Nevada, to plan and push through Congress a second Nevada reclamation project containing railroad land, this one north of Reno and relying on water from a proposed enlargement of Donner Lake in the California Sierra.[44]

A Strained Partnership

Already by 1910, however, the Truckee-Carson Reclamation Project, and with it the government-railroad partnership, was deeply troubled. The fundamental farm finance, cultivation, and environmental problems that had discouraged William H. Mills several years earlier continued unabated, indeed worsened markedly. Many, perhaps most, settlers were failing within only a season or two on the land and abandoning both government and railroad land in droves, often vanishing and leaving behind unpaid land, water, and tax bills. A damning, widely publicized report by a scientist at the Nevada Agricultural Experiment Station both documented the project's deep-seated difficulties and discouraged new farmers from taking up lands. The hardest blow to the project's reputation and future came in September 1910. Because of a severe water shortage brought about by long-term drought and the Reclamation Service's practice of opening up more land than it could reliably irrigate, the Department of the Interior, without notifying the Southern Pacific, precipitously suspended all new land entries in the project and, to conserve water, ceased issuing new water rights to purchasers of railroad land, including to persons who had already bought land. In effect, because of the terms of the 1906 and 1908 agreements, the secretary of the interior's order blocked all further railroad land sales.

Not a single acre was sold between September 1910 and the fall of 1914. The new policy, of course, also violated the Department of the Interior's 1908 promise that, in issuing water rights, it would treat railroad land buyers the same as others. Not until 1914, when the Reclamation Service completed the Lahontan Dam on the Carson River to increase water storage in the project, did land entry and the issuing of water rights resume.[45]

Nor did additional water from the new dam soothe relations between government and railroad. B. A. McAllaster, who took over negotiations with the Truckee-Carson Project upon his appointment in September 1908, was a worthy successor to William H. Mills. Experienced in western land, water, and agricultural matters from a long prior stint as chief land agent of the Union Pacific, McAllaster quickly became influential within the railroad on resource policy and proved to be an effective, flexible mediator with outside interests. Nevertheless, relations with the government became increasingly strained. As conditions on the project deteriorated, beginning even as early as 1910, a characteristic Department of Interior response was to resolve its problems by seeking advantage over the Southern Pacific, going so far on occasion as to attempt to appropriate railroad interests and property in the region. Most important, federal officials tried to make up their persistent water shortages by minimizing, delaying, and on occasion prohibiting irrigation of railroad lands. Astonishing turnover in personnel also weakened the government's grip on affairs in the Truckee-Carson Project, particularly between 1910 and 1917. The Department of the Interior frequently terminated employees or transferred them back and forth among various western projects, positions within the projects, or levels of administration on the projects or at offices in Portland, Denver, and Washington, blurring institutional memory, fragmenting leadership, and hindering coordination between various levels in the Reclamation Service and the Department of the Interior, and even on the project site. Between 1914 and 1917, for example, more than a half-dozen different project managers and "interim managers" succeeded each other in charge of local policies on the Truckee-Carson, with three men serving in 1917 alone; there were just as many different project engineers handling technical matters.[46] Repeatedly, reclamation officials misplaced records, lost track of agreements the agency had made with the railroad, reversed policies of their predecessors, neglected to inform the company of important decisions affecting railroad interests, and failed to respond to the railroad's inquiries, price lists, or requests for clarifications of vacillating policies. Often, they resorted to contacting the Southern Pacific Land Department for replacement documents, and McAllaster and other Southern Pacific people were required time and again to inform some reclamation officials of what others were doing or what the Service's own policies and pertinent laws were. Frequently, the railroad did not know who was in charge of what position in the Reclamation Service, and its inquiries to officials who had recently departed had to be answered by newly arrived persons who knew little about previous discussions and decisions. The railroad's agreements with predecessors had to be rediscovered or redrawn.[47]

When Lahontan water began to flow in September 1914 and the issuing of new water rights resumed, the Reclamation Service at first refused to provide railroad land buyers with water contracts. When McAllaster objected that this prevented the railroad from disposing of its land and discriminated against railroad land buyers in violation of the 1906 and 1908 agreements, new reclamation officials countered that they knew of no such agreements with the railroad. After McAllaster provided them with copies, they reluctantly, and with much delay, began to issue a few permits, but they also reduced the amount of railroad land eligible for future irrigation water from 12,000 to 2,000 acres.[48] Lahontan water did little, however, to quench long-standing shortages. To make up some of the shortfall, periodically over the next several years, local reclamation officials ceased issuing water contracts to buyers of railroad land, usually without informing the company, leaving innocent buyers high, and literally dry, and the railroad's land business in chaos. When some new subdivisions containing railroad land opened up for irrigation, the project prohibited the delivery of water to railroad sections altogether.[49] Department of Interior officials in Washington also attempted, unsuccessfully as it turned out, to get Congress to pass a law making the Reclamation Service's lien on lands in the project for water charges superior to the first mortgages the railroad held on its lands on time-payment contracts.[50] Because settlers continued to abandon farms, this would have amounted to a forced confiscation of much of the best, most irrigable railroad property in the Truckee-Carson Project. Finally, and most seriously for the future of the project, in 1914, to recoup some added costs of building and operating the Lahontan Dam and other needed facilities, the government raised the price of water rights from $30, already difficult for typical farmers to meet, to $60 per acre, or $4,800 for a typical farm containing eighty irrigable acres. Shortly afterward, in 1915, the Reclamation Service informed the railroad that it was revoking its approval of previous railroad land price lists. Its land prices had to be reduced, the railroad was told, in order to compensate for increased farm start-up costs caused by the government's higher water charges. This, in effect, transformed the small profits the company was making on its land sales into income for the project.[51] The Southern Pacific's objections to all of the above actions between 1914 and 1918 were routinely ignored or the Reclamation Service delayed responding, in some cases for a half-year or longer. The Service eventually reversed some of these policies, on occasion approving some railroad land price lists and reopening water rights to railroad land buyers, only sometimes to change its mind once again a few months or years later.

Partnership did produce some small progress, however, in reducing farm start-up costs for farmers. When it reopened land sales after Lahontan Dam started operating in the fall of 1914, the Southern Pacific further liberalized its standard time-payment plan, reducing the down payment on land from 20 to 10 percent, decreasing the annual interest rate on the remaining debt from 7 to 6 percent, and increasing the time of repayment from five to ten years. Only the interest on the remaining principal was due each year, with the first year's interest forgiven. The entire remaining principal was due only at the end of the tenth year, the assumption being that by that time the farm would be successful and the owner able to repay the loan or at least, with land values higher, to easily refinance the land. As in other Southern Pacific land-grant areas, almost all settlers purchased using the time-payment plan. In effect, the Southern Pacific was advancing farmers nearly all the capital necessary to purchase railroad land, bringing their initial land costs as low as or lower than on public land acquired from the government.[52] Then, in 1918, responding to frequent entreaties since 1906 from railroad land agents, the Reclamation Service reduced the money farmers had to pay for water rights in early years and doubled the time of complete repayment from ten to twenty years. After a down payment of 5 percent, farmers paid the rest in fifteen annual installments, but starting only after the fifth year. For all intents and purposes, the Reclamation Service began waiving water-rights charges for the first five years of cultivation.[53] Such examples of constructive cooperation notwithstanding, the relatively easygoing agreement and exchange of information between railroad and government during the project's earlier years were replaced by nearly constant confusion, conflict, delay in selling and settling railroad land, and, very important from the company's perspective, uncertainty.

Unsurprisingly, railroad land sales in the Truckee-Carson Project faltered. The Southern Pacific's prices remained low, with most irrigable parcels selling for between $4 and $7 per acre. A few tracts were above $10, but some were below $3.[54] Nevertheless, between 1914 and 1917, the company could sell, and buyers secure water rights for, only about 1,500 of the railroad's more than 23,000 irrigable acres in the project, for a total of about 3,600 acres since 1908, when the Reclamation Service first authorized sale of railroad land. Meanwhile, the longer the great majority of the railroad's land in the project could not be placed on the market and remained unsold, even according to the Department of the Interior, the more that increases in the Service's water charges and the local governments' higher property taxes depressed land sales.[55] Ironically, it was the railroad itself that was stuck for annual property taxes on the unsold acres, which rose dramatically as land values in the region increased with irrigation and development, cutting into the railroad's profits.[56] No complete figures survive, but the railroad's costs in selling and administering its lands in the Truckee-

Carson Project probably exceeded its small profits, and its land business there was running at a loss. Increased freight and passenger traffic, however, did compensate somewhat. As Charles W. Eberlein had warned higher company executives back in 1904, from the railroad's perspective, the government proved, indeed, to be "hard to deal with in land matters."[57]

The Parting of Ways

Relations between the Southern Pacific and the U.S. Reclamation Service reached a nadir in 1918 and 1919. During 1918 and through the middle of 1919, Truckee-Carson Project managers persisted in reneging on the 1906 and 1908 agreements by refusing to treat railroad land buyers equally with others in acquiring water rights and by failing to approve railroad price lists, or even to estimate a date when they might be approved. Only a handful of company-owned farms, no more than nine, were declared eligible to be sold and irrigated in 1918. By that time, some railroad land price lists had waited as long as thirteen years for approval. Then, in a public notice on October 1, 1918, the Service announced, without prior discussion with the Southern Pacific, that it was eliminating almost all remaining railroad lands from its list of lands to be irrigated in the future. After the fact, the Service justified these actions to the railroad's Land Department by citing the chronic shortage of water and its need to quiet controversies and lawsuits caused by opposition to the Service's assertion of a right to use Lake Tahoe as a storage reservoir up the Truckee River. The agency also claimed that it needed first to create a local public drainage agency to siphon off the rapidly rising groundwater and runoff from excess irrigation in the project, which was threatening to drown crop roots and pollute soil with alkali.[58] All of these problems, McAllaster and other Southern Pacific leaders were well aware, were unlikely to be resolved for many years, if ever. The Southern Pacific had reached the end of its patience.

In May 1919, Truckee-Carson Project managers announced approval for the Southern Pacific to sell only three of its many additional parcels but pressed the company to liquidate those particular farms immediately so that the government could also settle neighboring public lands to recoup its expenses for water connections in the district. This and other government communications at the time also complained that it was the railroad that was too slow to sell its lands. After consulting with higher executives, the obviously exasperated McAllaster wrote a curt reply on June 4: "Inasmuch as the United States Reclamation Service has required approximately thirteen years to say that it is ready to furnish water for the particular land referred to, Central Pacific Railway Company may be excused if it consumes sixty days within which to make necessary examinations and attend to the detail work necessary for placing the land upon the market." McAllaster went on to break off all further cooperation with the project in land sales. He announced that the railroad would immediately begin pricing its remaining lands on its own and putting them on the market without approval and consultation by the Reclamation Service. "Such lands will be sold as opportunity offers without any requirements being made by the Company that the purchaser obtain a water right from the United States and he may make such application . . . at his option when the Reclamation Service is ready to consider same."[59] When startled government officials pleaded with the railroad not to abandon the 1906 and 1908 agreements, McAllaster countered to project manager John F. Richardson that cooperation worked both ways and that the government had repeatedly refused to live up to its promise to provide water and to treat railroad land buyers equally. In the meantime, the railroad had been forced to withhold valuable land from the market, pay taxes, and incur other losses. To the Service's concern that the railroad's independent land sale would threaten the government's control by further fragmenting private land in the project among many owners, its ability to open up compact subdivisions in an orderly manner, and its power to enforce its requirement that those farmers who benefited from free use of groundwater and surface water seeping from the project's irrigation works had to buy water rights, McAllaster responded that in the future the Reclamation Service could solve those problems on its own. Indeed, the railroad's land agent charged Reclamation Service officials with lying when they said there was insufficient water to irrigate new railroad land. Company investigators had discovered that, at the same time as officials were claiming water shortages, they were connecting subdivisions without railroad lands to the waterworks, liberally providing water rights to non–railroad land buyers, and selling irrigation water to anyone, even if they had not acquired water rights or abided by acreage limitations or other technical project requirements.[60]

The railroad-government partnership to develop water and settle land along the lower Truckee and Carson rivers dissolved in June and July 1919. At a time of farm optimism caused by rising profits due to World War I crop-price increases, remaining irrigable Southern Pacific land in the project (that year renamed the Newlands Project) sold rapidly, although the company had raised prices about one dollar per acre. Within a year, vast tracts, perhaps as much as 20,000 acres, had been taken up by private parties, including virtually all potentially irrigable railroad land in the project. In the early 1920s, the company did retain 35,900 acres, but almost all was too infertile, uneven, elevated, or remote from ditches ever to be irrigated, or was reserved as future canal or reservoir sites. Unfortunately for the democratic social goals of federal irrigation, the Southern Pacific ceased acting as agent for the Reclamation Service in enforcing acreage, residence, and other legal and administrative requirements. Almost all the railroad's new farm units were small, less than 160 acres, and included about 80 acres of irrigable land, but a few were from 320 to 640 acres. While most railroad buyers lived in Fallon and other nearby communities, many were from as far away as Idaho. Buyers often made multiple purchases, with many tracts also passing to women, presumably wives or daughters, with the same last names as purchasers of adjacent farms. Undoubtedly, an unknown number of buyers also already had farms on government land in the project. Obviously, people were speculating in railroad land.[61] After 1919, the Reclamation Service was forced to contact the railroad's Land Department for the names of buyers so that it could track them down after the transactions and convince them to pay for water rights and abide by other project rules.[62]

A Productive Partnership

While it existed, the partnership between the Southern Pacific and the Reclamation Service had been important to the inception of federal irrigation. The railroad assisted in promoting and underwriting the movement on behalf of the concept of federal involvement in large-scale irrigation, as well as passage of the Reclamation Act of 1902. The company's promise of support figured strongly in the government's choice of the Truckee-Carson as the pioneer project. To that project, the Southern Pacific contributed information, expertise, free rights-of-way on company property, land at low cost for irrigation facilities, and some capital for infrastructure improvements such as bridges, culverts, and particularly the railroad's branch line into the district.[63] To further land settlement on that and other projects, the Southern Pacific fashioned a model agreement for selling and pricing private land in reclamation projects in a manner "analogous" to public land and cooperated with the Reclamation Service from 1906 through 1919 to bring railroad land sales under the jurisdiction of federal officials and into line with the project's residence and 80-acre requirements—which themselves owed their very existence in part to land agent William H. Mills's long-term campaigning for democratic, small-farm building. The railroad then acted as an enforcement agent of those and other project rules. The Southern Pacific also advertised and promoted government and railroad land sales in the Truckee-Carson area. Under this system of mutual administration, a modest amount of railroad land, perhaps as much as 4,000 acres, was sold, settled, and watered as small farms during the years before the company abandoned the agreements of 1906 and 1908. The railroad, through its low land prices combined with an inexpensive mortgage plan, capitalized initial costs for farmers, and pressed the government to increase farmers' chances for success by also, though belatedly, lowering high start-up costs by reducing water-rights charges in the first years and extending the repayment period.

Nevertheless, serious problems continued for reclamationists, railroaders, and settlers on the Truckee-Carson Project. Largely because the government failed to uphold its end of the bargain and to meet the railroad halfway, opportunities were missed to get federal reclamation off to a more secure start. The Reclamation Service's delays, indecision, confused organization, and haughtiness greatly reduced the extent of railroad land that could have been incorporated within the project, took away the government's ability to control the timing and pattern of settlement of a large amount of prime railroad land, and scuttled the railroad's proposed experimental farm, which might have encouraged sounder cultivation methods. Perhaps most important, the Southern Pacific, after 1910 but particularly after 1918, became skeptical of the future of the Truckee-Carson Project and the competence and trustworthiness of the people who ran it. Once converted from avid supporter into aggrieved, suspicious critic, the Southern Pacific performed perhaps its most powerful influence on the direction of reclamation, blocking the federal government's takeover of Lake Tahoe as a storage reservoir—thus permanently limiting the scope and success of the Truckee-Carson (Newlands) Project. In a larger sense, the Southern Pacific helped local people to begin imposing limits on the government's assertion of virtually unlimited water rights in the West.

The Lake Tahoe Controversy and Limits for Federal Reclamation

In the late nineteenth and early twentieth centuries, the Southern Pacific became more interested in Lake Tahoe, one of the West's largest, deepest, clearest, and most beautiful lakes. The lake sits six thousand feet high, nearly filling a forested basin in the Sierra Nevada straddling the border between California and Nevada. Before it exits California eastward into Nevada, the Truckee River flows into and then out of the lake, which stores, naturally, many millions of acre-feet of clean mountain water. The railroad benefited from increasing tourist travel to the lake, particularly after 1899, when the lumbering, lake-shipping, and resort-owning Duane L. Bliss family built the Lake Tahoe Railway and Transportation Company. The fifteen-mile narrow-gauge line connected the old Central Pacific overland mainline depot at Truckee up the Truckee River to the Blisses' Tahoe City steamboat pier at their luxurious, soon-to-be-completed Tahoe Tavern hotel. Tourists now had easy access to the burgeoning resorts of the lake's north shore, and by steamer around the lake. As with Monterey, Yosemite, Sequoia, Crater Lake, and other scenic attractions near its lines, the Southern Pacific began to feature Lake Tahoe in its travel promotional litera-

ture, and the company even contemplated investing in lakeside resort properties.[64] To foster natural scenic preservation as it had done in Yosemite, Sequoia,
and other places along its lines, the railroad in the late 1890s and early 1900s,
spearheaded by land agent William H. Mills, attempted to get Congress to create a giant national park in the region. When that proved unsuccessful, Mills
and his company had a hand in the establishment of the Tahoe and adjacent
national forests, which accomplished at least partial protection.[65] The Southern Pacific's emerging, lucrative passenger and freight trade in the district, and
much else, on the other hand, was jeopardized by the designs of the U.S. Reclamation Service on Lake Tahoe water.

Within a few years of beginning the Truckee-Carson Reclamation Project
in Nevada, downstream along the Truckee and Carson rivers, the Reclamation
Service ran out of water to meet the needs of farmers to whom it had sold land
and was forced to halt subdivision and sales of thousands of remaining acres
in the project. Under pressure from Nevada leaders and higher government
officials worried about the damaged reputation of the new agency, reclamation
managers looked west to Lake Tahoe as their "big fix." Beginning as early as
1903, the Reclamation Service moved to seize control of the lake's water and
the small, low dam at Tahoe City, California, across the lake's outlet into the
Truckee River, to erect a much higher dam, and to convert Lake Tahoe into a
vast irrigation reservoir.[66]

Formidable obstacles stood in their path. Reclamation Service officials at
first failed to comprehend the plan's implications. Implementation would have
necessitated a complete rearrangement of the environmental, as well as the social, economic, political, and legal, structures that underpinned life in the extended Lake Tahoe–Truckee River region. Drawing the lake down to meet
the Reclamation Service's greatly increased downstream needs would have annually exposed a wide "bathtub ring" of mud and boulders around the lake,
stranding beaches, piers, and resorts high and dry, rendering navigation dangerous if not impossible, and ending summertime recreational use.[67] No matter, because raising the dam and increasing water storage in the winter and
spring would quickly erode the shoreline and swamp much of the narrow plain
around the lake, destroying the beaches, homes, towns, and resort businesses
anyway.[68] Moreover, as studies by the Southern Pacific and the Lake Tahoe
Railway demonstrated, periodically sending the vastly larger quantity of water
down the narrow canyon of the Truckee River to reach the Truckee-Carson
Project would drown the riverside rail and industrial center at Truckee as well
as a dozen or more towns, many mills, factories, hydroelectric plants, and other
businesses dependent on the river, successful farms already operating adjacent
to the river in the Truckee Meadows just west of Reno, and parts of downtown Reno. The likely property destruction and damage or condemnation

The Lake Tahoe Railroad along the Truckee River between Truckee and Tahoe City, ca. 1910. Because its roadbed and bridges were never more than a few feet above the river's normal water line, the railway's very existence was jeopardized by federal irrigators' plan to convert Lake Tahoe into a giant reservoir. The railroad, with its allied Southern Pacific Company, led the opposition to the Bureau of Reclamation from the early 1900s into the 1920s. Courtesy Jim Johnson of Heritage Graphics, Grass Valley, California.

claims against the federal government, as well as the potential opposition, would be astounding.[69]

Nevertheless, the Reclamation Service forged ahead. Officials attempted to cajole or threaten lakeshore property owners to deed over their lands or to give permission to flood them, introduced bills into Congress to legalize the actions and to provide funds for construction and for land and business condemnations, and sought to force the dam owners to sell the dam to the government. By 1915, a condemnation suit, a settlement with the dam company, and a court decision—the famed Orr Ditch Decree apportioning water rights in the Truckee River—did give the Reclamation Service theoretical control of the existing dam, two feet of the lake's depth, and the river's flow out of the lake.[70] The Service immediately discovered in 1916, however, that even its raising and lowering of the vast lake by a mere two feet caused lakeshore and downstream flooding and property damage, unleashing another flurry of lawsuits against the government. Moreover, because of the prior rights of downstream users to the flow of the

Truckee River, the Service could rarely use its two feet unless it could cut the lake's natural rim, which it lacked the legal right to do.

From the beginning, protests erupted from lakeshore and riverside property owners, downstream water users, and the state of California, which had never recognized any right of Nevadans to the water of Lake Tahoe. Lawsuits and prohibitive injunctions stymied the Reclamation Service. Ultimately even some other federal authorities opposed the project, including the U.S. Attorney General's office, which emphatically and repeatedly advised that the scheme was an illegal, in fact unconstitutional, assault on established property rights and the sovereignty of the state of California. Also opposed were the U.S. Geological Survey, which judged the science behind the proposal as preposterous; chief forester Gifford Pinchot and the Department of Agriculture's U.S. Forest Service; the Army Corps of Engineers, whose mandate it was to protect the lake's navigability; the secretary of war; and even some higher officials in the Reclamation Service's parent agency, the Department of the Interior.[71]

From the early 1900s through the 1920s, local opponents, led by the powerful Bliss family and its Lake Tahoe Railway, were able to block most of the Reclamation Service's moves. They organized lakeshore property owners in 1913 into the Lake Tahoe Protective Association, instituted lawsuits and secured injunctions, protested to the secretary of the interior, defeated most funding bills in Congress, and on occasion resorted to vigilante action against the Reclamation Service. The state of California also filed suit in 1912 to halt the Service's plan, and the case dragged on into the 1930s.[72] Nevertheless, desperate for Lake Tahoe water, the Service persisted with a single-mindedness bordering on megalomania, justified apparently by its sense of righteous crusading.[73] As against the interests of upstream water users, the Reclamation Service countered by asserting the superior right of agricultural irrigators. "To the extent that we have a prosperous farming community in Nevada dependent upon increase of Tahoe storage," wrote Reclamation Service counsel John Truesdell to all major federal reclamation officials in 1918, "the summer resort and pleasure interests at the Lake will have to yield."[74] Some of the Service's leaders, in fact, went as far as to lay secret plans to act independently without legal authorization to quickly dredge and blast open the rim of the lake at the dam to create a de facto enlarged reservoir and then to resolve the political and legal fallout later in litigation. Such a strategy, if nothing else, would force Congress to provide funds for condemnations.[75]

The basic outline of what has come to be called the "Lake Tahoe Controversy" has been known for some time.[76] What has been overlooked by nearly all previous authors is that standing behind the opposition, and bearing a good share of the responsibility for the ultimate outcome of the conflict, was the Southern Pacific Company. From the railroad's viewpoint, not only was its growing, lucrative Tahoe tourist business and the larger traffic potential of the Lake Tahoe–Truckee River region threatened but also the company's own vital properties and facilities. The Central Pacific's old transcontinental road, still the lifeline to the East for Southern Pacific operations in central and northern California and the Pacific Northwest, ran eastward over Donner Pass, dropped sharply into the town of Truckee—where the company had located its most important Sierra crossing staging yard, water and fueling facility, and forest firefighting headquarters. From Truckee, the line continued east, paralleling the banks of the Truckee River, sometimes only a few feet above flood level, for the thirty miles down the steep, narrow river canyon to Reno. The route had been challenging to engineer and expensive to construct in the first place, and rebuilding it on higher ground also would greatly lengthen and steepen the line and make operations over it much costlier. Dismantling the critical Truckee yard and staging facilities—originally built on one of the only sizable stretches of level land in the region, again only a few feet above the flood-level of the Truckee River—and relocating it probably far eastward to Reno, would have increased the Donner Pass run, already one of the most arduous railroad hauls in the world, from twenty miles to more than fifty miles. Enormous strategic business advantage would have shifted to the Southern Pacific's traditional rivals for north Pacific Coast traffic, the Union Pacific, the Northern Pacific, the Great Northern, the Canadian Pacific, and the upstart Western Pacific, which in 1909 completed its own line just a short distance north of the Southern Pacific's route through the Sierra and into California. Without doubt, the single most valuable piece of property jeopardized by the Tahoe reservoir proposal was the Southern Pacific's mainline through the region.[77]

The Southern Pacific combated the Reclamation Service's proposal from its inception. Not that the railroad opposed the use of water for economic development. Not only had the Southern Pacific long supported many local irrigation movements, since 1902 the company had been cooperating closely with the Service itself in the planning, building, and sale of public and railroad land in the Truckee-Carson Project. Through a subsidiary, the Donner Lumber and Boom Company, the railroad had even built and for many years owned and operated the Tahoe outlet and Donner Lake dams to regulate water for downstream lumber mills and hydroelectric plants serving Reno.[78] But the company was dead set against the wholesale assault on the ecology and economy of the entire Tahoe-Truckee region planned by the Reclamation Service. Resisting repeated overtures by the Service to convert the railroad into an ally, William H. Mills, B. A. McAllaster, and other company leaders criticized the plan on scientific, economic, and environmental grounds and called on the government to abandon it, or at least scale it back. In one typical statement of the company's position, land agent McAllaster pleaded in 1919 with the manager of the

Truckee-Carson Project not to tamper with Lake Tahoe, which he praised as "one of the noted beauty spots of the Sierras" and increasingly a vacation destination for people all over the nation. "I think it true beyond all question," McAllaster warned, "that any attempt on the part of the Secretary of the Interior to so deal with the waters of Lake Tahoe as to destroy, or in anywise lessen the beauty of the Lake, will be strongly opposed by the people not only of California and Nevada, but of the United States in general." Intent on securing the railroad's support, reclamation leaders responded by inundating McAllaster with appeals for the company to change its mind. One Nevada irrigation official countered McAllaster's defense of the lake's natural qualities with a clear statement of the reclamation movement's sense of Manifest Destiny. "It is my firm belief that rain and snow water were primarily intended by the Creator to fructify our fields," he lectured the railroad executive. "And since God Almighty in creating the earth, took pains to form the mountains and valleys so as to cause Lake Tahoe to overflow into Nevada, He meant for us to have it, and the attempt by some California residents, to contravene God's design to me looks pitiful in the extreme."[79]

McAllaster remained unmoved by the appeal to divine will. Privy to extensive information gathered over nearly two decades by himself and other Southern Pacific experts on the region, McAllaster in October 1919 wrote a long report to his superior, vice president and chief counsel William F. Herrin. McAllaster reviewed the company's long and tangled relationships with the Truckee-Carson Project, including the collapse a few months earlier that year of the company's 1906 and 1908 agreements with the project to sell railroad land for irrigated farms. He also detailed Reclamation's broken promises and false assurances to the railroad that it had no intention of operating Lake Tahoe as a major storage reservoir and instead sought only minimal management over a small amount of water to alleviate rare drought conditions. McAllaster had acquired copies of confidential agency documents clearly demonstrating that, contrary to their toned-down public statements, reclamation officials actually were striving for virtually complete control of all of Lake Tahoe's water and fully intended, at least eventually, to take as much as they physically and legally could. Indeed, the agency had from the beginning proposed to do just that, and even in 1919 and 1920, despite nearly two decades of criticism and opposition to the plan, Reclamation engineers still were operating on the assumption that the proposed, enlarged Tahoe dam would send at least 2,500 second-feet of water down the Truckee River, even though they knew that property destruction occurred at 1,000 second-feet and that 1,600 second-feet was the maximum of known natural floods. If the reservoir were built, in the words of a Service engineer, "condemnation and payment of damages are therefore unavoidable."[80] To get around the limits on moving water imposed by the lake's natural rim and the narrow

Truckee River canyon, the Service, in fact, periodically contemplated a plan to tunnel from Nevada west through the Sierra to capture the lake directly from its bottom. In his October 1919 report, McAllaster advised Herrin that the Reclamation Service's enabling bills pending in Congress, which contained no limits and would in effect authorize the secretary of the interior to drain Tahoe, "would seriously injure the Lake as to scenic and resort attractions." Normally cautious and tentative in making policy recommendations to top company executives, McAllaster this time bluntly told Herrin that "in my opinion these Bills should be defeated."[81]

Although refraining from confronting the Reclamation Service publicly, the Southern Pacific worked behind the scenes to halt the reservoir plan. In addition to lobbying against the bills in Washington, the company, in cooperation with the Bliss family and its Lake Tahoe Railway, a quasi-subsidiary narrow-gauge line with which the Southern Pacific had always maintained a close relationship, repeatedly encouraged the lakeshore and downstream property owners to continue refusing to sign over their holdings or flooding rights to the Reclamation Service and to institute lawsuits if necessary.[82] Providing some measure of the success of the Bliss family and the two railroads in stiffening property owners' resistance, as of 1919, despite years of pressure and threats from the Reclamation Service, only thirty of 285 lakeshore property owners had given deeds or permission to the government to flood their lands to control the lake's level.[83]

Then, in a bizarre sequence of events in 1925 and early 1926, the Southern Pacific and its allied Lake Tahoe Railway outflanked the Reclamation Service. Government officials had always seen the Lake Tahoe Railway as the major barrier to success in their scheme.[84] The narrow-gauge ran virtually at the river's natural flood level in the canyon between Truckee and Tahoe City. The line was already plagued by periodic flood damage to roadbed, tracks, and bridges, while logs, brush, and other floating debris caused by the release of extra water down the river increasingly collected at bridges, constricting the river and aggravating the destruction.[85] What was worse, in order to exit up out of the river canyon and reach its terminus about a mile farther at the company's steamboat pier, the railroad was forced by the extremely narrow strip of level land at the river's outlet on the lake to have some of its tracks follow the beach and a low trestle just above the lake, with waves at high water literally lapping between the rails. Also crammed onto that strip were a small turntable and roundhouse essential to sending trains back to Truckee.[86] In addition, the railroad and its owners, the Bliss family, were the most aggressive and visible leaders of the opposition, openly encouraging and coordinating the complaints of lakeshore owners, the Reno hydroelectric utility, lumber mills using the Truckee's water, the California State Chamber of Commerce, and California congressmen, as well as the Southern Pacific behind the scenes.

The Lake Tahoe Railroad's rail and steamer terminal, a few feet above lake level, at the pier of the Tahoe Tavern Hotel, Tahoe City, 1908. In the mid-1920s, as part of its fight against the government's reservoir plan, the Bliss family sold out its interests to the Southern Pacific. Until the 1940s, the railroad operated the branch line, steamboats, and the hotel and resort. Courtesy Nevada Historical Society, Reno.

Clearly, from the Reclamation Service's perspective, the Lake Tahoe Railway had to go. For many years, the Service pressed the railroad to rebuild its line and terminal on higher ground, which, given the extreme ruggedness of terrain and narrowness of the Truckee canyon, was probably impossible from an engineering standpoint and certainly beyond the financial resources of the tiny, unprofitable company.[87] At first, the Service tried to maneuver the railroad to rebuild at company expense, but when the Blisses rebuffed them, the government offered first to share and then to pay the entire cost. The Blisses countered, however, that the government's estimated cost of relocation, $100,000, was only one-fifth of what would be necessary. Reclamation officials preferred, though, to take over the railroad and tear up its tracks, and had threatened the company repeatedly with condemnation and had introduced legislation in Congress, so far unsuccessfully, to provide authorization and funds. Not only would condemnation eliminate the irksome railroad, it would isolate the lake, discourage further resort development there, and intimidate other opponents. In the words of the Truckee-Carson Project's counsel, condemnation "might help somewhat to clear up the situation around Lake Tahoe and to convince the landowners and others that the Government means business if we immediately start suit to remove this railroad and press same vigorously."[88] The Lake Tahoe Railway, however, categorically refused to sell out, except at a price of $1 million, a prohibitive amount the company undoubtedly set only to mock the federal agency. Closing its line to Truckee would have stranded its lake steamers and Tahoe Tavern resort, just completed in 1901. Besides, the Bliss family had for decades resided in the Tahoe region, was committed to its future preservation as a natural lake, and opposed in principle its conversion into a storage reservoir. Particularly, the Blisses believed—justifiably—that the Service, once it had pushed the railroad out of the way either by relocation or condemnation, would immediately move to cut Tahoe's rim in order to increase the potential flow of irrigation water.[89]

As of early 1925, with a long-term drought raging in Nevada and the beleaguered Reclamation Service still lacking sufficient water to operate its downstream project, the conflict remained unresolved. In fact, continuous litigation had prevented any Tahoe water from being used on the Nevada project since 1919, and in the language of the Reclamation Service's annual report, land settlement and irrigation development on the recently renamed Newlands Project were being "retarded." In charge of the dam but able to use the lake as a reservoir only minimally and intermittently, and even then with resulting lakeshore and downstream damage, the agency remained determined to seize complete control of the lake's water. The opposition, however, led by the Bliss family and the Southern Pacific, was still powerful enough to forestall the reservoir plan.[90]

Not all the details of what happened next are completely known, but it is clear that either the Lake Tahoe Railway or the Southern Pacific, or both, devised a plan to trump the Reclamation Service, and then both companies cooperated to implement it.[91] As a narrow-gauge line unable to exchange rolling stock with the Southern Pacific, the Lake Tahoe Railway had labored under the extra costs, time, and inconvenience of unloading and reloading all passengers and freight at Truckee. For some time, the railway had contemplated converting to standard gauge, but it lacked the capital. All along, the Reclamation Service had fought the gauge-conversion because it would have raised the profitability and value of the railway greatly, far higher than the pending condemnation bills would allow and higher than Congress would ever be likely to appropriate for a condemnation suit. Flood damages to the standard-gauge railroad caused by the Service's operation of the lake dam would also multiply. Reclamation officials threatened the railway with an injunction if it tried to widen the gauge before a condemnation lawsuit could be launched. Then, in 1925, the Lake Tahoe Railway and the Southern Pacific engaged in a fast, but complicated, transaction. Through a subsidiary, the Southern Pacific bought the Blisses' Tahoe Tavern resort, the lake's most elegant. The company was now in the resort business on the lake. As a key to the bargain, the Bliss family, obviously eager to rid itself of a money-losing property, leased the Lake Tahoe Railway to the Southern Pacific for one dollar per year, with the proviso that the larger company immediately convert it to standard gauge. Upon completing the conversion, the Southern Pacific was to be given an option to buy the railroad for an additional one dollar. Stunned at having to confront a much more powerful foe and faced with the possibility that their reservoir plan was about to be scuttled, Department of Interior officials fumed and renewed their threats of injunctions against the gauge-conversion. When the Southern Pacific applied in the summer of 1925 for a permit to use some Reclamation Service land in the conversion, Secretary of the Interior Hubert Work opposed the project and refused to grant the permit, unless, that is, the company also relocated the line to higher ground.[92]

Undaunted, the Southern Pacific moved decisively to upgrade the line essentially in place, raise its traffic capacity, earnings, and value manyfold, and at the same time, block the Reclamation Service's Tahoe-reservoir plan. Determined to build anyway, without using Reclamation land, the Southern Pacific secured quick approval for conversion from the Interstate Commerce Commission. Then, in a dramatic feat reminiscent of the Central Pacific's epic race to beat the Union Pacific across the Great Basin in the 1860s, in a matter of weeks in early 1926, company engineers redesigned the line and construction crews realigned rights-of-way, widened bridges, beefed up roadbeds, and installed new heavier rails on the standard gauge. On May 1, 1926, Southern Pacific trains started operating up the river canyon between Truckee and Tahoe City and onto the rail-steamboat terminal pier at the Tahoe Tavern. Shortly thereafter, the Southern Pacific began offering through-trains to Lake Tahoe for tourists directly from San Francisco and other points. In 1927, the Bliss family transferred ownership of the railway to the Southern Pacific.[93]

The railroad and the Reclamation Service, now faced with the reality of a functioning, more valuable standard-gauge line blocking its path, did soon reach a measure of accommodation on some issues. In the fall of 1926, after a series of conferences among Southern Pacific and Lake Tahoe Railway leaders, Reclamation officials, and Nevada irrigationists, the Department of the Interior and the railroads struck a bargain that acknowledged the status quo. Reclamation acceded to a right-of-way across government lands at Lake Tahoe to accommodate more efficient location of the standard-gauge line as well as to a lease to the railroads on sixty-four acres, at $4,000 per year, for year-round resort use by the Tahoe Tavern Hotel and for additional trackage for the new Pullman service the Southern Pacific was introducing. The railroads, in turn, signed an important contract clause releasing the United States from claims for damages between Truckee and Lake Tahoe, when such damages were caused by releases or discharges of water from the lake.[94] Railroaders, resort operators, and federal reclamationists had agreed to coexist, but implicit in that agreement was the assumption that Lake Tahoe would never become a gigantic irrigation reservoir.

The back of its reservoir plan broken by the railways, the Reclamation Service never was able to mount another serious challenge to Lake Tahoe water, beyond the two feet of depth that in 1915 it had technically gained control over but could rarely use.[95] Also in 1926, the Service, in a sense conceding defeat of lofty original plans for the venture, scaled back the Newlands Project to less than one-fourth its original acreage, turned over much of the project's actual operation to the local Truckee-Carson Irrigation District, and shifted its attention away from Lake Tahoe and toward other sources of water to make up the shortage. Not until the completion of the large Boca, Stampede, and Prosser dams on the Truckee River's tributaries downstream from the town of Truckee from the 1940s to the 1960s did the irrigators, in the meantime renamed the U.S. Bureau of Reclamation, get more water for their beleaguered Nevada project. People worldwide now celebrate the region's beaches, resorts, alpine ranges, and remarkable sapphire and emerald waters as prime scenic attractions, but few today still remember back to when the Southern Pacific helped to save Lake Tahoe. Even more had been accomplished, however. Regional interests, led in part by the Southern Pacific, had successfully resisted the federal government's assertion of broad, dominant water rights, blazing a trail for other locales to follow in subsequent decades.

PART IV

Agriculture

11 "Evangel Train"

SCIENTIFIC AGRICULTURE

The Gospel Train Arrives

Each year between 1908 and 1912, a farm demonstration train co-sponsored by the Southern Pacific Company and the University of California College of Agriculture toured the rural districts of the state. Hundreds of times during this period, the train, with blue and gold banners unfurled along its sides, pulled into a country town surging with holiday excitement. Buggies, farm wagons, and automobiles lined the streets; throngs of farmers and their families, townspeople, and school children filled the depot and pressed against the tracks. When the railroad and university officials had debarked from the train to the serenade of a school band, local dignitaries stepped forth to deliver a flowery welcome, and the formal lecture program began. From the beds of flatcars, the station platform, or down the street in a church or lodge hall, the train's agricultural experts preached their gospel of scientific farming, higher earnings per acre, and revitalized rural life. Exhibit cars then opened, promptly filling with curious people milling among displays of crop pests, insecticides, irrigation valves, new seed varieties, and model farm kitchens, or watching demonstrations of the Babcock test or better ways to prune grapevines. After a stay of several hours, perhaps overnight with the addition of a longer evening program in larger towns, the train departed amid cheers and applause, heading for repeat performances ten or twenty miles down the line.[1] Not just in California but in the Southern Pacific's other western states during the first three decades of the twentieth century, similar joint railroad-university demonstration trains carried the revolutionary message of scientific agriculture to rural people.

Although also common across the United States, particularly in the Midwest and South,[2] farm demonstration trains and their popularity seem particularly incongruous in California, where anti-railroad sentiment had run high since the 1870s. Political and economic opposition to the Southern Pacific, however, was also intense at that time in Texas, Oregon, and Nevada, other states where the company operated demonstration trains. At the very inception of the trains in the early twentieth century, Progressive editors and politicians were using the company's reputed hostility toward farmers as a principal issue to inflame popular passions against the company. Coming, then, as it did during the climax of the anti-corporate Progressive era across the Far West and Southwest, the Southern Pacific's sponsorship of demonstration trains and general support for universities and modern agriculture in general appear out of character. Not only was the ostensible villain providing expensive assistance to farmers, a group whose welfare it was charged with ignoring, the company was also engaged with western land-grant universities in promoting the modern ideal of scientific efficiency, held by many historians to be a unifying principle of the Progressive movement. In addition to providing insights into an important facet of the agricultural history of the West, the story of the agricultural demonstration trains suggests that the Southern Pacific was not as hostile toward farmers' interests and Progressivism itself as historians have traditionally maintained. It also illustrates the ways in which railroad and university were similar and inter-related types of organizations that shared problems, values, relationships, and roles in the modernization of western agriculture.

Kindred Spirits: The Southern Pacific and the Land-Grant Colleges

The agricultural demonstration trains of the early twentieth century did not initiate the cooperation between corporation and college, nor were they, as some have charged, transitory public-relations stunts to blunt criticism of the Southern Pacific's other activities. They were, instead, the culmination of a long tradition of interaction that went back practically to the origins of the company and western land-grant universities and other scientific and agricultural agencies. In the 1860s and 1870s, when the various railroads that would ultimately unite into the Southern Pacific system were getting started, agriculture in parts of the older-settled West, including California, Texas, and Oregon, was beginning its evolution from pioneer cereal and open-range livestock production to more diversified, intensely farmed crops. The transition depended on the acquisition of more scientific knowledge about the unique potentials and problems of farming this region with different soils and climates, most of them arid or semi-arid. Scientific agriculture, nevertheless, did not develop easily in the West but only after a long, tortuous, uphill struggle against rival interests—miners and cattlemen, for example—as well as the small farmers' deep-seated traditionalism, lack of education and understanding of modern science, and suspicion of "city people" and "outsiders" in general. Ironically, as had also been

A Southern Pacific Railroad–Oregon Agricultural College farm demonstration train at Cottage Grove, Oregon, in the early 1900s. Courtesy Oregon Historical Society, Portland.

true in the East, much of the farmers' antipathy toward new ways was directed against the just-founded public land-grant universities, whose mission it was to improve agriculture. Not only were western legislatures stingy with financial support for higher education, increasingly influential farm groups like the Grange roundly attacked the colleges, particularly their schools of agriculture, for "wasting" public tax money on agricultural research, for teaching an "impractical curriculum" heavy on pure science and light on better ways to plow, and for luring rural students away from the farm life. Occasionally, farm critics went so far as to try to strip the universities of their public funding under the federal Morrill Land Grant College Act of 1862, or to abolish them outright and replace them with farm trade schools.[3]

With few friends and many enemies, the land-grant universities survived and expanded through support from a handful of urban interests, particularly the railroads, including the Southern Pacific. Like other western railroads, the Southern Pacific was a natural ally of agricultural researchers and educators and became an important partner in the establishment of scientific agriculture in the region.[4] Well-read and broadly educated as a rule, Southern Pacific people, particularly middle-level managers, shared the university experts' belief that human life could be improved by the organized application of intelligence through science and technology. Typically, Southern Pacific leaders in western states formed friendships and professional relationships with university people, socialized with them, met and corresponded with them frequently about mutual interests, and in some instances served the universities officially as regents and, in the case of Texas A & M, as acting president.

As a company, the Southern Pacific was committed to encouraging more modern agriculture as the cornerstone of corporate development policy.[5] If farmers could increase their volume of production per acre, shift to higher-value crops, and be assured of more reliable harvests—which were the promises of scientific agriculture—the company stood also to gain directly in terms of population growth and economic development along its lines, as well as increased company freight and passenger revenues and higher sales prices for its millions of acres of granted lands, a connection that was made as early as 1878 by William H. Mills, editor of the Southern Pacific–owned *Sacramento Record-Union,* and was reiterated over the years by many company officials.[6] Thus, from its founding in the 1860s, the company conducted agricultural research of its own and encouraged the founding and operation of public and private scientific agricultural organizations—including agricultural and horticultural societies, state and local inspection and regulatory agencies, and most especially the land-grant colleges with their experiment stations and farm extension programs. In the early twentieth century, in addition to continuing and sometimes increasing its support for these outside agencies, the Southern Pacific also instituted its own corporate-wide network of agricultural development departments to convince growers and the general public residing specifically in its service area of the advantages of scientific farming. The scope of the railroad's activities in agricultural research, education, and regulation varied from state to state and locale to locale according to time, the specific people involved, the extent and nature of work being done by rival railroads, and regional agricultural potentials, problems, and institutional structures. Nevertheless, from California north to Oregon and east to Texas, the Southern Pacific was a leader in the development of scientific agriculture.

As was true of other areas of corporate policy, the Southern Pacific's support for scientific agriculture first took shape during the 1860s and 1870s in California, the company's home ground, and spread as the railroad expanded into other states. In California, railroad and university were contemporaneous. The company consolidated its hold on the state's internal transportation system in the late 1860s and early 1870s, while the 1869 driving of the golden spike on the Central Pacific and the 1881 opening of the Southern Pacific Railroad to Texas completed transcontinental links to the east. To garner a federal subsidy under the provisions of the 1862 Morrill Land Grant College Act, the state legislature founded the University of California at a small urban facility in Oakland in 1868, but it was not until it moved to a spacious rural campus in Berkeley in 1873 that full operations began, particularly for its College of Agriculture.[7]

This was a pivotal time for the state, when the turbulent gold-rush world was being replaced by a more diverse, stable, social and economic order based particularly on farming.[8] Each fledgling agency—railroad and university—at once reflected and helped to bring about this transformation. Enticed by the profits to be made from land-grant sales and traffic in farm products, the Southern Pacific's expanding local lines opened millions of acres of fertile new land to settlement and its two transcontinental connections eventually brought farmers within reach of vast, ever-growing, out-of-state markets.[9] Hindering agricultural modernization and preventing farmers from taking full advantage of the new land and market potentials, however, were the state's unique and extremely localized patterns of climate, soils, water resources, and overall growing conditions. California was a veritable terra incognita to farmers, who were initially mystified by sandy desert lands, an absence of winter frost, and superabundant winter rains, followed by annual drought during the normal summer growing season. The University of California's College of Agriculture, through scientific research and education, could assist in resolving such problems. Thus, both the railroad and the university not only came to encourage new forms of agriculture, both also found their own institutional growth to be dependent on agricultural success. For the Southern Pacific, land-grant sales, traffic revenues, stock values, and to some extent the capital available for expansion ebbed and flowed with the fortunes of the state's farmers. For the university, the importance of developing agriculture, and especially the essential service to the state that could be provided by the College of Agriculture, became a powerful justification for increased support for the institution from a niggardly legislature.[10] Understandably, throughout the late nineteenth and early twentieth centuries, the Southern Pacific and the University of California undertook a variety of activities to improve farming.

Railroad Agricultural Research

For its part, in addition to subdividing and advertising its granted lands and organizing aggressive colonization programs for rural districts, the railroad applied its capital, personnel, technical resources, and growing organizational structure to compile agricultural information, to promote the introduction of new higher-value crops, and to experiment with ways to diversify and in other ways modernize farming. The Southern Pacific particularly exerted a powerful influence on the collection and dissemination of reliable agricultural information, which was essential to farming in California's varied, unique, and largely unknown environments. Beginning with the establishment in the mid-1860s of the first railway stations, many in unsettled or newly settled districts, the company systematically collected and tabulated agricultural data. The railroad used the information to encourage farm settlement and more traffic along its lines, to assist in advertising and selling its granted lands, and to make it easier to forecast rolling-stock requirements for future shipments. At the direction of the company's general superintendent Alban N. Towne, who took special interest in agricultural innovation, station agents periodically gathered local statistics on soils, irrigation methods, crop acreage, production per acre, shipments, and pests and diseases and sent these to company headquarters. The railroad tabulated the data, arranged it chronologically and by locality, used it internally for railroad operations, furnished it to agricultural scientists, and released it in papers and bulletins that were widely reprinted in the California press. The Southern Pacific's information was especially valuable to researchers and farmers because it was segregated down to the local level, which other, smaller, less extended agencies lacked the capacity to do. So that the company and general public might be alerted, railway agents were also instructed to report immediately by telegraph or telephone any freezes, floods, conditions of developing drought, and the appearance of new crop pests and diseases.[11] Periodically, as in 1886, the company ordered comprehensive resurveys of the agricultural resources, especially new developments, at hundreds of localities in all its tributary regions, including the Southwest, Great Basin, and Oregon.[12]

By the 1920s, the Southern Pacific's extensive agricultural reporting system had become an essential element of management, providing a basis for judging economic conditions along the lines, planning efficient movement of cars and equipment, and forecasting company earnings. Station agents throughout the Southern Pacific system, in April, June, and August of each year, submitted comprehensive reports on acreage planted in each crop, average yields, and threatening weather or pest outbreaks that could affect crops. These were supplemented by agents' periodic telegraphic reports of unusual conditions, as well as information from Pacific Fruit Express, the company's refrigerated car subsidiary, and the Bureau of Crop Estimates of the U.S. Department of Agriculture.[13]

At least as important as the agricultural data was the Southern Pacific's collection of weather records. For its own operations, the company needed accurate weather data. As railway stations were established in the 1860s and 1870s, usually far distant from the few, widely scattered government weather stations, modern weather instruments were installed and local agents were trained and began to take thrice-daily readings of temperature, precipitation, and wind velocity and direction. By 1877, in California alone, the railway was operating 83 weather stations, plus five water-temperature recording stations on the Sacramento and San Joaquin rivers, and the number expanded thereafter across the state and other Southern Pacific territories. Local agents tabulated weather information weekly or monthly and sent it to company headquarters, where it was assembled, printed, and distributed to such agencies as the U.S. Army Signal Corps, the U.S. Department of Agriculture, the U.S. Coast Survey, and the University of California, as well as to individual scientists, newspapers, and agricultural periodicals. The Southern Pacific established ongoing relationships with agencies, such as the U.S. Coast Survey, and scientists, such as George Davidson of the Coast Survey and the University of California, providing them on a regular basis with climate and other information for decades. In some instances, the railroad gathered data to the specifications of outside scientists and in other ways directly assisted their experiments.[14]

Chief land agent Benjamin B. Redding was particularly active in the accumulation and dissemination of climate as well as soil statistics. Building on systematic observations by local station and Land Department agents going back nearly a decade, Redding in 1877 compiled a detailed report on soil and climate characteristics of the San Joaquin Valley, which he provided to agricultural developers such as James Ben Ali Haggin and government agencies such as the U.S. Coast Survey.[15] Redding also incorporated his growing knowledge into an important, more comprehensive paper, "The Climate of California," first presented in late 1877 and early 1878 to meetings of the State Agricultural Society and the California Academy of Sciences. In maintaining that climate need not be a mystery, Redding applied both the railroad's voluminous local weather records and the general scientific meteorological literature to identify the patterns of California's climate, particularly the dramatic regional variations caused by the Alaska Current, coastal fogs and cloud banks, prevailing winds, storm tracks, and mountain-induced rain shadows. He may have been the first serious observer to demonstrate that in the still largely unsettled San Joaquin Valley, particularly the western side, contrary to the claims of local boosters and land developers, agriculture was impossible without irrigation. In the southern Central Valley, with average precipitation less than eight or nine inches annually, Redding concluded, farmers "hope in vain for rain." He advocated not only large public irrigation systems for the valley and other districts, a subject that Californians were just beginning to hotly debate, but also the establishment of a network of weather stations at local public schools. "Science," Redding believed, "by patient observation and intelligent research, can discover and interpret."[16] Widely reprinted, Redding's work remained for several decades the most influential summary of California's climate.[17]

In effect, into the early twentieth century, the Southern Pacific served as the unofficial "weather bureau" for California and much of the rest of its territory. Its climate statistics formed the basis for early agricultural research, the siting of agricultural experiment stations, and farm planning. Even when the U.S.

Weather Bureau was established in the Far West in the early twentieth century, it continued for some time to rely on statistics gathered at the far more numerous stations along the Southern Pacific's rail network. The railroad, operating through its local station agents, also assisted the Weather Bureau in broadcasting frost warnings to farmers.[18] The company worked with weather and agricultural agencies and growers' organizations to develop systems in California and Oregon for emergency shipment of oil to fuel smudge pots in frosted orchard districts.[19]

As the Southern Pacific pioneered in the gathering of agricultural and climatic information, the company also encouraged the introduction of new crops and cultivation methods into California and other territories. The railroad as an organization experimented with crops, as did many of its leaders acting as private citizens, and the company also worked with outside individuals and agencies to develop new, more reliable, and profitable crops, or crops that would allow the cultivation of hitherto unfarmable land. The Southern Pacific's involvement in agricultural experimentation dated back to the company's very founding. Although he worked primarily in the hardware and railroad businesses, Collis P. Huntington was a lifelong advocate and supporter of agricultural innovation. In the late 1850s and early 1860s, he helped organize the California State Agricultural Fair at Sacramento, and he was a member of the State Board of Agriculture. In 1862, while he was in Washington, D.C., lobbying for the passage of the Pacific Railway Act, Huntington, as agent of the state's Board of Agriculture, secured and shipped seed samples of new plant varieties from the U.S. Patent Office, including tobacco, for testing in California.[20] In 1870, Huntington initiated the first of the company's many agricultural experiments. Convinced that the millions of acres of Great Basin land acquired from the government by the Central Pacific Railroad was not worthless for agriculture, as most people inside and outside of the company insisted, Huntington arranged for the Smithsonian Institution and the U.S. Department of Agriculture to analyze and conduct cultivation experiments on soils from the railroad's lands, especially those tainted with alkali. He ordered samples taken and sent to Washington, D.C., from especially rainless points on the land grant between the Big Bend of the Truckee River in Nevada east to the Great Salt Lake.[21] Throughout his tenure as company executive, much of it spent in New York and Washington, Huntington repeatedly sent west new crops to improve farm production in his railroads' territory, and he encouraged his associates and underlings to do likewise.[22]

Central Pacific Railroad and Southern Pacific company president Leland Stanford, who was involved in scientific farming even before he arrived in California, engaged in agricultural experimentation on several of his landholdings from the 1860s until his death in 1893. In addition to being one of the most

Southern Pacific depot, hotel, and demonstration garden at Yuma, Arizona, 1900. Throughout its system, the company embellished station grounds with irrigated demonstration gardens in the hope of introducing new crops to increase farmers' profits and the railroad's traffic. Courtesy Huntington Library.

important scientific breeders of race horses, particularly trotters, on the West Coast, Stanford began many other farming ventures, insisting on introducing the most modern scientifically proven crop varieties and cultivation methods, hiring experts to advise and manage, and using advanced processing equipment. He converted his east San Francisco Bay Warm Springs farm and his vast estate at Vina, in the northern Sacramento Valley, into some of the most modern and productive vineyards in the state, and even the world. The Vina farm, especially, developed into a huge operation, and after experimenting unsuccessfully with dozens of different wine varieties, Stanford settled on fine brandy. Within a few years, the Vina farm grew into the largest maker of brandy in the world, and by the late 1880s was winning prizes in the United States and other countries.[23]

Many Southern Pacific leaders followed Huntington's and Stanford's examples, but none more avidly than land agent Benjamin B. Redding. Redding was the epitome of the nineteenth-century, self-taught, amateur scientist. Well-read in many fields, Redding was a patron and participant in scientific organizations such as the California Academy of Science and grower organizations such as the State Horticultural Society. He served on the California State Fisheries Commission, conducted his own scientific experiments, supported the experiments of others privately and through his railroad office, delivered numerous scientific papers, such as his noted work on California's climate, before bodies such as the Academy of Science and the State Agricultural Society, and published voluminously in the farm and general press. Although he made contributions in the fields of forestry, climate, Pacific Coast fishes, California Indian cultures, and ornithology, Redding's major interest was agriculture. He combined study of scientific literature with experimentation on the railroad's or his own lands to investigate subjects such as irrigation methods, citrus, grape-vine culture, and olive production.[24] He was one of the first to demonstrate that citrus, which had been confined to the warmer southern counties, could be grown commercially in the north as well. In 1876 in Sacramento County, he set out 1,200 orange trees, and additional lemon and lime trees, and by ceasing irrigation on August 1 to minimize growth of new foliage in the autumn, he got his trees to weather frosts down to 26 degrees.[25] Redding's olive experiments, however, were his major contribution to California agricultural diversification. By comparing California climates and soils to those of the world's premier olive-growing regions and then experimenting with the tree in Sacramento, Tulare, and San Diego counties, Redding demonstrated that much of the state, particularly inland valleys and foothills, was ideal for commercial production. He also promoted the importation of better European olive varieties.[26] Redding's experiments and writings helped to establish both citrus and olive cultivation as substantial industries in northern and central California by the early twentieth century.

Redding's successor as chief land agent after 1883, William H. Mills, continued Redding's tradition of promoting agricultural innovation. Mills studied new agricultural developments and maintained contacts with authorities in and outside the state looking for new crop varieties and cultivation techniques to improve farming in the area of the railroad's land-grant and service area. By coordinating with other company people, outside agricultural experts and agencies, and private growers, Mills served as catalyst for the importation and trial of countless new crops and methods. In 1906, for example, Mills was responsible for getting the Southern Pacific, the California State Board of Trade, of which he was the founder and leading light, and the U.S. Department of Agriculture to bring a newly discovered, drought-tolerant variety of Siberian alfalfa for trial in California and Nevada. The next year, he used the same network to introduce new dry-farming techniques.[27]

Other Southern Pacific land officials also assisted agricultural innovation. Between the 1870s and early 1900s, for example, Robert L. Fulton, land agent for the company's Great Basin territory, worked to introduce new sheep, grape, and alfalfa-hog industries into Nevada.[28] In the early 1900s, B. A. McAllaster, head land agent, and C. E. Wantland, district agent in Los Angeles and southern California, systematically kept track of new crops by reading farm journals, seed catalogs, research literature, and proceedings of farm meetings and worked to get them test-grown by the railroad or private farmers. In just one example, between 1911 and 1913, McAllaster and Wantland discovered a new variety of wheat being developed by a Wyoming seed company especially for high production under dry-farming methods, sent samples for experiments at the University of Nevada in Reno, and got the variety introduced into new dry-farming regions in Nevada and California.[29]

Ultimately, between the 1860s and the 1920s, the Southern Pacific also sought to introduce rice, rubber, sugar beets, milo maize, field peas, new varieties of alfalfa, and many other new, higher-value crops into portions of its territory.[30] Of special importance was the railroad's introduction into California's Coachella Valley in the 1890s of the first date palms, which when the trees began to mature in the early 1900s, produced one of the region's most important cash crops.[31] The railroad also supported the experiments of private farmers. Again in the Coachella Valley, it was the railroad that started the important table grape industry in 1900. The company paid Pat Gayle, who had been the first homesteader in the valley, $125 per month and bored a new well on his farm for him to grow different varieties of grapes on a two-acre test plot.[32] In one of its more unusual ventures into crop experimentation, the Southern Pacific, under McAllaster's direction, worked between 1908 and 1912 with the famous Santa Rosa plant-breeder Luther Burbank in an unsuccessful attempt to introduce his newly patented thornless cactus as a "naturally" growing fodder that promised to convert millions of acres of the railroad's nearly worthless desert land in southern California and the Great Basin into rich cattle pasturage.[33] Local railway station agents, such as Clarence M. Wooster, who managed the depot in Auburn, California, in the 1870s also pioneered orchard-planting and other higher-value land uses in their districts.[34]

Not content to let happenstance determine which new crops were tried, the Southern Pacific established numerous experimental and demonstration gardens, first in California and eventually throughout its territory. Although many of the railway's early facilities immediately started landscaping their grounds with samples of plants that could grow in local environments, more elaborate projects designed for experimentation and promotion of new crops soon developed, particularly under the aegis of the company's general superintendent Alban N. Towne, an avid agricultural promoter. As early as 1870, with Huntington's enthusiastic support, Towne ordered six half-acre plots along the lines plowed and planted in vegetables, fruit trees, and other potential crops. The company located the demonstration plots near water and installed irrigation works.[35] Railway gardens were also located strategically near many depots, which usually had their own water supplies and which served as local hubs of travel and business activity.

The railroad's first large, specialized experimental farm emerged shortly after the company built its line down California's lightly populated San Joaquin Valley. In 1875, near Tulare, the railroad put in an experimental tree ranch,

At his Santa Rosa, California, home and laboratory, ca. 1910, Luther Burbank greets Southern
Pacific traffic executive Charles S. Fee and his associate, James Horsburgh, Jr. (hat in hand). The
railroad worked closely with the famed plant-breeder to develop and introduce new farm crops
in lands along its rail lines. Author's collection.

irrigated from artesian wells, to test and propagate shade trees for rights-of-
way and stations in arid locales.[36] In the late 1870s, in the hope of providing
itself with an inexpensive supply of hardwood for ties, construction material,
and fuel, the Southern Pacific conducted a several-year-long experimental program of planting large tracts of land-grant land—again primarily in the San
Joaquin Valley—in eucalyptus trees imported from Australia. As other would-
be eucalyptus-boomers were discovering, however, the wood could not be cured
properly for the railroad's purposes and the groves turned out to be fire hazards and shelters for crop pests that invaded nearby farmers' fields. By the early
twentieth century, the railroad was tearing out most of its groves and prohibiting
the further cultivation of eucalyptus on its lands, except for occasional shade
or ornamental trees. Some railroad eucalyptus experiments, however, lasted until about 1920.[37]

　　Also in the 1870s, the railroad purchased land adjacent to the depot in the
San Joaquin Valley town of Merced and began experiments with orchard trees.

By the early twentieth century, the company's Merced demonstration plot was growing soft-shell almonds, royal apricots, white and black figs, Muscat grapes, Lisbon lemons, mission olives, navel oranges, Bartlett pears, American black walnuts, and English walnuts.[38] Other major experimental facilities were built in the 1880s at Indio and Yuma, Arizona, where the railroad had developed productive water facilities in southern California's Colorado Desert. The Indio demonstration farm, where company employees grew figs, grapes, melons, alfalfa, winter vegetables, and eventually dates, had an especially important impact on the start of modern agriculture in the Coachella Valley and other low-elevation desert regions in the Southwest.[39] By 1915, the Southern Pacific had instituted a systemwide policy of planting fruit- and nut-bearing trees and other "economic" plants at all of its stations and section houses as inducements to agricultural improvement, particularly in desert regions.[40]

The Southern Pacific's support was also essential to California's perennial combat against crop pests and diseases. When new crops, particularly fruits, were introduced from other farm regions in the late nineteenth and early twentieth centuries, a bewildering variety of pests and diseases tagged along, many of them, without natural local predators, flourishing in California's congenial environment. The threat was severe enough by the 1880s that pressure from scientists and organizations representing large-scale producers, such as the State Horticultural Society and the State Viticultural Society, prompted the legislature in 1883 to create the State Board of Horticulture to identify destructive fruit pests and diseases and eradicate them through inspections, quarantines, and crop-destruction orders. The general public was apathetic or hostile toward such controls, however. Many farmers and shippers evaded the rules, and into the first decades of the twentieth century, despite the adoption of stricter laws and vigorous campaigns to build support, the financially strapped and understaffed Horticultural Board and its few local agents could not enforce the orders effectively. By the early twentieth century as well, other specialized state agricultural agencies had assumed similar responsibilities, along with accompanying frustrations, in the control of diseased livestock and crops other than fruit.[41] As the carrier of most middle- and long-distance shipments and the employer of many agents in localities throughout the state, the railroad was central to inspection and quarantine enforcement. From the inception of the system, the company worked closely with local, state, and federal agricultural inspectors, faithfully advised them of arrivals of plants, trees, cuttings, seeds, and animals from out of state so that they could be inspected, fumigated, or destroyed if necessary, distributed information to farmers and shippers about quarantine orders, trained its station and yard workers and other employees in detection of tainted products and held them strictly accountable for "rigid enforcement" of state regulations, and stopped all suspicious cargoes until authorities could inspect them. By 1921, just the enforcement of plant quarantines, which the railroad enjoined its employees was "very important work," affected more than one thousand of the company's cars per day.[42]

Alliance with the University of California

While the Southern Pacific Company was gathering agricultural information and encouraging crop experimentation and agricultural modernization, the University of California's College of Agriculture, under the thirty-year deanship of the venerable Eugene W. Hilgard (from 1874 to 1904) and E. J. Wickson's ten-year tenure as dean (from 1904 to 1913), expanded its course offerings for agriculture students at its Berkeley campus. More importantly, the college, at Hilgard's direction, launched a program of experimentation in soil classification, viticulture, citrus production, crop disease and pest prevention, and irrigation techniques that culminated in 1887 in the establishment of a federally funded university agricultural experimentation station at Berkeley, followed by a chain of substations located in the state's numerous specialized environments. In 1906, the legislature created a new agricultural branch of the university, the State Farm and Farm School at Davis, in a more representative agricultural environment than chilly, foggy Berkeley. By the early 1900s, the university was also operating a well-organized extension service to broadcast research results to farmers through a variety of bulletins, school programs, and farmers' institutes. By helping put regional farming on a sounder scientific footing, the College of Agriculture's research and educational activities were important to the gradual conversion of pioneer farming into California's modern, highly specialized, and commercialized system, based on fruit and specialty crops.[43]

Ironically, work by the Southern Pacific and the University of California on behalf of agriculture, essential as it was to the economic development of the state, brought neither institution widespread public approval. Many Californians perceived both railroad and university as large, elitist, centralized, monolithic, and ominous concentrations of power, symbolic of the modern, large-scale organizations produced by industrialization. Operating as they did at the state, national, and even international levels and subject to little local control, railroad and university also appeared to many as outsiders, treading on local prerogatives.[44]

As a result, both railroad and university repeatedly collided with California's social, economic, and regional interest groups, whose specific needs and values clashed with those of the two larger-scale organizations. The growing antipathy of some groups toward the Southern Pacific is well documented by historians and does not require detailed recounting here. Suffice it to say that, by the early twentieth century, harnessing the "Octopus" had become the stock campaign slogan of politicians, farm organization leaders, labor union officials, business leaders, and urban reformers alike, and the anti-railroad issue had become the critical unifying theme in assembling the coalition of Progressives that took control of the legislature and elected Hiram Johnson governor in 1910.[45]

The unpopularity of the University of California, particularly its College of Agriculture, is neither as well known nor as well understood. As in the rest of the country, the university's overtures toward farmers from the 1870s through the 1920s aroused mostly apathy, if not outright hostility, especially among small-scale farmers and the country population in general residing outside the San Francisco Bay Area. Many critics charged that the university's Regents were deliberately shortchanging agricultural instruction by diverting Morrill land-grant funds to traditional academic departments. In 1874, shortly after the school's move to Berkeley, the newly organized California State Grange, encouraged and led by Ezra Carr, the university's sole professor of agriculture, launched the attack when it demanded that the legislature abolish the Board of Regents, which under the school's charter had autonomous authority, consolidate the university with the state's public school system under the control of the State Board of Education, and restructure the curriculum to give primary attention and financial support to "agricultural, mechanical, and industrial instruction." Although a joint investigative committee of the legislature concluded that the Regents and faculty had "done as well as any reasonable citizen could expect" to teach agriculture and to administer the land-grant funds, rural leaders well into the twentieth century continued to work to detach the College of Agriculture from the university or to shift federal land-grant support to a second, independent agricultural school in the interior, where practical instruction in farming would prevail.[46]

At the same time, other critics repeatedly attacked the College of Agriculture itself for being remote and elitist, its curriculum theoretical, impractical, irrelevant to ordinary farmers, and more likely to entice country youths into city careers than to teach them to become better farmers. Self-styled "practical farmers" and their supporters also ridiculed university experts, agricultural research, and scientific farming in general as inferior to tradition and intuition as guides to successful production. To such detractors, who must have constituted a sizable part of the farm population, agricultural courses and experiments were a waste of tax money; research bulletins, replete with jargon and arcane statistics, were naive regarding the "real" problems and limited resources of farmers; agricultural institutes and demonstrations were abstruse, condescending, and unrelated to actual local situations. As one farm leader complained in language that echoed for decades through the farm and country press, the College of Agriculture's extension programs implied that "we do not know our business."[47] Even university officials were driven to admit that because of "ignorance and conservatism," in the words of one pro-university editor, "there is still a good deal of skepticism on the part of the rural population as to the value of the work of our colleges."[48]

Although never as openly vilified as the Southern Pacific, the University of California and its College of Agriculture suffered from widespread public distrust that had considerable influence on the legislature. By the early twentieth century, because of insufficient funding, the College of Agriculture still did not have an adequate building on the Berkeley campus; available class and research facilities were crowded and dilapidated; and many much-needed experiments could not be begun or continued because of thin resources.[49] Still, into the 1920s, rural pressure groups persisted in attacking the university and the college, precipitating repeated legislative investigations, and sponsoring bills to abolish the university or to create rival institutions in the country.[50]

Unsurprisingly, similar institutional origins and political problems quickly drove the Southern Pacific and the College of Agriculture into close alliance. Especially in the early decades of the college's existence, before the Hatch Act of 1887 brought some federal assistance to agricultural research, legislative support for experiments was minimal, amounting only to a few hundred dollars per year. In addition, the college was deficient in staff, equipment, and branch facilities outside Berkeley to gather data about California's diverse microenvironments. The college also lacked the influence, both within the university and the state at large, to improve its position. Railway officials, who often shared the agrarian values and scientific commitment of the agricultural experts, were quite willing to use the company's financial, structural, and political resources and its personnel to sustain the fledgling school's research and educational programs.[51] Particularly from 1868 through the 1880s, railway patronage sometimes spelled the difference between failure and success for the college. For instruction and experimentation, for example, the school relied heavily on raw data being gathered by the Southern Pacific. The company's expanding records on elevation, rainfall, temperature, wind, soil characteristics, and water availability were provided to the college.[52] Southern Pacific officials, especially in the Land Department, also routinely supplied the scientists with seed, plant, and soil samples and contributed free shipping for chemicals, plants, and farm produce, as well as travel passes for faculty members doing agricultural work.[53]

The importance of railway-university cooperation was especially demonstrated during Hilgard's crucial early tenure as dean, while the university was still reeling from its bout with the Grangers and the legislature and when many of the College of Agriculture's programs were just taking shape. In the mid-

1870s, shortly after he arrived in Berkeley to replace the fired Ezra Carr, Hilgard formed a close relationship with land agent Benjamin B. Redding, who was also a university regent. Already well-versed on the subject of California's agricultural potential by virtue of his management of the company's Land Department and his own study and experiments, Redding offered his assistance to Hilgard, who was embarking on a pioneering classification of the state's soils and other agricultural resources, a project that Hilgard thought essential in establishing a basis for further research and in demonstrating the university's usefulness to skeptical farmers.[54] Redding provided information and samples from the railroad's collections, directed Hilgard to representative soil regions, and accompanied him on trips to inspect soils in the vicinity of the company's extensive land grant.[55]

When because of legislative indifference the professor was not given time and financial support to complete his study, Redding and L. M. Clement of the Track Department arranged for the Southern Pacific to assign one of its young civil engineers, Norman J. Willson, to work with Hilgard. Trained by the professor in the techniques of taking soil samples and making field observations, Willson, in what Hilgard described as "a somewhat arduous and solitary expedition," spent three months in 1880 trundling a handcar over most of the company's tracks in the state, stopping frequently to take samples and notes. According to Hilgard, Willson produced "a connected and reliable" set of four hundred soil samples, in addition to voluminous field notes on local rainfall and weather, natural plant cover, history of farm settlement, crop yields, irrigation methods and sources of irrigation water, and plant diseases that constituted "a most valuable, and in some respects unique, collection on the agriculture of the state."[56] Willson's samples persuaded Hilgard that his own initial "impressions regarding the upper valley of the San Joaquin were not very correct." He relied heavily on Willson's information, along with Southern Pacific climate data and several of Redding's published papers, to write his study of California soils and agricultural resources, published as part of the tenth census of the United States and one of the first landmarks of early California agricultural science and a critical step toward finally establishing some credibility for the College of Agriculture in the farm community.[57] The Southern Pacific distributed copies of Hilgard's report to help sell its granted lands in the Central Valley.[58]

Redding, who once told Hilgard that he believed the College of Agriculture's work had done "more to make the University popular than any other one thing," also interceded politically on behalf of the college.[59] He frequently defended the college's policies and appropriations before a cool Board of Regents and helped Hilgard plot lobbying strategy for dealing with an even more unfriendly state legislature. In only one of many such instances, Redding in 1880 used his influence with the Regents and the State Board of Viticulture to accelerate the College of Agriculture's important research program that eventually found a cure for the destructive grapevine pest *phylloxera,* which was on the verge of destroying the state's winemaking industries.[60]

Although Redding died in 1882, the Southern Pacific's support of the College of Agriculture persisted, and even increased, under his successors as land agent, William H. Mills and B. A. McAllaster, and other company leaders.[61] Through the early 1900s, the railroad continued to furnish the college with information, supplies, free transportation, monetary grants for experiments, and political intercession. The new and increasingly important work of agricultural extension especially benefited from railway assistance. Encouraged by new federal support and funding for extension services in the decades before and after 1900, the university expanded its publication program to get the results of research into the hands of working farmers and sponsored farmers' institutes, which varied from one-day meetings at Berkeley or one of the branch experiment stations to multi-day short courses on focused topics, such as irrigation or modern methods in general. Free or low-cost passes from the railroad greatly widened the range of dozens of the college' researchers, instructors, demonstrators, and farm institute workers. Local railway agents also distributed agricultural research bulletins and helped to advertise the institutes among farmers, and the railroad developed several programs under which farmers could take advantage of drastically reduced fares to attend the meetings.[62] The college regularly called on railway people with expertise in agriculture to make presentations to the institutes. William H. Mills was a particularly avid contributor. After a successful address in 1897, Mills told company president Collis P. Huntington that he believed the institutes to be "occasions of importance and dignity" that provided the company with the opportunity "to create a kindly feeling toward our people," and he vowed to accept all similar invitations in the future.[63] The Southern Pacific's own publications also attempted to build support for agricultural research and extension education. In the early 1900s, the company's new monthly magazine, *Sunset,* became a major forum for the staff of the College of Agriculture, other agricultural experts, and the cause of scientific farming generally.[64]

In the early 1900s, siding with most farmers' organizations, which had been agitating for decades for the establishment of a specialized agricultural facility for the university in the state's interior, Southern Pacific officials strongly supported the founding of a University Farm and Farm School for research and, as well, instruction in practical agriculture at the high school level. Strong opposition developed, however, including from some university leaders who feared the branch might one day develop into a separate and rival agricultural college.[65] Bills to create the University Farm failed to pass the legislature in 1901 and 1903. According to Peter Shields, the prime mover behind the proposal, when another bill came up for consideration in 1905, it was the railroad's Sacramento lobbyist, George Hatton, who delivered the twenty votes needed for passage.[66] After approval of the new school, William H. Mills and James Horsburgh, Jr., assistant general passenger agent and another strong advocate of the university and College of Agriculture, worked closely with the state commission empowered to choose a site. Mills was particularly instrumental in discouraging groups from isolated, atypical farming districts from pressuring the commission and thereby perhaps producing a stalemate.[67] Horsburgh worked to secure a representative site that would also further the company's interests. It would be "a great source of gratification to me personally, and place me in a stronger position with our people to help along similar lines in the future," he wrote to Dean E. J. Wickson, "if the farm might be located on the line of our road."[68] The final selection in 1906 of Davis, just west of Sacramento and adjacent to the railroad's main line between the San Francisco Bay and the interior, assured continued, close cooperation between the railroad and the university into and beyond the World War I era.[69]

Farm Demonstration Trains

By 1908, then, nearly four decades of mutual activities had produced well-established patterns of interaction between the Southern Pacific Company and the University of California. Developments culminating in the autumn of that year impelled the two institutions to launch their most formal cooperative effort, the agricultural demonstration train. Despite progress in some crops and regions, the early years of the twentieth century were troubled ones for many California farmers because of persistent problems of adjustment: rapid shifts in crops and technology toward increasing specialization, the expansion of expensive and problematical irrigation, the dispersed and uneven population distribution across an isolated rural landscape, a succession of bewildering plagues of pests and diseases, chaotic and rapidly changing markets, and the fact that many farmers continued to be new arrivals to the state, unaccustomed to California's unusual growing conditions. Moreover, in some traditional crops such as grains, soil exhaustion caused by continuous planting and poor cultivation methods cut sharply into production and profits. From the 1890s into the early 1900s, average wheat yield per acre fell drastically even while the price of wheat tumbled on world markets, causing great losses to farmers, arousing general concern about the viability of the state's cereal industries, and prompting the legislature in 1905 to order the College of Agriculture to study the causes and possible remedies for the crisis in grain production. Then, coming as it did on the heels of the devastating 1906 San Francisco earthquake and fire, the nationwide Panic of 1907 struck especially hard in California, toppling banks and weakening business and farming for several years.[70]

Adding to the concrete economic problems faced by the state's farmers and businesspeople, 1908 was a year of national malaise over the abandonment of the farms by young people and the generally bleak future of rural areas. The "Country Life Movement," the nationwide campaign encouraged by President Theodore Roosevelt to investigate and cure the problems that appeared to be sapping the vitality of farming districts, stimulated discussion throughout the California farm press. In the autumn of 1908, the president's Country Life Commission arrived to hold hearings and analyze the state's rural difficulties, embroiling the state in a heated debate over what was wrong with the farms and how to cure the ills of rural society.[71]

The Southern Pacific, also hit by the general business and agricultural turmoil, aggravated by a decline in tourism in the wake of the earthquake, found its freight and passenger revenues plummeting, particularly in rural areas. Declining traffic, company leaders were convinced, was caused by soil exhaustion and a failure of farmers to adopt new crops and methods.[72] At the same time, the Southern Pacific's public image had sunk to perhaps its lowest level with the 1901 publication of Frank Norris's novel *The Octopus,* which elevated political opposition in its wake, leading to the formation of the anti-railroad Lincoln-Roosevelt League in 1907 and a burgeoning movement to enact strong railroad regulation in the state. In the autumn of 1908, the Southern Pacific and other transcontinental lines raised eastbound rates on California products by ten cents per hundred-weight, igniting a firestorm of protest editorials and meetings that contributed in early 1909 to the legislature's passage of the state's first meaningful rate regulatory bill.[73] All of this foreshadowed the Progressive seizure of the legislature and governor's office after a fierce anti–Southern Pacific campaign in 1910 and the subsequent passage of much anti-railroad legislation.[74]

Meanwhile, the prestige of the University of California and its College of Agriculture remained low, particularly among farmers. The university continued to be subject to attacks and investigations, its funding was scant and unpredictable, and critics stalled the campaign for an agricultural college building in Berkeley and an expansion of the university's agricultural research and education.[75] Also, nationwide by the early 1900s, the deficiencies in traditional agricultural extension activities were becoming apparent. Few average farmers and farm children actually attended the farm institutes, and farmers commonly were unaware of or ignored the university's published research. Like the institute lectures, the scientific bulletins produced by researchers working on carefully controlled experimental plots were difficult for working farmers to understand and failed to take into account local and individual farm conditions.

Standard methods of providing agricultural extension services, which had relied on bringing the farmer to the university, were not working in California,
adduced College of Agriculture leaders; by 1908, the university became convinced that it had to go directly to the farmer.[76]

To improve California's agricultural outlook, as well as to alleviate their mutual political and public-image problems, leaders of the Southern Pacific and
the University of California's College of Agriculture held discussions over the
early fall of 1908. They were joined by officials of the State Horticultural Commission, which was itself continuing to encounter fierce farmer resistance to
its crop quarantines and diseased-crop destruction orders.[77] At a meeting on
October 21, an organizing committee headed by Paul Shoup, the railroad's assistant traffic manager, Warren T. Clarke, university professor and head of extension for the College of Agriculture, and J. W. Jeffrey of the Horticultural
Commission unveiled a plan for a farm demonstration train. Later, there would
be some debate over whether the railroad or the university deserved credit for
having originated the idea, but in truth such mobile farm extension schools
had already become commonplace since the 1890s in states to the east, notably
Iowa, Missouri, and Texas.[78] California's first demonstration train, however, was
to be the most ambitious to date because of the immensity of the state and the
diversity of its growing conditions and crop systems.

The enterprise was conceived of as a veritable "university on wheels," as it
became popularly known, or as university president Benjamin Ide Wheeler renamed it, "an Evangel train bringing to the farms of the state the gospel of a
better agriculture."[79] The College of Agriculture at Berkeley and Davis was to
determine the train's topics and general curriculum, develop the lectures, outfit
the special display and demonstration cars, and, along with the Horticultural
Commission, provide most of the educators and experts. The Southern Pacific
was to plan the itinerary and schedule, work with community business and
farm organizations and local rail agents to publicize the visits, furnish locomotives, redesigned freight, passenger, sleeping, and dining cars, equipment, food
and supplies, and train crew, and, of course, pay the bills. Working twenty-
four hours a day in late October and early November, the railroad dispatched
rail cars and automobiles to scour the state for samples of crops, pests, weeds,
livestock, and equipment for rapid shipment to Berkeley, where the special exhibition cars were being prepared.[80]

The Southern Pacific's news release announcing the train, published by newspapers statewide in late October, emphasized that the train's purpose was to ed-
ucate farmers about the benefits of scientific agriculture for their own operations. The train was to be "an object lesson for the farmers and land owners in
general, to show what is being accomplished by modern scientific agriculture
and all its kindred industries." In light of the ingrained suspicion that many

growers had about "book farming," the railroad and university were careful to stress the practicality of instruction aboard the train. The train would not propagate abstract theory but would bring the experts "to confer with the farmers and orchardists upon the ground and by discussion to bring out the practical needs of any one locality." Farmers, who were invited to come with questions pertaining to their own work, would get personalized "technical and expert information" directly from the people who had studied the wider problems. The scientists, for their part, would also gain something they had hitherto lacked, a better grasp of local situations and the actual needs of farmers.[81]

The first train left the University Farm at Davis to tour towns in the Sacramento Valley for nine days in early November 1908; other tours followed each month through the winter and early spring, until by May 1909 virtually all farming districts had been covered, from coastal to interior valleys and foothills, from Oregon south to the Imperial Valley. Aboard the first train were nearly twenty experts from the university, two of the state horticulturists, and Southern Pacific assistant passenger agent H. R. Judah, who was in charge. As time went on, to build support for the mobile demonstration project, its sponsoring institutions, and scientific agriculture in general, the railroad and university invited guests to ride the train and witness its work, including newspaper and farm-journal editors, local dignitaries, regional farm experts, and representatives of agricultural and business organizations. Even university president Wheeler, after a trial run, found the experience so exhilarating that he eventually became a regular participant, delivering enthusiastic orations on the virtues of scientific agriculture and the importance to the state of the university and its College of Agriculture before packed houses at dozens of rural towns. Some university people, such as Clarke and Dean of Agriculture Wickson, accompanied all the train's tours, but by the end of the season, almost every agricultural expert of the College of Agriculture and its experiment stations had served as a lecturer or demonstrator at one time or another.[82]

The lectures, demonstrations, and question-and-answer sessions given to visitors combined public relations efforts to build popular support for the university, Horticultural Commission, and railroad with attempts to impart detailed instruction aimed at improving farmers' productivity, profits, and life conditions through applied science. Each program started with short introductory talks by Wheeler, Clarke, and Wickson on the importance of scientific agriculture and the university's research and regular and extension classes. O. E. Bremner or another state horticulturist followed and discussed how, without inspections, quarantines, and, when necessary, crop-destruction orders, the state's orchard industries would be at the mercy of insects and disease blights. Passenger agent Judah, assistant freight agent C. J. Jones, or another Southern Pacific official closed by expounding on the unity of interest between the railroad and the people and the company's particular support for farmers. Each sponsor's representative tried to convince visitors of the value and sincerity of his agency's services, especially to farmers. Freight agent Jones, like President Wheeler, stretched rhetorical eloquence to the limits of credulity. Jones routinely stressed to farmers that the Southern Pacific, by what it was doing to support the train, was showing "that it has the good of the country at heart, and that it wants you to make money." His speeches fairly oozed with praise for the growers. "All I can say is that I am sorry for Virgil," he confided to San Joaquin County farmers. "If he had lived to see the Tokay grape as raised by Lodi growers, his poetry might today be loved by schoolboys."[83] When his turn came before the podium, passenger agent Judah tried to convince the audience to see the railroad as essentially a philanthropist.[84] State horticulturist Bremner found the railroad people particularly hard to take. "The oratorial general freight agent [Jones]," he reported to his agency with tongue in cheek, "turned loose broadside after broadside of such eloquence that it left the populous [sic] too amazed to counter."[85]

On the other hand, most of the lecture time at every stop was devoted to researchers and teachers expounding on such topics as soils and fertilizers, improving crop yields, viticulture, animal husbandry and veterinary science, orchard planting and care, apiculture, insects and crop diseases, truck gardening, farm machines, irrigation, and dry-farming.[86] Even the Southern Pacific's agents and crewmen, led by the head brakeman, after listening carefully to the presentations at the first stops, in the words of state horticulturist Bremner, could be found "haranguing . . . [crowds] of fifteen or more on the mystics of parasitism and the intricacies of fumigation methods" and directing visitors to the those experts who could provide more specialized advice.[87] Reflecting one of the specific farm problems behind the organization of the train, at most stops university professor George W. Shaw promoted a system university scientists had developed whereby crop rotation and alternate deep and shallow plowing could be used to preserve ground moisture, increase soil fertility, produce four cereal crops every three years, and expand yield 25 to 50 percent.[88] The passionate oratory, commented on in newspapers across the state, lent the demonstration train's visits a semblance to a religious revival. Indeed, biblical rhetoric and imagery enlivened many presentations. Not just university president Wheeler but other speakers—university, community, and railroad people alike—commonly referred to the train's message as a "gospel," proclaimed the necessity of the "conversion" of farming to the new pathways of science, and portrayed themselves as prophets in a great awakening of economic, social, and moral uplift.[89] For later reference by the trains' visitors or for those who had not attended, local newspapers often printed the lectures verbatim or condensed.[90]

In that autumn of 1908, the first joint university–Southern Pacific agricultural demonstration train through the Sacramento Valley was, in the words of

the *Marysville Appeal,* a colossal "success from every standpoint," attracting re-
spectable numbers of visitors, sometimes hundreds, at nearly every stop, as well
as earning accolades from farmers, newspaper editors, community leaders, and
dignitaries who had ridden aboard.[91] In fact, the crowds at some places were
so overwhelming that, before it headed out for subsequent trips, the train re-
treated to the University Farm at Davis, where the displays and general exhibition cars were remodeled to accommodate more people. Moreover, future
trains included additional lecturers and at least two more rail cars carrying constantly changing exhibits of crops and methods of specific value to the locales
being visited.[92]

As it made more ten-day to two-week trips in the winter and spring of 1909,
eventually covering the San Joaquin Valley, the Los Angeles area, the Imperial
and Coachella desert valleys, and coastal valleys from Ventura north to the San
Francisco Bay region, the demonstration train became increasingly localized,
reflecting the state's dramatically varied growing conditions and crop systems.
While traditional grain and animal industries and methods of combating the
region's notorious soil exhaustion had dominated discussion in the Sacramento
and northern San Joaquin valleys, when the train visited orange grove districts
around Riverside, local experts such as G. Harold Powell of the Southern California Pathological Laboratory at Whittier were taken aboard to give presentations on citrus pests, spraying methods and predatory insects used to control
them, and experiments being conducted on new and better varieties of oranges
and lemons.[93] At Gilroy, in the deciduous fruit district of the Santa Clara Valley south of San Jose, Professor Loughridge of the university advised farmers
on how to alter their local customs of weeding orchards and plowing fallow
fields in order to better preserve soil fertility and moisture.[94] In the Sonoma
and Napa valleys, presenters instructed viticulturists in the techniques of sul-
furing grape vines.[95]

Although in some communities fewer than one hundred persons attended
the train's demonstrations, in other places, despite the remodeling, crowds were
overflowing, requiring crews to open the car doors and windows so that those
left outside could at least hear the presentations. If anything, interest and attendance built with each successive trip. In the Sierra foothills, 1,500 people
passed through the exhibit cars at Lincoln, and farmers openly expressed surprise at knowledge and technology they had never encountered before, while
at Colfax and Dutch Flat, editors reported that almost all local farmers and
orchardists had attended.[96] The largest crowd in the San Joaquin Valley—
1,500—greeted the train at Dinuba, while four hundred to one thousand turned
out in other farm centers such as Sanger and Reedley.[97] At Beaumont, east of
San Bernardino and Riverside at the edge of the desert, the train's visit, timed
to coincide with St. Patrick's Day festivities, drew a huge crowd. At nearby Ban-

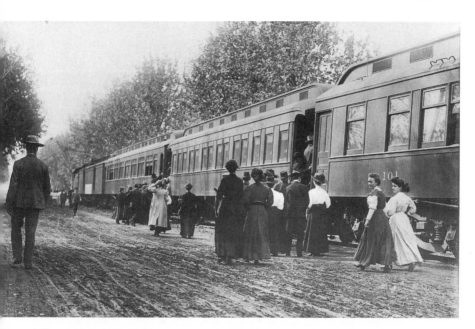

College students from California State Normal School visit the Southern Pacific–University of California agricultural demonstration train at Chico, ca. 1910. Courtesy Bancroft Library.

ning, virtually the entire town attended, including all the school children and a tribal delegation from an adjacent reservation, which a local editor said illustrated the Indians' "'true' spirited progressivism."[98] All in all, the touring university traversed most of the Southern Pacific's important routes in the state and was attended by more than 37,000 persons during the 1908–1909 season. According to Agriculture College dean E. J. Wickson, the enterprise cost the Southern Pacific about $300 per day to keep the demonstration trains on the road, or about $15,000 for the season.[99]

Despite lingering complaints about overcrowding and too-brief visits, the University of California–Southern Pacific Company farm demonstration tour of 1908–1909 was acclaimed by farmers, editors, and civic leaders across California. Scientists and trainmen alike testified that the trips were exhausting, with sometimes three or more stops per day, frequent night meetings, and grueling side trips by automobile or buggy to remote sites to investigate special farm conditions or new disease infestations. But even the university people were surprised at how effectively the train raised the enthusiasm of masses of ordinary farmers and other rural people for the message of scientific agriculture.[100] "The visit of the demonstration train to this vicinity," concluded the antirailroad *Sacramento Bee* in a typical response, "will no doubt do a whole lot of practical good to those who were fortunate enough to visit the train and hear the discourses."[101] After accompanying the train on several trips, President Wheeler in February 1909 reported on the train's success to a meeting of the university Regents and wired Southern Pacific president E. H. Harriman endorsing the train and asking the railroad to repeat it annually.[102]

Indeed, encouraged by overwhelming public response to the first year's effort, railroad and university did continue to dispatch California farm demonstration trains for three more travel seasons, in 1909–1910, 1910–1911, and 1911–1912. Each year, the touring university grew larger and more elaborate, involved more experimenters and educators, took to the road for more days, covered more rail mileage, visited more communities, and drew bigger crowds. By 1911–1912, the peak season, the demonstration trains traveled between 4,000 and 5,000 miles (nearly double the mileage of the first season), made 238 stops, and attracted about 102,000 visitors. In the 1910–1911 season, according to the U.S. Department of Agriculture and university president Wheeler, the Southern Pacific's California farm demonstration trains accounted for 40 percent of all such activity in the country.[103] According to a leading historian of agricultural extension, the $30,000 the Southern Pacific was spending annually on the train by 1910 was the largest such outlay by any American railroad.[104] Despite the expense, the railroad, like the university people, was enthusiastic about the demonstration trains' benefits to California and the company. "Much good was accomplished in bringing about improved tillage and better handling of crops," passenger traffic manager Charles S. Fee privately told an inquiring professor from Texas A & M University, "and in opening a freer channel of intercourse between the farmer and the agricultural experts at the University."[105]

Over the years, instruction dispensed aboard the University of California–Southern Pacific demonstration trains evolved in keeping with new farm needs and changing ideas of agricultural education. Each year, although the popular subjects of earlier trains were repeated, new topics were added to the curriculum, until the California trains were by far the most comprehensive mobile farm schools in the nation.[106] At a time when irrigated acreage was expanding dramatically, particularly in the burgeoning local public irrigation districts, for example, the train's experts devoted increased attention to irrigation methods and technology and approaches to cultivating and marketing irrigated crops.[107] Also, reflecting the influence of the Country Life Movement's focus on improving the social and cultural quality, not just the economic productivity, of rural living, later trains carried women professors from the College of Agriculture's Department of Home Economics to discuss improved food preparation, labor-saving devices, home life, and health issues—what was commonly referred to as "farm sanitation."[108] And, later trains attempted even more to tailor curriculum to the special questions pertinent to localities. During an outbreak of hog cholera in the San Joaquin Valley in early 1911, the train featured presentations on inoculating pigs with vaccine.[109] Working with local farm, civic, and business leaders, the railroad began to operate special passenger trains (with free fares) to bring more visitors from outlying districts to see the demonstration trains at their central stops.[110] More systematic effort was also made to cooperate with local school superintendents, principals, and teachers to assure more involvement by young people in the trains' activities.[111] When the train arrived in Chico in November 1911, for example, classes were dismissed at the high school and grammar schools, as well as the State Normal School, and all students were required to visit, take notes, and complete papers and projects based on information contained in the exhibits and lectures.[112]

The influences of the University of California–Southern Pacific Company farm demonstration trains are difficult to assess precisely because they cannot be isolated from the many complicated climatic, economic, institutional, and scientific and technological forces that were simultaneously reshaping farming in the state and nation. Then also, some of the trains' most significant improvements would have been long-term and not immediately apparent. Nevertheless, impressionistic evidence suggests that the trains were important in helping modernize California agriculture at a time of rapid transformation by keeping many farmers abreast of the great changes affecting their lives and livelihoods.

The demonstration trains' positive influences on agriculture were commonly attested to by scientists, editors, and local farm and business leaders. Some claims were general, such as the *Marysville Appeal*'s prediction of "a revolution in agriculture and horticulture in this garden spot of the Sacramento Valley," but there were plenty of concrete examples as well.[113] The rural, urban, and farm press frequently reported, sometimes even a year or more after a demonstration train's visit, specific ways that local growers had changed their methods as a result, with salutary effects. Presentations made aboard the trains of the 1908–1909 touring season, for example, were the direct stimulus for local public health campaigns resulting in ordinances or health department orders prohibiting tainted milk and creating fly and mosquito abatement programs in Marysville and Riverside.[114] At Arbuckle in the Sacramento Valley, a university scientist, while on a side trip from the first train, discovered that *phylloxera* infested old vineyards in the vicinity, causing farmers and local agricultural officials to mobilize quickly against the dreaded vine parasite. Within days, local vineyards had been inspected and many vines, in some cases whole vineyards, destroyed.[115] Also at Arbuckle, another expert identified a local epidemic killing more than one-half of the turkey-ranch stock as diphtheria, took the information and an infected bird back to Berkeley for study, and promised to return as soon as possible with recommended cures. Small wonder that the *Sacramento Bee* judged the train's visit "of inestimable value" to the district.[116]

Elsewhere, there were similar direct results from the first year's trains. Scientists also discovered more diseased vines near Roseville.[117] At Beaumont, then in the midst of a boom in planting apple orchards, university people gave growers "many valuable hints regarding methods of planting, cultivation, and irrigation of the crop" and particularly, advice on how they should go about choosing the best apple varieties for marketing and frost protection.[118] In the Imperial and Coachella desert valleys farther east, state horticulturists distributed thirty quarts of ladybird beetles to help farmers eradicate mealybugs devouring local cantaloupe and barley crops.[119] Also at El Centro in the Imperial Valley, when scientists learned that a carload of cotton seed was to arrive the next day to start what would one day become one of the region's most important crops, they warned local growers that extreme caution would be needed to prevent boll weevils from entering along with the seed. Consequently, upon arrival, the car was put under heavy guard while it was subjected to painstaking inspection.[120] At Ventura, university researcher J. B. Neff went to the area in advance of the train to take soil samples, and during the train's visit, scientists presented the results and advised farmers how to amend their humusdeficient soil for better production.[121] Years later, Southern Pacific passenger traffic manager Charles Fee recalled that the first train's visit to the San Joaquin, then in the midst of an epidemic, also had a direct influence on improved hog-cholera research, including the establishment of the State Hog Cholera Serum Laboratory.[122] Abundant such accounts followed in the wake of subsequent years' demonstration trains, and farmers attending the trains often attested to good results from suggestions received on previous visits.[123]

The California demonstration trains undoubtedly increased support for scientific agriculture among farmers and country people in general. Nationwide, according to a leading historian of agricultural extension, the trains were important in "dissolving rural suspicion of scientific agriculture and in awakening the farmer to its possibilities."[124] The California trains, for example, reached many more people than earlier extension methods—37,000 during the first year, compared to an annual average of just over 20,000 reached by all methods used in the state in the years leading up to 1908.[125] The train's organizers also believed that the train's effects were magnified because they attracted farmers remote from the few earlier farm-institute sites and because they seemed to influence particularly the more impressionable younger people, as well as the largest, most "progressive" farmers, who were most likely to serve as models to others. Also important was the conversion of country and agricultural editors, who had often been skeptical, if not openly hostile, to scientific agriculture. Many an editor, once taken aboard one of the demonstration trains to view modern farming methods firsthand, returned to announce, like the editor of the *Merced Sun,* that "the day of scientific farming is at hand." The train, he reported, was "the most emphatic argument that can be found of the necessity of combin-

Rural people jammed into the lecture cars as the Southern Pacific–University of California agricultural demonstration train toured the state, ca. 1910. Courtesy Bancroft Library.

ing scientific information with manual labor in the proper production of agricultural and horticultural crops." Farmers who continued to scoff that no "college man" or "city chap" could teach them anything, he warned, "are doing themselves a woeful injury."[126] In only one indication that farmers were heeding this type of advice, just the first two trips of the 1908–1909 touring season caused a trebling of the number of letters from farmers seeking assistance from the university's agricultural departments.[127]

Actually, all parties found positive results. For their part, experts aboard the train frequently admitted that they too had learned much about the realities of farming in California that would improve their work. The experience "has been an education to the instructors as well as the instructed," reported state horticulturist Bremner, "and we believe we know *more* now of *what* the people want, and that is just *what* we are going to try and give them."[128] One important likely repercussion of the train was that after 1910, criticism of the university and its College of Agriculture in the rural areas and in the legislature, although it never vanished, did diminish markedly, paving the way for increased funding for buildings and programs at Berkeley, Davis, and regional experiment stations.[129] The Southern Pacific also undoubtedly reaped some public relations benefits from its sponsorship of the demonstration trains. Many country and agricultural editors, for example, grudgingly admitted that whatever its other faults might be, the railroad was to thanked for its indispensable service on this occasion. Calling the demonstration train "a practical example of long-headedness of a big corporation," the editor of the anti–Southern Pacific *California Cultivator* wished "all honor to the Southern Pacific and University people who are joined in these efforts."[130] The *Santa Paula Chronicle* wrote that the train was a sign "that the Southern Pacific is trying to inaugurate a more liberal and popular policy."[131]

Not all was sweetness and light, however. Throughout these intensely anti-railroad years, the much-heralded arrival of the demonstration train sometimes provided an ideal setting for anti–Southern Pacific banners, mass protest meetings, and verbal assaults on the company by local editors and farm, business, and political leaders. Though much less common, there were even a few public denunciations of the College of Agriculture or the larger University of California. At Chico in November 1908, the Chamber of Commerce, which was working with the Southern Pacific to organize and publicize the train's first visit there, simultaneously scheduled a mass meeting the night before the arrival to attack the railroad's fare structure and the company's refusal to grant the town terminal privileges and rates, two issues that the town had been pressing, and the railroad evading, for more than five years. The meeting stole the headlines on the very day the train pulled into town. The chamber then used the publicity aroused by the meeting and the demonstration train to convene other protest gatherings and to start a boycott of the Southern Pacific.[132] At Fresno a few months later, Chester Rowell, one of the leaders of the anti-railroad Lincoln-Roosevelt League and later of the state's Republican Progressive faction, used the demonstration train's visit to launch an editorial attack on the company in the columns of his *Fresno Republican,* particularly singling out chief counsel, vice president, and head political organizer William F. Herrin for charges of monopolistic arrogance and political corruption.[133] The public-relations sword, it seems, could cut in many directions.[134]

As it turns out, so could the truth. Some people did not want to hear, and particularly did not want others to hear, the wisdom of the farm experts. While most farm communities welcomed advice calculated to improve production and profits, science occasionally ran afoul of regional booster strategies and entrenched vested interests, producing unexpected and heated controversies that took on ironic, comic-opera qualities. When the first demonstration train arrived in December 1908 at Modesto, for example, locals crammed into a lecture hall for a night session were stunned to hear the university's George W. Shaw pronounce (correctly) that "Stanislaus [County] land is too valuable for the planting of eucalyptus trees." It seems that the area, like much of the state, was then gripped by one of a succession of speculative eucalyptus-planting manias encouraged by local nursery growers, land-subdividers, and the San Joaquin Eucalyptus Company, which had set up a network of local offices near Modesto. Promoters claimed that a nationwide hardwood shortage would create a lucrative market for the agriculturally grown trees imported from Australia. Shaw's condemnation of the faddish industry, according to the *Modesto News,* "did not set well with the eucalyptus growers and enthusiasts of this vicinity." By the next day, agitation had spread among farmers and prominent citizens of Stanislaus County, who expressed amazement "that the learned professor should have made such a statement." Adolph Epstein, known locally as the "Eucalyptus King," and others vilified the professor as incompetent, some demanding that he apologize or resign.[135]

After the California agricultural demonstration train's 1911–1912 season, at its peak of popularity and attendance, although university and railroad organizers remained pleased with general results, they decided to end the project. Problems of overcrowding had persisted, inconveniencing visitors and leading some train managers to conclude that the fast pace of presentation, combined with the crush of people, many of them non-farmers, was watering down the scientific message. Moreover, the very format of the project prevented scientists from following up with any but a handful of individual farmers. Professors also grew weary of the trains' demanding regimen; for decades, agricultural scientists had been struggling to free themselves from just such stultifying routines and to shift their attention more to research.[136] At the same time, new approaches to providing agricultural extension services were emerging, particularly centering on locating resident farm agents in rural areas, who would rely on better roads and automobiles and even the use of motion pictures to keep in continuous contact with masses of farmers. Across the nation after 1912, university leaders and agricultural officials rapidly abandoned farm demonstration trains, and indeed all types of institutes. Even railroad people, their companies facing growing financial problems after 1912, came to believe that the demonstration trains, which certainly had served their purpose, had now outlived their usefulness. Indeed, the Smith-Lever Act, passed by Congress to provide federal funding for the county agent and new forms of farm extension, specifically prohibited the use of the money for demonstration trains.[137] With the summer 1912 retirement of College of Agriculture dean E. J. Wickson, who had since the beginning identified himself with the project, and his replacement by Thomas F. Hunt, described at the time as "new blood" from the east, the university and the railroad decided to ground the demonstration trains, at least as annual, comprehensive efforts to reach masses of farmers. Instead, in 1913, the university, in cooperation with local farm bureaus, established a network of county agricultural agents. The Southern Pacific, in keeping with its tradition of involvement in scientific agriculture, worked with the university in the new system, including providing free transportation for the agents.[138]

Farm demonstration trains, most of them organized and supported by the Southern Pacific Company, made occasional, brief revival tours in California. As early as February 1913, after severe January frosts had devastated southern orange and lemon groves, the railroad and university quickly dispatched a "Frost Educational Special" through Los Angeles, Orange, Riverside, and San Bernardino counties to advise growers how to prune, water, and fertilize in order to minimize the long-range tree damage and how best to weather freezes in the future. Following the highly successful citrus special, the university announced it had adopted a new theory of demonstration trains: "It is believed that by sending out trains to accomplish a special purpose and sending with the train qualified specialists, work of a higher character and of more lasting benefit can be achieved."[139] At stops in the citrus district, university officials took the opportunity to get the assembled growers and local leaders to sign petitions and adopt resolutions calling for the passage of a bill, then pending in the legislature, appropriating $385,000 to establish a university experiment station for citrus research. The creation that year of what became a renowned citrus experimentation center at Riverside testifies to the important role the University of California–Southern Pacific Company demonstration trains played in the advance of scientific agriculture in the state.[140] Over the next decade and a half, railroad and university teamed up a few more times, often with other companies such as the Northwestern Pacific, Union Pacific, or Santa Fe, to send out additional specialized trains.[141]

California's original demonstration trains had focused on problems of cultivation, but after World War I, the state's major agricultural problem ironically shifted to overproduction. In 1928, with farmers suffering serious, long-term losses from glutted fruit markets and declining crop prices, the College of Agriculture and the Southern Pacific organized another, and what appears to have been the final, comprehensive demonstration train aimed at teaching farmers how to boost their incomes by diversifying, especially by adding varied livestock sidelines and by forming marketing cooperatives. Nearly 50,000 persons visited the fourteen-car train during its tour.[142]

In the first decades of the twentieth century, the Southern Pacific continued to aid the University of California and its College of Agriculture in ways other than sponsoring farm demonstration trains. After 1910, the railroad lobbied in Sacramento and in other ways tried to increase support in the state for greater and more secure funding for the university, particularly the College of Agriculture. The railroad's work was especially important in obtaining approval for the construction of a large new building to house the college at the Berkeley campus (completed in 1912). Then, in 1914, the railroad cooperated with University of California staff, students, and alumni in their campaign for a state constitutional amendment to expand and stabilize university financing. The railroad urged its many employees and customers to vote for the amendment because it represented "a need of an educational institution that has a bearing on the welfare of the State and its industries, and because the passage of the amendment will be of especial benefit to the agricultural interests of the State." To the railroad, it was "an economic, not [a] political issue."[143] Acknowledging the railroad's assistance on this occasion, as well as decades of general support, the university Regents in 1914 passed a resolution formally thanking the company. The Regents directed their secretary to inform the railroad that "repeatedly, in the past, through its co-operation with the agricultural investigations and the agricultural extension work of the University, and through its aid to University extension in many forms, and through its always kindly attitude toward the University, the Southern Pacific has shown a much appreciated sympathy with the work of the University."[144]

Promoting Scientific Agriculture across the West

When it entered other states, in the interest of stimulating economic development and traffic for its lines, the Southern Pacific instituted the scientific agricultural programs it had pioneered in California. As had happened in the Golden State, the railroad became a leading defender, supporter, and shaper of state land-grant colleges and their agricultural research and education. Usually, the colleges were in towns served by the Southern Pacific, originally located there because of political pressure exerted by the company or a predecessor. The colleges' presence in its territory assured maximum railroad support. Also, as had been true in California, close interaction between railroaders and researchers and professors grew out of shared values, educational and professional experiences, commitments to social and economic progress through applied science, and in many cases friendships and family relationships. Although in California the company had focused on encouraging fruit and specialty-crops relying on irrigation, the Southern Pacific's agricultural development strategy in other states varied according to regional farm problems and potentials, marketing outlooks, and political and institutional arrangements.

In Nevada in the early 1870s, for example, it was the Central Pacific Railroad that donated the twenty-acre tract the state legislature required before it would found and build a state land-grant college. The University of Nevada opened in 1874 in the rail center and county seat at Elko, where the company had just installed a major water system and hoped to encourage irrigated farming.[145] Mining interests opposed to any public spending for agriculture immediately attacked the university, however, and many groups condemned the site as arid, unlikely to support extensive farming, and several hundred miles remote from most state residents in the environmentally more promising Reno and Carson City–Virginia City areas to the west. Crippled by low public esteem and legislative indifference and ridiculed by the state's farmers, the institution struggled during its first two decades, its leadership unstable and agricultural programs barely functioning. In 1885, the university relocated to the even more important Southern Pacific center of Reno, which the railroad was also subdividing and promoting through the Pacific Improvement Company. Problems persisted nevertheless, unresolved until the appointment in 1894 of the first effective president, Joseph E. Stubbs. Recommending Stubbs and heading the state-wide movement to lobby the Regents to hire him was Robert L. Fulton, prominent Nevada editor, businessman, civic leader, promoter of irrigation and agriculture, and the Southern Pacific's Great Basin land agent.[146] A lifelong friend of Fulton, the new president was also brother to Southern Pacific Company vice president and traffic manager J. C. Stubbs and to David M. Stubbs, general manager of the Big Four's Occidental and Oriental Steamship Company. A strong supporter of scientific agriculture, President Stubbs particularly built up the university's agricultural experiment station and farm extension programs. Through Fulton and Stubbs, the Southern Pacific backed the university in the legislature, furnished seed, soil, and materials for research, and provided subsidies for research and free transportation for the agriculture college's scientists and supplies, as well as for farmers participating in extension programs. Particularly, the Southern Pacific sponsored experiments in irrigation, dry-farming techniques, and crops suitable to water-short Nevada.[147]

Similar partnerships between gown and railroad pertained in Oregon. Oregon Agricultural College (later Oregon State University) benefited from the railroad's patronage, especially after 1900. Southern Pacific vice president and chief counsel William F. Herrin, among the Corvallis institution's first valedictory graduates, remained a loyal and active alumnus and friend, and John Knox Weatherford, one of the company's lead Oregon attorneys, served on the Board of Regents from 1897 to 1923.[148] Before, during, and after the Harriman Lines' merger, the railroad politically defended the college and its funding, organized campaigns to convince Oregon business leaders to support the college, subsidized agricultural research and extension programs, and assisted in starting up branch experiment stations in diverse environments, including one in southeastern Klamath Falls, also a Southern Pacific region. Particularly, the company provided capital contributions and publicity for the college's ambitious irrigation experiments, culminating in an important project in the 1920s and 1930s to encourage and finance small farmers in the Willamette Valley to install deep wells so they could diversify by irrigating field crops and orchards and adding new livestock sidelines.[149]

In Arizona Territory, the Southern Pacific, as early as the 1880s through land agent Mills, worked to introduce date palm culture to the Southwest desert, assisting and financing the importation of trees and cultivation studies by the U.S. Department of Agriculture. By the mid-1890s, the University of Arizona's fledgling Arizona Experiment Station, located in Tucson, the company's most important rail center in the state, had joined the project. With the railroad's support, the university's date palm experiments continued and expanded into the early 1900s, by which time the crop had become established in Arizona and in California's Coachella Valley.[150] During the 1890s and early 1900s, particularly after the 1895 appointment of civil engineer Epes Randolph as head of the Southern Pacific Railroad of Arizona, the company regularly contributed cash and free transportation to the university's agricultural programs. In fact during most years, the Southern Pacific was the only state railway making contributions of any sort or amount.[151] It furnished large grants to, among other new projects, the application of new agricultural machinery, surveys of alkali destruction of irrigated farmlands in the Salt River Valley, rangeland preservation and rehabilitation, calf-breeding, and most important, studies of irrigation by tapping underground river flows, which opened up farming in new desert regions.[152] The railroad's grant in 1906 of $5,000 to that irrigation research project, according to Arizona Experiment Station director R. H. Forbes, allowed the university to double the work-hours of scientists assigned, making it possible for the first time for progress to be made "in a very satisfactory manner."[153]

In its Atlantic System east of El Paso, where the company arrived in the early 1880s, the Southern Pacific's support for agricultural science, if anything, intensified. To Texas Agricultural & Mechanical College, located at College Station in the heart of Southern Pacific territory, the railroad again contributed cash, supplies, and transportation services, particularly free or low-cost travel for farmers attending the college's many extension courses, including segregated offerings for black farmers. E. J. Kyle, agriculture dean from 1911 to 1930, developed an especially close relationship with the Southern Pacific's subsidiary Houston & Texas Central, from which the college received abundant aid for research, extension courses, and demonstration trains.[154] The Southern Pacific's agricultural development work in Texas was particularly aimed at finding replacements for the state's troubled cotton-growing industry, particularly after the boll weevil struck in full force after 1903. In Texas, closer to concentrated eastern markets and with more rainfall and surface water, especially in central, eastern, and Gulf Coast areas, the railroad stressed shifting to such crops as rice, sugar, tobacco, and what it called "a balanced system of farming," in other words, traditional diversified production.[155]

In Texas, the railroad's political support proved to be crucial. Founded by the legislature in the early 1870s to take advantage of the federal Morrill Land Grant College Act, Texas A & M from the beginning was besieged on all fronts. As was generally true across the West, farmers, led by the Grange, denounced the college, first because it emphasized classical education, then after its reorganization in 1880 because it devoted resources to engineering as opposed to agriculture, and later because its agricultural programs stressed research instead of "practical farming." Distant and different agricultural regions also attempted to strip the college of its control of the state's sole experiment station in College Station and to substitute separate, independent experiment stations in their districts, which they temporarily succeeded in doing between 1909 and 1921. Meanwhile, the state's elite institution, the University of Texas, resentful of having to share the same state college fund, repeatedly spearheaded campaigns to close its rival and/or transfer its federally supported programs to Austin. Unending political pressure produced a succession of legislative investigations and radical reorganizations and disruptions of the college throughout the late nineteenth and the first three decades of the twentieth centuries.[156] The Southern Pacific's support helped the college to maintain its independence and at least minimal funding from the state.

This was particularly evident in the 1910s, in many ways the nadir in Texas A & M's history, which occasioned the most direct involvement by Southern Pacific people in a land-grant university. Enemies led by the University of Texas and its powerful allies mounted their most forceful attempt to gain control of the college, perhaps even shut it down. Leading the defenders of Texas A & M was Edward B. Cushing. One of the college's first engineering graduates, in 1880, Cushing had deliberately gone to work for the Southern Pacific in order to facilitate the railroad's assistance to his alma mater. A skilled and respected civil engineer, Cushing rose through the ranks to become the head of the railroad's construction in Texas and Louisiana between 1908 and 1915 and after that chief executive in charge of engineering, maintenance-of-way, construction, and valuation for the Atlantic System. An advocate of agricultural research and education and always seeking to improve the stature of his former college, Cushing founded the first strong alumni association in the 1890s, served as its president, and led campaigns to mobilize alumni to raise money and build political support for making Texas A & M completely separate from the state university at Austin, with independent state funding. In 1913, University of Texas partisans got a constitutional amendment on the state ballot (SJR 18) that would have, in effect, converted Texas A & M into a branch of the university, governed by its Board of Regents. Appointed to Texas A & M's Board of Directors, in 1913 Cushing became the board's president just in time to lead the college's fight for survival. When the governor, who openly favored the university, engineered the firing of Texas A & M's president, reducing the institution to chaos, Cushing stepped in as the de facto chief administrator, represented the college in Austin, revamped its financial system, and even underwrote the college's checks with his personal accounts when the governor and legislature refused to appropriate money for the college.[157] During the campaign against the constitutional amendment in June and July 1913, as Board of Directors president, Cushing rallied farm organizations, was interviewed by and wrote opinion pieces for newspapers, pressed the governor to keep politics out of his handling of Texas A & M matters, and orchestrated a successful drive that defeated the measure at the polls.[158] Although Cushing's several subsequent attempts to secure Texas A & M's complete independence failed, and it would only be achieved decades later, the college and its agricultural programs were at least preserved.[159] When he died in 1924, the *Houston Chronicle* praised Cushing as "one of . . . Texas A & M's staunchest supporters and greatest benefactors"; the *Houston Post* characterized the Southern Pacific engineer's lifelong service to his alma mater as "epochal."[160]

Across western states, the Southern Pacific was undoubtedly the most prolific provider of agricultural demonstration trains. Sometimes though, in states it did not dominate as thoroughly as in California, the company worked in conjunction with other railroads. Since the agricultural colleges generally were in Southern Pacific territory, however, the company usually took the lead working with the scientists to plan and organize the projects, collect displays, and schedule tours. Southern Pacific demonstration trains in Texas began in 1904. To start up the campaign against the boll weevil, the U.S. Department of Agriculture dispatched Seaman A. Knapp in January to establish a headquarters in Houston, the Southern Pacific's main terminal and port in the state. When Knapp called on the state's railways for support, the railroad was the first and most vigorous respondent.[161] In February, the company, in cooperation with Texas A & M, sent out the first of many trains taking Knapp, his dozens of assistants, college scientists, and the railroad's own agricultural consultants around the state, starting in Southern Pacific territory and then on to other railways, to investigate the problem and organize groups of local farmers to stop the weevil infestation. Particularly, the railroad paid much of the cost, publicized the meetings, and recruited farmers in many districts to allocate ten-acre experimental and model plots to be worked by Knapp's agents. The Southern Pacific supplemented the U.S. Department of Agriculture's work by broadcasting the government's and the company's own literature about the weevil across the state and organizing special informational programs at public schools.[162] Within a year or two, Knapp's traveling-agent system, begun in the Texas boll-weevil campaign, spread to other states and crops and became the basis for the Department of Agriculture's county agent program, central to farm extension in the twentieth century. Acknowledging that "our funds are not sufficient to do this work," Knapp thanked the Southern Pacific's Houston & Texas Central line and other railroads for getting the farm-agent system going and helping it spread.[163] Again in conjunction with Texas A & M and other state and federal agricultural agencies, sometimes by itself and sometimes working also with other rail lines, the Southern Pacific organized and sent out other Texas demonstration trains in specialized or general farm-improvement campaigns into the 1920s.[164]

In cooperation with state agricultural colleges, the Southern Pacific also ran demonstration trains extensively in Oregon and Arizona and a few times in Nevada and Louisiana, where the company had less trackage. In Arizona, after the Southern Pacific and the university assembled the train in Tucson and toured it throughout the company's southern lines, the Santa Fe took the entourage on its northern lines.[165] In Oregon, the Southern Pacific, with Oregon Agricultural College and sometimes Harriman Lines companies in the state, ran numerous general and specialized demonstration cars and entire trains from the 1900s into the 1920s. Focusing on crop diversification, the 1911 train was especially notable. Early that year, in a familiar replay of what happened throughout the West, numerous regional newspapers and business and agricultural groups critical of scientific agriculture and Oregon Agricultural College's work started a campaign to put a referendum on the 1912 ballot to abolish the college. Heading the pack was the University of Oregon, seeking to absorb the college, and of course its state and federal funding.[166] In the fall, when planning a larger, dramatic train tour covering more of the state, the Southern Pacific and the college aimed not simply at getting farmers to diversify and modernize production but more particularly at bolstering the reputation and political support for the college, especially in districts remote and eastward from Corvallis. Farm groups, commercial organizations, and newspapers—even begrudgingly the *Portland Oregonian,* a leader of the referendum drive—praised the 1911 train as an example of the valuable, practical contributions the Agricultural College, scientific agriculture in general, and the Southern Pacific were making to the state's farming. The referendum failed to make the ballot.[167]

Southern Pacific farm demonstration trains in all states were curtailed after the mid-1910s, when the congressional Smith-Lever Act and U.S. Department of Agriculture policy prohibited further federal agricultural college and experiment-station money from being used to support demonstration trains. The Southern Pacific and its region's agricultural colleges, at their own expense, continued to dispatch occasional special farm demonstration cars or trains through the Great Depression.[168] The railroad's general support for the colleges' research and instruction continued unabated.

12 "The Damndest Railroading You Ever Heard Of"

MARKETING THE PRODUCE OF WESTERN FARMS

Marketing Problems

Between the 1860s and the 1920s, the Southern Pacific Company participated in and helped to shape every facet of agricultural development in its territory. The mere building of new rail lines, coupled with the company's land-grant colonization programs, opened up regions to cultivation and settlement and stimulated land subdivision. At the same time, the railroad's promotion of irrigation brought water for people to farm dry land in new ways, or even to farm it at all. And the Southern Pacific's fostering of agricultural science and education increased and diversified production, particularly in higher-value specialty crops. By the early twentieth century, the company's territory, which stretched from rainy Oregon, down through semi-arid California, eastward across Great Basin and Southwest deserts, and out onto the humid Gulf Plains, was unequaled in the West, indeed the world, in variety of planted crops and yet-untapped agricultural potentials.

Ironically, though, for all the money and effort that land and water developers, farmers, scientists, and railroad people invested in expanding the *supply* of farm products through removing the impediments to successful agriculture, in many ways the region's most fundamental problem remained a restricted and unreliable *demand* for those goods. In fact, increasing production excessively or prematurely exacerbated the farmers' problems. The Far West and Southwest's relatively scant and slowly growing population constricted local and regional markets, rendering them easily glutted. There were also numerous hindrances to sending produce to the burgeoning urban and small-town markets of middle western and eastern America: the great distances of one to three thousand miles; a largely unpopulated, rugged, intervening landscape that elevated freight tariffs; high spoilage rates on shipments caused by freezes in winter and blistering heat in summer; and the farmers' and shippers' lack of information on market conditions and prices. Some markets were glutted with perishables, particularly the major distribution centers such as

Chicago where most produce was sent, while other markets distant from major cities suffered shortages. Often, commission merchants who bought the produce on consignment, not the farmers, captured whatever profits were to be had. Moreover, many new specialty crops emerging in the Far West and Southwest, such as California's oranges, raisins, dates, and prunes, were exotic, unfamiliar to American palates. Some farm products, like fresh winter fruits and vegetables, arrived out of season and without established demand. If they were familiar, like apples from the Pacific Northwest, products competed with cheaper, locally grown rivals and had to overcome a prevailing consumer prejudice against produce that was "foreign" and hence presumed not to be as fresh or nutritious.[1]

General regional marketing problems were compounded by the "boom" quality of many agricultural developments in Southern Pacific territory. In the case of oranges in southern California, for example, speculative land subdivisions in the mid-1870s and during the region's infamous "Boom of the Eighties" suddenly expanded grove acreage ahead of established marketing potential, especially for the winter-ripening navels. Predictably, when tens of thousands of acres of maturing groves began to spill fruit onto limited markets from the late 1880s into the early 1890s, oversupply quickly undercut prices, sometimes below what was necessary even to recoup production costs. That many of the new crops of California and elsewhere were perishable, with a small sales window, simply aggravated the region's problematical balance of supply and demand.[2]

Profitable agriculture in the Southern Pacific's far western and southwestern territory thus required the development of an unprecedented marketing apparatus: complex, interlocking technological systems for processing, storing, refrigerating, and shipping; advertising strategies and mechanisms to cultivate, change, and then manage consumer tastes; and perhaps most important, new types of organization necessary to assure efficient, profitable shipment and marketing and to coordinate the many, often divergent interest groups involved— growers, shippers, transportation companies, ice and equipment manufacturers, distributors, advertisers, and consumers. And all this apparatus had to operate over great distances and a wide geography to handle massive amounts of produce and at costs that made it accessible and profitable to all. From finding better ways to market southern California oranges, San Joaquin Valley raisins, Imperial Valley cantaloupes, Oregon deciduous fruit, and Texas rice, to causing veritable bergs of ice to materialize in the middle of scorching deserts, to devising essential new transportation and information systems, the Southern Pacific Company provided capital, expertise, technology, and structure to link the various elements of the marketing equation and to generate models for profitably selling western produce that helped lay the foundation of successful regional agriculture and larger economic development.[3]

In the Imperial Valley, ca. 1920s, University of Southern California athletes load blocks of ice into the Southern Pacific's Pacific Fruit Express refrigerator cars, probably loaded with cantaloupes. Refrigerated freight was one of the most important innovations Southern Pacific contributed to produce marketing. Not only did such seasonal workers supplement the railroad's regular labor force, the company's news release pointed out that the rugged work helped the young men "store up money and muscle during their vacation." Courtesy DeGolyer Library, Southern Methodist University.

The Southern Pacific and Farm Cooperatives

As was generally true of Southern Pacific land, promotional, agricultural, and environmental programs, the railroad's work in agricultural marketing took seminal form during its early years in California in the 1870s, attained some system there in the 1880s and 1890s, and matured and spread throughout the company's territory in the early decades of the twentieth century. While farmers were struggling in the period to overcome their traditional individual competitiveness and inter-regional rivalries, the railroad, for example, was one of the earliest, most consistent advocates of farmers' cooperation in marketing as well as in other aspects of their business. In 1875, just after he had founded the *Sacramento Record-Union,* co-owned by the Southern Pacific, editor William H. Mills, close associate of the Big Four, exhorted California farmers to join local chapters of the Grange, the state's first cooperative movement, which had just been introduced from the East.[4] Over the next two decades, including after 1883, when he became the railroad's chief land agent, Mills and his newspaper remained strong advocates of the Grange, particularly its cooperative business

activities. In 1889, when he addressed the national convention of Grange leaders, meeting in Woodland, California, Mills's enthusiastic praise for the organization earned him a rousing ovation.[5] Mills's strong identification with farmers' problems and movements led him in 1896 and afterwards to support the
presidential candidacy of William Jennings Bryan, joint nominee of the Democratic and Populist parties. Mills even gave Bryan free passes for campaign travel
along the railroad's lines, earning the land agent stern rebukes from his hard-
money Republican boss, Collis P. Huntington, and other Southern Pacific
officials.[6] Other railway leaders, most notably Central Pacific president Leland
Stanford and another executive, David D. Colton, also supported the organization and programs of the Grange as well as other farmers' cooperative movements of the 1870s through the 1890s.[7]

Although successful, long-lasting farm marketing cooperatives did not become established for two decades after the 1870s, the Southern Pacific over that
period worked to get farmers to band together to reduce overproduction and
to achieve greater coordination, and hence efficiency and profits, in harvesting, packing, shipping, and marketing. By the mid-1880s, when fruit production was rapidly emerging as California's leading agricultural industry and burgeoning amounts of fruit began to pour from the state's new orchards, the
problems of shipping and marketing had become clear to the railroad. From
the Southern Pacific's perspective, the absence of regional and statewide cooperative organization, and the resulting tendency of farmers to seek to make individual shipping arrangements, raised costs to farmers and the railroad alike
and discouraged production and traffic in fruit. Small, individual shipments
inhibited the company's attempts to reduce tariffs by systematizing traffic, making shipments predictable, and concentrating cargoes and packing and shipping facilities at certain points so the railroad could form regularly scheduled,
uniform, more efficient, more tightly packed, lower-cost fruit trains. Even the
simple lack of standardized shipping crates and packing methods, combined
with the necessity of bringing most fruit cars back from the East empty, typically reduced the actual paying cargo on shipments to a small fraction of car
space, greatly raising transportation costs and reducing profits to farmers and
the railroad.

By the mid-1880s, it had become company policy to encourage farm cooperatives to organize production, shipment, and marketing and to reserve more
profits to the farmers to encourage production and general economic development in the state. In 1885, Stanford and Central Pacific general manager Alban N. Towne played a major role in the calling of a series of growers' meetings across the state. At the meetings, Stanford and Towne provided information
on the economics of fruit handling, packing, shipping, and marketing, exhorted
the farmers to form a statewide fruit cooperative, and offered to reduce freight

charges for fruit sent to Chicago from the current standard of $800 for indi-
vidual cars to as low as $300 per car (special express time, at near–passenger
train speed) and $200 per car (regular freight time) for entire trains carrying
green fruit, contracted regularly and in advance by farm cooperatives. The meetings ultimately resulted in the formation of the promising, but short-lived, California Fruit Union, an organization of 800 of the state's leading growers who
proposed to contract in concert with the railroad for shipments and to sell their
fruit together through agents in the East.[8]

From the 1880s into the 1920s, the Southern Pacific continued to support
the farm cooperative movement. After assuming the position of chief company
land agent and promotional officer in 1883, Mills, until his death in 1907, was
the railroad's leading proponent of cooperatives, particularly to achieve reliable
profits from growing perishables, a philosophy he articulated in *Sacramento
Record-Union* editorials, numerous published papers on the subject, and
speeches before the California Agricultural Society, the state's leading commercial bodies, and other forums.[9] In the 1880s, the *Record-Union* also strongly
supported the formation of the California Fruit Union.[10] After 1900, *Sunset*
magazine and other company publications repeatedly urged farmers to set aside
their individual and local differences and to form regional and statewide cooperatives for more effective control of supply and demand for their products.
A 1904 *Sunset* editorial advised that proposed local farmers' organizations to
pick and pack fruit for shipment and a central statewide farmer-operated agency
to buy the produce from these local cooperatives and to advertise and sell it aggressively "would result in inestimable benefit to the fruit-growers of California." Into the 1920s, the company operated and financed large-scale mutual
marketing ventures with a host of farm cooperatives.[11]

From the 1870s into 1890s, the Southern Pacific also made some organizational and technological innovations of its own that began to ameliorate marketing problems. Some station agents, for example, organized farmers in their
localities to market collectively. In the 1870s, Auburn agent Clarence M. Wooster, who had established himself as an authority and unofficial adviser on orcharding, campaigned in his region for the planting of fruit varieties on the basis of their marketability and also served as the catalyst for the first cooperative
out-of-state marketing of fresh fruit. Wooster convened meetings of growers
in his office, and the informal group subscribed $800 to rent a rail car and at-
tach it to a passenger train to experiment with hauling green fruit directly to
Chicago at the highest possible speeds. Although the car was unrefrigerated,
the fruit took advantage of the natural cooling effect of the trip over the high
Sierra Nevada and arrived at its destination with some spoilage but in "fairly
good condition." According to Wooster, the cargo sold at "enormous prices,"
giving a "new zest to the fruit industry in all its lines" and paving the way for

later such shipments and eventually the special ventilator and refrigerator cars that revolutionized California agricultural marketing.[12]

The form of local, ad hoc cooperation that Wooster had pioneered spread to other parts of the state, particularly southern California, which experienced a fruit-planting boom from the 1870s into the late 1880s. As cooperative fruit marketing expanded, farmer and shipper associations become more structured and long-lasting, shipments larger, and the Southern Pacific's involvement more extensive and crucial. At first, following agent Wooster's lead, the railroad hooked up individual, unrefrigerated fruit cars to passenger trains for rapid transit east. That proved expensive and impractical for massive fruit shipments, however. By 1885, Stanford reported an average of four fast-freight cars per passenger train heading east during fruit-picking season, but the railroad found that the heavy cars were a serious drag on the trains, as well as a safety hazard.[13] Eventually, the company coordinated farmers and shippers for the dispatch of entire fruit trains, sent at near–passenger train speeds. On June 24, 1886, on the heels of the company's advertising victory for California fruit at the New Orleans expositions, the Southern Pacific dispatched the first deciduous fruit special east from Sacramento, a sixteen-car train of ordinary, unrefrigerated boxcars bedecked with flags and large placards advertising California fruit. Earlier that year, the railroad had sent the first orange special train east from Los Angeles.[14] Subsequently, other fruit trains headed east, as need arose, but without regular, established service during some periods. Until successful cooperatives began to emerge in the 1890s, farmers and shippers were insufficiently organized to contract in advance for entire trains of cars.[15] Throughout the late nineteenth and early twentieth centuries, often by taking the initiative itself to bring farmers in a region together for organized shipments, the Southern Pacific continued to improve and expand its service to the East and beyond. In 1892, the company instituted, and then in 1895 expanded, a scheduled and faster fruit freight service to Ogden across the Central Pacific. With the cooperation of the Union Pacific and eastern lines, the special trains of ventilator cars reached Chicago on the fifth morning after leaving Sacramento. Some shipments of green fruit connected at eastern ports with fast steamers for Great Britain.[16]

The Railroad as Advertiser of Western Products

The Southern Pacific's major nineteenth-century work in agricultural marketing was to advertise the virtues of California and far western produce, particularly fruit, in the growing urban centers of the Middle West and East. Such general advertising served several purposes: calling attention to investment opportunities within the railroad's territory, especially on the company's land grant;

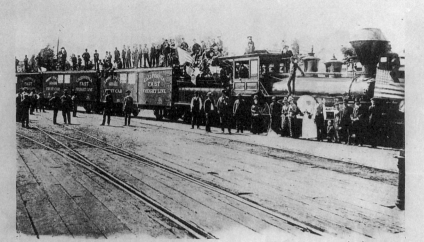

FIRST SPECIAL FAST FRUIT TRAIN
SHIPPED JUNE 24, 1886,
CHARTERED BY W. R. STRONG & CO. AND EDWIN T. EARL,
Fruit Packers and Shippers, Sacramento, California.

The first special fast fruit train left Sacramento on the Southern Pacific on June 24, 1886. Author's collection.

encouraging tourism to California and the other sunny Pacific Coast and south-western regions that yielded such abundant harvests even in winter; and, of course, expanding, even creating, demand for the region's products. All of these would serve to stimulate economic development and hence the railroad's freight and passenger traffic.

The cornerstone of the Southern Pacific's nineteenth-century advertising of western products was its program of sending lavish displays of California produce—particularly fruit—to eastern and European fairs. In fact, from the middle 1870s to, and even after, Chicago's Columbian Exposition of 1893, in the absence of much official state support, the railroad constituted the major agency organizing and financing displays of California's resources. Numerous Southern Pacific leaders, particularly Charles B. Turrill of the Passenger Department and chief land agent William H. Mills, became expert exhibition managers, frequently detailed by the company to assist state and local governments and private organizations in organizing displays.[17] Although the company mounted a small but credible display—indeed, the only noticeable representation—of California products at the Centennial Exposition, the country's first great world's fair, held in Philadelphia in 1876, the most influential Southern Pacific display was dispatched under Turrill's direction to the New Orleans World's

Fairs during the winters of 1884–1885 and 1885–1886. That large and innovative state exhibit, organized and financed almost entirely by the Southern Pacific,
featured a three-acre outdoor "California Park" of transplanted flowering and
fruit-bearing trees and shrubs, particularly citrus. Immense indoor arrangements
of fruit and vegetables were kept fresh and appealing with a continuous stream
of daily shipments the railroad collected and sent east. The quality of fresh winter produce impressed eastern visitors to the New Orleans expositions, and
southern California orchardists created a sensation by sweeping the prizes for
citrus, besting their heavily favored rivals from Florida.[18] The Southern Pacific
displays at the expositions of the mid-1880s were important promotional events
for California, indeed a turning point in the marketing of the state's fresh fruit.
The first extensive, well-publicized California displays in the East, they attracted
much attention, especially from correspondents who regularly commented on
the fair in the columns of eastern newspapers. Marketing impact was magnified
because fruit dealers in search of new sources of produce routinely attended
these and other eastern fairs.[19] Many observers, both in and out of California,
traced the state's real estate boom of the 1880s, the expansion of orange planting, especially in southern California, and the first consumer demand in the
East for the state's winter-ripening navel oranges and other fresh fruit to the
promotional successes at these exhibitions.[20]

Thereafter, the Southern Pacific became a major supporter of displays sent
from California and its other states to every important international exhibition, and to many smaller state fairs as well, including world's fairs at Chicago
in 1893, Atlanta in 1895, Paris in 1900, and St. Louis in 1904. In addition, the
railroad cooperated with private commercial groups to mount traveling or sta-
tionary exhibits of their communities' and regions' production. Particularly
significant was the Southern Pacific's partnership with the San Francisco-based
California State Board of Trade to organize and operate "California on Wheels,"
a festively decorated train touring the East carrying lecturers, promotional literature, and free samples of fresh fruit in the winters of 1888–1889 and 1889–
1890. Visited by more than one million people at stops in most states east of
the Rockies, "California on Wheels" was another of the initial promotional successes of the Golden State and its produce.[21] By creating its own displays and
assisting state government and private commercial organizations to stage exhibitions such as these, the Southern Pacific Company was the principal force in
California and the Far West stimulating and organizing the exposition movement and helping the region to fashion a more favorable image, attract visitors
and settlers, and expand markets for products, especially fruit.

In the twentieth century, Southern Pacific marketing efforts on behalf of
the fruit and other produce of California and the Far West expanded, became
structurally and technologically more sophisticated, and involved the railroad

more directly in coordinating individual farmers, cooperatives, shippers, and eastern distributors for profitable crop sales and the economic development of entire regions. When effective farm marketing cooperatives finally emerged in California after the 1890s, the railroad assisted them by continuing to encourage farmers to join, improving refrigeration technology, organizing complex icing and fruit express systems,[22] and sponsoring focused advertising campaigns to widen and manage markets for California and western fruit. As early as the mid-1880s, Southern Pacific promoters had written pamphlets and articles in eastern newspapers encouraging consumption of California fruit products. In 1887, for example, noted Southern Pacific booster and author Benjamin C. Truman wrote a long-running series on California wine, which appeared first in the *New York Times* and was widely reprinted. Experts judged the articles to be the best to date on the subject.[23] In the early 1900s, as the Southern Pacific's general booster programs and publishing on behalf of California and the Far West increased, the railroad's promotional monthly magazine, *Sunset,* and other Southern Pacific publications particularly focused on expanding the sales of California fruit. In 1899, *Sunset* inaugurated a monthly feature, "On the Use of California Fruit," contributed by Professor Charles H. Allen of San Jose, and repeatedly ran other articles aimed at marketing western products. Railroad publicity often aimed at changing the eating habits of the young. *The California Prune Primer,* a 1901 railroad pamphlet designed as a supplemental reader for elementary school children and sent by the company to 100,000 teachers across the country, created a mild sensation. Teachers and parents deluged the railroad with requests for extra copies. Within a few months more than 500,000 had been distributed. The outcome of this experiment led the company to issue other California "primers" with equal success. A large, widely circulating Southern Pacific pamphlet, *Eat California Fruit,* first issued in 1904 and republished in 1908, advised people to consume more California fruit because it was healthy, cheap, good tasting, and available fresh even in winter. The book also contained detailed instructions on peeling, preserving, and refrigerating fruit, including recipes for stewing and other ways of serving prunes, raisins, peaches, plums, pears, figs, nectarines, olives, olive oil, dates, citrus, and other distinctive California products. The Southern Pacific also aggressively promoted Oregon deciduous fruit crops, particularly between the early 1900s and the 1920s.[24]

The Southern Pacific and the Origin of Mass Produce-Marketing

The Southern Pacific's initial, general programs to publicize farm produce grew into major partnerships with growers' groups not only to advertise but also to organize packing, shipping, and marketing of their products. In 1907, the company inaugurated its first long-term marketing relationship, fittingly with a citrus cooperative, the California Fruit Growers' Exchange, which in 1893 had become the first successful California cooperative, ultimately inspiring in the early 1900s the emergence of a host of similar organizations for other crops, including raisins, walnuts, avocados, and deciduous fruits. Although the Fruit Growers' Exchange, originally restricted to the southern counties, had survived into the early 1900s and had even converted itself into a statewide organization of citrus producers, crop sales remained sluggish and prices paid to farmers low in the face of wildly multiplying harvests. In 1907, convinced that massive, organized marketing would stabilize and expand the mercurial citrus industry once and for all, Southern Pacific vice president E. O. McCormick approached his friend Francis Q. Story, president of the exchange, with the company's offer to match the cooperative's advertising budget in a concerted effort to increase eastern consumption of California oranges. Using McCormick's offer as leverage, Story was able to convince reluctant exchange directors to try advertising to solve the perennial problem of overproduction. Each committing $10,000 to the first year's five-month test campaign in Iowa, the railroad and the exchange cooperated over the winter of 1907–1908 to saturate that state with ads, lecturers, displays, posters, and "California Fruit Special" trains, all promoting the virtues of eating California oranges. By early 1908, the "Oranges for Health, California for Wealth" campaign had raised orange sales in Iowa by 50 percent. Such demonstrable success encouraged the railroad and exchange the next year to expand their program to the entire Middle West and other areas to the east and south. By the conclusion of the joint advertising campaigns in the 1910–1911 season, the railroad and exchange were each spending $100,000 per year; a healthy, expanding market for California oranges had been firmly established; sales east of the Rockies had climbed severalfold; crop prices to farmers had increased dramatically; the cooperative's "Sunkist" brand name had become a household word across the nation; the Fruit Growers' Exchange had become committed to advertising as a cornerstone of its business strategy; and, incidentally, a large migration from the Middle West to California had been stimulated. Some authorities consider the experiment of the railroad and exchange to have been the first saturation, consumer-product marketing campaign in history, paving the way for other efforts to establish brand names through massive advertising. Although their initial joint advertising venture ended in 1911, the Southern Pacific and California Fruit Growers' Exchange continued into the 1920s to mount shorter-term annual "Orange Week" campaigns in the East, which also featured California citrus displays and special promotional trains.[25]

The railroad reaped rich rewards of its own from its decades-long support of citrus marketing, which helps to explain the company's eagerness to enter into promotional partnerships with growers and shippers of many agricultural products. A 1920 Pacific Fruit Express review of Southern Pacific benefits from the citrus industry revealed that citrus shipments along the railroad's lines from California, mostly from southern districts, had increased from 1,000 carloads in 1886 to 7,500 in 1896, 30,000 in 1910, and 54,500 in 1917. With bearing orange and lemon grove acreage standing at 144,000, and with another 69,000 acres planted but not yet bearing, the company anticipated that within a few years its annual shipments of California citrus would soar to between 75,000 and 100,000 cars.[26]

Smaller-scale campaigns after 1900 assisted the organized growers of other fruits and specialty crops. In early 1909, for example, fresh from the successful orange campaign, the Southern Pacific suggested a joint advertising venture to the recently founded, Fresno-based cooperative, the Raisin Packers and Growers of California. The industry suffered markets as glutted as those of orange producers. Each year at railheads across the state, particularly Fresno, capital of the principal raisin district, many tons of "holdover crop"—surplus, deteriorating raisins—remained unshipped, sapping market prices and farm profits. At a growers' meeting convened in Fresno to deal with these problems, James Horsburgh, assistant general passenger agent and then the railroad's director of promotion, presented a plan for a nationwide "Raisin Day" campaign and pledged the railroad's financial and organizational assistance. A committee including representatives of the railroad, the raisin growers' cooperative, Fresno's Chamber of Commerce, and ultimately other commercial organizations in the state was established, and April 30, 1909, was set as the first Raisin Day. The group raised $30,000, and the Southern Pacific mobilized its agents and those of other railways nationwide, particularly sister Harriman Lines, to distribute ads, posters, displays, and samples of California raisins. On Raisin Day, dining cars and station restaurants of the Southern Pacific and other roads featured free helpings of dishes containing raisins, as did hotels in San Francisco, Los Angeles, and other major cities across the country. To heighten anticipation for the celebration, the Southern Pacific produced and sent one million copies of the *Raisin Primer* to the nation's schools. Follow-up advertising kept raisins before the public eye throughout the year. Raisin Day's success was as spectacular as the Sunkist orange campaign. After the event, raisin sales increased dramatically, the 1909 holdover crop being liquidated by the end of May. William Robertson, the secretary of the Raisin Day Committee, described the promotion to E. J. Wickson, dean of the University of California's College of Agriculture, as "a work which is probably the most colossal piece of advertising work ever attempted," an achievement, however, that "could not be carried through without the valuable support accorded by the railroads."[27] Into the 1920s, the celebration continued as an joint project of the Southern Pacific and the growers' cooperative. Beginning in 1911, raisin promoters added an annual April 30 "Raisin Festival," held in Fresno with the entire San Joaquin Valley participating, complete with parade, relays, pageants, and the coronation of the year's Raisin King. In 1920, cowboy film star Tom Mix was the reigning king. For decades, Horsburgh was revered throughout the valley as the "Father of Raisin Day."[28] The success of the idea—dedicating a day to a focused nationwide promotion of a product from the railroad's territory—led the Southern Pacific in subsequent years to create or participate in other such events, including an Orange Day and even a Pacific Northwest Salmon Day.[29] In the early twentieth century, the railroad also operated joint marketing ventures with growers of California prunes and cantaloupes, Oregon deciduous fruit, Texas Gulf Coast rice, and other fruit and specialty crops throughout Southern Pacific territory.

Pacific Fruit Express

In the early decades of the twentieth century, the Southern Pacific Company's technological and organizational contribution to modern western agricultural development climaxed in the founding of its refrigerator-car subsidiary, Pacific Fruit Express, and in the development of mass export of perishables from the West. Since the completion of the first transcontinental rail line in 1869, the generally slow and halting growth of technology and organization for shipping perishables had deterred the development of many potential fruit and vegetable crops in the West. At first, the railroad tried ordinary boxcars, resulting in extensive and costly spoilage. The Southern Pacific initially dealt with spoilage by fashioning new procedures to speed packing, handling, and passage eastward, such as attaching the cars to passenger trains, or at least faster "fruit specials." Such procedures remained useful but failed to solve the larger general impediments to mass shipping of perishables. For some time, American railroads had used specially designed ventilator cars relying on improved airflow to control produce temperature and reduce spoilage, and the Southern Pacific had acquired a few dozen of them as early as 1869. Effective only when the weather was moderate, however, they were restricted primarily to local shipments, and many types of perishables simply could not reach outside markets economically. Although increased demands from fruit growers in California and elsewhere impelled the company to put more ventilators into service in the late 1880s and early 1890s, the Southern Pacific maintained only a small fleet of the cars, a mere 992 in 1900. As early as the late 1860s, the company cooperated with shippers to build and experiment with refrigerator cars, using ice to cool produce, but the discouraging trials demonstrated that the technology was primitive and inefficient and that the cars were expensive to build and operate, especially in the absence of large-scale and widespread facilities to manufacture ice and to re-ice the cars while they were in transit.[30] Like other western roads, the Southern Pacific hesitated to venture into costly, non-railroad businesses such as ice-making. Moreover, railroads, including at first the Southern Pacific, typically served only a few isolated regions growing perishable crops, with narrow seasonal production insufficient to warrant railroad investments in specialized rolling stock and icing facilities.[31]

Tenacious shipping and marketing problems for perishable produce, along with the emergence of the large-scale meat-packing industry in the 1880s, opened up a niche for private refrigerator-car companies. In California, most prominent were the pioneer Armour Refrigerator Line and the later-comer Wells Fargo. The private companies furnished the rolling stock, ice, and icing facilities and contracted with the Southern Pacific to haul the cars to their destination. The business remained small scale, however—Wells Fargo, for example, instituted refrigerated service in 1898 and operated only one hundred cars in 1913—and it was restricted largely to isolated high-value shipments and unsuited for mass marketing of perishable crops.[32] Service provided by the small companies was often poor, provoking numerous complaints from shippers and growers. As of the early 1900s, according to the major historians of the subject, "there was no real organization for the transcontinental shipment" of perishables, and by far the majority of fruit was dispatched east green and/or during winter, with high spoilage continuing to cut into farmers' and shippers' profits and deterring increased production.[33]

Conditions changed rapidly after 1900, and the Southern Pacific played the key role in the establishment of technological and structural systems for export of perishables that revolutionized western agriculture.[34] Coincident with the expansion of irrigation in company territory, the production of perishables was increasing, and the small number of company ventilators and private refrigerator cars could not keep up with soaring demand for shipping. Company officials realized, moreover, that the growing of fresh fruit and vegetables opened up much untapped potential for regional economic development and future rail traffic. Combined after 1901 with the Union Pacific into the Harriman Lines, the Southern Pacific served a vast and varied hinterland with many expanding perishables-producing districts of different climates and harvest seasons, for the first time promising year-round, efficient and profitable employment for specialized cars and ice-making and icing facilities. At the same time, court verdicts, decisions by the Interstate Commerce Commission, and the Hepburn Act passed by Congress in 1906 made the railroads themselves legally responsible for fair charges for icing and refrigerated shipments, discouraging the carriers from relying on private refrigerator-car companies they could not control.

The Southern Pacific moved more aggressively than other lines to start a refrigerator-car subsidiary of its own. Sensing new opportunity and with vast resources at hand, President E. H. Harriman acted swiftly. In December 1906, he ordered the founding of the Pacific Fruit Express, jointly owned by the Southern Pacific and the Union Pacific, to handle the refrigerated shipments of both lines. Pacific Fruit Express immediately ordered 6,600 refrigerator cars ("reefers"), thus from the beginning entering the perishables transit business as the largest player in the West.[35]

Although at first the new company purchased ice from commercial manufacturers, it quickly established a large independent supply. In 1907 it purchased all the Armour Lines' ice-making and icing facilities in California, and in 1908 built the first unit of what would become a giant ice-making and car-icing facility at its new traffic division center in Roseville, twenty miles northeast of Sacramento. A large Pacific Fruit Express ice plant soon emerged also at Carlin, in northeastern Nevada.[36] In quick-fire succession, the company acquired or constructed natural or mechanical ice manufacturing and icing facilities at dozens of other sites across the Pacific Coast, Southwest, Great Basin, Rocky Mountain, and Great Plains regions. Ultimately, the company could ice, or re-ice, cars at, among other places, Roseville, Truckee, Fresno, Bakersfield, Los Angeles, Colton, El Centro, Brawley, and Calexico in California; Sparks, Carlin, and Las Vegas in Nevada; Yuma, Tucson, Phoenix, and Nogales in Arizona; Deming in New Mexico; El Paso in Texas; Ogden in Utah; Evanston and Laramie in Wyoming; and North Platte in Nebraska. From major manufacturing centers, ice was shipped in insulated boxcars and stored in warehouses to make possible the icing of cars at countless loading platforms throughout the western states.[37] The company soon built pre-cooling plants to simultaneously store and chill perishables before loading in order to reduce spoilage and the need for re-icing while the shipments were en route.[38]

Pacific Fruit Express embarked on a rapid expansion in rolling stock, icing capacity, and traffic that would not slow for decades, except for brief periods, during the few years of federal control of railroads during World War I and again after the onset of the Great Depression in 1929. The company handled 40,000 carloads annually as soon as 1908, its first full year of operation. By 1921, its fleet had grown to 19,500 reefers, carrying 142,000 loads of perishables, mostly eastward from western states; by 1923, 33,000 cars carried nearly 200,000 loads; by 1928, it fielded 40,000 refrigerator cars, most manufactured at extensive company-owned shops at Roseville and Los Angeles. Pacific Fruit Express reached its peak in traffic hauled in 1946, with 500,000 carloads.[39] By 1926, its investment in cars alone stood at $115 million.[40] Within a few years of operation, the

The Pacific Fruit Express's Roseville icing facility, ca. 1930. The largest ice plant in the world, it could service hundreds of refrigerator cars simultaneously and thousands per day. It was only one of many such centers on the Southern Pacific's perishable produce transportation system, the largest of its kind anywhere. Author's collection.

shipping company also became the largest producer of ice in the world, just as an adjunct of its main business of refrigerated hauling. In 1921, the company manufactured 1.4 million tons; by 1924, the annual production of just the Roseville ice plant, the largest in the world, had soared to 200,000 tons.[41] Although most Pacific Fruit Express shipments were from the Pacific Coast, particularly California, whose farmers were increasingly specializing in the growing of perishables for outside markets to the east, in the 1910s and 1920s the company expanded its business elsewhere, including Oregon and Washington—9,000 cars of perishables carried as early as 1913 from one Southern Pacific–affiliated Pacific Northwest line alone. Pacific Fruit Express then moved on to Nevada, Arizona, Mexico, and Texas, the Rio Grande Valley particularly.[42] The company also handled refrigerated shipping for rail companies beyond the original Harriman Lines. Its most important victory came in 1924, when it won the contract to operate all refrigerator cars over the Western Pacific, giving it control of all business in California except on the Santa Fe, which operated its own refrigerator-car subsidiary, with only 16,000 cars in 1923.[43] From its inception, although the Southern and Union Pacific roads owned the company in equal shares, by far most of the carloads originated along Southern Pacific lines. Reflecting this, when federal courts "unmerged" the two railroads in 1913, Pacific Fruit Express headquarters moved from Chicago, capital of the Harriman Lines, to San Francisco. By the early 1920s, the company had branch offices in Sacramento, Los Angeles, Portland, Ogden, Omaha, Houston, Kansas City, St. Louis, Chicago, St. Paul, Buffalo, New York City, Philadelphia, Boston, and Baltimore.[44]

Pacific Fruit Express's importance to revolutionizing western agriculture, however, was not simply a matter of its expanding fleets of reefers and carrying capacity, soaring ice production, and multiplying local facilities. The Southern Pacific and its refrigerator-car company used their combined size, structure, capital resources, and access to expertise to stimulate innovation in the science and organization of shipping and marketing of perishables, which was essential for large-scale regional agricultural development. Railroad and car company joined to experiment in refrigerated shipping, testing all manner of combinations of new car and crate designs, cooling techniques and equipment, shipping routes, crop varieties, and even farm harvesting, packing, and car-loading procedures, and then educating farmers and shippers in more efficient methods. By 1914, for example, thermographs, keeping a continual temperature record, had been installed in the cars to allow "ventilation clerks" to adjust car vents en route to best protect the shipment. The railroad's chief engineer's office kept the temperature charts as a permanent record of how shipments had been handled as well to provide data for further experiments.[45] In the 1910s and 1920s, in cooperation with the U.S. Department of Agriculture, the railroad and Pacific Fruit Express ran periodic test trips to discover more efficient shipping methods, routes, equipment, and temperature control. In just one of these in 1922, twelve test cars carrying cantaloupes were sent from the Imperial Valley via the Southern Pacific and eastern railroads to New York City, with a continuous record kept on all cars of temperature changes, spoilage, and the effects of different types of equipment. Other test trips improved knowledge of how to ship various crops, including potatoes, apples, lettuce, and table grapes, all of which became profitable industries along Southern Pacific lines.[46]

The Southern Pacific and Pacific Fruit Express also supplied the coordination that had hitherto been missing among the varied segments in the western perishables industry and that had delayed development.[47] In conjunction with the railroad as well as with a host of federal, state, and local agricultural agencies, the car company kept close watch on markets and prices for fruit and vegetables and shared information with growers and shippers. Immediately on the founding of Pacific Fruit Express, the two companies—first in California and later elsewhere—started convening meetings in producing districts of growers, crop cooperatives, shippers, rail officials, and refrigerator-car company leaders to work together to forecast crop production, establish shipping procedures and schedules, and order cars and ice.[48] The two companies developed a system for tracing Pacific Fruit Express cars on all other railroads through delivery and return, preventing delays and allowing shippers to be informed of the location of their produce daily so that cargoes might be quickly diverted to better markets. When eastern railroads took to delaying the return west of the company's empty rolling stock so that the valuable cars could be used along their own lines to deliver eastern perishables to market, the Southern Pacific mounted a nationwide force of "car detectives" to cruise eastern lines, spy out purloined Pacific Fruit Express cars in rail yards, and telegraph their location to Southern Pacific officials in San Francisco, who issued sharp protests to offending rival companies.[49] Even as Progressive politicians across the West were attacking railroads in their territory, the Southern Pacific and Pacific Fruit Express in the early decades of the twentieth century were demonstrating the mutual advantage of cooperation and forging close alliances among growers, shippers, and carriers, and in the process breaking down the animosities against the railroad.

The "Cantaloupe Deal"

The potential for the Southern Pacific and Pacific Fruit Express to encourage the growing of new perishable crops as well as to transform entire agricultural regions, is exemplified most dramatically in the spectacular emergence of the Imperial Valley cantaloupe industry. The crop was first planted in southeastern California's torrid, below-sea-level Imperial Valley and its northerly neighboring Coachella Valley as early as 1900 while the region was just beginning to be irrigated and settled. Prolific, fast growing, and flavorful when grown in hot climates, cantaloupes ripened in spring and early summer in the region, making them potentially a highly profitable crop to ship before eastern (and most western) fruits reached markets. As early as 1905, 237 carloads of cantaloupes moved from the valley, mostly the short distance westward to coastal cities via private refrigerator-car companies such as Wells Fargo. Formidable obstacles, however, blocked the path to large-scale production and particularly to eastern marketing. Bouts with crop pests, erratic irrigation-water supplies, and finally the great Imperial Valley flood of 1904–1907 discouraged growers from expanding production of this and other crops. Moreover, the fruit, among the most delicate grown in the West, spoiled rapidly and to ensure safe shipment had to be cooled quickly to 35 to 40 degrees, much colder than other crops.[50]

Handling a massive cantaloupe crop amounted to an unprecedented feat of refrigeration, which had to be accomplished in a concentrated harvest season, the six weeks or so around June 15, during which daytime temperatures usually exceeded 110 degrees—and as high as 130 degrees—cooling only slightly at night. Not only were there no large-volume icing stations in the valley or re-icing facilities along routes eastward across the Southwest deserts, the valley was isolated hundreds of miles from potential support bases in California and Arizona cities. Lacking also was any system or administrative machinery for importing the required vast quantities of reefers, and especially of ice, or for delivering cars and ice and picking up loaded reefers at the numerous small packing sheds and shipping platforms scattered along the valley's more than one hundred miles of rail track. Nor was there apparatus to deliver and sell large quantities of the fragile fruit during a small time-window without glutting markets and undermining prices.

Immediately after the founding of Pacific Fruit Express, the first major objective of the car company and its parent-partner Southern Pacific was to serve, administer, and expand the Imperial Valley cantaloupe crop, or the "cantaloupe deal," as railroaders came to know it affectionately, if also with a tinge of awe and apprehension. Within just a few years the combined companies had created the most administratively and technologically complex and sophisticated system to date for large-scale packing, refrigerating, shipping, and marketing of a farm crop, a prototype for similar systems for other crops and regions developed by the Southern Pacific and other parties into the mid-twentieth century.[51] Immediately after its founding, Pacific Fruit Express entered the valley. The railroad and the car company moved operations offices into the valley for the cantaloupe season, and additional employees, including executives, were detailed on temporary assignment for the duration of the harvest. Within a few years, about 1,000 employees—500 just to handle icing—seasonally bunked and dined at large boardinghouses the railroad built at Brawley, El Centro, and Calexico. Some railroad people made the annual trek to work the "cantaloupe deal" for decades. Railroad and refrigerator-car company began convening meetings, at first informal, of farmers, shippers, and transportation workers to plan the harvest. By the early 1920s, the meetings had grown more structured and numerous, regionally spread out to several localities, and specialized into separate gatherings for railroad people and crop producers.[52]

The Southern Pacific also had to improve the infrastructure in the remote, thinly settled region, including building nearly one hundred miles of additional branchlines plus innumerable sidings within a few years, serving the loading platforms of about sixty large growers and shippers. Occasionally, the railroad financed construction costs for packing sheds and loading platforms. Along the tracks, the company strung long-distance telephone wires for quicker communication and coordination. The partner companies developed a complex system for forecasting the crop months in advance, for importing and storing ice and empty reefers as far away as Yuma, Tucson, and even Mexico, for delivering empties and ice to the sidings, for pre-icing the empties just before loading, and then quickly collecting the filled and chilled cars for shuttling to Yuma for re-icing and composition into special cantaloupe trains for the East. To shelter the cars from the broiling sun and to reduce spoilage, much of the work took place during cooler nighttime hours, under huge floodlights designed and installed by the railroad. Each car was then re-iced between six and eight additional times on its journey east. During the "deal," Southern Pacific dispatchers were on order to give cantaloupe trains priority over all other types, resulting in uncanny delivery schedules. In 1927, for instance, of the 275 uniform cantaloupe trains the railroad sent eastward from Imperial Valley, all but eighteen made or bettered their scheduled arrival times at eastern destinations; *all* of the 153 trains dispatched to west-coast cities made or bettered delivery schedules. Over the course of the years, the railroad and the refrigerator-car company shaved hours, and then days, from the trip to the East; by 1927, shoppers could buy Imperial cantaloupes in Chicago stores on the seventh day after harvest. By the 1910s, the railroad had supplemented the fast-freight system with a method for telegraphically intercepting the trains en route and diverting individual cars to smaller spot markets where prices were higher.[53]

Stimulated by the aggressive intervention of the Southern Pacific and Pacific Fruit Express, Imperial Valley cantaloupe production and shipments soared, from 237 carloads in 1905 to 1,891 carloads in 1908, the car company's first full year of operation in the valley. By 1913, 3,500 carloads headed east with nearly 100 million cantaloupes aboard; 7,809 carloads by 1919, despite dislocation to growers and railroaders during World War I; by 1925, 14,500 carloads; and by 1931, 21,500 carloads, constituting half of all cantaloupes marketed in the United States. By 1927, nearly 40,000 acres of cantaloupes grew in the Imperial Valley, compared to less than 1,000 in 1905.[54]

The first cars left in mid-April and the last in mid-August, peaking during the four to six weeks around June 15. At the height of the season, 400 to 500 cars per day left the valley, the record being 647 cars on June 27, 1922. Four to six cantaloupe special trains headed east each day, and two west toward San Diego and Los Angeles, each normally containing 124 cars by the 1920s; the record 149-car cantaloupe train left for Chicago in 1927.[55] Since each car required 10,500 pounds of ice for initial cooling and 7,000 pounds for re-icing, the cantaloupes consumed veritable mountains of ice—200,000 tons annually in the valley by 1927.[56] "You think I didn't wear out some pencils down there, figuring out how much ice we're gonna use, what I've got in storage, all that!" recalled Pete Holst, who supervised cantaloupe icing after 1923. "You know, thirty thousand tons of ice wouldn't go very far when you used five thousand tons a day."[57]

During its several-month-long shipping season, the annual Imperial cantaloupe deal strained every physical and human resource of the Southern Pacific
and Pacific Fruit Express—rolling stock and locomotives, ice-making ability,
traffic capacity in yards and on routes in and out of the valley, and operating
workforce. The heat and never-ending labor took an especially heavy toll on
railroad employees unaccustomed to desert conditions. Executive Louis P. Hopkins, who from his headquarters in Los Angeles supervised all Southern Pacific
transportation east as far as El Paso, spent many cantaloupe seasons in the Imperial and Coachella valleys. With horror, he recalled the 125-degree heat. At
Indio, railroad managers slept in a contraption they affectionately dubbed "the
submarine," a horizontal metal tank with an opening in one end. One climbed
in and lay naked on a mattress, while cooling water drained over the tank all
night. In the Imperial Valley, according to Hopkins, they took showers and then
"flopped on the sheets without drying and an electric fan going full blast."
"Many nights," he remembered, "our sleeping period would be from 2:30 AM
to 4:30 AM. After ten weeks siege of this it was quite a relief to be headed toward
Los Angeles."[58]

At the same time, railroaders were keenly aware that they were pioneers, doing what no one had ever done before, expanding the technical and organizational limits of their industry. George R. McIntosh, general agent of Pacific
Fruit Express in Los Angeles, reported in 1922 that government officials and
others "have conceded . . . the handling of this crop, which must be harvested
and transported in the short space of six weeks, to be one of the greatest transportation accomplishments in the United States." Six years later, T. H. Williams,
assistant general manager of the Southern Pacific Company, viewed the "cantaloupe deal" as unique in American railroad history: "In all my railroad experience . . . I have never seen and I don't think it can be shown in the whole
United States where there is such an intense movement within such a short
time as this cantaloupe movement." It was, iceman Pete Holst boasted, "the
damndest railroading you ever heard of."[59]

Such supreme efforts obviously delivered huge profits to the Southern Pacific
and Pacific Fruit Express, and hence encouraged seemingly ever greater investments of capital and time and attempts at experimentation through the
1920s and 1930s. Although surviving records pay scant attention to specific profit
figures, indicative of the larger picture is the experience of the Southern Pacific's
tiny subsidiary, the San Diego & Arizona Railroad, which in 1928 earned
$182,000 in profit from carrying just 3,000 carloads of the valuable cantaloupes,
wholly within southern California.[60]

Soaring cantaloupe production, railroad profits, and regional development
could not have been achieved without close alliances among the many interests involved in the "cantaloupe deal." Minutes of the railroad's meetings for

growers and shippers indicate that they were typically cordial and collegial events, where railroaders, agricultural representatives, local and outside businessmen, and governmental officials acknowledged their mutual interdependence and cooperated to compromise differences and plan the harvest and shipment. Cantaloupe shipping leaders wrestled with manifold problems that invariably cropped up, such as scheduling, ordering ice and reefers, preventing thefts of melons from parked reefers, and, ironically, periodic cantaloupe price declines caused by overproduction, in other words excessive success. In 1925, for example, the group met under the cloud of falling cantaloupe prices and farm profits during the previous year and worked out a concerted plan, similar to what the Southern Pacific had done earlier with oranges and raisins, for a national saturation advertising campaign to promote the health benefits of eating the fruit, centered around a radio contest in which listeners guessed the number of seeds in a cantaloupe.[61] Praise for the Southern Pacific–Pacific Fruit Express system was loud and frequent from growers, government agricultural agencies, and local and outside newspapers.[62] In 1927, for example, the *Los Angeles Times* observed in a long feature story that the valley's cantaloupe crop, "the biggest, most rapidly handled, the most perishable and most concentrated freight deal in the world . . . stands as a model for other growing sections": "Growers and shippers from many sections of the United States have studied the methods of the Imperial Valley shippers and of the railroad as an example of the great degree of efficiency in handling such a [perishable] crop."[63]

The value of close cooperation between railroad, grower, and shipper was evident over and over again but perhaps never as clearly as during the ominous "car crisis of 1920." In that year, a national switchmen's strike, the ineptitude of federal officials still in wartime emergency control of American railroads, and the continuing practice of eastern railroads to deliberately delay the return of empty Pacific Fruit Express reefers back west combined to create a monumental 50,000-car shortage in California during June and July, threatening the entire Imperial cantaloupe harvest as well as other crops. It was only quickly called protest meetings in El Centro, Los Angeles, and Sacramento and aggressive, concerted pressure on the Interstate Commerce Commission, the American Railway Association, and eastern business groups from the Southern Pacific, Union Pacific, Pacific Fruit Express, growers, shippers, and western governmental officials that forced the eastern railroads to relinquish some reefers back to California. The Southern Pacific improvised new, more efficient crate designs, car-packing methods, and train movements east to make up the rest of the deficiency.[64]

Freight-hauling profits, increasing farm income, and soaring cantaloupe acreage encouraged the Southern Pacific–Pacific Fruit Express partnership to

Loading cantaloupes aboard the Southern Pacific at Fallon, Nevada, on the Truckee-Carson Reclamation Project, ca. 1915. Courtesy Nevada Historical Society, Reno.

transport the cantaloupe deal's system of careful organization and cooperation to other regions and then to other crops. Over the first few decades of the twentieth century, the railroad developed additional prosperous cantaloupe-producing districts with different ripening seasons, including the Yuma and Salt River valleys in Arizona; the Turlock area of California's northern San Joaquin Valley and the Huron-Westside district of the central San Joaquin (an especially productive area yielding 10,000 carloads of cantaloupes annually by the 1920s and 1930s); the Fallon and Fernley areas in the Truckee-Carson federal reclamation project and Lovelock and Mason, all in Nevada, which benefited especially from its monopoly on the autumn ripening season; and finally the Beeville, Texas, area. The cantaloupe system was also immediately adapted to other crops and by the 1920s was being used to encourage the growing of Imperial Valley lettuce and winter vegetables, both soon to emerge among the region's most profitable and long-lasting crops, and of table grapes, green fruit, and livestock throughout California and the Southwest, among other products.[65]

By 1929, the companies, working closely with farmers, cooperatives, and packers and shippers, had created a nationwide system for fast, efficient shipment, icing, and marketing for a great variety of fruits and vegetables. The Southern Pacific had built large export concentration points, with yards and ice-making and icing facilities, at Roseville in northern California, at Colton east of Los Angeles at the edge of the desert, at Yuma and Phoenix in Arizona, and at El Paso, which handled the largest volume of shipments.[66] By the 1920s, this was both the heart and central nerve center of the Southern Pacific Company. In 1920, 28 percent of all the railroad's revenues—$36 million in all—came from hauling the products of western orchards and farms.[67]

Packing Sheds, Texas Rice, Oregon Fruit, and Livestock

In the early decades of the twentieth century, the Southern Pacific Company's marketing services came to be characterized by four distinguishing features: publication of pamphlets, posters, and other mass-produced materials promoting consumption of local products; railroad sponsorship of lavish displays at U.S. and European expositions and at eastern transportation and business centers; coordination of individual growers, farm organizations, commodity cooperatives, and shippers to create more efficient and profitable packing, loading, refrigeration, and shipping systems for local products; and cooperation with those interests to mount and finance mass advertising and marketing campaigns. Also by the early twentieth century, specialized Southern Pacific agricultural and/or industrial departments, operating in the company's various regions and employing expert agents—some traveling, some headquartered at major transportation points—centralized management of the railroad's efforts to improve local production, shipping, and marketing.

One notable Southern Pacific practice, which was introduced in the 1890s and grew dramatically in the early 1900s, was the railroad's encouragement, through investing its lands and capital, of private or public facilities to ship or process local farm produce. Although the company itself sometimes built and operated such facilities, more commonly it lent farm cooperatives, processors, and shippers money—sometimes large sums—to finance spur rail lines to their establishments and to build packing sheds, loading platforms, warehouses, canneries, or refrigeration facilities. Often accompanying the loans were free or nominally priced leases to Southern Pacific lands on which to locate the improvements. Little or no interest was charged on the loans, which were repaid typically by small fees charged on future sales. Interest was suspended or occasionally the loans forgiven altogether, should local producers fall on hard times. In effect, the Southern Pacific was providing start-up capital, and assuming some of the risks, to create outlets for the produce of local farms. The practice was not without problems for the railroad. The loans tied up capital, and some of the growers' organizations and shippers proved unstable and failed to meet their agreements. Although in the early 1900s the railroad temporarily reduced the number of new loans granted, competition within the railroad industry in California forced the practice to be reinstated and indeed expanded. When the Union Pacific entered the state by acquiring control of the San Pedro, Los An-

geles, and Salt Lake Railroad in 1905, the new line started offering similar incentives to lure fruit and vegetable shippers away from the Southern Pacific
and Santa Fe lines. Shippers immediately began playing railroads against each
other to extract concessions and the most favorable subsidies of their packing
and loading facilities. The Southern Pacific and Santa Fe increased their loan
programs to meet the challenge from their traditional rival while reaching an
agreement between themselves to cooperate and not to compete for packing-
houses.[68] By the 1920s, the Southern Pacific and its subsidiary lines had outstanding loans to scores of fruit cooperatives, lumber companies, canneries, oil
refineries, water companies, and other interests throughout its territories, but
especially in California. Amounts varied from as low as a few thousand dollars
to as high as $1.5 million to one lumber company; many were for several hun-
dred thousand dollars. In only one typical example, in the early 1920s the Southern Pacific advanced the West Ontario (California) Citrus Association $205,402
to build warehouse and shipping facilities at Narod; $171,505 had been paid
back by 1930, at a rate that graduated from two cents per box shipped in the
first few years to four cents per box in 1930 and afterward.[69]

The agricultural marketing mechanisms it had pioneered in California, the
Southern Pacific transferred to the railroad's other regions, particularly Texas
and Louisiana, Oregon, and the Great Basin. For Texas and Louisiana, by the
early 1900s, the railroad had established a particularly aggressive agricultural
and industrial development department headquartered in Houston and New
Orleans and with local offices and specialized traveling agents operating
throughout the region. The department focused particularly on working with
classes of growers to promote more efficient and profitable outlets for their
products. In the early 1920s, for example, livestock agent Nat Parks organized
cattle raisers to develop ways to speed rail shipments of the live animals to
market, reducing weight-loss and the need for feeding en route and increasing profits to ranchers. Agents for other crops, including perishables, achieved
similar efficiencies and economies.[70] Between 1900 and the 1920s, Southern
Pacific agricultural and immigration agents S. F. B. Morse, Sam Houston Dixon,
J. C. Cooper, H. M. Mayo, H. H. Attwater, and John Howard organized exhibits of Texas and Louisiana products at expositions, promoted the development of farm organizations, worked with these groups to improve the railroad's
shipping and marketing services, and developed advertising campaigns and literature on behalf of regional products.[71] Southern Pacific agricultural development efforts in Texas and Louisiana focused particularly on encouraging more
intensive farming in order to raise new, more profitable, diversified specialty
crops, particularly after the boll weevil scourge in the early 1900s threatened
the main cotton crop. Southern Pacific exhibits, pamphlets, advertising campaigns, and marketing efforts urged the growing and consuming of fruits and

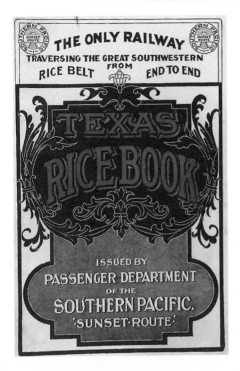

Cover of the *Texas Rice Book* (1893), one of many pamphlets the Southern Pacific produced to promote the growing and consumption of Texas and Louisiana rice. Courtesy DeGolyer Library, Southern Methodist University.

vegetables, tobacco, sugar, and especially rice, which the company promoted aggressively from the 1890s into the 1920s as a more reliable and profitable replacement for cotton along the Gulf Coast from the Mississippi River west and south practically to the Rio Grande.[72]

In the 1880s and 1890s, Southern Pacific agricultural department managers, land officials, and local station agents instituted a decades-long campaign to encourage rice production in Texas and Louisiana. The company sponsored cultivation experiments, developed markets for rice, and settled colonies of pioneer rice-growers on railroad land and land purchased for subdivision, particularly the famous Iowa Colony, near Lake Charles, Louisiana. One railroad agent and principal founder of the Iowa Colony, Sylvester L. Cary, headquartered at nearby Jennings, was tireless in converting former overflowed lands to rice cultivation. Rice industry historian Henry C. Dethloff has concluded that Cary, along with Jabez Bunting Watkins and the more famous Seaman A. Knapp, was one of "a triumvirate of promoters, entrepreneurs, and speculators who sometimes collectively, but mostly independently, stimulated the settlement of the [Gulf Coast] prairies and the development of agriculture." Cary came to be hailed throughout the Gulf Coast region as "Father Cary."[73] In promoting Texas and Louisiana rice production and consumption, the Southern Pacific worked closely with the officials of the Rice Association of America and the Texas-Louisiana Rice Farmers' Association.[74]

In contrast to the generally factual and objective Southern Pacific advertising materials promoting sales of the products of other regions, such as California and Oregon, the Texas publications pushing rice tended toward exaggeration, often bordering on pseudo-scientific quackery. The rice books, for example, proclaimed that eating rice, as compared to traditional American corn and wheat and especially meat, produced physically, mentally, and spiritually healthier people and even cured invalids. Experts who should have known better cooperated in the Southern Pacific publicity campaign. No less revered authorities than national agricultural extension official Seaman A. Knapp and his wife testified in Southern Pacific pamphlets to the multifold health benefits of Texas and Louisiana rice. Mrs. Knapp assured potential consumers that eating rice kept the Chinese "in perfect health," cured the ill and infirm, and improved the temperament—in contrast to beef, which produced too much "restless energy." "The quiet patience of the Chinese and Japanese is due to rice. Irritable and nervous people should eat rice."[75] Another railroad pamphlet claimed that a diet of rice and legumes was used by the body "with least labor to the organs of assimilation and elimination" and was "ideal for maintaining the human machine." Substituting rice for traditional corn and wheat "as the principal food for Southern people will tend to the development of a hardier race. It will decrease dyspepsia, malaria and mortgages."[76]

On its lines in Oregon, the Southern Pacific especially worked with growers and shippers to expand markets and improve shipping for deciduous fruit— particularly apples—which was becoming a booming regional business in the late nineteenth and early twentieth centuries. Methods similar to those pioneered to the south in California were used. One major improvement came in 1914, when the Southern Pacific introduced a new, faster service for fruit shipments from Oregon to the east. Fruit had generally moved north from the Willamette, Umpqua, and Rogue river valleys to Portland, and thence eastward. To the praise of fruit growers and shippers, the company opened new, through service south to Roseville east of Sacramento, and then east. By switching fruit trains to this faster route, and then cutting the holdover in Roseville to only three hours, compared to eighteen hours in Portland, the Southern Pacific was able to shave nearly a day from the running time from Oregon to the east— 7.5 days to Chicago, 10.25 days to New York City, nearly as fast as fruit from California—which could make a critical difference in spoilage and profits for refrigerated produce.[77]

Most prominent of the Southern Pacific marketers in Oregon during the early twentieth century was Amos A. Morse, special freight agent for the Southern Pacific and Union Pacific during the Harriman Lines era, from 1901 until his retirement in 1913. From Morse's manuscript collection, now at the University of Oregon, emerges the most detailed picture available of the impor-

tant development work being done by many Southern Pacific agents in boost-
ing sales and better shipping methods for crops—and thus railroad freight
revenues—in the company's territory from Oregon south to California and
West to Texas and Louisiana.[78] Morse gathered and managed exhibitions of regional products at expositions, actively sponsored the organization of farmers
and shippers, attended their conventions, and advised them about better marketing practices, ways to deal with overproduction, and how to cultivate sales
by raising the quality of produce shipped.[79] To the end of increasing sales of
farm products along the Harriman Lines, he traveled frenetically among the
agricultural districts of the Pacific Northwest, as well as California, and routinely in the northern part of the United States to the Great Lakes and across
Canada, making contacts with growers, shippers, and buyers, bringing them
together and negotiating agreements among them, as well as devising new shipping services, schedules, and lower tariffs to make the deals attractive to all parties. He kept constantly in touch with producers and buyers in his broad domain via circular and private letters, pamphlets, telegrams, and telephone. Morse
became famous in the Pacific Northwest for creating from nothing, virtually sin-
gle-handedly between 1907 and 1912, a new, profitable business for growers and
the railroad by sending Oregon and California produce to Canada. Hitherto,
the Santa Fe had monopolized the trade in citrus and other west-coast produce
to Canada, via its connection to Kansas City and from there north. By working out agreements, including provisions for lower tariffs, between growers, shippers, buyers, the Harriman Lines, and the Canadian Pacific Railway, Morse devised a faster, cheaper, new route for citrus and deciduous fruit to move from
California, Oregon, and Washington north through the Pacific Northwest to
a connection with the Canadian Pacific and then east, thereby doing an end-
run around the Santa Fe and garnering a significant share of the business. Between 1907 and his retirement in 1913, Morse regularly revisited the territory
along the new Canadian fruit marketing route, tending and expanding the
trade.[80]

On the Great Basin in the early twentieth century, the Southern Pacific developed shipping and marketing programs to assist the growers of new crops—
most notably cantaloupes and potatoes—being introduced in northern Nevada
on private and federally assisted reclamation and irrigation projects such as
the Truckee-Carson Project south and east of Reno.[81] Now under new competition from the Western Pacific, which completed its line from San Francisco Bay to Utah in 1909, the Southern Pacific had additional incentives to
hold and build freight business. Decades of disappointment trying to encourage farming in the arid, underdeveloped region, however, led the railroad
to put most of its marketing efforts into livestock production, the one "crop"
that the vast open desert and grassland ranges seemed able to yield in abun-

dance. An added benefit to the company was the possibility of increasing the tiny revenues then being derived from grazing leases to several million acres of the old Central Pacific land grant. Stretching in a nearly perfect checkerboard pattern of sections across much of northern Nevada and Utah, the railroad's land still lay mostly unsold and unused because of the region's aridity, as well as competition from the vast surplus of public land to which ranchers had free or cheap access before congressional passage of the Taylor Grazing Act in 1934.[82]

Across the northern Great Basin, from Reno east to the company's terminus at Ogden, the Southern Pacific in the early twentieth century worked with ranchers and shippers to improve movement and marketing of livestock, especially cattle and sheep. The company subsidized the building of loading pens, corrals, and watering facilities at strategic points along the line in Nevada and Utah and provided annual leases of one cent per acre per year to railroad land used for these improvements and to pasture livestock being held for shipment and sheep awaiting shearing. As agent Nat Parks was doing in Texas, the railroad consolidated livestock shipping into special trains operating on faster schedules to speed the animals east for more profitable sale.[83] The Southern Pacific also put its land grant to use in another way, not technically associated with marketing. When drought threatened to starve cattle and sheep herds elsewhere in its territory, as happened in California's San Joaquin and Salinas valleys in 1894, the railroad dispatched special trains to move the stock to better-watered ranges on its unused Great Basin land and charged freight charges only slightly higher than the cost of labor and fuel while waiving grazing fees.[84] By the early 1920s, in cooperation with the Union Pacific and Denver & Rio Grande railroads and federal agricultural officials, the Southern Pacific had built a centralized special terminal at Ogden for receiving livestock and grain from the vast basin and mountain region, locating milling and elevator companies and livestock processors, and reorganizing trains to more efficiently send grain and livestock and by-products to the rest of the country.[85]

The Southern Pacific's most innovative marketing service in the Great Basin, however, was the development of public trail corridors for driving livestock to market over the region's stretches of sparse grass and water, and across lands jealously guarded by competing owners. When the federal General Land Office refused to take action on the nagging problem, at the behest of ranchers and livestock associations, the railroad served as the coordinating agency. Between the early 1900s and the 1920s, company Land Department agents knowledgeable about the landscape laid out, mapped, marked, and maintained networks of livestock trails, sometimes one hundred or more miles long, complete with public-access grazing ranges and waterholes, that threaded from distant ranches down to central railheads across lands belonging to the railroad, the federal government, and cooperating private property owners.[86] By tailoring marketing programs to the potentials of the Great Basin, as it was doing in California, Oregon, and the Southwest, the Southern Pacific promoted not only increased and more reliable traffic revenues for itself but more successful agriculture, higher profits for farmers, and overall regional economic development and population growth.

PART V

Conservation

13 "Shall This Destruction Proceed?"

WILDERNESS PRESERVATION

The "Octopus" in the Garden

Many fail to realize that, at its inception in the late nineteenth century, natural resource conservationism was not a widespread or popular philosophy. Its principal proponents were a small cadre of artists, writers, naturalists, and occasionally local preservationists—political amateurs who were at first short on numbers, financial backing, and political savvy. To overcome public indifference and powerful opponents, conservationists sometimes allied themselves to stronger, more experienced and politically influential groups. On many questions, including the creation of national parks and forest preserves, western railroads provided the leverage to transform conservationist visions into actual laws and functioning programs.[1] Among the first and most vigorous corporate participants in the conservation movement was the Southern Pacific Company. In the late 1800s, John Muir and other wilderness preservation and resource conservation leaders formed partnerships with the Southern Pacific that lasted for decades and produced some of the landmark victories in the early wilderness preservation crusade, most notably the creation and expansion of Yosemite and Sequoia national parks and other natural reserves.[2]

At first glance, Southern Pacific interest in conservation appears incongruous. Even the simple construction and operation of railway technology constituted an unprecedented assault on natural ecological systems. Much of the early damage was to public lands adjacent to the transcontinental railway lines. Construction crews wantonly dug out and dynamited hillsides, filled in depressions and wetlands, altered or blocked watercourses, cut down whole forests, excavated sand and stone for construction materials, and slaughtered wild animals accidentally or for food or whim. Flooding and erosion were aggravated and wildlife patterns disrupted, sometimes seriously and permanently. Blasting and excavation conducted in the 1870s by the company's subsidiary California & Oregon Railroad while building its line north through California's Sacramento Valley, for example, silted rivers, destroyed fish-spawning grounds, and reduced or ended salmon runs.[3] Decades later in the early 1900s, the Southern Pacific's construction of the Lucin Cutoff—a raised, filled causeway across the Great Salt Lake—converted part of the vast inland dead sea into a freshwater reservoir by constricting the lake's circulation, dramatically altering the ecology of the shoreline and killing some salt-producing factories. Higher water levels and more severe and destructive flooding also resulted during rainy years, damaging shoreline property and businesses and threatening the causeway itself.[4]

In dry regions, despite the railroad's precautions, cinders and sparks from locomotives or crew campfires ignited great grass and forest conflagrations, which raged uncontrollably, burning down fences, farm crops, buildings, bridges, and other private and public property. On heavily traveled routes, the roadbed reeked from garbage thrown casually overboard by dining car workers and from human excrement flushed by countless train toilets directly onto the tracks. The trash heaps and open privies of line maintenance crews added to the stench, as did the creosote preservative saturating the rail ties. Barreling trains introduced deafening noise into quiet rural and town neighborhoods and killed and maimed wild animals, livestock, pets, and people as never before. Billowing wakes of dust, smoke, and ashes settled on adjacent vegetation and buildings and sometimes poisoned soil. Increasingly fenced and garbage-filled, the rights-of-way also impeded travel, except by invading hordes of rail-riding hoboes, who set fires and attacked nearby residents and their property. Rail rights-of-way also served as convenient pathways for other invaders: exotic plants, weeds, animals, crop pests, and diseases. By the end of the nineteenth century, some Southern Pacific and other western railroad rights-of-way through wilderness, rural districts, and cities had become wasteland corridors.[5] Historian John Stilgoe has characterized the American railroad right-of-way as a new sort of "trackside ecosystem," an extension into the countryside of the urban industrial zone, an essentially alien environment that was born and sustained through the disruption of older systems and that had by the turn of the nineteenth century "acquired mysterious, slightly sinister qualities" reflected in novels, popular literature, and movies.[6]

John Muir, a regular rider aboard the Southern Pacific, complained about the bleak outlook along rail lines. "Every train rolls on through dismal smoke and barbarous melancholy ruins," he wrote in 1901. Instead of issuing "gorgeous many-colored folders" proclaiming theirs to be the most "scenic route," Muir recommended, the railways should compete over which was "the route of superior desolation . . . the smoke, dust, and ashes route." Then, their advertisements could more truthfully read:

Come! Travel our way. Ours is the blackest. It is the only genuine Erebus route. The sky is black and the ground is black, and on either side there is a continu-

Clearing the right-of-way for the Southern Pacific's new Natron Cutoff in southeastern Oregon, 1923. Although its line construction devastated earth, forest, and animal life, the railroad was an important force for wilderness preservation and resource conservation in the West. Author's collection.

ous border of black stumps and logs and blackened trees appealing to heaven for help as if still half alive, and their mute eloquence is most interestingly touching. . . . The charring is generally deeper along our line, and the ashes are deeper, and the confusion and desolation displayed can never be rivaled. No other route on this continent so fully illustrates the abomination of destruction.[7]

Such jaundiced views on technology and progress might be expected from one such as John Muir, but he was not alone in condemning rail technology for violating natural and aesthetic values. Even loyal railroad officials could share the apprehension. One of these was William H. Mills, longtime head Southern Pacific land agent and vice president, a lifelong champion of progress through railroad construction, and also an authority on forestry. When in the early 1880s an eastern company proposed to build a tourist rail line right into Yosemite Valley itself, Mills, who was at that time also a leader of the California State Yosemite Valley Commission governing the park, was revolted and, although the proposed feeder line would likely have increased tourist traffic heading for Yosemite on the Southern Pacific, he wrote a scathing editorial in his *Sacramento Record-Union.* To bring a railroad into the valley, Mills argued, "would be to destroy all the picturesqueness and charm of the magnificent scenery, and to rob that marvelous valley of its poetry and majesty." "There should be no rushing, no grading down of hills, no prosaic cuttings and fillings, no jar and rattle of cars, no hideous shriek of engines." The valley should be entered in a quiet manner, "not from the clashing, roaring, sentiment-destroying standpoint of a railroad car." In short, Mills concluded, "we should regard the intrusion of a railroad into Yosemite Valley as the most inexcusable and monstrous act of Vandalism."[8]

Nor was the destruction confined to narrow rights-of-way. The railroads' heavy hand also transformed broader, hitherto natural or lightly disturbed landscapes tributary to the Southern Pacific and other lines. Access to the expanding rail marketing network impelled people everywhere to shift to new, more intensive and exploitative land uses. As typical railroad officials in that era of pioneer western settlement, Southern Pacific leaders did not leave such growth to chance. As is documented in earlier chapters in this book, they promoted farming, industry, urban development, and settlement throughout their territory. The railroad subdivided and improved its granted lands, attracted farmers to the land, financed new farms and other enterprises, platted fledgling towns, helped farms, mines, lumber mills, and other businesses increase production and markets, built itself or stimulated other parties to build large-scale water systems, and advertised the glories of the Far West in the East and Europe to attract immigrants and tourists. By the early 1900s, the company was spending well over one million dollars per year just on advertising its region, and it had become perhaps the leading booster of the West.[9]

The result wherever the tide of rail-induced development flowed was the transformation of natural into man-made—usually much disturbed—landscapes. Typically, wetlands were drained or filled, forests denuded to meet the demand for construction material and fuel, and undulating irregular lands were restructured into rectilinear surveys and then subdivided, leveled, fenced, stripped of native vegetation and wildlife, and converted to housing, commerce, industry, or monoculture of foreign crops. Even as natural rivers were being filled in, dried up, or rerouted, new types of water facilities—wells, reservoirs, irrigation canals, and drainage ditches—rearranged the waterscape, above and below ground, forcing new patterns for plant and animal life everywhere. Foreign species conquered the land, quickly constituting a majority of plants and animals in some thickly settled places. Within a few years of introduction, Southern Pacific rails had revolutionized vast stretches of California's Sacramento, San Joaquin, Salinas, Imperial, and Colorado valleys, Oregon's Willamette Valley, the Texas Gulf Plains, and countless desert, mountain, and Great Basin places. The transformative environmental effects of building large, transcontinental roads were compounded

Early rail construction methods relying on human labor and animal-driven machines were destructive enough, but later more "advanced" technologies intruded even more into nature. By the early 1900s, the Southern Pacific routinely deployed powerful steam shovels to do heavy excavation. This one was filling the High Trestle near Wolf Creek, Oregon, ca. 1900s. Author's collection.

by the rapid proliferation of small feeder lines, particularly logging railroads.[10] Like other railroads, the Southern Pacific greatly accelerated the process of exploiting resources, thus disturbing natural landscapes and driving back the wilderness all along the far-western frontier.[11]

Railroaders as Conservationists

While railroad construction and operation were upsetting environmental balances in some regions, enlightened corporate self-interest prompted Southern Pacific leaders to welcome, or even lead, many resource conservation programs. Despite vigorous conflicts with many groups in California and other states, particularly over freight rates, rail services, and political influence, Southern Pacific officials, like the leaders of other land-grant railroads, realized that the profits of the company depended on the economic and social well-being of its hinterland, especially the expansion and modernization of agricultural systems. The railroad's identification with the long-term public interest led it also to support

Intensive logging that spread along the Southern Pacific's Tillamook Branch in Oregon and its spin-off logging railways in the late nineteenth and early twentieth centuries brought deforestation and soil erosion. Author's collection.

many conservation programs in the late nineteenth and early twentieth centuries. Although they aggressively promoted development in low-elevation valleys near their rail lines, Southern Pacific leaders, taking the long-term view, realized that the company's complex needs and interests ultimately depended on balanced, efficient, renewable use of natural resources. For example, especially in the semi-arid Far West, the sale of railroad land and increased crop production, the source of most of the company's traffic, relied on irrigation water. The need to assure future water supplies led the company to support protection of forest watersheds, control of erosion and flooding, and management of water flow through streams, lakes, and reservoirs. The Southern Pacific's managers also understood that tourism and industry, two other important sources of rail revenues, also required a planned approach to using scarce resources, including scenic wilderness.[12]

Moreover, the extension of the American rail network to the West during and after the 1860s helped to create the cultural and economic milieu in which conservationism could for the first time flourish and spread. If the laying down of tracks blighted some immediate wilderness, the building of rail lines by the Southern Pacific and other companies through spectacular mountains and deserts and along rivers and ocean coasts, along with their advertising of the West and fostering of mass tourism, also encouraged a new conservationist ethic by opening up the region's wild beauties to a wider, influential middle-class public. Concurrent with the communications revolution born of mass journalism, quick telegraphic information transfer, and cheaper and better image-making, the first westbound trains carried a host of magazine and newspaper reporters, travel-account writers, and artists and photographers. Their numbers continued to grow until their places in depicting western natural beauties were taken by twentieth-century makers of movie and television entertainment. Some of the early promoters of western scenery were in the employ of the railroads, such as the Southern Pacific's own photographers Alfred Hart and Carleton E. Watkins and writers Charles Nordhoff and Benjamin C. Truman, who in addition to documenting new rail facilities, photographed and wrote of wondrous sights along the line to attract travelers and settlers. Entire sophisticated industries sprang up to take advantage of the seemingly insatiable market for western tourism. Railroads like the Southern Pacific cooperated with, indeed often even spawned, the new travel agencies, tour companies, itinerant lecturers, and resort hotels. The Southern Pacific recruited private investors to build tourist hotels along the company's lines or the railroad itself founded the resorts, most notably the famed Del Monte (1880) in scenic Monterey, California, the first and foremost of great nineteenth-century western railroad watering places. The travelers and settlers also included masses of invalids as well as others seeking the uplifting, allegedly curative powers of benevolent nature in the West.[13]

The subtle, complex influence of the western railroads on the American imagination—especially what came to be its characteristic celebration of wild nature—may be difficult to measure precisely, but it was most certainly substantial. According to Thurman Wilkins, biographer of John Muir, it was not until the building of the western lines that railroad-promoted sightseeing began to capitalize on the "wild and monumental scenery of the West. . . . and as a result of vigorous advertising, the trains brought enormous throngs of visitors to the western wilds, including the brand-new national parks. Tourism, then, proved a powerful means of popularizing wilderness during the latter part of the nineteenth century."[14]

More than simple corporate self-interest, however, led many Southern Pacific leaders to advocate conservationism. Well-educated pioneers in a modern, highly technical business, the railway's officials were well versed in new scientific ideas. Moreover, as prominent members of the business community, they had wide networks of friendship and professional association among scientists, artists, writers, and educators, the very groups most involved in early conservation movements. John Muir and Southern Pacific leaders, for example, had many mutual acquaintances by the 1870s and 1880s, particularly among California's cultured groups. With leaders from these other fields, Southern Pacific officials shared a rational, scientific worldview and the modern pursuit of "efficiency," as well as an older romantic faith in the spiritual benefits of communion with nature. Support for conservationism among the railroad's leaders, then, stemmed naturally from their private beliefs, as well as the changing needs of a dynamic company.[15]

Many of the railway's leaders, as a result, had long careers in environmental affairs, both as part of their Southern Pacific service and in their private lives. The persistence and diversity of their involvements cannot be explained completely as functions of the railroad's business interests. This was especially true of the three chief land agents: Benjamin B. Redding (1865–1882), William H. Mills (1883–1907), and B. A. McAllaster (1909–1933). These men administered the land grant and lent remarkable continuity to the company's resource policies. All three became recognized experts on soil, climate, forestry, irrigation, flood control, and wildlands preservation and management. They wrote and lectured on these topics, helped to advise, organize, or guide the activities of conservation groups, and sat as members or consultants with a number of government agencies with environmental concerns. Lesser company land agents scattered throughout Southern Pacific territory also promoted or attended forestry, agricultural, and water conferences, or participated in local conservation movements.[16] A number of Southern Pacific-supported conservation movements, in which these and other railroad leaders participated, particularly associated with land and water, have already been analyzed in previous chapters in this book: the fight to harness hydraulic-mining debris, the emerging public management of water supplies in the interest of long-term conservation as well as economic development, the halting of the great Colorado River flood of 1904–1907, and the encouragement of a scientific approach to agriculture that counted soil and fertility conservation among its principal objectives.[17]

The railroad's land agents were not alone in supporting and leading conservation movements. Between the 1890s and the 1920s, passenger department managers, such as James Horsburgh, Jr., and E. O. McCormick, worked for the founding of local and national parks and recreation facilities. The department's booster monthly magazine, *Sunset* (1898–1914), provided a major national forum for writers on water conservation, scientific forestry, and wildlife and wilderness preservation. Counsels in the law department, particularly W. W. Stow in the 1880s and early 1890s and William F. Herrin after the mid-1890s, lobbied on behalf of important environmental legislation. Even the top executives and owners, such as Leland Stanford, Charles Crocker, and Collis P. Huntington, donated funds and land to build or improve parks, including Golden Gate Park in San Francisco, Lake Merritt Park in Oakland, and Fresno's city park. E. H. Harriman, who controlled the Southern Pacific between 1901 and 1909, was an especially important patron of environmental science, forestry, and wilderness preservation. For decades, Harriman fought against the destruction of forests in his home state of New York. At his death, he bequeathed to the state for a public wilderness park a gigantic estate, which he had rescued grove by grove over the years from the timberman's ax.[18]

Never fully articulated or systematically codified, emerging Southern Pacific environmental policies were not always uniform or consistent. Policies evolved gradually from the 1860s through the early 1900s in response to specific events and issues with resource or environmental implications for the railroad. Often in the railroad's unsettled or thinly settled hinterland, with governments and other organized bodies weak, the Southern Pacific was the first to be faced with pressing environmental needs, and being the most structured and technologically advanced entity, was the first to be drawn into trying to find solutions. When conditions or the company's perceived interests changed, policies were also sometimes modified, even reversed. It was not uncommon for one branch of the railroad to favor one policy that benefited its particular facet of railroading, while other Southern Pacific people opposed that policy. Even regarding specific issues, corporate interests thus could be contradictory, ambiguous, or opposed to the preservation of the natural environment. This was true, for example, in the famous Hetch Hetchy controversy from 1905 to 1913, when the company's official and public support for San Francisco's search for more water overrode its traditional protectionism toward Yosemite National Park. Some Southern Pacific people, though, such as vice president and chief counsel William F. Herrin, continued to assist John Muir in fighting San Francisco's dam-building in the park.[19] In general, the Southern Pacific most often endorsed "utilitarian" conservation activities, which aimed at rational resource management to reduce waste and to contribute to balanced, long-term development. In many instances, however, the railroad supported "preservationism," the protection of undefiled wild nature. Many of the events recounted in this chapter transpired before the Hetch Hetchy controversy and other internecine battles of the early twentieth century had wrenched the conservation movement and splintered utilitarians and preservationists into hostile camps. That optimistic, romantic, and perhaps naive generation believed that it was possible to exploit resources more wisely in the interest of healthier development and to increase and democratize access to nature, while at the same time preserving wilderness and scenery.[20]

Indeed, Southern Pacific environmental policy fit no single category that historians have traditionally used to classify late-nineteenth and early-twentieth-century human behavior toward nature: free and unrestrained exploitation of resources, utilitarian conservationism of resources for long-term economic development, or wilderness preservationism. Instead, regarding specific times, events, and issues, the company's policies could reflect any one, or even more than one, of these modes of human resource use. In general, though, from the 1860s through the 1920s, the Southern Pacific shifted away from unrestrained exploitation, so evident in its construction phase. The railroad moved toward policies that, in the interest of sustained long-term development, stressed rational, scientifically based management of resources and natural systems on its own lands, other private parties', and the public's. To railroad people, this often meant also that natural systems—wilderness—had to be preserved against development. Certainly, Southern Pacific resource and environmental policies, as ambiguous and inchoate as they sometimes were, belie the old historical dogma that big business was antithetical to modern conservation and other Progressive-era reforms.[21] Despite incongruities in policies and actions, in the vacuum created by powerful anti-conservation interests, public indifference, and governmental weakness and inaction, the Southern Pacific often provided crucial publicity, financing, organization, leadership, and political support for conservation efforts in its territory from the 1860s through the early twentieth century.

The Battle for Yosemite National Park

One of the earliest, clearest, and most indicative examples of the Southern Pacific's importance in wilderness preservation and resource conservation was the partnership the railroad forged with John Muir and others for the creation of Yosemite National Park, one of the movement's major achievements. In 1864, the national government had closed Yosemite Valley to further public land sales and entrusted it to the guardianship of the state of California. Yosemite Valley thus became the first American wilderness preserve, for all intents and purposes the first "national park," although that specific term would not be used for years to come.[22] Nevertheless, by the 1880s, Muir and fellow devotees of Yosemite had become outraged at the extent to which pioneer development was already ravishing this unique glacial valley and the surrounding wilderness. Even though only a handful of wealthy tourists visited the isolated, state-managed park, neighboring ranchers poached on the high-elevation meadows above it with their voracious sheep (which Muir condemned as "hoofed locusts"). Loggers shaved the forests from the higher slopes, bringing down silt to clog the valley's rivers and lakes. Everywhere, carelessly set fires scorched meadows and woodlands. On the valley floor, farmers plowed, hayed, grazed livestock, and set out orchards in the very mist of majestic waterfalls, and campers cut down trees and littered the woods with trash. To reduce local flooding, enterprising settlers even took it on themselves to dynamite boulders and a granite ledge out of the Merced riverbed, speeding the stream's flow, weakening its banks, lowering the valley's water table, and encouraging invading trees and brush to choke out meadow grasses and wildflowers, to obscure scenic views of cliffs and waterfalls, and to greatly aggravate the wildfire danger. Blighted by erosion and cluttered with makeshift fences, run-down shacks, dusty, poorly maintained roads, and other human debris, Yosemite Valley was, in Muir's words, "a frowzy, neglected backwoods pasture."[23] Hamstrung by public apathy, political intrigue, stingy budgets, and interference from the legislature, the state Yosemite Valley Commission appeared powerless to halt this deterioration. In the late 1880s, Muir, aided by a small but dedicated crew of artists, writers, and scientists, began a struggle to save Yosemite by converting it into a true national park, under the direct management of the federal government.[24]

Formidable hurdles stood in their path. Americans were accustomed to exploiting resources as rapidly as possible. To most people, preserving wilderness was a new, strange, even unpatriotic idea. Moreover, powerful local interests strenuously opposed protecting Yosemite. Instead, they wanted free rein to log the forests or graze their livestock in the lush summer meadows. A host of park concessionaires also fought to retain their lucrative monopolies over lodging and transportation, while other developers proposed converting the valley itself into a gaudy tourist carnival along the lines of Niagara Falls. All of these groups preferred dealing with a lax, easily manipulated state commission rather than unpredictable federal authorities. With much influence in the state legislature, the governor's office, and Congress, the enemies of Yosemite preservation repeatedly blocked programs to increase protection of the region, to transfer it to federal jurisdiction, or to vote sufficient funds to enforce existing regulations. Like many other natural landmarks, Yosemite appeared doomed.[25]

The Southern Pacific's leaders had long appreciated the company's stake in preserving Yosemite. Aware of the park's importance as a tourist attraction, the railway had dispatched writers, artists, and photographers into the valley as early as the 1860s and had broadcast its beauties around the world in posters, photographs, and travel pamphlets.[26] In the 1870s, the company's people also began to assist John Muir in his conservation work, particularly the protection of Yosemite. When in the early 1870s he emerged from living in Yosemite, moved to the San Francisco Bay region, and took up a career of writing and lecturing, Muir reached out to a wider audience with his appeal for wilderness preservation, and he was willing to temper his earlier, more radical environmental and anti-industrial rhetoric somewhat in order to win converts to the cause. He was even coming to admire many of the businessmen who had brought progress and wealth to the people, and he appeared to feel comfortable with them. His writings made him a celebrity, not only in literary and scientific communities, but in business circles as well. Through his contacts, such as mentor Jeanne Carr, he met many business leaders, especially in the San Francisco area, including officials of the Southern Pacific Company, then the major corporation operating on the Pacific Coast. Just as they assisted other writers, artists, and scientists, company leaders from the mid-1870s onward also provided Muir with free rail passes and letters of introduction to influential businessmen, and in other ways supported him in his research, lecturing, and writing about the High Sierra.[27]

Some Southern Pacific executives were even more directly involved in preserving Yosemite. One was William H. Mills, the longtime railroad land agent and editor and the railroad's partner in the *Sacramento Record-Union*. Throughout his long public career in California, Mills was a staunch defender of farm interests and one of the West's early conservation leaders. Convinced that in the long run agriculture could only be expanded in this semi-arid state through comprehensive water management, Mills became one of the first promoters of public irrigation, scientific forestry, and mountain watershed preservation. In the late 1870s and early 1880s, Mills used the *Record-Union* to lead a journalistic war against hydraulic mining that helped bring about the ultimate prohibition of the dumping of mining debris into California's Central Valley streams.[28]

A close friend of Muir's early mentor, Jeanne Carr, Mills opened up the columns of the *Record-Union* to the great naturalist's first major public appeal for wilderness preservation. In 1876, only a year after he and the railroad had taken over the newspaper, Mills ran Muir's important article deploring the rampant obliteration of California's forests by grazing, lumbering, and carelessly set fires. Muir intended the piece to awaken legislators at the state capitol to the crisis looming in the mountains and to prod them into inaugurating a modern forestry program for the state, such as other countries had done. If the "waste and pure destruction" were not halted immediately, Muir predicted, soils would be irreparably eroded and irrigation waters would cease their flow. California

Many Southern Pacific pamphlets, such as this one from the 1870s, promoted tourist travel to Yosemite and other scenic points along the railroad's lines in California and the rest of its service area. Courtesy California State Railroad Museum, Sacramento.

would revert to barren desert, and "man himself will as surely become extinct as sequoia or mastodon, and be at length only a fossil." In recommending the "profoundly interesting article" to its readers, Mills's newspaper described Muir as "the California geologist . . . a practical man and a scientific observer."[29] Although Muir's warning had no noticeable impact on California's complacent and development-minded legislators, its message undoubtedly impressed Mills. For the next thirty years, Mills and the *Record-Union* were leaders in California in championing scientific forestry, fire control, and watershed and wilderness preservation to protect forests in California and the Far West.[30]

Beginning in 1879, Mills also served a long term on the state Yosemite Valley Commission. One of the few dedicated commissioners, Mills repeatedly fought against exploitation of the valley. A powerful member of the commission's executive committee, he led campaigns to enlarge the park, adopt comprehensive scientific management policies, increase the commission's authority and funds, crack down on violators of park regulations, break the monopoly of the concessionaires, and reduce transportation and lodging prices in order to open up the valley to more people. While Mills served on the commission, Southern Pacific civil engineers advised on the construction of roads, bridges, and other facilities in the valley, and the company supported efforts in the legislature that succeeded in temporarily increasing appropriations for Yosemite preservation. Despite being criticized, often justly, by Muir and other conservationists, the Yosemite Valley Commission in the 1880s, under the leadership of a few conservation-minded men like Mills and state engineer William Hammond Hall, did make some progress in overcoming the valley's complex ecological problems. Always respecting "the ability of the Indians to manage the valley" and believing them to be "the first commissioners," Mills interviewed local tribal members and early pioneers and discovered that natives had regularly and purposely burned the valley's grasses and thinned groves for centuries. Relying on this oral testimony, Mills in the 1880s got the commission to reinstitute such millennia-old native practices as systematic brush-clearing, controlled burning of meadows, and selective tree-cutting to avert uncontrollable forest fires and to preserve the valley's original open, park-like appearance. Ironically, Muir and other preservationists, failing to understand the Indians' integral involvement in the valley's ecology, denounced these actions as "unnatural" and in 1889 precipitated another in a long series of legislative investigations that sapped the commission's authority. Under Mills's leadership in the 1880s, the state's Yosemite Valley Commission pioneered these and other modern wilderness management techniques that would become commonplace in the twentieth century, including less invasive road-building, removing human interruptions of natural water flows, and subjecting concessionaires to stricter regulation, all practices that would be copied in Yellowstone and the later Yosemite national parks. Yosemite's enemies, however, by keeping the commission's legislative appropriations tiny, its power limited, and its membership filled by transient political appointees, thwarted most protectionist measures.[31]

Finally, in 1889, Mills resigned from the commission in frustration, convinced that current policies were only hastening the valley toward ruin. In a *Sacramento Record-Union* editorial, published at the beginning of the campaign to create a national park at Yosemite, Mills denounced the state's administration of Yosemite Valley as being guilty of "ignorance, stupidity and vandalism."[32] To his frequent correspondent Robert Underwood Johnson, conservationist editor of *Century Magazine* and Muir's close ally in early preservation battles, Mills confided that he had become "painfully conscious" that California had violated a "trust on behalf of the lovers of nature throughout the world" and that the management of Yosemite Valley should be "brought to the bar of public conscience."[33] Although Mills encouraged the efforts of Johnson and Muir to preserve the valley, he at first doubted that federal administration would bring any improvement and balked at the idea of relinquishing state control. In the 1890s, however, Mills was converted by Johnson and Muir into an ally in the movement to reorganize all the Yosemite region into a great national park.[34]

Muir and Johnson had hatched their scheme to return Yosemite Valley to federal control in 1889. Fearing that a direct assault on California's stewardship might wound local pride and provoke too much opposition, however, they concentrated first on preserving the higher-elevation territory surrounding the valley, which was still in national ownership.[35] To counter powerful opponents in California and the nation's capital, Muir and Johnson turned for help to Southern Pacific leaders. Grasping the importance of protecting watersheds and scenic wilderness, the railroad provided the political muscle to extend federal protection over the larger Yosemite region. On March 18, 1890, U.S. representative William Vandever of Los Angeles, probably acting at the request of Southern Pacific officials, introduced legislation into Congress to create Yosemite National Park. The measure allowed the state to retain authority over the valley itself and provided for a national park much smaller than the preservationists favored. Although they had had no role in introducing the proposal, Muir wrote influential articles about Yosemite for *Century Magazine* and he and Johnson testified before legislative committees in support of Vandever's bill and organized a campaign among eastern conservationist friends to pressure Congress for its passage.[36]

The Southern Pacific's lobbyists joined in. U.S. senator Leland Stanford, a builder and executive of the railroad, quietly encouraged the company's political friends to move the bill through Congress. Although Stanford did not move aggressively enough to suit Muir and Johnson, W. W. Stow, then chief Southern Pacific attorney and political organizer, labored among California's congressional delegation with greater results. Muir later recalled that "Mr. Stow in particular charged our members of Congress that whatever they neglected they must see that the bill for a National Park around Yosemite Valley went through."[37] Despite the efforts of Muir, Johnson, Stanford, and Stow, the Yosemite park bill languished in House committees through the summer of 1890, besieged by California interests opposed to protection of the Yosemite region. With Congress scheduled to adjourn on the first of October, the bill appeared lost for that session.[38]

When the Yosemite bill finally came up for consideration in September 1890, Daniel K. Zumwalt, the Southern Pacific's district land agent for the San Joaquin Valley, was in Washington attending to railroad land-grant business and promoting one of his pet projects, the formation of a national park in the giant-sequoia region, south of Yosemite. An agricultural and irrigation innovator and a devoted lover of wilderness, Zumwalt, through his friend and host in Washington, Congressman Vandever, was instrumental in getting the Yosemite legislation strengthened by enlarging the park beyond even Muir's initial proposal. Zumwalt also had the bill amended at the last minute to add provisions more than doubling the size of the giant-sequoia park. (The original measure creating Sequoia National Park, also supported by the Southern Pacific, had passed Congress in early September.) For nearly a month, Zumwalt marched from office to office in the capitol pushing for the passage of the amended Yosemite-

Sequoia bill before Congress adjourned. Finally, during the last two frenzied days of the session, both the House and Senate quickly took up and passed the bill in the scramble to finish their business. Vandever and the other floor managers allowed virtually no debate. The enemies of preservation were caught off guard, and the bill passed with few congressmen even comprehending its contents. Only hours later on October 1, President Benjamin Harrison signed the legislation creating Yosemite National Park. Most authorities credit Zumwalt with being the moving force behind both the amendment and the miraculous last-minute passage of the Yosemite-Sequoia bill, although historians have generally misconstrued his actions as motivated by some unspecified corporate greed.[39]

The victory had been a narrow one. With Congress preoccupied with tariff and election reforms and the park's opponents working hard to bury the legislation, only the dogged efforts of Yosemite's few supporters had succeeded in forcing the bill through that session. Just after the battle, Robert Underwood Johnson informed Muir that the park bill had passed "only through the hardest sort of following up" on the members of House and Senate committees.[40] The labors of Stanford, Stow, and especially Zumwalt had been invaluable. The railroad's assistance apparently puzzled Muir, who had anticipated opposition from the company. Like many Californians, he was still leery of political entanglement with the "Octopus." Later, when recounting the Yosemite victory during an 1896 address before the Sierra Club, Muir acknowledged that "even the Southern Pacific R.R. Co., never counted on for anything good, helped nobly in pushing the bill for this park through Congress."[41] Actually, in the 1890 session, the railroad had worked to pass legislation creating three wilderness preserves in California: Yosemite National Park, Sequoia National Park, and General Grant Sequoia Grove.[42]

The struggle to save Yosemite Valley had only begun, however. In the 1890s, environmental depredations continued unabated in the valley, and the state commission proved incapable of dealing with the problems. Meanwhile, Muir and his cohorts were impressed by the U.S. Army's success in driving poachers from the surrounding national park.[43] When a sympathetic governor, George C. Pardee, took office in 1904, Muir resumed the assault on state control of the valley. By this time, to build public interest in wilderness and to organize conservation battles, Muir had in 1892 founded the Sierra Club, with substantial support from business leaders. Southern Pacific executives were especially prominent among the Sierra Club's charter members, so much so that some other members less open-minded than Muir complained that the club's purity was tainted.[44] Led by Muir as president and William Colby as secretary, the club decided to press the California legislature to return the valley to the federal government for inclusion in the national park.[45]

The Southern Pacific's assistance was even more crucial to federal recovery of Yosemite Valley itself. Although Muir and the Sierra Club have generally been credited with engineering the transfer, the 1904 proposal to return the valley to federal jurisdiction did not actually originate with the great naturalist or the club. When he initiated the club's lobbying at the start of the state legislative session in December 1904, William Colby was surprised to discover that the California State Board of Trade had for nearly a year been at work in Sacramento and around the state on behalf of Yosemite Valley retrocession. Ancestor of the present-day California State Chamber of Commerce, the Board of Trade had been founded in 1887 largely through the efforts of Southern Pacific land agent William H. Mills. Composed of representatives from leading commercial bodies around the state, the Board of Trade had developed under Mills's guidance into a powerful advocate of tourism, immigration, agriculture, irrigation, and forest and wilderness preservation. At Mills's request, Muir himself had authored essays for inclusion in Board of Trade promotional pamphlets.[46] Now, a committee of the board led by Mills, who was by this time also a member of the California Redwood Commission formed to govern the new state park at Big Basin, was preparing a bill to protect Yosemite Valley by returning it to federal jurisdiction. After cordial conferences with Mills and his associates, Colby and Muir decided to withdraw the Sierra Club somewhat into the background and to defer to the Board of Trade, because in Colby's words, that organization was "a powerful body with a very large backing and all that we want to do is to see that the bill passes."[47]

Thus, the Board of Trade and the Sierra Club joined forces. Mills and Colby co-authored a retrocession bill, which they introduced into the legislature in January 1905.[48] At first, all went well. Relying on editorials in San Francisco's *Call* and *Chronicle* and other newspapers, as well as the State Board of Trade's contacts with local business organizations, Mills mobilized public opinion behind the measure. Ultimately, he was able to secure the backing of nearly every important newspaper and commercial body in the state.[49] Meanwhile, the Sierra Club marshaled dignitaries and scientists, including Muir himself, to lecture, pamphleteer, and testify before legislative committees denouncing the ruin of Yosemite under the state regime. The retrocession bill passed the Assembly easily on February 2.[50]

Trouble loomed in the Senate, however. There, the despoilers of Yosemite had dug in for a bitter struggle to retain the valley under state management. The opponents of retrocession were led by William Randolph Hearst's *San Francisco Examiner*, archenemy of the Southern Pacific, which harped on the theme of California's injured pride, and by a powerful state senator, John Curtin. Curtin, who had personally clashed with federal authorities over his rights to graze cattle in Yosemite National Park, was also retained as an attorney by the valley concessionaires to protect their interests. An early canvass of votes convinced Muir and Colby that the Senate would defeat the Yosemite bill by a wide margin. Thinking that amateurs like themselves could not compete with such professional adversaries, Muir and Colby feared defeat in January and February.[51]

At this juncture, Muir's cause benefited from close friendships he had developed in the early 1900s with two of the most powerful and controversial Southern Pacific leaders—Edward H. Harriman, who had purchased the railroad from the families of its builders and added it to his national transportation empire in 1901, and William F. Herrin, chief counsel, vice president, and infamous founder and operator of the "Southern Pacific political machine," which held considerable influence in California from the 1890s to the 1920s. Muir's relationship with Harriman especially demonstrates how far Muir had come since the 1870s toward making his peace with the industrial and corporate world. Having met the financier and railroad tycoon on the famous Harriman-sponsored Alaska expedition of 1899, Muir soon came to admire the man and his works, to appreciate Harriman's devotion to conservation and preservation causes, and to hold him and his family in genuine affection. The great naturalist corresponded regularly with the railroad magnate, traveled frequently under his passes or patronage, and spent a writing vacation with the Harriman family. In his letters, Muir often praised Harriman for his many business accomplishments and their service to mankind.[52] To console Harriman for his financial losses during the great national panic of 1907, for example, Muir wrote, "you have done a giant's work in the past years."[53]

When Harriman died in 1909, Muir was grief-stricken. Despite his own failing health, the exhausting battle to save Hetch Hetchy Valley from San Francisco's dam-building designs, his aversion to writing, and opposition from some of his anti-monopoly friends, Muir in 1911 penned a short memorial book on the life of E. H. Harriman.[54] Muir warmly praised Harriman as a "great builder," similar to the glaciers that had crafted Yosemite Valley:

> He fairly reveled in heavy dynamical work and went about it naturally and unweariedly like glaciers making landscapes—cutting canyons through ridges, carrying off hills, laying rails and bridges over lakes and rivers, mountains and plains, making the Nation's ways straight and smooth and safe, bringing everybody nearer to one another. He seemed to regard the whole continent as his farm and all the people as partners, stirring millions of workers into useful action, plowing, sowing, irrigating, mining, building cities and factories, farms and homes . . . Fortunes grew along his railroads like natural fruit.

Muir was grateful for Harriman's aid and friendship. "To him," he wrote, "I owe some of the most precious moments of my life."[55]

To rescue the 1905 Yosemite Valley retrocession bill in the California legislature, it was natural for Muir to turn to his close friend. Described by some contemporaries as "the most powerful man in America," Harriman ruled over a large financial and business empire, which by that time included the Southern Pacific, Union Pacific, and Illinois Central railroads, and he wielded considerable influence in the national Republican Party.[56] Aware that the railway president shared his concern for preserving wilderness, Muir asked in his letter of January 5, 1905, for Harriman's assistance in the Yosemite matter. After describing how California had "grossly mismanaged" the valley, Muir complained that the bill to restore the valley to federal control, though supported by virtually all Californians, was being blocked in the Senate by vested interests and the *Examiner*, which "with damnable perverted industry is trying to bury the truth beneath a sham storm of fables." Yosemite's welfare, Muir explained to Harriman, demanded strong federal protection, such as Yellowstone had received. "If you are like-minded, and can help us secure its passage," he implored, "I wish you would."[57]

Harriman responded quickly and decisively. Upon receiving Muir's letter, he sent telegrams to Muir assuring him of his support and to William F. Herrin, head of the Southern Pacific's Legal Department in San Francisco, directing him to mobilize the company's supporters in the legislature behind retrocession. As the railroad's chief counsel and lobbyist, Herrin was widely recognized as one of the most influential men in the state. An amateur naturalist and committed conservationist, he already knew Muir through a mutual friend, artist William Keith. Herrin undoubtedly welcomed Harriman's instructions. Herrin and his assistants journeyed and telephoned inconspicuously to Sacramento numerous times in January and February to work for the Yosemite bill, and the margin in the Senate narrowed.[58]

Nevertheless, when the bill neared a final vote in the Senate in late February, Colby's canvass still showed that it would lose by several votes. Just before the roll call on the bill on February 23, however, a group of pro-railroad senators suddenly switched sides, propelling Yosemite retrocession to victory *by one vote*. George Pardee, a conservationist governor, signed the bill reconveying Yosemite Valley to federal control. "You will probably note the Hand of Providence guiding matters through all this doubt," a jubilant Colby reported to Muir from Sacramento.[59]

Colby and Muir knew better. The hand of the Southern Pacific had been guiding matters. In explaining their triumph to Robert Underwood Johnson, Muir acknowledged that, despite favorable public opinion, vested interests were so deeply entrenched that "we might have failed to get the bill through the Senate but for the help of Mr. Harriman, though of course his name or his company were never in sight through all the fight."[60] Muir also wrote appreciative

letters to Harriman and Herrin. "Many thanks," he told Herrin, "for your Sacramento Yosemite work, the best thing ever done for the mountains and the world,
carrying blessings for everyone, and covering a multitude of real or imaginary
railroad sins." In March, Muir, Herrin, and William Keith lunched together
in celebration of their rescue of Yosemite Valley from venal state management.[61]

Muir and Herrin became fast friends and, toward the end of Muir's life, frequent companions. The two comrades tramped together across the San Francisco Bay hills, relaxed at Herrin's San Francisco home or at his forest retreat
on the slopes of Mount Shasta, one of Muir's favorite places, planned gatherings with Keith and other conservationist friends, or trundled off in Herrin's
private rail car to explore wilderness areas throughout the American West. Sharing Muir's reverence for nature, the railway attorney provided transportation
and political backing for Muir's preservation projects until the great naturalist's death in 1914.[62]

In 1905, however, the battle over Yosemite Valley was far from settled; the
front merely shifted to the other edge of the continent. To complete the transfer, Congress had to pass legislation accepting California's grant and adding the
valley to the national park. Despite strong support from Muir's friends, President Theodore Roosevelt and chief forester Gifford Pinchot, the Yosemite bill
faced an uncertain future. In the spring of 1906, California lumbermen, cattle
grazers, and valley concessionaires, once again led by state senator Curtin,
swarmed to Washington with proposals to prevent retrocession of the valley
and to reduce the national park's boundaries or to weaken park authorities' control over their businesses. Failing this, they hoped to delay congressional consideration until after the statute of limitations in California's bill expired. If
they could cause the valley to revert to state jurisdiction, they were confident
they could thwart future retrocession plans. Responding to these pressures, the
Republican Speaker of the House, Joe Cannon, on the pretext of governmental economy, refused to allow the Yosemite retrocession bill to come to a vote.
In the upper house, Senator Kittredge of South Dakota, acting on behalf of a
small local California railroad company seeking to protect its monopoly short
line up the Merced River Canyon to the valley's border, succeeded in getting
the measure bottled up in committee. A worried Colby wrote Muir that their
contacts in Washington believed the cause was doubtful. "It is a case of get the
bill through now or never," he warned.[63]

To break the impasse, Muir again called on Harriman. On April 8, he wrote
the Southern Pacific president asking for more assistance. "I will certainly do
anything I can to help your Yosemite Recession Bill," Harriman responded on
April 16.[64] Although he soon became preoccupied with personally directing the
railroad's relief efforts following the great San Francisco earthquake and fire,
Harriman contacted Cannon with a request that he free the Yosemite measure

Southern Pacific vice president, chief counsel, and political manager William F. Herrin (left) with John Muir in the early 1900s. The two became fast friends after Herrin and his company during 1904–1906 helped Muir secure passage of state and federal bills returning Yosemite Valley to the U.S. government for inclusion in Yosemite National Park. Courtesy Holt-Atherton Pacific Center for Western Studies, University of the Pacific, Stockton, California.

for a vote. In early May, Cannon reversed himself and released the bill onto the House floor, where it promptly passed. Harriman's intercession with Senate leaders also helped to clear the way in the upper house. On June 11, 1906, President Roosevelt signed into law the legislation accepting Yosemite Valley and preserving the national park's powers intact.[65] The decades-long struggle had finally ended. The precious valley had been saved, returned to federal jurisdiction, and merged into the national park for more modern and vigorous protection.

John Muir certainly deserves credit for having inspired and orchestrated the movement to protect the Yosemite, one of the great achievements of early conservationism. However, the consistent support of the Southern Pacific over four decades was also important, indeed critical. Without the company's assistance, the efforts of Muir, Johnson, and the Sierra Club might not have succeeded at all or might have produced only a tiny, highly developed, upper-class resort in a blighted valley surrounded by a denuded landscape. Yosemite National Park, as it is known and celebrated today, might never have come into being. The collaboration of "wilderness saint" and "robber baron" may have appeared anomalous to contemporaries and also to later historians, who have largely over-looked or misinterpreted it. Actually, it was rooted in a wide common interest in preserving forest watersheds and scenic wilderness.[66]

Daniel K. Zumwalt and Sequoia National Park

That same common interest between conservationists and railroaders led the Southern Pacific to take an important part in other far-western wilderness reser-vations, although none of the railroad's protection efforts equaled its Yosemite work in intensity or duration. San Joaquin Valley land agent Daniel K. Zum-walt's important role in congressional passage of the bill creating Sequoia Na-tional Park in early September 1890 and then in the tripling of the size of the preserve in the September 30 Yosemite-Sequoia bill has already been discussed in conjunction with his lobbying in Washington on behalf of the Yosemite park. In the same legislation, Zumwalt secured the creation of yet a third national park, General Grant Grove, adjacent to the Sequoia preserve.[67]

The question remains whether Zumwalt acted only as an individual or whether he also served as an agent of his company. As was true of many exam-ples of Southern Pacific involvement in conservation, including the work of many railroad leaders like William H. Mills, who labored in Yosemite over four decades, Zumwalt's support for Sequoia National Park merged personal and com-pany interests. An avid outdoorsman, a later member, guide, and benefactor of the Sierra Club, and one of the key Tulare County leaders who had for years been agitating for preservation of the giant sequoias in the Sierra to the east, Zumwalt went to Washington in the summer of 1890 as a community spokesman to work with the local congressman William Vandever to get the park created. It is clear, however, that he was also in Washington handling land-grant busi-ness for the Southern Pacific, to lobby the federal General Land Office to stop its delay of issuing patents to railroad granted land, and that the railroad paid the costs of his travel and weeks-long stay in the nation's capital. Unfortunately, Zumwalt's outgoing and incoming correspondence with railroad leaders dur-ing his trip and time in Washington is missing from the extensive collection of his papers in the records of the Southern Pacific Land Company in San Fran-cisco.[68] Thus, few details survive of the railroad's specific interests at that stage of formation of Sequoia National Park. The matter was discussed in general, however, in correspondence between Zumwalt and chief Southern Pacific Rail-road land agent Jerome Madden before and after the Washington trip, and it is clear that the company supported the creation of the park and that Zumwalt was also working on behalf of the company in getting the bill passed and then in having the park's area enlarged in the later Yosemite-Sequoia bill.[69]

The intriguing question is why. Earlier historians of Sequoia National Park, including Oscar Berland, Douglas Strong, and Lary Dilsaver and William Tweed, have with some surprise acknowledged Zumwalt's important role. Lacking direct evidence of the railroad's motivation, however, they have fallen back on the "Octopus" myth and have read into the railroad's support for the park some nefarious, if unknown, plot to thwart the public interest and to steal advantage for itself. Particularly, so the conjectured scheme goes, the Southern Pacific conspired in "deceit" to support the park because the resultant withdrawing of public timber land from sale and harvesting would have reduced competition for potential loggers working on the company's land grant elsewhere in Sierra forests.[70] Zumwalt's surviving letters, however, make it clear that there was nothing secret or complicated about the railroad's interests in Sequoia. They resembled the railroad's interests in Yosemite: forest and watershed preservation in general, and in particular the development of another national park near Southern Pacific lines to stimulate tourist travel. The railroad also wanted the park to be as large and dramatic as possible to compete with Yosemite and Yellowstone for travelers' attention. Based on precise information provided by Zumwalt, within days of Congress's actions, by October 10, 1890, the Southern Pacific's Passenger Department had already published and distributed a tourist map of the park. Demand quickly outstripped supply, however, and the railroad kept having to republish the map.[71] Soon dispatching artists and photographers to capture the wonders of the giant-sequoia groves, as it had done with Yosemite, the Southern Pacific made Sequoia National Park a staple among its featured tourist destinations.[72]

Lake Tahoe "National Park": A Lost Opportunity

Another example of the Southern Pacific's interest in scenic wilderness is the company's long-term effort to protect Lake Tahoe, which Mark Twain in the early 1860s had called "the fairest picture the whole earth affords." As early as 1867, even before the completion of the first transcontinental route, the Central Pacific Railroad had started running periodic excursion trains for winter sports enthusiasts from low-elevation California to the Donner Pass–Truckee–Tahoe region.[73] In the late 1890s and early 1900s, the railroad's vice president and land agent, William H. Mills, was one of the most influential publicists and lobbyists in a campaign to create a Lake Tahoe national park. Between the 1860s and the 1880s, spurred primarily by an insatiable demand for lumber and fuel on the Comstock Lode silver-mining district of western Nevada, the deforestation of Lake Tahoe's steep slopes and the surrounding central Sierra Nevada range was nearly complete.[74] Joining a chorus of cries against the ruination of one of the West's premier lakes and scenic paradises, Mills's *Sacramento Record-Union* as early as 1889 denounced the soil erosion, flooding, reduction in valuable watersheds, debauching of glorious scenic landscapes, and particularly the massive wildfires fueled by logging slash and dense, explosive dry underbrush that had grown up in place of the forests. "Witnesses fresh from the Lake Tahoe region inform us," the *Record-Union* reported, "that almost that entire section is a scene of desolation on account of the destruction of fires. . . . At the head of Emerald Bay last week a fire was raging of many miles extent, destroying the finest [remaining] park of tree growth in all that region."[75]

Although many individuals and groups had pushed, with some success, for preservation of the region since the 1880s, Mills and Nevada's U.S. senator William Stewart, for decades the Southern Pacific's steadfast spokesman in Congress, played the key roles in the eventual extension of federal protection.[76] Encouraged by President William McKinley's 1899 designation of a relatively untouched small slope southwest of the lake as the Lake Tahoe Forest Reserve, Stewart, aided and informed by his close associate Mills, in late 1899 introduced a bill into Congress to create a giant Lake Tahoe national park for even greater and more extensive protection of the region from further development. Opposition quickly mounted, particularly from local landowners who feared limitations on the exploitation of their properties, and others in California and Nevada, led by Southern Pacific nemesis the *San Francisco Examiner,* which claimed that the region's forest was too far gone to ever recover and that current federal public land law would provide a windfall for large landowners in the region, including the railroad, which would be allowed to exchange rugged or logged-over land for more valuable federal land elsewhere.

In the campaign for the park, Mills served as Stewart's adviser, particularly being responsible for having the senator enlarge the park beyond the Lake Tahoe Basin proper and deep into the Sierra west and north, even over the mountains' crest into the Pacific watershed, to preserve also the headwaters of the Sacramento Valley's American and Feather rivers. In this, Mills was particularly determined to stop the deforestation of the central Sierra at large and the resultant shrinkage of watersheds needed for downstream flood-control, irrigation, and electrical power generation. "Shall this destruction proceed?" he asked in a *San Francisco Post* article he authored to support the Tahoe national park proposal.[77] In addition to writing articles in newspapers and magazines favoring the park, Mills got the Department of the Interior to launch an investigation into the region's deforestation, and he had a series of documentary photographs taken and furnished for Stewart's use in promulgating the region's remaining beauties, as well as before-and-after sets of pictures illustrating the deleterious effects of tree-clearing. He also secured the support of numerous California and Nevada newspapers, of Robert L. Fulton, the Southern Pacific's

Great Basin land agent, who was particularly influential in Nevada, of California's congressional delegation, and of two powerful conservation organizations that Mills had helped to found and lead, the California State Board of Trade and the California Water and Forest Association.[78] Although opponents prevailed and defeated the national park bill in Congress, Stewart and Mills persisted over the next few years in pushing for Tahoe regional protection by keeping the issue to the forefront before Congress, the Department of the Interior, the press, and the public.[79] Ultimately, in 1905, with support from the Sierra Club and many conservation leaders but still against the desires of local residents, President Theodore Roosevelt signed a proclamation extending the existing small Lake Tahoe Forest Reserve over the entire central Sierra region and within the year also created four additional nearby reserves in central and northern California: the Plumas, Trinity, Klamath, and Lassen Peak national forests. Along with others, Mills and Stewart had effectively made their point about the importance of preserving west-coast forests.[80]

During the early 1890s, the Southern Pacific had also supported the establishment of the huge Sierra National Forest between Sequoia and Yosemite. Then, as described in chapter 10, in the 1910s and 1920s, the Southern Pacific, led by land agent B. A. McAllaster and chief counsel William F. Herrin, headed a coalition of regional groups in blocking the U.S. Reclamation Service from building a large dam on the Truckee River and converting Lake Tahoe into a vast storage reservoir to soothe the thirst of the faltering Truckee-Carson Reclamation Project in western Nevada. Although the Tahoe region did not become a national park, the railroad had left its mark in more limited, but still significant, preservation of the lake, land, and forest. Thus, by the early 1900s, including its work to preserve Yosemite, Sequoia, the Sierra National Forest, and the Lake Tahoe region, the Southern Pacific had had a hand in placing more than three hundred miles of the Sierra Nevada range under federal protection.

Other Wilderness Parks

Southern Pacific leaders contributed significantly to other wilderness preservation movements throughout the railroad's territory. In addition to leading efforts to set aside and protect Yosemite and the Lake Tahoe basin, William H. Mills was a founder of California's Big Basin Redwoods State Park in the early 1900s. One of a handful of large unlogged stands of coastal redwoods in the Santa Cruz Mountains and San Francisco Peninsula, Big Basin was the target of numerous preservation efforts by artists, scientists, and civic leaders in Santa Cruz and the Santa Clara Valley. In the early 1890s, Leland Stanford attempted unsuccessfully to buy several thousand acres of logging-threatened groves in the area to use as a botanical preserve for his fledgling university.[81] Then, in the early 1900s, painter Andrew Hill founded the Sempervirens Club to press the state legislature for a park at Big Basin. Aided by President David Starr Jordan of Stanford University (Leland Stanford was dead by this time), the club got a bill into the legislature. Assemblyman Grove L. Johnson, infamous leader of the Southern Pacific's corps of legislative partisans and father of later Progressive governor Hiram Johnson, took charge of the bill and was instrumental in getting it passed in 1901. Governor Henry Gage appointed Mills to the state commission founded to plan and govern the park, at first named California Redwood Park, and to arrange for the land purchase. As he had done two decades earlier while a Yosemite Valley commissioner, the railroad land agent attempted to introduce modern scientific management policies during his service on the Redwood Commission until his death in 1907. A major figure in the complex and controversial land purchase, he brought in outside experts such as National Forest director Gifford Pinchot to advise on governance and forestry policies, pressed new governor George C. Pardee to increase the park's preservation budget, and worked through U.S. senator George Perkins in Washington to get the federal government to withdraw from the sale and instead grant to the state three thousand adjacent acres for inclusion in the park.[82] Southern Pacific firefighting workers and equipment were crucial to averting the park's first crisis, the huge Santa Cruz Mountains forest fire of September 1904, which thanks in part to the railroad's efforts left Big Basin's most important redwood groves unscathed.[83] Big Basin became the first modern California state park and the beginning of a succession of state redwood preserves that in the late 1920s would be consolidated by the legislature into the California Department of Parks and Recreation.

In Oregon in the early 1900s, Southern Pacific vice president and director of passenger traffic E. O. McCormick was one of the principal movers in the creation of Crater Lake National Park, which was served by two of the railroad's lines in the southern part of the state. With he and his company being well-known supporters of the national parks, McCormick after 1916 was asked by the first national parks director, Stephen T. Mather, to take part in a group of influential scientific, political, and business leaders with conservationist credentials to lead a campaign for additional enlargement of Sequoia National Park to protect more big-tree groves.[84] The work in the late nineteenth and early twentieth centuries of McCormick, William H. Mills, W. W. Stow, Daniel K. Zumwalt, William F. Herrin, Edward H. Harriman, B. A. McAllaster, and many other of the railroad's people lends justification to national-parks historian Alfred Runte's conclusion that the Southern Pacific was "one of the most vigorous sponsors of natural scenery in general and West Coast national parks in particular."[85]

Indeed, as another historian, Richard West Sellars, has observed, the national parks developed as a result of a "cooperative effort between government and private business—notably railroad, automobile, and other tourist interests—to use the resources of publicly owned lands, particularly in the West." With respect to the government, wilderness promoters, and the railroads, Runte has characterized their work together as a "pragmatic alliance."[86] To that I might add that the Southern Pacific's participation in the alliance on behalf of creating parks was certainly "pragmatic," in that all groups, including the railroad, pursued their own perceived special interests, often economic. But, in the case of Southern Pacific leaders, most of them longtime westerners, it was more than a simple matter of pragmatism—or corporate welfare. Support for public parks was rooted also in a shared vision, a commitment to the diverse development and settlement of their region, including at the same time, however, the preservation of some of its vast, unique wilderness.

In a way, that pragmatic alliance forged at the birth of Yosemite National Park continues to operate more than a century later. In the summer of 1999, the Wildlands Conservancy, a private, non-profit preservation group, transferred 14,000 acres of California desert land to the U.S. Department of the Interior for inclusion within the recently redesignated and enlarged Joshua Tree National Park, formerly a national monument, east of Los Angeles. The Conservancy had purchased the land for $2.5 million from Catellus Development Corporation, which chose to sell the land for preservation rather than to improve it or to sell it to other private developers, which presumably could have increased the value of other nearby company land. Later in 1999, the Conservancy and congressional leaders negotiated another deal with Catellus for the purchase of an additional 487,000 acres, at a price of $56 million, to add to the park or the holdings of the U.S. Bureau of Land Management. The transfer included 200,000 acres of habitat critical to endangered species such as the desert tortoise, the desert bighorn sheep, and the Bigelow cholla cactus. Then, in 2003, the Conservancy and California U.S. senator Dianne Feinstein arranged for Catellus to transfer to the Bureau of Land Management another 62,000 acres of sections of desert and mountain land between the Salton Sea and the Colorado River. Much of the intervening checkerboard of all this land was still in public ownership, making possible for the first time the uniform management and preservation of a large portion of the Mojave and Colorado deserts. The principal party to the land deals, Catellus, is the successor corporation to the Santa Fe Pacific Land Company, which was successor to the Southern Pacific Land Company, which was successor to the Southern Pacific Railroad Land Department. In the 1860s Congress had originally granted the land to the railroad to encourage construction.[87]

14 "Putting Our Properties on the Most Conservative and Scientific Basis"

RESOURCE CONSERVATION

Early Railroad Resource Policies

Over the late nineteenth and early twentieth centuries, the Southern Pacific Company compiled a distinguished record of support for wilderness and scenic-land preservation in the American West. But the railroad's involvement in public lands and resources management did not stop there. No less significant, if somewhat less visible, was the company's contribution to utilitarian conservationism, or the development of more efficient resource use, including on public lands, for sustained, long-term economic development. As is examined in preceding chapters, the Southern Pacific began to encounter resource problems affecting itself and the broader public immediately upon construction of its lines in the 1860s and 1870s. Its own and the larger pioneer society's water-supply and flood-control needs led the company to become an active leader in water development, water conservation, and California's abolition of hydraulic mining. As early as the 1860s and 1870s, protecting the value of its land grant as well as land the federal government had not yet patented to the railroad, led the company to establish patrols to catch squatters and poachers stealing timber, stone, sand, water, and other resources. The guilty parties were warned, and if they failed to desist, prosecuted. The company also required persons leasing or settling on railroad land preparatory to purchasing it to leave trees, stone, soils, and water intact.[1]

Possessing diverse and complex interests, the company also became immediately embroiled in many other resource issues, including some that seem far afield from the railway business, such as wildlife management. By 1878, for example, the Southern Pacific had already tried various methods to eradicate the exploding population of invading ground squirrels that were damaging road-beds and granted lands. Years of fruitless efforts, and consultation with experts, however, convinced the railroad that, in the words of Southern Pacific Railroad land agent Jerome Madden, "it is almost impossible to permanently exterminate . . . [the squirrels] and the area of the Company's lands infested is so great that . . . [the company is] unwilling to incur the great expense consequent upon the proper attempt to do the matter thoroughly." The Southern Pacific Railroad's board of directors ordered the extermination programs discontinued and restricted employees from cooperating with outside parties seeking the railroad's help in getting rid of the rodents.[2]

Apparent even in the relatively simple case of ground-squirrel eradication, as well as in more complex water-development and flood-control questions that always were arising, the major outlines of Southern Pacific resource-management policy were already taking form in the 1870s, and they became more fully elaborate and systematic with each passing decade. Although the company's approaches to resources evolved slowly in response to situations as they arose and although they changed over time and were not always consistent, certain general principles were clear from the beginning.[3] First, resource policy was rooted in the company's assessment of what furthered its business interests, which were, of course, constantly changing and becoming more diverse. Second, the railroad's policy often also reflected the involvement of the railroad's leaders, particularly middle-level managers and experts, in broader conservation issues and movements outside of the company. Third and increasingly important, in formulating its position on given issues, the railroad relied on expertise and scientific analysis—gathering systematic data, conducting elaborate studies, and doing careful cost-benefit evaluations—accomplished either by its own growing staff of engineers and scientists or consultants hired for specific projects. Fourth, the railroad increasingly preferred rational management of resources for long-term profit for itself, and more stable and predictable future development in the company's territories. Although the railroad first applied long-term scientific management to its own lands and resources, it also encouraged other private parties and the public to adopt such approaches. Fifth, the Southern Pacific particularly came to favor, at least by the early twentieth century, coordinated, centralized management of land, water, and resource questions in the hands of public authorities. Sixth, in the absence of effective control of resources by government or other private agencies, the railroad was often drawn, usually reluctantly, into performing functions for the broader society—organization, finance, application of science and technology, and coordination of diverse interests to achieve common goals— that are now considered to be the domain of government. And when government did assume authority over those functions, it was often the Southern Pacific that worked to bring it about and helped shape government programs. As was true of the railroad's pioneering roles in promoting scientific agriculture and marketing agricultural produce, and especially in the development of town waterworks and regional irrigation systems, so it was with broader resource conservation. Cautious, pragmatic, and flexible in its approach, the Southern Pacific offered a measure of coordination and stability to western

A Southern Pacific fire train and crew at Truckee, California, 1925. Firefighting technology was an important Southern Pacific contribution to Western forestry. Visible are devices that Southern Pacific engineers and shops fabricated and introduced along the company's western lines: specially designed water-pumping locomotive, extra-large water tanker cars, portable canvas hoses that could be attached in sections to quench fires as far as one thousand feet away, and an adapted hydraulic-mining-type water cannon, or "monitor" (top right face of locomotive), which could launch a powerful, saturating column of water along the tracks. Author's collection.

resource use that often left lasting structures even after the company was no longer directly involved.

Scientific Forestry

A case in point is the Southern Pacific's influence on the development of forestry. Even before conservationist William H. Mills rose to leadership of the railroad's Land Department, the Southern Pacific was introducing modern forestry practices onto its lands and encouraging others to shift to sustainable forest uses. In the year after the driving of the Golden Spike completed the Central Pacific's transcontinental connection, the railroad began a wide-ranging, systematic tree-breeding and -planting program for shade and windbreaks along its rights-of-way and around its stations and other facilities, to assure its own supply of hardwood for ties and other construction needs, to control erosion and to reforest denuded slopes adjacent to its tracks, and to donate to parks and other public and private properties in the company's station towns. The program was initiated in 1870 by Charles Crocker and Central Pacific general superintendent

Alban N. Towne. Collis P. Huntington, who also adhered to the then-common, but now-discredited, belief that planting trees would increase rainfall, sent prodigious quantities of seed from the East. In California by the late 1870s, the company operated four major nurseries. The largest, at Chico, in the Sacramento Valley, annually shipped more than 400,000 eucalyptus, walnut, oak, locust, cypress, and persimmon trees for planting onto railroad lands. Early experiments focused on growing and transplanting black locust and especially eucalyptus.[4]

The eucalyptus experiments were the most elaborate and long-lasting. By the mid-1870s, the railroad was operating several experimental tree ranches specializing in testing, raising, and transplanting eucalyptus in the San Joaquin Valley near Tulare, where the company was also pioneering techniques for artesian well-drilling.[5] Although the ranches sent tens of thousands of trees for transplanting, experiments with using the wood for ties and construction proved disappointing, and as early as 1885 the company contemplated shutting down the eucalyptus project and selling the land. In the early 1900s, however, the San Joaquin tree ranches were still in operation.[6] Under the management of an employee named Scupham, the railroad conducted an even more ambitious eucalyptus and catalpa growing and transplanting program at its nursery in Oakland, from which by 1877 it had already dispatched 40,000 trees to shade 400 miles of its right-of-way throughout California as well as "to ensure exemption of travelers from the autumnal fevers prevalent on the treeless plains of the Pacific slope."[7]

While it was building its first line through the Coachella and Imperial valleys in 1876, the Southern Pacific began an ambitious plan to protect its right-of-way in the region from wind erosion, drifting sand, and blistering sun by building artificial sand-dune shelters and planting ground covers and belts of tamarisk trees. Such revegetation programs could be long-lived. As late as the 1960s, the railroad was still maintaining the Coachella and Imperial valley planting project and experimenting with improvements to it.[8] In the early twentieth century, along the Oregon Coast, in the Point Conception and Santa Barbara Channel areas of southern California, and along other coastal rights-of-way where blowing sand and shifting dunes troubled rail lines, the Southern Pacific worked with scientists from Oregon State University and garden designers from San Francisco's Golden Gate Park to plant grasses, ground covers, shrubs, and trees to shield rights-of-way. On the leeward side of the tracks, the railroad reclaimed land for agricultural uses.[9]

Despite the earlier failure of eucalyptus to provide a useful building material, another planting craze in California in the early 1900s rekindled Southern Pacific interest in the tree. New railroad executives and lower-level managers, dispatched from the east by the Harriman Lines to bring the Southern Pacific

Land Department into conformity with practices used on the Union Pacific (and who were unfamiliar with the disappointments of the 1870s and 1880s), began new experiments in eucalyptus culture. Particularly important leaders were Charles W. Eberlein, a New Yorker whom the Harriman Lines designated as its "acting land agent" to restructure the department between 1902 and 1908, and B. A. McAllaster, who embarked on a long, successful tenure at the head of the department in 1908, when he was transferred from the Union Pacific.[10] The railroad hired Leslie W. Symmes, a professor and eucalyptus expert at the University of California in Berkeley, who traveled the state evaluating eucalyptus experiments, examined the company's lands, and developed a series of reports from 1907 to 1909 on how the company might use different varieties of the tree in forested land-grant regions, not only to increase their value and salability but also to provide a source of wood for its own use. Particularly, the company became convinced, demonstration plots would show eucalyptus to be a potential local crop, thereby increasing land-grant values and sales in arid regions.[11]

Based on Symmes's sanguine recommendations, beginning in 1909, the Southern Pacific greatly expanded its still-operating but small-scale eucalyptus projects, first in the Imperial Valley, then in the San Joaquin Valley, and then elsewhere in California, as well as along the company's lines in Mexico. Unfortunately, the new experiments only rediscovered that the wood from the tree was a poor construction material, that local water supplies were generally insufficient to irrigate the trees properly, that the groves harbored crop pests that invaded nearby farm fields and provoked the ire of farmers, and that the economics of eucalyptus culture was almost always unprofitable. In Mexico, even more bizarre problems developed. Of the 11,500 young trees set out along rights-of-way in 1910 and 1911, those that were not killed by frost at high elevations, root-rot in swampy places, and alkali poisoning in deserts, were devoured by lizards, and less than 10 percent survived in 1914.[12] Although the astute and realistic McAllaster and other Land Department experts became quickly disillusioned with the experiments and wanted to end them in 1914, railroad president William J. Sproule insisted that they continue. Two years of pressure from McAllaster and other executives, however, finally convinced Sproule in 1916 to order all the company's eucalyptus projects halted and the affected lands reopened for sale.[13] As was the case with the railroad's attempt at ground squirrel eradication and its entanglement with numerous failed irrigation projects in its territories, not all Southern Pacific resource policies worked.

On the other hand, the company had more success in its management of natural forests. Under the direction of William H. Mills from 1883 to 1907, the Land Department introduced modern conservation methods on its forested land grant in the Sierra Nevada and in Oregon. A longtime student and promoter of scientific forestry as editor of the *Sacramento Record-Union* and as a member of the California state Yosemite Valley Commission, and now in charge of one of the largest expanses of forests in the United States, Mills presided over the introduction on the land grant of brush-clearing and controlled burning, or "light-burning" as it was then called, to simulate naturally occurring fires in order to reduce fuel build-up and wildfire dangers. Mills also adopted measures to prevent erosion and timber poaching. To preserve the forests and protect the scenic value of its rights-of-way to encourage tourism, the Southern Pacific at Mills's direction by the early 1890s had instituted a policy of prohibiting logging on its own lands immediately adjacent to rail lines and also of buying the trackside lands of private parties or trading them for company tracts remote from the lines.[14]

For long-term preservation of woodlands, the Southern Pacific, as was indicated by Mills's efforts to create the Tahoe National Forest after 1899, also supported the founding of national forests in California and the rest of the Far West. One of the railroad's major problems in its forests was the checkerboard pattern of land tenure. With the railroad's one-mile-square sections alternating with sections owned by the federal government or private parties, systematic management and fire protection were complicated, if not impossible. The railroad often bought and sold or exchanged land with other parties to make as much of its land as contiguous as possible. In the late 1890s the Southern Pacific was the first railroad to try—at first unsuccessfully, as it turned out—to get the federal government to start a land-exchange program with the land-grant lines. In the early 1900s, however, the Southern Pacific again took the lead in helping chief national forester Gifford Pinchot formulate and secure congressional legislation that eventually allowed railroads to swap their lands within the limits of national forests with the federal government for intervening public sections elsewhere in the railroads' land-grant areas.[15] To encourage the spread of scientific forestry, Mills himself worked with outside agencies, including the Yosemite Valley Commission, the California Redwood Commission governing Big Basin State Park, of which he was a member, and the California Water and Forest Association, of which he was a major founder and leader. To learn new methods, interact with other parties, and to affect the future of woodlands management, Mills, his successors, and other lesser Land Department agents and experts routinely attended and made presentations and introduced proposals at national, state, and local forestry and conservation meetings.[16]

In the early twentieth century, the Southern Pacific expanded its efforts to modernize forestry on its lands. The Land Department consulted in particular with chief national forester Gifford Pinchot in instituting a comprehensive scientific forestry plan.[17] About 1900, the railroad's Land Department began to contract with consulting foresters to survey and evaluate the railroad's wooded lands and to provide advice on forest management. This was followed, beginning in 1907, by the hiring of a staff of railroad foresters, because, in the words of acting land agent Charles W. Eberlein, "the cost of services of a competent forester is nothing compared to the results that would be immediately obtained from such employment." Under the supervision of the Land Department, a chief company forester coordinated teams of field experts and a network of forest wardens, local residents hired by the company to work part-time traversing its forest lands, apprising it of conditions, and keeping watch for fires. The railroad sought to hire its foresters from the ranks of young men educated in American university forestry schools and field-trained in Gifford Pinchot's newly created federal Forest Service. In addition to continuing fire prevention and suppression practices long in use on the railroad's lands, the company in its more comprehensive forestry program introduced such policies as scientific grading and mapping of all timber lands according to timber quality, maturity of growth, and marketability, scheduling for sale first the best, most mature timber, and insisting (through deed reservations and other means) that land buyers use logging practices that did not injure new growth, cause erosion, or otherwise disturb watercourses, watersheds, or adjacent unlogged lands. Accompanying these new practices was an aggressive program of exchanging railroad land sections with the government and other large-scale owners of intervening forest lands for more comprehensive and systematic management. Land exchanges were essential so that, according to acting land agent Eberlein, "our timber may be collected into solid bodies which will greatly enhance the value of the timber and reduce the danger of destruction from fires or wind." In contrast to most other land-grant roads, since its first reception of granted forest lands, the Southern Pacific had refrained from selling logging rights to its lands and instead adopted a strict policy of selling timber only with the land. As a result, in the early 1900s, the company possessed practically no cut-over land. The small amount of such logged land still on company property rolls, however, was put into reforestation.[18] In the early 1900s, the Southern Pacific developed the basis of complex, modern forestry programs used to manage the railroad's lands into the 1980s.

The Railroad and the Forest Service

Typically sharing ownership of lands with the federal government in the national forests in a checkerboard pattern, the Southern Pacific, while developing its forestry program, became involved in the management of national forests as soon as they began to be created in the early 1890s. By 1909 the railroad's lands had been included within eighty-eight new national forest reservations or later additions to existing national forests established since 1892 in California, Oregon, Nevada, and Utah. By far the majority were recent products of Theodore Roosevelt's presidential proclamations between 1901 and 1909. Thus, relations with the new national forests, administered by the U.S. Department of Agriculture, were no small matter. To guard its interests, the company vigilantly watched the operations of the national forests, proposals to create new ones, and the emerging early federal forestry policies.

Friction invariably developed between railroad and public forest goals, policies, and people. National Forest Service supervisors, for example, soon took to asserting their right to control railroad lands within the reserves, and even neighboring company lands outside of the preserves, going as far as to try to regulate or to prohibit altogether the railroad's leases to private parties for grazing and other uses on its own odd-numbered land sections. The Forest Service also sometimes tried to restrict access by the railroad or its tenants or buyers to company lands. The Department of the Interior's General Land Office, for its part, periodically attempted to close unsurveyed lands within the national forests to further patenting to the railroads. The Southern Pacific viewed this as, in effect, an illegal abrogation of large portions of its land grants. In general, the railroad's Land Department executives particularly chafed at the wide administrative discretion that early federal forest officials sought to exercise in an era of experimentation and precedent-building. That agency officials in Washington, D.C. or on the scene often lacked the knowledge and local experience possessed by railroad land and forest experts only compounded the potential conflicts. Government policies often appeared to the railroad to be unscientific, arbitrary, contradictory, ambiguous, vacillating, and ungrounded in actual local conditions and past practice. In the absence of clear law and administrative procedure, decisions even by low-level forest officials often took years to appeal or adjust to diverse local conditions and the interests of railroads and other landowners within the national forests. There were also differences of philosophy and technique in forest management, for example in fire protection. The Forest Service became increasingly and adamantly committed to suppression as its favored fire-management method, while the Southern Pacific still favored controlled burning to minimize larger, more damaging conflagrations.[19] These and other issues emerging in the national forests explain why the company, though it was generally supportive of the founding of the public forests in principle, was also vigilant in keeping track of and trying to shape the development of policies in the reserves as well as eager to exchange its forest reserve land sections for public land elsewhere in the railroad's grant areas.[20]

Despite what might be seen as natural, predictable differences over larger

policies, Southern Pacific and federal foresters, finding themselves thrown together on a rugged terrain that refused to respect the artificial survey grid imposed upon it, discovered virtue in cooperation. In starting up their programs
in the 1890s, Forest Service people, generally latecomers to the forests, routinely
relied on the railroad for maps and other forest data that the company had been
collecting sometimes for decades. Soon, however, the railroad came to realize
that some of the information the Forest Service was amassing was more current and reliable than its own and sought reciprocal assistance from the government. Through the early decades of the twentieth century, in dozens of
national forests in the Far West, the Southern Pacific and the Forest Service developed comprehensive and ongoing programs for sharing information, including maps, cruise reports of timber quality and value, surveys of erosion and
pest damage, grazing-lands conditions and carrying capacity, and alerts about
the activities of timber, grazing, and mining poachers. Information exchange,
as both the railroad and the federal government fully realized in fostering and
continuing the programs, greatly expanded each party's fund of reliable knowledge regarding its lands, prevented duplication of effort, encouraged more encompassing and long-term study of the forests, saved time and money, and in
many ways enhanced the effectiveness of public and railroad forestry. Sharing
information led the Southern Pacific and the Forest Service also to cooperate
in programs to reduce erosion and watershed damage, to crack down on overgrazing and poaching, and to designate, map, mark, and maintain public railways for sheep and cattle drives through the national forests.[21]

Battling the Pine-bark Beetle

An example of the long-lasting, comprehensive, cooperative programs essential
in shared management of forests was the pine-bark-beetle campaign of the early
decades of the twentieth century. In the wake of droughts during the early 1900s,
infestations of pine-bark beetles spread throughout far-western forests, killing
trees and dramatically increasing the threat of wildfires, particularly in northern California and Oregon. Southern Pacific land agents, timber cruisers, and
fire wardens, the most numerous and organized forest observers in some regions,
were generally the first to discover and track the movements of the insects.[22] Immediately realizing the major threat to company interests, the railroad, particularly after the infestation worsened dramatically in 1910 and 1911, took the lead
in developing a cooperative approach to combating the pests. In the words of
land agent B. A. McAllaster, the Southern Pacific committed itself to pest eradication "because the timber stand of the Pacific Coast is largely tributary to its
rail lines and does now and will for indefinite years to come constitute a mate-

rial part of the traffic for such lines . . . [and] because of its deep interest in the protection and maintenance of the timber stand of the coast country."[23]

Even before 1910, the company instituted a comprehensive program of regularly surveying pest damage, alerting federal and state foresters and entomological research and control agencies, and convening regular local and region-wide meetings of government experts, political leaders, and private timber owners to develop cooperative information-sharing and eradication programs. In general, the Southern Pacific served as the detection network, collecting information on the insects' movements, communicating it to research agencies at the University of California and elsewhere for analysis, experimentation, and recommendations. National and state forestry agencies managed most of the eradication programs, removed infected trees, and burned the slash. Over years, indeed decades, railroad and public foresters and scientists maintained virtually day-to-day contact in combating the beetle and other forest threats.[24] Costs were shared, usually prorated among public agencies, private parties, and the railroad according to acreage owned in the affected districts. Almost always, the Southern Pacific, having concluded that even remote infestations would ultimately spread to its lands, furnished half or more of the funds, even if it had little or no holdings in the affected locales. The company also pressured other private landowners—who trusted that in an emergency the government and the railroad would pick up the bill—to pay their share. Grateful federal foresters maintained that the company's avid public support, even more than its monetary contributions, enhanced the prestige and the legitimacy of the beetle-eradication program and increased the government's leverage in getting smaller-scale private forest owners to cooperate and contribute. In 1911, just after the inception of the cooperative program, one of them termed the Southern Pacific's backing "the key to the situation," and a year later wrote McAllaster that "it is only through this general recognition [that your company lends] that there is any hope of stopping the great waste of forest resources from insect depredations."[25] The Southern Pacific also made contributions to far-western forestry associations to finance conferences on forest pest control.[26]

Although these ad hoc voluntary programs succeeded in controlling, though not eradicating, the insects in some areas, railroad and public foresters were convinced by 1920 that only long-term, well-funded, compulsory insect-eradication programs could deal with the pine-bark beetle, along with other insect pests and diseases that were now known to be endemic in the forests. In the early 1920s, under the aggressive lead of McAllaster, who was also a member of the influential California Forestry Committee, the Southern Pacific wrote, had introduced, and lobbied through laws first in Oregon and then in California creating comprehensive state-funded programs of research, regulation, and eradication of forest pests.[27] Modeled after the Oregon law, the California system, which passed the legislature and became effective in August 1923, required landowners to eradicate forest pests on their holdings and to notify the state forester of infestations on their lands and adjacent lands, and authorized the state forester to declare zones of infestations and to enter and remove infected trees on the lands of owners who refused to undertake eradication. To recoup expenses to the public, the law gave the state a first lien on the property of un-cooperating owners, foreclosable in ninety days.[28]

Not content with action just on the state level, the Southern Pacific, again spearheaded by McAllaster—for whom the attack on the pine-bark beetle had risen to the level of a personal crusade—and by chief corporate counsel William F. Herrin, worked in 1923 and 1924 with western forestry associations and tim-ber companies and lobbied Congress to augment the annual appropriation to the National Forest Service by $125,000 to increase insect control in the federal forests.[29] Congressmen acknowledged that the Southern Pacific's efforts were in-strumental in securing the necessary funds.[30] The railroad also pushed for tougher state and federal quarantines on the transport of infected lumber products and live trees, even taking on and defeating nursery industry lobbyists who tried to abolish the quarantines. When the quarantines went into effect, as long as trees and lumber moved primarily by rail, which was still true as late as the 1920s and 1930s, the Southern Pacific served as a principal enforcement agency. As it had been doing for diseased fruit and fruit trees since the 1880s, the railroad trained its land, forestry, station, and yard agents and directed them to inspect lumber and tree cargoes, to stop infected products from moving on the company's lines, and to notify public authorities of diseased shipments.[31] As was happening in the same period regarding irrigation development in countless local water dis-tricts, as well as in federal reclamation projects such as the Truckee-Carson Project in western Nevada, the evolution of modern land and resources policies in many far-western state and national forests, in a real sense, resulted from a partner-ship between government agencies and the Southern Pacific Company.

Firefighting

The same need to protect land-grant forests and rail traffic in lumber products motivated the Southern Pacific to take the lead in the introduction of modern fire-prevention in the Far West. However, especially since most Southern Pacific territories were arid or semi-arid, wildlands fire directly jeopardized company assets even more valuable than forests. Potentially threatened were cars and lo-comotives, roadbeds and ties, massive wooden bridges and trestles, and main-tenance structures and water facilities along the lines everywhere. Especially vulnerable were stations, shops, roundhouses, warehouses, administrative offices, and employee housing in countless forest towns, particularly along the old Central Pacific's lifeline from California to the east across the Sierra Nevada and the company's connection to the Pacific Northwest through northern California and Oregon mountains. The approximately fifty miles of wooden snowsheds and wood-shored tunnels in the vicinity of Donner Pass, unique among American railroads, presented even greater dangers. Once ignited by derailments or collisions, sparks from smokestacks, wheels, or hot brakes, or forest fires burning down on them, snowsheds and tunnels quickly erupted into infernos, burning out of human control. Borne on strong winds spawned by the blaze, fireballs and superheated air surged through the tunnels, incinerating everything in their path and turning the shafts into giant flame-throwers, spouting fire dozens of feet out the openings, sometimes spreading the fires to the wildlands. Much property damage, injury, and loss of life resulted. In Southern Pacific lore, tunnel or snowshed fires were the most terrifying dangers facing employees. One executive had a heart attack after riding out such a fire in his private car; another was driven into an insane asylum. Cave-ins often followed the fire explosions, closing mainlines and blocking traffic for days and sometimes weeks. The railroad's costs in reconstruction and lost or delayed traffic were enormous. Such fearsome episodes occurred frequently in the late 1860s and early 1870s, particularly in the Sierra Nevada, where in 1869–1870 alone, the first year of full operations on the Donner Pass route, 4,000 feet of snowshed were lost in one fire and 1,200 in another. In response, the Southern Pacific erected what was certainly the most modern, comprehensive, widespread, technologically sophisticated—and expensive—fire-combat system in the American West until well into the twentieth century.[32]

The railroad organized its fire department in the late 1860s, while still building the Central Pacific line over Donner Pass and eastward across the Great Basin. By 1869, specially outfitted fire-trains were stationed permanently, first at Truckee, just east of Donner Pass, and then west through the most fire-prone stretch of the Sierra Nevada at Summit Station (itself in a snowshed gallery), Cisco, and Emigrant Gap. The railroad remodeled locomotives—the first one was the *Grey Eagle*—to pump water through hoses from extra-large water tanker cars or from trackside streams and lakes.[33] For instantaneous response, rotating, trained firefighting crews kept the trains at the ready year round and under steam around the clock during the fire season from May through November. As the Southern Pacific sent its tracks into other forested regions, particular northward through northern California mountains and the Santa Cruz Mountains between San Jose and Monterey Bay to the south, additional fire trains and crews were detailed, including along branch lines throughout Oregon. By the end of the century, the company's fire-trains guarded hundreds of miles of vulnerable rights-of-way and railroad property across the Far West and as far east

The *C. P. Huntington* on firefighting duty in 1892. The third Central Pacific Railroad locomotive in the early 1860s, shortly later reborn as Southern Pacific Railroad number 1, the diminutive wood-burner was unsuited to the longer and heavier trains of subsequent years. By century's close, the company had replaced the catcher with a flaming burner and relegated the locomotive to end its days in ignominious fashion clearing weeds from rights-of-way. In the 1920s, however, the venerable *C. P. Huntington,* its historical significance finally realized, was restored for exhibition. Today it is featured at the California State Railroad Museum in Sacramento. Courtesy DeGolyer Library, Southern Methodist University.

as Texas and Louisiana. A major fire facility at Dunsmuir, on the Shasta Division in northern California, for example, in the early twentieth century boasted not only a standard fire-train and crew but also a huge water plant, one of the largest in the Southern Pacific system, with 400,000 gallons of daily output, installed especially to fill fleets of firefighting tanker cars. Also at Dunsmuir, the railroad operated its training school for fire crews.[34]

Through the post–World War II period, the Southern Pacific's firefighters and equipment also served as a front line of public defense against wildlands fire in its regions. Railroad firemen fought on their own or assisted public and private agencies in combating blazes in forests and grasslands, private structures, and towns, sometimes far from the rail lines. Many a mountain town without its own water system or professional fire department was saved from annihilation. In 1887, for example, railroad crews defeated a fire that would have destroyed Colfax, about halfway between Sacramento and the Sierra summit. In fire-prone Truckee, Southern Pacific fire trains saved the town from major fires seven times in the settlement's first ten years and continued to provide protection against scattered blazes into the mid-twentieth century.[35]

As it did with its water facilities and refrigerated cars, the Southern Pacific constantly improved its firefighting technology and organization. For more than a half-century, the company's famed Sacramento Shops designed and manufactured a continuing succession of new equipment: tools, toolboxes, locomotive retrofit kits, and larger and more efficient firefighting pumps, hoses, nozzles, and tankers and other special cars for the fire trains.[36] By the 1920s and 1930s, a standard Southern Pacific fire train included a locomotive with pumps for tapping water in tankers or from streams or other local supplies, several large nozzles similar to hydraulic-mining "monitors" and capable of launching streams of water hundreds of feet, two tank cars with combined capacity of 12,500 gallons, hand tools, ladders, portable telephones, chemical fire extinguishers, and a thousand feet of hose to quench fires far from the tracks.[37] The railroad also modified its snowsheds, first by installing 150-foot-long cast-iron sections every half-mile to retard the fires' spread. When that failed to deter the firestorms, the company substituted movable metal snowshed sections that during the summer fire season telescoped on wheels into the permanent structures, creating open-space firebreaks that proved more successful. In the twentieth century, the wooden sheds were gradually rebuilt in flame-resistant concrete, the last of them replaced in the 1980s. Along the most vulnerable stretches of track, beginning in the early 1870s, the railroad strung telegraph and then telephone lines, with terminals every mile. Twenty-four hours a day, watchmen walked the lines, hourly telegraphing or telephoning conditions to firefighting stations. During high-danger seasons on particularly vulnerable forested rights-of-way, special motor cars carrying firefighting crews and equipment followed all trains.[38]

In 1876, the Southern Pacific installed its most spectacular fire-detection facility, the Red Mountain lookout station. Located high in the Sierra Nevada atop a bald peak two miles north of and 2,000 feet above the station town of Cisco, the fire lookout afforded a nearly fifty-mile view of the Central Pacific's right-of-way and surrounding forest over Donner Pass. In what may have been the first modern fire lookout in the Far West, the railroad placed two powerful, European-designed telescopes with pointer mechanisms that tracked the location of fires on easily read maps. Two-man crews kept watch around the clock between May and November, telephoning half-hourly reports down to the fire station at Cisco. The railroad operated the Red Mountain lookout until 1934, when the last of the wooden snowsheds in its purview was torn down.[39] According to a company survey, by 1930, the Southern Pacific's fire department was protecting railroad property and forests and private and public lands in seven states; systemwide, ninety-three locomotives had been retrofitted and were operating as firefighters. As a result, although according to company officials

Abandoned but remarkably well preserved Red Mountain fire lookout station, photographed in 1991. Installed in 1876, the station, outfitted with state-of-the-art maps, telescopes, and communications equipment, guarded the Southern Pacific's mainline through the Sierra Nevada until the 1930s. The white horizontal line across the mountainside, left center, is a modern, cement snowshed that replaced the original, vulnerable wooden version. Photograph by Richard J. Orsi, author's collection.

the railroad still had a "fire prevention and control problem of immense magnitude," its fire-loss per mile was less than one-half the average for all steam railroads in the United States.[40] Stephen J. Pyne, the major historian of wildland fire, has judged the Southern Pacific's firefighting system to be "exemplary" among far-western railroads, especially in encouraging technological innovation in wildland fire control.[41]

In the decades from 1890 to 1930, as the Southern Pacific broadened its program to protect the company's and the general public's wooded lands, fire prevention and control emerged as one of the major dimensions of railroad forestry. The local residents hired as part-time rangers to keep watch over railroad forests served primarily, at least at first, as fire wardens. Across Southern Pacific territory in Oregon and California, these agents were responsible for detecting and alerting the company to fire hazards, such as lumbering slash in nearby forests and trash, dead trees, and excessive grass and underbrush accumulating along the rights-of-way. At the direction of the company's Land Department, local railroad fire wardens hired crews and saw to the elimination of hazards. By 1900, the railroad was systematically removing combustible material and plowing firebreaks along its fire-prone rights-of-way; employees were also instructed not to burn trash during dry seasons. When wildfires did occur, the local railroad wardens formed firefighting crews and supervised the suppression. During large blazes, company land agents from San Francisco, even on occasion William H. Mills and B. A. McAllaster, arrived to take charge, sometimes spending weeks on the scene. During times of high fire danger, the company employed special fire patrols to keep round-the-clock vigilance.[42] To discourage fires on lands adjacent to rail lines, whether caused by rail operations or not, the Southern Pacific launched publicity campaigns to convince other landowners to remove fire hazards and to maintain firebreaks, particularly abutting the rights-of-way. When its local fire wardens alerted the company to hazards on adjoining private lands, railroad officials sent out letters advising property owners of the problems and recommending methods of removal.[43]

As was the case with the control of the pine-bark beetle and other forest issues in the early twentieth century, the Southern Pacific developed close, cooperative fire-prevention and suppression programs with public and private forest interests and agencies. In fact, it was combating the fire problem together that often led the way to closer cooperation on broader forestry questions. With fire matters at that time handled mostly by local and state authorities, the Southern Pacific worked most intimately with them, as opposed to the U.S. Forest Service. When first instituted in the early decades of the twentieth century across the Southern Pacific's forested regions in Oregon and California, specific fire-prevention and suppression systems varied locally and changed constantly. In some places, voluntary associations of landowners, the earliest form of control, established fire patrols and fought blazes; in others, local and county governments were responsible for various voluntary or compulsory programs. Increasingly, though, state government assumed greater authority for centralized, mandatory, publicly operated fire control. Whatever the local system, the Southern Pacific was an important participant, if not the original instigator of organized efforts. Railroad fire wardens shared information and worked cooperatively with local, private, and state fire rangers; they and Southern Pacific fire-trains and crews fought fires together with other interests on a regional basis, with the railroad people often arriving at a fire front first and with the most advanced equipment. In some cases, railroad fire rangers, numerous, experienced, and already mobilized, were themselves also designated as the public fire officials. In California by the 1910s, for example, the State Department of Forestry was appointing local Southern Pacific forest agents as official state fire wardens, responsible for ordering controlled burns and issuing fire permits in the vicinity of rail lines. In 1925, after extending the state's contract with the railroad for another five years, state forester M. B. Pratt commended the railroad–state wardens for having worked "very carefully . . . and in an efficient

manner" and for "materially reducing the number of fires."[44] With large landholdings and other assets to protect, an awareness of the important regional
interests at stake, and sufficient financial resources, the railroad generally paid
a large share of the costs of cooperative programs. In the case of California, for
example, in the 1920s, the Southern Pacific was paying one-third of the salaries
of state fire rangers working in counties near its lines and its land grant during
the fire season between May and October.[45]

Devoted to the cause of forest protection, land agent B. A. McAllaster, from
his appointment in 1908 until retirement in 1933, was an influential leader in
the creation of organized, state-operated fire systems in the Far West. For all
the local efforts of the railroad to fight regional fires, sometimes cooperatively
with other groups, McAllaster by 1912 had come to believe that, just as in the
case of municipal police and fire departments, only centralized, publicly operated, tax-supported, mandatory programs could provide effective wildlands fire
control. While the railroad considered its fire department adequate for its own
needs in the immediate vicinity of rights-of-way, the same could not be said
for the wide areas of granted land stretching ten, twenty, or more miles away.
Becoming more frequent and destructive as forest areas were developed, fires
often spread over wide territories, engulfing, threatening, and requiring suppression efforts not just on the railroad's lands but also private properties and
public jurisdictions. Funds raised locally, often through voluntary contributions
by only a few large landowners such as the railroad, proved inadequate to support permanent, compulsory fire systems with modern equipment. As a result,
fire control was effective in a few districts, haphazard in most, and nonexistent
in others. McAllaster believed that state administration and financing of
firefighting was essential to the protection of forests for lumbering, water storage, recreation, and wilderness preservation. In California, the land agent's general views were shared by a host of local and state foresters as well as lumber
companies, although their sharp disagreements regarding means stalled the
enactment of a centralized state firefighting system.[46]

In 1912, the California State Conservation Commission, newly created by
the state's ruling Progressives, convened a meeting of contending lumbering
and forestry interests to try to forge an agreement on firefighting. The commission invited McAllaster, who was well known and trusted by the state's lumbering establishment, to submit a proposal for discussion at the meeting.
McAllaster's proposal, which one historian termed "the most concrete plan for
state action," called for the creation of fire districts throughout the state to operate under the supervision of the state forester to undertake both long-term
fire prevention and, when fires occurred, suppression.[47] The state forester would
appoint district wardens, or rangers, who would establish and manage the local fire systems as well as build and operate fire lookout stations. On the the-

ory that firefighting was in everyone's interest, not just the specific owners on whose lands the fires occurred, the program would be financed by a combination of general local property taxes and state appropriations. McAllaster's plan for local districts under state jurisdiction met the problem of widely varying local fire conditions and the objections of many contending interests and served as the basis for discussion at the meeting and, with modifications, became the recommended legislation introduced by the Conservation Commission into the legislature later in 1912.[48] However, some lumber interests, particularly owners of redwood lands in wetter, less fire-prone areas, continued to oppose any system with mandatory taxes, and for the next four legislative sessions the bill fell either to Governor Hiram Johnson's veto or the legislature's refusal to approve use of state funds for local firefighting.[49] Only in 1919, when the problem of forest fires during a drought period had become monumental, did conflicting interests overcome their differences and a bill similar to McAllaster's proposal become law. Under the law, the state forester was to establish and govern local fire-control districts supervised by forest wardens (rangers), with the costs borne by the state. Fire protection in California was revolutionized by the 1919 act, with the state finally gaining centralized control.[50]

With a state firefighting apparatus in place, McAllaster in 1920 helped to organize the California Forestry Committee, on which he served as an influential member for ten years. Composed of representatives from major lumbering companies and other businesses, university forestry departments, and state and federal forestry agencies, this unofficial group worked to conduct inquiries and publish reports on forest issues, to mediate conflicts and forge consensus among the contending forest interests, and to advise the state forester on broad-ranging matters, particularly concerning fire control and most especially the still-hot controversy between light-burning and fire-suppression advocates. In one of its many investigations, the Forestry Committee raised private funds and, through McAllaster's leadership, sponsored a series of experiments, mostly on Southern Pacific forest lands, to evaluate various fire-control methods. The Forestry Committee's 1923 report on light-burning, which pronounced the practice to be of only marginal use, was important in quieting the controversy and paving the way for the adoption of fire suppression as the preferred method nationwide. On several subsequent occasions, McAllaster and other Southern Pacific forestry experts attempted to revive interest in light-burning, but to no avail. C. Raymond Clar, leading historian of California forestry, concluded that, as a mediating force to avert stalemate in the legislature and as a "clearing house for opinions on proposed legislation," the California Forestry Committee "earned an honorable place" at a critical juncture in the development of forestry in the state.[51] When the Forestry Committee disbanded, McAllaster was appointed by the governor in 1931 to the newly constituted official State Board of Forestry to oversee the management of the state's forests. Serving variously as temporary chairman and vice chairman and presiding effectively at many of the Board of Forestry's meetings, McAllaster continued to further the cause of forestry into the 1930s.[52]

The Southern Pacific as Environmental Mediator

The Southern Pacific became involved in countless environmental and resource issues beyond its forests, and, as has been documented in this and other chapters, the company had a substantial influence on the development of environmental and resource law, policy, and institutional development in the Far West. One service for the broader community that the railroad was often called upon to perform, in the absence of clear laws and public agencies to take responsibility, was to mediate among contending environmental and resource interest groups. This was evident in the Southern Pacific's attempts in many locales to get conflicting water users to set aside their disagreements in order to cooperate in larger, more viable irrigation districts.[53] Mediation also characterized the railroad's work in scientific forestry and fire control. Southern Pacific efforts sometimes succeeded in reducing conflict and in creating more efficient resource programs, but sometimes, as was true of Mojave River irrigation, peacemaking efforts went for naught. Sometimes, too, they exposed conflicts of interest and policy within the Southern Pacific itself, which could immobilize the company and certainly limit its constructive conservationist role. Such was the case in the controversy that broke out after 1910 between northern Sacramento Valley copper-mining and agricultural interests.

In the early 1900s, sulfur dioxide fallout from proliferating copper smelters near Redding blighted a large and widening belt of land downwind and eastward across the Sacramento Valley and into the foothills.[54] Soil was poisoned, and crops, range grass, and timber were killed, ruining farmers, ranchers, and lumbermen. Although there were no state laws or agencies controlling air pollution, two hundred agriculturalists formed a Farmers' Protective Association, sued the refineries, and won a federal court decision in the summer of 1910 ordering the smelters to install devices on smokestacks to filter out the sulfur dioxide. When the majority of mining companies refused to abide by the injunction at all, and the few that did installed filters that proved inadequate, farmers and other local residents, lacking state regulatory laws or agencies to appeal to, approached the Southern Pacific Land Department for assistance. They asked particularly for the railroad's intercession in getting the smelters to abide by the court order and, failing that, financial support for a broader lawsuit to shut down the refineries.[55] Although he and his company were basically sympathetic to the farmers, B. A. McAllaster followed established policy and ordered a succession of investigations to survey the damage and determine the actions and points of view of farmers and smelting companies. The company's agents reported vast devastation and financial ruin to many landowners, not to mention $150,000 in damage to 80,000 acres of Southern Pacific forested land.[56] With the smelter owners intransigent, McAllaster went to top executives and secured their approval for a $1,500 contribution to the farmers' lawsuit.[57] McAllaster also sent copies of the railroad's smoke-damage surveys to the State Conservation Commission and tried, unsuccessfully, to get the state to intervene in the case and press the smelters to filter the smoke properly.[58] Moreover, infuriated at the damage to their property, railroad leaders began to prepare a lawsuit of their own to protect land-grant values, but further surveys disclosed that because it was impossible to determine which of the independent smelters were causing the damage, the railroad's case would be unwinable.[59]

McAllaster's attempts to convince smelter owners to reach agreement with the farmers and to reduce the air pollution had no effect, in part because not all railroad officials shared his sympathy for the farmers. When Southern Pacific support for the farmers' lawsuit was praised lavishly in the Redding community, irate smelter owners protested to top railroad executives that the company was showing favoritism toward farmers and asked for like support for their defense against the lawsuits. They reminded the rail leaders that the mines spent $43,000 per month freighting their copper on Southern Pacific lines. They also complained to the railroad's Traffic Department, which in turn took a stand against the Land Department's support for the farmers.[60] The dispute, with the railroad now in the middle, dragged on for several years. Additional Land Department investigations determined that the damage was worsening, with the affected area expanding at the rate of ten miles a year.[61] Nevertheless, company officials struggled to decide which of their conflicting corporate interests should prevail and failed to act further.[62] Finally in July 1914, with the company sharply divided against itself, the matter was submitted to company president William Sproule, who ruled that the Southern Pacific "should remain neutral and not give subscriptions to either the smelters or the farmers' organizations."[63] The railroad's aid was sorely missed; in 1915, the U.S. district court in San Francisco dismissed the farmers' lawsuit and allowed the smelters to remain open.[64] Hamstrung by internal company division, Southern Pacific intervention had failed to affect the outcome.

Rangeland Management

In other cases, however, the railroad's mediation among contending parties sometimes created important and lasting resource-use systems. In the late nineteenth and early twentieth centuries, from the Southern Pacific's viewpoint, the problems of management in the vast rangelands granted to the company along the old Central Pacific route in the Nevada and Utah Great Basin were analogous to those in California and Oregon forests. The semi-arid or desert region was broken and rugged, water scant and scattered, and the grass cover sharply uneven according to differences in soil, moisture, and elevation. Isolated from urban markets, lacking in agricultural potential, and virtually unpopulated, this immense region remained largely undeveloped, with little public or railroad land sold, or even used—except, that is, for large-scale, open-range cattle and sheep grazing. However, with the huge land surplus, free access to public land, and absence of any conservationist administrative structure and land-use regulation, ranchers lacked incentives to use the land wisely and instead overgrazed at will on the federal lands, clashed with one another over access to scarce grass and water, adamantly resisted any attempt by the Department of the Interior to regulate or charge fees for grazing, and poached on Southern Pacific land. In addition, as was the case in national forests, national reclamation projects, and local irrigation districts, the checkerboard land pattern and the accompanying lack of clearly marked boundaries defeated attempts by government and railroad to manage Great Basin land. Similar situations prevailed over much of the Southern Pacific's territory in Arizona, New Mexico, and western Texas, although except for Texas, the company had little or no granted land in those areas.[65]

By the early 1900s, the Southern Pacific, like increasing numbers of conservationists and public land officials, had begun to favor federal regulation of grazing on open public lands in the Far West, including the requirement for leases and fees. The railroad advocated regulated grazing as a way to end the free use of public land, and hence to encourage ranchers also to buy or lease railroad land, but also for conservation reasons, as a means of lessening overgrazing and promoting long-term organization and stability in cattle and sheep grazing, and hence more secure traffic revenues. At first, railroad land agents viewed regulation and leasing as difficult or impossible to achieve because of the strong opposition of ranchers and western political leaders, and the company refrained from publicly pushing the plan and thus alienating livestock producers. "This change is looked upon with considerable distrust and disfavor," acting land agent Charles Eberlein reported to higher executives in 1907. While affirming that regulation and leasing of public lands would be favorable to railroad interests, he felt he had to be "very careful not to express any opinion in the matter of the leasing of the public lands, as the Railroad Company is looked upon as an interested party, and any opinion or action taken by the Railroad Company would be looked on as hostile by either cattlemen or sheepmen and probably be distrusted by all."[66] Although early leasing measures failed Congress, the idea grew in support among conservation interests, and similar bills were introduced every few years over the next three decades. The Southern Pacific continued to support the concept of regulation of grazing and the lease system but continued to keep in the background while tracking legislation carefully.[67] The company was concerned that the various proposals contained contradictions that could undermine their effectiveness and injure railroad interests: unrealistically high fee schedules, arbitrary lease limitations that would not allow enough acreage to ranchers on dry lands incapable of supporting large numbers of animals, and the absence of protections for leaseholders from homesteaders filing claim to their leased land. "The result would be the enforced decrease of live stock products of the United States," land agent McAllaster warned chief counsel William F. Herrin in 1914. McAllaster repeatedly advised higher executives to lobby for changes to the bills, none of which passed.[68]

By the 1920s, the Southern Pacific believed even more strongly in the importance of centralized grazing-land management and leasing and began to take more public positions on the issue. Alarmed at the rapid deterioration of misused western grazing lands, company officials began to place more importance on the resource conservation benefits of regulation and leasing. Attorney Harry H. McElroy, of the Law Department, El Paso Division, stated it best in 1925 when alerting Herrin, his superior, to ominous conditions on the grazing lands of the Southwest. McElroy reported that

> the destruction of the grass and vegetation on the public lands has been very far reaching in its effects, but it has been destructive not only of the cattle growing industry but also of our reclamation and irrigation projects. Recent investigations have shown that the sanding of our irrigation streams and reservoirs is directly attributable to the erosion caused by overgrazing of the public lands in the drainage area of such streams.

Confessing he had "become quite a partisan in favor of the public domain control," McElroy recommended that the railroad lobby more vigorously and try to change public opinion to bring about grazing regulation. He considered it a matter "of self-preservation for us to advocate the control and leasing of the public domain," and he advised Herrin that he did not "believe the railroad would antagonize the cattle industry by favoring the control of public domain or presenting its views and the data in support thereof to the public and to Congress."[69]

In the early 1920s, the Land Department opened a campaign to convince stockmen in its territory of the necessity of buying and leasing public and railroad rangelands in order to protect the lands' productivity and to assure long-term predictability. The campaign included a series of articles written by the department in the *Nevada Stockgrower* during 1921. The company tried also to establish close contact with the stockraisers' associations in order to provide what influence it could.[70]

From the railroad's perspective, particularly troubling about the federal leasing programs being proposed at the time was their failure to acknowledge that over much of the railroad land-grant area, federal land sections alternated with railroad sections in the familiar checkerboard pattern. A leasing system for only the even-numbered public sections would create great management difficulties for both railroad and government. For example, railroad land was for sale while government land was not. How could the railroad ever sell its land if prospective buyers could not be assured of access to intervening public sections? Conversely, how could grazers lease public sections if they could not guarantee that they could buy or lease the intervening railroad sections? Particularly in rugged, isolated landscapes that defied the boundaries on paper surveys, and where available water was widely scattered, any workable management program had to encompass both intervening land systems as well as water supplies.[71] When a grazing lease bill surfaced in Congress in 1925, at McAllaster's recommendation, the Southern Pacific tried to get it amended to include both railroad and public land in the regulation and leasing program.[72] The company also tried to get other land-grant railroads to make common cause to have future grazing bills amended to take into account the checkerboard pattern in land-grant areas.[73] To deal with the problem of the checkerboard pattern, McAllaster also suggested that the company approach the government with a land-exchange offer to make federal and railroad grazing lands whole and allow for comprehensive management under both land systems.[74] Grazers of cattle and sheep remained bitterly opposed to leasing, however; the 1925 bill failed to clear committee, and the stalemate in Congress lasted into the early 1930s.[75] Not until 1934, when the Great Depression had swelled livestock surpluses, ruined prices, and driven ranchers to bankruptcy or near-bankruptcy, did opposition to range control and leasing wane enough to allow congressional passage of the Taylor Grazing Act, which ushered in a new era of grazing regulation.[76]

Livestock Drive-Trails

While stalemate blocked the adoption of an overall program of range management during the early decades of the twentieth century, the Southern Pacific mediated among various feuding cattle, sheep, and federal interests to bring a measure of organization to northern Great Basin grazing lands. On February 20, 1904, acting land agent Charles W. Eberlein wrote to general manager Julius Kruttschnitt warning of an unacknowledged crisis looming on the western ranges and urging the company to develop livestock drive-trails through federal and railroad grazing lands in northern Nevada and Utah. Federal leasing and regulation of ranchlands were in the offing, he predicted, and it would increase the sale or leasing of railroad lands near the tracks. Eberlein and Great Basin land and livestock leaders were concerned that as the open range became more engrossed, shipping points along the Central Pacific's mainline through the largely roadless region would be blocked off from trail drives from deep in the hinterland, cutting seriously into livestock production and railroad traffic. Lacking grass and water for their traveling herds, let alone permission to cross the range of others, distant ranchers would be unable to reach the rail line. The problem would be more serious for sheepherders, who needed even more grass and water and wider throughways for their slow-moving herds and who faced sometimes violent opposition from cattlemen, who refused access even across public range. Both sheepmen and cattlemen, moreover, had to migrate their herds seasonally over great distances, generally from lower, warmer, and drier early-maturing ranges to the south to the higher, cooler, and wetter ranges with later-ripening grasses to the north. This meant crossing, from south to north, the Central Pacific's right-of-way. Permanent, public drive-ways were urgently needed, Eberlein warned, and since the federal General Land Office lacked the means, the mandate, and the will to create them, it was in the vital future interest of the region, its livestock producers, and the corporation itself, for the railroad to do it. He recommended that the company immediately determine its present and future livestock shipping stations and reserve land and water sources from sale in the vicinity of those points for the future use of herds being held for shipment. The railroad should also reserve corridors of odd-numbered sections from sale or lease and mark north-south public drive-trails through its land grant and across the Central Pacific line, as well as trade its remaining unclaimed indemnity lands with the federal government for fragments of public land on the even sections to make the trails continuous and wide enough for large herds of cattle and sheep.[77] Kruttschnitt agreed, and the Southern Pacific immediately moved to implement a trailway plan. Livestock trail reservation clauses were inserted thereafter into leases and deeds issued to persons acquiring granted lands in northern Nevada and Utah.[78]

The project proved much more vast than Eberlein anticipated, however. In fact, the Great Basin trail-drive system that eventually emerged, along with the company's forestry and fire protection and water development programs, turned out to be among the railroad's most ambitious and complex efforts at resource management. At first the problems were overwhelming: large-scale grass, water, and topographic surveys and maps had to be completed, and then repeatedly tested and revised; clashing local ranching interests, particularly cattle and sheep raisers, had to be mollified and brought into agreement; delicate

negotiations had to be conducted with private landowners and the General Land
Office to trade, purchase, or lease lands or grant easements to make the trails
continuous. Then, just as some progress occurred, San Francisco's earthquake
and fire of April 1906 destroyed the railroad's headquarters building at 4th and
Townsend streets, taking with it almost all the Land Department's maps and
other papers. Over the next several years while the Land Department franti-
cally reconstructed its records, work on the trailways stayed on hold. The death
of William H. Mills in 1907 and the revolving door of acting chief land agents
further stymied the project.[79]

Not until 1908, when B. A. McAllaster, who was a strong supporter of the
program, took over land operations, did the trail plan get back under way. Working in conjunction with federal land surveyors, the Southern Pacific in 1908 located and opened a few trails marked with posts leading the way to some major rail shipping points, with a goal of one day having north-south trails every
forty to sixty miles over the nearly 500 miles from Reno east to the Great Salt
Lake.[80] Over the next several years, many new trails were surveyed, negotiated
with local livestock interests and federal land officials, marked with posts, and
placed in operation down to railhead shipping points, some of which were
served by up to a half-dozen trails from different directions. The railroad publicized the corridors and distributed printed maps and instructions to local livestock raisers.[81] By 1912, a widespread network of dozens of railroad-managed
trails, twenty to fifty miles long and at least a half-mile wide, was bringing cattle and sheep herds down to many points on the Central Pacific, among them
Halleck, Wells, Preble, Fenelon Station, Deeth, Elko, Metropolis, Montello, and
Golconda Station in Nevada and Kelton and Lucin in Utah. McAllaster reported to higher executives that the trails were an immediate success and new
ones were being added "as fast as our examination work progresses."[82]

The Southern Pacific was also building new stockyards, loading docks, and
watering facilities of its own at shipping stations, as well as subsidizing private
livestock shippers to locate there. As it was doing in Texas and other livestock-
producing regions, the company was simultaneously centralizing, systematizing, and reducing time and freight tariffs on livestock shipments originating in
Nevada and Utah.[83] Railroad reports by 1912 indicated that the livestock trails
were being used far beyond expectations. At Lucin each autumn, between sixty
and seventy-five bands of sheep arrived from the north over just one trail, for
an annual total of about 250,000 head; other trails averaged between 250,000
and 300,000 head of sheep per year. The Halleck station shipped 800 cars of
sheep per year; Carlin, 600. Traffic in cattle was also high. At all points, almost
all livestock shippers used the Southern Pacific's trails to reach the tracks.[84]

The trails did not operate without problems, though. Conflict between cattle and sheep raisers abated only somewhat, even after the Southern Pacific live-

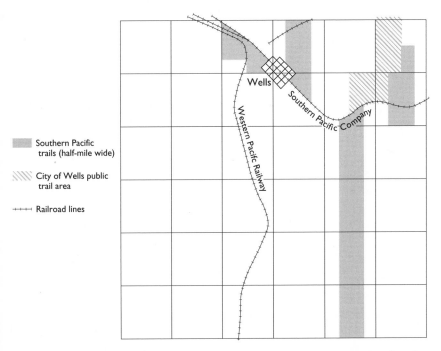

Central Pacific Railroad land grant near Wells, Elko County, Nevada, showing sections the railroad withdrew from sale and combined with public land from the Department of the Interior to form a livestock drive-trail reserve, 1910s–1920s. The railroad developed, mapped, and managed dozens of such trails, allowing ranchers to drive herds of cattle and sheep to railheads in Nevada and Utah. Adapted from Central Pacific, "Land-Grant Map Books" (mss. 1907 and subsequent years). Courtesy California State Railroad Museum, Sacramento.

stock trails began to operate, and the railroad repeatedly had to negotiate among the cattlemen and sheepmen, as well as feuding cattle ranchers competing for grass and water. Ultimately, the company resorted to separating the sheep from the cattle by widening many of the corridors used heavily by sheepherders, to as much as a mile wide in the case of one trail into Elko.[85] Some farmers complained that the unoccupied pathways harbored rabbits and other crop pests, and the company sent investigators and tried to control the pests. Some drovers reported that the routes were located incorrectly, and the railroad was always adjusting routes to meet the needs of users.[86] When a specific parcel of railroad land was being sold or leased, as happened rarely, field agents resurveyed local needs and rerouted the trail around the land. As assistant chief land agent F. W. Houtz put it, the company wanted "to consider the possible future requirements as well as present necessities."[87]

Perhaps most significant from the company's perspective, the far-flung trail-reservation system consumed a staggering amount of railroad land, keeping it indefinitely off the market, while of course local taxes continued to be due. Typically, the trails ran from corner to corner over odd-numbered railroad land sections, with only occasional small pieces of former government or private land on the even-numbered sections stitched together for a throughway. A meticulous company study indicated that as of the spring of 1918, in Nevada alone, 234,300 acres of railroad land were tied up in the trails, and the company was paying about $10,000 in local property taxes annually on the land.[88] These problems aside, however, the Southern Pacific had coordinated varied interests in devising and imposing a new, flexible land-use system on a difficult landscape, a trail-driving and livestock-marketing network of immense value to the railroad, growers, and the region. As it turned out, the livestock trail system also had unexpected duration.

After the Southern Pacific's livestock trail system had been operating successfully for nearly ten years, the federal government belatedly took an interest in the matter of livestock trails across the closing public domain. In 1917, G. E. Hair, an agent of the General Land Office, Department of the Interior, which had custody of public land in the Great Basin, arrived in the region to develop livestock trails in keeping with a congressional act of 1916. In meeting local stockmen, Hair was surprised to discover that the Southern Pacific was already operating an effective driveway network. Hair approached land agent McAllaster with an offer to cooperate with the railroad in the creation of a federally operated, expanded trail network, based on the railroad's existing system and adding government sections to extend, straighten, and shorten the trails. He asked also for copies of the railroad's maps and other information to assist in planning the new trails.[89] Obviously eager to cooperate, McAllaster immediately assured Hair of the railroad's assistance, sent the available maps as requested, had his office staff update the information, and a month later sent the government agent a second, revised set.[90]

Building the complicated new combined system took almost as long as it had taken the railroad to plan its trails in the first place. For nearly two years, Hair and McAllaster and their staffs worked closely; eventually, Hair moved his office to San Francisco, apparently in part to facilitate communication with the railroad. Hair made proposal after proposal, sent the maps for revision to the railroad's experts who knew the local situation better, and then produced yet new drafts that incorporated railroad suggestions. In effect, the railroad's land experts had veto power over the location of the trails. In many cases, it was railroad field agents who actually rode the proposed trails to test and revise them on the scene.[91]

Both the government and the railroad stood to gain from the deal that was worked out. The Department of the Interior received the railroad's maps, backlog of experience, and use of its office staff and field agents to plot and investigate the routes, as well as the company's goodwill with livestock producers.

The railroad also agreed to reserve its lands in the trail from sale or lease indefinitely, though not forever. If it needed to dispose of a parcel of land (which as it turned out happened very rarely), the company agreed to require a trail deed-reservation from the buyer or to replace the tract with another piece of railroad land. The Southern Pacific also benefited in a substantially expanded trail system feeding its shipping stations, particularly extending farther into the hinterland beyond the limits of the land grant, as well as freedom from the responsibility and much of the cost for operating and continually maintaining the trails. Most important, the new driveway system relied more heavily on government sections, freeing many thousands of acres of railroad land for sale or lease. On just three of the revised trails, the number of Southern Pacific land sections involved in the trail decreased from 27 to 17 on one, 20 to 9 on another, and 16 to 9 on the third. About 210,000 railroad acres would still be involved in the entire new system, but then there would be many more trails, and they would be longer.[92]

Finally, in April 1919, the government and the railroad reached agreement on the trail system, and both agencies took action to reserve land along the trails and start their operation.[93] After turning direct supervision of the trails over to the Department of the Interior, the Southern Pacific Land Department, as before, continued to work with livestock raisers and their organizations to maintain order and efficiency and to reduce conflict in the industry. Land agents arbitrated trespass disputes involving herds on the public livestock trails, tried to get lawsuits for damages between stockmen settled out of court, and perennially were called upon to mediate between feuding cattlemen and sheepherders.[94] Fresh from its success with the Department of the Interior, the Southern Pacific negotiated with the Department of Agriculture to create similar cooperative livestock driveways for cattle and sheep through the national forests in the Far West.[95] Cordial relationships appear to have prevailed between the railroad and the General Land Office in their ongoing dealings regarding the planning and operation of livestock trails, in contrast to the often strained relationships the railroad had with that same agency over land-grant patents, with the Reclamation Service over water development, and to a lesser extent with the Forest Service over forestry policy. Cooperation was clearly in each party's interest. Each depended on and had much to gain from the other. Also, the agreement on the trails was mutual, flexible, and impermanent, with either party free to modify or step away from it.

Although conceived of as temporary, interagency cooperation on the livestock trails continued for an unexpectedly long time. As late as 1950, the trails, despite having been constantly rerouted around newly established ranches, farms, and settlements, were still in use, and the railroad's lands in the trails continued to be reserved from sale or lease. In 1949, the Southern Pacific informed the Department of the Interior that it wished to dispose of some of the reserve, but only the acreage, not specific tracts that were part of the trails. The company would sell pieces of land, but only subject to the approval of the government and with the proviso that the buyers would be required to exchange the land with the government for equivalent acreage away from the trails. The Department of the Interior indicated its favor, and sales began. By 1953, the railroad had disposed of all but 60,000 of its more than 200,000 acres in the original livestock trail reserve. Sales stopped at that point, and railroad and government continued to cooperate in the operation of the trail.[96] As had been true of urban and rural water facilities and firefighting and forestry programs, a complex land- and resource-use system of great importance to livestock raisers and the Great Basin region as a whole had begun as a private, railroad-initiated program, only to be transformed with Southern Pacific assistance into an ongoing function of government.

The Southern Pacific and Western Resources: A Conclusion

Over the full diversity of its resource-related activities—land-grant settlement, water development, agricultural modernization, wilderness preservation, and management of forests, grasslands, and other natural resources—the Southern Pacific Company had undergone great transformation between the 1860s and the 1930s. Evolving corporate interests, as well as the personal identification of Southern Pacific officials with the broader public welfare of the regions in which they lived, led the railroad quickly to outgrow the pioneer resource-exploitation phase of rail line construction and to move toward long-term conservation of resources and preservation of wild natural landscapes—on its own and increasingly on public and other private lands. In developing its policy approaches to resource issues, the company relied more and more on science and expertise. Even in the late nineteenth century, but especially after 1900, the railroad also encouraged the expansion of regulatory law and centralized public management of land, water, and other resource matters. But, when the growth of the public regulatory function was lacking or delayed, the Southern Pacific, pursuing its corporate interest of expanding and more reliable profits, sometimes furnished organization and conflict resolution within its territory, resulting in ongoing private resource-management programs. When these programs, as often happened, were converted into permanent public functions, the railroad typically helped to bring about and shape the new agencies or programs.

In some of those transitions of resource policy, the Southern Pacific moved in step with changes in the broader society, particularly during the so-called Progressive Era after 1900. In some transitions, however, the railroad moved ahead, particularly of people and groups within its own service area in the Far West and Southwest, leading the way toward and helping to institute more reasoned, long-term, sustainable resource-use policies and programs. Often the most organized entity in its territory, the Southern Pacific provided capital, technology, structure, mediation, and, most importantly, leadership, in assisting the broader society to resolve resource issues. In the process, the railroad left a legacy of more effective business practices, laws, public agencies, and cooperative arrangements among contending interests as well as more enlightened attitudes toward nature and its use and preservation.

Epilogue

This book has not been just about important people thinking great thoughts and erecting great structures. It is also a story of simple things, what some historians have called "stuff": iron rails, tunnels, snowsheds, accounting ledgers, surveyors' chains, tourist pamphlets, farm schools, water pumps, irrigation canals, rainfall gauges, soil samples, oranges, raisins, rice, ice, cantaloupes, eucalyptus trees, fire hoses, pine-bark beetles, and livestock trails. Such items may seem inconsequential in shaping history. Yet, as archaeologist James Deetz and others have shown, in such mundane, apparently uncomplicated things hide insights into a broader and more complex and important world, waiting for us to unlock them.[1]

It was through things such as these that the Southern Pacific Railroad dramatically affected the course of human affairs in its territory. By its mere construction, but also by its designed programs, the railroad encouraged land subdivision, promoted settlement, altered land use and agricultural production, increased access to water, located towns, transformed regional landscapes, and opened up opportunities for countless others to create new enterprises with similar effects. In addition to affecting what people did and how they did it, the Southern Pacific sought to reshape "nature" for more efficient human use, even while helping to protect some of it as wilderness preserves. Inherent in the stories of small things is the centrality of Southern Pacific Railroad's activities to the history of its region, and its formative impact on the development of the American West.

In the post–World War II era, American railroads entered a long decline from which they have yet to emerge. The causes are many. Among them have been some external to the industry: financial aftershocks from the pre-war Great Depression; the deepening love affair of Americans with motor vehicles; and inhospitable, even counterproductive, government regulations. But some of the industry's woes have been self-imposed—for example, the industry's earlier overbuilding and its defensive, conservative, retrenching response to competition, such as in its deliberate killing of rail passenger traffic. Decline thus became its own self-fulfilling prophesy.

One of the most afflicted companies was the Southern Pacific Railroad. Several decades of falling traffic and rail revenues, problematic investments in non-rail businesses, and disposal of assets to raise cash had greatly weakened the company by the early 1980s. The Southern Pacific Company was ripe pickings for more aggressive, better-financed competitors. And come they did, like sharks to a dying seal. First, the Santa Fe in 1983 effected a merger of the two holding companies, only to have the Interstate Commerce Commission disallow the combination of the two parallel railroads as a restraint on trade. Then, in 1988, the Santa Fe, having shorn the Southern Pacific Company of some of its most valuable assets, such as its Land Company, spun off the money-losing Southern Pacific Railroad to the Denver & Rio Grande. Finally, in 1996, the ancient nemesis, the Union Pacific, bought and absorbed the Southern Pacific Railroad. All along, in what two historians have described as a "piece-by-piece dismantling of a once-viable railroad," the new owners shuttered Southern Pacific offices in the Far West, "retired" old-time employees with their institutional memories, sold or ripped out many lines, liquidated additional valuable assets, and threw out vast quantities of records carrying the corporation's history.[2] The Southern Pacific was scheduled to lose even its name and identity on September 11, 1996. At 9:00 A.M. on that day, the Southern Pacific Railroad, in the early twentieth century the world's largest transportation system and the most important single corporation in the history of most of its territory, was no more. When the final freight train moving under the railroad's name arrived at its destination in San Luis Obispo, the locomotive engineer sent out a parting message over the railroad's radio network: "This is the last sunset for the SP. Good night SP and thanks for the memories."[3]

A Note on Manuscript Sources

This study of Southern Pacific Company history is based on three decades of research, primarily in manuscript and document collections, many of which historians have never examined or have not exploited extensively. In some cases, the collections have been opened to scholars only recently. The most important of these manuscript resources are listed below. Also, I have described and evaluated these and other specific collections further where their materials are pertinent in the chapter notes, which follow at the end of the book.

- Southern Pacific Company Records, extensive segments of which are publicly available at the California State Railroad Museum and Archives, Sacramento; the University of Texas, El Paso; Arizona State University; the University of Oregon; the Oregon Historical Society; and the San Diego Historical Society.

- Southern Pacific Company Records in the company archives and records warehouses in San Francisco and Houston. Particularly significant in San Francisco were the nineteenth- and twentieth-century records of the Executive Department, the Corporate Secretary, the Public Relations Department, the Legal Department, and the Southern Pacific Land Company. The latter includes the virtually complete business correspondence (1869–1900) of Daniel K. Zumwalt, company land agent for the San Joaquin Valley, which contains much new information on general Southern Pacific land-grant policies and the famous Mussel Slough tragedy of 1880.

- The National Archives, Washington, D.C., particularly records of the Department of the Interior (General Land Office) and the Attorney General pertaining to federal governmental relationships with western railroads.

- The National Archives Regional Center, Denver, particularly the records of the U.S. Bureau of Reclamation (Reclamation Service).
- The State Libraries and Archives of California, Oregon, Nevada, Arizona, New Mexico, and Texas.
- The Collis P. Huntington Papers, Syracuse University, and in microfilm edition.
- The Henry E. Huntington Biographical File, Henry E. Huntington Library, San Marino, California. Numerous other Huntington Library collections pertaining directly to Southern Pacific history have also been examined.
- The Pacific Improvement Company Papers and the Timothy Hopkins Transportation Collection, Stanford University.
- The William Mahl Papers, Barker Texas History Center, University of Texas, Austin (Mahl was one of the principal architects of the integrated Southern Pacific system from 1882 to 1913).
- Imperial Irrigation District Library and Archives, El Centro, California.
- Harry T. Corey Papers, University of California, Los Angeles (Corey was the Southern Pacific civil engineer in charge of the California Development Company's irrigation works in the Imperial Valley).
- Truckee-Carson Irrigation District (Truckee-Carson Reclamation Project; later, Newlands Project) Records, Nevada Historical Society, Reno.
- Institutional archives of the following universities, particularly of their presidents' offices and colleges of agriculture: University of California, Berkeley; University of California, Davis; University of Nevada, Reno; Oregon State University; University of Arizona; New Mexico State University, Las Cruces; University of Texas, Austin; and Texas A&M University.
- Numerous other collections of manuscripts, photographs, and other materials pertaining to Southern Pacific Company history among the holdings of institutions across the Far West, including California State Railroad Museum, Sacramento; Henry E. Huntington Library, San Marino, California; Bancroft Library, University of California, Berkeley; Stanford University; Santa Barbara Historical Society; San Diego Historical Society; Tulare County Library, Visalia, California; Kings County Library, Hanford, California; Yolo County Library, Woodland, California; Holt-Atherton Pacific Center for Regional Studies, University of the Pacific, Stockton, California; Oregon Historical Society, Portland; University of Oregon, Eugene; Nevada Historical Society, Reno; Arizona Historical Society, Tucson; University of Arizona, Tucson; Arizona State University, Tempe; New Mexico State University, Las Cruces; DeGolyer Library, Southern Methodist University, Dallas; University of Texas, El Paso; University of Texas, Austin; Barker Texas History Center, Austin; San Antonio Public Library, San Antonio; Institute of Texan Cultures Library, San Antonio; and Houston Public Library, Houston.
- I also made extensive use of the library of the State Historical Society of Wisconsin, Madison; the Newberry Library, Chicago; and the library of California State University, Hayward.

Notes

Abbreviations for Collections and Repositories

BL   Bancroft Library, University of California, Berkeley

CPH   Collis P. Huntington Collection, Arents Research Library, Syracuse University

CRRM   California State Railroad Museum Library and Archives, Sacramento

DG   DeGolyer Library, Southern Methodist University, Dallas

HEH   Henry E. Huntington Biographical File, Henry E. Huntington Library, San Marino, CA

HL   Henry E. Huntington Library, San Marino, CA

IID   Imperial Irrigation District Library and Archives, El Centro, CA

JMP   John Muir Papers, Holt-Atherton Center for Regional Studies, University of the Pacific, Stockton, CA

NA-W   National Archives, Washington, DC

SP-A   Southern Pacific Company, Letter Press Books . . . , Washington, DC, Attorneys (67 vols., 1866–1908), Southern Pacific Land Company Records, San Francisco

SP-CS   Southern Pacific Company, Corporate Secretary's Files, Southern Pacific Company Records, San Francisco

SP-E   Southern Pacific Company, Executive Department Permanent Files, Southern Pacific Company Records, San Francisco

SP-H   Southern Pacific Company Records, Houston

SP-L   Southern Pacific Land Company Records, San Francisco

SP-PR   Southern Pacific Company, Public Relations Department Permanent Files, Southern Pacific Company Records, San Francisco

SU   Department of Special Collections, Stanford University

TCID   Truckee-Carson Irrigation District Records, Nevada Historical Society, Reno

USBR   U.S. Bureau of Reclamation Records, National Archives, Denver

UTA   Barker Texas History Center, University of Texas, Austin

ZC-SP   Daniel K. Zumwalt Correspondence, Southern Pacific Land Company
          Records, San Francisco

1   Building the Southern Pacific Company

The quotation in the chapter title is from Collis P. Huntington, in George Kraus, *High Road to Promontory: Building the Central Pacific (now the Southern Pacific) across the High Sierra* (Palo Alto: American West Publishing Company, 1969), 72. In late 1863, a grim Huntington expressed concern about his railroad's ability to surmount California's Sierra Nevada and complete the transcontinental line.

1. Peter R. Decker, *Fortunes and Failures: White Collar Mobility in Nineteenth-Century San Francisco* (Cambridge: Harvard University Press, 1978), 32–59, 147–59; Ward McAfee, *California's Railway Era, 1850–1911* (San Marino: Golden West Books, 1973), 15ff.; Gerald D. Nash, *State Government and Economic Development: A History of Administrative Policies in California, 1849–1933* (Berkeley: Institute of Governmental Studies, University of California, 1964), 1–136; James J. Rawls and Richard J. Orsi, eds., *A Golden State: Mining and Economic Development in Gold Rush California* (Berkeley: University of California Press, for the California Historical Society, 1999), passim, but especially chap. 12 by A. C. W. Bethel, "The Golden Skein: California's Gold-Rush Transportation Network," 250–75; William Deverell, *Railroad Crossing: Californians and the Railroad, 1850–1910* (Berkeley: University of California Press, 1994), 1–33.

2. Richard V. Francaviglia and Jimmy L. Bryan, Jr., "'Are We Chimerical in this Opinion?' Visions of a Pacific Railroad and Westward Expansion before 1845," *Pacific Historical Review* 71 (May 2002): 179–202; and D. W. Meinig, *The Shaping of America: A Geographical Perspective on 500 Years of History; Vol. 3: Transcontinental America, 1850–1915* (New Haven: Yale University Press, 1998), 1–28; for California, McAfee, *California's Railroad Era*, 15–43. California U.S. senator William Guin introduced an unsuccessful transcontinental railway bill in 1853.

3. James John Campilio, "A History of the Sacramento Valley Railroad up to 1865" (M.A. thesis, University of Southern California, 1934); Robert O. Briggs, "The Sacramento Valley Railroad" (M.A. thesis, Sacramento State College, 1954).

4. James E. Vance, Jr., *Geography and Urban Evolution in the San Francisco Bay Area* (Berkeley: Institute of Governmental Studies, University of California, 1964), 36–47; Mel Scott, *The San Francisco Bay Area: A Metropolis in Perspective,* 2nd ed. (Berkeley: University of California Press, 1985), 39–70.

5. Carl I. Wheat, "A Sketch of the Life of Theodore D. Judah," *California Historical Society Quarterly* 4 (September 1925): 219–70; Helen Hinckley, *Rails from the West: A Biography of Theodore D. Judah* (San Marino: Golden West Books, 1969).

6. On the origin and construction of the Central Pacific Railroad, I have relied especially on Kraus, *High Road to Promontory;* Robert Edgar Riegel, *The Story of the*

Western Railroads: From 1852 through the Reign of the Giants (Lincoln: University of Nebraska Press, 1964 [1926]), 1–94; *Southern Pacific's First Century: Indexed Edition* (San Francisco: Southern Pacific Public Relations Department, 1955), 3–15; David Haward Bain, *Empire Express: Building the First Transcontinental Railroad* (New York: Viking Penguin, 1999); David Lavender, *The Great Persuader* [Collis P. Huntington] (Garden City, NY: Doubleday, 1970); Maury Klein, *Union Pacific: The Birth of a Railroad, 1862–1893* (Garden City, NY: Doubleday, 1987); John Hoyt Williams, *A Great and Shining Road: The Epic Story of the Transcontinental Railroad* (New York: Times Books, 1988); and John Debo Galloway, *The First Transcontinental Railroad: Central Pacific, Union Pacific* (New York: Simmons-Boardman, 1950). In general, I will not make further reference to these books in the following notes, but the story, which is inherently chronological, can be followed in all of the works. Collis P. Huntington left two unpublished and hitherto unnoticed accounts of his role in the founding and building of the Central Pacific: Huntington to James Speyer, New York, December 6, 1899, and Collis P. Huntington Autobiographical Materials, "Central Pacific" (ms.), 29ff., both in box 238, *CPH.* According to Huntington, it was he, intrigued by Judah's inchoate scheme, who agreed to finance the incorporation of the company and the initial survey and who recruited the original eight investors, including Hopkins, Stanford, and Crocker.

An obvious omission from the above list is Stephen E. Ambrose, *Nothing Like It in the World: The Men Who Built the Transcontinental Railroad, 1863–1869* (New York: Simon & Schuster, 2000), a recent best-seller, though much criticized by reviewers familiar with railroad and western history. Error-ridden and generally unreliable, the work also depends too often on weak sources and labors under an unfortunate, unsupportable prior agenda: to celebrate and exaggerate the contributions of the engineers like Judah, who technically designed the road, while demonizing the financiers and businessmen, such as the Big Four, who, though sullied in deed and reputation, were nevertheless much more responsible for the eventual completion and operation of the transcontinental. Ambrose qualified his judgment somewhat in *To America: Personal Reflections of an Historian* (New York: Simon & Schuster, 2002), chap. 4, published posthumously.

7. Lavender, *Great Persuader;* Norman E. Tutorow, *Leland Stanford: Man of Many Careers* (Menlo Park, CA: Pacific Coast Publishers, 1971), and *The Governor: The Life and Legacy of Leland Stanford,* 2 vols. (Spokane: Arthur H. Clark Co., 2004); Bunyan Hadley Andrew, "Charles Crocker" (M.A. thesis, University of California, Berkeley, 1931); Ralph Cioffi, "Mark Hopkins, Inside Man of the Big Four" (M.A. thesis, University of California, Berkeley, 1951); B. B. Redding, *A Sketch of the Life of Mark Hopkins* (San Francisco: A. L. Bancroft & Co., 1881); Kraus, *High Road to Promontory,* 294–300.

8. The Central Pacific's difficulties with finance, engineering, labor, political and business rivalries, light traffic, shortages, and high supply and equipment prices were reviewed by longtime company chief engineer William Hood, "Building Southern Pacific Lines," *Southern Pacific Bulletin* (May 1924): 34.

9. Stuart Daggett, *Chapters on the History of the Southern Pacific* (New York: Augustus M. Kelley, 1966 [1922]), 16; Lavender, *Great Persuader,* 99. Actually, Judah knew little about railroad finance and construction costs, and even his revised construction-cost estimates were again wrong. Although the final figures are elusive, the cost of building

the Central Pacific as far as Nevada turned out to be much more than Judah's estimate of $13 million, probably at least twice as much. See, for example, Williams, *Great and Shining Road,* 283–87, for discussion of Congress's Pacific Railroad Commission's 1888 estimate for the entire road to Ogden of $36 million, which was probably substantially less than the true cost. In 1867, Huntington reported that the cost of building through the mountains alone would total $15 million, and somewhat over $30 million as far as Nevada; Kraus, *High Road to Promontory,* 187–88.

10. McAfee, *California's Railroad Era,* 57ff.; Deverell, *Railroad Crossing,* 1–56.

11. Wallace D. Farnham, "The Pacific Railroad Act of 1862," *Nebraska History* 43 (September 1962).

12. Carter Goodrich, *Government Promotion of American Canals and Railroads, 1800–1890* (New York: Columbia University Press, 1960); Nash, *State Government and Economic Development,* 10–26, 42–62.

13. Deverell, *Railroad Crossing,* passim, esp. 28–33, 126ff.; McAfee, *California's Railroad Era,* 62ff.

14. *Sacramento Union,* January 8 and 9, February 23 and 27, 1863.

15. Kraus, *High Road to Promontory,* 62–71; Lavender, *Great Persuader,* 136–40; Williams, *Great and Shining Road,* 62–68.

16. Walton Bean, *California: An Interpretive History* (New York: McGraw-Hill, 1968), 214; Ambrose, *Nothing Like It in the World,* 116–17.

17. Even the adulatory Stephen E. Ambrose acknowledged that Judah made serious engineering errors and could lie, cheat, bribe, and practice conflict of interest with the best of them; *Nothing Like It in the World,* 71, 75, 103–104, 124. See also Lavender, *Great Persuader,* 106–110. Richard White, "Information, Markets, and Corruption: Transcontinental Railroads in the Gilded Age," *Journal of American History* 90 (June 2003): 19–43, analyzes corruption, especially the manipulation and falsification of financial information, by the transcontinental railways, and particularly by Huntington and the other associates.

18. Collis P. Huntington, quoted in Kraus, *High Road to Promontory,* 72; Lavender, *Great Persuader,* 141; *Sacramento Union,* October 27, 1863.

19. Detail about supplies, operating equipment, and machinery Huntington bought, how he shipped it around Cape Horn or overland, costs, and problems finding supplies in the required great volume, arranging for shipping, and making payments, including enormous federal Civil War sales taxes, is in valuable, little-known documents at *CRRM,* especially "Record of Invoices in New York by Collis P. Huntington," vols. 1–4 (ms., 1863ff.). Almost all Huntington's shipments were by the dangerous sea route around the Horn, which took at least four to six months. The Central Pacific lost millions of dollars' worth of supplies when ships sank or were disabled and had to be towed to foreign ports, where they were commonly condemned, sometimes along with their cargoes. Even if they survived condemnation, the railroad's shipments had to be unloaded and reloaded into other hulls, causing added delay, expense, and supply shortages at the construction front; see also Hood, "Building Southern Pacific Lines," 3–4.

20. Lavender, *Great Persuader,* 180–81, 190ff., 203ff.; White, "Information, Markets,

and Corruption," 19–43. Huntington's reputation, in Julius Grodinsky, *Transcontinental Railway Strategy, 1869–1893: A Study of Businessmen* (Philadelphia: University of Pennsylvania Press, 1962), passim, for example 24ff., 41ff.; Dolores Greenberg, *Financiers and Railroads, 1869–1889: A Study of Morton, Bliss & Company* (Newark, NJ: University of Delaware Press, 1980), 178ff.; Wallace D. Farnham, "Shadows from the Gilded Age: Pacific Railwaymen and the Race for Promontory—or Ogden?" in *The Golden Spike,* ed. David E. Miller (Salt Lake City: University of Utah Press, 1973), 1–22.

21. Construction techniques and equipment used over the Sierra and across the Great Basin can be viewed in hundreds of documentary photographs taken by Alfred A. Hart, the Central Pacific's official photographer; see Mead B. Kibbey, *The Railroad Photographs of Alfred A. Hart, Artist* (Sacramento: California State Library Foundation, 1996). For Andrew J. Russell's photos of the Union Pacific's construction across the Great Plains and Rockies, see Barry B. Combs, *Westward to Promontory: Building Across the Plains and Mountains* (Oakland: Crown Publishers, with the cooperation of the Oakland Museum and Union Pacific Corporation, 1986).

22. *Sacramento Union,* March 26 and April 26, 1864.

23. Theodore Judah had conceived of the Dutch Flat Road as a constant outlet and source of business for the Central Pacific, as well as an aid to rail construction through the rugged Sierra Nevada. The road served both purposes well; Thomas Frederick Howard, *Sierra Crossing: First Roads to California* (Berkeley: University of California Press, 1998), 168–74.

24. George Kraus, "Chinese Laborers and the Construction of the Central Pacific," *Utah Historical Quarterly* 37 (1969): 41–57; Alexander P. Saxton, "The Army of Canton in the High Sierra," *Pacific Historical Review* 35 (1966): 141–52; Ping Chiu, *Chinese Labor in California, 1850–1880: An Economic Study* (Madison: State Historical Society of Wisconsin, 1963); Williams, *Great and Shining Road,* 94–100.

25. Historians commonly state that the Central Pacific fired its Chinese workers upon completion of the line, and they blame California's depression beginning in late 1869 and the labor and anti-Chinese agitation that followed on the flooding of the labor market by the unemployed workers; Bean, *California: An Interpretive History,* 220. Actually, the company did not release its workers, or at least very many of them, because from mid-1869 onward it continued to employ thousands of Chinese for maintenance, operations, to rebuild hastily constructed portions of the transcontinental line, and to build many new lines, such as the Southern Pacific and California & Oregon railroads. Many of the same Sierra crews, and under the same foremen, in the 1870s built the Southern Pacific Railroad down the San Joaquin Valley and through southern California, and in the 1880s constructed the company's Texas and Oregon lines, resulting in great efficiency and speed; Hood, "Building Southern Pacific Lines," 4; Alexander Saxton, *The Indispensable Enemy: Labor and the Anti-Chinese Movement in California* (Berkeley: University of California Press, 1971), 66. Regarding Texas, see Alton K. Briggs, "The Archeology of 1882 Labor Camps on the Southern Pacific Railroad in Val Verde County, Texas" (M.A. thesis, University of Texas, Austin, 1977), passim, esp. 1–39; Southern Pacific Railroad, "Chinese Workers [in Texas]" (Chinese file No. 24, "Railroads"), Institute of Texan Cultures, San Antonio; and Edward J. M. Rhoads, "The

Chinese in Texas," *Southwestern Historical Quarterly* 81 (July 1977): 8–12, and (January 1978): 1–36. A longtime company engineer who worked on Central Pacific construction, Joel O. Wilder, described the continued employment of the Chinese crews and the retirement of the last surviving Sierra workers as late as the 1920s, in his reminiscences, "My Half Century of Railroad Service," *Southern Pacific Bulletin* 9 (August 1920): 7. Manuscript pay records of Southern Pacific lines throughout the Far West and Southwest attest to the many Chinese who remained with the company; located at *CRRM,* the Oregon Historical Society, Portland, and the Arizona State University Library, Tempe.

Myths commonly associated with the railroad's Chinese workers include the oft-repeated, likely apocryphal, story that, to chip out ledges for the Central Pacific along high Sierra cliffs, the Chinese were lowered over the edges of the precipices to work from hanging baskets, often falling to their deaths. No credible firsthand evidence supports this notion, and much evidence, not to mention common sense and the laws of physics, contradicts it. For a recent, straightforward passing-along of the false Chinese-in-the-basket tale, along with other myths about the Central Pacific's Chinese, see Ambrose, *Nothing Like It in the World,* 149–65, esp. 156–57.

26. Donald Warrin and Geoffrey L. Gomes, *Land as Far as the Eye Can See: Portuguese in the Old West* (Spokane: Arthur H. Clark, 2001), 134–41.

27. Joel Wilder, "My Half Century of Railroad Service," *Southern Pacific Bulletin* 9 (October 1920): 22–23, and (November 1920): 23–25; Hood, "Building Southern Pacific Lines," 3–4; Clarence M. Wooster, "Meadow Lake City and a Winter at Cisco in the Sixties," *California Historical Society Quarterly* 18 (1939): 149–56, and "Early Days on the Mountain Division," 23 (1944): 117–22; George Kraus, "Central Pacific Construction Vignettes," in *Golden Spike,* ed. Miller, 45–61.

28. *Sacramento Union,* April 8, 1867, February 20, 1869; for problems caused by snow blockades of Donner Pass, see *Sacramento Record-Union,* March 17, 18, 20, and 21, 1882.

29. *Sacramento Union,* August 30, September 2, November 30, and December 9, 1867; John R. Signor, *Donner Pass: Southern Pacific's Sierra Crossing* (Menlo Park, CA: Golden West Books, 1985), 11–50.

30. Klein, *Union Pacific: The Birth of a Railroad,* 1–234.

31. *San Francisco Bulletin,* May 8 and 11, 1869; *Alta California* (San Francisco), May 8, 11, and 12, 1869; *Sacramento Union,* May 10, 11, and 27, 1869; Kraus, *High Road to Promontory,* 262ff.; Bain, *Empire Express,* 645–72; special centennial issues of the *Utah Historical Quarterly* 37 (Winter 1969) and *The American West* 6 (May 1969).

32. Leland Stanford to Collis P. Huntington, telegram, Promontory, May 11, 1869, and Mark Hopkins to Huntington, Sacramento, June 11, 1869, *CPH.* Hopkins went on to defend the public ceremony as valuable for the company because of the many "enthusiastic individuals" who praised the achievement and expected a celebration. He also justified Stanford's taking the limelight. Because Stanford had "shoveled the first dirt" in taking on the railroad's opponents, Hopkins thought, "there was a propriety, as well as sound policy in his driving the last spike & a gold one." Stanford returned Huntington's dislike in kind; see Lavender, *Great Persuader,* 228.

33. Decker, *Fortunes and Failures,* 159ff.

34. Grodinsky, *Transcontinental Railway Strategy*, 30–32; Tutorow, *Stanford*, 115–17; Lavender, *Great Persuader*, 285ff.

35. Charles Crocker, into the late 1870s, opposed Huntington's strategy of expansion and consolidation. In 1877, he wrote Huntington that he was "sick of building more roads" and threatened not to approve any more expenses other than for operations. "I am for getting out of debt," he advised. Crocker also worried that, because of the growing political opposition to the company, it was "a very bad policy" for the Big Four to own all the railroads in California. At least regarding politics, Crocker was prophetic. See Crocker to Huntington, San Francisco, May 25 and November 22, 1877, in Mark Hopkins et al., *Letters from Mark Hopkins, Leland Stanford, Charles Crocker, and David D. Colton to Collis P. Huntington, from August 27th, 1869, to December 30th, 1879* (New York: John C. Rankin Co., 1891), 95, 153–59.

36. *Oakland Daily Transcript*, October 30 and November 6, 8, and 9, 1869; Beth Bagwell, *Oakland, The Story of a City* (Novato, CA: Presidio Press, 1982), 50–62. For the completion of the key link between Sacramento and San Francisco Bay, the Western Pacific, see *Sacramento Union*, June 3 and 20, 1867, and April 2 and 4, 1868, and *Alta California* (San Francisco), April 3, 1868.

37. John H. Kemble, "The Big Four at Sea: The History of the Oriental and Occidental Steamship Company," *Huntington Library Quarterly* 3 (April 1940): 330–58.

38. The Big Four's acquisitions of California rail lines were listed in *Sacramento Union*, January 1, 1871. The records of dozens of these subsidiaries of the Central Pacific, later the Southern Pacific Company, are at *CRRM*. For expansion in the 1860s and 1870s, including details and dates of acquisitions and mergers, see Southern Pacific Company, Executive Department, "Historical Data . . . Central Pacific Railway" (typescript, 1943), *SP-E; Southern Pacific's First Century: Indexed Edition*, 15ff. and 25–26. For the building of the California & Oregon up the Sacramento Valley, see William Harland Boyd, *The Shasta Route, 1863–1887: The Railroad Link between the Sacramento and the Columbia* (New York: Arno Press, 1981), 28–40.

39. On the Big Four's acquisition of the Southern Pacific Railroad, see Southern Pacific Company, "Historical Memoranda" (typescript, ca. 1960s), *SP-CS*.

40. Detail about construction methods, materials, machinery, prices, wages, and subcontracting in building early Central and Southern Pacific roadbeds, tracks, stations, shops, hotels, employee housing, waterworks, and other railroad facilities is in the financial records for construction of the San Joaquin Valley and southern California segments by the Contract and Finance Company, the Big Four's successor to Crocker and Co.; Contract and Finance Company, Financial Records, "Day Book, 1873–1875," and "Timber Day Book, 1873–1874," mss., *CRRM*. Also evident is how the Big Four maximized personal profits from construction. The associates' Southern Pacific Railroad paid the associates' Contract and Finance Company to build its rail lines. The Contract and Finance Company in turn bought its lumber, paint, hardware, tools, and much of its machinery from Sacramento's Huntington-Hopkins Hardware Store (owned, of course, by Huntington and Hopkins), often spending hundreds if not thousands of dollars *per day* during construction periods; see, for example, "Timber Day Book," 138ff. For reminiscences of a worker who built the valley line, see Clarence M. Wooster, "Build-

ing the Railroad down the San Joaquin in 1871," *California Historical Society Quarterly* 18 (1939): 22–31; for rail construction down the valley and urban and agricultural effects, see Richard Harold Smith, "Towns along the Tracks: Railroad Strategy and Town Promotion in the San Joaquin Valley, California" (Ph.D. diss., University of California, Los Angeles, 1976), 113–282.

41. *Alta California* (San Francisco), August 10, 1876; *Sacramento Record-Union,* August 11, 1876; Bill Yenne, *Southern Pacific* (Greenwich, CT: Bison Books, 1985), 34–39; *Southern Pacific's First Century: Indexed Edition,* 18–19 and 24–25 for photos of the Tehachapi Loop; John Signor, *Tehachapi (Southern Pacific-Santa Fe)* (San Marino: Golden West Books, 1983), passim; William D. Middleton, *Landmarks on the Iron Road: Two Centuries of North American Railroad Engineering* (Bloomington: Indiana University Press, 1999), 89–92.

42. *Sacramento Record-Union,* August 23, September 6 and 7, 1876; *Alta California* (San Francisco), September 5 and 6, 1876; *Los Angeles Evening Express,* September 6, 1876; Marie Harrington, *A Golden Spike* (Mission Hills, CA: San Fernando Valley Historical Society, 1976); Phil Serpico, *Railroading through the Antelope Valley* (Palmdale, CA: Omni Publications, 2000), 11–96.

43. Robert M. Fogelson, *The Fragmented Metropolis: Los Angeles, 1850–1930* (Cambridge: Harvard University Press, 1967), 46–58; Robert Glass Cleland, *The Cattle on a Thousand Hills: Southern California, 1850–1880* (San Marino: The Huntington Library, 1964), 224–26. A good account of early railroads in Los Angeles, including the Los Angeles & Independence and its eventual purchase by the Southern Pacific in 1877, is Paul R. Spitzzeri, "The Road to Independence: The Los Angeles and Independence Railroad and the Conception of a City," *Southern California Quarterly* 83 (Spring 2001): 23–58. On the line between Los Angeles and its harbor, see John W. Robinson, *Southern California's First Railroad: The Los Angeles & San Pedro Railroad, 1869–1873* (Los Angeles: Dawson's Book Shop, 1978). For the Southern Pacific's entry into Los Angeles, the city's subsidy, and the railroad's conversion of that city from cow town into metropolis, see Larry Mullaly and Bruce Petty, *The Southern Pacific in Los Angeles, 1873–1996* (San Marino: Golden West Books and Los Angeles Railroad Heritage Foundation, 2002), 11ff.

44. *Sacramento Record-Union,* April 16, 25, and 28, May 22 and 28, October 1, 5, and 10, 1877; *San Francisco Bulletin,* February 12 and 17, 1877, September 10, 1878; "Resolution of the Mayor and Common Council of the Village of Yuma, April 14, 1877," and "Articles of Agreement between Yuma Village and Phineas Banning; Assignment to the Southern Pacific Railroad, April 14, 1877," Banning Company Collection, *HL;* *Arizona Sentinel* (Yuma), March 18, May 27, August 5, November 25, 1876, March 3, 1877. The Southern Pacific Railroad's construction across the Tehachapis, through Los Angeles, eastward across the desert, and to Yuma, as well as competition with Tom Scott of the Pennsylvania Railroad for control of the southern transcontinental route, were discussed by Collis P. Huntington and the Big Four's junior associate in California, David D. Colton, in the infamous "Colton Letters," the originals of which are in the Collis P. Huntington–David Colton Correspondence, 1876–1879, *HEH.* The original letters, by the way, contain many minor and a few major variations from the versions that most

historians have used, those published by the *San Francisco Chronicle,* December 23, 1883, and republished by other anti-Southern Pacific papers across the country during Mrs. Colton's sensational lawsuit against the surviving members of the Big Four.

45. *Southern Pacific's First Century: Indexed Edition,* 30–31, 37; Loren Nicholson, *Rails across the Ranchos* (Fresno: Valley Publishers, 1980), passim; and John R. Signor, *Southern Pacific's Coast Route* (Wilton, CA: Signature Press, 1995); David F. Myrick, "Santa Barbara County Railroads: A Centennial History," *Noticias* [Santa Barbara Historical Society] 32 (Summer-Fall 1987): 1–63.

46. Daggett, *Chapters,* 140–41, lists many branches extended from the company's main lines in California by the end of the 1870s.

47. Just in California, the Southern Pacific system acquired large federal land grants to four of its railroads: the Central Pacific, the California & Oregon, the Western Pacific, and the Southern Pacific. In the 1880s, the company acquired the federal land grant of the Oregon & California in Oregon, as well as state grants of a dozen Texas predecessor lines. See chapters 3, 4, and 10 regarding the tangled relationships between the railroad and, for example, the U.S. Department of the Interior occasioned by the federal land grants. For the connection between subsidies and the railroad's corruption of politics and finance, see White, "Information, Markets, and Corruption," 19–43.

48. Collis P. Huntington to David Colton, April 12, 1875, Huntington Collection, Mariner's Museum, Newport News, Virginia, quoted in Grodinsky, *Transcontinental Railway Strategy,* 299; Lavender, *Great Persuader,* 318–28.

49. *San Francisco Bulletin,* September 10, 1878, February 4, March 28, May 14, June 25, 1879, March 30, November 5, 1880; *Arizona Sentinel* (Yuma), October 12, November 23, 1878, January 4, February 8, September 27, 1879, March 20, 23, 27, September 4, 1880, January 14, 1882; *Arizona Star* (Tucson), March 25, September 10, 1880; *Phoenix Herald,* October 4, 1879.

50. *Alta California* (San Francisco), March 9, 12, and 22, 1880; *Sacramento Record-Union,* March 9, 10, and 19, 1880; *Arizona Star* (Tucson), March 25, 1880, March 24, 1881. For construction and early operation of the Southern Pacific in Arizona and New Mexico, see David F. Myrick, *Railroads of Arizona, Vol. I: The Southern Roads* (Berkeley: Howell-North Books, 1975), passim, esp. 13–138 and 164ff. (on Huntington's rivalries with Tom Scott and Jay Gould over control of the route from Arizona to Texas), which also contains numerous useful historical and contemporary photographs; Myrick, *New Mexico's Railroads: An Historical Survey* (Golden, CO: Colorado Railroad Museum, 1970), 58–94; Myrick, "Notes on Railroad Construction in Arizona, New Mexico, and Texas" (ms., September-October 1966), *SP-PR; Southern Pacific's First Century: Indexed Edition,* 17 and 20. From Tucson, the railroad also received a right-of-way and land for a station and yards; "Deed for Land Transferred from City of Tucson to Southern Pacific Railroad Company" (ms. copy, August 25, 1879), Southern Pacific Railroad Papers, Arizona Historical Society, Tucson.

51. *Southern Pacific's First Century: Indexed Edition,* 20–21; Mildred L. Jordan, "Railroads in the El Paso Area" (M.A. thesis, University of Texas, El Paso, 1957), 103–31.

52. *San Antonio Express,* January 13, 1881; *San Francisco Call,* January 13, 1883; *Sacramento Record-Union,* January 13, 1883; *Southern Pacific's First Century: Indexed Edition,*

20–25; Jordan, "Railroads in the El Paso Area," 103–31; Earle B. Young, *Tracks to the Sea: Galveston and Western Railroad Development, 1866–1900* (College Station: Texas A & M University Press, 1999), passim, esp. 4–6, 46–47, 85–92, 101–21; Grodinsky, *Transcontinental Railroad Strategy,* 170–73; Lavender, *Great Persuader,* 336.

53. *Sacramento Record-Union,* January 14, March 22, 1882, January 13 and 26, 1883; *San Antonio Express,* January 12, 1883; *El Paso Herald,* October 4, 18, November 22, 1882; *Southern Pacific's First Century: Indexed Edition,* 25.

54. Charles S. Potts, *Railroad Transportation in Texas* (Austin: University of Texas Press, 1909), 45–51; S. G. Reed, *A History of the Texas Railroads* (Houston: St. Clair Publishing Co., 1941), passim, esp. 190–282; S. G. Reed, "Southern Pacific System in Texas," in *The Handbook of Texas,* ed. Walter Prescott Webb (Austin: Texas State Historical Association, 1952), 2:641–43; Joseph L. Bart, Jr., "The Southern Pacific System in Texas," in *The Handbook of Texas: A Supplement* (Austin: Texas State Historical Association, 1976), 905; Southern Pacific Company, *A Hundred Years of Progress,* A Souvenir Reprint from the *Southern Pacific Bulletin (Texas and Louisiana Lines),* May–June 1951; "Southern Pacific Lines in Texas and Louisiana," in "Historical Memoranda" (typescript, ca. 1960s), II, chap. 7, 1–8, the "official" corporate history of the Atlantic System lines, *SP-CS;* H. M. Mayo, "History of the Southern Pacific Lines in Texas" (typescript, ca. 1927), Southern Pacific Company, Public Relations Department Historical File, *SP-H;* "Corporate History of the Galveston, Harrisburg and San Antonio Railway and Predecessor Companies as of June 30, 1918" (typescript, ca. 1918), Southern Pacific Company, Public Relations Department Historical File, *SP-H;* Claude Elliott, "The Building of the Southern Pacific Railroad through Texas" (M.A. thesis, University of Texas, Austin, 1928), passim; Robert S. Maxwell, *Whistle in the Piney Woods: Paul Bremond and the Houston, East and West Texas Railway* (Texas Gulf Coast Historical Association, Publication Series, vol. 7, no. 2, November 1963), 46–50, 62–63; Clifford R. Morrill [superintendent of El Paso Division, 1919–1939], "Railroad History: El Paso Division, Southern Pacific" (typescript, Texas A & M University Library, 1971), copy at *DG;* and important manuscript incorporation papers, merger agreements, and corporate histories of twenty Texas railroads that had merged into the Galveston, Harrisburg & San Antonio (SP) by 1918, Houston & Texas Central Railroad Company Collection, 1876–1918, especially "Corporate History of the Galveston, Harrisburg & San Antonio Railway Company" (typescript, Houston, June 30, 1918), *DG.*

55. James P. Baughman, *Charles Morgan and the Development of Southern Transportation* (Nashville: Vanderbilt University Press, 1968), 223–35; Southern Pacific Company, "History of the Morgan Line" (mimeo, 1948), passim, esp. 7–8, *SP-E;* Richard V. Francaviglia, *From Sail to Steam: Four Centuries of Texas Maritime History, 1500–1900* (Austin: University of Texas Press, 1998), 128ff., 221ff., 235ff., 262ff., for the general history of the Morgan Steamship Line; *S.S. Mumus, the Palatial New Passenger Steamer of the Southern Pacific Atlantic Steamship Lines, Plying between New Orleans and Havana, Winter Season, 1906–07* (New Orleans: Passenger Traffic Department, Southern Pacific Atlantic Steamship Lines, 1907), for contemporary detail on the company's steamer service around the Caribbean and to the east coast. The Morgan Line continued to expand

and buy out other shipping companies well into the twentieth century, before the Southern Pacific shut it down in the early 1940s. For Southern Pacific steamships, ferries, and riverboats, see Don L. Hofsommer, *The Southern Pacific, 1901–1985* (College Station: Texas A & M Press, 1985), 150–55. See also, Grodinsky, *Transcontinental Railway Strategy,* 170–73, 298–301, for insights into the Huntington-Gould rivalry for control of Texas and southern transcontinental rail markets, culminating in the important agreement of 1881 that helped secure the Southern Pacific Company's stable and prosperous future development. According to Grodinsky, 301, Huntington's consolidation of Southwest and Texas/Louisiana rail and steamship lines was so successful that they carried most transcontinental traffic through the region by the mid-1880s.

56. C. E. Bretherton [vice president of Oregon and California line], "Suggestions for Proposition to the Holders of the First Mortgage Bonds, Oregon and California Railroad Company" (ms., marked confidential, London, October 24, 1884); Collis P. Huntington to Henry Villard, New York, June 2, 1884, in Oregon and California Railroad Company, *Report of the President to the Stockholders* (July 21, 1884), 7; Oregon and California Railroad, Board of Directors, "Minute Books" (ms., 8 vols., 1870–1929, index accompanies each volume), esp. vol. 3: minutes of meeting of June 8, 1887, vol. 4: minutes of meetings of October 3, December 5–6 and 26, 1887, and March 26, April 10, and June 11, 1888; all in Southern Pacific Collection, Oregon Historical Society, Portland. Also *The Money Market Review* (a European periodical), February 26, 1887, copy in the Frank Bryson Gill Papers, ms. 1591, box 4, folder 7, Oregon Historical Society; and for the early history of the Oregon line, John Tilson Ganoe, "The History of the Oregon & California Railroad," *Oregon Historical Quarterly* 26 (1926): 236–83, 330–52.

57. *Sacramento Record-Union,* April 10 and 16, June 20 and 23, September 7, 1883, August 15, 1884, August 4 and 30, 1886, January 13, March 18 and 29, May 4, 10, 27, and 30, June 1, October 19, November 21, and December 17, 19, and 20, 1887; Papers Relating to the . . . Southern Pacific Company's Linkage of the Oregon and California and the . . . California and Oregon Railroad at Ashland . . . December 17, 1887 (one port.), *BL;* George B. Abdill, *This Was Railroading* (Seattle: Superior Publishing, 1958), 85ff.; Boyd, *Shasta Route,* 88–100; D. C. Jesse Burkhardt, *Backwoods Railroads: Branchlines and Shortlines of Western Oregon* (Pullman: Washington State University Press, 1994), 1–52, 77–124, 139–44.

58. Daggett, *Chapters,* 142ff., 360ff.; Lavender, *Great Persuader,* 339ff., 344ff.

59. *San Francisco Bulletin,* April 1, 1885; *San Francisco Call,* April 1 and 2, 1885; *San Francisco Examiner,* April 2, 1885; *Sacramento Record-Union,* April 1, 2, and 14, 1885.

60. *Southern Pacific's First Century: Indexed Edition,* 31–32; George T. Clark, *Leland Stanford: War Governor of California, Railroad Builder, and Founder of Stanford University* (Stanford: Stanford University Press, 1931), 338ff.; Lavender, *Great Persuader,* 341–42, 344; Grodinsky, *Transcontinental Railway Strategy,* 298–301; and Daggett, *Chapters,* 140–53. In 1889, a reporter asked Huntington, then in San Francisco, about Stanford. "Stanford is East, but he does not do any railroad work," sneered Huntington. "He is a politician now. He leaves all railroad matters to the rest of us"; *San Francisco Bulletin,* March 27, 1889.

61. Lavender, *Great Persuader,* 206–207, 228, 252, 273–74, 344ff.; Clark, *Stanford,* 436–37; Tutorow, *Stanford,* 263–70, and *The Governor,* 807–50.

62. *San Francisco Chronicle,* April 11, 12, 16, and 17, 1890; *San Francisco Call,* April 11, 12, 16, and 17, 1890; *San Francisco Bulletin,* April 9, 1890; *Sacramento Bee,* April 10, 1890. The revolution in Southern Pacific leadership was generally unpopular with Californians, who still saw former Civil War governor Stanford favorably, more devoted than Huntington to the public's welfare; Clark, *Stanford,* 436ff.; Lavender, *Great Persuader,* 359ff.; Daggett, *Chapters,* 217–19; Tutorow, *Stanford,* 263–70.

63. Historians often characterize Huntington as an ogre. "He ran the CP and then the SP like a medieval king," Stephen F. Ambrose recently wrote; *Nothing Like It in the World,* 379. Clearly, Huntington was nothing of the sort toward his employees. His correspondence includes many long letters to and from lower executives, with his staff often expressing frank opinions contrary to their boss's. While Huntington insisted on personal loyalty, he encouraged independence of thought and action in his subordinates, solicited their opinions on important matters, and frequently took their advice, even if it ran against his own inclinations. According to Southern Pacific comptroller William Mahl, who worked closely with Huntington and knew him as well as any associate, Huntington's genius as a manager was to find excellent men to run parts of the railroad, to set general policy, and then to give subordinates freedom and respect in achieving objectives: Huntington "allowed all his men all possible latitude, indicating to them only the general policy to be observed . . . leaving them to work out the details to insure the desired ends"; Mahl, "Memoirs" (ms., 1913), passim, esp. F-17–21, William Mahl Papers, *UTA.*

64. *Oakland Tribune, San Francisco Bulletin, San Francisco Examiner, San Francisco Chronicle,* July 16, 1895; Hubert Howe Bancroft, "Life of Alban N. Towne, Prepared for the Chronicles of the Builders of the Commonwealth and Material for its Preparation, 1886–1891" (16 folders), *BL.*

65. *Southern Pacific's First Century: Indexed Edition,* 32.

66. Alfred D. Chandler, *The Visible Hand: The Managerial Revolution in American Business* (Cambridge: Belknap Press of Harvard University Press, 1977), 124–25.

67. Daggett, *Chapters,* 252–53, 255–56, 258–59, 292, 354–63; Hofsommer, *Southern Pacific,* 26–27. Maury Klein describes Stubbs as a "traffic genius," while discussing Harriman's elevation of Stubbs to head of traffic for the entire Union–Southern Pacific system in *The Life and Legend of E. H. Harriman* (Chapel Hill: University of North Carolina Press, 2000), 273–75.

68. Mills's activities as head land agent and his influence over the company's land, water, agricultural, wilderness preservation, and resource-conservation policies are covered in the following chapters. From about 1887 through 1898, Mills also managed the land subdivisions of the Big Four families under the subsidiary firm, the Pacific Improvement Company. Though largely ignored today, Mills was also one of Huntington's major political advisers. His voluminous correspondence with Huntington between 1883 and the president's death in 1900 is preserved especially in two collections: *CPH,* also in a microfilm edition; and *HEH.* A short biography is "Memorial Ascription to the Late William H. Mills," in California State Board of Trade, *California: Resources*

and Possibilities . . . (San Francisco, 1907), 61–62. Two historians have examined Mills's importance in the Southern Pacific Company: on irrigation policy, see Donald J. Pisani, *From Family Farm to Agribusiness: The Irrigation Crusade in California and the West, 1850–1931* (Berkeley: University of California Press, 1984), 17, 294, 297; on political organizing, see Deverell, *Railroad Crossing,* passim.

69. Truckee office: Guy Coates, "Truckee's Early Physicians were a Courageous Breed," *Sierra Sun* (Truckee), March 6–12, 2003.

70. Even at the beginning, its work force of fifteen thousand paid the railroad's hospital insurance fund nearly $10,000 monthly.

71. *Sacramento Union,* April 23, 1869; Central Pacific Railroad Company, *Annual Report . . . 1873* (Sacramento, 1873), 8; J. Roy Jones, M.D., *The Old Central Pacific Hospital* (Sacramento: Western Association of Railway Surgeons, 1960), esp. 5ff.; Jones, *Memories, Men and Medicine: A History of Medicine in Sacramento* (Sacramento: Society for Medical Improvement, 1950), passim, esp. 140ff., 156–57; Henry J. Short, *Railroad Doctors, Hospitals and Associations: Pioneers in Comprehensive Low Cost Medical Care* (Upper Lake, CA: H.J. Short, ca. 1986); Walter Light, *Working for the Railroad: The Organization of Work in the Nineteenth Century* (Princeton: Princeton University Press, 1983), 209; Charles E. Rosenberg, *The Care of Strangers: The Rise of America's Hospital System* (New York: Basic Books, 1987), 113–14, which cites the Central Pacific Railroad hospital as the major example of the emergence of industrial hospitals.

72. *Statement of the Workings of the Railroad Hospital at Sacramento, California, for the Year 1883* (Sacramento: H. S. Crocker & Co., 1884), 9–11.

73. Short, *Railroad Doctors,* 5ff.; Hofsommer, *Southern Pacific,* 174.

74. Short, *Railroad Doctors,* 35ff.; Hofsommer, *Southern Pacific,* 112–13, 174.

75. "Southern Pacific Hospital Department" (ms. map, ca. 1951), *CRRM;* Short, *Railroad Doctors,* 18ff.

76. Collis P. Huntington to J. W. Garrett, president, Baltimore & Ohio Railroad, New York, December 19, 1882, and Huntington to A. B. Nixon, New York, February 1, 1883, *CPH;* Jones, *Old Central Pacific Hospital,* 19ff.; Short, *Railroad Doctors,* 1; Hofsommer, *Southern Pacific,* 251.

77. "William Mahl," *Railway Age* 64 (May 17, 1918): 1260; "William Mahl, Vice-President and Comptroller of the Union Pacific and Southern Pacific Systems" (United Press Syndicate, Bio-Press Service Release No. 1031, ca. 1909), copy in box 2E462, William Mahl Papers, *UTA;* also in Mahl papers, his manuscript "Memoirs" (1913), a useful, if somewhat chaotic, autobiographical document of the inner workings of American railroad companies in the era. Mahl held responsible financial positions under three important railroad entrepreneurs, Huntington, Tom Scott, and Edward H. Harriman. One historian appreciating Mahl's importance is Don Hofsommer (see a short biography in his *Southern Pacific,* 26).

78. T. W. Pierce, president of the Galveston, Harrisburg & San Antonio Railroad, to E. G. Thompson, assistant superintendent, Galveston, Harrisburg & San Antonio Railroad, New York, April 13, 1882; E. H. Miller, Jr., secretary, Southern Pacific Company, to Collis P. Huntington, San Francisco, March 30, 1885; Huntington to Mexico International Railroad Company, New York, September 13, 1888; all in Mahl Papers, *UTA.*

79. Mahl, "Memoirs," passim, esp. F-13–15, Mahl Papers, *UTA.*

80. William Mahl, "Gould System, Southern Pacific Company, and Union Pacific Railway: Mileage, Bonds, and Stocks, December 15, 1890" (ms.); Mahl, "Earnings and Expenses per Mile of Road: Southern Pacific, Union Pacific, Missouri Pacific, and Atchison, December 15, 1890" (ms.), *HEH.*

81. For Mahl's work with the Pacific Improvement Company, and that company's role in Southern Pacific financial stability, see Mahl, "Memoirs," G-1ff. Borrowing heavily to support the rail lines, the Pacific Improvement Company itself owed $36 million in 1893. Although its assets exceeded a whopping $90 million, more than enough to cover its loans, the company had such severe cash-flow problems in meeting its debt payments in 1893 and 1894 that it was saved only by the Big Four interests' personal guarantees of its notes and emergency borrowing from sugar magnate Claus Spreckels. For a history of the company, see Daggett, *Chapters,* 133–35; also, chapter 5.

82. Audit and reorganization and the final separation of the Pacific Improvement Company from the Southern Pacific is discussed in chapter 5.

83. David F. Myrick, "Refinancing and Rebuilding the Central Pacific, 1899–1910," in Miller, *Golden Spike,* 85–117; *Southern Pacific's First Century: Indexed Edition,* 32–33; Daggett, *Chapters,* 395–424.

84. Mahl, "Memoirs," F-22.

85. Ibid.

86. *San Francisco Examiner,* October 1, 1895.

87. Collis P. Huntington to William Mahl, Raquette Lake, New York, August 28, 1898, R30.1, *SP-PR.*

88. "Death Calls William F. Herrin, Chief Counsel," *Southern Pacific Bulletin* 16 (April 1927): 5–6; also, Herrin autobiographical documents in the Oregon State University archives.

89. John P. Young, *Journalism in California* (San Francisco: Chronicle Publishing Co., 1915), 279.

90. Kruttschnitt biography: Kruttschnitt, "Memorandum" (typescript, November 3, 1922), File 090.3–9, Pt. 5, "Consolidation of Railroad's New York Office Files"; and *Testimony of Julius Kruttschnitt, November 22, 1922, Before the Interstate Commerce Commission, Finance Docket No. 2613, In the Matter of the Application of the Southern Pacific Company to Acquire Control by Lease and by Stock Ownership of Central Pacific Railway Company* (Washington, DC: Government Printing Office, 1922); both in *SP-E.* See also, *San Francisco Bulletin,* April 7, 1897; *New York Post,* October 4, 1924; *Southern Pacific Bulletin* 13 (November 1924): 11–12; Hofsommer, *Southern Pacific,* 25–89, passim; *Southern Pacific Bulletin* 14 (May 1925): 3–6.

91. Hofsommer, *Southern Pacific,* 115–16; *Southern Pacific Bulletin* 14 (May 1925): 3.

92. James Thorpe, *Henry Edwards Huntington: A Biography* (Berkeley: University of California Press, 1994), passim, esp. 88–145, 155–64; William B. Friedricks, *Henry E. Huntington and the Creation of Southern California* (Columbus: Ohio State University Press, 1992), passim, esp. 30–47.

93. *San Francisco Examiner,* August 22, 1895.

94. See, for example, *San Francisco Call,* May 6, 1897.

95. Bruce A. MacGregor, *South Pacific Coast: An Illustrated History of the Narrow Gauge South Pacific Coast Railroad* (Berkeley: Howell-North Books, 1968), passim., esp. 190ff.

96. For expansion: Charles F. Crocker to Collis P. Huntington, San Francisco, May 18, 1888, *CPH;* for locations and construction and acquisition dates of these and many railroad properties, see *Southern Pacific's First Century: Indexed Edition,* passim; for the Coast Route specifically, see Nicholson, *Rails through the Ranchos,* passim.

97. *Southern Pacific's First Century: Indexed Edition,* 33–34, 39, 47–48; Neill C. Wilson and Frank J. Taylor, *Southern Pacific: The Roaring Story of a Fighting Railroad* (New York: McGraw-Hill, 1952), 123ff.

98. Burkhardt, *Backwoods Railroads,* passim; Reed, *Texas Railroads,* passim; and "The Southern Pacific System in Texas," in Webb, *Handbook of Texas,* 2:641–43.

99. See Klein, *Harriman,* 255.

100. "Historical Data . . . Central Pacific Railway" (ms., 1943), 9ff., *SP-E;* Hofsommer, *Southern Pacific,* 9ff.; Klein, *Harriman,* 217–21; Daggett, *Chapters,* 425–30; and *Southern Pacific's First Century: Indexed Edition,* 34–37; *Sacramento Record-Union,* February, 1, 1901; *San Francisco Call,* January 29 and February 2, 1901; *San Francisco Chronicle,* February 3, 1901; and follow-up articles and editorials in these and other California newspapers in days and weeks following. Harriman had earlier tried to buy the Central Pacific's line from Ogden west to San Francisco to assure control for the Union Pacific of the entire transcontinental line, but Huntington had refused to sell. A full account of the failure of Henry E. Huntington, Collis's choice for his successor and the odds-on favorite to assume the presidency of the Southern Pacific, to be chosen to lead the company by the bankers in control, and the subsequent decision of the Huntington heirs to sell their stock, is in Thorpe, *Henry Edwards Huntington,* 155–64. More knowledgeable than anyone else about the Southern Pacific's financial affairs, William Mahl, in his "Memoirs" (ms., 1913), F-17–21, also wrote of the changing power structure within the company after Huntington's death and the confusion, conflict, and drift in management, paving the way for the ascendancy of the company's bankers and the Harriman takeover.

101. Hofsommer, *Southern Pacific,* 9–52; Klein, *Harriman,* 217ff., passim; Lloyd J. Mercer, *E. H. Harriman: Master Railroader* (Boston: Twayne Publishers, 1985), 67–87.

102. Klein, *Harriman,* xiii–xiv. The Harriman Lines actively propagated the notion among the contemporary public that it was modernizing the Southern Pacific and making it more public-spirited; for examples of this common newspaper view, see *San Francisco Chronicle,* March 6, May 7, 9, and 14, and October 10, 1903. *Pacific Rural Press* (San Francisco), September 18, 1909, in mourning Harriman's death said he had "made the attitude of the Southern Pacific toward the producers and producing interests of the state . . . distinctly different from its old policy and behavior. It seemed to rejoice in the prosperity of the State's industries, rather than [be] envious of them." For impressive statistics on the Harriman Lines' rebuilding of the Southern Pacific and its higher productivity, see Mercer, *Harriman,* 67–87.

103. "Historical Data . . . Central Pacific Railway" (ms., 1943), 9ff., *SP-E,* the company's account of the modernization; Hofsommer, *Southern Pacific,* 14ff.; Klein, *Har-*

riman, 254–63, 280–82; George Kennan, *E. H. Harriman: A Biography,* 2 vols. (Boston: Houghton Mifflin, 1922), 1:232–85. For the Lucin Cutoff, Middleton, *Landmarks on the Iron Road,* 42–44; David Peterson, *Tale of the Lucin: A Boat, A Railroad and the Great Salt Lake* (Trinidad, CA: Old Waterfront Publishing, 2001), 43–105. For the Montalvo Cutoff on the Southern Pacific Railroad's coast line from Santa Barbara into Los Angeles, see Myrick, "Santa Barbara County Railroads," 60.

104. Kennan, *Harriman,* 1:235–85; Mercer, *Harriman,* 67–87.

105. John H. White, *The Great Yellow Fleet: A History of American Railroad Refrigerator Cars* (San Marino: Golden West Books, 1986), 149ff.; Anthony W. Thompson, Robert J. Church, and Bruce H. Jones, *Pacific Fruit Express* (Wilton, CA: Central Valley Railroad Publications, 1992), passim; see also the account of Pacific Fruit Express in chapter 12.

106. Don Hofsommer says the same in *Southern Pacific,* 13. William Mahl, who continued as the chief comptroller of the Harriman Lines, held that, before Harriman took over, the Southern Pacific was "well-maintained," stood in "fine physical condition," was well-managed, possessed talented leaders in Henry E. Huntington and Julius Kruttschnitt, and having, in contrast to other major railways, survived the Panic of 1893, was financially sound; Mahl, "Memoirs" (ms., 1913), F-17–21.

107. Chief Southern Pacific engineer William F. Hood, who under Huntington planned and under Harriman completed, the improvements, wrote an account in a 1920 letter to retired Southern Pacific Great Basin land agent Robert L. Fulton. It was in 1898, for example, that Huntington ordered the construction of the Lucin Cutoff across the Salt Flats and Great Salt Lake; Hood had completed the engineering and had nearly finished purchasing the heavy-duty steam shovels and other equipment and acquiring the right-of-way when Huntington died in August 1900. Work was then suspended until November 1901, when Harriman ordered it resumed; William Hood to Robert L. Fulton, San Francisco, January 6, 1920, Robert L. Fulton Correspondence and Papers, Nevada Historical Society, Reno. Hood's biography: "Mr. Hood Retires to Seek New Problems," *Southern Pacific Bulletin* 10 (June 1921): 13–15, 20. In 1922, longtime Southern Pacific executive and then chairman Julius Kruttschnitt testified to the Huntington-era origins of the modernization projects before the Interstate Commerce Commission, only in greater detail about all of the Southern Pacific improvements. Kruttschnitt also said that the Union Pacific's previous engineering and construction of bridges, roadbeds, embankments, and other physical facilities had been inefficient and more costly than the Southern Pacific's more modern practices, and after he "was made [Harriman Lines] director of maintenance and operations [in 1904] the Southern Pacific specifications were adopted on the Union Pacific, and most of them are in effect there today"; Kruttschnitt, "Memorandum," and *Testimony before the Interstate Commerce Commission,* 18–21, 26ff.

108. Hofsommer, *Southern Pacific,* 25ff.; Klein, *Harriman,* 267ff. The role of Southern Pacific executives in organizing the Harriman Lines' management system was also emphasized by John F. Hippin, "A Wall Street Man and a Western Railroad: A Chapter in Railroad Administration," *Bulletin of the Business Historical Society* 23 (September 1949): 117–48. Julius Kruttschnitt later testified before the ICC that the Harriman

Lines' management was composed primarily *not* of Union Pacific men, but of former Southern Pacific executives, who then modernized Union Pacific policies and physical plant; Kruttschnitt, "Memorandum," passim, and *Testimony before the Interstate Commerce Commission*, passim, esp. 29ff. "It is significant," the Southern Pacific chairman noted, "that every man he [Harriman] selected for . . . jurisdiction over the combined systems, which embraced the greatest mileage ever, was selected from the Southern Pacific staff. The head of the accounting department came from the Southern Pacific; the head of the construction department . . . ; the head of the law department . . . ; the head of the maintenance department . . . ; the head of the operating department . . . ; the head of the traffic department. . . . Under Mr. Harriman's directions these officers introduced on Union Pacific lines Southern Pacific methods and practices, whose excellence had been proven in their previous positions, and these were used until the properties were unmerged . . . in 1913."

109. For fuller account, see chapter 6.

110. Regarding land-grant policy and the Harriman Lines' loss of the Southern Pacific's Oregon & California Railroad land grant, see chapter 5. Tensions between executives of hitherto rival companies have been common in railroad mergers; see, for example, the troubled New York Central–Pennsylvania Railroad merger of the early 1960s, described in Richard Saunders, *The Railroad Mergers and the Coming of Conrail* (Westport, CT: Greenwood Press, 1978).

111. Hofsommer, *Southern Pacific*, 51–52.

112. See draft agreement for transfer by the Southern Pacific to the Union Pacific of its lease on Central Pacific line, ca. January 1, 1913; "Southern Pacific-Union Pacific Dissolution Agreement, 1912–1913," box 13, *SP-E.*

113. Hofsommer, *Southern Pacific*, 52–53. Southern Pacific president William Sproule later said that he and his associates had acquiesced to the Union Pacific's pressure "simply as an expedient."

114. A collection of draft agreements, letters, telegrams, memoranda, and clippings discloses the internal debate among the future executives of the soon-to-be-revived Southern Pacific in 1912 and 1913, and their transition from forced acceptance of the loss of the Central Pacific to intransigent opposition; "Southern Pacific-Union Pacific Dissolution, 1912–1913" [includes ensuing court cases and ICC applications to 1923], boxes 13–14, *SP-E.* For the debate in 1912 and 1913, see especially Julius Kruttschnitt to William S. Lovett, January 24, 1913; Kruttschnitt to William Sproule, telegram, April 28, 1913; Lovett to George Wickersham, January 16, 1913; W. A. Worthington to Kruttschnitt, January 25, 1913; William F. Herrin to Kruttschnitt, February 3, 1913; "Memorandum" (ms., February 7, 1913).

115. The Southern Pacific managers' secret campaign in 1913 to keep the Central Pacific, while they were still subject to Harriman bosses, and their cooperation with outsiders, particularly the California State Railroad Commission, also opposed to the Union Pacific's plan, was outlined by Don Hofsommer in a paper he delivered to a conference on railroad history, sponsored by the University of California Inter-campus Economic History Group at the California State Railroad Museum, Sacramento, in November 1987.

116. Unidentified newspaper clipping, September 14, 1913, Teal Scrapbook, "Rail-

road Matters, 1906–1915," 181, in Oregon Collection, University of Oregon Library, Eugene; *Atlanta Journal,* February 28, 1913; Hofsommer, *Southern Pacific,* 54–56.

117. For letters, reports, clippings, pamphlets, court decisions, and briefs pertaining to the Southern Pacific's defense in the courts and its ICC application to retain control of the Central Pacific, the company's alliances with outside business and governmental agencies throughout its territory, and the Union Pacific's continued attempts to acquire the line, see "Southern Pacific-Central Pacific Case," boxes 10–12; and also "Consolidation of Railroads" (New York office files); *SP-E.* Full internal histories of the "unmerger" and the struggle for control of the Central Pacific are in "Historical Data . . . Central Pacific Railway," 13ff., and "Historical Memoranda" (typescript, ca. 1960s), I, chap. 13, both in *SP-E.* See also *Petition before the Interstate Commerce Commission in the Matter of the Application of the Southern Pacific Company to Acquire Control by Lease and by Stock Ownership of the Central Pacific Railway* (New York: Charles P. Young Co., October 10, 1922); Hofsommer, *Southern Pacific,* 54–55, 78–89; Daggett, *Chapters,* 432–40; and *Southern Pacific's First Century: Indexed Edition,* 41–42.

118. C. A. Ryan, "History of the San Diego and Arizona Eastern Railway Company" (mimeo, San Francisco, 1944), the Southern Pacific's official account; and Southern Pacific Company, "History of the San Diego and Arizona Eastern Railway Company" (ms., 1937), a full analysis containing copies of key documents, letters, contracts, and lawsuits related to the complicated Southern Pacific financing and subsidy of the railroad and its final purchase in 1916; both in *SP-E.* Also Robert M. Hanft, *San Diego and Arizona: The Impossible Railroad* (Glendale, CA: Trans-Anglo Books, 1984); Patrick W. O'Bannon, "Railroad Construction in the Twentieth Century: The San Diego and Arizona Railway," *Southern California Quarterly* 61 (Fall 1979): 255–90; and John A. Wilson, "Formidable Places: Building a Railroad in the Carriso Gorge," *Journal of San Diego History* 40 (Fall 1994): 179–97, an engineering and construction study based on company records. The San Diego Historical Society holds the well-indexed, extensive corporate archives of the San Diego & Arizona Railroad, valuable also for general Southern Pacific Company history.

119. Southern Pacific Company, "History of the Northwestern Pacific Railroad" (mimeo, 1937), the official account, *SP-E;* for the Northwestern Pacific and other twentieth-century additions to the Southern Pacific, Hofsommer, *Southern Pacific,* passim, esp. 45ff. In 1929, the Southern Pacific bought out the Santa Fe's interest and owned the Northwestern Pacific solely thereafter.

120. *Southern Pacific Bulletin* 13 (August 1924): 5–6, (October 1924): 7, (November 1924): 3–10, (December 1924): 9–10; Hofsommer, *Southern Pacific,* 98ff.; Gustav L. Seligman, "The El Paso and Northeastern Railroad System and Its Economic Influence in New Mexico" (M.A. thesis, New Mexico State University, 1958), the history of the predecessor line to the El Paso & Southwestern, and Seligman, "The El Paso and Northeastern Railroad's Economic Impact on Central New Mexico," *New Mexico Historical Review* 61 (July 1986): 217–31; Myrick, *Railroads of Arizona,* 1:241–46; Myrick, *New Mexico's Railroads,* 66–94; William A. Keleher, *The Fabulous Frontier: Twelve New Mexico Items,* rev. ed. (Albuquerque: University of New Mexico Press, 1962), 278ff.

121. Daniel Lewis, "The Empire Strikes Out: Mexican Nationbuilding and the Fer-

rocarril Sud-Pacifico de Mexico, 1880–1951" (Ph.D. diss., University of California, Riverside, 1997); *Southern Pacific's First Century: Indexed Edition,* 33–34, 39, 47–48; Wilson and Taylor, *Southern Pacific,* 123ff.; John Kirchner and John Signor, *The Southern Pacific of Mexico and the West Coast Route* (San Marino: Golden West Books, 1986). The Mexican government bought the line from the Southern Pacific in 1951. Records of the Southern Pacific de Mexico are at *HL;* Dan Lewis, "SP de Mexico Collection . . . 1909–1951: Finding Aid" (Huntington Library, June 1997), is an excellent description. After 1900, the Southern Pacific also bought and extended other Mexican companies, especially southern extensions of the railroad's Texas lines.

122. *Southern Pacific Bulletin* 3 (March 1, 1915): 3, and (March 15, 1915): 1.

123. Southern Pacific Company, Valuation Department, "Corporate History of the Southern Pacific Company and Proprietary Companies Comprising the Pacific System as of June 30, 1916" (typescript, San Francisco, 1919), ms. 1113, Southern Pacific Company Collection, Oregon Historical Society, Portland. A response to ICC Federal Valuation Order No. 20, this valuable document summarizes information on the incorporation of 158 predecessor companies, dates of construction of each segment of line, dates opened for traffic, ownership chains, leases, contracts, agreements, legal papers, current valuation (as of 1916), location of corporate records, and sources for the information in corporate annual reports, government documents, newspapers, etc. A photodocumentary of operations across Southern Pacific lines in the United States, ca. 1920s–1930s, at the peak of its reach and influence, is the Roland E. Collons Scrapbooks, Southern Pacific vols., *DG.* For the company's auto ferries, see Southern Pacific Company, *Four Auto Ferries on San Francisco Bay* (San Francisco: Southern Pacific Company, April 18, 1928); Southern Pacific Golden Gate Ferries, Ltd., Collection of Photographs (in California, Oregon, and Texas), ms. A1985; and Southern Pacific Company, Golden Gate Ferries, Ltd., Traffic Department, Scrapbooks (ca. 1928–1937), ms. A1994; all in *DG.*

2   Men of Vision

1. *Alta California* (San Francisco), December 15, 1866; also in Ivan Benson, *Mark Twain's Western Years* (Palo Alto: Stanford University Press, 1938), 211–12. Some of the information in this chapter appeared in other form in Richard J. Orsi, "*The Octopus* Reconsidered: The Southern Pacific and Agricultural Modernization in California, 1865–1915," *California Historical Quarterly* 54 (Fall 1975): 197–220.

2. Richard J. Orsi, "Railroads in the History of California and the Far West: An Introduction," *California History* 70 (Spring 1991): 4–9; James J. Rawls and Walton Bean, *California: An Interpretive History* (New York: McGraw-Hill, 1998), 173–94. Even before the railroad's completion, Henry George warned that monopoly, inequity, and uncertain fortunes would be the bitter price of the transcontinental in "What the Railroad Will Bring Us," *Overland Monthly* (October 1868).

3. William Deverell, *Railroad Crossing: Californians and the Railroad, 1850–1910* (Berkeley: University of California Press, 1994), passim; Ward McAfee, *California's Railroad Era, 1850–1911* (San Marino: Golden West Books, 1973), passim. Anti-railroad clip-

pings, pamphlets, cartoons, 1870s–1890s, are in the Timothy Hopkins Transportation Collection, container 7, folders 1–3; and Stanford Family Scrapbooks, vols. 7 and 26; both at *SU;* also John R. Robinson, *The Octopus: A History of the Construction, Conspiracies, Extortions, Robberies, and Villainous Acts of the Central Pacific, Southern Pacific of Kentucky, Union Pacific, and Other Subsidized Railroads* (San Francisco, 1894).

4. Frank Norris, *The Octopus* (New York, 1901), book 1, chap. 1; W. H. Hutchinson, "Prologue to Reform: The California Anti-Railroad Republicans, 1899–1905," *Southern California Quarterly* 44 (September 1962): 175–218; David B. Griffiths, "Anti-Monopoly Movements in California, 1873–1898," *Southern California Quarterly* 52 (June 1970): 93–121; McAfee, *California's Railroad Era,* passim. More balanced is Deverell, *Railroad Crossing,* passim; and regarding conflict with rural interests, Michael Magliari, "Populism, Steamboats, and the Octopus," *Pacific Historical Review* 58 (November 1989): 449–70.

5. For the Southern Pacific's negative impact on California land and agriculture, William L. Preston, *Vanishing Landscapes: Land and Life in the Tulare Basin* (Berkeley: University of California Press, 1981); Ellen Liebman, *California Farmland: A History of Large Agricultural Landholdings* (Totowa, NJ: Rowman and Allanheld, 1983), 36–43, 67–71; Stephanie S. Pincetl, *Transforming California: A Political History of Land Use and Development* (Baltimore: Johns Hopkins University Press, 1999), 5, 20–22. Popular writers take their cue from historians. Joan Didion, throughout the entirety of her recent personal, family, and historical memoir of California, uses the supposed tyranny of the Southern Pacific railroad as her book's central metaphor. Not only did the Southern Pacific distort land distribution and farming toward monopolization but, even more broadly, she claims the railroad was responsible for beginning the state's central contradiction, what she terms "the pauperization of California," its "mortgaging" of itself and its people to corporate empires; see Didion, *Where I Was From* (New York: Alfred A. Knopf, 2003), passim, esp. dust jacket, 24–25, 40–48, 87–90, 182–83. See also, Rebecca Solnit, *River of Shadows: Eadweard Muybridge and the Technological Wild West* (New York: Viking, 2003), passim, esp. 66ff., 167ff., 180ff. For myths about Southern Pacific land-grant policies, see chapter 3.

6. See Robert Glass Cleland, *From Wilderness to Empire: A History of California,* rev. ed. by Glenn S. Dumke (New York: Alfred A. Knopf, 1962), 173–75, 190–92, 235–46; Andrew Rolle, *California: A History,* 2nd ed. (New York: Thomas Y. Crowell, 1969), 337–46, 358ff., 421–22, 430ff., 457ff.; Walton Bean, *California: An Interpretive History* (New York: McGraw-Hill, 1968), 220ff., 298–311, and 320–25 (most anti–Southern Pacific passages remain in later editions coauthored by James Rawls), and *Boss Ruef's San Francisco* (Berkeley: University of California Press 1952), 3–5, 32–35, 146, 158, and 146–52; Stuart Daggett, *Chapters on the History of the Southern Pacific* (New York: Augustus M. Kelley, 1966 [1922]), passim; John W. Caughey, *California: A Remarkable State's Life History* (Englewood Cliffs, NJ: Prentice-Hall, 1970), 320–24 , 398–99, and 407–13; Royce D. Delmatier et al., *The Rumble of California Politics, 1848–1970* (New York: John Wiley & Sons, 1970), 125ff., 134, 158; Spencer C. Olin, Jr., *California's Prodigal Sons: Hiram Johnson and the Progressives, 1911–1927* (Berkeley: University of California Press, 1968), passim; Richard W. Barsness, "Railroads and Los Angeles: The Quest for a Deep-Water

Port," *Southern California Quarterly* 47 (December 1965): 379–94; George E. Mowry, *The California Progressives* (Berkeley: University of California Press, 1951), chap. 1 and passim. Conflict of interest between the Southern Pacific and farmers, often highlighted by the Mussel Slough incident, has been a particularly consistent theme; see chapter 4 and Richard J. Orsi, "Confrontation at Mussel Slough, 1880," chap. 13 of *The Elusive Eden: A New History of California,* by Richard B. Rice, William A. Bullough, and Richard J. Orsi (New York: McGraw-Hill, 1996 and 2002 editions). For Nevada, Russell R. Elliott, *History of Nevada* (Lincoln: University of Nebraska Press, 1973), 157–69 and 239–51; James W. Hulse, *The Silver State: Nevada's History Reinterpreted* (Reno: University of Nevada Press, 1991), 114–32; Sally Zanjani, *The Unspiked Rail: Memoir of a Nevada Rebel* (Reno: University of Nevada Press, 1981). For Texas, James L. Haley, *Texas: From Frontier to Spindletop* (New York: St. Martin's Press, 1985), 249ff.; Larry D. Hill, "Texas Progressivism," in *Texas through Time: Evolving Interpretations,* ed. Walter L. Buenger and Robert A. Calvert (College Station: Texas A & M University Press, 1991), 232ff.; T. R. Fehrenbach, *Lone Star: A History of Texas and the Texans from Prehistoric to the Present* (New York: Da Capo Press, 2000), 418ff., 604ff., and 622ff.

7. For more balanced accounts, Earl Pomeroy, *The Pacific Slope: A History of California, Oregon, Washington, Idaho, Utah, and Nevada* (New York: Alfred A. Knopf, 1968), 100ff., 175–76, and 335ff.; Caughey, *California,* 343–47, on some railroad land-promotion programs; Ward M. McAfee, "Local Interests and Railroad Regulation in California During the Granger Decade," *Pacific Historical Review* 38 (February 1968): 51–66; W. H. Hutchinson, "Southern Pacific: Myth and Reality," *California Historical Society Quarterly* 48 (December 1969): 325–34; Gerald D. Nash, "The California Railroad Commission, 1876–1911," *Southern California Quarterly* 44 (December 1962): 287–305; David Lavender, *The Great Persuader* [Collis P. Huntington] (Garden City, NY, 1970); Lloyd J. Mercer, "Land Grants to American Railroads: Social Cost or Social Benefit?" *Business History Review* 43 (Summer 1969): 134–51; R. Hal Williams, "The Railroad in California Politics: The 1890s," in Williams, *The Democratic Party and California Politics, 1880–1896* (Stanford: Stanford University Press, 1973), chap. 9; Deverell, *Railroad Crossing.* Also, Orsi, "Railroads in the History of California and the Far West," 2–11.

8. Collis P. Huntington–Mark Hopkins Correspondence, vols. 1–5, esp. letters August 23, September 28, and October 29, 1872, and February 15, March 3, and March 10, 1873, *SU;* Lavender, *Great Persuader,* 130, 181ff., 293ff., and 376–77; Julius Grodinsky, *Transcontinental Railway Strategy, 1869–1893: A Study of Businessmen* (Philadelphia: University of Pennsylvania Press, 1962), 16, 41ff., and 56ff. Southern Pacific leaders often privately acknowledged that their fortunes depended on economic progress and population growth in the railroad's territories; see Hopkins to Huntington, San Francisco, November 8, 1873, in Hopkins et al., *Letters from Mark Hopkins, Leland Stanford, Charles Crocker, Charles F. Crocker, and David D. Colton to Collis P. Huntington, from August 27th, 1869, to December 30th, 1879* (New York: John C. Rankin Co., 1891), 51–53; Huntington to David D. Colton, New York, November 27, 1875, January 8 and February 12, 1877, and February 2, 1878, in *Ellen M. Colton vs. Leland Stanford, et al.,* 17 vols. (privately printed, 1883–1884), 4:1687–88, 1753, 1756, and 1846 (a copy of this published trial transcript can be found at *HL*); Huntington to W. C. Wickham, New York, December 13, 1882,

and February 16 and December 23, 1883, and to A. N. Towne, New York, January 18, 1884, and to Brewster, Cobb and Estabrook, New York, February 12, 1884, and to Thomas A. Quilelle, New York, March 21, 1884, and to E. B. Waite, New York, March 22, 1884, and to Lewis A. Hyde, New York, July 25, 1885, all in *CPH*. To an 1892 gathering of Southern Pacific Company executives in San Francisco, Huntington said: "I want all of you, gentlemen, to remember that in the prosperity of California itself lies the secret of our own success"; in *San Francisco Examiner,* April 24, 1892.

9. Bureau of the Census of the U.S. Department of Commerce and the Social Science Research Council, *The Statistical History of the United States from Colonial Times to the Present* (Stanford, CT, n.d.), 12–13; Commonwealth Club of California, *The Population of California* (San Francisco: Parker Publishing Co., 1946), 21. For economic problems, Gerald D. Nash, *State Government and Economic Development: A History of Administrative Policies in California, 1849–1933* (Berkeley: Institute of Governmental Studies, University of California, 1964), 1–224; Paul Wallace Gates, ed., *California Ranchos and Farms* (Madison: State Historical Society of Wisconsin Press, 1967); Robert Glass Cleland and Osgood Hardy, *March of Industry* (San Francisco: Powell Publishing Co., 1929); and Richard J. Orsi, "Selling the Golden State: A History of Boosterism in Nineteenth-Century California" (Ph.D. diss., University of Wisconsin, Madison, 1973), 1–113, on economic and social problems delaying population growth and comparison of California growth rates to other states, 1850–1900.

10. Central Pacific Railroad Company, *Annual Report . . . 1881* (San Francisco, 1882), 40, and *Annual Report, 1883* (1884), 50; Lavender, *Great Persuader,* 320ff.; E. A. Kincaid, "The Federal Land Grants of the Central Pacific Railroad" (Ph.D. diss., University of California, Berkeley, 1922), chap. 15; Walter A. McAllister, "A Study of Railroad Land-Grant Disposal in California with Reference to the Western Pacific, the Central Pacific, and the Southern Pacific Railroad Companies" (Ph.D. diss., University of Southern California, 1939), 109–10; Ralph Kauer, "The Workingmen's Party of California," *Pacific Historical Review* 13 (September 1944): 278–91; Bean, *California,* 219–43; Rice, Bullough, and Orsi, *Elusive Eden,* chap. 15.

11. Southern Pacific Company, *Annual Report . . . 1894* (San Francisco, 1895), 87 and 122, and *Annual Report, 1896* (1897), 7, 26, 29, and 58; McAllister, "Land-Grant Disposal in California," 457 and 485; Lavender, *Great Persuader,* 369ff.; Donald E. Walters, "Populism in California, 1889–1900" (Ph.D. diss., University of California, Berkeley, 1952); Griffiths, "Anti-Monopoly Movements," 93–121.

12. On land-grant roads, James B. Hedges, *Henry Villard and the Railways of the Northwest* (New Haven: Yale University Press, 1930), and "Promotion of Immigration to the Pacific Northwest by the Railroads," *Mississippi Valley Historical Review* 15 (September 1928): 183–203; Paul Wallace Gates, *The Illinois Central Railroad and Its Colonization Work* (Cambridge: Harvard University Press, 1934); and Richard Overton, *Burlington West: A Colonization History of the Burlington Railroad* (Cambridge: Harvard University Press, 1941); Morris N. Spencer, "The Union Pacific Railroad Company's Utilization of Its Land Grant with Emphasis on Its Colonization Program" (Ph.D. diss., University of Nebraska, 1950); William S. Greever, *Arid Domain: The Santa Fe Railway and Its Western Land Grant* (Stanford: Stanford University Press, 1954), and "A Com-

parison of Railroad Land Grant Policies," *Agricultural History* 25 (April 1951): 83–90; special issue, *Agricultural History*, "The Role of Railroads in Agricultural Development," 21 (October 1957); Wallace Farnham, "Railroads in Western History: The View from the Union Pacific," in *The American West: A Reorientation,* ed. Gene M. Gressley (vol. 32, University of Wyoming Publications, 1966), 95–109; Sig Mickelson, *The Northern Pacific Railroad and the Selling of the West* (Sioux Falls, SD: Center for Western Studies, 1993); Roy V. Scott, *Railroad Development Programs in the Twentieth Century* (Ames: Iowa State University Press, 1985); Leslie E. Decker, *Railroads, Lands, and Politics: The Taxation of the Railroad Land Grants, 1865–1827* (Providence, RI: Brown University Press, 1964). For railroad executives' identification of their companies' interests with their areas' population growth and economic development and their preference for quick sales of land grants, at low prices, and to small-scale resident farmers, Thomas C. Cochran, *Railroad Leaders, 1845–1890: The Business Mind in Action* (Cambridge: Harvard University Press, 1953), 151–52, and "Land Grants and Railroad Entrepreneurship," *Journal of Economic History* 10 (supplement 1950): 53–67. On rivalry between the Southern Pacific and other roads, L. L. Waters, *Steel Trails to Santa Fe* (Lawrence: University of Kansas Press, 1950), 71–74 and 127–42; Lewis B. Leslie, "A Southern Transcontinental Railroad into California: The Texas and Pacific Versus the Southern Pacific, 1865–1885," *Pacific Historical Review* 5 (March 1936): 52–60; articles in *California History* 70 (Spring 1991): William F. Deverell, "The Los Angeles 'Free Harbor Fight,'" 12–29; Don L. Hofsommer, "For Territorial Dominion in California and the Pacific Northwest: Edward J. Harriman and James J. Hill," 30–45; Edward Leo Lyman, "From the City of Angels to the City of Saints: The Struggle to Build a Railroad from Los Angeles to Salt Lake City," 76–93. Although his company did not possess a federal land grant, James J. Hill of the Great Northern Railway also shared the development philosophy of Southern Pacific leaders, supporting land subdivision, small-scale farming, scientific agriculture, and irrigation in his northern hinterland from Minnesota to Washington; Clair Strom, *Profiting from the Plains: The Great Northern Railway and Corporate Development of the American West* (Seattle: University of Washington Press, 2003), passim.

13. *Alta California* (San Francisco), August 22, 1882; Alonzo Phelps, *Contemporary Biography of California's Representative Men,* 2 vols. (San Francisco: A. L. Bancroft & Co., 1882), 2:77–83.

14. The nature of the relationship between the *Sacramento Record-Union* and the Southern Pacific has long been conjectured. Veiled references to ownership of the *Record-Union* among the letters of the Big Four led historians to conclude that the railroad controlled the newspaper; see Huntington-Hopkins Correspondence, March 16, 1872, August 22, 1873, February 25 and March 18, 1875, and April 10 and 26, 1876, *SU;* Huntington to David D. Colton, April 27, 1876, published as part of the "Colton Letters," *San Francisco Chronicle,* December 17, 1883; Cerinda W. Evans, *Collis Potter Huntington,* 2 vols. (Newport News, VA: The Mariners' Museum, 1954), 1:185–90; Norman E. Tutorow, *Leland Stanford: Man of Many Careers* (Menlo Park, CA: Pacific Coast Publishers, 1971), 132; George T. Clarke, *Leland Stanford* (Stanford: Stanford University Press, 1931), 286–89, 303–307, and 430–31; Robert L. Kelley, *Gold vs. Grain: The Hydraulic Mining Controversy in California's Sacramento Valley, A Chapter in the Decline in the*

Concept of Laissez Faire (Glendale, CA: Arthur H. Clark Co., 1959), 124ff.; Rolle, *California*, 428. How control was maintained has been unknown. While inspecting records of the Pacific Improvement Company, formed by the families of the Big Four, and other Southern Pacific records, I found documents indicating the Big Four set up Mills in the early 1870s as proprietor and editor of the *Sacramento Record* to counteract the anti-railroad *Sacramento Union*, financed his buyout of the *Union* in February 1875, and continued to subsidize the new combined paper by grants from the Pacific Improvement Company and the Southern Pacific until the early 1900s, when E. H. Harriman absorbed the railroad. The Pacific Improvement Company advanced funds to Mills in exchange for half interest in the Sacramento Publishing Company, publisher of the *Record-Union;* Pacific Improvement Company, "Index to Minutes, 1878–1904," Pacific Improvement Company Records, folio 78, vol. 6, *SU.* The paper turned out to be a huge expense. In the 1870s, for example, the Big Four paid the newspaper a *weekly* subsidy of $500, or $26,000 per year. By the end of 1878, including the subsidy since 1875, the purchase price, and paid-off loans, they had paid Mills and the newspaper's company a grand total of $274,339; Crocker to Huntington, San Francisco, December 2, 1878, in Hopkins et al., *Letters,* 226. After becoming the railroad's land agent in 1883, Mills moved to San Francisco but retained management of the *Record-Union.* Dictating to a stenographer, Mills actually wrote the editorials for the paper, as well as later for the *San Francisco Post,* which the railroad also controlled; *San Francisco Examiner,* June 29, 1900. When he wrote to Governor Pardee in 1902 objecting to the planned state display in St. Louis, Mills enclosed a clipping from the *Record-Union* with the comment that "the editorial expressions of the 'Record-Union' have my full approval"; Mills to George C. Pardee, San Francisco, December 29, 1902, Pardee Correspondence, *BL; San Francisco Call,* November 22, 1895. As late as 1903, two years after the Harriman Lines had taken over the Southern Pacific, Mills, still land agent, continued to manage and write editorials for the *Record-Union,* and the Southern Pacific owned the paper, though the stock was in Mills's name. In 1903, the new Harriman Lines management of the Southern Pacific Company billed the Sacramento Publishing Company for $43,000 in "moneys advanced" and transferred the paper's ownership to the Pacific Improvement Company as part of the agreement separating the two Big Four–founded companies; Sacramento Publishing Company, "Minutes," 48–49, in Pacific Improvement Company Records, container 467; Charles W. Eberlein, "Memorandum: Southern Pacific" (typescript, ca. 1903) and Eberlein to William D. Cornish, Portland, May 9, 1903, Eberlein Correspondence, *SP-L.*

15. *San Francisco: Its Builders, Past and Present* (San Francisco: S. J. Clarke Publishing Co., 1913), 1:343; *San Francisco Chronicle,* May 25, 1907.

16. For Madden, see Phelps, *Contemporary Biography,* 2:46–50. For Hoag obituaries, *Sacramento Record-Union, Sacramento Bee,* and *San Francisco Call,* April 24, 1898. On Turrill, documents in Turrill Papers, *BL.* For Horsburgh, John P. Young, *Journalism in California* (San Francisco: Chronicle Publishing Co., 1915), 279.

17. Railroad officials' development ideas resembled those of many nineteenth-century western leaders, including Henry George and Caspar T. Hopkins, who opposed the Southern Pacific. See Charles A. Barker, "Henry George and the California Background

of Progress and Poverty," *California Historical Society Quarterly* 24 (June 1945): 97–115; Caspar T. Hopkins, *Common Sense Applied to the Immigration Question* (San Francisco: Turnbull and Smith, Printers, 1869); Claude R. Petty, "John S. Hittell and the Gospel of California," *Pacific Historical Review* 24 (February 1955): 1–16; Gerald D. Nash, "Henry George Reexamined: William S. Chapman's Views on Land Speculation in Nineteenth Century California," *Agricultural History* 33 (July 1959): 133–37; Nash, *State Government and Economic Development,* 63–80 and 139–58; Orsi, "Selling the Golden State," passim, esp. 1–113; Gerald L. Prescott, "Farm Gentry vs. the Grangers: Conflict in Rural America," *California Historical Quarterly* 56 (Winter 1977/78): 328–45; William D. Rowley, *Francis G. Newlands: Reclamationist and Reformer* (Bloomington: Indiana University Press, 1995); Donald J. Pisani, *To Reclaim a Divided West: Water, Law, and Public Policy, 1848–1902* (Albuquerque: University of New Mexico Press, 1992).

18. Leland Stanford, "Opening Address of the Annual Fair of the State of California Agricultural Society, Sacramento, September 26, 1863," *Transactions of the California State Agricultural Society During the Year 1863* (Sacramento, 1864), 49.

19. Redding's essays on agriculture include "Sanitary Influence of Trees," *Resources of California* (San Francisco), February 1882; "The Olive in Tulare County," *Pacific Rural Press* (San Francisco), July 10, 1880; "Influence of Irrigation on Citrus Trees," *Pacific Rural Press,* August 16, 1879; "Cost of Wheat Production," *San Francisco Bulletin,* January 2, 1880; "Oranges and Olives," *San Francisco Bulletin,* January 30, 1880; "The Climate of California," *Transactions of the California Agricultural Society, 1878* (1879), 129–34. Hoag, before joining the railroad, was agricultural editor of leading newspapers and secretary of the California State Agricultural Society. His writings include "Agricultural Review," *Transactions of the California Agricultural Society, 1874* (1875), 245–52; "Orange Culture in California Society," *Transactions of the California Agricultural Society, 1879* (1880), 132–38; "History of the State Agricultural Society of California," *Transactions of the California Agricultural Society, 1879* (1880), 176–211. For his travels and speeches made as the railroad's immigration commissioner, *Sacramento Record-Union,* May 9 and 19, and June 5, 9, and 23, 1883. For Fulton's career in Nevada agriculture, irrigation, and civic affairs, Barbara Richnak, *A River Flows: The Life of Robert Lardin Fulton* (Incline Village, NV: Comstock-Nevada Publishing Co., 1983), esp. 72. For Zumwalt, *ZC-SP;* Kathleen E. Small, *History of Tulare County, California,* 2 vols. (Chicago: S. J. Clarke Co., 1926), 2:462–65; James M. Guinn, *History of the State of California and Biographical Record of the San Joaquin Valley* (Chicago: Chapman Publishing Co., 1905), 632.

20. W. H. Mills, "Annual Address Delivered Before the State Agricultural Society of California . . . Sacramento, September 18, 1890," *Transactions of the California Agricultural Society, 1890* (1891), 184–208, also, *Sacramento Record-Union,* September 19, 1890, and other papers; Mills, "Marketing of California Fruits," *Californian Illustrated Magazine* 2 (October 1892): 703–708.

21. W. H. Mills, "Annual Address," passim, and "Marketing of California Fruits," passim; Mills and Edwin K. Alsip, *Report on the Columbus, Ohio, Exhibit* (San Francisco: California State Board of Trade, 1888), 8–9. In reports as railroad land agent, Mills linked regional and company progress to specialized agriculture: Central Pacific

Railroad Company, *Annual Report, 1882* (1883), 60–64, and *Annual Report, 1887* (1888), 72–73; also his address before the Los Angeles Chamber of Commerce, in Los Angeles Chamber of Commerce, *An Account of the First Annual Banquet of the Los Angeles Chamber of Commerce* (Los Angeles: Kingsley and Barnes, Printers, 1893), 46–47. The *Sacramento Record-Union* promoted horticulture and specialized farming, 1875–1900s; policy editorial, February 22, 1875; also January 1, 1876, special issue.

22. Lavender, *Great Persuader,* 363 and 426.

23. Southern Pacific Company, *Annual Report, 1892* (1893), 26–27, *Annual Report, 1894* (1895), 33, and *Annual Report, 1896* (1897), 28. See also, *Speech of C. P. Huntington at the Annual Dinner, Southern Pacific Company, San Francisco, May 16, 1900, on "California— Her Past, Present and Future"* (n.p., 1900), 6ff.

24. James Horsburgh, Jr., "Colonization Efforts," in California Development Board, Counties Committee, *Bulletin Number Nine* (January 1911), 17; E. O. McCormick, "The Southern Pacific's Part in the Development of the West," *Southern Pacific Bulletin* 3 (October 1, 1915): 1–2; W. B. Scott [president, Southern Pacific Sunset–Central Lines], *Texas and Her Railroads* (Houston: Southern Pacific Sunset–Central Lines, April 5, 1914), 13.

25. *Sacramento Record-Union,* January 1 and 3, and March 4, 22, and 23, 1876, February 22, March 9, July 31, and August 3, 7, and 28, 1878, many issues October, November, and December 1881, and January 15, 1883; Kelley, *Gold vs. Grain,* 75–129, 145, 174, and 216. In his July 31, 1878, editorial Mills charged that, with agriculture now the dominant interest, the state's laws should change to protect farmers. Mining's defenders attacked the *Record-Union's* stand; *Alta California* (San Francisco), August 2, 1878; *Nevada City Transcript,* August 6 and 7, 1878. Kelley hints that the railroad also got one of its "controlled" judges to rule favorably to farmers in the key federal case. See chapter 9 for a more complete account of hydraulic mining.

26. *Sacramento Record-Union,* April 1, 1875, August 30 and September 5, 1888; *Alta California* (San Francisco), April 19, 1875; and *Sunset* 4 (April 1900): 246, and 14 (November 1904): 90. For detail on assistance to farm organizations, see chapter 12.

27. Gates, *California Ranchos and Farms,* passim; Nash, *State Government and Economic Development,* 63–80 and 139–58.

28. See, in *Sunset:* Charles H. Shinn, "Experimental Agriculture in California: The University of California Stations, United States Department of Agriculture," 8 (November 1901): 15–19; H. Morse Stephens, "University Extension in California," 10 (March 1903): 439–46; Leroy Anderson, "What Modern Farming Means," 10 (March 1903): 456–58. Until the railroad sold it, *Sunset* ran articles promoting modern agriculture in nearly all issues, 1899–1915.

29. For agricultural science and colleges, see chapter 11.

30. Central Pacific Railroad Company, *Lands of the Central Pacific Railroad of California* (Sacramento, 1868), 14–15. Identical wording was in the company's land pamphlets, 1870s–1880s, and in annual land-agent reports; see also Collis P. Huntington to L. E. Payson, Washington, DC, September 5, 1891, Collis P. Huntington Letterbook 6, *HEH.*

31. See William H. Mills to James G. Fair, San Francisco, January 2, 1884, in *San Francisco Bulletin,* February 14, 1884, and to San Francisco Board of Trade, San Fran-

cisco, February 4, 1884, in *San Francisco Merchant,* February 15, 1884, and testimony to
U. S. Pacific Railway Commission, *Testimony Taken By the United States Pacific Railway Commission,* 8 vols. (Washington, DC: Government Printing Office, 1887), 5:2413.

32. *San Francisco Call,* February 16, 1884; *Sacramento Bee,* January 19, February 1, 13, and 16, 1884; *Marysville Appeal,* January 24 and 31, 1884; *Colusa Sun,* February 9, 1884; *Red Bluff Sentinel,* February 4 and 5, 1885; *Sacramento Record-Union,* February 20, 21, 23, 26, and 27, and March 12, 1884.

33. For the railroad's land development and sales, see chapters 3–6.

34. B. B. Redding, "Immigration and How to Promote It," *The Californian* 5 (January 1882): 60; *Alta California* (San Francisco), November 30 and December 1, 1881.

35. Horsburgh, "Colonization Efforts," 17; also W. H. Mills, first report as land agent, Central Pacific Railroad Company, *Annual Report, 1882* (1883), 60–64; his introduction to California State Board of Trade, *California: Early History, Commercial Position, Climate, Scenery, Forests, General Resources . . .* (San Francisco, 1897–1898), 4–5; his pamphlet, *The American Question* (San Francisco, ca. 1886), 8ff.; and his "Annual Address" to the Agricultural Society, 1890. Many Southern Pacific leaders promoted subdivision of large estates into small farms; see Collis P. Huntington to David D. Colton, New York, April 29, 1878, in *Colton vs. Stanford,* 4:1825.

36. Tutorow, *Stanford,* 33, 47, 50–51; Barker, "Henry George and the California Background," 98–99; *Sacramento Record-Union,* March 21, 27, and 31, and April 19, 1890; for B. B. Redding, *Alta California* (San Francisco), December 21, 1869.

37. For Mills's earlier attack on land monopoly, *Sacramento Record,* May 16, 1870; also Henry George, *Our Land and Land Policy* (San Francisco: White and Bauer, 1871); Charles A. Barker, *Henry George* (New York: Oxford University Press, 1955), 190–91; David Lavender, *California: A Centennial History* (New York: W.W. Norton, 1976), 122; for California land monopoly, Ellen Liebman, *California Farmland: A History of Large Agricultural Landholdings* (Totowa, NJ: Rowman and Allanheld, 1983), 6–28.

38. See *Sacramento Record-Union,* January 16, May 24, 1877, August 26, 1879, March 29, October 27, 1890; *San Francisco Bulletin,* March 26, October 25, 1890. Henry Huntington, assistant to the president, Southern Pacific Company, after inspecting the Sacramento and San Joaquin valleys, also denounced land monopoly; *Sacramento Bee,* May 20, 1891.

39. William H. Mills, *California Land Holdings* (San Francisco, 1892); also *Sacramento Record-Union,* April 14, 1892; *Oakland Times,* April 8, 1892; *Bakersfield Californian,* June 2, 1892; Mills to C. P. Huntington, San Francisco, June 4, 1892, enclosing speech and clippings, *CPH.* Mills similarly addressed the California State Board of Trade, also widely reported, *Sacramento Record-Union,* March 29, 1890, and *San Francisco Bulletin,* March 26, 1890. His other attacks on land monopoly included *The American Question,* passim; Mills to *San Francisco Call,* San Francisco, published January 13, 1896; Mills, "California Agricultural Lands," *San Francisco Call,* December 19, 1897; and Mills, "What [Spanish/Mexican] Land Grants Did to California," in *San Francisco Call,* July 9, 1905. Under his management, the *Record-Union* denounced land monopolists for depopulating rural districts; see editions of February 22, 1875, and October 3, 1891.

40. *Sacramento Record-Union,* August 26, 1879; *California Patron,* September 6, 1879. At the recent constitution convention, Grange delegates had defeated a clause proposed by Workingmen's Party delegates for the new California constitution that would have placed legal limits on the farm acreage any one person could own.

41. Charles Nordhoff, "California III.—Its Products and Productiveness," *Harper's* 45 (July 1872): 255–67; Southern Pacific Railroad, *Lands of the Southern Pacific Railroad* (1880), 101–102 and 112ff., and, in 1883 edition, 116–17 and 127ff.; Pacific Coast Land Bureau, *California Guide Book: Lands of the Central Pacific and Southern Pacific Railroad Companies* (San Francisco: Pacific Coast Land Bureau, ca. 1882), passim; Bernhard Marks, *Small-Scale Farming in California: The Colonization System of the Great Valley of the San Joaquin in Central California* (San Francisco: Crocker & Co., ca. 1890), passim; *Sacramento Record-Union,* February 27, 1875, July 13 and 14, 1877, and August 23, 1888. *Sunset* also promoted agricultural colonies and small farms; see A. J. Wells, "The Romance of the Fresno Ranch: An Old Time Principality Being Broken up for Colonization," 22 (May 1909): 557–59, and "Slicing the Great Ranchos," 23 (August 1909): 219–21; "Carmichael Colony in the Heart of California," 26 (May 1911): 576–77, and other articles in this issue. For analysis of the railroad's encouraging small-scale farms colonies, see chapters 3–5.

42. Nash, *State Government and Economic Development,* 76–79; Cleland and Hardy, *March of Industry,* 197–216; Paul S. Taylor, "Water, Land, and People in the Great Valley," *The American West* 5 (March 1968): 24–29 and 68–72.

43. For Southern Pacific promotion of water systems and irrigation, see chapters 7–10. For Mills on irrigation, *Sacramento Record-Union,* January 3 and March 4, 1876; Mills, "Annual Address," 201ff.; Mills, *The Hydrography of the Sacramento Valley* (San Francisco: California State Board of Trade, 1904); *San Francisco Call,* June 6 and July 4, 1904; Mills to George C. Pardee, San Francisco, February 3, 1903, Pardee Correspondence, *BL;* California State Board of Trade, *Reclamation of Arid Lands by Irrigation: Report of the Committee on Arid Lands of the California State Board of Trade* (San Francisco, 1889); *San Francisco Call,* April 12, 1899, reporting his speech to the Board of Trade on smaller farms, horticultural development, and agricultural diversity to be gained from irrigation. Mills also promoted forest conservation to preserve watersheds for future irrigation needs; see *Sacramento Record-Union,* August 26, 1882, January 1 and 15, 1883. In addressing the Water and Forest Association of California, which he had helped found, he presented statistics showing that, if lumbering in California was not controlled, watersheds and irrigation potential would shrink, causing future depressions. Indeed, Mills argued, California not only had to save remaining forests but plant new ones; *San Francisco Call,* December 15, 1900. For other Southern Pacific leaders, on irrigation and conservation, B. B. Redding, "Influence of Irrigation on Citrus Trees," *Pacific Rural Press* (San Francisco), August 16, 1879; Redding, "The Climate of California," *Transactions of the California Agricultural Society . . . 1877* (1878), 123–40, widely reprinted in state newspapers and reports for the rest of the century, for example *California Patron* (state Grange newspaper), February 6, 1878, and *Resources of California* (San Francisco), January and February 1887 and December 1888; I. N. Hoag, letters to *Sacramento Record-Union,* published May 9, 19, and June 9, 1883, April 4, 1885, and June 5, 1886; Collis P. Huntington,

"Annual Report of the President," in Southern Pacific Company, *Annual Report, 1892* (1893), 26–27; Jerome Madden, *California: Its Attractions for the Invalid, Tourist, Capitalist, and Homeseeker* (San Francisco: H. S. Crocker, 1890), 22ff. In the 1870s, Redding was also a member of the State Fisheries Commission, one of California's first conservation agencies, and he wrote often about zoology, ornithology, forestry, and botany; see Redding to R. W. Waterman, San Francisco, October 22, 1876, and January 3, April 28, November 17, and December 22, 1879 (on the introduction of plants and fish into southern California), Waterman Family Papers, *BL*. For his writings on climate, agriculture, and natural history, California Academy of Sciences, *In Memoriam: Benjamin B. Redding, Born January 17th, 1824, Died August 21st, 1882* (n.p., n.d.).

44. B. A. McAllaster to William F. Herrin, San Francisco, December 5, 1912, and April 16, September 11, and October 8, 1913; McAllaster to President William Sproule, October 8, 1913, and November 9, 1914; Herrin to Sproule, December 5, 1912, file 539, *SP-L;* McCormick, "The Southern Pacific's Part in the Development of the West," 1–2, address to the 22nd International Irrigation Congress, Stockton, California, September 13, 1915.

45. *Sunset* encouraged irrigation and resource conservation: see E. T. Perkins (U.S. Reclamation Service engineer), "Redeeming the West: Present Status of Government Irrigation Projects . . . ," 16 (November 1905): 3–25; C. J. Blanchard (U.S. Reclamation Service), "Redeeming the West—The Klamath Project," 17 (September 1906): 207–14, and "Uncle Sam's New Farm," 19 (September 1907): 487–92; G. K. Swingle, "Chaining the Sacramento," 17 (October 1906): 453–55; and "Redeeming the Arid West—Some Results of the Recent National Irrigation Congress at El Paso," 14 (February 1905), a large section with articles promoting irrigation in California, by Alexander McAdie (U.S. Weather Bureau), E. A. Sterling (U.S. Bureau of Forestry), and Governor George C. Pardee. *Sunset's* policies on irrigation, in January 1905, p. 308. Also H. T. Payne, "Game Birds of the Pacific," 22 (January 1909): 65–73; Sumner W. Matteson, "Saving the Buffalo," 21 (October 1908): 498–503; George H. Maxwell, "Save the Forests and Store the Floods," 9 (May 1902): 42–43; E. A. Sterling, "The Use of Forest Preserves," 19 (May 1907): 10–17.

46. For Mills's belief that public irrigation water should be restricted to small farms, especially his 1891 Irrigation Congress speech introducing the acreage limitation idea to the congress, *San Francisco Bulletin,* September 23, 1891; *Sacramento Record-Union,* September 18, 19, 21, and 24, 1891; Mills to Governor George Pardee, San Francisco, October 5, 1904, Pardee Correspondence, *BL*. For Mills's role in the 160-acre principle's evolution, Taylor, "Water, Land, and People," 29. For the company and egalitarian distribution of water, see chapters 9–10.

3   Land-Grant Myths

The quotation in the chapter title is from Southern Pacific Railroad Washington, DC, attorney Henry Beard, who thus advised Collis P. Huntington as the company fought the U.S. Department of the Interior over its proposed route and land grant; Beard to Huntington, August 21, 1869, vol. 6, *SP-A*.

1. Robert S. Henry, "The Railroad Land Grant Legend in American History Texts," *Mississippi Valley Historical Review* 32 (September 1945): 171–94; reprinted and analyzed in Carl N. Degler, ed., *Pivotal Interpretations of American History,* 2 vols. (New York: Harper and Row, 1965), 1:36–60. Henry's article remained controversial. The *Mississippi Valley Historical Review* published comments by other historians in subsequent issues; a session evaluating the paper was held at the 1946 annual conference of the Mississippi Valley Historical Association; and it continued to be discussed in scholarly journals. Critics, while admitting that earlier historical works had greatly exaggerated the federal land grants, doubted that the grants had been effective use of public resources, as opposed to distributing the land directly to small-scale farmers. For critics, see comments by David Maldwyn Ellis, Robert E. Riegel, and Edward C. Kirkland published in *Mississippi Valley Historical Review* 32 (1946): 557–76; and Paul Wallace Gates, "The Railroad Land-Grant Legend," *Economic History* 14 (Spring 1954): 143–46. Henry's article, and criticisms of it, were again reprinted in Vernon Carstensen, ed., *The Public Lands: Studies in the History of the Public Domain* (Madison: University of Wisconsin Press, 1968), 121–79. My findings, summarized in following chapters, regarding the land grants of the Southern Pacific Company, particularly in California, strongly support Henry's charge that, in general, historians have seriously exaggerated the size of the federal grants. They have also misunderstood or failed to study thoroughly their actual influences on land tenure and overlooked the important services railroads such as the Southern Pacific provided in developing, subdividing, advertising, and quickly settling agricultural land and facilitating the emergence of small-farm units.

2. Eminent social scientist Paul S. Taylor, a passionate advocate of small-scale farming and critic of national policies encouraging land monopoly, in critiquing land and water monopoly in California's Central Valley, illustrated the land monopoly he charged had resulted from railroad land grants (all in the state had gone to various Southern Pacific subsidiaries) by publishing a map based on an 1875 campaign poster by an early anti-railroad political party, the People's Independent Party. The party's map (see p. 66, this book), based on the same seriously exaggerated and misleading Department of the Interior maps that Robert Henry exposed, was widely reprinted in anti-railroad literature of the nineteenth century, and has been naively borrowed by some recent journalistic and scholarly critics of the Southern Pacific's grants. Depicting half of the state, including practically all valuable, low-elevation, well-watered land, as having been given to the company, including most of the coast south of the San Francisco Bay region and all the Los Angeles area, the map visually exaggerates the actual land granted by between 400 and 1000 percent and depicts grants along hundreds of miles of rail line for which no land grants were ever made. Even a casual evaluation by a qualified economist/ sociologist such as Taylor should have exposed the map as a fraud; Taylor, "Water, Land, and People in the Great Valley . . . ," *American West* 5 (March 1968): 24–29, 68–72. The map, which duped contemporaries as well as recent historians and geographers, continues to mislead the general public. The Oakland Museum exhibits one today as a period artifact, without commentary as to its veracity.

3. Geographer Ellen Liebman's argument that the Southern Pacific's grants and land policies delayed settlement, discouraged small farmers, and dramatically furthered land

monopoly in California, based it appears largely on a misreading of a flawed 1923 dissertation and a 1917 undergraduate course paper, contains so many minor and major factual errors and significant faulty conclusions that it would not be possible to critique it fully here. Enough to say that her account bears little resemblance to what actually happened. Suggestive of the problems are her statements that the land grants delayed settlement because the railroad line went "for the most part" through unsurveyed territory, and because of that and the fact that the land could not be surveyed and thus provided to settlers until the line was located since the federal government "used the railroad line as a baseline [for the survey]," land was kept out of settlement and hence monopolized later by the company and other speculators. California public land, of course, was indeed surveyed one or two decades *before* the Southern Pacific even existed or any of its lines contemplated, and the very notion of the ubiquitous federal rectilinear survey being based on impermanent, curving rail lines that the companies were forever moving, straightening, bypassing, tearing out, etc., is preposterous in the extreme; the rail lines were *not* used as "baselines." See Ellen Liebman, *California Farmland: A History of Large Agricultural Landholdings* (Totowa, NJ: Rowman and Allanheld, 1983), 36–42.

4. In his otherwise excellent environmental history of the San Joaquin Valley, *Vanishing Landscapes: Land and Life in the Tulare Lake Basin* (Berkeley: University of California Press, 1981), 102ff., 130–31, geographer William L. Preston alleged that the railroad grant delayed settlement and agricultural development, discouraged small-scale farming, and encouraged land monopoly. His analysis suffers from narrow, dated, mostly secondary sources; for Southern Pacific land policies in the region, for example, he relies exclusively on Frank Norris's 1901 muckraking piece of fiction, *The Octopus*. To prove the traditional case against the land grants, Preston also compared maps of two sets of federal survey townships (squares, six miles on a side, containing thirty-six one-mile-square sections). The first set of two were what might be called "homestead townships" (those containing the towns of Visalia and Hanford) where Preston said lands were "selected under provisions of the Homestead Act or cash entry." For comparison, the second set of two of what might be called "railroad townships" (near Pixley and Corcoran), within the Southern Pacific's land-grant area, depicted areas where Preston said land was "available more cheaply and in larger blocks (e.g., railroad land grants and Swamp and Overflowed Lands)." By counting the number of farmsteads at various dates, Preston claims to show that there were far fewer farms in the railroad townships than in the homestead townships, and moreover, that there were even fewer, and hence presumably larger, farms established on the odd-numbered railroad sections, as compared to the even-numbered public sections, within the railroad townships. Problems are rife in the comparison, including his failure to account for the townships' varied settlement dates, water supply and irrigability, crops, and land prices, all of which affect subdivision and the size of farmsteads. More troublesome are the two "homestead" townships, which he meant as controls. The Visalia district was *not* a "homestead" township at all: it was settled and the land taken up in the early 1850s, more than a decade before the passage of the Homestead Act. The Hanford township is even more problematical: it is not only *not* a "homestead" township, it was smack in the middle of the rail-

road's land grant. In fact, it was the most famous railroad township, site of the notorious Battle of Mussel Slough. Moreover, the number of farms on the *odd-numbered railroad sections* in the Hanford (railroad) township on Preston's map is significantly greater, and the farms presumably smaller, than on the public sections. The result is that the maps do not prove at all that Southern Pacific grants and land policies discouraged small-scale farming, but if anything, the reverse, that they fostered it.

5. The core myths that follow about Southern Pacific Company land grants are abstracted from numerous writings by scholars and non-scholars. These ideas have gained such acceptance that authors often do not even bother to cite supporting evidence. Many accounts also contain factual errors, including incorrect dates, land statistics, prices, provisions of rail land-grant laws, and even spellings of names, caused most likely by the fact that authors rarely have consulted primary sources; I will not address myself to these minor errors. A limited selection of examples includes those written by Paul Taylor, Ellen Liebman, and William Preston, cited above, and also Oscar Lewis, *The Big Four* (New York: Ballantine Books, 1971 [1938]), 280ff.; Carey McWilliams, *California: The Great Exception* (Berkeley: University of California Press, 1999 [1949]), chap. 6, esp. 90ff., in which he uses the land grants to the Southern Pacific as a major example, indeed cause, of "The Rape of the Public Domain"; Stephen Schwartz, *From West to East: California and the Making of the American Mind* (New York: The Free Press, 1998), 105ff.; Stephanie S. Pincetl, *Transforming California: A Political History of Land Use and Development* (Baltimore: Johns Hopkins University Press, 1999), 5ff., 20–22, 77–78; Richard Maxwell Brown, *No Duty to Retreat: Violence and Values in American History and Society* (New York: Oxford University Press, 1991), chap. 3; Robert V. Hine, *The American West: An Interpretive History,* 2nd ed. (Boston: Little, Brown and Co., 1984), 168ff., 177ff., 184–85; Ted Simon, *The River Stops Here: Saving Round Valley, A Pivotal Chapter in California's Water Wars* (Berkeley: University of California Press, 2001), 86–87; Richard W. Behan, *Plundered Promise: Capitalism, Politics, and the Fate of the Federal Lands* (Washington, DC: Island Press, 2001), esp. 110; Donald Worster, *Rivers of Empire: Water, Aridity, and the Growth of the American West* (New York: Pantheon Books, 1985), 101–102; Howard A. DeWitt, *California Civilization: An Interpretation* (Dubuque, IA: Kendall/Hunt Publishing Co., 1979), 160, 195–96; Walton Bean, *California: An Interpretive History* (New York: McGraw-Hill, 1978), 187ff.; David Lavender, *California: A Bicentennial History* (New York: W. W. Norton, 1976), 122–23; Warren A. Beck and David A. Williams, *California: A History of the Golden State* (Garden City, NY: Doubleday, 1972), 254–60; Warren A. Beck and Ynez D. Haase, *Historical Atlas of California* (Norman: University of Oklahoma Press, 1974), chap. 67, which publishes (and even exaggerates further) the flawed 1875 People's Independent Party railroad land-grant map; John W. Caughey and Norris Hundley, Jr., *California: History of a Remarkable State* (Englewood Cliffs, NJ: Prentice-Hall, 1982), 226–27; Jerry A. O'Callaghan, *The Disposition of the Public Domain in Oregon* (Washington, DC: Committee on Interior and Insular Affairs, U.S. Senate, 1960), 100–101. More journalistic and popular, and generally more seriously distorted, versions include Philip Fradkin, "Southern Pacific Changing 'Octopus' Image," *Los Angeles Times,* April 16, 1972, which also uncritically reprints the 1875 fraudulent map; George L. Baker, "The Kingdom of

the Railroads," *The Nation,* March 12, 1973, passim, esp. 334, 338–39; Hal Rubin, "Who Owns California," *California Journal,* June 1981, 221–23; Joel Kotkin and Paul Grabowicz, *California, Inc.* (New York: Avon Books, 1982), 21; and what may be the most deficient of all, John Ross and Tim Redmond, "The Octopus Revisited," *San Francisco Bay Guardian,* October 19–26, 1983.

6. Values, prices, and land disposal details, later in this chapter.

7. The railroad's varied regional land-grant geographies, most of them contrasting to the classic checkerboard pattern, are clear from detailed manuscript maps of the Southern Pacific Company's grants, made by the company's Land Department while reconstructing records after the San Francisco earthquake and fire of 1906: Central Pacific Railroad, "Land Grant Map Book" (ms., ca. 1906–1940s), vols. 1 and 2, and Southern Pacific Railroad, "Land Grant Map Book" (ms., ca. 1906–1940s), vols. 1–4; *CRRM.* Also for southern California, "Lands Granted to the Southern Pacific Railroad Company, Now Southern Pacific Land Company" (map, February 1, 1914), sheet 6, California State Archives, Sacramento. On the geographical implications of the unique Texas state railroad land-grant system, S. G. Reed, *A History of Texas Railroads* (Houston: St. Clair Publishing Co., 1941), 129–87; Reed, "Southern Pacific System in Texas," in *Handbook of Texas,* ed. Walter Prescott Webb (Austin: Texas State Historical Association, 1952), 2:642–43; Reed, "Public Aid to Railroad Construction," *Handbook of Texas,* 2:430–31; Robert S. Maxwell, *Whistle in the Piney Woods: Paul Bremond and the Houston, East and West Texas Railway* (Texas Gulf Coast Historical Association, 1963), 23–24; A. F. Muir, "The Buffalo Bayou, Brazos, and Colorado Railway Company, 1850–1861" (M.A. thesis, Rice Institute, 1942), 78–79; Southern Pacific Company, "Taxes, 1894" (ms.), and Houston & Texas Central Railway Co., "Register of Land Patents" (ms.), *SP-H;* Lee Van Zant, "State Promotion of Railroad Construction in Texas, 1836–1890" (Ph.D. diss., University of Texas, Austin, 1967), 105–32; Thomas Lloyd Miller, *The Public Lands of Texas* (Norman: University of Oklahoma Press, 1972), 95–105.

8. See Taylor, "Water, Land, and People in the Great Valley"; Fradkin, "Southern Pacific Changing 'Octopus' Image."

9. Luther Conant, Jr., *The Lumber Industry, Part 1: Standing Timber* (Washington, DC: Department of Commerce and Labor, Bureau of Corporations, January 20, 1913), 15–16.

10. *San Francisco Call,* February 28, 1913.

11. Robert Bradley Jones, *One By One: A Documented Narrative Based upon the History of the Oregon and California Railroad Land Grant in the State of Oregon* (Maryhurst, OR: The Source Magazine, ca. 1973), 19, 162–71 (bibliography of similar exaggerated sources).

12. Kotkin and Grabowicz, *California, Inc.,* 21.

13. Ross and Redmond, "The Octopus Revisited."

14. See Beck and Williams, *California,* 258; James J. Rawls and Walton Bean, *California, An Interpretive History,* 7th ed. (New York: McGraw-Hill, 1998), 178; William W. Robinson, *Land in California: The Story of Mission Lands, Ranchos, Squatters, Mining Claims, Railroad Grants, Land Scrip, Homesteads* (Berkeley: University of California Press, 1948), 157.

15. Some of Ross and Redmond's statistics are worse, amounting to 500–2500 percent exaggerations; see my critique published in *San Francisco Bay Guardian,* December 7, 1983.

16. F. W. Sercombe, "Report of Examination of Central Pacific Railway Company Land Department Accounts . . . September 22nd, 1865, to November 30th, 1903, Inclusive" (typescript, San Francisco, May 1904), in Sercombe to Erastus Young, San Francisco, June 16, 1904; and Sercombe, "Statement Showing the Progress Made in Auditing the Accounts of the Southern Pacific Railroad Company's Land Department, from July 12th, 1871, to June 30th, 1903" (typescript, San Francisco, October 1, 1903); Charles W. Eberlein Correspondence, *SP-L.*

17. Southern Pacific Land Department, "Lands Granted to the Southern Pacific Railroad Company in California" (ms., November 9, 1907), File 654, *SP-L.*

18. For sales and markets, later in this chapter.

19. Exact acreage in various Southern Pacific lines' grants is elusive. Based on public documents, historian Benjamin Hibbard concluded in 1924 that grants to the Central Pacific, Southern Pacific, California & Oregon, and Oregon & California roads totaled (as of 1923) about 20,850,000 acres; Hibbard, *A History of the Public Land Policies* (New York: The Macmillan Company, 1924), 264. He, however, includes in the totals much land the company never actually owned: such as acreage granted, but never patented; land later lost in federal lawsuits, such as over the Atlantic & and Pacific overlap case; the entire grant assigned to the Central Pacific by the Western Pacific Railroad when the Big Four bought out that line in the 1860s; and land that was later confiscated by the federal government such as mineral lands, Mexican land-grant lands, and the 2.8 million acres lost in the Oregon & California lawsuit. Internal Southern Pacific records summing up land-grant history to 1965 used the following figures, rounded off: theoretical maximum total, including confiscated lands, 21,112,000 acres; acreage not received or released to the federal government, 3,430,000; resulting net patents received, 17,679,000. By 1965, however, the company had sold 13,899,000 acres of that, leaving its holdings at about 3,780,000 acres. See Southern Pacific Company, "Historical Memoranda" (ca. 1965), vol. 1, chap. 3, p. 10, *SP-E.* A useful, statistical, financial, and legal summary of Southern Pacific federal land-grants, extensively documented in federal records, is David F. Myrick, "Land Grants: Aids and Benefits to the Government and Railroads and to the Southern Pacific Company" (mimeo, October 28, 1969), in my collection as well as numerous libraries, including *CRRM.*

20. *Sacramento Union,* August 16, 1867.

21. Redding biography, California Academy of Sciences, *In Memoriam: Benjamin B. Redding, Born January 17th, 1824, Died August 21st, 1882* (n.p., n.d.); *Sacramento Record-Union,* August 22 and 25, 1882; Alonzo Phelps, *Contemporary Biography of California's Representative Men,* 2 vols. (San Francisco: A. L. Bancroft, 1882), 2:77–83; Ella Sterling Mighels, *The Story of the Files: A Review of California Writers and Literature* (San Francisco: Cooperative Printing Co., 1893), 253–55.

22. *Sacramento Union,* August 16, 1867.

23. For early land programs, 1860s–1870s, land agent reports in *Annual Reports,* Central and Southern Pacific railroads; *Sacramento Union,* August 16, 1867. Madden biog-

raphy, Phelps, *Contemporary Biography,* 2:46–50; G. W. Sullivan, *Early Days in California* (San Francisco, 1888), 1:98–100; *Weekly Commercial Record* (San Francisco), June 13, 1889; mss. in Jerome Madden Papers, *BL,* including appointment documents and railroad power of attorney.

24. B. B. Redding to D. K. Zumwalt, Sacramento, September 25, 1873, *ZC-SP.*

25. For local land-agent system, two extant ms. collections: *ZC-SP* and B. B. Redding–W. C. Belcher correspondence (1870s), Central Pacific Railroad Land Department Letters, *CRRM.* For some Fulton papers, Nevada Historical Society, Reno. Fulton biography, Barbara Richnak, *A River Flows: The Life of Robert Lardin Fulton* (Incline Village, NV: Comstock-Nevada Publishing Co., 1983). Zumwalt remained with the Southern Pacific until the company released him during the 1893 national depression. His maps, documents, and thousands of incoming and outgoing letters are the best single source on day-to-day operations of the railroad's land business. For agents' duties, salaries, and lines of authority, esp. B. B. Redding to Zumwalt, Sacramento, October 19 and November 4, 1870, and May 20, 1871, Jerome Madden to Zumwalt, San Francisco, July 13, 1887, and Zumwalt to Madden, Visalia, October 30, 1878; *ZC-SP.* Zumwalt biography as respected Tulare County community leader, church elder, reformer, philanthropist, and agricultural and irrigation developer, in Kathleen E. Small, *History of Tulare County, California* (Chicago: S. J. Clarke Publishing Co., 1926), 1:323, 2: 463–65; *Visalia Delta,* November 3, 1904. For the Texas Southern Pacific Land Department (1880s–1920s), letters and account books, *SP-H.*

26. Documents, File 935, "Land Examiners in the Mojave Desert," *SP-L,* esp. F. L. Mary to B. A. McAllaster, Cottonwood, CA, February 26, 1911, Mary to Fred W. Houtz, Kramer, CA, April 28, 1911, and McAllaster to E. E. Calvin, San Francisco, April 24, 1911. For tribulations of surveying railroad land grants in rugged terrain, J. J. Bowden, *Surveying the Texas and Pacific Land Grant West of the Pecos River,* Southwestern Studies Monograph No. 46 (El Paso: Texas Western Press, University of Texas at El Paso, 1975).

27. This notion frequently surfaced in the nineteenth-century anti-railroad press and has been borrowed by scholar-critics of the Southern Pacific's land policy;see Liebman, *California Farmland,* 40–41; Ralph J. Roske, *Everyman's Eden: A History of California* (New York: Macmillan, 1968), 488–89; O'Callaghan, *Disposition of the Public Domain in Oregon,* 100–101.

28. The consistency of the policy over such a long period is clear from following the issue of land-patenting through nearly complete collections of internal discussions among company leaders, letters among railroaders and to and from federal land officials, reports on unpatented lands, and other documents. I have not found a single document testifying that the company sought to delay the patenting process, and innumerable documents to the contrary. See especially what appears to be the complete outgoing correspondence (67 vols.) of the Southern Pacific's Washington, DC, attorneys handling land-grant matters with the Department of the Interior, *SP-A;* many letters and copies of letters in the records of the company's San Joaquin Valley land agent, D. K. Zumwalt, *ZC-SP;* and the hundreds of letters dealing with land patents to and from Collis P. Huntington, who supervised the activities of the Washington

attorneys from his office in New York and maintained a regular correspondence on the subject with the railroad's other executives, land agents, attorneys, congressmen, federal officials, and U.S. presidents, *CPH.*

29. Many letters in *SP-A* describe the activities of land speculators contesting Southern Pacific patents in Washington and the railroad's efforts to counter them, particularly 1860s–1870s. By no means did the railroad win all contests; see Henry Beard, Southern Pacific attorney, Washington, DC, to B. B. Redding, Washington, November 23, 1867, vol. 4, describing a protracted controversy involving hundreds of thousands of acres in California and Nevada that the railroad happened to win; Beard to Redding, Washington, November 11 and 16, 1868, Beard to Joseph Wilson, commissioner, General Land Office, Washington, November 11, 1868, and Beard to Charles McLaughlin, Washington, November 15, 1868, vol. 6., describing a vast scheme by speculators to bribe government land agents and surveyors in the Sacramento and San Joaquin valleys to get them to falsely classify dry land as "swamp and overflowed" land, which would have denied it to railroad and opened it to rival entry by speculators. See also vol. 6, for the critical role that California land speculators led by William S. Chapman played in getting the Department of the Interior in the late 1860s to declare the grant to the Southern Pacific Railroad to be illegal and to threaten to restore the land to entry by others. Though the land remained reserved for the company, Interior's order itself was declared to be illegal and was countermanded by Congress, with the assent of the California state legislature. The land was patented to the railroad company, but the controversy clouded patents and titles to the grant and gave a pretext later for a massive invasion of San Joaquin Valley railroad land by squatters and speculators, climaxing in the famous 1880 Battle of Mussel Slough; O. H. Browning, secretary of the interior, to Wilson, Washington, DC, July 14, 1868 [copy], Beard to Redding, Washington, July 18, 1868, Beard to Collis P. Huntington, Washington, July 18, 21, 27, and 30, and August 1, 1868.

30. To lobby the Department of the Interior and other federal agencies, secure patents, and represent the company in title contests and court cases, Huntington in the mid-1860s retained several Washington, DC, attorneys. D. A. Chambers, Henry Beard, John Boyd, and Jonathan Bloss served as point men, coordinating land-grant legal activities of the company's land agents and executives. Huntington was their principal company contact, and he traveled often from New York to aid them in Washington, 1865–1900; many letters to and from the attorneys in *CPH,* some indexed in the collection's guide, and letters in *SP-A.*

31. Even some historians critical of the Southern Pacific have acknowledged that the General Land Office caused the patent delays; Stuart Daggett, *Chapters on the History of the Southern Pacific* (New York: August M. Kelley, Publishers, 1966 [1922]), 56–58. Some historians sympathetic to squatters on Southern Pacific lands also charge that Interior's delays increased squatterism; see James L. Brown, *The Mussel Slough Tragedy* (1958), 18ff. and 32ff. For problems of federal administration of the railroad and other internal improvement grants, particularly the government's patenting delays, Paul W. Gates, *History of Public Land Law Development* (Washington, DC: Government Printing Office, 1968), chap. 14, esp. 379–80; Leslie E. Decker, "The Railroads and the Land Office: Administrative Policy and the Land Patent Controversy, 1864–1896," *Mississippi*

Valley Historical Review 46 (March 1960): 679–99; Harold H. Dunham, "The General Land Office, 1875–1890," in Carstensen, *Public Lands*, passim, esp. 186–87; and Dunham, *Government Handout: A Study in the Administration of the Public Lands, 1875–1891* (New York: Edwards Brothers, 1941), passim.

32. The pace of government patenting did pick up in the mid-1870s, and the railroads began to receive more list-approvals, though not without delays. Chronic delays continued, however, climaxing from the mid-1880s into the 1890s, as discussed later in this chapter. For the nature of the problem, evident in initial delays in Central Pacific lists of patents, and the railroad's persistent prodding of the Department of the Interior, E. B. Crocker to Collis P. Huntington, Sacramento, January 10, 14, and 31 and February 21, 1867, *CPH;* Henry Beard to B. B. Redding, Washington, DC, November 28, 1867, vol. 5, Beard to Redding, June 5, 1868, vol. 6, and Beard to Redding, Washington, July 30, 1869, vol. 8, *SP-A.* Department of the Interior records contain numerous documents testifying to the Southern Pacific's pressure from the outset to get its patents; see, for example, Leland Stanford to John B. Usher, secretary of the interior, Sacramento, February 20, 1864, J. M. Edmunds, commissioner, General Land Office, to James Harlan, secretary of the interior, Washington, DC, July 12 and August 17, 1865, Huntington to Usher, Washington, DC, February 11 and 28, 1865, Beard to O. H. Browning, secretary of the interior, Washington, DC, September 6, 1866, RG 48 (598: 33), *NA-W;* more letters in (598: 33) and (598: 34), particularly Beard to Joseph S. Wilson, commissioner, General Land Office, Washington, DC, March 26, 1870, which reviews continuing patenting breakdowns, presents statistics on Central Pacific patents to date, and reiterates the railroad's objections to delays. For Nevada and Utah, Willis Drummond, commissioner, General Land Office, to Columbus Delano, secretary of the interior, February 26, 1873, (598: 39). The General Land Office, overwhelmed and fearful of patenting too much land to the railroad companies, instituted many procedures—including endless buck-passing, requirements for reviews and re-reviews of decisions by different levels of officials, and time-consuming presidential signatures on the final approval papers—that also seriously delayed patents. Beginning in 1869, for example, the office arbitrarily started issuing patents for only one-half of each odd-numbered land section the Central Pacific and Union Pacific roads applied for, withholding the other half to secure the completion of the first transcontinental line. That route, of course, was completed in May 1869, but the one-half withholding rule remained in place, causing confusion and redundant work for the railroad and local land office officials, until late 1874, when President Ulysses S. Grant ordered the procedure discontinued; "Memo Regarding Secretaries of the Interior's Orders on Issuing Patents to Railroads" (ms., unidentified author, ca. 1870), and Beard to Columbus Delano, secretary of the interior, Washington, DC, March 24, 1871, RG 48 (598: 39), and Delano to President Ulysses S. Grant, Washington, DC, November 11, 1874 (598: 40). As the above correspondence suggests, from the late 1860s through the early 1870s as many as a dozen men revolved quickly through the offices of commissioner of the General Land Office and secretary of the Department of the Interior, many reversing the policies of predecessors, changing procedures and criteria for decisions, confusing even their agencies' staffs, and aggravating the business logjams.

33. For land-grant railways, James B. Hedges, *Henry Villard and the Railways of the Northwest* (New Haven: Yale University Press, 1930); Paul Wallace Gates, *The Illinois Central Railroad and Its Colonization Work* (Cambridge: Harvard University Press, 1934); Richard Overton, *Burlington West: A Colonization History of the Burlington Railroad* (Cambridge: Harvard University Press, 1941); William S. Greever, *Arid Domain: The Santa Fe Railroad and Its Western Land Grant* (Stanford: Stanford University Press, 1954); Sig Mickelson, *The Northern Pacific Railroad and the Selling of the West* (Sioux Falls, SD: Center for Western Studies, 1993); William S. Greever, "A Comparison of Railroad Land Grant Policies," *Agricultural History* 25 (April 1951): 83–90; special issue, *Agricultural History,* "The Role of Railroads in Agricultural Development," 31 (October 1957); Roy V. Scott, *Railroad Development Programs in the Twentieth Century* (Ames: Iowa State University Press, 1985), esp. chap. 2. The Southern Pacific's land administration was consistent with other western roads, which were becoming increasingly standardized and professionalized.

34. U.S. Pacific Railway Commission, *Testimony Taken By the United States Pacific Railway Commission,* 8 vols. (Washington, DC: Government Printing Office, 1887), 5:2413; see also, B. B. Redding to D. K. Zumwalt, Sacramento, April 15, 1872, *ZC-SP.*

35. B. A. McAllaster to William F. Herrin, San Francisco, February 15, 1923, File 976, *SP-L.*

36. The following analysis of Southern Pacific land-grant development and sales is constructed from documents in extensive manuscript collections from which I will cite only a few representative examples below. The collections are *ZC-SP; SP-A;* the Cash and Day Books and Journals of the Southern Pacific Railroad and the Central Pacific Railroad Land Departments in the 1870s and 1880s, many volumes of Land-Grant Map Books of the Southern Pacific Railroad and the Central Pacific Railroad, ca. 1906 and updated in following years, and the Central Pacific Railroad Land Department Letters, all at *CRRM;* and *CPH.* Railroad land pamphlets and ads were also consulted, as well as Central Pacific and Southern Pacific railroads' annual reports, and after 1884, the Southern Pacific Company's.

37. See letters of instruction, B. B. Redding to D. K. Zumwalt, esp. February 25, 1871, April 15 and October 19, 1872, January 24, 1873, and March 12, April 1 and 21, 1875, *ZC-SP.*

38. The Land Department gave district land agents such as D. K. Zumwalt detailed maps of already subdivided railroad properties for sale, almost always in one-eighth to one-half sections, with specific instructions regarding how each parcel was to be sold and for what price. Each parcel had to be sold whole; "Land Plat Book, 1879–1892," *ZC-SP.* The company turned away would-be purchasers seeking only small tracts containing water, trees, etc.; for the policy, B. B. Redding to Zumwalt, San Francisco, July 23, 1875, *ZC-SP.* In refusing an application to buy only half of one 160-acre tract, Zumwalt explained that the railroad did *not* sell small tracts that controlled resources; instead, the entire parcel had to be taken whole, "on account of valuable water privileges"; Zumwalt to N. Johnson, Visalia, May 30, 1881, and Jerome Madden to Zumwalt, San Francisco, May 25, 1881.

39. The policy of rapid land dispersal to actual, small-farm settlers was followed with

few exceptions on all Southern Pacific lines during the entire period from the 1860s through the early twentieth century, except during the Harriman Lines interlude from 1901 to 1913. For unequivocal statements, B. B. Redding to D. K. Zumwalt, April 15, 1872, and Redding, "Railroad Lands . . . Central Pacific Land Department . . . Sacramento, 1867," guideline for railroad land agents, copy appended to Redding to Zumwalt, February 25, 1871, *ZC-SP.* Collis P. Huntington's statement of the same policy is in Southern Pacific Railroad Company, *Annual Report, 1875* (1876), 9. Redding's quotation is from his letter to Zumwalt, San Francisco, April 29, 1875, *ZC-SP.* Redding had explained the policy to Zumwalt time and again, but Zumwalt was still uncertain how to apply it to the many kinds of disputed claims to Southern Pacific land. Exasperated at Zumwalt's continued failure to comprehend the basic principle, Redding was particularly direct and emphatic in this letter.

40. B. B. Redding to D. K. Zumwalt, April 15, 1872, *ZC-SP.*

41. In its land-grant program through the early twentieth century, the company sought to thwart speculation in its lands, which would have defeated the goal of rapid settlement by small-scale farmers, agricultural and town development, and increased rail traffic. In many letters over twenty years instructing San Joaquin Valley district land agent D. K. Zumwalt, Southern Pacific Railroad land agent Jerome Madden frequently warned Zumwalt to refuse the applications of speculator-buyers. "I do not like that sort of thing [speculation]," he wrote on November 11, 1881. "I want the purchaser to have the full benefit of R.R. prices, without the intervention of anybody else. . . . You shall take every opportunity of frowning down this class of claimants"; also letters of December 1, 1881, and April 21, 1887, and B. B. Redding to Zumwalt, Sacramento, April 15, 1872.

42. From the 1860s to the 1910s, public advertisements and internal railroad sources testify to very low prices, often many-fold lower, than charged by contemporary and scholarly critics of the company and of rail land-grants in general. Pricing policy frequently came up, for example, in private correspondence between regional land agents and the central Land Department offices; B. B. Redding to W. C. Belcher (Marysville, CA, agent for the company's California and Oregon Railroad grant), March 17 and October 1, 1873, and January 19, March 21, and April 28, 1874, which discussed standard prices for various types of fairly well-watered Sacramento Valley land between $2.50 and $10 per acre; Central Pacific Railroad Land Department Letters, *CRRM.* The great majority of the Southern Pacific Railroad's more arid, though potentially fertile, San Joaquin Valley land was priced between $2.50 and $5.50 per acre, except small areas on town edges and a few regions already being irrigated and considered more valuable but still seldom priced more than a few dollars above $10; B. B. Redding to D. K. Zumwalt, San Francisco, April 21, 26, and 29 and November 5, 1875, and Zumwalt "Land Plat Book, 1879–1892," containing prices of all the railroad's valley lands, *ZC-SP.* Complete daily records of all land transactions, 1870s–1880s, record low prices on the railroad's land almost everywhere in the San Joaquin Valley, where much of the most fertile company land was located. For the nearly one hundred land sales between February 1 and 28, 1882, for one representative example, almost all had prices under $5 per acre, with prices between $3 and $4.50 being by far the most common; between 1882 and 1885,

prices were between $2 and $6, with some remote and arid land selling for as little as $1; Southern Pacific Railroad Company, Land Department, "Journal, 1882–1885," vol. 1, p. 1ff., and vol. 2, pp. 35ff.; Southern Pacific Railroad Company, Land Department, "Day Book, 1871–1882," vol. 2, esp. 151, 179ff., and 274–75, *CRRM.* In Nevada, 1868–1900, almost all land that sold, most of it in the irrigable Truckee Meadows around Reno, sold for between $2 and $5 per acre; Central Pacific Railroad, "Land Sales, 1868–1900" (ms., n.d.), Nevada Historical Society, Reno.

43. Sercombe, "Central Pacific Railway Company Land Department Accounts, 1865–1903"; Sercombe, "Accounts of Southern Pacific Railroad Company's Land Department, 1871–1903." For land policies, grading, and pricing, Richard J. Orsi, "Confrontation at Mussel Slough, 1880," chap. 13, *The Elusive Eden: A New History of California,* by Richard B. Rice, William A. Bullough, and Richard J. Orsi (New York: McGraw Hill, 1996 and 2002 eds.).

44. Khaled Bloom, "Land Speculation in the Pioneer San Joaquin Valley," *Agricultural History* 57 (July 1983): 297–307.

45. *Sacramento Union,* August 16, 1867; Central Pacific Railroad Company, *Annual Report, 1879* (San Francisco, 1880), 45–49; Central Pacific Railroad Company, *Railroad Lands in California and Nevada* (Sacramento, 1872), 17–18; Walter A. McAllister, "A Study of Railroad Land-Grant Disposal in California with Reference to the Western Pacific, the Central Pacific, and the Southern Pacific Railroad Companies" (Ph.D. diss., University of Southern California, 1939), 232ff. and 268ff.; B. A. McAllaster (Land Commissioner of the Southern Pacific Company) to E. A. Kincaid, San Francisco, October 22, 1920, in Kincaid, "The Federal Land Grants of the Central Pacific Railroad" (Ph.D. diss., University of California, Berkeley, 1922), appendix to chap. XV.

46. A 1876 California Grange survey pegged farm interest rates at between 12 and 24 percent; *California Patron,* December 13, 1876.

47. *Sacramento Union,* August 16, 1867; Central Pacific Railroad Company, *Annual Report, 1872* (1873), 39–40, *Annual Report, 1881* (1882), 50–51; Southern Pacific Railroad Company, *Annual Report, 1876 and 1877* (San Francisco, 1877), 49–64, and *Annual Report, 1881* (1882), 45–51; Kincaid, "Land Grants of the Central Pacific," appendix. For time-payment contracts, Day Books and Cash Books of the Southern Pacific and Central Pacific Railroads, 1870s-80s, *CRRM;* "Day Book, 1871–1882," vol. 2, 172ff., for example, records the charges in many such sales using 7-percent interest, 1881–1882.

48. A community leader and philanthropist, D. K. Zumwalt often interceded with San Francisco executives on behalf of needy land buyers; see Zumwalt to Jerome Madden, Visalia, esp. August 1880–January 1881, during drought and crop failure in the San Joaquin Valley, and March 28 and April 15, 16, 20, and 25, 1881, February 16 and March 7, 1883, and October 23 and 31, 1885, and Madden to Zumwalt, San Francisco, April 10, 1879, and January 4 and 12, March 15, and April 25, 1881, *ZC-SP.* Madden almost never refused Zumwalt's entreaties, even when settlers were seriously behind in payments or had given the railroad trouble in the past. Arranging for payment extensions and refinancing was an important duty of the railroad's district land agents. The railroad dealt with delinquent contract holders in several ways, all of which aimed at keeping the farmers on the land, or at least preserving their investments in previous princi-

pal payments and improvements. In one plan, railway land agents found buyers for defaulted contract holders' farms. In another, contract holders could remit some of their
land back to the company and refinance the retained portion for an additional five years
at the original price. In yet another, buyers reassigned the contracts to the company
and then leased back their farms for small fees or crop shares; they could then reapply
to purchase the lands at a later date, at the original price; in *ZC-SP,* Madden to Zumwalt,
San Francisco, April 10, 1879, September 2, October 21, and November 27, 1880, January 4, March 9 and 15, 1881, and Zumwalt to Madden, Visalia, April 17 and 28, April
20, 1881, February 16, March 7, 1883, October 23, 1885, September 16, 1886, and April
13, 1887. At all cost, the Southern Pacific avoided foreclosing and dispossessing serious
land buyers who had fallen on hard times. On April 10, 1879, land agent Madden
instructed Zumwalt to reassure delinquent purchasers that "the Company will not be
hard on them. . . . During my whole connection with the R.R. Co., I have never known
it to sell out any individual who has purchased land from it," he explained. "These people
need not be alarmed: the fair thing will be done." The railroad helped buyers capitalize their lands in two other ways: by offering land buyers employment on the railroad
during idle farm seasons; and, until the Interstate Commerce Commission prohibited
it in 1887, by selling prospective land buyers "land-seeker tickets," refundable toward
the purchase price, for them and families to search for railroad lands; *Alta California*
(San Francisco), February 26, 1868; Madden to Zumwalt, San Francisco, April 24, 1885,
April 9, 1886, and January 25, 1888, *ZC-SP.* Looked at another way, the railroad's credit
plan was even more favorable to persons seeking to enter farming. If land purchasers,
after their down payment, made the low annual interest payments instead of leasing
similar private land for the going rent of $1 to $2 per acre per year, they could save
enough after five years to nearly, or wholly, pay off the rest of the principal, plus sometimes to pocket additional cash. In the typical farm purchase discussed in the text (80
acres at $5 per acre, 10-percent interest), the annual interest payment of $32 was considerably less than an $80 to $160 yearly (market-rate) rental; between $48 and $128
could have been saved annually. Land values in the San Joaquin Valley also commonly
increased from a few dollars to between $20 and $40 per acre with improvements and
settlement, raising the buyers' profits yet more.

49. Kincaid, "Land Grants of the Central Pacific," appendix.

50. For lease terms, Jerome Madden to D. K. Zumwalt, San Francisco, December
27, 1876, and March 2, 1885; H. B. Underhill (of the Contract and Finance Company)
to Zumwalt, San Francisco, November 22, 1874; *ZC-SP.* For examples of leases, many
letters to and from Zumwalt, *ZC-SP;* and Southern Pacific Railroad Company, Land
Department, "Day Book, 1871–1882," vol. 1, 136ff. and 206ff., and esp. "List of Farming Leases Issued During December 1881 [the month that leases were signed]," in "Day
Book," vol. 2, 354–67, *CRRM.*

51. Jerome Madden to D. K. Zumwalt, San Francisco, June 30 and October 27, 1880,
and Zumwalt to Madden, Visalia, December 22, 1880, and October 14, 1886, *ZC-SP.*
The railroad also helped cash-strapped crop-share farmers by paying them $2 to $4 per
ton to haul the company's portion of their crop shares to the nearest railroad station;
see Madden to Zumwalt, San Francisco, October 7, 1884.

52. Poaching, especially by sheepmen, including those who rented small pieces of railroad land to use as bases for their migrating herds, was constant in lightly settled places such as the San Joaquin Valley and the Great Basin. The Southern Pacific took steps to prevent it, including lawsuits and hiring agents to follow sheep herds; Jerome Madden to D. K. Zumwalt, December 22, 1879, February 10 and 17, 1880; *ZC-SP.* For herders' use of leases to monopolize water, Madden to Zumwalt, November 3, 1880.

53. Jerome Madden to D. K. Zumwalt, San Francisco, June 3 and July 25, 1881, *ZC-SP.* The railroad viewed leasing as a temporary expedient. "The Company wants to sell, not to lease," Madden instructed Zumwalt in the above letter. "A great many persons would never buy if assured that their leases would be renewed from year to year." On the other hand, the company sought to protect lessees from losing crops when their leaseholds were sold to others. C. H. Wilson of the Tulare County area did not renew his lease to a half-section in the fall of 1881 and, following its policy, the railroad sold the land to another person. However, when informed that Wilson had already sown a crop, Madden wrote to Zumwalt that "it would be a most ruinous hardship to sell from under him," and that in the "exercise of mercy," the company was renewing Wilson's lease after the fact for another year, voiding the new sale contract, and refunding the purchase price to the buyer; Madden to Zumwalt, October 27, 1881.

54. Jerome Madden to D. W. Parkhurst, San Francisco, November 30, 1880 (copy), *ZC-SP;* B. A. McAllaster to G. W. Luce, San Francisco, April 24, 1913, Grazing Folder, *SP-L.* In the latter document, land agent McAllaster reported to higher executives that John G. Taylor, a sheep raiser near Winnemucca, NV, had for years leased 400,000–500,000 acres of company land. For other large Great Basin livestock lessors, Central Pacific Railroad Land-Grant Map Books, ca. 1906 and following years, *CRRM.*

55. Frequently, odd-numbered sections that were reserved for the railway in its land-grant area when the company filed its map and that should have been closed to all subsequent forms of settlement had not been accurately designated by the Department of the Interior in Washington, had not been communicated accurately, *or even at all,* to the local land offices, or, as appeared to be most often the case, had been incorrectly entered by local land officials on maps that other settlers used to locate and file their claims. Washington land officials also sometimes delayed months or even years in informing district land offices of the locations of patents issued to the railroad, leading local offices to continue to approve illegal rival claims by homesteaders, preemptors, and cash purchasers to the railroad's lands. Often, as well, local land officials did not carefully check even those maps that were accurate and thus allowed innocent settlers to file invalid claims against land the railroad already had title to, in some cases had already sold to other parties. The reverse also happened: Department of Interior or local land officials failed to eliminate prior homestead or preemption claims or purchases from the railway's selection lists, and thus gave patents to the company for lands to which settlers already held prior rights. For federal problems administering railroad and other internal improvement grants, Decker, "Railroads and the Land Office," 679–99; Gates, *History of Public Land Law Development,* chap. 14, esp. 379–80; and Dunham, "The General Land Office, 1875–1890," passim, esp. 186–87, who concluded that the "machinery for handling them [land grants] remained inefficient, antiquated, and

inadequate." According to Dunham, inefficiency, fraud, and corruption in the General Land Office also extended down to the district land offices; mistakes were common, resulting in endless litigation. Some historians critical of the Southern Pacific's dealings with rival land claimants blame the Department of the Interior's bungling of patents and claim-filings for much of the conflict; Brown, *The Mussel Slough Tragedy,* 18ff. and 32ff.; for the same from a historian unsympathetic to squatters, Barbara M. Bristow, "Mussel Slough Tragedy: Railroad Struggle or Land Gamble" (M.A. thesis, Fresno State College, 1971), 39ff. Department of Interior records also testify to the government's inept handling of Southern Pacific Company railroad patents. Sources on numerous patenting problems, particularly delays, have already been cited above for the Central Pacific. The department also made many serious errors, including protracted delays, in handling Southern Pacific Railroad lands. Federal officials frequently had to void patents for small tracts or huge bodies of railroad-owned land illegally issued to settlers or states, as well as patents wrongly issued to the company. Reluctant to admit even obvious mistakes, the Department of the Interior tended to reject appeals by the railroad companies. Contests, hearings, appeals, reappeals, and reversals resulted in further delays, losses to all parties, and much bad feeling toward the railroad. For the Southern Pacific Railroad, letters and reports in RG 48 (598: 220–30), *NA-W.* Also, for patenting problems of all Southern Pacific companies, see, from *SP-A:* Henry Beard to B. B. Redding, Washington, September 13, 18, and 19, and October 27, 1866, Beard to Joseph S. Wilson, commissioner, General Land Office, Washington, DC, September 21, October 10, 12, and 13, 1866, Beard to Collis P. Huntington, Washington, DC, October 2, 1866, vol. 2; Beard to Redding, Washington, DC, May 30 and June 5, 1868, vol. 6; Beard to J. A. Williamson, commissioner, General Land Office, Washington, DC, January 26 and 27 and March 8, 1877, February 18, 1878, and April 12, 1879, vol. 3; Beard to Williamson, Washington, DC, March 29, August 12 and 16, 1880, Beard to Carl Schurz, secretary of the interior, Washington, DC, November 20, 1880, Beard to N. C. McFarland, commissioner, General Land Office, Washington, DC, February 5, 1880, vol. 4; Beard to L. M. Slackslager, commissioner, General Land Office, Washington, DC, March 27, April 3 and 22, 1889, Beard to John W. Noble, secretary of the interior, May 15 and 16, 1889, and many other letters to federal land officials, 1889–1894, a period when the Department of the Interior deliberately obstructed the patenting process and indeed encouraged the giving of patents to squatters on the railroad's land grant, vol. 13.

56. For this routine procedure, Jerome Madden to D. K. Zumwalt, San Francisco, September 2, 1885, *ZC-SP.*

57. Many letters, *SP-A,* among Land Department executives, local land agents, and the company's Washington attorneys; and B. B. Redding to D. K. Zumwalt, San Francisco, August 21, September 6, and October 4, 1875; *ZC-SP.*

58. Henry Beard to B. B. Redding, Washington, DC, May 25 and June 5, 1868; also, Beard to Redding, September 13, 19, 20, and 25, 1866, Beard to Joseph S. Wilson, commissioner, General Land Office, Washington, DC, September 21 and 24, 1866, Beard to J. A. Williamson, commissioner, General Land Office, December 19, 1876, December 9, 1879, February 24, 1880, Beard to U. J. Baxter, acting commissioner, General Land

Office, June 6, 1876, Beard to N. C. McFarland, commissioner, General Land Office, August 17, 1881, December 28, 1882 (in which Beard reiterated to Interior that it was "not the desire of the Railroad Company to contest cases where there appears to be any substantial merit whatever [on behalf of the settler], upon mere questions of law"), vol. 2, *SP-A.* Also, B. B. Redding to D. K. Zumwalt, Sacramento, October 19 and December 27, 1870, and January 19, 1871, *ZC-SP,* letters of instruction prohibiting contests against legitimate settlers, even if their claims were technically flawed.

59. The railroad reached amicable compromises with many contestants by offering to sell the disputed tracts to the settlers for whatever their costs would have been had they homesteaded or purchased public land from the government, which within the railway grants, since most contestants were would-be preemptors, was usually the "government price" of $2.50 per acre. Such settlers also took advantage of the railroad's liberal time-payment plan, which meant that they immediately needed only 20 percent of the price, instead of the full cost, which would have been due on purchase from the government. In the late 1860s, the railroad went even further, advertising widely in newspapers and circulars offering settlers having conflicting homestead or preemption claims on company lands a rock-bottom price of $1.25 per acre if they would withdraw their claims; Elihu Johnson to O. H. Browning, secretary of the interior, Antioch, CA, February 1, 1869, RG 48 (598: 37), *NA-W.* In those agreements, the railroad's agents and attorneys handled all the paperwork for the settlers, and if by some chance the railroad's title to the land was later invalidated for some other reason, agreements with settlers promised full refunds of their land payments; Jerome Madden to William La Motte (one of the contesting claimants), San Francisco, January 31 and February 26, 1885, and Madden to D. K. Zumwalt, San Francisco, April 7 and May 12, 1885, and November 5, 1887. Sometimes, as in 1875 in the San Joaquin Valley, the Southern Pacific filed mass abandonments of its rights to lands that settlers were occupying and cultivating but where the settlers' claims were technically flawed; B. B. Redding to D. K. Zumwalt, San Francisco, September 6 and 30, 1875; all in *ZC-SP.* Settling with rival claimants was company policy throughout the land-grant area; Redding letters to Marysville district agent Edward A. Belcher, especially throughout January and February 1873, when several dozen conflicts were being resolved with settlers; also February 1, March 25, April 16, July 18, and October 1, 28, and 31, 1873, Central Pacific Railroad Land Department Letters, *CRRM.*

60. For details and goals of the railroad's land conflict hearings, B. B. Redding to D. K. Zumwalt, April 15, October 2, October 19, 1872, January 24, 1873, and March 2, April 1, 9, 21, and 29, June 29, July 19, 21, 1875, *ZC-SP.*

61. Squatterism was ubiquitous in California throughout the nineteenth century from the Gold Rush on; Robinson, *Land in California,* 111–32; Donald J. Pisani, "Squatter Law in California, 1850–1858," *Western Historical Quarterly* 25 (Autumn 1994): 277–310. Squatterism generated much violence, especially in rural areas, among rival squatters as well as between squatters and legitimate landowners. In far southern San Diego County during the 1870s and 1880s, for example, land conflicts elevated the number of homicides for the county to rates approaching those of Bodie, the legendary mining town; squatter violence in rural areas sometimes ended in mass gun battles with nu-

merous deaths, similar to what happened in Southern Pacific country at Mussel Slough; see Richard W. Crawford, "The Records of Local Government and California History," *California History* 75 (Spring 1996). For tactics and types of organizations employed by frontier squatters, many of which were used against the Southern Pacific, Gates, *History of Public Land Law Development,* 66–68, 116–17, 152–65; Malcolm J. Rohrbough, *The Land Office Business: The Settlement and Administration of American Public Lands, 1789–1837* (New York: Oxford University Press, 1968), 14–16, 92–96, 229–30; Hildegard Binder Johnson, *Order Upon the Land: The U.S. Rectangular Land Survey and the Upper Mississippi Country* (New York: Oxford University Press, 1976), 64–66; Allan G. Bogue, *From Prairie to Cornbelt: Farming on the Illinois and Iowa Prairies in the Nineteenth Century* (Chicago: University of Chicago Press, 1963), chap. 2; and Benjamin Horace Hibbard, *A History of the Public Land Policies* (New York: The Macmillan Co., 1924), chap. 11.

62. See B. B. Redding to D. K. Zumwalt, Sacramento, December 10, 1870, February 25, 1871, and October 14, 1872, and San Francisco, April 21, 1875, and April 10, 1876; Henry Beard to Zumwalt, Washington, September 22, 1872; Jonathan Bloss to Redding, Washington, March 31, 1876; Bloss to Jerome Madden, Washington, July 6, 1876; Zumwalt to Madden, Visalia, April 29 and November 19, 1886; and Madden to Zumwalt, San Francisco, May 5, 1886, *ZC-SP.*

63. Department of Interior records also refer often to squatters and their methods on Southern Pacific lands; J. S. Wilson, commissioner, General Land Office, to Register and Receiver, Marysville, CA, Government Land Office, Washington, DC, March 12, 1867, RG 48 (598: 35), *NA-W,* and hundreds of other references after the 1860s in RG 48 (598: 36, 37, 38, 39, and 40ff.). Rival claimants to Southern Pacific lands generally came in after Interior had reserved the land for the railroad and the railroad had started building its line and had raised land values dramatically. Then they tried, by hook or crook, to concoct evidence of settlement prior to the railroad's grant. Squatters were tenacious, in some cases trying many strategies, legal pretexts, and even fictitious names to push claims that the department had already rejected. Such contests commonly dragged on in appeals for five to ten years, with the Interior Department, controlled by new political appointees, frequently abandoning its own precedents and reversing earlier decisions, sometimes more than once in the same case. Sometimes, squatters transferred their rights back and forth from person to person in order to reopen rejected claims. Many, if not most, contestants to the railroad's patents were clearly speculators, their claims rejected because railroad or government agents turned up evidence that they were illegally prosecuting more than one preemption or homestead claim under their own or assumed names. Some individuals filed many claims involving much acreage over long periods and sometimes in different locales. Some squatter-speculators carefully researched government land records, cheaply bought quit-claim deeds to masses of old, usually flawed or expired, prior homestead or preemption claims, faked continuous settlement by those original filers to show that the land should have been excluded from the railroad's grant, and then filed simultaneous abandonments of those claims and their own new homestead, preemption, military bounty, or cash entry claims to large tracts of land; J. A. Williamson, commissioner, General Land Office, "Deci-

sion in the Case of William Barry vs. Central Pacific R.R. Co., Sacramento, California" (July 22, 1878), RG 48 (598: 43). Squatters who did succeed in getting the department to accept their preemption or cash-entry claims commonly paid the land fees in
discounted scrip, a favored medium of speculators; S. S. Burnett, commissioner, General Land Office, to Register and Receiver, Government Land Office in Sacramento,
Washington, DC, August 5, 1875, RG 48 (598:41). Squatter tenacity, ingenuity, and un-
scrupulousness were astounding. In one extreme, but not atypical case, a half-dozen
men, to steal a tract first from the government and then the railroad company, conspired in a tangled plot of fraud and perjury stretching from 1857 to 1881, when government land agents uncovered the swindle and the secretary of the interior rejected
the claim; J. A. Williamson, "Decision in the Case of James C. Hert vs. Central Pacific
Railroad Co., Sacramento District, California" (September 23, 1880, affirmed by the
secretary of the interior, March 17, 1881), RG 48 (598: 45). Williamson, "Decision of
March 9, 1878 . . . in Case of Central Pacific R.R. Co. vs. State of California . . . " (598:
43), is an instance of a failed attempt by California to acquire thousands of acres of railroad land.

64. For poachers, D. K. Zumwalt to Jerome Madden, Visalia, February 15 and March
7, 1877, and March 19, 1888; Madden to Zumwalt, San Francisco, December 22, 1879,
February 10 and 17 and November 3, 1880, August 17, 1881, and August 18, 1885, ZC-SP.

65. B. B. Redding to D. K. Zumwalt, San Francisco, June 24, 1875, and Jerome Madden to Zumwalt, San Francisco, August 18, 1876, and July 15, 1881, ZC-SP.

66. For Texas, A. B. Doucette, "Report on Texas and New Orleans Lands in Jefferson, Liberty, and Hardin Counties" (ms., 1903); R. E. Taukersley, Southern Pacific land
agent in Dallas, to C. C. Gibbs, chief Southern Pacific Texas land agent, Dallas, May
19, 1890; Gibbs to E. H. Carter, Southern Pacific land agent in Waco, January 1, 1899;
Carter to Gibbs, November 23, 1900; George M. Williams to Gibbs, San Antonio, June
24, 1903; SP-H.

67. B. B. Redding to D. K. Zumwalt, San Francisco, April 21, 1875, ZC-SP.

68. See, for example, D. K. Zumwalt to Jerome Madden, Visalia, April 29 and
November 19, 1886, and Madden to Zumwalt, San Francisco, May 5, 1886, ZC-SP.

69. Henry Beard, Southern Pacific Washington, DC, attorney, to B. B. Redding,
Washington, November 29, 1869, SP-A, an early example of the railroad's losing appeals
before the Department of the Interior; Beard advised the company in this letter that
the railroad would have to fight hard for all cases before the department, and these routine early defeats would mean that future cases would be even harder to win. See also,
B. B. Redding to D. K. Zumwalt, Sacramento, June 8 and 18, 1872, ZC-SP. For an
important early dispute with the Department of the Interior, in which the Southern
Pacific in a single case lost hundreds of protests against late entries allowed by the land
office on odd-numbered Western Pacific Railroad sections in the northern San Joaquin
Valley, see U.S. Land Office, San Francisco, "Arthur St. Clair Denver, et al., vs the Western Pacific Railroad Company" (November 11, 1872), Railroadiana (Western U.S.A.)
Collection, HL. The General Land Office had reserved the land originally to be patented
to the railroad, then several years later superimposed a recently legalized large reservation for a Mexican-era land grant onto the railroad's grant and eliminated the odd sec-

tions from the railroad's reservation (which just by itself was of dubious legality). When the Mexican grant was not ultimately surveyed in that place, instead of restoring the odd sections to the railroad's land grant, the land office, as had become its standard practice by the early 1870s, reopened the tracts to settlement by others. The company protested, lost, and the decision became a precedent for subsequent land-office decisions regarding conflicts between the railroad's grant and Mexican ranchos. In the 1870s, however, the Department of the Interior reversed itself at least twice on its rules for handling railroad grants in Mexican rancho areas, first, in the above case, ruling the ranchos superseded railroad rights, then, in its infamous 1874 "Dillingham Decision," that sections in rancho reservations not ultimately surveyed into the ranchos reverted to the railroad, then, after the U.S. Supreme Court's decision in *Newhall v. Sanger* (1877), ruling that those same sections did *not* revert to the railroad but were to be restored to the public domain for entry by others. Meanwhile, the railroad, possessing what appeared to be valid patents, had in good faith sold much of the land, and hundreds of innocent purchasers lost their titles.

70. A. St. Clair Denver, land attorney, to J. Chauncey Hayes, Washington, March 8, 1884, enclosing copy of L. Harrison, acting commissioner of the General Land Office, to Denver, Washington, DC, March 6, 1884, and Denver to Hayes, March 25 and 26, 1884, Denver-Hayes Letters, *BL;* and numerous documents in Department of Interior Records, RG 48 (598:33–46), *NA-W,* esp. J. Wright Johnson to Carl Schurz, secretary of the interior, Bellota, San Joaquin County, September 18, 1880 (598: 45); S. S. Burdette, commissioner, General Land Office, to Register and Receiver, Marysville, CA, Government Land Office, Washington, DC, November 7, 1874, "Decision of the Commissioner of the General Land Office of November 7, 1874, In the Case of William O Hennessy vs. Hugh Burns and the Central Pacific Railroad Co. and the Oregon Railroad Co."; and Commissioner, General Land Office, to Schurz, Washington, DC, August 21 and October 15, 1874, all in (598: 42); "Petition of [20] Settlers on Lands Excluded from Survey of Los Pocitas [sic.] Rancho, California to Carl Schurz, Secretary of the Interior" (June 1, 1878); H. F. Crane to Newton Booth, U.S. senator from California, San Francisco, June 10, 1878; J. A. Williamson, commissioner, General Land Office, to Schurz, Washington, DC, June 12, 1878; John Pope Hodnett, attorney, to Schurz, Washington, DC, July 31, 1878; Williamson to Hodnett, Washington, DC, August 1, 1878; and Williamson, "Decision of the Commissioner, General Land Office in the Case of William Barry vs. Central Pacific R.R. Co., Sacramento, California" (July 22, 1878), all in (598: 43); and Commissioner of the General Land Office, "Papers on Appeal in Case of T. D. Holladay vs. the Southern Pacific Railroad Company . . . Los Angeles District, California" (October 20, 1880), RG 48 (598: 230). Also, B. B. Redding to W. C. Belcher, Sacramento, May 7, 1870, Central Pacific Railroad Land Department Letters, *CRRM;* Henry Beard to J. A. Williamson, commissioner, General Land Office, Washington, DC, September 20, 1876, June 8 and 12, 1877; and Carl Schurz, secretary of the interior, to Williamson, Washington, DC, August 30, 1878 (copy), vol. 6; all in *SP-A.*

71. For intense squatterism in the mid- and late 1880s caused by the Department of the Interior's moratorium on patents to the Southern Pacific, as well as the company's protests and actions in response, Jerome Madden to William A. J. Sparks, commissioner

of the General Land Office (copy), San Francisco, November 3, 1885; Madden to D. K. Zumwalt, San Francisco, December 8, 1875, May 5 and 8 and July 31, 1886, September 30, October 22, and November 3, 1887, July 10, 1888, January 12, 16, 23, and 25, April 27, June 5 and 19, July 11, and November 18, 1889, May 27 and June 5, 1890, January 31, 1891, and October 12, 1892; Zumwalt to Madden, Visalia, December 12, 1885, October 11, 17, 19, and 29, 1887, January 21, 1888, January 16 and 28, March 14, 23, and 28, and June 26, 1889, January 3 and May 29, 1890, December 31, 1891; Madden to Collis P. Huntington (copy), San Francisco, May 21, 1890; in *ZC-SP;* also *Sacramento Record-Union,* March 21, 1889.

72. Collis P. Huntington to L. E. Payson, Washington, DC, September 11, 1891, Collis P. Huntington Letterbook 6 (1891), *HEH;* Henry Beard to John W. Noble, secretary of the interior, Washington, DC, November 10, 1891; and "Lists of Central Pacific R.R. Co. Lands under California and Oregon Grant Pending in Government Land Office, Unpatented" (ms., December 22, 1891); in vol. 13, *SP-A.*

73. *San Francisco Examiner,* December 5, 1896; *San Francisco Chronicle,* December 5, 1896, and March 26, 1900; *Southern Pacific Bulletin* 4 (January 1, 1916): 2.

74. Gates, *History of Public Land Law Development,* 365–66; David M. Ellis, "The Forfeiture of Railroad Land Grants, 1867–1894," *Mississippi Valley Historical Review* 33 (June 1946): 27–60.

75. For the local land office's active solicitation of adverse filings on the railroad's grant near Victorville, on the Mojave Desert, see William H. Gordon, field agent, Southern Pacific Land Department, to B. A. McAllaster, Barstow, CA, April 22, 1911; McAllaster to Register and Receiver, U.S. Land Office in Los Angeles, San Francisco, April 28, 1911, File 935, *SP-L.*

76. For taxation practices of county governments, Leslie E. Decker, *Railroads, Lands, and Politics: The Taxation of Railroad Land Grants, 1864–1897* (Providence, RI: Brown University Press, 1964).

77. Henry Beard to L. A. Graff, commissioner, General Land Office, Washington, DC, October 21, 1889, vol. 13, *SP-A.*

78. W. E. Glendinning to B. A. McAllaster, Ft. Myers, CA, February 16, 1911, Fire Protection File, *SP-L.*

79. See Jerome Madden to D. K. Zumwalt, San Francisco, August 17, 1881, *ZC-SP.*

4   The Mussel Slough Affair

1. Frank Norris, *The Octopus: A Story of California* (New York: Doubleday & Co., 1901). Norris did little and hurried research on the actual event. Anxious to finish the book in order to raise money to pay for his marriage and honeymoon, he surveyed a few anti-railroad sources, relying heavily on error-filled accounts in San Francisco newspapers, especially the anti–Southern Pacific *San Francisco Chronicle.* He also relied on pamphlets settlers had distributed to build support for their cause and on local legend that had grown up about the event. For his skimpy research, see Oscar Cargill, "Afterward" to the Signet edition of *The Octopus* (New York: New American Library, 1964),

459–69. Not only did he know little about the actual event, but his knowledge of general land and agricultural systems was flawed in the extreme, as was his understanding of how railroads, including the Southern Pacific, actually operated; Morton Rothstein, "Frank Norris and Popular Perceptions of the Market," *Agricultural History* 56 (January 1982): 50–66. Norris's information and misinformation was filtered through his own hyperbolic imagination and prose. The novel misrepresented every important facet of the event, including the geography and pattern of land tenure in the area, the sequence of settlement, the character of the participants, the legal issues, and the kind of agriculture practiced by the farmers in question. Norris was not the first to take literary license. Historian and philosopher Josiah Royce had earlier written a novel even more loosely based on the incident, *The Feud of Oakfield Creek* (1887). Garbled versions of the incident provide literary and artistic plot to the present day; see Oakley Hall's *Ambrose Bierce and the Queen of Spades: A Mystery Novel* (New York: Penguin Books, 1998), first published by the University of California Press. Anti–Southern Pacific political cartoonists frequently depicted the railroad as oppressing the Mussel Slough settlers: see Richard B. Rice, William A. Bullough, and Richard J. Orsi, *The Elusive Eden: A New History of California* (New York: McGraw-Hill, 2002 ed.), 253; Ed Salzman and Ann Leigh Brown, *The Cartoon History of California Politics* (Sacramento: California Journal Press, 1978), 30ff. Salzman and Brown maintain that the most famous of these political cartoons, Edward Keller's "The Curse of California," printed in the satirical *Wasp,* August 19, 1882, which depicted the Southern Pacific as a giant "Octopus" strangling Mussel Slough settlers and other groups of Californians, "may well have been" the "single most important cartoon in California history." Present-day historical song writer-singers Keith and Rusty McNeil, even in the twenty-first century, entertain audiences around California with their story and song about Mussel Slough, "A Hayseed Like Me," the details of which bear little resemblance to what actually happened; Keith and Rusty McNeil, *California Songbook, With Historical Commentary* (Riverside: WEM Records, 2001), 48–49. For thorough, insightful analysis of the centrality of novelists such as Norris in the creation of the powerful, popular myth of Mussel Slough, see the anthology edited by literary historian Terry Beers, *Gunfight at Mussel Slough: Evolution of a Western Myth* (Berkeley and Santa Clara: Heyday Books and Santa Clara University, 2004), passim. "It is," Beers writes, "the novelists who most effectively embedded the event in our collective memory. And even if the details are just plain wrong—or perhaps skillfully embellished—the truth that will prevail lives in novels more than history books" (p. 247).

2. Many histories of the railroad, land, agriculture, the San Joaquin Valley region, and generally of California, published and unpublished, have included versions of the story. In addition to great variation among the various versions, most works lack significant original research in primary sources, particularly in manuscripts and documents associated with the Southern Pacific, although these are available. Among published accounts, once again varied and generally error-ridden, one notable example is Oscar Lewis's *The Big Four,* a widely read book with many errors of fact and substance, from which many later writers borrowed; see last chapter, "Monopoly," for discussion of Mussel Slough (New York: Alfred A. Knopf, 1938, and many subsequent editions).

Walton Bean's popular textbook, *California, An Interpretive History* (New York: McGraw-Hill, 1968), in a passage, pp. 226–28, repeated intact in several subsequent editions of that venerable survey history, incorporated many errors in retelling the story. Among those, Bean's accusation that Collis P. Huntington was the most ardent advocate of fleecing the settlers, demanding that they be forced to pay "what the land was worth," appears to have been invented out of whole cloth, by Bean or some unknown predecessor. In fact, as letters in the readily available Huntington Collection at Syracuse University and on microfilm make clear, Huntington favored compromise with the settlers (whom he viewed as innocent dupes of their leaders), even if the railroad lost money (see discussion and documentation in this chapter). James J. Rawls, author of numerous excellent revisions of the book since Bean's death, has deleted the charge against Huntington from recent editions, but other errors remain. Other examples of traditional accounts are William W. Robinson, *Land in California* (Berkeley: University of California Press, 1948), 159–60; Ralph J. Roske, *Everyman's Eden: A History of California* (New York: Macmillan, 1968), 388–90; T. H. Watkins, *California: An Illustrated History* (New York: Weathervane Books, 1973), 222–31; Ward McAfee, *California's Railroad Era: 1850–1911* (San Marino: Golden West Books, 1973), 117–18, 174–76; William L. Preston, *Vanishing Landscapes: Land and Life in the Tulare Lake Basin* (Berkeley: University of California Press, 1981), 131; Spencer C. Olin, Jr., *California Politics, 1846–1920: The Emerging Corporate State* (San Francisco: Boyd and Fraser Publishing Co., 1981), 42–43; John W. Caughey and Norris Hundley, Jr., *California: History of a Remarkable State* (Englewood Cliffs, NJ: Prentice-Hall, 1982), 280–81; Stephen Schwartz, *From West to East: California and the Making of the American Mind* (New York: The Free Press, 1998), 105–12. For recent, extreme examples of distorted, factually incorrect versions of the Mussel Slough conflict, passed off as history, see Mark Arax and Rick Wartzman, *The King of California . . . : J. G. Boswell and the Making of a Secret American Empire* (New York: Public Affairs, 2003), 77–78; and Joan Didion, *Where I Was From* (New York: Alfred A. Knopf, 2003), 38–51.

3. Beverly J. Armento and Gary B. Nash et al., *Oh California* (Boston: Houghton Mifflin, 1991), 162–77, 190–201, includes an inaccurate version of the Mussel Slough conflict, uses Mussel Slough settlers as the leading example of big business's exploitation of farmers in that period, and for evidence quotes *The Octopus,* identified only as "a book," not as a work of fiction.

4. See local historian James L. Brown, *The Mussel Slough Tragedy* (privately printed, 1958), which cites and reprints valuable sources and contains a more or less objective account of events leading up to and occurring during the battle, and Richard M. Brown, "California Conflict and the American Dream," chap. 3 in his *No Duty to Retreat: Violence and Values in American History and Society* (Norman: University of Oklahoma Press, 1991), 87–127. James L. Brown's deep sympathy for the cause of the so-called "settlers," however, often leads him to assert pro-settler conclusions even in the face of his own evidence to the contrary. The event in Richard M. Brown's eyes is a typical "Western Civil War of Incorporation," and the Mussel Slough "settlers" become his principal illustration of local pioneer resisters to what he describes as "the drive to incorporate the West in the interest of the conservative, consolidating authority of capital in a

market economy"—in this instance a "land-closure campaign carried on by the Southern Pacific Railroad and its clients"—which he finds to be at the root of much of the mass violence on the frontier (pp. 92–93). As this chapter and other chapters in my book show, the railroad's land policies were the antithesis of a "land-closure campaign" and the great majority of the "settlers" were in reality squatter-speculators, many of them recently arrived outsiders, and, in effect, themselves "incorporators," or at least would-be incorporators. William Deverell's *Railroad Crossing: Californians and the Railroad, 1850–1910* (Berkeley: University of California Press, 1994), 56–57, and esp. 137ff., is a balanced, accurate account and is particularly distinguished for its analysis of Norris's *The Octopus,* the book's origins, Norris's research and writing, the novel's inaccuracies ("real drama but a sketchy and unreliable version of events"), and, nevertheless, its continuing influence on historians. Also reliable, especially in its insightful analysis of Norris's novel and other fictional accounts, is George L. Henderson, *California and the Fictions of Capital* (New York: Oxford University Press, 1999), 123–49. There are about a half-dozen master's theses about the battle, most of them narrow, incompletely researched, and of limited use. Two stand out for their extensive research in local land, tax, and other records, though reaching opposite conclusions regarding whether or not the settlers were, or were not, squatters: Barbara M. Bristow's work critical of the settlers, "Mussel Slough Tragedy: Railroad Struggle or Land Gamble" (M.A. thesis, Fresno State College, 1971), and Richard L. Rollins's basically pro-settler "The Mussel Slough Dispute: An Inquiry Based on the Census and Real Property Evidence" (M.A. thesis, California State University, Hayward, 1990). Also more subtle and even-handed in its analysis, especially of the railroaders' actual property interests and points of view, is Beers, *Gunfight at Mussel Slough,* although in its introductory historical analysis of the event, which provides the factual context for literary analysis, the book ignores the all-important chronological sequence of settlement, the central legal issue (the railroad's very title to its land grant), and the fact that the majority of the railroad's contestants were squatter-speculators, and not innocent homesteaders and land buyers; passim, esp. 1–15.

5. See McAfee, *California's Railroad Era,* 118, 175, and index; Olin, *California Politics,* index.

6. The squatters purposely cultivated this image, now ubiquitous in traditional histories; William Conlogue, "Farmers' Rhetoric of Defense: California Settlers Versus the Southern Pacific Railroad," *California History* 78 (Spring 1999): 40–55, 73–76.

7. For a more detailed account of the sequence of events outlined here, see my "Confrontation at Mussel Slough, 1880," chap. 13 in Rice, Bullough, and Orsi, *The Elusive Eden* (1988, 1996, and 2002 eds.); and James L. Brown's pro-squatter *Mussel Slough Tragedy,* generally reliable factually.

8. Traditional historical accounts commonly mix up the ownership of the Southern Pacific Railroad and attribute the route change to the Big Four as yet another example of their scheming greed and monopolistic economic and political power. For only one detailed, if largely erroneous, version of the route controversy in the late 1860s, relying on virtually no direct primary sources, see David J. Bederman, "The Imagery of Injustice at Mussel Slough: Railroad Land Grants, Corporation Law, and the 'Great Conglom-

erate West,'" *Western Legal History* 1 (Summer/Fall 1988): 242ff. He states unambiguously that the Southern Pacific Railroad was incorporated in 1865 while "under the control of the 'Big Four,' who were directors of the Central Pacific Railroad," the first transcontinental. The Big Four, Bederman goes on, were proposing to build this second, southern line east, to file the revised route, and to acquire the land grant in order "to capture all of this transportation [transcontinental] market." In reality, the Big Four did not acquire the Southern Pacific railroad until 1868, had nothing to do with the route change and the seeming "land grab," and only stepped into the controversy in its late stages. Continuing to press the railroad's interests, however, the Big Four did secure the reconfirmation of the route and the land grant in 1869 and 1870. The original owners of the company changed the route for many reasons, including the one commonly attributed, to acquire more land in the grant, and particularly more fertile, valuable land in the San Joaquin Valley capable of attracting more settlement and hence more railroad traffic revenue. The central coast region was also more rugged, colder and foggier, largely already owned by large Mexican-era ranchos, and at that time not agriculturally promising. Moreover, several extremely mountainous stretches, particularly the Cuesta Pass north of San Luis Obispo and Point Conception west and north of Santa Barbara, were considered at the time difficult if not impossible to build rail lines across. Plagued by engineering, labor, and financing problems on that coast route to Los Angeles, the Southern Pacific was not able to complete it until the early 1900s. San Joaquin Valley counties, on the other hand, obviously favored the route change through their region and lobbied strongly on its behalf. Shortly after the route and land-grant controversy had been resolved, Willis Drummond, then commissioner of the General Land Office, advised the Senate Committee on the Pacific Railroad that the route change was advantageous for settlers and the development of California because the coast route, largely already held within large Mexican-era ranchos, contained virtually no public land for settlement, whereas there was much unoccupied public land along the new route: "The change of route would, therefore, so far as the interests of settlers are concerned be to their advantage and accommodate an area of better country than that along the original line"; see Drummond to B. R. Cowan, acting secretary of the interior, Washington, April 15, 1872, Records of the General Land Office, Record Group 48 (598: 221), *NA-W.* On the Big Four's purchase of the Southern Pacific Railroad, see David Lavender, *The Great Persuader* [Collis P. Huntington] (Garden City, NY: Doubleday, 1970), 190ff., 210ff., 264–67; for the Department of the Interior's handling of the route change and land-grant controversy, 1866–1871, see next note.

9. The tug of war from 1867 to 1871 over the legality of the railroad's revised route and land grant among the Interior Department, the Southern Pacific, the Congress, the Johnson and Grant presidential administrations, the California state legislature, and rival speculators seeking to acquire the railroad's land along its route for themselves, can be followed in several manuscript collections:

(1). The records of the General Land Office, the Department of the Interior, and the Department of Justice, *NA-W.* See esp. General Land Office, in RG 48 (598: 220): T. G. Phelps, president, Southern Pacific Railroad, to Secretary of the Interior, September 28, 1866; Henry Beard to Secretary of the Interior Orville H. Browning, July

23 and 25, 1868; copy of U.S. Senate resolution affirming Southern Pacific's new route and land grant (July 25, 1868); W. S. Rosecrans to Browning, Washington, August 15, 1868; in (598: 221): Joseph S. Wilson, commissioner, General Land Office, to Register and Receiver, San Francisco Government Land Office, Washington, November 12, 1869; I. M. Howard, chairman of Senate Committee on Pacific Railroad, to Secretary of Interior J. D. Cox, Washington, December 14, 1869; copy of California legislature's act amending the Southern Pacific Railroad's charter to allow for the new route, signed by Gov. H. H. Haight on April 4, 1870; William M. Stewart, Cornelius Cole, Thomas Fitch, James A. Johnson, A. A. Sargent, and L. B. Axtell (congressmen) to Cox, Washington, DC, April 23, 1870; copy of U.S. Congress, "Joint Resolution Number 55 Concerning the Southern Pacific Railroad of California, June 28, 1870," directing the secretary of the interior to issue patents to the railroad along the revised route, while reserving rights of prior settlers; and various memoranda indicating actions of the secretaries of the interior and the land office regarding the railroad's route and land grant.

(2). *CPH:* Both incoming and outgoing correspondence contain dozens of letters between Huntington and his associates in California, congressmen, and the company's Washington attorneys, especially Henry Beard, about the route change and land-grant verification; see Mark Hopkins to Huntington, Sacramento, August 12, 1869, Leland Stanford to Huntington, Sacramento, November 8, 1869, Huntington to Secretary of the Interior Cox, New York, July 2, 1870, which reviews the controversy, Isaac E. Gates (Huntington's assistant) to Beard, New York, April 12, 1872.

(3). *SP-A* vol. 6, contains dozens of letters, 1868–1871: esp. Browning to Wilson, Washington, July 14, 1868 (copy); Beard to B. B. Redding, Washington, July 18, 1868 (discusses the work of speculators, whom he called "the scrip men," in getting Browning to revoke the railroad's land-grant reserve), and November 13 and 18, 1868; Beard to Huntington, Washington, July 18, 1868 (also discusses actions of rival speculators), July 21, 27, 30, August 1, 3, 4, 14, 15, 20, 1868, September 15, 1868; Beard to Browning, Washington, July 23, 25, August 6, September 21, October 9, 14, 1868; vol. 8: Beard to Redding, Washington, July 30, August 12, 13 (discusses land speculators working to defeat the railroad's land grant), 26, October 23, November 12, December 21, 1869; Beard to Huntington, Washington, July 30, August 7, 11, 21, 24, October 23, November 2, 3, 4, 11, 12, 15, December 15, 16, 1869, March 4, 1870; Beard to Lloyd B. Tevis, Washington, August 11, 14, September 21, November 12, December 16, 17, 1869; Beard to W. T. Otto, acting secretary of the interior, Washington, August 23, 1869; Beard to James H. Storrs, Washington, September 18 (discusses specifically speculator William F. Chapman's leadership of the opposition to the railroad's land grant), October 2, 9, 1869; Beard to Joseph Wilson, November 3, 1869; vol. 3: Beard to Carl Schurz, secretary of the interior, Washington, April 11, 1878 (one of the most important letters in the collection, reviews the legal history of the Southern Pacific's land grant and lists important documents affirming the route and the railroad's right to its land grant).

What is most essential here is that the issue was settled by 1870, with the legality of the new route and the railroad's land grant formally ratified by Congress, the U.S. Department of the Interior, and the state legislature. Also, the Department of the Interior, even while reversing itself several times regarding the route's legality, did maintain the land reserve for the railroad, and despite attempts of rival speculators to have the reservation revoked, it remained in effect throughout the debate. The ultimate resolution of the route in 1869 and 1870 by Congress and the state legislature was covered, along with reprinted major documents, by San Francisco's *Alta California*, November 14 and December 19, 1869, and February 27 and March 12, 1870. The *Alta* also reported that the speculators lobbying to get the railroad's land grant reopened to other settlement were prepared to buy all the land on the first day it was available for sale, December 19, 1869. For Huntington's role in getting the resolution through Congress, Lavender, *Great Persuader,* 264–67, 283–84.

10. The Southern Pacific Railroad Company did not even publish its first land pamphlets until 1876, when it began to prepare to sell the most valuable portion of its San Joaquin Valley grant, the Mussel Slough district. Before that, the Department of the Interior, despite pleadings from the company, had refused to deliver many patents for San Joaquin Valley land. Thus, the expensive publication and distribution of these substantial books would not have been warranted; see Southern Pacific Railroad Company of California, *The Lands of the Southern Pacific Railroad Company of California: Their Situation, Soil, Climate, Vegetation, Present and Prospective Values, Price, and the Terms Under Which They Are Offered for Sale* (San Francisco: Southern Pacific Railroad Company of California, 1876 [also eds. in 1877, 1880, 1882, and 1883]). By the time of the first pamphlet's publication, the squatters had already established their claims in the area, and for several years had been attacking the railroad's land title. The squatters' later quoting of the company's land pamphlets, which actually only promised settlers on its lands throughout California prices from $2.50 per acre "and upwards," as proof for their accusation that the railroad was price-gouging them and violating an implied contract, was a last-minute, desperation tactic when their title challenges had been rejected by the Department of the Interior and the federal courts. Even if that $2.50 price had been a fixed price for all the railroad's land, which the pamphlet's wording makes clear was *not* the case, it was in fact very close to the low prices (average about $3 per acre) that the railroad did indeed charge for the great majority of its land in the state; some was actually on sale for as little as $1 per acre. See the discussion of the Southern Pacific's land prices in chapter 3. For the Department of the Interior's delay in furnishing patents for the railroad's San Joaquin Valley land and the start up of the company's land advertising and sales in the area, see B. B. Redding to D. K. Zumwalt, San Francisco, February 11 and 17, 1875, *ZC-SP.* In 1875, the Southern Pacific began receiving patents only along its mainline south from Goshen to Delano, but it did not receive Mussel Slough region patents until it had completed its line through that area, in 1877.

11. In an 1880 letter to the *Visalia Delta,* republished in one of the squatters' own pamphlets defending their position, one of Doyle's new neighbors in Grangeville, Mary E. Chambers, described the early mechanics of squatterism openly: "In the fall of 1869, we were living in Placer county, my husband at that time being in the employ of the Central Pacific Railroad Company. [With his] being away from home all the time, I was anxious that he should get land somewhere and settle down, and make us a home. At that time we heard of this land in Tulare [County] being forfeited by the railroad company . . . , and that it was to be thrown open for pre-emption and homestead set-

tlement. I therefore persuaded Mr. Chambers to go and locate, and in November, 1869, he came here and located on railroad lands; then came back, bought an outfit and moved his family December 26th, arriving in Tulare January 7, 1870." The newcomers, she says, were opposed and harassed in any way they could by "the stock men," prior settlers in the region, mostly on the even-numbered sections, who ranged their livestock on the squatters' grain. Chambers, for her part, despised "these stock raisers as an indolent people . . . [who] never made an effort to cultivate the soil; but we, with our energy and perseverance, would make the wilderness to blossom and bear." Later in 1870, the Chambers family expanded their squatter foothold by occupying yet more adjoining railroad land and turning over their first claim to Mary Chambers's brother and his family: "In the latter part of July or the first of August of the same year, we moved on to the quarter section of land adjoining the one we now occupy, my brother, Arch McGregor [one of those killed at the battle in May 1880] taking up the one we are now on. He took this up in preference to government land (of which there was plenty to be taken at that time) because it joined ours"; Settlers' Committee, *The Struggle of the Mussel Slough Settlers for Their Homes! An Appeal to the People; History of the Land Troubles in Tulare and Fresno Counties; The Grasping Greed of the Railroad Monopoly* (Visalia: Delta Printing Establishment, 1880), 15–16. Throughout their filings of homestead, preemption, and other claims and appeals with the Land Office, and later court cases, the squatters asserted that they had initially settled their claims between 1867 and the mid-1870s, sometimes even later, clearly after the railroad had filed its map with the Department of the Interior and the odd-numbered sections had been closed to further settlement.

12. For Doyle's own account of squatting and leading the movement to acquire title to the railroad's land, Eugene L. Menefee and Fred A. Dodge, *History of Tulare and Kings Counties, California* . . . (Los Angeles: Historic Record Company, 1913), 110–12; Doyle biography on 81–82.

13. Doyle and his squatter-clients closely guarded their secret contracts, and though they were formally printed on standard, fill-in-the-blank forms and their existence was open knowledge in the region, the company had trouble getting hold of a copy. Finally, land agent Zumwalt in the fall of 1876 secured printed copies from a local resident sympathetic to the railroad and angered by the problems the squatter boom was causing in the area and sent copies to the railroad's headquarters in San Francisco as well as to the company's law firm in Washington, DC; two letters from Zumwalt to Jerome Madden and to John B. Bloss, Visalia, December 6, 1876, Madden to Zumwalt, San Francisco, December 8, 1876, B. B. Redding to Zumwalt, San Francisco, May 1, 1877, and Printed Contract Between J. J. Doyle and Mussel Slough Settlers [in this case, one F. Eggleston] (ca. 1876), filed with incoming letters of November 1876, *ZC-SP.* When they soon discovered that the railroad had a copy of the contract, the squatters, furious because disclosure of such contracts and Doyle's personal financial interest in defeating the railroad's land title would weaken their case, took extreme retaliatory measures against the man who had leaked the contract, one E. F. Littlepage. Within a month, his business destroyed by a squatter boycott and his life and his family's threatened, the desperate Littlepage decided to move to Los Angeles. Impoverished and unable to sell his prop-

erty in the area, he appealed to Zumwalt for transportation passes and moving expenses, which the railroad provided, in Zumwalt's words, because Littlepage's service to the company "was very valuable" and "I don't know how else it [the contract] could have been obtained"; Zumwalt to Redding, Visalia, November 11 and 18, 1876, and Madden to Zumwalt, San Francisco, December 19, 1877.

14. There are many Interior Department records, *NA-W,* regarding the mass claims of the Mussel Slough settlers; see, for the department's rationale, in RG 48 (598: 225), J. A. Williamson, commissioner of the General Land Office, to Carl Schurz, secretary of the interior, Washington, September 11 and 20 and October 4 (two letters), 1877; in RG 48 (598: 226), J. M. Armstrong, acting commissioner, General Land Office, to Register and Receiver, Visalia, CA, Washington, DC, December 17, 1878 (two letters), Armstrong to Carl Schurz, Washington, DC, December 2, 1879, and to Register and Receiver, Visalia, Washington, DC, August 6 (two letters), 1879; in RG 48 (598: 229), Williamson to Schurz, Washington, March 24, 1880, and Armstrong to Register and Receiver, Visalia, May 31, 1879; in RG 48 (598: 330), Acting Commissioner to Schurz, Washington, October 12, 1880. Letters rejecting the claims were published in later squatter pamphlets, along with the squatters' rationale in contesting the railroad's land titles, such as Settlers' Grand League, *Petition: A Statement of Facts on Behalf of Six Hundred Actual Settlers, in Tulare and Fresno Counties, To the Citizens of the United States of America* (Hanford: The Public Good, 1878). The *Visalia Delta,* August 30, 1878, published a special supplement printing the correspondence between the squatters, their attorneys, and the Department of the Interior, including the letters rejecting the claims. John J. Doyle's own accounts appeared in Menefee and Dodge, *History of Tulare and Kings Counties,* 110–12, and Kathleen E. Small, *History of Tulare County,* 2 vols. (Chicago: S. J. Clark Publishing Co., 1926), 1: 177–80. Squatter challenges to the railroad's land titles in the district frequently came up in the railroad's land department correspondence in the early and mid-1870s; see B. B. Redding to D. K. Zumwalt, San Francisco, February 11, 1875, and April 13, 1876, *ZC-SP.* Beginning about 1874 and continuing even after the battle in May 1880, the squatters repeatedly tried to file mass claims to the same tracts that had already been rejected by the Department of the Interior, each time using different pretexts, such as under the homestead, preemption, desert, timber culture, cash-entry, and other federal land laws; see in *ZC-SP,* Zumwalt to Jerome Madden, Visalia, July 2, 1877, and Madden to Zumwalt, San Francisco, July 5, 1877.

15. Defending their "homes" from the predatory corporation was the standard rationale for their actions in their numerous statements and publications; Settlers' Committee, *Struggle of the Mussel Slough Settlers for Their Homes;* Members of the League of Settlers, "Petition to His Excellency, Rutherford B. Hayes, President of the United States" (September 9, 1880), in U.S. Department of Justice, Record Group 60, General Records of the Department of Justice: Records Relating to the Mussel Slough Affair, 1880–1881: Letters and Telegrams Received (microfilm reel, National Archives, Washington, DC, 1956), *BL.*

16. For farming and irrigation practices in Mussel Slough country during and after the 1870s, Preston, *Vanishing Landscapes,* 130–44. Grain and hay were still the major

crops in 1880. That the squatters were raising hay and grain, which did not require or even repay the use of irrigation, is demonstrated by the fact that, in the aftermath of the battle, from May through July 1880, when the Mussel Slough squatters started acquiring their claims legally from the railroad, many started out by leasing their land, almost always paid for by shares of crops already standing on the claims. Universally, the crops the farmers shared with the railroad were grain and hay that had already been sown and had been watered with natural rainfall over the winter and was nearing harvest; see many letters reporting dozens of new leases to the squatters, written by land agent Daniel K. Zumwalt to his superior Jerome Madden, in May through July 1880, for example, May 21, 1880; also Charles Crocker, "Agreement with Businessmen's Committee of Hanford and Lemoore" (ms., San Francisco, May 15, 1880), copy enclosed in Madden to Zumwalt, San Francisco, May 21, 1880, which provided for and described the crop shares of grain and hay, ZC-SP. The leases were also recorded, along with the crop-share payments in grain and hay, in Southern Pacific Railroad Land Department, "Journal and Day Book" (1879–1881 vol.), CRRM.

17. Bristow, "Mussel Slough Tragedy," 22ff.; letter from an anti-squatter farmer in the district, The Argonaut (San Francisco), April 23, 1881.

18. Such was the case, for example, with Henry D. Brewer, whose eviction from his claim on railroad land touched off the battle in May 1880. Brewer's railroad claim, though plowed and sown in grain, was unfenced and unimproved in any other way. Ironically, the gunplay actually took place on his adjacent legally owned farm, where he had located his buildings, fences, well, and irrigation ditches. Brewer had also been buying, subdividing, and selling other land in the vicinity on the even-numbered public land sections; Bristow, "Mussel Slough Tragedy," appendices, and 102 (for Brewer's legitimate land deals) and 116–17 (for land deals by squatter leaders Thomas Jefferson McQuiddy, William W. Flewelling, and S. E. Biddle [who moved in and out of the squatter camp], and W. J. McQuiddy); also, for location of squatter claims by the McQuiddys and Biddle, D. K. Zumwalt, "Land Plat Book, 1879–1882" (ms., Township 18 S, Range 22 E map), ZC-SP. Even the pro-squatter James L. Brown's Mussel Slough Tragedy, 62–65, describes Brewer's other land dealings, his legal homestead on the even-numbered section adjacent to his railroad land claim, and the fact he had made no improvements, other than the wheat crop, on the railroad claim. Railroad district land agent Zumwalt also conducted several surveys of improvements on squatter claims, and found that very little of value was actually located on the disputed tracts. He also found that squatters were often claiming more than one railroad tract, sometimes alleging homestead or preemption rights to railroad land, when in fact they already had their one legal homestead or preemption claim on even-numbered public land sections; about Zumwalt's researches regarding the holdings and improvements of adverse claimants in the area, see B. B. Redding to Zumwalt, San Francisco, April 13, 29, and May 6, 1876, ZC-SP. Even the pro-squatter newspaper, the Visalia Delta, April 27, 1876, observed that there were no improvements on the squatters' claims to railroad land, noting matter-of-factly that such improvements would obviously be unwise since the claimants lacked titles to the tracts.

19. Bristow, "Mussel Slough Tragedy," 42–43, and appendices listing all district land sales; letter from an anti-squatter farmer, in The Argonaut (San Francisco), April 23, 1881.

20. See Bristow, "Mussel Slough Tragedy," esp. 48ff. and appendices, for all non-railroad Mussel Slough land sales, 1870s–1880s, from Tulare and Fresno county records; unimproved land in the area commonly sold for more than $20 per acre. The railroad's alleged prices were exaggerated by contemporaries and historians in other ways. For example, the *San Francisco Chronicle* on March 31, 1879, complained the railroad was *overcharging* the squatters about $3,200 *apiece* for their lands, which was, again, an exaggeration of 100 percent or more. At a realistic actual average railroad price of $15 per acre, the *entire* cost of an 80-acre claim would have been only $1,200, total, while 160 acres would have cost only $2,400. The actual sale prices for the railroad's Mussel Slough lands, which in almost all cases were only one-quarter to one-half the figures that squatters later claimed in order to appeal to public sympathy, are in manuscript "Map and Plat Books," *ZC-SP;* see particularly "Land Plat Book, 1879–1892," maps for Township 18S, Range 21E (which lists squatter militia chief Thomas Jefferson McQuiddy's claim as being priced at $13.50 per acre, Henry Brewer's claim at $19, and John J. Doyle's claim at $20), 20E, and 22E. Many letters from Zumwalt to chief land agent Jerome Madden in that collection reporting land transactions in the Mussel Slough area noted the exact prices; typical letters of October 14, 15, and 19, 1878, for example, mentioned prices per acre for numerous sales of $5.50, $8, $10, $12, $16, $17.50, $18, and $20. Virtually no land transactions reported by Zumwalt for the district from 1877 through 1880 listed a price higher than in the lower $20 range per acre; the very few exceptions were a handful of tiny suburban lots within or immediately adjacent to the sites of Hanford, Lemoore, and other towns. Each sale, with price and terms, was also recorded in the "Day Books" and "Cash Books" of the Southern Pacific Land Department for the 1870s and 1880s, at the *CRRM.* The "Day Book, 1871–1882," vol. I, pp. 322 and 336, describes a particularly indicative 1880 sale by the railroad, to one William B. Cullum of a quarter section (160 acres) of prime land, which was only one-quarter mile north of the Hanford town and straddled the main irrigation canal of the Mussel Slough Ditch Company, yet sold for only $19.50 per acre; the right-of-way for the canal was reserved from the sale, in keeping with the railroad's policy of encouraging irrigation. Walter Crow, a Southern Pacific land buyer and one of the persons killed in the May 1880 battle, told relatives that he had acquired his land for $20 per acre (Southern Pacific Railroad "Day Books" listed it more precisely as $19 per acre), with only one-fifth down payment. Crow also said that he considered the land to be already worth $40 per acre, unimproved, and he advised relatives also to buy railroad land because it was a great bargain; see James L Brown, *Mussel Slough Tragedy,* 80; *Alta California,* May 14, 1880. The greatly exaggerated prices claimed by the squatters and early anti-railroad newspaper reports, which historians have uncritically accepted, were incorporated in public statements and pamphlets squatters published after the battle to justify their actions. In general, the prices squatters claimed started out in the $30- to $60-per-acre range (see *San Francisco Chronicle,* December 8, 1878) and grew larger with time, until by the time reminiscences and memorials were beginning to appear in the early twentieth century, some statements had inflated the figures to nearly $100 per acre; see *San Francisco Examiner,* March 31, 1900. All are gross exaggerations. For analysis of how the squatters employed standard yeoman images and arguments, some of them untrue, to change public opin-

ion, see Conlogue, "Farmers' Rhetoric of Defense," 40–55; also Settlers' Committee, *Struggle of the Mussel Slough Settlers for Their Homes,* and Members of the League of Settlers, "Petition to His Excellency, Rutherford B. Hayes, President of the United States."

21. Some historians have stated that the Southern Pacific not only charged the Mussel Slough settlers outrageously high prices, but in addition, when the land was opened for sale, the company immediately put the land up for public auction, for sale to the highest bidder; see, for one example, Roske, *Everyman's Eden,* 389. No evidence supports this allegation. At no time did the company ever auction off the Mussel Slough, or any other, portion of its land grant. Instead, following the company's established policy, it graded and sold its land for firm, advertised prices.

22. John J. Doyle was an official of both the Grand League and the Workingmen's Party, as well as a friend of Denis Kearney, the violence-mongering founder and president of the Workingmen's Party. In 1879, invited by the Grand League, Kearney gave impassioned speeches to large crowds in the Mussel Slough country in which he exhorted the squatters to fight to protect their lands from the railroad. "Murder the red-eyed monsters," he shouted to roars of approval, and he promised to lead an army of forty thousand San Francisco workers to protect squatters from the railroad; James L. Brown, *Mussel Slough Tragedy,* 40–41; letter from an anti-league farmer in the region, *The Argonaut* (San Francisco), April 23, 1881.

23. Richard M. Brown, *No Duty to Retreat,* 101ff., and James L. Brown, *Mussel Slough Tragedy,* 45ff., though James Brown denies a direct connection between the League and the violence. There can be no doubt that the squatters threatened and perpetrated violence against the railroad and its land buyers. Incidents were described in detail in letters from railroad land agent Zumwalt to his superiors in San Francisco; see, for example, Zumwalt to Jerome Madden, Visalia, January 4, 1879, *ZC-SP;* Zumwalt even transmitted a partial list of the names of the masked men participating in a raid on the farm of a Southern Pacific land buyer. A particularly violent episode, in which a tenant and his family on land bought from the railroad were awakened at night, kidnapped, and their house and possessions burned by Grand League vigilantes, was reported in the *San Francisco Chronicle,* December 8, 1879. The squatters' sending of letters of banishment, along with the names of those being banished, was described in the *Chronicle,* May 12, 1880; the same article noted that the League's "members have made several domiciliary visits recently in disguise" to back up its orders against buyers of railroad land. Other reports of squatter violence and threats of using armed force against railroad employees and land buyers appeared in the *Chronicle,* March 7, 17, and 31, 1879, and in a letter by Southern Pacific land agent Jerome Madden, published in *Pacific Rural Press* (San Francisco), April 12, 1879. Squatter violence was also described and decried by an anti-squatter farmer, writing in a letter to *The Argonaut* (San Francisco), April 23, 1881.

24. D. K. Zumwalt to Jerome Madden, Visalia, November 28, 1878, and Madden to Zumwalt, San Francisco, May 22, 1880, *ZC-SP.* Zumwalt was afraid to purchase the weapon, a Colt revolver, locally, so Madden bought it for him in San Francisco and sent it to Visalia by confidential courier.

25. James L. Brown's pro-squatter *Mussel Slough Tragedy,* 40ff. and 84–85, contains

abundant detail from numerous firsthand sources about the Grand League's activities and the long-term conflicts and factionalism in the region, particularly between the earlier-arrived, and wealthier, cattle raisers and irrigators and the newly migrated squatters. Older and deep-rooted intra-community feuds and conflicts of interests of long standing, which had for years erupted into livestock slaughters, fence and crop burnings, shootings, and other acts of violence, became aggravated and subsumed into the rivalry for railroad land; see also, Bristow, "Mussel Slough Tragedy," 12ff. and 52ff., for the best account of local divisiveness. Similar local conflict was attested to by early county histories of the Mussel Slough region published in the few years before or after the 1880 battle; see *History of Tulare County, California* (San Francisco: Wallace W. Elliott & Co., 1883); *History of Kern County, California* (San Francisco: Wallace W. Elliott & Co., 1883), 219–21. From the inception of the land controversy with the railroad, the region was never united against the company. Some local residents continued to buy railroad land. Setbacks to the squatters' cause were followed by periods when some squatters themselves settled with the railroad and legalized their holdings through buying or leasing the land. The Grand League retaliated against defectors by boycotting and threatening them; see Jerome Madden to D. K. Zumwalt, San Francisco, April 24 and May 8, 1880, *ZC-SP.*

26. Southern Pacific leaders at both the local and higher levels closely followed the mounting squatter violence. Increasingly, company officials grew fearful, not only for the safety of the railroad's local property and employees' lives, but because reports from buyers who pulled out of land deals convinced the company that the specter of squatter violence was drying up its land business in the area and the larger San Joaquin Valley. Local land agent Zumwalt believed that "some such work [violence] will be done," and on his advice, the company dispatched from San Francisco an undercover detective to protect company property and lives and to gather evidence about squatter violence. This was necessary, in Zumwalt's words, to "get facts and threats for future use—they talk plainer now than they will after their work is done"; see D. K. Zumwalt to Jerome Madden, Visalia, March 12, April 30 (the above quotes are from this letter), May 23, 1878, and January 4, 1879, and Madden to Zumwalt, San Francisco, March 15, April 3, and May 5, 1878, *ZC-SP;* Charles Crocker to Collis P. Huntington, San Francisco, November 30, 1878, *CPH.*

27. For the railroad's public defense of its land titles and prices, see Jerome Madden's "The Greatness and Littleness of Land Grabbing," *Pacific Rural Press* (San Francisco), April 12, 1879, letter responding to the *Press*'s earlier article supporting the squatters, published March 22, 1879.

28. Huntington had from the beginning thought that the squatters were mostly innocent, naive persons being duped by demagogic leaders. In the interest of the railroad's public goodwill and to avert political reprisals, Huntington opposed aggressive actions against the squatters. Instead, he advised that the railroad should compromise and reduce its land prices, even to the point of losing money, if the squatters would acknowledge the validity of the company's land titles. In 1876, he wrote to his close friend and partner Mark Hopkins that "it is of no use to get a privilege to go into a long litigation about it" and "it occurs to me that some arrangement might be come to

with these squatters as to the amount they shall pay the Company when it is decided they are on its lands. If it is possible, get them to pay something, even less than their value, so as to avoid litigation"; Huntington to Hopkins, Washington, DC, April 10, 1876, *CPH,* also in Huntington-Hopkins Correspondence, 8:143, *SU,* and quoted in Cerinda W. Evans, *Collis Potter Huntington,* 2 vols. (Newport News, VA: Mariners' Museum, 1954), 1: 289–90; also in the *CPH:* Huntington to Shellabarger and Wilson, New York, May 27, 1880, and Charles Crocker to Huntington, San Francisco, May 7, 1880 (an important letter that, on the eve of the battle, reviewed the differences between the hard-liner Crocker on the one hand, and Stanford and Huntington, who favored compromise and selling the land to the squatters at low prices if they would acknowledge the railroad's land title), and Huntington to Crocker, New York, May 17, 1880. In his May 7, 1880, letter, Crocker said "I feel clear, so far as I am concerned, that our true policy is to assert our rights and maintain them at any hazard or reasonable expense." Until talked out of it by other Southern Pacific leaders, Crocker even advocated hiring and arming a private army to go down and protect the marshals evicting squatters; see his May 7 letter to Huntington.

29. The Southern Pacific's hesitance, its desire not to enflame matters further, and its reluctant decision that test eviction lawsuits were its only recourse against the squatter violence were discussed in numerous letters between Zumwalt and Madden between October 1878 and April 1879, especially Zumwalt to Madden, Visalia, November 1 and 2, 1878, and Madden to Zumwalt, San Francisco, November 4, 1878, and January 18 and 30, 1879, *ZC-SP.* The company at first sought eviction only of squatter leaders. "It would not be right to oppress the poor and the ignorant," Madden wrote Zumwalt on February 15, 1879. "It is the advisers and those who head the antirailroad movement that the company wishes to make an example of." See also the long review of the company's quandaries, its concern about squatter violence, and its motives in the lawsuits, in Charles Crocker to Collis P. Huntington, San Francisco, November 30, 1878, and Huntington to Crocker, New York, December 16, 1878, *CPH.* In agreeing to Crocker's decision to start a few test cases against squatter leaders, Huntington reasoned that "it is best for them as well as for us that they know soon that we shall stand for our rights." It was only in the spring of 1879, when informants told the company that the squatters were signing a pact to resist with force all evictions, one by one, no matter the result of test cases, that the company instituted masses of lawsuits; see Jerome Madden, writing in *Pacific Rural Press* (San Francisco), April 12, 1879, and Southern Pacific attorney Delos Lake, writing in the *Sacramento Record-Union,* May 17, 1880. The squatters' pact in response to the lawsuits, to resist with force any attempt by the railroad to possess its lands, was published in the *San Francisco Chronicle,* March 7, 1879.

30. Attorney David J. Bederman's article, "Imagery of Injustice at Mussel Slough," 237–89, which is critical of Sawyer's decision in the railroad's pivotal first eviction case, against Pierpont Orton, is flawed by errors of historical fact and law, particularly regarding the sequence of events, the facts and the later debate over the legality of the Southern Pacific's route change and results of the controversy, the manner and timing of squatters arriving on the land (almost all of whom arrived *after* the railroad's

title to the land attached in 1867), the law and operating procedures of the Department of Interior in reserving railroad land grants and dealing with conflicts with prior settlers, the issues in the Orton case, and the Department of the Interior's specific rationale for denying the squatters' claims. For a sounder historical treatment, see John Larimore, "Legal Questions Arising from the Mussel Slough Land Dispute," *Southern California Quarterly* 58 (1976): 75–94; also a short account of eviction litigation, James L. Brown, *Mussel Slough Tragedy,* 54–56, and many documents associated with the evictions and illustrating the rationales on all sides reprinted in the book's appendix, 134–48. The Orton case was *Southern Pacific Railroad* v. *Orton,* 32 F. 457 (1879). In reaching his decision, Sawyer closely applied the precedents set in an earlier U.S. Supreme Court case involving the land grant of the Northern Pacific Railroad, *Schulenberg* v. *Harriman,* 88 U.S. 44 (1874), in which the high court ruled that a perfect title to its grant passed to the company when its route was fixed and a map filed with the Department of the Interior. Also, once the title passed to a railroad, only judicial or congressional action, and not the actions of officials such as secretaries of the interior, could invalidate that title. California newspapers reported the Orton decision; see *San Francisco Call,* December 18, 1879. For the Southern Pacific's reaction to the decision, see Charles Crocker to Collis P. Huntington, San Francisco, December 16, 1879, *CPH.*

31. Jerome Madden to D.K. Zumwalt, San Francisco, February 3, 6, and 7, 1880, *ZC-SP.*

32. A person attending a squatters' meeting to discuss Stanford's visit and proposed settlement reported to Zumwalt that the squatters "think now they will be made a present of all land in Mussel Slough, or nearly"; B. Donager to Zumwalt, Hanford, March 23, 1880, *ZC-SP.* The correspondence and reports of meetings between squatter leaders and Crocker and Stanford to work out the compromise were published, along with the squatters' accusation that the railroad had caused its failure, in Settlers' Committee, *Struggle of the Mussel Slough Settlers for Their Homes,* 22–29. Although James L. Brown, *Mussel Slough Tragedy,* and other sources have descriptions of the failed attempt by Stanford to arrange a compromise, the best account, the one most relying on many primary sources, including letters passing among the Big Four, is Norman Tutorow, *Leland Stanford: Man of Many Careers* (Menlo Park, CA: Pacific Coast Publications, 1971), 104–107. Tutorow, like all others, including myself, could not determine why the compromise fell apart. Apparently, the public positions of both parties had so hardened by that time that neither group would, or could, back down far enough to satisfy their opponents.

33. The railroad's actions in the few weeks before the battle were reviewed in long statements company officials made to newspapers following the battle, along with correspondence with railroad land buyers who were demanding possession of their holdings; *Alta California* (San Francisco), *San Francisco Call,* and *San Francisco Chronicle,* May 12, 1880; Charles Crocker to Huntington, San Francisco, May 7, 1880, *CPH,* best sums up the railroad's position on the eve of the battle, and the company's reasoning in asking the court for a few test-case evictions.

34. Eyewitnesses disagreed on who actually fired first, but most charged that rail-

road land buyer Mills Hartt, a well-known hothead, had been the one. The first to draw
and brandish weapons, however, were clearly the members of the squatter militia.

35. This brief account of the battle was constructed as best as possible from a number of sources (not all of which agree in all details), including James L. Brown's *Mussel
Slough Tragedy,* 59ff., U.S. marshal Alonzo W. Poole's account published in San Francisco's *Alta California,* May 12, 1880, and especially the detailed sworn statement dictated the next day by Southern Pacific land-grader William Clark in Charles Crocker's
San Francisco office, appended to Crocker to Huntington, San Francisco, May 12, 1880,
CPH. After the company reduced his salary in 1890 for poor performance, Clark had
a falling out with his employers. To compensate him for lost earnings, he entreated company officials to recompense him monetarily for the suffering and danger he had lived
through while grading lands in the Mussel Slough country. When they refused, Clark
a few years later, in two letters to Collis P. Huntington bordering on extortion, threatened that, if he were not paid, he would publish versions of what had happened in the
battle that were unfavorable to the railroad. The account of the battle he gave Huntington in his letter of January 29, 1896, however, is nearly identical to that in his 1880
statement. Huntington refused to pay him off after the first letter, but there is no record
whether or not Huntington did pay eventually, but to do so would have been unlike
the Southern Pacific president; Clark to Huntington, San Jose, January 29, 1896, Mussel Slough Vertical File, Tulare County Historical Library, Visalia; Huntington to Clark,
New York, November 15, 1895, *CPH;* Mary Anne Terstegge, "Mussel Slough," *Los Tulares: Quarterly Bulletin of the Tulare County Historical Society,* No. 146 (December 1984):
2–4. Witnesses reported that one of the railroad land buyers, Walter Crow, a crack shot,
killed several squatters while returning their gunfire. Crow did not die at the battle scene,
however. Having made his escape, he was murdered later a mile or more away, shot in
the back from point-blank range. Although Clark's killer's identity was an open secret
in the area, no one was ever arrested for the crime. Some wounded squatters also died
later of their wounds. Squatters killed Mills Hartt, the other railroad land buyer, at the
battle; he was one of the first shot.

36. At Hanford, into the 1970s, a yearly historical celebration entitled "Homecom-
ing," held in early May, centered around the Mussel Slough conflict and battle. The
event was marked by special issues of newspapers and speeches and testimonials by surviving squatters and their descendents, over the years retelling the story of the railroad's
defrauding of the innocent Mussel Slough settlers until it developed into a local founding myth; there are many clippings from past newspapers of these events in Hanford
and other communities, as well as other commemorations, in vertical files on Mussel
Slough at the Tulare County Library in Visalia and the Kings County Library in Hanford; see *Lindsay Gazette,* September 24, 1948, *Dinuba Sentinel,* August 1, 1963, and July
1, 1976, *Fresno Bee,* August 22, 1948, May 2 and December 4, 1949, and January 26,
1950, *Modesto Bee,* December 16, 1954, *Visalia Times Delta,* August 9, 1952, and June
25, 1959, *Hanford Sentinel,* March 30 and April 6 and 13, 1957 (a series of articles on the
episode), and *Los Tulares: Quarterly Bulletin of the Tulare County Historical Society,* No.
26 (March 1956): 4. A many-day-long centennial memorial of the Mussel Slough affair
itself was held in Hanford in May 1980; see "Mussel Slough: A Centennial," a large

special issue of *Hanford Sentinel,* May 12, 1980. Literary works "memorializing" the Mussel Slough squatters were numerous over the next half-century; Irving McKee, "Notable Memorials to Mussel Slough," *Pacific Historical Review* 17 (February 1948): 19–28; Gordon W. Clarke, "A Significant Memorial to Mussel Slough," *Pacific Historical Review* 18 (November 1949): 501–504; James L. Brown, *Mussel Slough Tragedy,* 11–20, and Brown, "More Fictional Memorials to Mussel Slough," *Pacific Historical Review* 26 (November 1957).

37. Immediately after the battle, squatters applied in droves to the company to buy or lease their claims legally. For those persons, the company withdrew lawsuits, cancelled unpaid fines, and if the fines had been paid, counted the fines as payments toward purchase or lease. See Charles Crocker to Collis P. Huntington, San Francisco, May 26 and 28, 1880, and Huntington to Crocker, New York, May 29, 1880, *CPH;* for the agreement and orders to the local land agent to honor the new prices and terms, see Jerome Madden to D. K. Zumwalt, San Francisco, May 21, 25, 26, and 27, and June 1, 3, 5, and 14, 1880; Charles Crocker, Agreement with Committee of Businessmen from Hanford and Lemoore (May 15, 1880), enclosed in above May 21 letter from Madden; Crocker to Zumwalt, San Francisco, telegrams, May 24 and 25, 1880; Crocker to S. E. Biddle, San Francisco, June 1, 1880 (copy), *ZC-SP;* for the many squatters who legalized their claims, see dozens of letters reporting sales or leases, Zumwalt to Madden, June 1880 through summer 1881; in only one letter, to Ben Donager, the railroad's Hanford station agent, June 19, 1880, Zumwalt transmitted sixty-one such leases to be sent by special courier to San Francisco. Many squatters who temporarily leased their lands started converting the leases into purchases, June–November 1880; in those cases, lease payments were counted toward the purchase price. These transactions were also recorded in the Southern Pacific Railroad Land Department, "Day Book, 1871–82," 1: 378ff., and "Journal, 1882–1885," 1: 73ff., into the mid-1880s, *CRRM.* Also, *Visalia Delta,* extra edition, June 2, 1880, covered the compromise arrangement. The railroad continued to negotiate agreements for purchase or lease with a diminishing number of former squatters for years. As late as 1887, the company was still trying to assist a few former squatters to clear their records by helping them find buyers who would buy the lands, as well as pay the overdue court judgments from their lost eviction lawsuits; Zumwalt to Madden, November 11, 1887, *ZC-SP.*

38. Indicative of the problems encountered in evicting the holdout squatters, even the dedicated U.S. marshal Poole continued to have difficulty serving eviction writs after the battle through 1881. Well-known by now, Poole would be immediately recognized upon his arrival, and word would spread quickly about his movements. Observers dogged his tracks. Some squatters flatly refused to leave the properties, local officials refused to arrest them, and residents refused to work for him, or even rent him the buggies, wagons, and horses he needed to remove whatever property squatters had from their illegal claims. Poole tried sending assistant marshals and employees from San Francisco to accomplish the evictions, but when they received the same treatment and were threatened with death, Poole, fearing for their lives, recalled them to San Francisco; Marshal A. W. Poole to Wayne MacVeagh, Attorney General, San Francisco, April 5,

1881, as well as Poole's other telegrams and letters, in U.S. Department of Justice, Records Relating to the Mussel Slough Affair, 1880–1881: Letters and Telegrams Received (microfilm reel, National Archives, Washington, DC, 1956), *BL*. In those instances when authorities were successful in dismantling buildings and moving possessions to the edges of public roads, teams of squatters followed openly behind them and quickly reassembled the buildings and moved the evicted persons back onto their claims; James L. Brown, *Mussel Slough Tragedy*, 107–108.

39. A letter from an anti-League farmer discussed opposition to the squatters in *The Argonaut* (San Francisco), April 23, 1881. The pro-squatter *Visalia Delta*, April 22, 1881, printed a letter opposing the squatters and the League from a group calling itself the "Farmers' Club." The League was still active as late as 1887; Jerome Madden to D. K. Zumwalt, San Francisco, January 10, 1887; Zumwalt to Madden, Visalia, April 19 and 23, 1881, *ZC-SP.*

40. Menefee and Dodge, *History of Tulare and Kings Counties*, 801–802; James M. Guinn, *History of the State of California and Biographical Record of the San Joaquin Valley* (Chicago: Chapman Publishing Co., 1905), 602; William Hammond Hall, *Detail Irrigation Map: Lemoore and Hanford Sheet* (Sacramento: California State Engineering Department, 1885), California State Archives, Sacramento (the same map, as well as adjacent sheets, also lists names of other former Southern Pacific contestants, now farming former railroad land on odd-numbered and/or on even-numbered public sections); Richard M. Brown, *No Duty to Retreat*, 120–22.

41. Into the late 1880s, squatters continued to buy and sell claims against the railroad. After the battle, some even approached the Southern Pacific to buy or lease their own claims legally, in exchange for the company's dropping its court cases against them and cancelling court fines, while secretly trying also to buy from the company the lands being claimed by neighboring squatters who were refusing to come to terms. The railroad refused such applications; even after all that had happened, the company still insisted on giving squatters the chance to buy their claims legitimately and clear their records. See D. K. Zumwalt to Jerome Madden, Visalia, October 29 and November 1, 1880, and Madden to Zumwalt, November 3 and 13 and December 30, 1880, and August 2, 1881, *ZC-SP;* Southern Pacific Railroad Company Land Department, "Day Book, 1871–1882," 2: 22, 41, *CRRM.*

42. D. K. Zumwalt to Jerome Madden, Visalia, April 4, 1889, and Madden to Zumwalt, San Francisco, April 9, 1889, *ZC-SP.*

5   Land-Grant Development

The quotation in the chapter title is from James Horsburgh, Jr., passenger agent of the Southern Pacific, who in addressing the California Development Board in 1911, envisioned a better society in California of "well-tilled little farms" toward which the state and the railroad should build; Horsburgh, "Colonization Efforts," California Development Board, Counties Committee, *Bulletin Number Nine* (January 1911), 17.

1. Central Pacific Railroad Company, *Lands of the Central Pacific Railroad Company of California* (Sacramento: H. S. Crocker & Co., 1868, 1870 and 1872 editions); Southern Pacific Railroad Company, *The Lands of the Southern Pacific Railroad Company of California* (San Francisco, 1876, 1877, 1880, and 1883 editions).

2. Collis P. Huntington to Mark Hopkins, New York, October 23, 1873, and Isaac Gates to S. A. Burnah, New York, October 18, 1873, Huntington-Hopkins Correspondence, *SU;* David Lavender, *The Great Persuader* (Garden City, NY: Doubleday, 1970), 294–95.

3. California Immigrant Union, *All About California and the Inducements to Settle There* (San Francisco, 1870), 14; *Alta California* (San Francisco), April 23, 1875; Edna M. Parker, "The Influence of the Southern Pacific Railroad on Settlement in Southern California, 1876–1890" (M.A. thesis, Mills College, 1936), 63ff.; Thelma Kesseli, "The Railroad as an Agency of Settlement in California, 1870–1890" (M.A. thesis, University of California, Berkeley, 1948), 55ff.

4. Pacific Coast Land Bureau, *California Guide Book: The Lands of the Central Pacific and Southern Pacific Railroad Companies* (San Francisco, ca. 1882), passim; for Easton and the Land Bureau, H. H. Bancroft, *Chronicles of the Builders of the Commonwealth,* 5 vols. (San Francisco: The History Company, 1890–1891), 4: 492–529; *Alta California* (San Francisco), January 1, 1890.

5. Walter Alexander McAllister, "A Study of Railroad Land-Grant Disposal in California, with Reference to the Western Pacific, the Central Pacific, and the Southern Pacific Railroad Companies" (Ph.D. diss., University of Southern California, 1939), 454–58 and 482–86; Leslie E. Decker, *Railroads, Lands, and Politics: The Taxation of the Railroad Land Grants, 1864–1897* (Providence, RI: Brown University Press, 1964), 109–10.

6. Central Pacific Railroad Company, *Annual Report, 1877* (1878), 12; also land agents' annual reports in the annual reports of the Central and Southern Pacific Railroads, 1870s–1880s; on the dubious profitability of the Central Pacific's land grant, Lloyd J. Mercer, "Land Grants to American Railroads: Social Cost or Social Benefit?" *Business History Review* 43 (Summer 1969): 134–51.

7. Southern Pacific Railroad Company, *Annual Report, 1881* (1882), 49, *Annual Report, 1882* (1883), 44–45; *Alta California* (San Francisco), October 5, 1881.

8. Annual reports of the Central/Southern Pacific railroads, 1870s–1880s.

9. Central Pacific Railroad, *Annual Report, 1873* (1874), 40ff.; early land pamphlets, Central/Southern Pacific railroads.

10. McAllister, "Study of Railroad Land-Grant Disposal," 253ff. and 285ff. For Tevis-Haggin's acquisition of railroad land, as well as tactics used by them and other speculators to engross estates from the Desert Land Act and other entries on public land along the Southern Pacific Railroad's San Joaquin Valley route, see Donald J. Pisani, *From Family Farm to Agribusiness: The Irrigation Crusade in California and the West, 1850–1931* (Berkeley: University of California Press, 1984), 195–203.

11. Gerald D. Nash, "Henry George Reexamined: William S. Chapman's Views on Land Speculation in Nineteenth Century California," *Agricultural History* 33 (July 1959): 133–37.

12. Decker, *Railroads, Lands, and Politics,* 103ff. and 243–45; Paul Wallace Gates, *The*

Illinois Central Railroad and Its Colonization Work (Cambridge: Harvard University Press, 1934), 158ff.

13. The land transaction between the Central Pacific and Charles McLaughlin and other original owners of the Western Pacific was public knowledge; see *Alta California* (San Francisco), October 3, 1869; Lavender, *Great Persuader,* 185–88; George Kraus, *High Road to Promontory: Building the Central Pacific across the High Sierra* (Palo Alto: American West Publishing Co., 1969), 172–79. For the deal, see Central Pacific executive E. B. Crocker to Collis P. Huntington, Sacramento, March 29 and April 26, 1867, and January 28, 1869, and Leland Stanford to Huntington, San Francisco, April 6, 1867, *CPH.* For the legal history of the Western Pacific grant and railroad's transfer of its lands to McLaughlin, see C. F. Impey, commissioner, Southern Pacific Land Company, to Guy V. Shoup, Southern Pacific executive, September 17, 1934, File 837, *SP-L;* nearly seventy years after the original transaction, some land just patented by the Department of the Interior was being deeded to McLaughlin's estate. Obituaries of McLaughlin and descriptions of his land activities, in *Oakland Tribune,* December 13 and 14, 1883. For the purchase of the San Francisco & San Jose, which involved Southern Pacific Railroad lands, see Huntington to Mark Hopkins, January 20, 25, and February 9, 1870, and to Lloyd Tevis, January 26, 1870, in Huntington, *Letters from Collis P. Huntington to Mark Hopkins, Leland Stanford, Charles Crocker, E. B. Crocker, Charles Frederick Crocker, and D. D. Colton from August 20, 1867, to March 31, 1876,* 3 vols. (NY: privately printed, 1892–94), vol. 2; Hopkins to Huntington, Sacramento, November 13, 1872, *CPH;* Lavender, *Great Persuader,* 275–76. The records of Southern Pacific Railroad land transfers to Tevis-Haggin during the 1870s appear in various entries in the Day Books and Cash Books of Southern Pacific Railroad Land Department, *CRRM;* also letters in *ZC-SP,* for example, Jerome Madden to D. K. Zumwalt, San Francisco, November 10, 1876.

14. McAllister, "Study of Railroad Land-Grant Disposal," 290ff.; Alice Carothers, "The History of the Southern Pacific Railroad in the San Joaquin Valley" (M.A. thesis, University of Southern California, 1934), passim; Richard Harold Smith, "Towns along the Tracks: Railroad Strategy and Town Promotion in the San Joaquin Valley, California" (Ph.D. diss., University of California, Los Angeles, 1976), passim.

15. Central Pacific Railroad Company, *Annual Report, 1877* (1878), 47–50, and *Annual Report, 1878* (1879), 53–56.

16. With the exception of the few, occasional, very large sales explained above, during all periods on the Southern Pacific Railroad, for example, nearly all sales were for small tracts, between 40 and 160 acres being by far the most common (constituting virtually all sales near the rail line), farms between 160 and 320 acres being infrequent, and sales of 640 or more acres being rare; Southern Pacific Railroad Company, Land Department, "Journal, 1882–1885," vols. 1 and 2, and Southern Pacific Railroad Company, Land Department, "Day Book, 1871–1882," *CRRM;* D. K. Zumwalt, "Land Plat Books, 1869–1893," showing that almost all railroad land near the rail line was subdivided and sold in small parcels, *ZC-SP.*

17. As agricultural and land historians have long established, even after passage of the Homestead Act in 1862, free homesteading of good agricultural land was more

"fancy" than fact, with speculators and other engrossers getting the lion's share of valuable tracts before actual homesteaders could ever get to the land. Moreover, Congress in passing railroad land-grant bills prohibited homesteads within the areas of the grants and doubled the minimum purchase price for public land on the even-numbered sections, to $2.50 per acre. Homesteading was thus *not* a realistic alternative to buying good land at low prices from the railroads within their grant areas; Fred A. Shannon, *The Farmer's Last Frontier: Frontier Agriculture, 1860–1897* (New York: Holt, Rinehart and Winston, 1945), 51ff.; Paul W. Gates, *History of Public Land Law Development* (Washington, DC: Government Printing Office, 1968), chaps. 16 and 17. In California, particularly in the vicinity of the Southern Pacific's land grant in the San Joaquin Valley, much public land was acquired first by speculators; Paul Wallace Gates, "The Homestead Law in an Incongruous Land System," *American Historical Review* 41 (July 1936): 652–81, Khaled Bloom, "Pioneer Land Speculation in California's San Joaquin Valley," *Agricultural History* 57 (July 1983): 297–307.

18. *San Francisco Bulletin,* July 21, 1884; *Sacramento Record-Union,* July 22, 1884; Capay Valley Land Company land contracts, Pacific Improvement Company Records, Containers 278–294, *SU.*

19. Julius Grodinsky, *Transcontinental Railway Strategy, 1869–1893: A Study of Businessmen* (Philadelphia: University of Pennsylvania Press, 1962), 41ff., 56ff., 208ff., and 397ff.

20. For the 1883 advertising and land promotion program, chapter 6.

21. Charles F. Crocker to William Hammond Hall, San Francisco, January 22, 1891, William Hammond Hall Collection, California Historical Society, San Francisco; Hall's career in irrigation, in Gerald D. Nash, *State Government and Economic Development: A History of Administrative Policies in California, 1849–1933* (Berkeley: Institute of Governmental Studies, University of California, Berkeley, 1964), 189–90.

22. Marks's biography, Irena Penzik Narell, "Bernhard Marks: Retailer, Educator and Land Developer," *Western States Jewish Historical Quarterly* (Fall 1975): 26–38; Wallace W. Elliott and Company, *History of Fresno County, California* (San Francisco, 1882), 111ff. and 219–21; Virginia E. Thickens, "Pioneer Agricultural Colonies of Fresno County," *California Historical Society Quarterly* 25 (March 1946): 26ff.; *California Patron* (Grange), February 14, 1877; Bernhard Marks, *Small-Scale Farming in California* (San Francisco: Crocker & Co., ca. 1889); *Alta California* (San Francisco), November 21 and December 19, 1889, and January 1, 1890; *San Francisco Chronicle,* January 7, 1890; *Resources of California,* December 1889.

23. *San Francisco Post,* October 13, 1884; *San Francisco Chronicle,* January 16, 1885.

24. Collis P. Huntington to Albert Gallatin, New York, July 9, 1886, *CPH.*

25. Collis P. Huntington to James B. Houston, July 13, 1882; David Lubin to Huntington, February 1 and March 16, 1891; Jerome Madden to David Lubin, February 11, 1891, *CPH.*

26. For the Doukhobors and their migration, George Woodcock and Ivan Avakumovic, *The Doukhobors* (London: Faber and Faber, 1968), passim, esp. 130ff.; James Frederick Church Wright, *Slava Bohu: The Story of the Dukhobors* (New York: Farrar and Rinehart, 1940), passim, esp. 103–86; Aylmer Maude, *A Peculiar People: The Doukhobors*

(New York: Funk & Wagnalls, 1904), passim; Carl Addington Dawson, *Group Settlement: Ethnic Communities in Western Canada* (Toronto: Macmillan, 1936), 1–91.

27. Collis P. Huntington to Henry E. Huntington (telegram), New York, July 23, 1900, *HEH.*

28. Henry E. Huntington to Collis P. Huntington, February 15, July 10 and 16, and August 11 and 13, 1900; Collis to Henry, February 20 and July 16 and 27, 1900, *HEH.*

29. Henry E. to Collis P. Huntington, Los Angeles, December 15 and 16, 1899, and February 15, March 1 and 6, July 10, and August 11 and 13, 1900; Collis to Henry, New York, December 21, 1899, and February 20, March 6, July 16, 17, 23, and 27, 1900, *HEH.* The contemplated move to California, in Woodcock and Avakumovic, *Doukhobors,* 168ff. and 225ff.

30. *San Francisco Examiner,* January 9, 11, 12, February 3 and 16, and April 7, 1900; *San Francisco Call,* January 12, February 9, 1900; *San Francisco Chronicle,* January 11–16, 1900. The *Los Angeles Times, Record, Herald,* and *Express,* almost every day, January 11 through February 1900.

31. Henry E. to Collis P. Huntington, February 15 and March 1, 1900, and telegram, San Francisco, July 16, 1900; Collis to Henry, New York, February 20 and March 6, 1900, and telegrams, July 19 and 23, 1900, *HEH; San Francisco Chronicle,* January 16, 1900. On the Southern Pacific's problem hiring immigrant laborers, *San Francisco Examiner,* April 7, 18–23, June 29–30, October 20, and November 1, 1900; *San Francisco Chronicle,* June 30, 1900; and *San Francisco Call,* July 2, 1900. Collis P. Huntington, the principal proponent of the colonization plan, also died in August 1900.

32. Woodcock and Avakumovic, *Doukhobors,* 168ff. and 225ff.

33. Harry J. Carman and Charles H. Muller, "The Contract and Finance Company and the Central Pacific Railroad," *Mississippi Valley Historical Review* 14 (December 1927): 326–41; Stuart Daggett, *Chapters on the History of the Southern Pacific* (New York: August M. Kelley, Publishers, 1966 [1922]), 133–35; Lavender, *Great Persuader,* 328; Norman E. Tutorow, *Leland Stanford: Man of Many Careers* (Menlo Park, CA: Pacific Coast Publishers, 1971), 110ff.

34. Richard White, "Information, Markets, and Corruption: Transcontinental Railroads in the Gilded Age," *Journal of American History* 90 (June 2003): 38–40, for the Western Development Company's siphoning funds from the Central Pacific to the Big Four.

35. Records of the Pacific Improvement Company, esp. container 26, folder 201, *SU;* for resort hotels, including Hotel Del Monte in Monterey, Castle Crag north of Redding, California, the El Carmelo in Pacific Grove, and the Arcadia in Santa Monica, Collis P. to Henry E. Huntington, New York, August 10 and December 23, 1893, and Henry to Collis, San Francisco, August 5, 1893, among other letters between the two, 1893–97, *HEH; San Francisco Bulletin,* February 24, 1900. For the Pacific Improvement Company, see also chapter 1.

36. "Pacific Improvement Company—Report for Year Ending December 31, 1897" (ms., New York, January 17, 1898), *CPH.*

37. *San Francisco Call,* April 26, 1894, and February 20, 1901; *San Francisco Exam-*

iner, April 26, 1894; *San Francisco Chronicle,* April 27, 1894; Earl Pomeroy, *In Search of the Golden West: The Tourist in Western America* (New York: Alfred A. Knopf, 1957), 114.

38. Smith, "Towns along the Tracks," passim; McAllister, "Study of Railroad Land-Grant Disposal," 290ff.; Kesseli, "Railroad as an Agency of Settlement"; Donald G. Davis, "Material Relating to the Effect of the Southern Pacific Railroad on the Settlement and Urbanization of the San Joaquin Valley" (typescript, Berkeley, CA, 1964), *BL;* Carothers "Southern Pacific in the San Joaquin," 44ff.; George H. Tinkerham, *History of Stanislaus County, California* (Los Angeles, 1921), 94.

39. William S. Chapman to C. H. Huffman, San Francisco, March 28, 1872, Huntington-Hopkins Correspondence, *SU;* Kathleen E. Small, *History of Tulare County, California* (Chicago, 1926), 1:502; Smith, "Towns along the Tracks," passim. In developing market towns, the railroad, through its holding company, often bought up private lands as town sites before actually constructing the lines, and then ran the lines through those sites. Its own land-grant sections would not be released by the government until long after construction, too late for town-site selection, and by the time the line was built, speculators would have seized the best sites on private and public land. For Pacific Improvement Company town properties and town-building activities, see Central Pacific Railway, "Town Lot Sales, 1868–1900" (ms., ledger, n.d.), Nevada Historical Society, Reno; E. B. Ryan, Southern Pacific Railroad Tax Department, to D. K. Zumwalt, San Francisco, July 10, 1890, which reviews properties in more than a dozen San Joaquin Valley Pacific Improvement Company towns, *ZC-SP.* For town-building in the upper Salinas Valley, Loren Nicholson, *Rails across the Ranchos* (Fresno: Valley Publishers, 1980), 74–76; *San Luis Obispo Tribune,* February 19 and April 19, 1889.

40. Pomeroy, *In Search of the Golden West,* 19–23; *Sacramento Record-Union,* August 26, 1882; *San Francisco Bulletin,* January 20, 1880; Charles Crocker to Collis P. Huntington, San Francisco, October 28, November 3, 13, and 21, and December 11 and 15, 1879, Mark Hopkins et al., *Letters from Mark Hopkins, Charles Crocker, Charles F. Crocker, and David D. Colton to Collis P. Huntington from August 27th, 1869, to December 30th, 1879* (New York: John C. Rankin Co., 1891), 313–19; for the Pacific Improvement Company's work during and after the 1880s in the Monterey Peninsula area, see also Connie Y. Chiang, "Monterey-by-the-Smell: Odors and Social Conflict on the California Coastline," *Pacific Historical Review* 73 (May 2004): 192ff.; and John Walton, *Storied Land: Community and Memory in Monterey* (Berkeley: University of California Press, 2001), 150–82.

41. Pomeroy, *In Search of the Golden West,* 113–14; Lucy Neely McLane, *A Piney Paradise by Monterey Bay: Pacific Grove* (San Francisco, 1952), 9ff.; Collis P. Huntington to Charles Crocker, New York, May 3, 1880, *CPH.* For the Pacific Improvement Company's Monterey water supply, see chapter 8.

42. *San Francisco Call,* January 20, 1901; Pacific Improvement Company, *Hope Ranch: A Story of Two-Thousand Acres of Wooded Land and a Prophesy of Its Future* (San Francisco: H. S. Crocker Co., 1908).

43. Pacific Improvement Company, *Pebble Beach, Monterey County, California* (San Francisco: H. S. Crocker Co., 1909); El Verano Improvement Association Records, in Pacific Improvement Company Records, container 25a, *SU.*

44. Tom Gregory, *History of Yolo County, California* (Los Angeles, 1913), 54ff. and 108ff.; William O. Russell (ed.), *History of Yolo County, California* (Woodland, CA, 1940), 227ff.; *Woodland Mail,* January 15, 1890.

45. J. I. McConnell (ed.), *Yolo County, California* (Woodland, CA, 1887), 68–69; *Sacramento Record-Union,* July 7 and 28, 1887.

46. Capay Valley Land Company Records, Pacific Improvement Company Records, containers 278–294, esp. Capay Valley Land Company, "Cash Book, 1887–1897," container 293, "Minutes, 1887–1920," container 280, and "By-Laws" (June 1, 1887), container 278, *SU.* A company advertisement, in *Sacramento Record-Union,* September 21, 1891.

47. Mills's report on the company, in *Woodland Mail,* February 28, 1891; also *Sacramento Record-Union,* September 21, 1891; *Alta California* (San Francisco), January 1, 1890; Southern Pacific Company, *Annual Report, 1891* (1892), 27; Mills's reports, in letters to Collis P. Huntington, San Francisco, January 30, 1892, and January 27, 1898, *CPH;* to the last letter, Mills appended "Capay Valley Land Company, Statement to January 1st., 1898."

48. Capay Valley Land Company, "Cash Book," *SU;* Southern Pacific Company, *Annual Report, 1891* (1892), 27; land contracts, Capay Valley Land Company Records, *SU;* and William H. Mills to Collis P. Huntington, San Francisco, January 30, 1892, *CPH.*

49. *Woodland Mail,* January 15, 1890, and February 28, 1891; Gregory, *History of Yolo County,* 54ff. and 64–65.

50. *Woodland Mail,* January 15, 1890, and February 28, 1891; *Sacramento Record-Union,* November 17, 1889, and September 21, 1891; Russell, *History of Yolo County,* 227ff. and 293–94; Western Co-Operative Colonization and Improvement Company, *History and Description of the Tancred Colony* (n.p., n.d.); William H. Mills to Collis P. Huntington, San Francisco, May 16, 1893, and Mrs. W. B. Bayley to Huntington, Rumsey, May 20, 1893, *CPH;* Mills, *Map of Portions of Central California: Showing the Geographical Situation of Capay Valley in Yolo County, the Principal Towns and Their Railroad Connections* (San Francisco, 1892).

51. William H. Mills to Collis P. Huntington, San Francisco, January 18, March 22, and May 16, 1893, *CPH.*

52. Sonoma Valley Improvement Company, "Journals and Ledgers, 1890–1913," Pacific Improvement Company Records, containers 48–53 and 25a, folder 191g, *SU; Sacramento Record-Union,* September 21, 1891.

53. C. F. Crocker to Collis P. Huntington, February 7, 10, and 19 and March 2, 1887, and William H. Mills to Crocker, February 3, 1887 (copy), *CPH.* The Southern Pacific and the Santa Fe also competed to purchase the ranch for a right-of-way; Robert Glass Cleland, *The Irvine Ranch* (San Marino: The Huntington Library, 1966), 92–94.

54. On the Crocker-Huffman property, see chapter 8. For these and other land deals, see C. L. Wilson to Collis P. Huntington, Lincoln, California, December 9, 1893, and March 5, 1894; William H. Mills to Huntington, San Francisco, May 4, 1893; Charles F. Crocker to Huntington, San Francisco, December 29, 1890; *CPH.* For a rationale for subdividing ranch land into farms, see Huntington to Mills, New York, February 11 and 21, 1887; and Huntington to F. S. Douty, Pacific Improvement Company, New York,

December 4, 1890, all in *CPH*. Huntington, working closely with land agent Mills, appears to have been the driving force, envisioning not only personal profits but also development, population growth, and cultural maturity for California, and he repeatedly took his partners to task for their timidity and lack of follow-through in acquiring likely properties before rivals beat them to the punch; for his ideas on subdividing open range into farms and the role he planned to play, see Huntington to Mills, October 28, 1892, in *San Francisco Examiner,* November 3, 1892.

55. *Houston Post,* January 27 and February 3, 5, 6, 10, and 14, 1904, for the railroad's farm-colony subdivisions in Texas.

56. *Houston Post,* February 13, 1904.

57. The Pacific Improvement Company borrowed half a million dollars from Claus Spreckels in 1893 to save itself from failure; Charles F. Crocker to Collis P. Huntington, San Francisco, October 5, 1893, *CPH*. Many letters in *CPH* from Crocker to Huntington from 1893 until Crocker's own death several years later testify to the Crocker-Stanford faction's unrelenting pressure on Huntington to dissolve the Pacific Improvement Company, as well as the families' arrangements in the Southern Pacific Company; see letters of May 23, June 14, 17, 18, 23, and 28, August 3, and November 15 and 24, and December 22, 1893, and January 9, 1894; F. S. Douty, Pacific Improvement Company executive, to Lowell White, San Francisco, September 14, 1893, and Douty to Huntington, September 25, 1893; and Speyer and Co. to Huntington, New York, December 6, 1893, and March 3, 1894, for cash-flow shortages that caused creditors to foreclose on loans and sell securities the Pacific Improvement Company had deposited with them as collateral. For the Pacific Improvement Company's financial difficulties, 1893–94, see also, William Mahl, "Memoirs" (ms., 1913), G-1ff., William Mahl Papers, *UTA*. For conflict between the Crockers and the Huntingtons over the Pacific Improvement Company, see also Henry E. to Collis P. Huntington, April 5, 1896, and Collis to Henry, April 21, 1896 and June 28 and July 19, 1898, *HEH*. The companies' travails and conflicts among the associates were frequent sources of glee to San Francisco's usually anti–Southern Pacific newspapers; see *Examiner,* March 27–31, and April 2, 10, and 26, 1894, and November 7 and 8 and 29, 1895, and March 30, April 10, 11, and 12, 1896, February 1, 1897; *Chronicle,* March 18, 19, 29, 30, and April 27, 1894, and December 5, 1895; *Bulletin,* March 28–29, 1894, January 27 and February 1, 1897; and *Call,* March 28–30 and May 18, 1894, March 27, 1897.

58. Collis P. Huntington to William H. Mills, Washington, DC, April 23, 1896, *CPH*.

59. For conflict between the Crocker-Stanford faction and the Huntingtons, see James Thorpe, *Henry Edwards Huntington: A Biography* (Berkeley: University of California Press, 1994), 88–121; *San Francisco Examiner,* March 30, 1896.

60. William H. Mills to Collis P. Huntington, San Francisco, December 15 (two letters), 16, 17, and 27, 1897, and January 13, 18 (two letters), 25, and 27, and February 7 and 21, 1898; Mills to H. E. Huntington, San Francisco, December 29 and 31, 1897; and Collis P. Huntington to Mills, New York, December 22 (two letters) and 24, 1897, and January 5 and February 3, 5, and 16, 1898; *CPH;* Henry to Collis, San Francisco, December 17, 1897, *HEH*. On the controversy over Mills's supposed insider land deals with Henry, see *San Francisco Examiner,* April 19, 1896, and *San Francisco Call,* April 27, 1896.

61. William Mahl, "Statement Showing Cost and Interest of Roads Constructed by Pacific Improvement Company Since January 1, 1892 . . . to June 30, 1898" (ms., ca. 1898); Mahl to F. S. Douty, June 27, 1898, Mahl to Henry E. Huntington, September 30, 1898, Mahl to Thomas Hubbard, August 15, 1898 (containing the audit of the financial relationship of the two companies); Henry E. Huntington to Mahl, October 11, 1898; Hubbard to Mahl, June 13 and September 8, 1898; Collis P. Huntington to J. L. Wilcutt, February 10, 1899; Collis to Mahl, Raquette Lake, New York, August 28, 1898, in which he instructed Mahl on conducting the audit and told Mahl to separate the accounts of the two companies "exactly right and equitable so that one company may not gain and another lose in the adjustment"; all in File R195.2, *SP-PR.* By 1898, Collis P. Huntington thought the Pacific Improvement Company had outlived its usefulness; Collis to Henry, New York, July 19, 1898, and also, Collis to Henry, New York, June 28, 1898, for Collis's order for an audit of the Pacific Improvement Company, *HEH.*

62. *San Francisco Examiner,* November 15, 17–20, and December 5 and 12, 1899; *San Francisco Call,* November 15, 16, and 25, December 5 and 12, 1899; *San Francisco Bulletin,* November 27 and December 5, 1899.

63. McAllister, "Study of Railroad Land-Grant Disposal," 396–97.

64. Ibid., Appendix O and X; Southern Pacific Company's annual reports, 1880s–1890s.

65. For the Harriman Lines' land-grant policy and the attack on old-time Southern Pacific officials, see William D. Cornish Office Files and the Charles W. Eberlein Correspondence, two collections in *SP-L;* see Eberlein to Cornish, San Francisco, August 11, 18, 28, 1902, and May 29, June 5 and 13, July 1, 8, and 24, August 3 and 9, 1903, Eberlein to William H. Mills, letter and telegram, New York, December 8, 1902, and Mills to Eberlein, San Francisco, November 17 and December 1 and 8, 1902, Cornish to Eberlein, New York, August 17, 1903, Eberlein Correspondence; Cornish to Julius Kruttschnitt (assistant to President Harriman), New York, August 1, 1902, Eberlein to Cornish (en route in Texas), September 11, 1902, Kruttschnitt to Cornish, San Francisco, March 12, 1903, Cornish Office Files. Eberlein's September 11, 1902, letter particularly clarifies his marching orders from Harriman and Cornish, the Harriman Lines' sweeping changes in Southern Pacific land policy, Eberlein's criticism of the Southern Pacific's land policies, and his personal contempt for Jerome Madden and William H. Mills, whom he frequently accused of being incompetent and probably dishonest old men. Also running through Eberlein's criticisms is a familiar strain of east coast elitism, a ridicule and haughty dismissal of the Southern Pacific leaders as old-fashioned western provincials, out of step with modern, efficient business practices. "These fellows all pull back in the harness," he wrote Cornish in the above-cited July 24, 1903 letter. Madden, he described as "very old and extremely hide-bound in all his ideas," with a "sluggish consciousness"; Eberlein to Cornish, San Francisco, August 28, 1902, Eberlein Correspondence. Mills, he criticized for his "nervous and intensely theoretical temperament"; Eberlein to Cornish, September 11, 1902, Cornish Office Files. He branded Madden, Mills, and indeed also Union Pacific land agent B. A. McAllaster and all other Harriman Lines western land officials as "dismal failures" and "automatons"; Eberlein to Cornish, San Francisco, August 9, 1903, Eberlein Correspondence. But, also

about Mills, Eberlein warned, "we shall be in an awkward fix if Mills flies the track and pulls out and there is grave danger he may"; Eberlein to Cornish, San Francisco, July 15, 1903, Eberlein Correspondence. For the campaign to oust Mills for dishonesty, its failure, and the Harriman people's worry about the damage he might do if he left the company, see Eberlein's August 9, 1903, letter, and Cornish to Eberlein, New York, August 17, 1903, Eberlein Correspondence.

66. "Claims Against Pacific Improvement Company" (mss., letters among executives re. Pacific Improvement Company and Southern Pacific relationships, Executive Department File); William Mahl, "Pacific Improvement Company Claims Against Southern Pacific Company" (ms., April 28, 1903); "Memo for Mr. Mahl: Pacific Improvement Company Settlement, July 12, 1903" (ms., March 30, 1910); Julius Kruttschnitt to A. D. Shepard, May 7, 1903, Kruttschnitt to E. H. Harriman, New York, September 23, 1902, and Thomas H. Hubbard to Mahl, New York, July 30, 1902; all in File R195.2, *SP-PR.*

67. For newspaper leaks, see *San Francisco Post,* over which Mills had long had influence, July 8, 1903, and a full and inflammatory report in *San Francisco Examiner,* July 15, 1903; *Oregon Journal,* November 26, 27, and 28, 1905. About the Oregon newspaper leaks, see William D. Fenton, Southern Pacific attorney, to William F. Herrin, Portland, November 28, 1905, Cornish Office Files, *SP-L.*

68. For opposition to Eberlein and the new policies, especially by Mills and Herrin, see numerous manuscripts in various collections in *SP-L;* esp. Julius Kruttschnitt to William D. Cornish, San Francisco, February 9 and March 12, 1903, Cornish Office Files. See also, William H. Mills to Charles W. Eberlein, San Francisco, December 8, 1902, in which Mills provides a comprehensive statement of the California executives' arguments against the no-sale policy; Eberlein to Cornish, telegram, Portland, September 14, 1904, and November 4, 1905; William F. Herrin to Cornish, San Francisco, March 27, 1905; Eberlein Correspondence. In a letter to Cornish on August 9, 1903, Eberlein complained that "I can't even dictate a letter in safety," forcing him to write and mail all his correspondence personally; Eberlein Correspondence. The ingenious tactics used by many western Southern Pacific leaders, including Mills, William F. Herrin, and it seems almost all company people in Oregon, to ignore, countermand, and usurp Eberlein's authority and thwart his mission are catalogued in his long letter of complaint to Cornish, Portland, November 11, 1905. About his old-time Southern Pacific executive opponents, Eberlein wrote: "This is such a tight corporation. Every man below Mr. K[ruttschnitt] stands shoulder to shoulder to down the impudent foreigner [Union Pacific officials like himself] and defeat his purposes"; Eberlein to Cornish, San Francisco, July 24, 1903, Eberlein Correspondence.

69. That the old Southern Pacific leaders' obstructionist tactics worked, especially in confusing the Harriman men, raising opposition to their efforts within and outside the company, and exacerbating public discontent with the railroad, is evident from Charles W. Eberlein to Julius Kruttschnitt and Eberlein to William D. Cornish, San Francisco, July 15, 1903, and Cornish to Kruttschnitt, New York, July 20, 1903, Cornish Office Files, *SP-L.*

70. William D. Cornish to William H. Mills and Charles W. Eberlein, telegram,

New York, April 10, 1907, and Cornish to Eberlein, New York, April 10, 1907, Cornish Office Files; Mills to Cornish, April 11, 1907, File 610; Mills to Cornish, San Francisco, April 20, 1907, Cornish Office Files, which presents a full review and rationale of Southern Pacific mineral rights policies back to the 1880s; Cornish to Julius Kruttschnitt, New York, April 18, 1907, Cornish Office Files; all in *SP-L*. For Mills's campaign to revoke the Harriman Lines' new land policies, in which he secretly enlisted sympathetic and influential outsiders, including California state mineralogist Lewis E. Aubury, see File 976, *SP-L;* esp. Mills to S. G. Weston, Oakland, May 18, 1906, Weston to E. H. Harriman, Elko, NV, June 5, 1906, Cornish to Mills, New York, June 13 and December 3, 1906, and February 25 and April 10, 1907, Mills to Cornish, Oakland, June 20, July 18, November 24 and 26, 1906, and April 1, 1907, Mills to Aubury, September 11, 1906, Aubury to Mills, July 14, 1906, Mills to William F. Herrin, February 12, 1907, Cornish to Herrin, February 16, 1907.

71. Charles W. Eberlein to E. H. Harriman, New York, April 20 and May 7, 1908, and Eberlein to William D. Cornish, May 13 and June 5, 1908, Eberlein Correspondence, *SP-L*.

72. For unique homestead provisions of the Oregon & California land grant, see Gates, *History of Public Land Law Development,* 456–57. Southern Pacific sales practices during the 1880s and 1890s are evident from the approvals of land-sales transactions by the Oregon & California Railroad Company, Board of Directors, in its "Minutes" (ms.), vol. 4:1ff., 15, 123ff., 162ff., 174ff., 213ff., 347ff., and vol. 5:47ff., 61; Oregon Historical Society, Portland.

73. Oregon & California Railroad Company, Board of Directors, "Minutes," vol. 5:61, 105–109, 116, 129ff., 207ff., 213, 229, 288–89, 336ff., Oregon Historical Society, Portland; William H. Mills to Charles W. Eberlein, San Francisco, November 17 and December 1 and 8, 1902; Eberlein to Mills, telegram and letter, New York, December 1, 1902; Eberlein Correspondence, *SP-L*.

74. Gates, *History of Public Land Law Development,* 602–603. The governor of Oregon at the time was George E. Chamberlain. In 1907, he was also president of the International Irrigation Congress, which was meeting at Sacramento. When Chamberlain objected to the land-sale withdrawal to Southern Pacific president E. H. Harriman, Harriman not only refused to revoke the policy, but announced in a congress address that the railroad would hold onto the lands at least for another twenty to fifty years as a reserve to ensure the company's future access to construction materials. "We have given this much thought," Chamberlain recalled Harriman's having said, "and when the time comes we intend to have a reserve with which we can maintain these great transportation lines for those who come after, that they not accuse us of wasting the resources which we had at our command." According to Chamberlain, Harriman's private statement and his public speech convinced Oregon interests that they could not get the Southern Pacific to alter its policy, and they immediately shifted to pressuring the federal government to revoke the land grant; see the 1916 testimony of Chamberlain, by then a senator from Oregon, in U.S. Congress, House Committee on Public Lands, *Oregon & California Land Grants: Hearings . . .* (Washington, DC: Government Printing Office, 1916), 143–44.

75. For Mills's objections to withholding Oregon & California lands from sale, particularly the potential backlash from Oregonians, see his letters in the Eberlein Correspondence and Cornish Office Files, *SP-L;* esp. Mills to Charles W. Eberlein, December 8, 1902, Eberlein Correspondence. For conflict between Eberlein and Mills and Herrin over the Oregon & California lands, see Eberlein to William D. Cornish, telegram, Portland, September 14, 1904, and November 4, 1905, and many letters that passed among Eberlein, Herrin, and Julius Kruttschnitt in 1905. Harriman's assistant, Kruttschnitt, an old Southern Pacific man, was gradually converted to support Mills's position. Regarding opposition to the new Oregon & California land policy by Herrin, E. E. Calvin, and even Harriman-loyalist Kruttschnitt, see Herrin to Kruttschnitt, San Francisco, December 4, 1905; Kruttschnitt to Cornish, Chicago, December 21, 1905, Cornish Office Files. For the company's complex political problems caused by its Oregon & California land policy, see Eberlein to Cornish, and many attachments of letter-copies and clippings, December 7, 1905, Eberlein Correspondence.

76. For the U.S. Supreme Court's decision, see *Portland Oregonian,* June 27, 1915, and days following, esp. June 30, July 1, 2, 18, September 18, 1915; *Portland Journal,* September 19, 1915; *Oregon & California Railroad* v. *United States,* 238 U.S. (June 21, 1915); Ferris Act (39 Stat., 218, June 9, 1916); *Oregon & California Railroad* v. *United States,* 243 U.S. 549 (April 23, 1917); *United States* v. *Oregon & California Railroad,* 8 Fed. 2d 645 (September 15, 1925). For the uproar in Oregon against the Harriman Lines' ending of land sales, see newspaper clipping file, "Oregon and California Railroad Land Case," box 4, James Withycombe Papers (the state governor at the time), Oregon Historical Society, Portland; and Joseph Nathan Teal Scrapbooks Relating to Portland and Oregon Politics, 1894–1912, volume on "Railroad Matters, 1906–1915," Oregon Collection, University of Oregon Library, Eugene; *Portland Journal,* November 26, 27, and 28, 1905. For the *Portland Oregonian*'s leadership of the movement, Leslie Scott (editor, *Oregonian*), to Professor F. G. Young, Portland, April 16, 1907, Southern Pacific Collection, Oregon Historical Society, Portland; *Oregonian,* January 13, February 2, April 13 and 14, 1907. For general history of the land sales withdrawal and ensuing confiscation, see McAllister, "Study of Railroad Land-Grant Disposal," Appendix O and X; Daggett, *Chapters on the History of the Southern Pacific,* 449–53; David Maldwyn Ellis, "The Oregon and California Railroad Land Grant, 1866–1945," *Pacific Northwest Quarterly* 34 (October 1948): 261–62; Willis Chatham Hawley, *The Oregon and California Land Grant: Speech in the House of Representatives, May 24, 1916* (Washington, DC: Government Printing Office, 1916); Louis F. Bean, *The Oregon and California Land Grant: Remarks of . . . in the House of Representatives on House Bill No. 302, February, 1917* (Salem, OR: State Printing Dept., 1917); Abraham Walter Lafferty, *Oregon and California Land Grant Suit . . . Speech in the House of Representatives . . . July 15, 1911* (Washington, DC: Government Printing Office, 1911), and *A. W. Lafferty in Historic Fight to Save O. & C. Land Grant for Oregon* (Portland, 1952); U.S. Congress, House Committee on Public Lands, *Oregon & California Land Grants: Hearings . . . ,* and U.S. Congress, Senate, *Hearing before the Subcommittee of the Committee on Public Lands, Sixty-Fourth Congress, First Session, on S.B. 30 [Oregon & California Railroad Lands],* two of the best sources of primary evidence; Robert Bradley Jones, *One by One: A Documented Nar-*

rative Based upon the History of the Oregon and California Railroad Land Grant in the State of Oregon (Maryhurst, OR: The Source Magazine, ca. 1973), passim; Jerry A. O'Callahan, *Disposition of the Public Domain in Oregon* (Washington, DC: Committee on Interior and Insular Affairs, U.S. Senate, 1960), 37–47; Elmo R. Richardson, *BLM's Billion Dollar Checkerboard: Managing the Oregon and California Lands* (Santa Cruz, CA: Forest History Society, 1980). For the company's perspective, William Sproule, *The Southern Pacific's Position in the Oregon-California Land Controversy* (ca. 1916); *Southern Pacific Bulletin* 4 (January 15, 1916): 7, which published a defense by company counsel Peter F. Dunne, and esp. (April 1, 1916): 3, which reprinted President William Sproule's statement. Essentially, the company maintained that, as courts had always held, the passage of the 1869 land-grant act by Congress had conveyed clear land title to the railway, and other provisions in the act were merely incidental to that; that position was, in fact, upheld by the U.S. Supreme Court in its 1915 rejection of the government's suit. For the railroad's own detailed internal history of the Oregon & California land debacle, see Southern Pacific Company, "Historical Memoranda" (ms., ca. 1960s), vol. I, chap. 5, and also chap. 3, *SP-E.* In the 1916 "revestiture" bill, Congress reimbursed the Southern Pacific for its equity in the lands up to the $2.50-per-acre maximum sale price for the land allowed in the land-grant act, minus the amount the railroad had already received in land sales. After ten years of negotiations and lawsuits, the federal district court for Oregon awarded the railroad $1,723,470, while another company holding a mortgage on the lands received something over $2 million; see "Oregon & California Land Grant Accounting Suit" (1925–1928), File 075, Box 29, *SP-E,* esp. William Sproule to A. D. McDonald, New York, June 10, 1926; *Portland Oregonian,* June 26, 1926.

77. Two valuable collections pertaining to Southern Pacific land history were brought to San Francisco after the 1906 earthquake and fire to reconstruct the Land Department's records: the D. K. Zumwalt Correspondence, *ZC-SP,* and the 67-volume "Letter Press Books . . . Washington, D.C., Attorneys" (1866–1907), from several firms of attorneys on retainer, *SP-A.* Other collections were moved from corporate headquarters in New York. The reconstructed map books of Southern and Central Pacific lands are now at *CRRM.*

78. From 1869 to 1879, B. A. McAllaster had lived in Kansas, where he studied agricultural science. In 1882, he went to work for the Land Department of the Union Pacific Railway in Kansas City. In 1890, he was appointed head of that department, succeeding his father in that position, and he moved to Omaha. Experienced and knowledgeable in the field of arid-lands farming, McAllaster was one of the early and vociferous critics of the then fashionable, now discredited, "rain-follows-the-plow" theory that boosters used to lure farmers out onto the dry Great Plains. He also was one of the leaders of the irrigation congress movement. McAllaster's background fitted him well to follow in the tradition of B. B. Redding and William H. Mills. For his transfer to head the Southern Pacific Land Department, see *Omaha Bee,* September 20, 1908; for autobiographical information, a letter he wrote to the secretary of agriculture, state of Kansas, San Francisco, July 24, 1917, File 621A; he reviewed the circumstances of his appointment and the confusion that beset Southern Pacific land policies from 1906

to 1910 in a long report to Paul Shoup, San Francisco, October 29, 1926, File 976A; all in *SP-L.*

79. McAllaster recalled the details of the reversion to traditional Southern Pacific sales policies and his role in affecting the change in a letter he wrote to Paul Shoup, San Francisco, October 29, 1926, File 976A, *SP-L;* also letters passing among McAllaster, William F. Herrin, Julius Kruttschnitt, E. E. Calvin, R. S. Lovett, and E. H. Harriman in 1908 through 1910, and as late as 1919, also in Files 976 and 976A, document the success of old Southern Pacific executives, led by newcomer McAllaster and once again aided by influential outsiders, including Lewis Aubury, California state mineralogist, in gradually liberalizing the Harriman Lines' no-sales policies; see esp. McAllaster to Lovett, San Francisco, June 10, 1909, Lovett to McAllaster, New York, June 19, 1909, and Lovett to Lt. Gov. D. S. Dickerson of Nevada, New York, June 5, 1909, and Herrin to McAllaster, August 13, 1910.

80. The company reiterated and explained its traditional land sales and develop-ment policies in an editorial in *Southern Pacific Bulletin* 2 (June 15, 1914): 4. For the basic patterns of Southern Pacific land programs and the major policy decisions through the 1960s, see Louis Frandsen (head of the Natural Resources Department, Southern Pacific Land Company), "Resume . . . Land Department" (ms., ca. 1968); Southern Pacific Company, "Historical Memoranda" (ms., ca. 1960s), chap. 15; and "His-tory of Southern Pacific Land Company's Real Estate" (ms., 1972), all in *SP-E.* For an analysis of mid-twentieth-century land operations by a somewhat critical outside jour-nalist, see Philip Fradkin, "Southern Pacific Changing 'Octopus' Image over Owner-ship of Land," *Los Angeles Times,* April 16, 1972.

81. The railroad's account of the land-grant effects of the transportation acts of 1940 and 1946 is Southern Pacific Company, "Historical Memoranda" (ca. 1960s), vol. 1, chap. 4, 1–4, *SP-E;* see also, John F. Stover, *American Railroads* (Chicago: University of Chicago Press, 1961), 88–91.

82. *Southern Pacific's First Century,* indexed edition (San Francisco: Southern Pacific Public Relations Department, 1956), 102. For the debate within the company over the redirection of land policy, see "Withdrawal of Grant Lands from Sale" (1948–1952), box 29, *SP-E,* esp.: D. J. Russell to A. T. Mercier, November 29, 1948, and August 10, 1949; C. J. McDonald, "Memorandum" (ms., November 29, 1948), "Memorandum" (ms., December 1, 1948), and "Memorandum for File" (ms., August 22, 1949); Mc-Donald to A. T. Mercier, February 16 and July 15, 1949; and W. Prince Catlin to L. Frand-sen, August 3, 1949; and Frandsen, "Resume . . . Land Department," 6ff. Frandsen, who was appointed head of the Natural Resources Department of the Land Company in the summer of 1949 and took part in the final discussions and decision, character-ized the railroad's new stance toward its lands as "a change from a policy of liquida-tion to one of management." Exceptions were to be made, however, when the price of the land was considered high enough to warrant sale or when there were special cir-cumstances, such in as the 1952 sale of 260,000 acres (price: $362,000) to the federal government for the expansion of Joshua Tree National Monument in southern Cali-fornia's Mojave Desert; see McDonald to Frandsen, August 11, 1949, and Frandsen to

L. B. Young, March 24, 1952, "Withdrawal of Grant Lands from Sale" (1948–1952), box 29, *SP-E*. Sporadic land sales continued, the company's total former land-grant acreage declining to about 4 million by the 1960s and 3 million by 1980, producing a stream of sales and, increasingly, rental revenue. In 1983, during its ill-fated takeover of the Southern Pacific (holding) Company, the Santa Fe management immediately merged the Southern Pacific Land Company with its own real estate subsidiary to create the Santa Fe Pacific Land Company, which was shortly spun off as the Catellus Development Corporation, which still exists. When the Interstate Commerce Commission predictably disallowed the merger of the two parallel railroads as a restraint on trade, the Southern Pacific Transportation Company (in other words the railroad part of the operation) was sold, though now greatly weakened by having been shorn of its more profitable assets, particularly the land grant. This left some observers to wonder whether the seizure of the Land Company had been the real objective of the Santa Fe all along. In 1981, for example, the former land grant had yielded $81.4 million in income to the Southern Pacific Company, compared to only $16.8 million from rail operations; *San Francisco Business Journal,* February 1, 1982. For the attempted merger, see Don L. Hofsommer, *The Southern Pacific, 1901–1985* (College Station: Texas A & M University Press, 1986), 318–23, though it went to press before the ICC's rejection of the merger.

6   Promoting the Far West

1. *San Francisco Post,* July 11, 1878; also unidentified clipping, filed with July 1874 clippings, *Stanford Family Scrapbook,* vol. 7:98, *SU*.

2. Richard C. Overton, *Burlington West: A Colonization History of the Burlington Railroad* (Cambridge: Harvard University Press, 1941), 111ff., 139ff., 190ff., 226ff., 237ff., 329; Morris N. Spencer, "The Union Pacific Railroad Company's Utilization of Its Land Grant with Emphasis on Its Colonization Program" (Ph.D. diss., University of Nebraska, 1950), 18ff., 85ff.

3. Stuart Daggett, *Chapters on the History of the Southern Pacific* (New York: August M. Kelley, Publishers, 1966 [1922]), 56ff.; Leslie E. Decker, *Railroads, Lands, and Politics: The Taxation of the Railroad Land Grants, 1864–1897* (Providence, RI: Brown University Press, 1964), passim; B. B. Redding, "Report of the Land Department of the Southern Pacific Railroad Company to the President and Directors of the Southern Pacific Railroad Company" (ms., Sacramento, June 30, 1873), Hopkins Documents, vol. 2:26, Timothy Hopkins Transportation Collection, *SU;* W. H. Mills's land agent reports, Central Pacific Railroad Company, *Annual Report, 1887* (San Francisco, 1888), 69–73, and *Annual Report, 1888* (1889), 118–20.

4. Collis P. Huntington–Mark Hopkins Correspondence, 1870–1874, vols. 1–5, *SU,* esp. letters of August 23, September 28, and October 29, 1872, and February 15, March 3 and 10, 1873; Daggett, *Chapters,* 169ff.; Julius Grodinsky, *Transcontinental Railway Strategy, 1869–1893: A Study of Businessmen* (Philadelphia: University of Pennsylvania Press,

1962), 16ff., 41ff., and 56ff.; David Lavender, *The Great Persuader* (Garden City, NY: Doubleday, 1970), 130, 181ff., 293ff., and 376–77; Norman E. Tutorow, *Leland Stanford: Man of Many Careers* (Menlo Park, CA: Pacific Coast Publishers, 1971), 114–18; Walter A. McAllister, "A Study of Land-Grant Disposal in California with Reference to the Western Pacific, the Central Pacific, and the Southern Pacific Railroad Companies" (Ph.D. diss., University of Southern California, 1939), 307–55; James L. Brown, *The Mussel Slough Tragedy* (1958), passim; also, chapters 3 and 4 in the present volume for additional discussion of Mussel Slough and other conflicts with squatters.

5. *Alta California* (San Francisco), October 5, 1881; *San Francisco Bulletin,* May 21, 1883.

6. *People and the Railroad; Tourists and Settlers . . . They Came to See and to Stay! Central Pacific Railroad (forerunner of Southern Pacific Company)* (North Highlands, CA: History West, in cooperation with the California State Railroad Museum and the Pacific Coast Chapter Railway & Locomotive Historical Society, 1981) is a potpourri of drawings, photographs, ads, pamphlet covers, and snippets from Southern Pacific publications and other writings about the railroad's promotional activities, primarily in California, from the 1860s through the 1950s.

7. U.S. Pacific Railway Commission, *Testimony Taken By the United States Pacific Railway Commission,* 8 vols. (Washington, DC: Government Printing Office, 1887), 6:3423ff.

8. Collis P. Huntington to Mark Hopkins, New York, January 29, 1872, and Charles Nordhoff to Hopkins, Santa Barbara, April 16, 1872, Huntington-Hopkins Correspondence, *SU;* Nordhoff, "California," *Harper's* 44 (May 1872): 865–81, 45 (June 1872): 65–81 and (July 1872): 255–67; Franklin Walker, *A Literary History of Southern California* (Berkeley: University of California Press, 1950), 107–108; also article on Nordhoff, *Dictionary of American Biography.* Nordhoff's Southern Pacific commission and his writings about California are the subject of Carol J. Frost's "Golden State" (ms., 1996), in the possession of this author, a chapter from Frost's projected biography of Nordhoff.

9. D. M. Berry to Dr. Thomas B. Elliott, Los Angeles, September 5, 1873, Elliott Papers, *HL;* Walker, *Literary History,* 107.

10. Walker, *Literary History,* 109–10; *New York Times,* January 30, February 20, March 13, and April 24, 1887; quotation from the *Tribune,* in *Los Angeles Times,* June 9, 1887. A Truman biography, in *Dictionary of American Biography* and an obituary in *Los Angeles Times,* July 19, 1916; also, Gary F. Kurutz, *Benjamin C. Truman: California Booster and Bon Vivant* (San Francisco: Book Club of California, 1984). The Southern Pacific disbanded its literary bureau and dismissed Truman in 1889, when the Boom of the Eighties had busted and California and the railroad were suffering from a recession; Collis P. Huntington to Ben C. Truman, New York, November 25, 1889, and February 25, 1890, *CPH.*

11. *Sacramento Union,* June 4, 1869; Robert Louis Stevenson, *Across the Plains* (New York: Charles Scribner's Sons, 1892).

12. *Southern Pacific Bulletin* 10 (February 1921): 20.

13. *Reno Gazette,* March 28, 1879.

14. Another description of the cars and trains and what it was like to travel on them

was left by George Trepanier, a retired conductor, in *Southern Pacific Bulletin* 10 (November 1922): 30.

15. *Carson City Appeal,* February 13, 1875.

16. *Nevada State Journal* (Reno), October 1, 1873; *Reno Gazette,* July 22, 1876.

17. Collis P. Huntington to E. H. Miller, New York, November 2, 1872, and Huntington to Mark Hopkins, New York, December 2, 1872, Huntington-Hopkins Correspondence, *SU.*

18. Henry G. Hanks, "History of Former World's Fairs or International Expositions, Compiled from Various Sources," in California State Mining Bureau, *Fifth Annual Report of the State Mineralogist* (Sacramento, 1885), 22–25, reprinted in *California World's Fair Magazine* 1 (April 1892): 17–22; Collis P. Huntington to Mark Hopkins, New York, June 8, 1876, and J. A. Johnson to Huntington, Philadelphia, June 6, 1876, Huntington-Hopkins Correspondence, *SU;* Land Office, Central Pacific and Southern Pacific R.R. Companies, B. B. Redding Land Agent, *Circular* (ca. 1876), announcing the railroad's exhibition at the Centennial and providing instructions for persons wanting to contribute displays for the company to send to Philadelphia; Richard J. Orsi, "Selling the Golden State: A Study of California Boosterism" (Ph.D. diss., University of Wisconsin, Madison, 1973), chap. 2, part 3.

19. *California Patron,* January 17, 1877; Hanks, "History of Former World's Fairs," 22–25; I. E. Gates to Mark Hopkins, New York, June 8, 1876, Huntington-Hopkins Correspondence, *SU.*

20. *Inter-Ocean* (Chicago), October 1 and 14, 1883; *Sacramento Record-Union,* March 25, 1884; California Immigration Commissioner, Chicago, Illinois, *California: The Cornucopia of the World* (Chicago: Rand McNally & Co., 1883), 75–76; *San Francisco Call,* January 13, 1896.

21. W. G. Kingsbury, *A Tour Through Texas and California in 1884* (London, 1884), 23; *Sacramento Record-Union,* November 20, 1884; Charles B. Turrill, *Californian Notes* (San Francisco, 1876), and *Deuteronomy Brown: A Real Estate Transaction* (1888); Charles B. Turrill to Leland Stanford, San Francisco, July 1, 1889, Leland Stanford Correspondence, vol. 2, Leland Stanford Papers, *SU;* see also, Charles B. Turrill Papers, *BL,* passim.

22. *El Dorado Republican* (Placerville), July 19, 1884; *Oroville Register,* September 25, 1884; *Resources of California* (San Francisco), December 1884; *San Francisco Bulletin,* November 13 and December 5, 1884; Southern Pacific Company, *Catalogue of the Products of California, Exhibited by the Southern Pacific Company, at the North, Central, and South American Exposition New Orleans, November 10th, 1885, to April 1st, 1886* (New Orleans, 1886), passim, written by Turrill; *The Rural Californian* (Los Angeles) 7 (November 1884): 202; A. Andrews, *Report of A. Andrews, United States Commissioner for California at the World's Industrial and Cotton Centennial Exhibition, New Orleans, Louisiana, December 16, 1884, to June 1, 1885* (Sacramento, 1886), 7–8; *Sunday States* (New Orleans), January 4, 1885; *New Orleans Picayune,* January 13, 1885; *New Orleans Times-Democrat,* January 20 and May 8, 1885; *Journal of Commerce* (San Francisco), January 15, 1885; Orsi, "Selling the Golden State," chap. 2, part 3.

23. *California Spirit of the Times* (San Francisco), May 2, 1885; *Southern Pacific Com-*

pany Circular Number 23, Office General Passenger Agent (San Francisco, October 20, 1885); *North, Central, and South American Exposition Gazette,* September and November 1885; Southern Pacific Company, *Catalogue,* 16–20; *San Francisco Chronicle,* April 4, 1886; *Daily States* (New Orleans), December 2, 1885, January 3 and 7, 1886; *New Orleans Times-Democrat,* December 23, 1885.

24. *Alta California* (San Francisco), April 14, 1885; *San Francisco Chronicle,* April 13, 1885; *San Francisco Post,* April 6, 1885; Southern Pacific Company, *Catalogue,* passim; *New Orleans Picayune,* December 31, 1885, and February 5, 1886; *Evening Wisconsin* (Milwaukee), January 19, 1885; *Louisville Times,* October 16, 1885; *Louisville Commercial,* October 16, 1885; *Daily States* (New Orleans), January 4, 1885; *Buffalo Courier,* January 22, 1885; *New Orleans Times-Democrat,* February 25, 1888; Los Angeles Board of Trade, *Los Angeles City and County . . . Including Annual Report for . . . 1885* (Los Angeles, 1885), 17ff.; Benjamin Truman, "The Fruits of California," *New York Times,* April 13, 1887; Charles Dwight Willard, *The Herald's History of Los Angeles* (Los Angeles: Kingsley-Barnes and Neuner Co., 1901), 326; Norton P. Chipman, *Report upon the Fruit Industry of California: Its Growth and Development and Present and Future Importance* (San Francisco: California State Board of Trade, 1889), 15.

25. *Los Angeles Herald,* May 23, 1885; *San Francisco Report,* June 19, 1885; *The San Franciscan,* January 23, 1886; *Sacramento Bee,* January 26, 1886; *San Francisco Examiner,* March 31, 1885; *St. Louis Republican,* April 12, 1885; *Phoenix Herald,* April 2, 1885; *New Orleans Times-Democrat,* February 11, 1885.

26. *California Spirit of the Times,* February 14, April 11, 1885.

27. *San Francisco Post,* April 6, 1885; *San Francisco Bulletin,* December 5, 1884; *Kern County Gazette* (Bakersfield), December 13, 1884; *Los Angeles Herald,* February 14, 1885; Los Angeles Board of Trade, *Annual Report* (1885), 30ff., *Annual Report* (1886), 34–35.

28. Los Angeles Board of Trade, *Annual Report* (1885), 30ff., and *Annual Report* (1886), 34–35.

29. *California Patron,* February 27, 1886, and March 20, 1886; the disputed editorial, in *New Orleans Picayune,* February 5, 1886. Appreciation for the Southern Pacific's displays also in *Journal of Commerce* (San Francisco), January 15, 1885; *Resources of California,* December 1884; *San Francisco Report,* January 29, 1885; *San Francisco Merchant,* May 22, 1885; *Woodland Call,* May 8, 1886; *Santa Cruz Courier,* November 19, 1886; *Sacramento Bee,* May 15, 1886; *Woodland Democrat,* May 6, 1886; *Santa Clara Valley* (San Jose), April 1, 1885; and *Phoenix Herald,* April 2, 1885.

30. *San Francisco Call,* May 2 and June 18, 1901, on Buffalo exhibit; for many more, see James Horsburgh, Jr., "Colonization Efforts," in California Development Board, Counties Committee, *Bulletin Number Nine* (January 1911), 18–20; *San Francisco Chronicle,* November 12, 1910.

31. *San Francisco Call,* January 13 and 14, 1901; *Sunset* 4 (November 1899): 27; Los Angeles Chamber of Commerce, *The Members' Annual* (Los Angeles, 1900), 18.

32. W H. Mills and Edwin K. Alsip, *Report on the Columbus, Ohio, Exhibit* (San Francisco: California State Board of Trade, 1888), passim; J. A. Filcher, "California's Exhibit at the Atlanta Exposition," *Overland Monthly* n.s. 27 (April 1896): 387–401; "Board of Trade and the Railroad," *Overland Monthly* n.s. 27 (May 1896): 575–76;

Southern California Immigration Association, *Report of the Managers of the Chicago Citrus Fair* (Los Angeles, 1886), passim; Los Angeles Chamber of Commerce, *Members' Annual* (1899), 21.

33. *California World's Fair Magazine* 1 (June 1892): 60ff.; *Journal of Commerce* (San Francisco), April 28, 1892; Charles B. Turrill to J. A. Filcher, San Francisco, April 29, 1892, Turrill to Irwin C. Stump, San Francisco, June 7, 1892, and Turrill to California World's Fair Commission, San Francisco, June 13, 1892, and letters written during 1892 and 1893 concerning his management of the preliminary display, Turrill Papers, *BL*.

34. California World's Fair Commission, "Proceedings of Committees and Minutes of Meetings (1891–1894)," 3 vols. (ms.), 1:10ff., 67, and 77, California State Archives, Sacramento; telegram, Charles B. Turrill to W. H. Mills, San Francisco, April 28, 1892, Turrill Papers, *BL*. Mills also served as an advisor to Governor Pardee on state promotional matters; Mills to George C. Pardee, San Francisco, December 29, 1902, February 18 and 22, 1903, February 19 and March 10, 1904, Pardee Correspondence, *BL*.

35. California Midwinter International Exposition, Executive Committee, *California Midwinter Exposition . . . Information for Intending Exhibitors* (San Francisco, 1893), inside cover.

36. *Portland Oregonian,* November 28, 1901; Henry F. Reed, "Official History of the Lewis and Clark Centennial Exposition Held at Portland . . . 1905" (typescript, 1908), 70ff., Oregon Historical Society, Portland; "Standing Committees of the Board of Directors, Lewis and Clark Exposition, Appointed and Approved October 16, 1903" (typescript), Abbot Low Mills Papers, box 7, Oregon Collection, University of Oregon. For the Southern Pacific's exhibition program in Texas, see *Houston Post,* February 3, 1904.

37. Southern Pacific Company, Pacific System, "Record of Conventions, Meetings, and Expositions upon the Pacific Coast and Summer Tourist and Homeseekers' Excursions, 1897–1916" (typescript, 1916), File R195.7, *SP-PR.* For the Southern Pacific's massive movement of 25,000 attendees to the National Convention of the Christian Endeavor Society in San Francisco in July 1897, see Henry E. Huntington to Collis P. Huntington, San Francisco, July 10, 1897, and Collis to Henry, London, July 26, 1897, *HEH;* the railroad formed fifty-nine special trains to carry the passengers from Ogden to the coast, an unprecedented dense movement necessitating the invention of a new traffic control system.

38. Orsi, "Selling the Golden State," passim, esp. 114–234.

39. For Southern Pacific assistance in founding the Immigration Association of California, B. B. Redding, "Immigration, and How to Promote It," *The Californian* 5 (January 1882): 53–60; *Alta California* (San Francisco), October 28, 1881. For the Sacramento Valley's Immigration Association of Northern California, *Pacific Rural Press* (San Francisco), September 20, 1884; *Sacramento Record-Union,* September 16 and 19, 1884. Mills and the State Board of Trade, *Resources of California,* April 1890; California State Board of Trade, *California: Resources and Possibilities; Seventeenth Annual Report of the California State Board of Trade for the Year 1906* (San Francisco, 1907), 61.

40. California Immigrant Union, "Certificate of Incorporation" (ms., 1869), California State Archives, Sacramento; *San Francisco Bulletin,* October 9, 1869, and October 17, 1871; *Alta California* (San Francisco), October 14, 1872; W. H. Mills to *San Fran-*

cisco Call, published in *Call,* January 13, 1896; Norton P. Chipman, *Annual Report of General N. P. Chipman, President, California State Board of Trade* (San Francisco, 1896), 7–8; California Promotion Committee, *Bulletin Number Five* (June 1907), 19.

41. *Alta California* (San Francisco), April 19, 1875.

42. Chipman, *Annual Report* (1896), 7–8; California State Board of Trade, *Annual Report, 1906* (1907), 61; Mills and Alsip, *Report on Columbus Exhibit,* passim; *San Francisco Call,* January 13, 1896; *Resources of California,* March 1889.

43. *Alta California* (San Francisco), October 28, 1881; *San Francisco Call,* December 4, 1884; *San Francisco Bulletin,* December 2, 1884, December 1, 1885, and December 7, 1886; Immigration Association of California, *Second Annual Report* (San Francisco, 1884), 3; Chipman, *Annual Report* (1896), 7–8; *Resources of California,* April 1890.

44. Filcher, "California's Exhibit at the Atlanta Exposition," 390ff.; Southern California Immigration Association, *Chicago Citrus Fair,* passim; Los Angeles Chamber of Commerce, *Members' Annual* (1899), 21.

45. Mills and Alsip, *Report on Columbus Exhibit,* 11–12; California State Board of Trade, *Catalogue of the Natural Products of California Compiled by the State Board of Trade to Accompany Its Travelling Free Exhibit Known as "California on Wheels"* (San Francisco, ca. 1890), and *Two Grand Tours of . . . California on Wheels Under the Auspices of the California State Board of Trade and the Southern Pacific Company* (San Francisco, December 1889); *Resources of California,* January and December 1889, and April 1890; *San Francisco Call,* January 13, 1896; and Chipman, *Annual Report* (1896), 1; *Southern Pacific Bulletin* 8 (May 1924): 14. A report on the first year of "California on Wheels" by the railroad's exhibit manager, E. McD. Johnstone, in his letter to General Passenger and Freight Agent T. H. Goodman, San Francisco, September 28, 1889, "California on Wheels" folder, File R197.7, *SP-PR.* The *Sacramento Record-Union* reported on the second exhibit during August and September 1890, esp. September 30, 1890. For "California on Wheels" and produce marketing, see chapter 12.

46. Chipman, *Annual Report* (1896), 7–8; *San Francisco Call,* January 13, 1896; *Overland Monthly* n.s. 27 (May 1896): 575–76.

47. Charles Dwight Willard, *A History of the Chamber of Commerce of Los Angeles, California* (Los Angeles: Kingsley-Barnes and Neuner, 1899), 80ff. and 95–96; Los Angeles Chamber of Commerce, *Members' Annual* (June 1895), 4ff. (1900), 18, and (1912), 17–20; Norman S. Stanley, *No Little Plans: The Story of the Los Angeles Chamber of Commerce* (Los Angeles: Reprinted from Southern California Business, 1956), 8ff.

48. *Sacramento Bee,* November 25, 1886; *Sacramento Record-Union,* December 5, 1884; Immigration Association of California, *Second Annual Report* (1884), 7.

49. In *Sunset:* Will S. Green, Sacramento Valley Dev. Ass., "California's Inland Empire—The Sacramento Valley," 8 (April 1902); Colvin B. Brown, Stockton Chamber of Commerce, "Millions in Potatoes," 9 (May 1902); T. S. Hocking, Stanislaus County Board of Trade, "Sunny Stanislaus," 9 (August 1902); A. J. Wells, "A Valley County," 23 (December 1909), and "An Orange Empire: San Bernardino County," 24 (January 1910).

50. For more on *Sunset* and its Homeseekers' Bureau, see later in this chapter.

51. Caspar T. Hopkins, "California Recollections of Caspar T. Hopkins," *California Historical Society Quarterly* 27 (June 1948): 169–71; *San Francisco Bulletin,* December 5, 1885.

52. *San Francisco Call,* January 13, 1896; Chipman, *Annual Report* (1896), 7–8; California Development Board, Counties Committee, *Bulletin Number Nine* (January 1911), 20.

53. *Alta California* (San Francisco), April 23, 1875; Edna M. Parker, "Influences of the Southern Pacific Railroad on Settlement in Southern California, 1876–1890" (M.A. thesis, Mills College, 1936), 63ff.; Thelma Kesseli, "The Railroad as an Agency of Settlement in California, 1870–1890" (M.A. thesis, University of California, Berkeley, 1948), 55ff.

54. Gerald D. Nash, *State Government and Economic Development: A History of Administrative Policies in California, 1849–1933* (Berkeley: Institute of Governmental Studies, University of California, Berkeley, 1964), 160–62; John S. Hittell, *The Commerce and Industries of the Pacific Coast of North America* (San Francisco, 1882), 159–60.

55. San Francisco Board of Trade, *Report of Special Committee on the Inter-Oceanic Canal: "The Key to the Pacific"* (San Francisco, 1880); *Sacramento Record-Union,* October 3, 1891.

56. Willard, *History of the Chamber of Commerce,* 126ff., and *The Free Harbor Contest at Los Angeles* (Los Angeles: Kingsley-Barnes and Neuner, 1899); Richard W. Barsness, "Railroads and Los Angeles: The Quest for a Deep-Water Port," *Southern California Quarterly* 47 (December 1965): 379–94; William F. Deverell, "The Los Angeles 'Free Harbor Fight,'" *California History* 70 (Spring 1991): 12–29; and Robert M. Fogelson, *The Fragmented Metropolis: Los Angeles, 1850–1930* (Cambridge: Harvard University Press, 1967), 108ff. On chambers of commerce in the Progressive movement, George E. Mowry, *The California Progressives* (Berkeley: University of California Press, 1951), passim.

57. *San Francisco Chronicle,* December 15, 1907. A later, similar resolution failed; *San Francisco Chronicle,* November 15, 1908.

58. See Collis P. Huntington to J. B. Hayne (LeHavre, France), New York, December 18, 1882, *CPH.*

59. Land agent reports, in annual reports of the Central Pacific and Southern Pacific railroads, 1870s–1880s.

60. Southern Pacific Railroad Company, *Annual Report, 1881* (1882), 49, and *1882* (1883), 44–45.

61. Mills biographies and obituaries, in San Francisco's *Examiner, Call,* and *Chronicle,* and the *Sacramento Record-Union,* May 25, 1907; *San Francisco, Its Builders, Past and Present* (San Francisco: S. J. Clarke Publishing Co., 1913), 1:343–45.

62. *San Francisco Bulletin,* May 12, 1883, *San Francisco Call* and *Alta California* (San Francisco), May 22, 1883.

63. Hoag obituaries in *San Francisco Call* and *Sacramento Bee,* April 23, 1898, and *Sacramento Record-Union,* April 24, 1898; Mrs. Eliza P. Robbins Crafts, *Pioneer Days in the San Bernardino Valley* (Redlands, 1906), 167–68; *An Illustrated History of Southern California* (Chicago: Lewis Publishing Co., 1890), 546–49; autobiographical sketch, in *Sacramento Record-Union,* January 2, 1882.

64. Central Pacific Railroad Company, untitled circular (San Francisco, April 20, 1883), by I. N. Hoag, in Eugene W. Hilgard Family Papers, *BL;* reprinted in *Sacramento Record-Union,* May 17, 1883; *San Francisco Bulletin,* May 21, 1883, and *Call,* May 22, 1883.

65. Charles B. Turrill to George Davidson, San Francisco, June 11 and 14, 1883, Davidson Collection, *BL.*

66. *Sacramento Record-Union,* May 9 and 19, June 9, 1883; *San Francisco Bulletin,* May 21 and 24, 1883; *San Francisco Call,* May 22, 1883; *Alta California* (San Francisco), May 22, 1883.

67. On Southern Pacific's Chicago California Immigration Office, esp. Isaac N. Hoag, "Letterbook, 1883–1884," *HL,* esp. reports on his activities in Hoag to T. H. Goodman, September 10, 19, and 20, October 3, November 23, and December 15, 1883, and February 14, 1884; also draft letter to an unknown recipient in 1884, pp. 487–97. Also California Immigration Commissioner, *California: The Cornucopia of the World* (1883 and 1886); *Sacramento Record-Union,* June 23, 1883, and March 19, 1884; *Inter-Ocean* (Chicago), October 1 and 14, 1883, for railroad's exhibit at Illinois State Fair.

68. *Sacramento Record-Union,* May 19, 1883, March 19, and 25, 1884; *People's Cause* (Red Bluff), September 26, 1884. On Hoag's expenses, see Hoag to T. H. Goodman, November 23, 1884, Hoag, "Letterbook, 1883–1884," *HL.*

69. *Sacramento Record-Union,* April 24, 1898, and *Bee,* April 23, 1898; *Free Press* (Redding), June 4, 1887; *Visalia Delta,* June 23, 1887; Althrop Publishing and Mailing House, *California: All About the Golden State* (Chicago, ca. 1888), back cover.

70. W. G. Kingsbury, *Emigration: An Interesting Lecture on Texas and California* (London: G. W. Sparks, Printer, 1883), and *A Tour Through Texas and California in 1884; San Francisco Call,* January 13, 1896; Lucie Morris, "The History of the Town of Lancaster, Center of the Antelope Valley, California" (M.A. thesis, University of Southern California, 1934), 17ff.; Richard Starr, "History of Antelope Valley, California" (M.A. thesis, University of Southern California, 1938), 101ff. For biographical information on the colorful, if occasionally checkered, career of W. G. Kingsbury, native New Yorker, peripatetic self-taught dentist and/or physician, Texas agriculturist, and longtime London land and immigration agent during the 1870s and 1880s, for the predecessor Galveston, Harrisburg, & San Antonio, later Southern Pacific, see S. W. Geiser, "Men of Science in Texas, 1820–1880," *Field and Laboratory* 27 (July 1957): 115–16; and John Henry Brown, *Indian Wars and Pioneers of Texas* (Austin: L. E. Daniell, ca. 1890), 552.

71. *Wasp* (San Francisco), May 23, 1883; *San Francisco Chronicle,* May 28, 1883; *Sacramento Record-Union,* May 31, 1883.

72. *Solano Republican* (Vacaville), March 21, 1884.

73. *Sacramento Record-Union,* May 31, 1883.

74. *Oakland Times,* reprinted in *Sacramento Record-Union,* May 23 and 25, 1883; *San Francisco Call,* May 27, 1883; also *San Francisco Bulletin,* May 24, 1883; *Alta California* (San Francisco), May 22 and 27, 1883; *Rural Californian* 6 (December 1883): 250; *Yolo Democrat* (Woodland), November 1883, clip in California Scrapbook 16, *HL; Antioch Ledger,* July 14, 1883; *Sacramento Record-Union,* May 17, 23, 25, and 31, 1883, and March 25, 1884.

75. Central Pacific Railroad, *Annual Report, 1881,* 14, *Annual Report, 1882,* 20, and

Annual Report, 1883, 22; E. A. Kincaid, "The Federal Land Grants of the Central Pacific Railroad" (Ph.D. diss., University of California, Berkeley, 1922), appendix; U.S. Pacific Railway Commission, *Testimony,* 6:3601.

76. Annual reports of Central and Southern Pacific railroads through 1884; annual reports of the Southern Pacific Company after 1884; Kincaid, "Federal Land Grants of the Central Pacific," chap. 15; and Decker, *Railroads, Lands, and Politics,* 109–10.

77. See I. N. Hoag to T. H. Goodman, December 9, 10, 12, 13, and 24, 1883, Hoag, "Letterbook, 1883–1884," *HL;* Collis P. Huntington to A. C. Hutchinson, August 18, 1885, and Hutchinson to Huntington, October 24 and 30, 1885, *CPH.*

78. For swindles against Englishmen in Antelope Valley, *Los Angeles Herald,* December 24, 1885; *Lancaster News,* December 12, 1885; Collis P. Huntington to W. G. Kingsbury, New York, October 26, 1885, *CPH.*

79. The "placing out," or "transportation," of British youths, common since the 1700s, resembled an American phenomenon of the late nineteenth and early twentieth centuries, the "orphan trains" that eastern missionary societies dispatched west to resettle poor, wayward, uncared-for, or orphaned urban children, many of them immigrants; some went to California and other Southern Pacific territories; Marilyn Irvin Holt, *The Orphan Trains: Placing Out in America* (Lincoln: University of Nebraska Press, 1992), passim, and esp. 76 and 105. Holt discusses the British origins, which U.S. originator Charles Loring Brace used as the model for American practices, on pp. 44–45; for the British children being sent to Iowa, see Curtis Harnack, *Gentlemen on the Prairie* (Ames: Iowa State University Press, 1985). The British practice persisted into the 1930s and 1940s; a Fairbridge Farm School, also troubled by abuse of children, operated in British Columbia from 1935 to 1947; see, for reference to it, *Victoria Times Colonist* (British Columbia), August 20, 2001, A9.

80. See *San Francisco Chronicle,* January 7 and 9, 1886; *San Francisco Bulletin,* January 8, 1886.

81. *San Francisco Chronicle,* January 7 and 9, 1886; *San Francisco Bulletin,* January 8, 1886. Kingsbury, as a matter of fact, had long exasperated his Southern Pacific superiors, who questioned his reliability, honesty, and frugality with the railroad's money. He also became personally involved in various separate land and colonization businesses, some on the shady side, including as an investor in 1879 in a business to solicit funds from charities and investors to profit from settling poor Englishmen on Texas farms; see Texas Farm and Freehold Union, *Abridged Prospectus . . .* (London, ca. 1879). On the railroad's doubts about Kingsbury's competence as its European agent, see Collis P. Huntington to A. C. Hutchinson, New York, August 18, 1885, and Hutchinson to Huntington, New Orleans, October 24, 1885, *CPH.* From 1881 through Kingsbury's dismissal in late 1885, Huntington frequently had to resolve problems caused by Kingsbury and complaints about his work from within and outside the company, including charges of misrepresentation.

82. Collis P. Huntington to L. G. Thompson, New York, February 24, 1886, *CPH.*

83. *San Francisco Chronicle,* January 7, 1886; Collis P. Huntington to W. G. Kingsbury, New York, October 28 and December 7, 1885, and January 7 and 18, 1886; Huntington to A. N. Towne, New York, January 5, 1885; Huntington to Arthur Livermore

(U.S. Consul, Londonderry, Ireland), New York, January 5 and 13, 1886; Huntington to T. H. Goodman, New York, January 6, 1886; Huntington to L. G. Thompson, New York, February 24, 1886, *CPH.*

84. One incident involved another wayward agent, John C. Morrison, whom the company had hired to recruit Germans for land-grant settlement. Morrison ran up dubious expenses, refused to follow directions or to report on his operation, and broke off relations with Kingsbury, who was supposed to supervise him from London. The protracted "Morrison Affair" of 1882–1883 touched off the Southern Pacific's growing disillusionment with Kingsbury and the foreign agent system generally; Collis P. Huntington to A. N. Towne, New York, September 27 and November 27, 1882; Isaac E. Gates to W. G. Kingsbury, New York, February 1 and March 1 and 20, 1883; Gates to Morrison, New York, February 2 and March 2, 1883; Gates to T. H. Goodman, New York, March 7, April 16 and 30, and October 4, 1883; *CPH.* The Fresno scandal was the last straw.

85. Collis P. Huntington to W. G. Kingsbury, New York, November 15, and 26, 1887, *CPH.*

86. Earl Pomeroy, *In Search of the Golden West: The Tourist in Western America* (New York: Alfred A. Knopf, 1957), 3–138; John E. Baur, *The Health Seekers of Southern California, 1870–1910* (San Marino: The Huntington Library, 1959); Paul F. Allen, "Tourists in Southern California, 1875–1903" (M.A. thesis, Claremont Graduate School, 1940); John Cooper Packard, Jr., "The Role of the Tourist Hotel in California Development to 1900" (M.A. thesis, University of Southern California, 1953).

87. *San Francisco Call* and *Examiner,* May 2, 1901; Horsburgh biography, in John P. Young, *Journalism in California* (San Francisco: Chronicle Publishing Co., 1915), 279.

88. See Charles Nordhoff, *California: For Health, Pleasure, and Residence* (New York, 1872), and *A Guide to California, the Golden State* (London, 1883); Benjamin C. Truman, *Tourist's Illustrated Guide to the Celebrated Summer and Winter Resorts of California* (San Francisco, 1883), and *Homes and Happiness in the Golden State of California* (San Francisco, 1885).

89. Southern Pacific Company, *California South of the Tehachapi,* 5th ed. (San Francisco, 1901); Southern Pacific Company, Passenger Department, *North Bay Counties California* (San Francisco, 1909), *Lake Tahoe* (San Francisco, 1902), *Imperial Valley, California, Where Water Has Worked Miracles* (1916), *California Resorts Along the Coast Line and in the Santa Cruz Mountains* (San Francisco, 1901). For an example of Texas publications, Southern Pacific Company, *Press Expressions for the Consideration of Everyone Interested in Texas* (Houston: Passenger Department, Sunset Route, ca. 1906). For analysis of Southern Pacific Texas pamphlets, Patrick J. Brunet, "'Can't Hurt, and May Do You Good': A Study of the Pamphlets the Southern Pacific Railroad Used to Induce Immigration to Texas, 1880–1930," *East Texas Historical Journal* 16 (1978): 35–45. Like the railroad's promotional literature about other regions, Texas pamphlets, compared to the hyperbole of western booster material in general, were restrained and objective, emphasizing factual presentations of land values and farm-production statistics. They stressed the great opportunities in Texas, but also that investment capital and hard work were required. Nevertheless, Texas was portrayed as an incipient paradise, where civi-

lization was replacing the fading frontier. Discussion of problems such as racial tensions was avoided. Over time, Southern Pacific pamphlets become even less exaggerated and more realistic and detailed. Brunet's generalizations also apply to the great volumes of Southern Pacific promotional literature for California, Oregon, Nevada, and Arizona.

90. Southern Pacific Company, *Southern Pacific Sketch Book* (San Francisco, 1890), *California for Health, Pleasure and Profit: Why You Should Go There* (San Francisco, 1894), *California for the Tourist* (San Francisco, 1910); Horsburgh, "Colonization Efforts," 18–20.

91. Walton Bean, *California: An Interpretive History* (New York: McGraw-Hill, 1968), 249.

92. *Sunset* 1 (May 1898) to 4 (December 1899).

93. *Sunset* 1 (October 1898) to 2 (October 1899), 6 (February 1901) to 11 (June 1903), and 17 (August 1906) to 18 (January 1907); 14 (February 1905), 18 (November 1906), 11 (August 1903), 22 (January 1909); and another passenger department pamphlet, A. J. Wells, *Plea for Old California Names* (San Francisco, 1905).

94. *Sunset* 3 (June 1899) and 15 (September 1905); *San Francisco Chronicle,* January 1, 1904, and January 1, 1905; Horsburgh, "Colonization Efforts," 18–20.

95. *Sunset* 17 (June 1906): passim, (September 1906): 237–43, (October 1906): 301ff., 18 (April 1907): 501–54, 20 (April 1908): 513–62, 22 (April 1909): 326ff.; Southern Pacific Company, *San Francisco Imperishable* (San Francisco, 1906), and *San Francisco Hotels and Reconstruction,* a monthly magazine; W. H. Mills, *Influences that Insure the Rebuilding of San Francisco* (San Francisco, 1906), also in *San Francisco Call,* May 13, 1906.

96. Horsburgh, "Colonization Efforts," 18–20, "How the Railroad Helps: What the Southern Pacific Company is Doing for California," *San Francisco Chronicle,* January 1, 1904, and "Telling the World About California: How the Southern Pacific Is Doing It," *San Francisco Chronicle,* January 1, 1905. The Bureau's California promotional booklets include Arthur Dunn, *Kern County, California* (San Francisco, 1914); Sacramento Valley Development Association, *Sacramento Valley, California* (San Francisco, 1911); M. E. Dittmar, *Shasta County, California* (San Francisco, 1915); and W. Russell Cole, *Sonoma County, California* (San Francisco, 1915).

97. Records, correspondence, and pamphlets of the *Sunset* Homeseekers' Bureau are in the William Bittle Wells Papers, Oregon Collection, University of Oregon Library, Eugene; see Wells, "The Story of My Life" (typescript, Portland, ca. 1957), 104–27, and Wells, "Wells Outline" (vol. 2), passim, esp. 10–25; p. 172 of the scrapbook, "Wells Outline" (vol. 2), holds a letter from Paul Shoup, assistant general passenger agent, Southern Pacific, to Wells, San Francisco, December 3, 1906, establishing the bureau. Also in the Oregon Collection is Wells's report on his bureau's activities, *Report, Bureau of Community Publicity, Passenger Department, Oregon-Washington Railroad and Navigation Company, Southern Pacific—Lines in Oregon, for Fiscal Year Ending June 30, 1911* (Portland: Sunset Magazine Homeseekers' Bureau, 1911). Wells's papers are also at the Oregon Historical Society in Portland, see Wells, "Record of William Bittle Wells" (typescript), 35–46, and Wells, "Reflections and Reminiscences of a Long Life" (typescript), 20–22; ad recruiting communities for the bureau's programs appeared, *Portland Ore-*

gonian, March 22, 1908. Wells's many pamphlets include the first one, *Medford, Oregon, and the Rogue River Valleys: The Land of Plenty* (Portland: Commercial Club of Medford, 1907), *Oregon: The Land of Opportunity* (Portland: Sunset Homeseekers' Bureau, 1909), *Yamhill County, Oregon* (Portland: Yamhill County Development League and Sunset Magazine Homeseekers' Bureau, ca. 1910), *Walla Walla Valley, Washington* (Walla Walla: Walla Walla Commercial Club, 1910), *How to Get to Buhl, Idaho* (Portland: Sunset Homeseekers' Bureau, ca. 1910), and *Hood River, Oregon* (Portland: Hood River Commercial Club and Sunset Magazine Homeseekers' Bureau, 1910), a copy of which Wells inscribed in his collection at the University of Oregon as having reached "the 'high water' mark of publication by the Bureau."

98. *Sunset* 32 (January 1914): 194–200, (February 1914): 434ff., and later issues; Horsburgh, "Colonization Efforts," 18–20.

99. "How the Railroad Helps," *San Francisco Chronicle,* January 1, 1904. For the railroad's rationale in selling *Sunset,* see September 1914 issue. Overall history, in *Sunset Magazine: A Century of Western Living, 1898–1998* (Stanford: Stanford University Libraries, 1998), passim, esp. "The Southern Pacific Launches a New Magazine to Develop Its Market," pp. 77ff.; Charles William Mulhall, Jr., "Sunset: The History of a Successful Regional Magazine" (M.A. thesis, Stanford University, 1955); Paul Johnson (ed.), *The Early Sunset Magazine, 1898–1928* (San Francisco: California Historical Society, 1973); *Sunset Magazine: A Century of Western Living, 1898–1998* (Stanford and San Francisco: Hoover Institution, Stanford University, and California Historical Society, 1998); a popular history in May 1998 centennial issue of *Sunset,* esp. 84ff. Facts about Southern Pacific ownership, including tables of data on advertising, articles, readership, salaries, and printing costs, are in "Southern Pacific Company, Pacific System, *Sunset Magazine*" (typescript, n.d.), File R195.5, *SP-PR;* for financial information, advertisers, production costs, and the railroad's subsidy, see *Sunset* Magazine Financial Records, *CRRM,* esp. "Cash Book" (May-December 1906) and "Cashier Sunset Magazine General Ledger . . . December 1909."

100. James Horsburgh to George Pardee, San Francisco, May 9, 14, 18, 19, 20, and 25, 1904, Pardee Correspondence, *BL.*

101. *Sunset* 2 (February 1899): 74, 4 (February 1900): 167, and (March 1900): 207; *San Francisco Chronicle,* January 1, 1904, and January 1, 1905; Horsburgh, "Colonization Efforts," 18–20.

102. *Southern Pacific Bulletin* 5 (May 15, 1917): 5.

103. See *Southern Pacific Bulletin* 10 (April 1921): 31.

104. "Truckee—The Home of the 'Frozen North' Films," *Southern Pacific Bulletin* 11 (December 1922): 16–18. Among Southern Pacific–facilitated films was Charlie Chaplin's classic, *The Gold Rush;* Guy Coates, "Chaplin movie has special place in Truckee history," *Sierra Sun* (Truckee), November 14–20, 2002.

105. Southern Pacific Company, *Homeseekers' Excursions to California* (1901), a pamphlet at *CRRM; Sunset* 6 (January 1901): 105 and (February 1901): 123, 7 (June–July 1901): advertising section, 11 (September 1903): 579; *San Francisco Call,* November 5 and 14, 1907, August 9, 1908, and November 20, 1911; an earlier reduced-fare plan, in *San Francisco Call,* September 13, 1896; "How the Railroad Helps," *San Francisco Chron-*

icle, January 24 and May 9, 1901, and January 1, 1904; Horsburgh, "Colonization Efforts," 18–20; "How the Southern Pacific Company Brings Tourists and Settlers to the West," *Southern Pacific Bulletin* 11 (October 1922): 5; *Southern Pacific Bulletin* 1 (November 20, 1913): 3, and 2 (February 15, 1914): 1; *Homeseekers' Fares to Texas, 1911* (Houston: Passenger Department, Sunset Route, 1911), Ephemera Collection, *DG.*

106. Annual reports of the Southern Pacific Company, 1888–1911.

107. "Telling the World About California: How the Southern Pacific is Doing It," *San Francisco Chronicle,* January 1, 1905.

108. See *California For the Settler* (San Francisco: Southern Pacific Company, 1922), and new editions most years, 1890s–1920s. Arizona materials: cf. *The New Arizona: A Brief Review of its Resources, Development, Industries, Soil, Climate, and Especially its Advantages for Homemaking* (San Francisco: Passenger Department, Southern Pacific Company, 1897, 1902, 1907, and 1911 editions); *Tucson, Arizona* (San Francisco: Sunset Magazine Homeseekers' Bureau, ca. 1912); *Southern Arizona—Enchanted Land* (San Francisco: Southern Pacific Company, 1928); and *Southern Arizona for the Settler* (San Francisco: Southern Pacific Company, 1929).

109. *Southern Pacific Bulletin* 11 (September 1922): 23 and (October 1922): 3–5, 14 (November 1925): 6, 16 (August 1928): 17.

110. California Development Board, Counties Committee, *Bulletin Number Nine* (January 1911), 20.

7   Pioneer Water Developer

The quotation in the chapter title is from *Southern Pacific Bulletin* (February 1920), p. 22, commenting on the railroad's nagging difficulty in finding adequate water. Chapter 7 is a revision and expansion of an earlier essay in *California History* 70 (Spring 1991).

1. Donald Worster, *Rivers of Empire: Water, Aridity, and the Growth of the American West* (New York: Pantheon Books, 1985), investigates aridity, especially in Southern Pacific regions.

2. Donald J. Pisani, *From Family Farm to Agribusiness: The Irrigation Crusade in California and the American West, 1850–1931* (Berkeley: University of California Press, 1984), xi; and Pisani, "Enterprise and Equity: A Critique of Western Water Law in the Nineteenth Century," *Western Historical Quarterly* 18 (January 1987): 15–37; Robert G. Dunbar, *Forging New Rights in Western Waters* (Lincoln: University of Nebraska Press, 1983); Thomas E. Malone, "The California Irrigation Crisis of 1886: Origins of the Wright Act" (Ph.D. diss., Stanford University, 1965); Mary Ellen Glass, *Water for Nevada: The Reclamation Controversy, 1885–1902* (Carson City: University of Nevada Press, 1964); John M. Townley, *Turn This Water into Gold: The Story of the Newlands Project* (Reno: Nevada Historical Society, 1977); Karen L. Smith, "The Campaign for Water in Central Arizona, 1890–1903," *Arizona and the West* 23 (Summer 1981): 127–48; Erwin Cooper, *Aqueduct Empire: A Guide to Water in California, Its Turbulent History, and Its Management Today* (Glendale, CA: The Arthur H. Clark

Co., 1968); Gordon R. Miller, "Shaping California Water Law, 1781–1928," *Southern California Quarterly* 55 (Spring 1979): 9–42; Arthur Maas and Raymond L. Anderson, . . . *and The Desert Shall Rejoice: Conflict, Growth, and Justice in Arid Environments* (Cambridge: MIT Press, 1978), 1ff. and 147ff.; Norris Hundley, Jr., *Water and the West: The Colorado River Compact and the Politics of Water in the American West* (Berkeley: University of California Press, 1975); Catherine Miller, "Riparian Rights and the Control of Water in California, 1879–1928: The Relationship Between an Agricultural Enterprise and Legal Change," *Agricultural History* 59 (January 1985): 1–24; and Douglas R. Littlefield, "Water Rights during the California Gold Rush: Conflicts over Economic Points of View," *Western Historical Quarterly* 14 (October 1983): 415–34.

3. On the Southern Pacific's alignment with other private interest groups on water and other conservation and environmental preservation questions, Richard J. Orsi, "*The Octopus* Reconsidered: The Southern Pacific and Agricultural Modernization in California, 1865–1915," *California Historical Quarterly* 54 (Fall 1975): 197–220, and " 'Wilderness Saint' and 'Robber Baron': The Anomalous Partnership of John Muir and the Southern Pacific Company for the Preservation of Yosemite National Park," *The Pacific Historian* 29 (Summer/Fall 1985): 136–56.

4. Alfred D. Chandler, Jr., *The Visible Hand: The Managerial Revolution in American Business* (Cambridge: Harvard University Press, 1977), 79–205.

5. For the tank-car system used during early construction on the Southern Pacific system, Special Commissioners, Central Pacific Railroad of California, "Report of Condition, Equipment, etc., of the Central Pacific Railroad of California, January 25, 1869" (typescript copy), 22, Southern Pacific Company Records, Railroad Commissioners' Reports, 1866–1874, *CRRM*.

6. Mark Hopkins to Collis P. Huntington, Sacramento, February 14, 1867, *CPH*. Stephen E. Ambrose, in his *Nothing Like It in the World: The Men Who Built the Transcontinental Railroad, 1863–1869* (New York: Simon & Schuster, 2000), 195–96, attributes curious, similar, but not identical, language to Hopkins, in a letter to Collis P. Huntington, February 24, 1866, which he indicates was found at *CPH*. My date for the Hopkins letter of 1867, and my precise wording, are certain, directly from a photocopy of the original at *CPH*.

7. Suggestive of how expensive hauling water cars could be for the railroad, in the early twentieth century, after the 1903 completion of the Lucin Cutoff west of Salt Lake City, and before the company tapped springs miles distant and built a water plant to serve the line in 1916, a water train had to be sent in daily to serve local stations at a cost of $125 per day, per station, or roughly $50,000 per year, per station. If such a per-station water-hauling cost were to be extended to even a small portion of the company's hundreds of stations, it is easy to comprehend the Southern Pacific's powerful financial incentives for building many, elaborate water stations; H. G. Butler, consulting engineer, "Report to Mr. E. B. Welles on the Value of the Water Rights of Southern Pacific Company (Pacific System) as of June 30, 1916" (typescript, San Francisco, November 12, 1924), 70, Legal Files, box 8, folder 15, San Diego and Arizona Railroad Collection, San Diego Historical Society; Butler's survey of the history

and current state of sixty water stations is one of the best sources on the railroad's vast water system.

8. *Mining and Scientific Press* (San Francisco), January 17 and March 21, 1885; *Arizona Sentinel* (Yuma), April 12, 1879; David F. Myrick, *Railroads of Nevada and Eastern California,* 2 vols. (Berkeley: Howell-North Books, 1962–3), 1:18, and 2:770–71, 887–88, and 840; Myrick, *Railroads of Arizona,* 2 vols. (Berkeley: Howell-North Books, 1975), 1:105–107; Alan Hensher, *Ghost Towns of the Central Mojave* (Los Angeles: The Author, ca. 1979), 10ff.; David Grosh Thompson, . . . *The Mohave Desert Region: A Geographic, Geologic, and Hydrologic Reconnaissance* (Washington, DC: Government Printing Office, 1929), 229–30 and 269–72.

9. Linda Sanford, " 'You Put Your Roots Deep Around Here': A History of Tule Lake Basin, California" (graduate course paper, History 3505, California State University, Hayward, November 28, 1995), 59, this author's collection; Samuel Dicken, *The Legacy of Ancient Lake Modoc: A Historical Geography of the Klamath Lakes Basin, Oregon and California* (Eugene: University of Oregon Bookstore, 1985).

10. *Elko Independent,* May 30, 1874; Edna B. Patterson et al., *Nevada's Northeast Frontier* (Sparks, NV: Western Print and Publishing, 1969), 545 and 577.

11. Butler, "Report," 36ff.; *Reno Gazette,* May 2, 1882, surveying Southern Pacific water experiments in Nevada. Ambrose, *Nothing Like It in the World,* 309, described how during 1868 and 1869 construction across the dry Great Basin, the company bored tunnels into distant mountains to tap underground water and then piped it miles to trackside water stations, from which it was shipped by water cars and then wagons to the construction front.

12. For the Southern Pacific's Tulare artesian-well project, see chapter 11; report on the Tulare wells by C. E. Grunsky, assistant state engineer, in *Sacramento Record-Union,* January 1, 1884; *Tulare Register,* August 24, 1883; *San Francisco Post,* clipping, late June 1883, Southern Pacific Scrapbooks, vol. 13, *HEH;* "Tulare's First 100 Years," centennial edition *Tulare Advance-Register* (Tulare: Tulare Advance-Register, 1972); Thomas H. Thompson, *Official Historical Atlas of Tulare County* (Tulare, 1892). Richard H. Smith, "Towns Along the Tracks: Railroad Strategy and Town Promotion in the San Joaquin Valley, California" (Ph.D. diss., University of California, Los Angeles, 1976), 205–207, notes water facilities in valley towns. For 1870s water systems built along the lines down the San Joaquin Valley and across Tehachapi Pass, southward to Los Angeles, and eastward across the desert to the Colorado River, see Railroad Commissioners' Reports, 1866–1874, box 1, Southern Pacific [San Jose to Mojave file], passim, Southern Pacific Company Records, *CRRM.*

13. Thompson, *Mohave Desert Region,* 212 and 221; Butler, "Report," 106–107; Phil Serpico, *Railroading through the Antelope Valley* (Palmdale, CA: Omni Publications, 2000), 23.

14. Charles Crocker to Collis P. Huntington, April 30, 1877, in Mark Hopkins et al., *Letters from Mark Hopkins, Leland Stanford, Charles Crocker, and David D. Colton to Collis P. Huntington from August 27th 1869, to December 30th, 1879* (New York: John C. Rankin Co., 1891), 88; Huntington to Crocker, New York, April 19, 1877, *CPH; Indio News,* January 27, 1966.

15. *Arizona Sentinel* (Yuma), April 13 and 27, 1878; Myrick, *Railroads of Arizona,* 1:27–30; C. G. Ekstrom, "History of the Yuma Water Plant" (typescript, ca. 1940), Arizona Historical Society, Yuma.

16. *Arizona Sentinel* (Yuma), April 12 and May 20, 1879, and February 18, 1882; *Arizona Star* (Tucson), November 30, 1881; Charles Crocker to Collis P. Huntington, San Francisco, February 7, 1879, in Hopkins et al., *Letters to Collis P. Huntington* (1891), 256; Walter C. Mendenhall, *Ground Waters of the Indio Region, California, with a Sketch of the Colorado Desert,* Department of the Interior, U.S. Geological Survey, Water-Supply Paper 225 (Washington, DC: Government Printing Office, 1909), 7, 40ff.; Frank Adams, *Progress Report of Cooperative Irrigation Investigations in California, 1912–1914,* Bulletin No. 1, California State Department of Engineering (Sacramento: State Printing Office, 1915), 71–74. *Reno Gazette,* May 2, 1882, reviewed the railroad's experiments with artesian wells.

17. *Arizona Star* (Tucson), November 30, 1881; Myrick, *Railroads of Arizona,* 1:105–107; Frank D. Reeve, *History of New Mexico,* 3 vols. (New York: Lewis Historical Publishing Co., 1961), 2:248.

18. *Arizona Star* (Tucson), November 30, 1881; R. G. Skerritt, "Water Stations in the Arizona Desert: Oil-Engine Compressors Raise Water from Deep Wells for Locomotives of the Southern Pacific Lines," *Compressed Air Magazine,* September 1929, pp. 2867–70.

19. For summaries of operations in important regions and major water plants in the early twentieth century: Butler, "Report," 1–160 (60 major stations in California, Nevada, Utah, and Oregon); "Location of Water Tanks between San Diego and Imperial Valley" (typescript, December 3, 1918), San Diego and Arizona Railroad Collection, Engineering Series, box 20, folder 13, San Diego Historical Society; and "Record of Machinery at Locomotive Water Supply Pumping Stations (Western Division)" (61 water stations in east San Francisco Bay area and southern Sacramento and northern San Joaquin valleys) (January 1, 1938, Southern Pacific Drawings, no. 4484), "Table: Water Supply Stations" (northern and central California) (1956, Southern Pacific Drawings, no. 5914), and Southern Pacific Company, "Analysis of Water Supplies—El Paso Division—Atlantic System—Aug. 1898" (17 facilities in southwest Texas) (ms. drawing), all at *CRRM;* U.S. Interstate Commerce Commission, Division of Valuation, "Engineering Report upon the Southern Pacific in State of New Mexico" (blueprint, 1922), 20–23, Governor Mechem Papers, Special Reports, New Mexico State Archives, Santa Fe. For Texas, Clifford R. Morrill (superintendent, El Paso Division, 1919–39), "Railroad History: El Paso Division, Southern Pacific" (typescript copy, Texas A & M Library, 1971), 42ff., copy at *DG,* ms A1994 1954c. For Oregon, A. T. Mercier to William F. Hood, Portland, December 16, 1918, copy in Engineering Series, box 20, folder 13, San Diego & Arizona Railroad Collection, San Diego Historical Society.

20. Butler, "Report," 101–105.

21. Ibid., 126–31.

22. Ibid., 71ff.

23. Southern Pacific Lines, "Ogden Water Service Lines, August 20, 1931," Southern Pacific Drawings, *CRRM.*

24. "Proposed Pumping Plant, Water Pumping Station, Sacramento" (October 25, 1912, and June 14, 1913), Southern Pacific Map No. 571, *CRRM*. The Fresno plant, opened in 1930, plumbed a deep, pure well for a locomotive watering station and a large Southern Pacific ice plant and refrigerator car icing facility; *Southern Pacific Bulletin* (December 13, 1930).

25. Southern Pacific Drawings 96 ("Combined Pumphouse and Water Treating Plant: Elevations, Plan, Section"), 3364 ("Mixing Vats for Water Purifying Plants Used on 200 Gallon Chemical Tanks"), 839 ("7200-gallon Wooden Tank, Water Car for Fire Service"), and 6536 ("Motor and Feed Regulator for Automatic Water Treating Plants"), and "Analysis of Water Supplies—El Paso Division—Atlantic System—August 1898" (ms. drawing), all at *CRRM*.

26. Butler, "Report," 18–22, 59–60. For the railroad's distribution system at Wells, see "City of Wells, Elko County, Nevada, Layout, Water Mains and Hydrants, Sewers, Manholes and Flushtanks" (March 8, 1928), SP Drawings No. 3422, *CRRM*.

27. Butler, "Report," passim.

28. Ibid., 95–96.

29. Southern Pacific Map No. 3066, "Napa Junction, Proposed New Water Supply . . . " (January 1931), *CRRM*.

30. Butler, "Report," 38ff.

31. Gustav L. Seligman, "The El Paso & Northeastern Railroad System and Its Economic Influence in New Mexico" (M.A. thesis, New Mexico State University, 1958), 15ff.; Robert H. Sholly, "Alamagordo, New Mexico: A Case Study in the Dynamics of Western Town Growth" (M.A. thesis, University of Texas, El Paso, 1971), 13ff.; David F. Myrick, *New Mexico's Railroads: An Historical Survey* (Golden: Colorado Railroad Museum, 1970), 62, 71, 88, and 93.

32. Documents Relative to the Bonito River Reservoir and Pipeline, Bon 1–2, Southern Pacific Legal Department, El Paso Files, Southern Pacific Company Collection, University of Texas, El Paso; J. L. Campbell, "The Water Supply of the El Paso and Southwestern Railway from Carrizozo to Santa Rosa, New Mexico," *Transactions of the American Society of Civil Engineers* 70 (December 1910): 164–89; *Southern Pacific Bulletin*, November 1, 1924, p. 8; Dorothy Jensen Neal, *Captive Mountain Waters: A Story of Pipelines and People* (El Paso: Texas Western Press, 1957), passim; Mildred L. Jordan, "Railroads in the El Paso Area" (M.A. thesis, University of Texas, El Paso, 1957), 204–206; William A. Kelleher, *The Fabulous Frontier: Twelve New Mexico Items,* rev. ed. (Albuquerque: University of New Mexico Press, 1962), 310ff.

33. Robert M. Hanft, *San Diego & Arizona: The Impossible Railroad* (Glendale, CA: Trans-Anglo Books, 1984); Patrick W. O'Bannon, "Railroad Construction in the Twentieth Century" (typed course paper, University of California, San Diego, June 14, 1977, Dr. Scheiber's class), copy at San Diego Historical Society.

34. O'Bannon, "Railroad Construction," 34.

35. San Diego and Arizona Railroad Collection, Construction Series, box 23, folders 1–15, and box 24, passim, San Diego Historical Society; "Reservoir and Pipeline Filing," Legal Files, box 18, folder 6, on railroad acquisition of water permits from the U.S. General Land Office, 1924–1933.

36. Engineering Series, box 20, folder 13 (correspondence of the Engineering Department regarding maintenance of water facilities, 1918–1921), San Diego and Arizona Railroad Collection, San Diego Historical Society, esp. Thomas F. O'Connell (master mechanic) to J. R. Lowe (superintendent), San Diego, March 1, 1920; O'Connell to L. J. Masson (auditor), San Diego, August 5, 1920; and Lowe to Carl Eichenlaub (engineer), San Diego, February 14, 1921. The extensive documentation of the San Diego & Arizona's water systems in the Engineering Series and the Construction Series provides the clearest picture of water problems railroads faced in building and operating in the arid West and how the company attempted to overcome these difficulties with technology and organization.

37. For the use of steam shovels and their drain on the railroad water supply, San Diego and Arizona Railroad Collection, Construction Series, box 24, esp. folder 15 (about construction of the line between San Diego and the Imperial Valley, 1920), San Diego Historical Society; and "Water Report for Coyote Wells, July 1920" (Engineering Series, box 20, folder 13). For chemical treatment plants, U.S. Interstate Commerce Commission, Division of Valuation, "Engineering Report" (1922). For water production at sixty stations as of 1916, Butler, "Report," 1–6.

38. *Arizona Sentinel* (Yuma), February 18, 1882; *Houston Post,* February 4, 1897; *The Oasis* (Nogales, AZ), May 28, 1898; *El Paso Herald,* October 24, 1901; Skerritt, "Water Stations in the Arizona Desert," 2867–70; William Ashton Hawkins to William H. Mills, Salt Lake City, March 3, 1907, File 727, and L. E. Johnson to B. A. McAllaster, San Francisco, April 5, 1911, File 433, *SP-L.* For Southern Pacific cooperation with the agricultural colleges' irrigation experiments, see chapter 11. For acquisition of new water rights, Butler, "Report," passim; and "Reservoir and Pipeline Filing," Legal Files, box 18, folder 6, San Diego and Arizona Railroad Collection, San Diego Historical Society. For chemical testing systems, "Analysis of Water Supplies—El Paso Division—Atlantic System—August 1898," Southern Pacific Drawing No. 6554, *CRRM.*

39. Arizona Corporate Commission, Motor Transportation Commission, Rate Division, "Steam Railway Companies' Comparative Monthly Reports of Revenues and Expenses for the Years 1913–1914," Arizona State Archives, Phoenix.

40. Butler, "Report," passim; U.S. Interstate Commerce Commission, Division of Valuation, "Engineering Report" (1922), passim.

41. Documents Relative to the Bonito River Reservoir and Pipeline, Bon 1–2, Southern Pacific Legal Department, El Paso Files, Southern Pacific Company Collection, University of Texas, El Paso; *El Paso Times,* April 5, 1931; Neal, *Captive Mountain Waters,* 26ff.; Seligman, "El Paso and Northeastern Railroad System," 15ff.; Kelleher, *Fabulous Frontier,* 310ff.

42. *Southern Pacific Bulletin,* February 1920, p. 22.

43. Butler, "Report," 62–63, 92.

44. *Arizona Sentinel* (Yuma), April 27, 1878.

45. W. Q. Barlow to E. O. McCormick, San Francisco, July 19, 1918, and C. J. Blanchard to McCormick, Hazen, NV, June 23, 1918, File 610B, *SP-L.*

46. Ekstrom, "Yuma Water Plant."

47. Neal, *Captive Mountain Waters,* 26ff.; Seligman, "El Paso and Northeastern Railroad System," 15ff.; Kelleher, *Fabulous Frontier,* 310ff.

48. See "Table: Water Supply Stations" (1956), Southern Pacific Drawings No. 5914, *CRRM.*

8 Private Irrigation

The quotation in the chapter title is from assistant California state engineer C. E. Grunsky, commenting on the Southern Pacific's Tulare County artesian wells; *Sacramento Record-Union,* January 1, 1884.

1. Regarding the Southern Pacific and the Colorado River and Imperial Valley, 1900–1920s, see Imperial Irrigation District, Board of Directors, "Minutes," 2 vols. (1911–1917), *IID;* File 372 ("California Development Company"), and File 426A ("Imperial Irrigation District"), *SP-L;* H. T. Cory, "Irrigation and River Control in the Colorado River Delta," American Society of Civil Engineers, *Transactions* 76 (1913): 1204–1571; A. J. Wells, "Capturing the Colorado," *Sunset* 18 (March 1907): 391–404; George Kennan, *The Salton Sea: An Account of Harriman's Fight with the Colorado River* (New York: Macmillan, 1917); M. J. Dowd, "Arizona vs. California: History of the Imperial Irrigation District" (typescript, 1956), chaps. 7 and 8, *IID;* Robert G. Schonfeld, "The Early Development of California's Imperial Valley," *Southern California Quarterly* 50 (September 1968): 279–307, and (December 1968): 395–426; Don L. Hofsommer, *The Southern Pacific, 1901–1985* (College Station: Texas A & M Press, 1986), 32–34.

2. See George E. Mowry, *The California Progressives* (Berkeley: University of California Press, 1951), 1–22; Walton Bean and James J. Rawls, *California: An Interpretive History* (New York: McGraw-Hill, 1983), 166–285; Spencer C. Olin, Jr., *California Politics, 1846–1920: The Emerging Corporate State* (San Francisco: Boyd & Fraser Publishing Co., 1981), 27–71; Robert V. Hine, *The American West: An Interpretive History* (Boston: Little, Brown, 1984), 168–70; Arrell Morgan Gibson, *The West in the Life of the Nation* (Lexington, MA: D.C. Heath, 1976), 465–69.

3. Alfred R. Golzé, *Reclamation in the United States* (Caldwell, ID: The Caxton Printers, 1961), 14–15. Robert G. Dunbar, *Forging New Rights in Western Waters* (Lincoln: University of Nebraska Press, 1983), all but ignores the railroads. Donald C. Jackson has presented some information on the Santa Fe's support for dams; Jackson, "Ed Fletcher, the Santa Fe Railway, and Phoenix's Cave Creek Flood Control Dam," in *Fluid Arguments: Five Centuries of Western Water Conflict,* ed. Char Miller (Tucson: University of Arizona Press, 2001), 251–75. Historians of railways have done only somewhat better: Roy V. Scott, in *Railroad Development Programs in the Twentieth Century* (Ames: Iowa State University Press, 1985), 21, 80, 101–102, and 113, briefly describes a few examples of railway promotion of irrigation, particularly by the Great Northern in the Pacific Northwest and northern Great Plains; also, Scott's "Land Use and American Railroads in the Twentieth Century," *Agricultural History* 53 (October 1979): 688–89. Nevertheless, virtually all scholarly histories of western railroads, including studies of

individual corporations, overlook water development and irrigation; for an important recent exception, see Claire Strom, *Profiting from the Plains: The Great Northern Railway and Corporate Development of the American West* (Seattle: University of Washington Press, 2003), passim, esp. 66ff. See also, Richard J. Orsi, "*The Octopus* Reconsidered: The Southern Pacific and Agricultural Modernization in California, 1865–1915," *California Historical Quarterly* 54 (Fall 1975): 204–206.

4. Norris Hundley, Jr., *The Great Thirst: Californians and Water, 1770s-1990s* (Berkeley: University of California Press, 1992 and 2001 editions), passim.

5. Russell R. Elliott, *Servant of Power: A Political Biography of Senator William M. Stewart* (Reno: University of Nevada Press, 1983), 112; also John M. Townley, "Reclamation in Nevada, 1850–1904" (Ph.D. diss., University of Nevada, Reno, 1976), 66–68; William L. Kahrl, ed., *The California Water Atlas* (Governor's Office of Planning and Research and California Department of Water Resources, 1978), 39.

6. Donald J. Pisani, *From Family Farm to Agribusiness: The Irrigation Crusade in California and the American West, 1850–1931* (Berkeley: University of California Press, 1984), 291ff., and *To Reclaim a Divided West: Water, Law, and Public Policy, 1848–1902* (Albuquerque: University of New Mexico Press, 1992), 86–87 and 289–90; Donald Worster, *Rivers of Empire: Water, Aridity, and the Growth of the American West* (New York: Pantheon Books, 1985).

7. Pisani, *To Reclaim a Divided West,* 87 and 186ff.

8. Pisani, *From Family Farm to Agribusiness,* passim, and *To Reclaim a Divided West,* passim, esp. preface, chap. 1, and 327–36.

9. For community organization needed in irrigation systems, Arthur Maas and Raymond L. Anderson, . . . *and the Desert Shall Rejoice: Conflict, Growth, Justice in Arid Environments* (Cambridge: MIT Press, 1978), 1ff. "Riparianism" and "appropriationism" are explained in chapter 9; see esp. note 3.

10. Alfred D. Chandler, Jr., *The Visible Hand: The Managerial Revolution in American Business* (Cambridge: Harvard University Press, 1977), 79–205; regarding the innovative activities of railroads and their effects on general American economic and institutional development, see also Glenn Porter, "Industrialization and the Rise of Big Business," in *The Gilded Age: Essays on the Origins of Modern America,* ed. Charles W. Calhoun (Wilmington, DE: Scholarly Resources, 1996), 10ff.

11. See Collis P. Huntington, "Annual Report of the President," Southern Pacific Company, *Annual Report . . . 1892* (1893), 26–27; Orsi, "*The Octopus* Reconsidered," 204–206.

12. See Benjamin B. Redding, "Influence of Irrigation on Citrus Trees," *Pacific Rural Press* (August 16, 1879); I. N. Hoag, letters in *Sacramento Record-Union,* May 9 and 19 and June 9, 1883; Jerome Madden, *California: Its Attractions for the Invalid, Tourist, Capitalist, and Homeseeker* (San Francisco, 1890). Redding bibliography, in California Academy of Sciences, *In Memoriam: Benjamin B. Redding, Born January 17th, 1824, Died August 21st, 1882* (n.p., n.d.). Also, pamphlets written by federal irrigation experts and published by the railroad, such as Samuel Fortier (U.S. Department of Agriculture), *Irrigated Agriculture: The Dominant Industry of California* (San Francisco, 1905), and J. B. Lippincott (U.S. Reclamation Service), *Irrigation of the Sacramento Valley: An*

Address at the Reception for the Congressional Irrigation Committee at Red Bluff, California, June 15, 1905 (San Francisco, 1905).

13. See in *Sunset:* George H. Maxwell, "Save the Forests and Store the Floods," 9 (May 1902): 42–43; E. T. Perkins (U.S. Reclamation Service engineer), "Redeeming the West: Present Status of Government Irrigation Projects . . . ," 16 (November 1905): 3–25; C. J. Blanchard (U.S. Reclamation Service), "Redeeming the West—The Klamath Project," 17 (September 1906): 207–14; G. W. Swingle, "Chaining the Sacramento," 17 (October 1906): 453–55; "Redeeming the Arid West—Some Results of the Recent National Irrigation Congress at El Paso," 19 (February 1905), a large special collection of articles promoting irrigation by Alexander McAdie of the U.S. Weather Bureau, E. A. Sterling of the U.S. Forest Service, and California governor George C. Pardee. For the magazine's editorial policy favoring irrigation, see January 1905 issue (p. 308).

14. Orsi, "*The Octopus* Reconsidered," 204–206, and " 'Wilderness Saint' and 'Robber Baron': The Anomalous Partnership of John Muir and the Southern Pacific Company for the Preservation of Yosemite National Park," *The Pacific Historian* 29 (Summer/Fall 1985): 142. For Fulton's promotion of irrigation, see Fulton collection at the Nevada Historical Society Library, Reno; Barbara Richnak, *A River Flows: The Life of Robert Lardin Fulton* (Incline Village, NV: Comstock-Nevada Publishing Co., 1983); William D. Rowley, *Francis G. Newlands: Reclamationist and Reformer* (Bloomington: University of Indiana Press, 1995); examples of Fulton's speeches and writings promoting irrigation, see *Reno Gazette,* November 21, 1878, February 10, 17, and 19, 1883, November 17, 1904, and June 17, 1905, and *Nevada State Journal* (Reno), June 18, 1905.

15. See *Sacramento Record-Union,* January 3 and March 4, 1876; William H. Mills, "Annual Address Delivered before the State Agricultural Society of California . . . Sacramento, September 18, 1890," *Transactions of the California State Agricultural Society during the Year 1890* (Sacramento, 1891), 184–208, reprinted *Sacramento Record-Union,* September 19, 1890; William H. Mills, *The Hydrography of the Sacramento Valley* (San Francisco: California State Board of Trade, 1904); *San Francisco Call,* June 6 and July 4, 1904; William H. Mills to Governor George C. Pardee, San Francisco, February 3, 1903, Pardee Correspondence, *BL.*

16. California State Board of Trade, *Reclamation of Arid Lands by Irrigation: Report of the Committee on Arid Lands of the California State Board of Trade* (San Francisco, 1889); *San Francisco Call,* April 12, 1899, on a Mills speech to the Board of Trade promoting irrigation for smaller farms, horticultural development, and agricultural diversity.

17. A California delegate, Mills addressed the International Irrigation Congress of 1891 with a plea for public finance and management of irrigation and for strict limitation on land that could be irrigated with public water; *San Francisco Bulletin,* September 23, 1891; *Sacramento Record-Union,* September 24, 1891, also September 18, 19, and 21, 1891; Mills to Governor George C. Pardee, San Francisco, October 5, 1904, Pardee Correspondence, *BL;* Paul S. Taylor, "Water, Land, and People in the Great Valley," *The American West* 5 (March 1968): 29.

18. For Mills's work in forestry, parks, and wilderness preservation, see chapters 13–14;

Orsi, "'Wilderness Saint' and 'Robber Baron,'" passim, and *The Octopus* Reconsidered," 205.

19. C. E. Grunsky, assistant California state engineer, in *Sacramento Record-Union,* January 1, 1884; *Tulare Register,* August 24, 1883; *San Francisco Post,* clipping, late June 1883, Southern Pacific Scraps, vol. 13, *HEH;* "Tulare's First 100 Years," centennial ed. *Tulare Advance-Register* (Tulare: Tulare Advance-Register, 1972); Thomas H. Thompson, *Official Historical Atlas of Tulare County* (Tulare, 1892).

20. *Los Angeles Times,* October 24, 1893; *San Francisco Bulletin,* June 15, 1887, and July 7, 1888; *San Francisco Merchant,* August 3, 1888; *Los Angeles Herald,* October 24, 1893; *Indio: Its Climate and Resources* (M. L. Requa, 1893); Walter C. Mendenhall, *Ground Waters of the Indio Region, California, with a Sketch of the Colorado Desert,* Department of the Interior, U.S. Geological Survey, Water-Supply Paper 225 (Washington, DC: Government Printing Office, 1909), passim, esp. 7 and 45ff.; *Indio Daily News,* January 27, 1966.

21. *Los Angeles Times,* June 8, 1913; David Gosh Thompson, . . . *The Mohave Desert Region: A Geographic, Geologic, and Hydrologic Reconnaissance* (Washington, DC: Government Printing Office, 1929), 317 and 330; Frank D. Reeve, *History of New Mexico,* 3 vols. (New York: Lewis Historical Publishing Co., 1961), 2:248.

22. Pisani, *From Family Farm to Agribusiness,* 102–28.

23. Richard J. Orsi, "Confrontation at Mussel Slough," in Richard B. Rice, William A. Bullough, and Richard J. Orsi, *The Elusive Eden: A New History of California* (New York: McGraw-Hill, 2002), chap. 13; Pisani, *From Family Farm to Agribusiness,* 102–103, 122–24, and 191; Maas and Anderson, *Desert Shall Rejoice,* 146–274, esp. 152 and 157ff.; Richard Harold Smith, "Towns along the Tracks: Railroad Strategy and Town Promotion in the San Joaquin Valley, California" (Ph.D. diss., University of California, Los Angeles, 1976), passim, esp. 248–82; William Hammond Hall, *Topographical and Irrigation Map of the San Joaquin Valley* (Sacramento: State Engineering Department, 1886), sheets 2, 3, and 4, copy California State Archives.

24. Maas and Anderson, *Desert Shall Rejoice,* 157ff.; Smith, "Towns along the Tracks," 153–60; Pisani, *From Family Farm to Agribusiness,* 122–24; Bernhard Marks, *Small-Scale Farming in Central California: The Colonization System of the Great Valley of the San Joaquin* (San Francisco: Crocker & Co., 1888), passim; Virginia Thickens, "Pioneer Agricultural Colonies of Fresno County," *California Historical Society Quarterly* 25 (March 1946): 17–38, (July 1946): 169–77. On Haggin and the Kern County Company, Pisani, *From Family Farm to Agribusiness,* chap. 8; Norman Berg, *History of the Kern County Land Company* (Bakersfield, CA, 1971); Hundley, *Great Thirst* (1992), 91ff.

25. Southern Pacific Railroad Company, Land Department, "Journal, 1882–1885," 1:83–84, *CRRM.*

26. Southern Pacific Railroad Company, Land Department, "Day Book, 1871–1882," 1:179, *CRRM;* sales contracts, *ZC-SP.*

27. Regarding Stanford, Norman E. Tutorow, *Leland Stanford: Man of Many Careers* (Menlo Park, CA: Pacific Coast Publishers, 1971), passim.

28. For Fulton's water projects, esp. with Newlands, see Richnak, *A River Flows,* pas-

sim, esp. 36–98; Rowley, *Francis G. Newlands,* passim; Pisani, *To Reclaim a Divided West,* 198–203; *Reno Gazette,* October, 21, 1889. Fulton's obituary stressed his importance in pioneering Nevada irrigation; *Nevada State Journal* (Reno), October 27, 1920, also, October 25 and 26, 1920.

29. Pisani, *From Family Farm to Agribusiness,* chap. 5, esp. 120.

30. Kenneth R. McSwain, *History of the Merced Irrigation District* (Merced: Merced Irrigation District, 1978), 1–4.

31. For the meeting, and Davidson's report of April 15, 1877, *San Francisco Mail,* May 10, 1877; *Farmers' Canal Company of Merced County . . . Professor Davidson Reports in Favor of a Proposed Plan* (San Francisco: Bacon & Co., 1877).

32. *San Francisco Bulletin,* September 12, 1885; Oscar Lewis, *The Big Four* (New York: Ballantine Books, 1971 [1938]), 86.

33. "A Great Irrigation Scheme," by "BCT" (perhaps Benjamin C. Truman), *San Francisco Bulletin,* September 12, 1885; *Sacramento Record-Union,* January 29, 1886; *San Francisco Post,* January 27, 1886; *Alta California* (San Francisco), December 19, 1889; *San Francisco Call,* December 9, 1893; Crocker-Huffman Land and Water Company, *Merced County, California* (San Francisco: Murdock Press, ca. 1903); Bernhard Marks, *Small-Scale Farming in Central California: The Colonization System of the Great Valley of the San Joaquin* (San Francisco: Crocker & Co., 1888), esp. last page; Corwin Radcliffe, *History of Merced County* (Merced: A. H. Cawston, Publisher, 1940), 176–86; McSwain, *Merced Irrigation District,* 5–7; Huffman biography, John Outcalt, *History of Merced County, California, with a Biographical Review . . .* (Los Angeles: Historic Record Co., 1925), 417–19.

34. Smith, "Towns along the Tracks," 277.

35. *San Francisco Call,* September 9, 1893; McSwain, *Merced Irrigation District,* 7ff. Crocker-Huffman and Pacific Improvement companies' projects under Mills, in *San Francisco Call,* March 22, May 2, 1894; *San Francisco Examiner,* May 5, 1894.

36. Crocker-Huffman Land and Water Company, *Merced County,* passim; *San Francisco Call,* May 25, 1913.

37. McSwain, *Merced Irrigation District,* 9–38; *History of Merced County, California* (San Francisco: Elliott and Moore, Publishers, 1881), 179–80; Delores J. Cabezut-Ortiz, *Merced County: The Golden Harvest* (Windsor Publications, 1987), 43, 47, and 49; Radcliffe, *History of Merced County,* 176–86; Outcalt, *History of Merced County,* 333–59; Smith, "Towns along the Tracks," 276–77; C. E. Grunsky, *Irrigation Near Merced, California* (Washington, DC: Government Printing Office, 1899), 34–37.

38. On Monterey Peninsula developments, Pacific Improvement Company, *Pebble Beach, Monterey County, California* (San Francisco: H. S. Crocker Co., 1909); Lucy Neely McLane, *Piney Paradise by Monterey Bay: Pacific Grove* (San Francisco: Lawton Kennedy, 1952), 9ff.; Earl Pomeroy, *In Search of the Golden West: The Tourist in Western America* (New York: Alfred A. Knopf, 1957), 113–14; Augusta Fink, *Monterey County: The Dramatic Story of Its Past* (Santa Cruz, CA: Western Tanager Press, 1982), 122–34, 166–76, and 198. On Hope Ranch, *San Francisco Call,* January 20, 1901; Pacific Improvement Company, *Hope Ranch: A Story of Two-Thousand Acres of Wooded Land and a Prophesy of Its Future* (San Francisco: H. S. Crocker Co., 1908); and Harold Chase, *Hope Ranch*

(Santa Barbara: Santa Barbara Historical Society, 1963). For various projects, records of subsidiaries, Pacific Improvement Company Records, *SU;* see also chapters 1 and 5.

9   Public Irrigation

The quotation in the chapter title is from Collis P. Huntington, commenting on irrigation development in California's Imperial Valley; *San Francisco Bulletin,* May 3, 1893; *San Francisco Call,* December 14, 1893.

1. Donald J. Pisani, *To Reclaim a Divided West: Water, Law, and Public Policy, 1848–1902* (Albuquerque: University of New Mexico Press, 1992), 104–108; Norris Hundley, Jr., *The Great Thirst: Californians and Water, 1770s–1990s* (Berkeley: University of California Press, 1992), 85–97. For litigation between holders of riparian and appropriation rights, especially between the Miller-Lux and Haggin-Tevis interests over control of Kern County water *(Lux v. Haggin)*, M. Catherine Miller, *Flooding the Courtrooms: Law and Water in the Far West* (Lincoln: University of Nebraska Press, 1993), passim.

2. For support of western railroaders—especially James J. Hill of the Northern Pacific and Collis P. Huntington—for George Maxwell's National Irrigation Association, lobbying for federal support for public irrigation, Pisani, *To Reclaim a Divided West,* 288–90; esp. note 68 on p. 290.

3. Donald J. Pisani, *From Family Farm to Agribusiness: The Irrigation Crusade in California and the American West, 1950–1931* (Berkeley: University of California Press, 1984), 129–53, 220ff.; Hundley, *Great Thirst,* 63–110; Robert Kelley, *Gold vs. Grain: The Hydraulic Mining Controversy in California's Central Valley—A Chapter in the Decline of Laissez-Faire* (Glendale, CA: Arthur H. Clark Co., 1959). Put simply, "riparian rights," a feature of Anglo-American common law, assured the rights of downstream owners of land along streams to full flow and water quality in those streams. Largely derived from water laws designed for developing mining operations in the arid West, the "appropriation doctrine" allowed upstream water-rights owners to divert water from streams for "beneficial use" and convey it to distant lands without returning it for the use of downstream landowners.

4. *Sacramento Record-Union,* March 7, April 24 and 30, and May 4, 5, and 7, 1877; Pisani, *From Family Farm to Agribusiness,* 140–47.

5. Pisani, *From Family Farm to Agribusiness,* 129–252, notes some Southern Pacific involvement in the early debate; see 138–44.

6. Robert Kelley, "Taming the Sacramento: Hamiltonianism in Action," *Pacific Historical Review* 34 (February 1965): 21–49, and *Battling the Inland Sea: American Political Culture, Public Policy, and the Sacramento Valley* (Berkeley: University of California Press, 1989); Marvin Brienes, "Sacramento Defies the Rivers: 1850–1878," *California Historical Quarterly* 58 (1979).

7. For specific quotations, *Sacramento Record-Union,* July 29, 1878, and November 17, 1877. For some anti-hydraulic-mining and general anti-mining articles and editorials in the paper, 1875–1884, see esp. July 29, 30, and 31, and August 3, 7, 8, 9, 10, 13, and 28, 1878; also December 24 and 28, 1875; January 1, 3, 17, and 29, March 4, 22, and

23, April 1, 1876; February 6, 1878; April 9 and 28, and November 13, 1880; almost all issues in October, November, and December 1881; and January 15, 1883. See Pisani, *From Family Farm to Agribusiness,* 166–67, for *Record-Union's* criticism of water monopoly by miners.

8. Kelley, *Gold vs. Grain,* 75–129, 145, 174, and 216; Kelley was unaware of the newspaper's connection to the railroad. Pisani concluded that the newspaper "led the editorial attack on hydraulic mining"; see *From Family Farm to Agribusiness,* 162ff., esp. 163. See *Sacramento Record-Union,* August 28, 1878, for the newspaper's efforts to organize anti-debris groups.

9. *Sacramento Record-Union,* February 3 and March 4, 1878. Flood-caused traffic blockades plagued the railroad; Alban N. Towne to Collis P. Huntington, February 4, 1881, *CPH.*

10. *Alta California* (San Francisco), July 21, 1877, July 26, 30, and August 2, 7, 1878; *Nevada City Transcript,* August 6, 7, 1878; *Sacramento Record-Union,* March 28, July 31, August 3, 13, 1878; Kelley, *Gold vs. Grain,* 123ff.

11. Kelley, *Gold vs. Grain,* 245. Kelley also implies that the Southern Pacific privately used its influence with Judge Sawyer.

12. *San Francisco Call,* June 6 and July 4, 1904; William H. Mills, *Hydrography of the Sacramento Valley* (San Francisco: California State Board of Trade, 1904), passim. Mills and his newspapers often advocated comprehensive state water management; *Sacramento Record-Union,* May 5, 6, 8, 17, and 22, 1875; December 13 and 28, 1880; January 3 and 6, 1881; March 19, 22, and 28, April 1, 11, 15, 18, 19, and 21, and August 6, 1890; Mills to Governor George C. Pardee, San Francisco, February 3, 1903, Pardee Correspondence, *BL.*

13. See *Sacramento Record-Union,* April 26 and 27, 1875.

14. Pisani, *From Family Farm to Agribusiness,* 166–90; *Sacramento Record-Union,* April 9 and 28, and November 13, 1880; records of the State Engineer's office, California State Archives; William Hammond Hall's biennial reports to the state legislature, 1878–88, published in *Appendix to the Assembly and Senate of the State of California;* and *Miscellaneous Reports of the State Engineer, 1880–1888,* 2 vols., California Room, California State Library.

15. See *Sacramento Record-Union,* May 5, 6, 18, and 22, 1875.

16. *Sacramento Record-Union,* May 5, 6, and 8, 1875.

17. *Sacramento Record-Union,* February 27, 1885. The *Record-Union* frequently opposed weakening riparian rights protections for downstream landowners, including via local-irrigation-district legislation; see editorial of May 23, 1881. For the paper's campaign against the Fresno bills, see February 27 and March 3, 11 (special issue reprinting the legislative debate), 12, and 14, 1885; Pisani, *From Family Farm to Agribusiness,* 220ff. Other newspapers, especially San Francisco's *Examiner,* attacked the *Record-Union* for its opposition to the bills, the *Examiner* going as far as to denounce the Sacramento paper as an enemy of irrigation, which Mills's newspaper vehemently denied; *Record-Union,* editorial, March 3, 1885.

18. The Southern Pacific Scraps, *HEH,* are an important resource of the company's history, particularly relations with the press and outside parties. See vol. 4, for Mills's

original 1873 *Sacramento Record* editorials promoting a state irrigation system. For Mills's role as the Southern Pacific's lead-man in press and political matters, see William Deverell, *Railroad Crossing: Californians and the Railroad, 1850–1910* (Berkeley: University of California Press, 1994), passim, esp. 90, 124, and 130.

19. Pisani, *From Family Farm to Agribusiness,* 252ff.; Hundley, *Great Thirst,* 98ff.; Thomas E. Malone, "The California Irrigation Crisis of 1886: Origins of the Wright Act" (Ph.D. diss., Stanford University, 1965), passim; Frank Adams, *Irrigation Districts in California, 1887–1915* (Sacramento, 1917).

20. Pisani, *From Family Farm to Agribusiness,* 256–81; Hundley, *Great Thirst,* 100–101; *San Francisco Examiner,* November 17, 1896.

21. In the early twentieth century, the Land Department began to review all water-rights applications made to the California State Department of Public Works for conflicts with the company's; see W. H. Kirkbride to W. F. Herrin, January 2, 1924, and B. A. McAllaster to Herrin, San Francisco, January 8, 1924, File 383, *SP-L.* For an egregious example of a public water agency's (the Coachella Valley Storm Water District) trespassing on company lands and rights-of-way to avoid compensating the railroad $48,000 for property losses, see File 1175A.

22. As early as 1890, the railroad was paying taxes to many new districts, including the Tulare Irrigation District, the Sunset Irrigation District, and the Tipton Irrigation District; see D. K. Zumwalt to E. B. Ryan, Visalia, April 11, 1891, and March 8, 1892; and Jerome Madden to Zumwalt, San Francisco, March 9, 1892, and Zumwalt to Madden, Visalia, March 12, 1892; *ZC-SP.*

23. For a list of court cases, B. A. McAllaster, "Memorandum for Mr. Sharpe," September 29, 1909, in File 383, *SP-L.*

24. See B. A. McAllaster to William F. Herrin, San Francisco, February 15, 1915, File 440, *SP-L.*

25. File 440, "Alessandro Irrigation District," *SP-L,* esp. B. A. McAllaster to William F. Herrin, San Francisco, February 7, 1910, and April 9, 1913; Herrin to McAllaster, San Francisco, April 11, 1913; P. T. Carter to D. V. Cowden, Riverside, January 9, 1913; Purrington and Adair to Cowden, Riverside, February 5, 1913; Purrington and Adair to McAllaster, Riverside, March 4 and September 10, 1913; *Oakland Tribune,* October 13, 1911. Regarding the more complicated Perris District case, File 385, "Perris Irrigation District," esp. John D. Works to Charles W. Eberlein, Los Angeles, January 31, 1908; Office of Equitable Investment Co. to Property Owners of the Perris Irrigation District, Los Angeles, March 31, 1913; B. A. McAllaster to John F. Lowe, San Francisco, December 30, 1914, and to W. F. Herrin, San Francisco, February 15, 1915; Perris Irrigation District to Southern Pacific Company, Perris, October 10, 1916; *Coachella Valley News* (Indio), December 20, 1912; *San Francisco Examiner,* April 3, 1914.

26. *San Francisco Chronicle,* June 17, 1891.

27. *San Francisco Chronicle,* June 7, 1891.

28. William H. Mills to A. B. Hotchkiss, San Francisco, January 27, 1892, and Collis P. Huntington to Mills, New York, January 16, 1892, reprinted in unidentified newspaper clipping, ca. February 1892, Southern Pacific Scraps, vol. 19, *HEH.*

29. Pisani, *From Family Farm to Agribusiness,* 256, 278, and 335–80.

30. For Southern Pacific relationships with the districts, here and below, see letters, reports, and legal documents in many files concerning the districts, *SP-L,* nos. 387ff.

31. Invariably, after investing much time and money, the company found projects to resettle the urban poor on irrigation developments to be poorly planned, the economics impossible, and the settlers unsuited for farm-making; the few that even got started failed quickly; File 965, "Re Plan to Put Men on Small Farm Acreages," *SP-L.* Southern Pacific leaders also became skeptical of Carey Act projects; File 435, "Mary's River Irrigation Project," and File 772, "Carey Act," esp. B. A. McAllaster to William F. Herrin, February 15, 1915.

32. Although courted by district organizers, the Southern Pacific had its lands and operating property excluded, and in some cases sued irrigation districts to avoid entangling railroad interests in projects that were unfeasible or did not benefit the company. Such was the case with the unsuccessful Palmdale and Little Rock irrigation districts north of Los Angeles and the Deer Creek Storm Water District; see D. V. Cowden to B. A. McAllaster, San Francisco, August 19, 1919; McAllaster to Paul Shoup, San Francisco, October 5, 1923; File 411, *SP-L;* also, File 421, "Palmdale Irrigation District."

33. For the Southern Pacific's relations with districts, see Files 387ff., *SP-L;* also File 383, "Wright Law Irrigation Districts in California," esp. B. A. McAllaster, "Memorandum for Mr. Sharpe," September 29, 1909; reports rail officials compiled on water resources and the districts: W. H. Kirkbride to W. F. Herrin, January 2, 1924; and Charles W. Eberlein to John D. Works, San Francisco, January 23, 1908, File 374.

34. See F. W. Houtz to F. J. Evans, San Francisco, December 13, 1913, File 411, *SP-L.*

35. File 411, "Little Rock Creek Irrigation District, Antelope Valley," *SP-L;* esp. F. J. Evans, "Report on the Development of Antelope Valley, May 1st, 1912, to Dec. 1st, 1913" (typescript, December 1913); "Southern Pacific Land Company Sales Between May 1, 1912, and Dec. 1, 1913: Antelope Valley" (ms., December 26, 1913); W. S. Gelette, "Report on the Alkali and General Soil Conditions of . . . Antelope Valley for the Land Department, Southern Pacific Company" (typescript, 1916); B. A. McAllaster to H. W. Mongold, San Francisco, May 25, 1915; McAllaster to Paul Shoup, October 5, 1923; and D. V. Cowden to McAllaster, August 19, 1919.

36. J. W. Wilson to Land Department, Southern Pacific Company, Indio, March 11 and 23, 1911; B. A. McAllaster to Wilson, San Francisco, March 21, 1911; Fred Hill, "Memo" (April 6, 1911); McAllaster, "Memo" (March 25, 1911); File 429, *SP-L.*

37. File 504, *SP-L:* esp. E. A. Hardy to B. A. McAllaster, Orland, January 21 and February 1, 1917; McAllaster to A. D. Schindler, San Francisco, March 12, April 20, and June 24, 1918, and to E. F. Mitchell, San Francisco, March 12, April 20, May 10, and June 21, 1918, and to W. F. Herrin, San Francisco, April 13 and June 10, 1918; D. V. Cowden to McAllaster, San Francisco, April 18, 1918; Schindler to McAllaster, April 24, 1918; and Mitchell to McAllaster, April 25, 1918; *Fresno Republican,* January 3, 1917; *San Francisco Call,* September 17, 1917.

38. Such mediation occurred in the Tulare and Lindsay-Strathmore districts, which during the 1910s and 1920s fought in and out of courtrooms over dividing the water of the Kaweah River in the central San Joaquin Valley. The Southern Pacific for years

worked to fashion a compromise or to merge the districts so as to build a larger-capacity reservoir to serve the needs of both. All efforts failed; when in 1924 and 1926 courts ruled in favor of the Tulare District's water rights, vigilantes destroyed a Lindsay-Strathmore irrigation dam; File 398, "Tulare Irrigation District," *SP-L,* esp. Paul Shoup to W. F. Herrin, B. A. McAllaster, et al., San Francisco, May 17, 1924; Paul Shoup to F. W. Webster, San Francisco, June 6, 11, and 12, 1924; J. H. Dyer to Shoup, San Francisco, June 10, 1924; McAllaster to Shoup, June 11, 1924; also *San Francisco Chronicle,* June 11, 1925, and March 6 and April 12 and 14, 1926.

39. *Sacramento Record-Union,* April 15, 18, 19, 21, 24, and August 6, 1890, and September 21, 1891; *San Francisco Call,* April 12, 1899; File 876, "California State Board of Trade—Misc. Correspondence with William H. Mills [1906–1907]," *SP-L;* Mills to Governor George C. Pardee, San Francisco, February 3, 1903, Pardee Correspondence, *BL;* Mills, *Hydrography of the Sacramento Valley,* passim; Pisani, *From Family Farm to Agribusiness,* 294–356.

40. On the Arrowhead Company, see John W. Robinson, *The San Bernardinos: The Mountain Country from Cajon Pass to Oak Glen: Two Centuries of Changing Use* (Arcadia, CA: Big Santa Anita Historical Society, 1989), 119–28.

41. *Los Angeles Examiner,* February 27, 1911, for Pasadena.

42. For 1908–1919, in File 1003, "Mojave River Irrigation District Project Near Victorville . . . ," *SP-L,* esp.: B. A. McAllaster to W. F. Herrin, San Francisco, January 13, 1917, and to C. F. Gutridge, San Francisco, January 23, 1917; J. Q. Barlow to McAllaster, San Francisco, January 12, 1917; C. E. Wantland to McAllaster, Los Angeles, August 8, 1917. Also, *Victor Valley News-Herald* (Victorville), May 22, 1914, and February 16, 1917; *Los Angeles Examiner,* October 1, 1916; *San Bernardino Sun,* January 4, 1917; *Los Angeles Times,* February 6, March 25, and August 8, 1917.

43. File 1003, *SP-L:* Frank O. Miller to W. F. Herrin, Riverside, October 30, 1908; B. A. McAllaster to Herrin, San Francisco, November 4, 1908, and to Fred Hill, San Francisco, November 5, 1908, and to Oswald Wilson, San Francisco, May 23 and 29, 1914, and Hill to McAllaster, San Francisco, January 14, 1914. File 428: McAllaster, "Memo" (March 9, 1911), and McAllaster to Herrin, San Francisco, March 9, 1911.

44. William H. Gordon to B. A. McAllaster, Barstow, February 27, 1911; McAllaster, "Memo" (March 9, 1911); and McAllaster to W. F. Herrin, San Francisco, March 9, 1911; File 428, *SP-L.*

45. Railroad leaders frequently discussed among themselves and with irrigation organizers the dangers of local divisions; see B. A. McAllaster to A. A. Hoehling, San Francisco, June 1, 1918, and to Madison Marine, San Francisco, December 26, 1918, and McAllaster, "Memo" (December 19, 1919), File 1003, *SP-L.* Also, *Victor Valley News-Herald,* August 8, 1919.

46. For the first two decades of railroad involvement, see B. A. McAllaster's letter to Paul Shoup, San Francisco, February 21, 1921, File 1003A, *SP-L.*

47. B. A. McAllaster to D. V. Cowden, San Francisco, May 27, 1918, File 1003, *SP-L.*

48. Alfred Barstow to Paul Shoup, Los Angeles, February 15, 1921; B. A. McAllaster to Shoup, San Francisco, February 21, 1921; Hubert Francis Petre to McAllaster, Los Angeles, March 4, 1921; Frank M. Van Ness to McAllaster, Pasadena, February 22 and

March 15, 1921; and McAllaster to Van Ness, San Francisco, March 8, 1921; File 1003A, *SP-L.* References below are to File 1003A.

49. Dix Van Dyke to B. A. McAllaster, Daggett, March 18, 1921, and McAllaster to Van Dyke, San Francisco, May 2, 1921.

50. B. A. McAllaster to Dix Van Dyke, San Francisco, May 2, 1921.

51. C. E. Wantland to B. A. McAllaster, Los Angeles, September 2 and 29 and October 19, 1921.

52. C. E. Wantland to B. A. McAllaster, Los Angeles, October 19, 1921; McAllaster, "Memorandum" (November 29, 1921).

53. B. A. McAllaster, "Memorandum" (November 29, 1911); McAllaster to D. V. Cowden, San Francisco, November 30, 1911; Cowden to McAllaster, San Francisco, December 2, 1921; Norman F. Marsh to McAllaster, Los Angeles, ca. December 1, 1921; and J. B. Lippincott, "Report on Mojave Irrigation District Sent to the Secretary of the Interior" (ms., November 15, 1921).

54. B. A. McAllaster to W. E. Tussing, San Francisco, December 6, 1921, and February 8, 1922, and to W. F. Herrin, San Francisco, December 16, 1921, and January 6, 1922; Herrin to Paul Shoup, San Francisco, December 20, 1922, and January 14, 1922, and to McAllaster, San Francisco, February 2, 1922; Shoup to Herrin, San Francisco, December 29, 1921; and "Copy of Resolution Passed by Board of Directors, Mojave River Irrigation District, Meeting of February 12, 1922" (typescript).

55. W. E. Tussing to B. A. McAllaster, Los Angeles, June 27 and December 4, 1922, and May 8 and 10 and August 13, 1923; Paul Shoup to McAllaster, San Francisco, September 22, 1922, and from Los Angeles, September 29, 1922; McAllaster to Shoup, San Francisco, September 30, and October 2, 5, and 10, and December 30, 1922; McAllaster, "Memorandum" (typescript, October 3, 1922).

56. B. A. McAllaster to W. E. Tussing, January 11, 1923; Tussing to McAllaster, Los Angeles, January 15 and 24, 1923.

57. B. A. McAllaster to W. F. Herrin, San Francisco, January 22, 1924, and to W. E. Tussing, San Francisco, January 24, 1924; Herrin to McAllaster, San Francisco, January 22, 1924; Tussing to McAllaster, Los Angeles, January 14, 1924.

58. B. A. McAllaster to W. E. Tussing, San Francisco, June 16, 1924, and to J. H. R. Parsons, San Francisco, April 1, 1925; Tussing to McAllaster, Los Angeles, March 30, 1925; and Parsons to McAllaster, San Francisco, April 4, 1925.

59. W. E. Tussing to B. A. McAllaster, Sacramento, February 15, 1922, April 10 and 11, 1924; McAllaster to C. F. R. Ogilby, San Francisco, April 16, 1924, and to Tussing, San Francisco, April 16, 1924, and to W. F. Herrin, October 15, 1923, and to Guy V. Shoup, San Francisco, June 4, 1930; Ogilby to McAllaster, Washington, DC, April 24 and May 31, 1924, and May 16, 1929.

60. B. A. McAllaster, "Memorandum" (typescript, March 17, 1926); W. E. Tussing to McAllaster, Los Angeles, May 17, 1929; T. McAllaster to Guy V. Shoup, San Francisco, January 19, 1939; and to D. V. Cowden, San Francisco, February 21, 1939; also, *San Francisco Chronicle,* December 22, 1927.

61. T. McAllaster to Paul de Ford, San Francisco, September 1, 1944, and de Ford to McAllaster, September 22, 1944.

62. *San Francisco Bulletin,* May 3, 1893; *San Francisco Call,* December 14, 1893; Colorado River Irrigation Company, *Map of the Colorado Desert, Sonora Mesa, and Delta of the Rio Colorado, 1893* (Jersey City, NJ: J. Hart, 1893); M. J. Dowd, *History of the Imperial Irrigation District and the Development of the Imperial Valley* (El Centro, CA: Imperial Irrigation District, 1956), 7–8; also "Contract No. 11,322 [between the Southern Pacific Railroad Company and the Colorado River Irrigation Company], December 8, 1893" (ms.); Southern Pacific Land Company, "Survey South of the 3rd Standard Parallel . . . " (ms., n.d.); and B. A. McAllaster, "Abstract of the Testimony of W.H.H. Hart [January 1, 1898], in Relation to Contract 11322, Taken from Page 2167, Volume V. of Transcript of Record, Case of S.P.R.R. Co. et al. vs. U.S. of A., Involving Texas Pacific Overlap" (ms., October 29, 1913); all in File 426A, *SP-L.*

63. Dowd, *History of the Imperial Irrigation District,* 8–30; Norris Hundley, Jr., *Water and the West: The Colorado River Compact and the Politics of Water in the American West* (Berkeley: University of California Press, 1975), chap. 2; Charles Robinson Rockwood, *Born of the Desert* (Calexico: Calexico Chronicle, Publisher, 1930 [1909]). Manuscripts on the Southern Pacific's involvement in the Imperial Valley, 1900 through the 1920s, are in Imperial Irrigation District, Board of Directors, "Minutes," 2 vols. (1911–1917), Imperial Irrigation District Library, El Centro, CA; and File 372 ("California Development Company") and 426A ("Imperial Irrigation District"), *SP-L.* See also H. T. Cory, "Irrigation and River Control in the Colorado River Delta," American Society of Civil Engineers *Transactions* 76 (1913): 1204–1571; Cory and W. P. Blake, *The Imperial Valley and Salton Sink* (San Francisco: John J. Newbegin, 1915); A. J. Wells, "Capturing the Colorado," *Sunset* 18 (March 1907): 391–404; George Kennan, *The Salton Sea: An Account of Harriman's Fight with the Colorado River* (New York: Macmillan, 1917); M. J. Dowd, "Arizona vs. California: History of the Imperial Irrigation District" (typescript, 1956), chaps. 7 and 8, Imperial Irrigation District Library, El Centro; Robert G. Schonfeld, "The Early Development of California's Imperial Valley," *Southern California Quarterly* 50 (September 1968): 279–307, and (December 1968): 395–426; Don L. Hofsommer, *The Southern Pacific, 1901–1985* (College Station: Texas A & M Press, 1986), 32–34. A recent work on the Imperial Valley is William deBuys (photographs by Joan Myers), *Salt Dreams: Land and Water in Low-Down California* (Albuquerque: University of New Mexico Press, 1999), 71ff. For a recent analysis of the episode from the point of view of the Southern Pacific's president at the time, Edward H. Harriman, see Maury Klein, *The Life and Legend of E. H. Harriman* (Chapel Hill: University of North Carolina Press, 2000), 376–85, 390–91. The account that follows of closing the Colorado River break relies on these sources, along with others that are cited.

64. Helen Hosmer, "Imperial Valley: Triumph and Failure in the Colorado Desert," *The American West* 3 (Winter 1966): 34–49, 79; deBuys, *Salt Dreams,* 71ff., particularly vivid on the California Development Company's speculative nature, financial shakiness, careless engineering, and fraudulent, or nearly fraudulent, activities.

65. Sam E. Andrews, "Report of Investigations Showing Valuation of Land and Other Properties Liable to Destruction Had the 1906–7 Break in Colorado River Not Been Closed by the Southern Pacific Company" (typescript, 1924), 38–41, File 426A, *SP-L;*

C. E. Grunsky [consulting engineer to the U.S. Reclamation Service], "Lower Colorado River and Salton Basin" (ms. [copy], October 1, 1906), and Grunsky to the Honorable Director of the Geological Survey, Washington, DC, April 4, 1906 [copy], *IID*. For the Colorado River flood, 1905–1907, see esp. the account by H. T. Cory, the principal Southern Pacific engineer in charge of fighting the flood, "Irrigation and River Control in the Colorado Delta," passim. Manuscripts and an excellent collection of photographs taken by Cory and others to record the flood and the Southern Pacific's efforts to combat it, are in the H. T. Cory Collection, Department of Special Collections, University of California, Los Angeles, Library. See also, deBuys, *Salt Dreams,* 92ff., and 108ff. for the "cutting-back" phenomenon.

66. See *Arizona Star* (Yuma), March 15, 16, 23, May 21, 1884.

67. For the Southern Pacific's pioneering scientific study of the 1891 (and the recurring 1892) flood, see esp. *San Francisco Chronicle,* August 24, 1891; Cory, "Irrigation and River Control in the Colorado River Delta"; *San Francisco Chronicle,* June 29 and 30, July 2, 4, 8, 9, 11, 1891; *San Francisco Examiner,* July 14, 15, and 16, 1891; *New York Herald,* July 14, 1891; *Los Angeles Herald,* August 16, 1891; *Arizona Enterprise* (Florence), July 18, 1891; and *Report of the International Boundary Commission—United States and Mexico, 1891–1896, Part 1 and 2* (Washington, DC: Government Printing Office, 1898), 27. DeBuys, *Salt Dreams,* 65–70, also reviews the 1891 flood, but overlooks the Southern Pacific's role in flood surveying and analysis.

68. Charles W. Eberlein to W. H. Mills, San Francisco, December 16, 1903, and to Julius Kruttschnitt, January 12, 1904; File 372, "California Development Company," *SP-L.* Southern Pacific engineer H. T. Cory, who managed the California Development Company's irrigation system, also described the company's weaknesses in "Irrigation and River Control in the Colorado River Delta," 1231ff. and 1251ff.

69. Dowd, "Arizona vs. California," chap. 7; Hofsommer, *Southern Pacific,* 32ff.; Cory, "Irrigation and River Control in the Colorado River Delta," 1291ff.; Klein, *Harriman,* 378–79. DeBuys, *Salt Dreams,* 101ff., implies (with scant evidence) that the Southern Pacific plotted all along to take over the California Development Company in order to monopolize water and control the economy and development of the valley, and that the "loan" was a thinly veiled attempt to cover up its tyranny. Company documents cited above (note 68), along with sources that are cited below, demonstrate that this was not the case.

70. Descendent of the fabled Virginia family and a friend of Mark Twain, Randolph had a distinguished career as a civil engineer and executive with the Southern Pacific and its related line, the Pacific Electric in Los Angeles; "The Honored Career of Epes Randolph Closes," *Southern Pacific Bulletin* 10(September 1921): 13–14; Nat McKelvey, "The Indomitable Epes Randolph," *Trains* (July 1950): 44–49; and Olney Anderson, Jr., "Epes Randolph" (typescript, n.d.), Arizona Historical Society, Tucson. Cory had given up a professorship of engineering at the University of Cincinnati to become Randolph's assistant in Tucson in managing the railroad's lines in Arizona and Mexico and served as chief engineer of the California Development Company from 1905 to 1916; George Kennan, *E. H. Harriman: A Biography,* 2 vols. (Boston: Houghton-Mifflin, 1922), 2: 125; also manuscripts in the Cory Papers at the Department of Special Collections, UCLA.

71. Howe's vivid dispatches to the *Los Angeles Times* captured the flood's stunning, destructive power; for selections, see Andrews, "Report of Investigations." DeBuys, *Salt Dreams,* 104ff., is a gripping short account of the Southern Pacific's closure of the Colorado River; also, Klein, *Harriman,* 379–85, 390–91.

72. For the federal government's incapacity and its dependence on the railroad, see C. E. Grunsky (engineer to the U.S. Reclamation Service) to the Director of the Geological Survey, Washington, DC, April 4, 1906 [copy], *IID;* also correspondence between President Theodore Roosevelt and E. H. Harriman, quoted and summarized in Klein, *Harriman,* 384–85, 390–91.

73. E. H. Harriman to John Muir, February 20, 1907, *JMP.*

74. For the dramatic closing of the last break, see esp. *San Diego Union,* February 12, 1907; Dowd, "Arizona vs. California"; and for the best source, upon which other accounts generally draw, Cory's own comprehensive record in "Irrigation and River Control in the Colorado River Delta," 1291ff., and "Testimony of Harry Thomas Cory, Southern Pacific Company . . . vs. United States of America, No. E-352, in the Court of Claims of the United States" (typescript, 1927), 665, box 3, document 307, Cory Papers, Department of Special Collections, UCLA; Robert L. Speery, "When the Imperial Valley Fought for Its Life," *Journal of San Diego History* 21 (Winter 1975): 1–25. President Roosevelt's promised reimbursement caused drawn-out wrangling between the railroad and the government over the legitimacy and then the amount of the railroad's claim against the federal government. Luckily for future historians, the prosecution of its claim required the company to amass documents, manuscripts, and oral testimony regarding its activities in the Imperial Valley and in irrigation generally; see esp. Files 372 and 426A, *SP-L.* Finally, in 1930, the railroad received just over $1 million, less than one-half of its claim. For litigation over the claim, see Isidore B. Dockweiler, *In the Court of Claims of the United States: Southern Pacific Company vs. the United States of America, No. E-352, Plaintiff's Brief* (Los Angeles: Parker, Stone & Baird Co., ca. 1928); and esp., "Colorado River Break: Claim against U.S. Government, 1924–1934," box 28, file 345–1, and Isidore B. Dockweiler to Guy V. Shoup, Los Angeles, April 4, 1930, *SP-E.*

75. For the Southern Pacific's management and improvement of the California Development Company's irrigation system, Cory, "Irrigation and River Control in the Colorado River Delta," 1369ff.; Dowd, *History of the Imperial Irrigation District,* 36ff.; and a virtually day-to-day summary in "Abstract: Epes Randolph's Files Regarding Colorado River Problems, Boulder Canyon Dam and All American Canal, January 1910 to August 1921" (typescript, ca. 1920s), File 089–4, box 28, *SP-PR.* Cooperation between the Imperial Irrigation District and the Southern Pacific to improve water facilities was constant after 1911 and often came up in "Minutes" of the Board of Directors of the Imperial Irrigation District, *IID;* for cooperation to seal yet another Colorado River flood in 1914, see "Minutes" for April 9, 14, 18, 21, 22, and 23, May 12 and 26, and June 2 and 9, 1914; also, many documents in File 426A, *SP-L.* The railroad also contracted with the Reclamation Service to repair and rebuild federal levees along the Colorado; "Agreement between the Southern Pacific Company and the Government [U.S. Reclamation Service] for Work along the Colorado River" (ms., 1915), *SP-PR.*

76. Andrews, "Report of Investigations," 17; Frank Adams (University of Califor-

nia agricultural scientist), "Imperial [Irrigation District]" (typescript, February 2, 1929), 3ff., File R10–1, *SP-PR; Los Angeles Times,* October 30, November 29, and December 25 and 30, 1913, and January 4 and March 1, 1914.

77. Rumors of a railroad conspiracy to monopolize water and control the valley were particularly spread by W. H. Holabird, the court-appointed receiver of the bankrupt California Development Company's properties, who from 1909 to 1916 was constantly attempting to wrest control over the water system from the Southern Pacific and the Imperial Irrigation District and to install the other creditors as the owners; see *Los Angeles Times,* September 29, 1912, May 29, 1914, and April 15, May 9, and June 19, 1915, and *Los Angeles Examiner,* July 10, 1913, and June 20, 1915. Groups of landowners in the valley, however, often expressed their preference for the railroad over the development company as permanent water manager. For example, the *Los Angeles Times,* a sometimes opponent of the railroad, reported on May 23, 1909, that "practically all the Imperial Valley ranchmen anticipate the making of many improvements in the present irrigation system if the Southern Pacific company assumes formal control of the California Development Company's plant." Historians who have assumed the railroad intended from the beginning to seize the water system include Robert Schonfeld, "The Early Development of California's Imperial Valley," *Southern California Quarterly* 50 (December 1968): 395ff.; Hosmer, "Imperial Valley," 47; Donald Worster, *Rivers of Empire: Water, Aridity, and the Growth of the American West* (New York: Pantheon Books, 1985), 197–201; and deBuys, *Salt Dreams,* 101ff.

78. File 426A, Southern Pacific Land Company Records, San Francisco: W. F. Holt to E. E. Calvin, Redlands, August 11, 1910; Calvin to J. Kruttschnitt, San Francisco, August 10, 1910, and to W. H. Herrin, August 13, 1910; B. A. McAllaster to Herrin, San Francisco, August 18, 1910. From the inception, company officials routinely planned for eventual Southern Pacific capitalization of the proposed irrigation district. Los Angeles land agent C. E. Wantland, for example, wrote to E. E. Wade (assistant general passenger agent in San Francisco) on December 19, 1911, that "the Southern Pacific has been the guardian angel of the Valley, saved it from destruction and will, I imagine, have to take bonds for what it has invested in the canal system, and probably supply additional money."

79. *Coachella Valley News* (Indio), July 28, 1911; Dowd, *History of the Imperial Irrigation District,* 49ff.; Adams, "Imperial," 5ff.

80. File 426B, *SP-L:* B. A. McAllaster, "Statement of Amounts Expended by Southern Pacific Company in Connection with California Development Company Matters" (ms., October 7, 1925), and "Memorandum" (ms., October 5, 1925); T. O. Edwards to McAllaster, San Francisco, October 6, 1925; and McAllaster to Edwards, San Francisco, October 3, 1925. File 426A: "Agreement Between the Southern Pacific Company and the New Liverpool Salt Company, 1915" (typed copy, dated November 11, 1915); "Agreement Between the Southern Pacific Company and the Imperial Irrigation District, December 28, 1915" (typescript copy); and Guy V. Shoup, "Memorandum of Securities and Documents Delivered to the Imperial Irrigation District, June 22, 1916, Pursuant to Agreement between the Southern Pacific Company and Imperial Irrigation District Dated December 28, 1915" (typescript, August 14, 1916). File 372: William Sproule to

T. O. Edwards, Los Angeles, October 9, 1916 (on the railroad's discounting of Imperial Irrigation District bonds). Also, "Agreement between Southern Pacific Company and Imperial Irrigation District, Dated February 8th, 1915," File R195.73, *SP-PR.* For the Imperial Irrigation District's view of the complex, but cooperative, negotiations and planning between the railroad and the district for the Southern Pacific's purchase of the California Development Company, the transfer to the Imperial district, and the railroad's financing of that purchase, see Imperial Irrigation District, Board of Directors, "Minutes," vol. 1, esp. almost all meetings from July through November 1912, January 15, March 11 and 13, May 2, 13, and 27, June 10, July 8 and 31, August 12, September 24, October 14, 17, and 24, November 11 and 21, and December 9, 1913, January 2, 5, and 13, March 3, April 8, May 12, July 28, October 6, 20, and 27, November 2, 10, 24, 25, and 30, December 8, 18, and 28, 1914, February 9, August 10 and 24, October 13, November 18 and 27, 1915, and January 4, February 1, 3, and 10, 1916, *IID;* also, *Los Angeles Examiner,* July 10, 1913, and October 10, 1915; *Los Angeles Times,* February 13, May 9, and June 19, 1915, February 9 and April 3, 1916; *San Francisco Call,* January 9, 1913, and February 2, 1916; *San Francisco Post,* December 1, 1913. In the early 1900s, another western railroad, the Northern Pacific, similarly fostered and financed a local irrigation district; Dorothy Zeisler-Vralsted, "The Role of the Northern Pacific Railroad in the Development of the Kennewick (Washington) Irrigation District" (paper delivered at meeting of the Western Historical Association, New Haven, Connecticut, October 1992).

81. See Files 426.1 and 426.2, *SP-L,* esp. B. A. McAllaster to Sam E. Andrews, April 4, 1927; and C. E. Impey to M. J. Dowd, July 7, 1938; also, *El Centro Press,* November 22, 1926.

82. "Agreement Between the Southern Pacific Land Company and the Imperial Irrigation District, June 22, 1916" (typescript copy), File 426A, *SP-L.*

83. *Los Angeles Times,* August 17, 1916; *El Centro Progress,* August 27, 1916.

84. The flooding of Southern Pacific lands by surplus irrigation and drainage water flowing into the expanding Salton Sea was the most persistent disagreement between railroad and water agency. At first, the 1916 agreement, coupled with private negotiations and compromises, resolved difficulties. But, by the mid-1920s, with the sea still rising and inundating more and more company land and with the irrigation district still insisting on its right to flood as much land as it needed and still taxing the railroad on the submerged and useless lands, the company determined that its long-term property rights were endangered and sued the district; *San Diego Union,* March 2, 1924; File 426B, *SP-L,* esp. B. A. McAllaster to W. H. Herrin, April 17, 1924; Herrin to McAllaster, April 21, 1924; Sam E. Andrews to McAllaster, Colton, CA, April 25, 1924. File 426C: McAllaster to Guy V. Shoup, San Francisco, January 29, 1930.

85. File 426A, *SP-L:* Alfred Kohlberg to B. A. McAllaster, San Francisco, February 5, 1916; McAllaster to Guy V. Shoup, San Francisco, February 8, 1916; C. E. Wantland to McAllaster, Los Angeles, August 31, 1917; and many letters exchanged between McAllaster and Earl C. Pound of Brawley, January–February 1917. The railroad had always opposed careless, willy-nilly expansion of irrigated land in the valley without

thought to stable water supplies; see Kohlberg to McAllaster, San Francisco, ca. February 1916, and esp. McAllaster to Shoup, San Francisco, February 8, 1916, in which the land agent laid out in detail the long-held railroad policy and advised a superior executive that he would like to see more land irrigated in the valley, "but if there is no more than sufficient water supply for the lands now adjacent to constructed ditches then I think it would be a mistake."

86. B. A. McAllaster to W. F. Herrin, San Francisco, June 14, 1919, File 426A, *SP-L;* also, McAllaster to Herrin, February 26, 1917; Herrin to McAllaster, February 21, 1917; Phil Swing (attorney for the Imperial Irrigation District) to Herrin, El Centro, February 19, 1917; telegram, Paul Shoup to Julius Kruttschnitt, San Francisco, July 22, 1919. The 1917 bond issue alone increased Southern Pacific taxes on its lands $10,000 per year, the 1919 issue an additional $35,000 per year. See also, *El Centro Progress,* January 5 and February 11, 1917.

87. Sam E. Andrews to B. A. McAllaster, Colton, September 23 and October 7, 1923, and September 15, 1925; McAllaster to D. V. Cowden, October 25, 1923; F. H. McIver (secretary-treasurer of the Imperial Irrigation District) to McAllaster, El Centro, October 1, 1923; and McAllaster, "Memo" (October 1, 1923), all in File 426B, *SP-L.* See also, Board of Directors, Imperial Irrigation District, *Imperial Irrigation District: Information* (December 1925), 1–2. The Imperial Irrigation District's new revenue system based on land taxes shifted an even larger share of the region's irrigation costs to the railroad than is immediately apparent, since the company owned much land in the district but did not farm any of its vacant land grant, and thus used no water and could not benefit from elimination of water charges. On the prices of railroad land in the area in 1916, see McAllaster to Cowden, San Francisco, April 19, 1916; C. E. Wantland to Arthur E. Hull, Los Angeles, April 18, 1916; and Southern Pacific Land Company, "Imperial Irrigation District, Patented and Unpatented Lands" (typescript, 1916), all in File 426A. The railroad's development of sophisticated freight and marketing programs for cantaloupes and other crops is discussed in chapter 12; shipping figures for 1923, in J. T. Saunders to G. W. Boschke, San Francisco, November 2, 1926, box 28, file 089–4, *SP-E.*

88. *San Diego Union,* March 2, 1924.

89. Stuart Salisbury to B. A. McAllaster, Los Angeles, February 21, 1919, and McAllaster to Salisbury, San Francisco, February 26, 1919, File 426A, *SP-L;* see also chapter 10.

90. In 1924, B. A. McAllaster publicly promised the Imperial Valley Farm Lands Conference that the railroad would "work enthusiastically for the furtherance of suitable plans for the control of the Colorado River by the construction of dams and reservoirs whereby the water supply of the Valley will be stabilized and the danger of another flood such as was experienced in 1906 will be permanently done away with"; *San Diego Union,* March 1, 1924. For the Southern Pacific's building of branch lines and shoring up of river levies to assist in the construction and operation of Reclamation Service Colorado River projects, see David M. Myrick, *Railroads of Arizona: Vol. I: The Southern Pacific* (Berkeley: Howell-North Books, 1975), 419–30. For Southern Pacific lobbying and other political support for the Yuma and Boulder Canyon and other projects,

see Pisani, *From Family Farm to Agribusiness,* 308ff. "Colorado River Problem and Proposed Boulder Canyon Dam" (1926), file 089–4, box 28, *SP-E,* contains correspondence and reports illustrating the company's motives and actions regarding the Imperial Valley and Colorado River regions: to secure the Boulder Canyon Project, company vice president Paul Shoup in 1926 started the campaign to press the federal government to build the dam, working closely with U.S. Reclamation commissioner Ellwood Mead, Secretary of Commerce Herbert Hoover, and Harry Chandler, editor of the *Los Angeles Times;* see Paul Shoup to William Sproule, San Francisco, January 28, 1926; W. H. Kirkbride to J. H. Dyer, January 28, 1926; George W. Boschke to Shoup, San Francisco, September 29, 1926; Russell Chase to Boschke, September 25, 1926.

91. "Mexico California Development Company Lands in Mexico, 1917–1926," File 611A-D, *SP-L;* Louis B. Frandsen, "Resume . . . Land Department," Appendix "Mexican Lands" (typescript, ca. 1968), *SP-E.*

10   Federal Reclamation

The quotation in the chapter title is from Charles W. Eberlein, writing to William D. Cornish, San Francisco, February 18, 1904, File 610, *SP-L.*

1. Donald J. Pisani, *To Reclaim a Divided West: Water, Law, and Public Policy, 1848–1902* (Albuquerque: University of New Mexico Press, 1992), 273–336; William D. Rowley, *Reclaiming the Arid West: The Career of Francis G. Newlands* (Bloomington: Indiana University Press, 1996), passim.

2. See chapters 3 and 5; Richard J. Orsi, "*The Octopus* Reconsidered: The Southern Pacific and Agricultural Modernization in California, 1865–1915," *California Historical Quarterly* 54 (Fall 1975): 196–220.

3. For the early Truckee-Carson and other federal projects, William Joe Simonds, "The Newlands Project (Third Draft)" (Denver: Bureau of Reclamation History Program, 1996, Bureau of Reclamation website, 2001), esp. 1–11; John M. Townley, *Turn This Water into Gold: The Story of the Newlands Project* (Reno: Nevada Historical Society, 1977), 1–60; Donald J. Pisani, "Conflict over Conservation: The Reclamation Service and the Tahoe Contract," *Western Historical Quarterly* 10(April 1979): 167–90; Pisani, *To Reclaim a Divided West,* 322–36; Pisani, "State vs. Nation: Federal Reclamation and Water Rights in the Progressive Era," *Pacific Historical Review* 51 (August 1982): 165–87; Pisani, *From Family Farm to Agribusiness: The Irrigation Crusade in California and the American West, 1850–1931* (Berkeley: University of California Press, 1984), 281ff.; Pisani, *Water and American Government: The Reclamation Bureau, National Water Policy, and the West, 1902–1935* (Berkeley: University of California Press, 2002), passim., esp. 32–64, 96–122; James W. Hulse, *The Silver State: Nevada's Heritage Reinterpreted* (Reno: University of Nevada Press, 1991), 227–33; Paul Wallace Gates, *History of Public Land Law Development* (Washington, DC: Government Printing Office, 1968), 661ff.; Robert G. Dunbar, *Forging New Rights in Western Waters* (Lincoln: University of Nebraska Press, 1983), 52–54.

4. B. A. McAllaster to F. H. Newell, San Francisco, December 3, 1923, File 610B,

SP-L; Newell, "Federal Land Reclamation . . . ; 1. Origin, Problems and Achievements of Federal Land Reclamation," *Engineering News-Record* 91 (October 25, 1923): 666–73.

5. I have been able to locate only brief mentions of the Southern Pacific's involvement in the Truckee-Carson Project, other than minor allusions to the railroad's building of spur lines; see Townley, *Turn This Water into Gold,* passim. The semi-official history, Simonds's "The Newlands Project" (1996), does not mention the existence of a rail line through the region. The only major historian to acknowledge the role of the western railroads in national reclamation is Donald J. Pisani, and his focus is on efforts especially of the Great Northern and the Southern Pacific to promote the irrigation congress movement and passage of the 1902 act; see "George Maxwell, the Railroads, and American Land Policy, 1899–1904," in Pisani, *Water, Land, and Law in the West: The Limits of Public Policy, 1850–1920* (Lawrence: University Press of Kansas, 1996), 102–18, originally in *Pacific Historical Review* 63 (May 1994): 177–202; Pisani, *To Reclaim a Divided West,* 288ff.

6. Mary Ellen Glass, *Water for Nevada: The Reclamation Controversy, 1885–1902* (Reno: University of Nevada Press, 1964), 33–36. For Irrigation Congress tours run by the railroad of its Indio farming and irrigation experiment station in the Colorado Desert, see *Los Angeles Times,* October 24, 1893, and *Los Angeles Herald,* October 24, 1893. The company continued to support irrigation congresses after 1902; *Southern Pacific Bulletin* 3 (September 1, 1915): 7. In June 1905, when the gates were first opened to release water onto farmlands in the Truckee-Carson Project, the Southern Pacific ran a special train to the site and paid part of the expenses of the celebration and a tour by a joint congressional committee on irrigation to witness the event and visit western projects; land agent Robert L. Fulton officiated at the kickoff banquet; *Reno Gazette,* June 17, 1905.

7. Pisani, "George Maxwell, the Railroads, and American Land Policy," and *To Reclaim a Divided West,* 288–94; and Claire Strom, *Profiting from the Plains: The Great Northern Railway and Corporate Development of the American West* (Seattle: University of Washington Press, 2003), 59ff. I am deeply indebted to Dr. Pisani for providing information on railroads' promotion of the National Reclamation Act.

8. For Mills's attack on federal irrigation, see especially a 1901 article in *Water and Forest,* a periodical of the Water and Forest Association of California, which Mills had helped found to promote state irrigation; strategically reprinted in Congressman Frederick Newlands's home territory, *Reno Gazette,* December 10, 1901, while the Newlands Act was pending in Congress.

9. Conflict between the state and federalist factions surfaced at the 1896 Irrigation Congress; *Reno Gazette,* December 23, 1896. For the conflict, and especially Mills's role, see Pisani, *From Family Farm to Agribusiness,* 283–99; Glass, *Water for Nevada,* 45. Mills's quote, from his article in *Water and Forest,* reprinted *Reno Gazette,* December 10, 1901. James J. Hill, perhaps the most aggressive railroader in pushing for the National Reclamation Act, eventually came to share many of Mills's criticisms of the law and its application once it had gone into effect and exposed the problems inherent in early federal irrigation; Strom, *Profiting from the Plains,* 66ff.

10. Robert. L. Fulton, "Irrigation and Its Future in Nevada," *Reno Gazette,* June 17,

1905. For Fulton's other irrigation speeches, writings, and activities, some in association with Newlands, see *Reno Gazette,* November 21, 1878, February 10, 17, and 19, 1883, January 28 and August 19, 1889, August 20, 1900, November 17, 1904, and *Nevada State Journal* (Reno), June 18, 1905; Barbara Richnak, *A River Flows: The Life of Robert Lardin Fulton* (Incline Village, NV: Comstock-Nevada Publishing Co., 1983), 59–98; Rowley, *Reclaiming the Arid West,* 52–53, and "Forests and Water Supply: Robert L. Fulton, Science, and U.S. Forest Policies," *Nevada Historical Society Quarterly* 37 (Fall 1994): 215–24. I am deeply indebted to Dr. Rowley for furnishing information regarding Fulton's work and the larger issues of reclamation.

11. Charles Walcott, director, U.S. Geological Survey, to E. H. Harriman, Washington, DC, December 3, 1906, File 610, *SP-L;* also, Frederick H. Newell to E. T. Perkins, Washington, DC, May 20, 1908 (enclosing "Memorandum to E. T. Perkins"), box 18L, *TCID.* Walcott's letter and Newell's memorandum review the discussion at the 1902 meeting, including the decision to make Truckee-Carson the first federal project.

12. Three collections document this railroad-agency partnership: the Truckee-Carson Irrigation District Records, *TCID* (though the district was a local irrigation agency to which the Reclamation Service turned over operation of the project's water distribution system in 1926, the records contain manuscripts pertaining to the early federal management); *SP-L,* esp. Files 609 and 610 A-D; and the U.S. Bureau of Reclamation Records, *USBR.*

13. I am not the first to employ this characterization. Pisani, in *From Family Farm to Agribusiness,* 316, used it to describe the general relationships between the Reclamation Service and local interests. The Southern Pacific certainly fit the pattern.

14. See discussion, end of this chapter, regarding the Service's failed attempt to convert Lake Tahoe into a storage reservoir.

15. William F. Hood to L. H. Taylor, San Francisco, December 28, 1905, and January 4 and 9, 1906; Taylor to Hood, Hazen, NV, January 2 and 12, 1906, box 18L, *TCID.* For railroad cooperation with the Forest Service and other agencies, chapter 14.

16. William H. Hood to William F. Herrin, San Francisco, October 19, 1906 (copy), and L. H. Taylor to Chief Engineer, Reclamation Service [Frederick H. Newell], October 20, 1906, box 18L, *TCID.*

17. See documents, file "Acquisition of Lands . . . Southern Pacific Railway through 1911," Record Group 115, Entry 3, box 685, 1–9, *USBR,* esp. Frederick H. Newell to Charles D. Walcott, Washington, DC, November 15, 1905; Walcott to E. H. Harriman, Washington, November 12, 1905; Julius Kruttschnitt to Walcott, New York, November 23, 1905; and Newell to L. H. Taylor, Washington, November 24, 1905. Kruttschnitt's letter to Walcott served as authorization for subsequent transfers at $1.25 per acre years later, despite Land Department executives' objections that the lands' value had increased greatly; also copies of many above letters, particularly Kruttschnitt's letter, in File 609, *SP-L;* also D. H. Chambers to William D. Cornish, Washington, July 7, 1906, and Cornish to William H. Mills, New York, July 9, 1906; Kruttschnitt to E. E. Calvin, New York, November 23, 1905; Newell to B. A. McAllaster, Washington, August 25, 1911; A. P. Davis, acting director, Reclamation Service, to Kruttschnitt, Washington,

November 11, 1911; Kruttschnitt to William Sproule, New York, November 8, 1911; McAllaster to Newell, September 13 and December 12, 1911; McAllaster to W. F. Herrin, San Francisco, November 16, 1911; Herrin to Sproule, San Francisco, November 23, 1911.

18. R. M. Patrick (assistant district counsel, U.S. Bureau of Reclamation), to B. A. McAllaster, Fallon, NV, February 13, 1919, File 609, *SP-L;* quotation, from Patrick's letter.

19. E. S. Hopson, supervising engineer, Reclamation Service, Portland, to B. A. McAllaster, Portland, May 28, 1912; McAllaster to Hopson, June 1 and 11, 1912; and D. W. Cole to McAllaster, Fallon, NV, November 29, 1912, File 609, *SP-L.*

20. See chapters 3 and 5.

21. A. J. Wells, *Nevada* (San Francisco: Passenger Department, Southern Pacific Company, 1911), 13. Other company promotional materials for the region also defended the acreage limit and residence rules; see Central Pacific Railway Company, *Railroad Land for Sale; Irrigable Lands within the Truckee-Carson Project in the State of Nevada . . .* (San Francisco: Land Department, 1908); A. J. Wells, *The New Nevada: The Era of Irrigation and Opportunity* (San Francisco: Passenger Department, Southern Pacific Company, 1908), 27–31; Southern Pacific Company, *Government Lands in Nevada* (San Francisco: Passenger Department, 1908), 8–10. *SP-L* contains no documents objecting, even privately within the railroad, to the acreage-limitation and general residence rules, and many documents, public and private, favoring the rules; for the railroad's view, see Charles W. Eberlein to William D. Cornish, San Francisco, February 18, 1904, File 610; B. A. McAllaster to William F. Herrin, San Francisco, April 27 and July 1, 1914, File 610C; and McAllaster to Herrin, May 26, 1924, File 743.

22. B. A. McAllaster to William F. Herrin, San Francisco, July 1, 1914, File 610C; and McAllaster to Herrin, May 26, 1924, File 743, *SP-L;* also many documents, File 757, "Reclamation and Water Rights," esp. McAllaster to A. A. Jones, first assistant secretary, U.S. Department of the Interior, San Francisco, May 5, 1915.

23. Frederick H. Newell to L. H. Taylor, Washington, DC, June 23, 1903, box 18L, *TCID.*

24. Charles W. Eberlein to William D. Cornish, February 18, 1904, File 610, *SP-L;* also in file is the original of Bien's letter proposing the second plan, Morris Bien to Eberlein, Washington, December 5, 1903; copy in RG 115, Entry 3, box 685, *USBR.*

25. Charles W. Eberlein to Julius Kruttschnitt, San Francisco, February 18, 1904, File 610, *SP-L.*

26. Interior's expectations from the railroad, see Morris Bien to Charles W. Eberlein, December 15, 1903, File 610, *SP-L.*

27. L. H. Taylor to William H. Mills, Hazen, NV, May 11, 1906; Mills to William D. Cornish, Oakland, November 13, 1906; "Contract Between Central Pacific Railway Company and Purchasers of Land in the Truckee-Carson Project" [1906]; File 610, *SP-L.* Also Mills to Taylor, San Francisco, April 10 (enclosing copy of William F. Herrin to Mills, San Francisco, April 4, 1906), May 16, July 6, and September 11, 1906; Taylor to Mills, Hazen, July 10 and 30, 1906; Morris Bien to Taylor, Salt Lake City, August 20, 1906 (enclosing agreement between the railroad and the government, "The United States

Should Agree with the Central Pacific Railway Company that:"); box 18L, *TCID;* box 18L also contains a sales contract copy.

28. J. L. Willcutt to William H. Mills, Oakland, September 11, 1906; Mills to William D. Cornish, Oakland, November 13, 1906; "Resolution Adopted by the Board of Directors of the Central Pacific Railway Company, September 8, 1906" (typescript); all in File 610, *SP-L.* Also Mills to L. H. Taylor, San Francisco, September 11, 1906, box 18L, *TCID.*

29. D. A. Chambers to Director, U.S. Geological Survey, Washington, DC, September 24, 1906, File 610, *SP-L.*

30. C. A. Hitchcock to Reclamation Service and Director of the U.S. Geological Survey, Washington, DC, November 3, 1906, and to D. A. Chambers, November 3, 1906 (copies), File 610, *SP-L.*

31. William H. Mills to William D. Cornish, Oakland, November 13, 1906, File 610, *SP-L.*

32. Charles Walcott to William D. Cornish, Washington, DC, December 11, 1906, and to E. H. Harriman, Washington, DC, December 3, 1906; Cornish to William H. Mills, New York City, December 26, 1906; Mills to Cornish, San Francisco, January 2, 1907, File 610, *SP-L.* It took years of Southern Pacific land officials' entreaties for the Reclamation Service to send the information, including the vital maps of specific parcels of railroad land that would be irrigated, and even then the information was often incomplete or inaccurate; see Frederick H. Newell to L. H. Taylor, Washington, DC, September 23, 1905, which lists at least two years of conferences and items of correspondence between the government and the railroad over the questions of maps and specific tracts to be irrigated; Mills to Taylor, San Francisco, November 23 and December 27, 1905; Charles W. Eberlein to Taylor, San Francisco, November 24, 1905; Taylor to Mills, Hazen, NV, December 10 and 28, 1905, box 18L, *TCID.* Letters from railway officials pressed for precise maps, so they could sell the land quickly, and warned of problems caused by delay; reclamation officials explained why they did not have the information yet, lacked the manpower to make the maps, could not send maps for various reasons, or could send only general tentative maps. Actually, as late as April 1906, when negotiations with the railroad were far advanced, the Reclamation Service itself did not have accurate, detailed maps of the project area, particularly regarding which land sections were in public, private, and railroad ownership, and was in turn pressing the General Land Office of the U.S. Department of the Interior for the maps; see L. H. Taylor to Frederick H. Newell, Hazen, NV, April 2 and 30, 1906, box 18L, *TCID.*

33. Frederick H. Newell to L. H. Taylor, Washington, DC, September 23, 1905, box 18L, *TCID.*

34. For dickering, 1907–1908, over railroad land prices, see William H. Mills to William D. Cornish, San Francisco, January 2, 1907; Mills to Robert L. Fulton (telegram), San Francisco, December 31, 1906; Fulton to Mills (telegram), Reno, December 31, 1906; Mills to L. H. Taylor, San Francisco, January 15, 1907; Taylor to Mills, Fallon, NV, February 4, 1907 (copy also in box 18L, *TCID*); Mills to Cornish, San Francisco, March 4 and 22 and April 11 and 20, 1907; F. C. Radcliffe to Cornish, San Francisco, May 13, 1908; File 610, *SP-L.* Project managers, however, continued to follow their agreement

with Mills, and to survey, classify, and evaluate additional subdivisions of railroad land; none was freed for sale, however, pending Washington officials' approval of the agreement; Thomas Means, engineer, Truckee-Carson Project, to Radcliffe, Fallon, NV, September 28, 1907. Also, Means, *The Truckee-Carson Irrigation Project: A Letter of Information for Home Seekers* (Fallon, NV: U.S. Reclamation Service, November 1, 1907). Correspondence in *TCID* testifies to federal officials' confusion over the sale of railroad land. Compounding the problem was Mills's death, his replacement Radcliffe's failure to act with dispatch, and project engineer Taylor's replacement by Means, who knew little of what had transpired and had a predisposition against the railroad. Also, so many persons in the company and the government were involved in the approval of railroad price lists that no one knew the entire story or took responsibility for a resolution. The informal cooperation between Mills and Taylor no longer smoothed interagency work; see Frederick H. Newell to Means, Washington, DC, April 8 and May 20, 1908; Means to Newell, Fallon, NV, April 16, 1908; Newell to William D. Cornish, Washington, DC, April 25 and May 20, 1908; Means to E. T. Perkins (of the Reclamation Service), Fallon, April 29 and May 13, 1908; Perkins to Means, Yuma, AZ, May 6, 1908; Newell to Perkins, Washington, DC, May 20, 1908 (enclosing an important document, "Memorandum to E. T. Perkins," reviewing railroad-government communications about land prices and sales), box 18L.

35. William H. Mills to William D. Cornish, San Francisco, January 2, 1907, File 610, *SP-L*.

36. William H. Mills to William D. Cornish, San Francisco, April 20, 1907; also Mills to Cornish, April 23, 1907; File 610, *SP-L*. Cornish and company attorneys and lobbyists in Washington did discreetly attempt to change reclamation policy along the lines Mills suggested but were warned that the secretary of the interior would rebuff any attempt by the railroad to exert influence, openly or covertly; B. A. McAllaster to A. A. Hoehling, Jr., in Washington, DC, San Francisco, December 12, 1908, and Hoehling to McAllaster, Washington, DC, December 22, 1908.

37. William H. Mills to L. H. Taylor, San Francisco, January 15, 1907; Mills to Frederick H. Newell, director, U.S. Reclamation Service, Washington, DC, San Francisco, April 25, 1907; File 610, *SP-L*. The government's rejection of Mills's request that it defer settlers' payments for the first two years was delivered in L. H. Taylor to Mills, May 22, 1907, a few days after Mills died. The Department of the Interior's failure, or unwillingness, to acknowledge some of the economic and social realities and contradictions inherent in its programs, and which undermined the success of federal irrigation, was due in part, according to Donald J. Pisani, to "the personality and philosophy of Frederick Haynes Newell," the second and long-term director of the Bureau of Reclamation, who was devoted to traditional individualistic values, maintained that the farmers' failures were their own fault, "despised government paternalism," and was reluctant "to provide more assistance to the desert homemakers"; Pisani, "Reclamation and Social Engineering in the Progressive Era," *Agricultural History* 57 (January 1983): 46–63.

38. At the time, Southern Pacific land business itself was confused and halting, partly because of internal conflicts over land policy brought about by the Harriman Lines'

takeover of the company and mostly because the 1906 San Francisco earthquake and fire destroyed company records, including land maps and sales records, which took several years to reconstruct from files all over the country. The early 1900s dismissal of Jerome Madden, longtime land agent specifically for the Southern Pacific Railroad, and Mills's death in May 1907, aggravated the situation by interrupting institutional memory. Seemingly inept, F. C. Radcliffe, Mills's successor, was replaced in September 1908 by B. A. McAllaster. Transferring from the Union Pacific, McAllaster restored order and effectiveness to the department and remained as land agent until 1933; see J. L. Willcutt to F. C. Radcliffe, San Francisco, September 28, 1908, File 610, *SP-L*. For the 1906 catastrophe's effect on Southern Pacific land management in the Truckee-Carson Project, see also B. A. McAllaster to Thomas H. Means, San Francisco, October 18, 1909, box 18L, *TCID*.

39. For experimental farm, William H. Mills to William D. Cornish, San Francisco, March 4 and April 20 and 23, 1907; Mills to Frederick H. Newell, April 25, 1907; Mills to Morris Bien, May 7, 1907; F. C. Radcliffe to Cornish, San Francisco, November 20, 1907, and June 5 and July 6, 1908; Cornish to Radcliffe (telegram), New York City, May 28 and June 29, 1908; File 610, *SP-L*.

40. Frederick H. Newell to William D. Cornish, Washington, DC, May 20, 1908, box 18L, *TCID*.

41. For negotiations and the agreement, see comprehensive history of Southern Pacific relations with the U. S. Department of the Interior on the Truckee-Carson Project, in B. A. McAllaster to William F. Herrin, San Francisco, July 1, 1914, File 610, *SP-L*. Also, F. C. Radcliffe to William D. Cornish, San Francisco, November 20, 1907, May 13, 1908; Cornish to Radcliffe (telegrams), New York City, November 15, 1907, and May 28, 1908, and letter, June 11, 1908; Central Pacific Railway Company, "Resolutions Adopted by the Board of Directors, June 20, 1908" (typescript). See also McAllaster to Thomas H. Means, project engineer, Truckee-Carson Project, San Francisco, July 13, 1909; and Means to McAllaster, Fallon, NV, July 15, 1909; box 18L, *TCID*.

42. F. C. Radcliffe to William D. Cornish, San Francisco, July 6 and 25, 1908; B. A. McAllaster to William F. Herrin, San Francisco, July 1, 1914; File 610, *SP-L;* Radcliffe, *Railroad Land for Sale; Irrigable Lands within the Truckee-Carson Project in the State of Nevada for Sale by the Central Pacific Railway Company* (San Francisco: Land Department, August 21, 1908); *Government Lands in Nevada* (San Francisco: Passenger Department, Southern Pacific Company, 1908); Wells, *New Nevada*. Actually, although it had no land yet to sell, the railroad had been promoting the project for some time; *Uncle Sam's Nine Million Dollar Nevada Farm* (San Francisco: Southern Pacific Company, 1907).

43. Report on company lands in the Truckee-Carson Project in B. A. McAllaster to William Sproule, San Francisco, January 12, 1915, File 610, *SP-L*. Correspondence in box 18L, *TCID,* suggests a smooth relationship with the railroad through September 1910. On the project in 1908, Townley, *Turn This Water into Gold,* 36.

44. C. E. Wantland to Francis G. Newlands, July 25, 1911; Wantland to B. A. McAllaster, Denver, August 4, 1911; Newlands to Wantland, Washington, DC, July 29, 1911; "Memo for Mr. McAllaster" (September 5, 1911); File 436, *SP-L*.

45. Townley, *Turn This Water into Gold,* 49; B. A. McAllaster to William Sproule,

San Francisco, January 12, 1915, File 610, *SP-L;* see also many exchanges between McAllaster and reclamation officials, October 1, 1910 and subsequent dates, box 18L, *TCID; Los Angeles Times,* August 26, 1914. Some Southern Pacific promotional materials were even rewritten after 1910 to disclose the project's problems to prospective buyers; Wells, *Nevada,* 5, 8ff., and 33ff.

46. "Official Line-up, Newlands Irrigation Project" (1905–1921), Contents File, *TCID.*

47. For local and higher Reclamation Service officials' confusion and vacillation regarding earlier agreements with the railroad and price lists and their dependence on information from B. A. McAllaster and other railroad leaders, see McAllaster to D. W. Cole, Truckee-Carson project engineer, San Francisco, July 9, 1914; Cole to Project Manager, Truckee-Carson Project, Fallon, NV, August 3, 1914; W. A. Ryan, comptroller, U.S. Reclamation Service, Washington, DC, to C. J. Blanchard, Reclamation Service, Fallon, Washington, DC, August 14, 1915; Edward S. Taylor, counsel, U.S. Reclamation Commission, Portland, to Chief Counsel, U.S. Reclamation Service, Portland, Portland, February 2, 1916; R. M. Patrick, assistant district counsel, U.S. Reclamation Service, to McAllaster, February 13, 1919; box 18L, *TCID.* Dozens of similar exchanges illustrate the persistent problems of memory and communication, 1910–1919, in File 610, *SP-L.*

48. Frederick H. Newell to B. A. McAllaster, Washington, DC, August 21, 1914; McAllaster to W. A. Ryan, comptroller, U.S. Reclamation Service, San Francisco, September 3, 1914; File 610, *SP-L.* Also D. W. Cole to McAllaster, Fallon, NV, August 26, 1914; box 18L, *TCID.*

49. See B. A. McAllaster to F. G. Hough, project manager, U.S. Reclamation Service, Fallon, San Francisco, February 9, 1918; D. S. Sturmer, acting project manager, to McAllaster, Fallon, February 25, 1918; File 610, *SP-L;* also Frederick H. Newell to McAllaster, Washington, DC, August 21, 1914; McAllaster to W. A Ryan, comptroller, U.S. Reclamation Service, Washington, DC, San Francisco, September 30, 1914.

50. B. A. McAllaster to William F. Herrin, San Francisco, March 25, 1912, File 610, *SP-L.*

51. B. A. McAllaster to William Sproule, San Francisco, January 15, 1915; A. P. Davis, chairman, U.S. Reclamation Commission, to McAllaster, Washington, DC, July 26, 1915; McAllaster to William F. Herrin, San Francisco, December 18, 1915; McAllaster to O. P. Morton, district counsel, U.S. Reclamation Service in Portland, San Francisco, December 27, 1915; File 610, *SP-L.* And Edward S. Tyler, district counsel, U.S. Reclamation Commission in Portland, to McAllaster, Portland, May 20, 1916, box 18L, *TCID;* copies of these and many exchanges between railroad and reclamation officials, 1910–20, are in both Southern Pacific Land Company and the Irrigation District's records.

52. B. A. McAllaster to D. W. Cole, Truckee-Carson project manager, San Francisco, July 9, 1914 (copy also in box 18L, *TCID*), and telegram to Frederick H. Newell, August 18, 1914; "List of Lands for Sale by the Central Pacific Railway Company in the Truckee-Carson Project; Terms of Sale; Ten Years' Credit; 6% Interest" (Central Pacific Railway Land Department, ca. 1918); File 610, *SP-L.* For example, on a typical eighty-acre farm selling for $5 per acre, or a total of $400, the buyer paid only $40 down and no interest the first year, and only an interest payment of $21.70 at the end of each of the next nine years. At the end of the tenth year, the interest payment for that year

would be due, in addition to the remaining principal on the loan, $320. Actually, even if farmers on land for which the railroad held the mortgage could not make interest payments in a given year, or even the final balloon principal payment at the end of the contract, they generally did not have their land foreclosed and retaken by the company. Since the 1870s on its land grants, for distressed land-buyers who were honestly attempting to farm, the Southern Pacific waived annual interest payments or extended the terms of loans, in some cases indefinitely. The company's policy was to avoid foreclosure; see chapter 3.

53. Department of the Interior, "Public Notice: Newlands Project, formerly Truckee-Carson Project" (Washington, DC, April 23, 1919), copy in File 610, *SP-L*.

54. "List of Lands for Sale by the Central Pacific Railway Company in the Truckee-Carson Project; Terms of Sale; Ten Years' Credit; 6% Interest" (Central Pacific Railway, ca. 1918), File 610, *SP-L*.

55. B. A. McAllaster to F. G. Hough, Truckee-Carson project manager, San Francisco, February 9, 1918; C. S. Blanchard, statistician, U.S. Reclamation Service, to C. E. Wantland, Washington, DC, December 27, 1917, File 610, *SP-L*.

56. B. A. McAllaster to William Sproule, San Francisco, September 4, 1913, and to William F. Herrin, July 1, 1914, File 610, *SP-L*.

57. "Statement Showing Status of All Irrigable Lands to December 31, 1917," in "Annual History . . . Truckee-Carson Project" (1917), 112 and reverse, box 563, RG 115, *USBR*. From 1908, when railroad land was first authorized for sale, until fall 1910, when sales had to be halted, 2,140 acres were sold, and none between late 1910 and late 1914. By 1917, an additional 1,500 acres had been sold, for a total of about 3,600 acres; also B. A. McAllaster to William Sproule, San Francisco, January 12, 1915, File 610, *SP-L*.

58. B. A. McAllaster to Project Manager, Truckee-Carson Project, San Francisco, November 2, 1918; John F. Richardson, project manager, to McAllaster, Fallon, NV, November 6, 1918; D. S. Stuver, acting project manager, to McAllaster, Fallon, November 16, 1918; Central Pacific Land Department, "Abstract from the Report of the Secretary of the Interior for the Year Ending June 30, 1918, Page 97" (ms., 1918); Stuver to McAllaster, Fallon, April 5 and May 10, 1919; File 610, *SP-L*. Copies of most of these documents, as well as others similar, are in box 18L, *TCID;* there, see also McAllaster to Stuver, San Francisco, April 19, 1918; Stuver to McAllaster, Fallon, April 25, 1918; Richardson to McAllaster, Fallon, May 27, 1918.

59. D. S. Stuver, acting project manager, to B. A. McAllaster, Fallon, NV, May 10, 1919, File 610, *SP-L;* McAllaster to Stuver, June 4, 1919, box 18L, *TCID*, copy in File 610, *SP-L*.

60. D. S. Stuver to B. A. McAllaster, Fallon, NV, June 10, 1919; McAllaster to Stuver, San Francisco, June 13, 1919; John F. Richardson, project manager, to McAllaster, Fallon, July 1 and 24, 1919; McAllaster to Richardson, San Francisco, July 3 and 30, 1919; copies in File 610, *SP-L*, and box 18L, *TCID*. Characteristically, behind the scenes, officials at the Truckee-Carson Project had again lost their records on their agreements with the railroad and had no idea what the specific terms were. They had to ask higher Interior authorities for information and guidance; Richardson to Project Manager, Truckee-Carson Project, Fallon, July 1, 1919, box 18L, *TCID*.

61. B. A. McAllaster to John F. Richardson, San Francisco, February 20, 1920; File 610, *SP-L.*

62. "Price List, Central Pacific Railway Lands in Truckee-Carson Project" (ms., October 15, 1919); B. A. McAllaster to William F. Herrin, San Francisco, July 19, 1920, and March 29, 1924; John F. Richardson to McAllaster, Fallon, February 11, 1920; McAllaster to Richardson, February 20 and September 28, 1920; Richardson to McAllaster, Fallon, February 20 and April 25, 1922; McAllaster to Richardson, San Francisco, February 11 and April 22, 1922; File 610, *SP-L;* copies of most of above, box 18L, *TCID.*

63. Although the railroad no longer cooperated with the government in land sales, after 1919 it did support expansion of the project's facilities and provide large additional tracts of land at low prices for planned reservoir and other sites, such as the proposed, but expensive and never built, Spanish Springs reservoir: John F. Richardson, project manager, to B. A. McAllaster, Fallon, February 18 and 25 and March 8, 1921, May 23 and June 13, 1923, and February 8, 1924; McAllaster to Richardson, San Francisco, February 24 and March 19, 1921, and June 7, 1923; Brooks Fullerton, counsel, U.S. Reclamation Service, to McAllaster, San Francisco, September 16, 1921, and March 1 and July 15, 1922; McAllaster to Fullerton, San Francisco, February 9, 1922; also letters among Elwood Mead, commissioner of the U.S. Bureau of Reclamation, Paul Shoup, vice president, Southern Pacific Company, McAllaster, and other company and federal officials re. Spanish Springs reservoir, 1924–1926; File 610, *SP-L.*

64. Sessions S. Wheeler, with William W. Bliss, *Tahoe Heritage: The Bliss Family of Glenbrook, Nevada* (Reno: University of Nevada Press, 1992), esp. 53ff. for the building and operation of the Lake Tahoe Railroad; also, Owen F. McKeon, *The Railroads and Steamers of Lake Tahoe* (South Lake Tahoe, CA: Lake Tahoe Historical Society, 1984), 8–22; David F. Myrick, *Railroads of Nevada and Eastern California,* 2 vols. (Berkeley: Howell-North Books, 1962–63), 1:430–36.

65. For Lake Tahoe national park and national forest, see chapter 13.

66. Townley, *Turn This Water into Gold,* 47–52; Pisani, "Conflict over Conservation." The Reclamation Service announced its intentions to appropriate the lake's waters in a notice of its water rights issued in May 1903: L. H. Taylor, for the secretary of the interior, "Loc. Water Right, United States" (May 21, 1903), copy in William W. Bliss Records, Special Collections, University of Nevada, Reno, Library, box 10, folder 370. The Service in the early 1900s concluded that, unless Lake Tahoe could be used as a reservoir, water shortages could occur in any year in the project, and for that reason, as early as 1908, the Service contemplated halting the subdivision and sale of additional land until it could control the lake's water; Thomas R. Means, project engineer, to D. C. Henney, supervising engineer, Fallon, NV, October 16, 1908, Entry 3, Project Files, box 676, 1–11, *USBR.*

67. When the Tahoe reservoir would be drawn down, some property, particularly all the shoreline around Emerald Bay, would be permanently cut off from the lake. In the absence of roads, water transportation was the only means of travel around the lake. Illustrating what would happen is a photograph of the hundreds-of-yards-wide ring of muck and boulders around the lake in 1924, when during a drought the U.S. Reclamation Service pumped water over the dam to serve downstream irrigators; Edward B.

Scott, *The Saga of Lake Tahoe,* 2 vols. (Pebble Beach, CA: Sierra-Tahoe Publishing Co., 1957 and 1973), 2:239 and 241.

68. California newspapers and state officials particularly denounced the environmental effects of the plan and made constant attempts to turn public opinion against it and to stop it in Congress and the courts. For an artist's rendition of how unattractive the lake would look after becoming a reservoir, see *San Francisco Bulletin,* July 29, 1920. See also, *The Argonaut* (San Francisco), March 20, 1920. California sued in 1912 to establish state ownership of lands under Lake Tahoe below the high-water mark and to remove the dam across the lake's outlet into the Truckee River (*People of California v. Truckee River General Electric Co.*). The case was moved from California to federal courts and dragged into the 1930s, clouding the future of the lake and the Reclamation Service's reservoir plan; "Newlands Project History, vol. 18, 1927," Entry 10, box 382, 19–23, *USBR.*

69. The environmental and economic arguments for and against the Reclamation Service's turning Lake Tahoe into a reservoir, including the views of the Southern Pacific, the Lake Tahoe Railway and Transportation Company, and its owners, the Bliss family, are illustrated in documents in boxes 14 and 16, *TCID.* The Lake Tahoe Railway's objections were set forth in successful litigation it instituted in 1905 to obtain a Placer County (CA) superior court injunction prohibiting the Reclamation Service from building its dam and sending more water down the Truckee River; Lake Tahoe Property owners to Secretary of Interior Ethan Hitchcock, San Francisco, June 16, 1905, and various court papers for *Lake Tahoe Railway and Transportation Company versus Edward Malley, et al.,* box 1, folder 61, William W. Bliss Records, University of Nevada, Reno. Environmental problems caused by water diversion along the Truckee River between Lake Tahoe and Pyramid Lake are depicted in impressionistic essays and photographs in Robert Dawson, Peter Goin, and Mary Webb, *A Doubtful River* (Reno: University of Nevada Press, 2000).

70. For the Lake Tahoe controversy, Douglass Strong, *Tahoe: An Environmental History* (Lincoln: University of Nebraska Press, 1984), 98–106; Townley, *Turn This Water into Gold,* 47–53 and 113–17; George and Bliss Hinkle, *Sierra Nevada Lakes* (Indianapolis: Bobbs-Merrill, 1949), 337ff.; Simonds, "Newlands Project," esp. 3–11.

71. For opposition from the U.S. Attorney General, see Ottamar Hamele, acting chief counsel, "Opinion of Acting Chief Counsel, U.S. Reclamation Service, in Reply to Confidential Memorandum dated October 20, 1919, from the Department of Justice Relative to the Use of Lake Tahoe Water as a Storage Reservoir for the Newlands Irrigation Project, Nevada" (typescript, marked "Confidential, Not for Public Inspection," October 28, 1919), and J. F. Truesdell and George A. H. Fraser, Department of Justice, "Confidential Memorandum . . . and General Consideration of Urgent Lake Tahoe Problems" (typescript, Washington, DC, July 7, 1920), box 14, *TCID.* The Department of Justice went as far as to advise the Reclamation Service that, despite its 1915 purchase of the dam, even its current modest regulation of the lake's level was indefensible in court. The Service had "no right at present to use the lake as a storage reservoir as against the state of California," and the Department of Justice advised no further litigation of the Service's "untenable" position. For opposition from other

officials, see secretary of war Newton D. Baker to John B. Payne, secretary of the interior, Washington, May 13, 1920, box 14; on the Army Corps of Engineers, *Sacramento Bee,* June 2, 1920; for the state of California's vehement official opposition, Ottamar Hamele, acting chief counsel, U.S. Reclamation Service, to District Counsel Burr in San Francisco, Washington, undated but April 1920, box 14. Conflict with the Army Corps of Engineers, stemming from the Corps's mission of protecting the navigability of Lake Tahoe, was reviewed in John F. Truesdell, Reclamation Service counsel, to F. E. Weymouth, chief of construction, U.S. Reclamation Service, Los Angeles, May 13, 1919, Entry 3, Project Files, box 677, 1–11, *USBR.* For complex interplay of competing ideologies and interests plaguing the Reclamation Service's Tahoe reservoir plan, including opposition from other federal agencies, particularly the Forest Service, see Pisani, "Conflict over Conservation," esp. 173ff. Pisani's *To Reclaim a Divided West,* esp. 333–36, demonstrates that such conflicts over water policy, including among contending regions, interests, and even federal agencies themselves, were endemic in public irrigation.

72. "Newlands Project History, vol. 18, 1927," 19–23, Entry 10, RG 115, *USBR.* The legal and other problems emanating from the proposed takeover of Lake Tahoe, particularly conflicts with the state of California, were reviewed in a report by supervising engineer Morris Bien, "Memorandum for the Director, U.S. Reclamation Service, April 22, 1911" (typescript), Entry 3, Project Files, box 676, 1–11; see also "Copy of Memorandum Concerning Lake Tahoe" (ca. 1911), box 676, 1–11; and "Memorandum of Principal Correspondence Relative to Securing Control of Lake Tahoe Outlet and Associated Documents" (n.d.) and John F. Truesdell, Reclamation Service counsel, "Memorandum re. Lake Tahoe Situation, August 1, 1918: Physical Situation; What the U.S. Wants; Legal Rights" (ca. 1918), box 677, 1–11; and other documents in boxes 677–83, esp. "Claims of the State of California to Waters of Lake Tahoe thru April 1914," box 681, 1–1113, and "Claim of State of California to Waters of Nevada," Entry 7, Project Files, Administration through 1929, box 790, 435.04. Protests of Lake Tahoe property owners, led by the Lake Tahoe Protective Association, are in Entry 3, Project Files, box 682, 1–1114, 1–1115 (esp. letters from California congressman, conservationist, and Lake Tahoe property-owner William Kent), and 1–1122, and in box 683, 1–1122, and in box 791.

73. John F. Richardson, Truckee-Carson project manager, to George A. H. Fraser, special assistant to the U.S. Attorney General, Fallon, NV, October 20, 1919, box 14, *TCID.* The Reclamation Service's determination to continue pressing to get control of Lake Tahoe, even in the face of powerful government opposition and its own shaky legal position, is clear from many other documents in 1919 and 1920 in boxes 14 and 15. The rationale and protest activities of the opponents, particularly the Bliss family interests, are documented in many letters, scientific studies, reports, and legal papers, stretching from the early 1900s into the 1930s, in the William W. Bliss Records, University of Nevada, Reno, particularly the 1905 lawsuit documents in box 1, folder 61, as well as in papers in box 3, folder 213, box 4, folder 227, and esp. in boxes 10 and 11, folder 370. *USBR* also contains abundant evidence of the protests, particularly of Tahoe shoreline owners led by the Bliss family, and the resultant meetings, conferences with

opponents, and lawsuits; see especially the various annual project histories after 1908 of the Truckee-Carson (Newlands) Project, Entry 10, boxes 561–63 and 380–82, esp. "Annual Project History . . . Truckee-Carson Project, 1918," 206–17, and "Annual Project History . . . Newlands Project, 1921," 175–81.

74. Truesdell, "Memorandum re. Lake Tahoe Situation, August 1, 1918."

75. Truckee-Carson project director John Richardson put it this way: the government should "proceed with the work of channel excavation until stopped by injunction and then fight the matter out in the courts"; Richardson to the Director of the U.S. Reclamation Service, Fallon, NV, September 1, 1920, and other documents, box 14, *TCID*. For the project's plans to take over lakeshore property, see James Munn and J. F. Richardson, "Estimate of Cost of Securing Right of Way Around Lake Tahoe for Regulation of the Lake for Storage Purposes" (typescript, marked "Confidential, Not for Public Inspection," October 1919), box 14. The Service also planned and began to make "improvements" to the Truckee River below Lake Tahoe in anticipation of the eventual removal of the Lake Tahoe railroad and other obstacles "to provide for full utilization of Lake Tahoe"; "Annual Project History . . . Newlands Project, 1920," Entry 10, box 381, 50, *USBR*.

76. Townley, *Turn This Water into Gold,* 47–52; Hinkle and Hinkle, *Sierra-Nevada Lakes,* 336–45; Strong, *Tahoe: An Environmental History,* 98–106; Pisani, "Conflict over Conservation," passim. For the Bliss family's role, including incidents of vigilantism, see Wheeler and Bliss, *Tahoe Heritage,* 87–93. For a contemporary review of events from the government's perspective, U.S. Reclamation Service, "Statement of Facts Regarding Lake Tahoe and the Reclamation Service" (typescript, July 30, 1930), box 16G, *TCID*. Also W. Turrentine Jackson and Donald Pisani, *Lake Tahoe Water: A Chronicle of Conflict Affecting the Environment, 1863–1939* (Davis: University of California, Institute of Governmental Affairs, 1972).

77. The rationale of the Southern Pacific and Lake Tahoe Railway is illustrated in documents in boxes 16 and 16H, *TCID;* see C. T. Bliss, vice president and general manager, Lake Tahoe Railway, to John H. Richardson, Truckee-Carson project manager, San Francisco, February 18, 1919; Richardson to the Commissioner, U.S. Reclamation Service, Fallon, NV, August 12 and October 24, 1925; Richardson to E. J. Foulds, attorney, Southern Pacific Company, Fallon, NV, October 24, 1925. Also, Richardson to Chief of Construction, U.S. Reclamation Service in Denver, Fallon, NV, August 12, 1919; C. T. Bliss to secretary of interior Franklin K. Lane, San Francisco, November 20, 1919; and John F. Truesdell, Reclamation Service counsel, to F. E. Weymouth, U.S. Reclamation Service in Denver, Denver, November 29, 1919; box 14; also *Reno Gazette,* August 7, 1919, and *The Argonaut* (San Francisco), March 20, 1919.

78. Title abstracts document the Central Pacific Railroad's ownership of the Donner Lumber and Boom Company, which built and operated the Lake Tahoe dam, and that across Donner Creek at its outlet from Donner Lake, 1870s to early 1900s, when the railroad sold the dams to Reno's power company, the Truckee River General Electric Company; Entry 3, Project Files, box 676, 1–11, *USBR*.

79. For the railroad's opposition to the Tahoe reservoir idea, see documents in File 610D, *SP-L,* esp. for above references, B. A. McAllaster to John F. Richardson, San Fran-

cisco, July 30, 1919, and Richardson to McAllaster, August 13, 1919; copies in box 18L, *TCID*. The quoted irrigation official was Edmund Dietz in a letter to McAllaster, Northam, NV, August 9, 1919, box 18L.

80. Consulting engineer D. C. Henny and engineer J. F. Richardson to Chief of Construction, Bureau of Reclamation, Reno, NV, February 4, 1920, Entry 7, box 791, 435.07, *USBR*. From the early 1900s through the 1920s, reclamation officials, in internal communications, routinely assumed they would acquire all the water they could use from the lake. In counsel John Truesdell's words, for example, the government sought to "enlarge the [Truckee] river channel so that it can . . . draw from the Lake and transport to the Truckee Canal as much water as it wants to use on the project" and to elevate the dam to "have such control of the Lake when it rises at the time of high water, as to be sure to fill the Lake to the point determined upon, and not overfill it"; Truesdell, "Memorandum re. Lake Tahoe Situation, August 1, 1918."

81. See B. A. McAllaster's long review of the railroad's involvement in the controversy, to William F. Herrin, San Francisco, October 29, 1919, File 610D, *SP-L*. The Service clearly was seeking enormous quantities of Lake Tahoe and Truckee River water, far more than it was willing to admit publicly. Its original 1903 announcement of its water right, for example, asserted its right to *all* of the unappropriated flow of the Truckee River and announced its intention to raise the outlet dam to a height of twenty feet (it was then only about eight feet), and to deepen the channel leading to the dam (and hence to cut the lake's rim) to a depth of twenty feet, and to send as much as 3,000 second-feet of water down the river for irrigation purposes. Thus, in effect, the Reclamation Service's proposed dam would impound up to *forty feet* of the lake's depth and send a devastating tide of water down the river, triple its natural flood threshold. The Tahoe Railway's studies showed that even 1,000 second-feet caused severe flooding and damage to its bridges and roadbed. See Taylor, "Loc. Water Right, United States."

82. Illustrating the close association of the company and the Bliss interests, for example, the headquarters of the Lake Tahoe Railway were in the San Francisco's Southern Pacific building. B. A. McAllaster and other company leaders were in frequent communication with the Blisses about the Lake Tahoe matter and other mutual resort, tourism, and railroad concerns. It is possible, perhaps even likely, that the Southern Pacific had furnished capital to build and operate the struggling narrow-gauge line and had some influence over its policies, as was the case with some other ostensibly independent feeder lines. From the Tahoe line's inception, the Southern Pacific did grant it privileges that amounted to financial subsidies. When the Bliss family built its Tahoe Tavern Hotel in Tahoe City in 1901, the Pacific Improvement Company, the Southern Pacific's land-development subsidiary, furnished the Blisses a large tract of lakeshore land for a token payment. The Southern Pacific routinely gave leases to the Lake Tahoe Railway, again for token payments, for locomotives, rolling stock, and construction and operations equipment, as well as substantial land, trackage, a depot, and freight storage and office buildings adjacent to the Southern Pacific depot at Truckee; in one of many such leases, for example, a narrow-gauge locomotive, a baggage car, and three coaches cost the Lake Tahoe line only $10 per year, while *all* the tracks and buildings at Truckee cost a total of only $5 per annum. See Deed and Agreement for Sale of Prop-

erty by the Pacific Improvement Company to the Lake Tahoe Railway and Transportation Company, 1901 and 1902, William W. Bliss Records, box 1, folder 37, and
Leases with Southern Pacific Company for Rolling Stock, Use of Track Facilities at
Truckee, and the Use of a Crane and Coal Bucket, 1910–1913, box 1, folders 48–50, University of Nevada, Reno. Numerous documents in File 610D, including McAllaster's
October 29, 1919, report to William F. Herrin, *SP-L,* testify to the railroad's ongoing
opposition to the Tahoe reservoir plan.

83. John F. Richardson to B. A. McAllaster, Fallon, NV, August 13, 1919, box 18L,
TCID.

84. Truckee-Carson project manager John F. Richardson told his bosses: "Chiefly
through the opposition of Mr. W. S. Bliss and his friends and associates our efforts have
been futile and uncertainty still darkens every hope of an early and favorable settlement."
Because of the railroads' power Richardson recommended in that letter a temporary halt
in the quest for control of Lake Tahoe, but his superiors rejected his advice and ordered
him to keep pressing for condemnation suits; Richardson to Chief of Construction, U.S.
Reclamation Service in Denver, Fallon, NV, November 29, 1919, box 18L, *TCID.*

85. Myrick, *Railroads of Nevada and Eastern California,* 1:430–36.

86. For a 1904 photograph of precarious end-of-the-line conditions, Tahoe World
and Sierra Sun, *The Truckee & North Lake Tahoe Historic Picture Album* (Portland, OR:
Piedmont Publishing, 1998), 78; for other photos, Scott, *Saga of Lake Tahoe,* 1:37, 49,
and 55, and 2:219, 247, and 279.

87. See John F. Truesdell to F. E. Weymouth, chief of construction, U.S. Reclamation Service, Denver, August 7, 1919, box 14, *TCID.* The Department of Justice, on the
other hand, doubted that the Lake Tahoe Railway would bow to the Service's pressure
to relocate its line voluntarily at its own expense and warned that the line would stay
in place and that the Service would one day be liable for extensive flood damage.

88. R. M. Patrick, district counsel, to Chief Counsel, Bureau of Reclamation, Fallon, NV, December 20, 1918, Entry 3, box 682, 1–116, *USBR.* Documents pertaining
to the Service's rationales and strategies re the Lake Tahoe Railroad are in Entry 3, box
182, 1–1116, "Negotiations with the Lake Tahoe Railway Co. for Purchase of Lands and
Raising of Tracks, Bridges, etc.," esp. L. H. Taylor, supervising engineer, to Director,
Reclamation Service, Fallon, NV, July 5, 1907; F. Weymouth, chief of construction, to
Director and Chief Engineer, Reclamation Service, Klamath Falls, Oregon, October 6,
1916; A. P. Davis, director and chief engineer, to Lake Tahoe Railway and Transportation Co., Fallon, NV, April 29, 1917, and Davis to John F. Truesdell, Fallon, February
14, 1917; C. T. Bliss, vice president and general manager, Lake Tahoe Railway, to Davis,
Tahoe, California, May 16, 1917, and to secretary of interior Franklin K. Lane, San Francisco, November 20, 1919; W. S. Bliss to Elmwood Mead, commissioner of reclamation, San Francisco, February 3 and 24, 1925.

89. Boxes 14 and 16 of *TCID* contain numerous documents illustrating the Reclamation Service's concentration on the Lake Tahoe Railway as the major obstacle; see
John F. Richardson to the chief of construction of the Reclamation Service in Denver,
Fallon, NV, November 29, 1919, box 14. On the Bliss family's commitment to preserving
the region, Wheeler and Bliss, *Tahoe Heritage,* passim. Documents in *USBR* also illus-

trate the railroad-government conflict, esp. in Entry 3, box 682, 1–116; see R. M. Patrick to Chief Counsel, Fallon, NV, December 20, 1918; Chief of Construction to Director, "Report of changes in Lake Tahoe Railway and Transportation Company Railroad below Lake Tahoe outlet—Truckee-Carson Project, Nevada," December 24, 1918; engineer James Munn and project manager John F. Richardson to Chief of Construction, Fallon, NV, December 19, 1918; R. M. Patrick, "Memorandum for Files" (Fallon, NV, January 25, 1919), a long, telling account of a series of contentious meetings between railroad and reclamation leaders, during which both sides frankly expressed their opposing views toward Lake Tahoe and the Truckee River; and C. T. Bliss to John F. Richardson, San Francisco, February 18, 1919, with attached copy of Resolution Passed by the Lake Tahoe Railway Board of Directors, January 20, 1919. The board announced its categorical opposition to "any agreement" with the government because, among other objections, such agreement "would be on the basis of permitting the Reclamation Service cutting the natural rim of Lake Tahoe."

90. "Annual Report . . . Newlands Project" (1925), 8–9, RG 115, box 382, *USBR.*

91. Wheeler and Bliss, *Tahoe Heritage,* 98–99, say that the Blisses approached the Southern Pacific with the proposal, and that may have happened. Another account implies that both parties contributed to formulating the plan; McKeon, *Railroads and Steamers of Lake Tahoe,* 18–19. In any case, the larger railroad quickly carried out the action.

92. Hubert Work, secretary of interior, to C. T. Bliss, Washington, DC, August 29, 1925, and Bliss to Work, Tahoe, California, September 4, 1925, William W. Bliss Records, box 11, folder 370, University of Nevada, Reno.

93. For conversion to standard gauge: McKeon, *Railroads and Steamers of Lake Tahoe,* 18–19; Wheeler and Bliss, *Tahoe Heritage,* 98–99; Myrick, *Railroads of Nevada and Eastern California,* 1:430–36; for a photograph, Scott, *Saga of Lake Tahoe,* 2:222. The Southern Pacific operated the railroad until 1942, when automobile competition and declining rail traffic during World War II brought about its closure. For additional information on the Lake Tahoe Railroad's history, see documents in the Lake Tahoe Railroad Collection, *CRRM.*

94. "Annual Project History . . . Newlands Project" (1926), 1ff., 6–7, Entry 10, box 382, *USBR;* also "Lease—U.S. of America to Lake Tahoe Company" (October 19, 1926); Elwood Mead, commissioner, U.S. Bureau of Reclamation, to the Secretary of the Interior, Washington, DC, November 6, 1926, and "Lease—U.S. of America to the Lake Tahoe Company . . . " (October 19, 1926), Entry 7, Project Files through 1929, box 763, 223.01; Mead to Secretary of the Interior, Washington, DC, January 15, 1927, Entry 7, box 791, 435.07; Mead to Ray T. Baker, Washington, DC, January 7, 1926, and L. V. Pinger, secretary, Truckee-Carson Irrigation District, to Mead, telegram, Fallon, NV, February 12, 1926, box 764, 223.01; *Fallon Standard* (Nevada), October 20, 1926.

95. In 1934, the Nevada irrigators did make another half-hearted attempt at breaking the lake's rim, though it is not known if the Reclamation Service played any direct role. The incident is famous in Tahoe lore. Crews and steam shovels Nevadans sent secretly to dredge the outlet channel were detected by the Bliss family and other Tahoe City residents and stalled by civil disobedience and vigilantism until a sheriff arrived with an injunction; Wheeler and Bliss, *Tahoe Heritage,* 89–91.

11 Scientific Agriculture

The phrase in the chapter title, "Evangel Train," was University of California president Benjamin Ide Wheeler's name for the agricultural demonstration trains jointly operated by the university and the Southern Pacific.

1. Composite description of a California demonstration train visit, from Warren T. Clarke, "The Agricultural and Horticultural Demonstration Train," *Pacific Rural Press,* January 14, 1911, and "Sending the College to the Farmer—How the Demonstration Train Delivers Knowledge in Car-Load Lots," *Sunset* 30 (April 1913): 383–89; *The University of California Chronicle* 11 (April 1909): 186–87, 14 (January 1912): 111, and 15 (April 1913): 292; O. E. Bremner, "Humors of the Demonstration Train," *Third Biennial Report of the Commissioner of Horticulture of the State of California for 1907–1908* (Sacramento: State Printer, 1909), 126–29; *Sacramento Bee,* December 12, 1908; *Sacramento Union,* November 17 and 18, 1908; *San Jose Herald,* May 23, 1909; *Woodland Democrat,* November 9, 1910; *Pacific Rural Press,* March 27, 1909; *San Francisco Call,* February 9, 1909; "An Agricultural College on Wheels," *Riverside Press,* March 12 and 16, 1909; and *California Cultivator,* March 18 and June 3, 1909, and March 3, 1910.

2. For other regions, Roy V. Scott, *The Reluctant Farmer: The Rise of Agricultural Extension to 1914* (Urbana: University of Illinois Press, 1970), 176–83, *Railroad Development Programs in the Twentieth Century* (Ames: Iowa State University Press, 1985), 39–44 and 93, and "Railroads and Farmers: Educational Trains in Missouri, 1902–1914," *Agricultural History* 36 (January 1962): 3–15; Jacob A. Swisher, "The Corn Gospel Trains," *The Palimpsest* 28 (November 1947): 321–33; John Hamilton, *The Transportation Companies as Factors in Agricultural Extension,* U.S. Department of Agriculture, Office of Experiment Stations, Circular 112 (Washington, DC: Government Printing Office, 1911), 3, 6–14; Chu Chang Liang, *Industrial and Agricultural Development Departments of American Railroads* (Peiping, China, 1933), 107–15 and 153.

3. For farmers' opposition to agricultural colleges and scientific agriculture, Scott, *Reluctant Farmer,* 1–103; Charles E. Rosenberg, "Science, Technology, and Economic Growth: The Case of the Agricultural Experiment Station Scientist, 1875–1914," *Agricultural History* 45 (January 1971): 1–20; Clayton S. Ellsworth, "Theodore Roosevelt's Country Life Commission," *Agricultural History* 34 (1960): 155–72; William L. Bowers, *The Country Life Movement in America, 1900–1920* (Port Washington, NY: Kennikat Press, 1974), 111ff.; Donald B. Marti, "The Purposes of Agricultural Education: Ideas and Projects in New York State, 1819–1865," *Agricultural History* 45 (October 1971): 271–83; Lawrence R. Veysey, *The Emergence of the American University* (Chicago: University of Chicago Press, 1965), 14–15; Richard S. Kirkendall, "The Agricultural Colleges: Between Tradition and Modernization," *Agricultural History* 60 (Spring 1986): 3–21; Alan I. Marcus, "The Ivory Silo: Farmer-Agricultural College Tensions in the 1870s and 1880s," *Agricultural History* 60 (Spring 1986): 22–36.

4. Railroads strongly supported universities and scientific agriculture; Scott, *Railroad Development Programs,* chaps. 1–3, esp. 36ff.

5. See chapter 2; and my "*The Octopus* Reconsidered: The Southern Pacific and Agri-

cultural Modernization in California, 1865–1915," *California Historical Quarterly* 54 (Fall 1975): 196–220.

6. *Sacramento Record-Union,* August 10, 1878.

7. For the university's history, Verne A. Stadtman, *The University of California, 1868–1968* (New York: McGraw-Hill, 1970); William Ferrier, *Origin and Development of the University of California* (Berkeley: Sather Gate Book Shop, 1930); Mary Lee Mayfield, "The University of California Agricultural Experiment Station, 1868–1924" (M.A. thesis, University of California, Davis, 1966); and Ann Foley Scheuring, with Chester O. McCorkle and James Lyons, *Science & Service: A History of the Land-Grant University and Agriculture in California* (Berkeley: Regents of the University of California, Division of Agriculture and Natural Resources, 1995).

8. Gerald D. Nash, *State Government and Economic Development: A History of Administrative Policies in California, 1849–1933* (Berkeley: Institute of Governmental Studies, 1964); Lawrence J. Jelinek, *Harvest Empire: A History of California Agriculture* (San Francisco: Boyd and Fraser Publishing, 1983); Richard B. Rice, William A. Bullough, and Richard J. Orsi, *The Elusive Eden: A New History of California,* 3rd ed. (New York: McGraw-Hill, 2002), 231–309; and Claude T. Hutchinson, *California Agriculture* (Berkeley: University of California Press, 1946).

9. See chapter 12; and Orsi, "*The Octopus* Reconsidered," passim.

10. See *Davis Enterprise,* January 30 and February 27, 1909; E. J. Wickson, "The University at Large in the State," *California Cultivator,* April 2, 1908, 379 and 407, and "Agricultural Education in California," *California Cultivator,* October 22, 1908, 391–92 and 401; *San Francisco Call,* editorial, February 13, 1909; Stadtman, *University of California,* 141–54; Mayfield, "Agricultural Experiment Station," 23–25 and 34–35.

11. *San Francisco Bulletin,* March 16 and April 12, 1877, January 19, 1880, and May 2, 1886; *Pacific Rural Press,* February 28, 1880 (including report on oranges, wine, brandy, and grain in the San Gabriel Valley, by H. V. Slosson, local station agent); *Sacramento Record-Union,* January 29, 1886; *San Francisco Post,* January 27 and 30 and February 5, 1886; *Southern Pacific Bulletin* 1 (December 31, 1913): 3, and 10 (February 1921): 29, and (May 1921): 30.

12. See survey reports, *Sacramento Record-Union,* January 29, 1886; and *San Francisco Post,* January 27 and 30 and February 5, 1886; *San Francisco Bulletin,* April 12, 1877.

13. "The Value of the Crop Report," *Southern Pacific Bulletin* 9 (July 1920): 27.

14. *San Francisco Bulletin,* January 25 and 30, 1878; unidentified clipping, 1878 newspaper, carton 6, "California Weather Clippings," Eugene W. Hilgard Papers, *BL;* John Corning (assistant general superintendent, Central Pacific Railroad) to George Davidson (U.S. Coast Survey), San Francisco, March 9 and 15, 1872, S. S. Montague (chief engineer, Central Pacific Railroad) to Davidson, San Francisco, August 12, 1872, January 29, 1873, January 23, 1874, December 30, 1878, January 16, 1879, and weekly from January 20 to May 17, 1879, B. B. Redding to Davidson, San Francisco, November 14, 1879, E. M. Johnstone (Passenger Department) to Davidson, January 3, March 1, and November 2, 1887, William F. Hood (chief engineer, Southern Pacific Company), to Davidson, February 2 and October 4, 1887, December 23, 1889, May 15 and October 20, 1890, January

3, 1895, and May 1, 1908, Davidson Collection, *BL;* University of California, College of Agriculture, Agricultural Experiment Station, *Report . . . 1895–1897* (Sacramento, 1898), 414; "A Railway Weather Bureau and Its Value to the Public," *Sunset* 1 (June 1898): 35; *Pacific Rural Press,* January 18, 1879, and January 1883. Hilgard of the University of California's College of Agriculture used the Southern Pacific's weather data back to the 1860s as the basis for his analysis of California's climates and their potentials for agriculture, published with the U.S. Census for 1880; Hilgard, *Report on the Physical and Agricultural Features of California . . . ,* U.S. Census Report, 10th Census, 1880, 6 (1883), 10–12.

15. B. B. Redding to George Davidson, November 13 and 15, 1877, Davidson Collection, *BL.*

16. Redding, "The Climate of California," *San Francisco Bulletin,* January 25, 1878.

17. Redding, "The Climate of California," in *Transactions of the California State Agricultural Society . . . 1877* (Sacramento, 1878), 123–40, and *San Francisco Bulletin,* January 25, 1878; reprinted, *The California Patron* (Grange), February 6, 1878; *Pacific Rural Press,* January 26, 1878; *Resources of California,* January, February 1887, December 1888.

18. *Southern Pacific Bulletin* 15 (May 1926): 13.

19. *Southern Pacific Bulletin* 2 (April 15, 1914): 1, 7 (February 1929): 14, and (March 1929): 4.

20. David Lavender, *The Great Persuader* [Collis P. Huntington] (Garden City, NY: Doubleday, 1970), 74, 109; *Sacramento Union,* April 10, 1862.

21. Collis P. Huntington to B. B. Redding, New York, March 29, May 5, and June 20, 1870; Huntington to Commissioner of Agriculture, Department of the Interior, New York, July 6, 1870; Alban N. Towne to Huntington, May 17 and June 10, 1870; *CPH.*

22. Lavender, *Great Persuader,* 426, discussing Huntington's letter to land agent William H. Mills, October 29, 1894, about introducing foreign crops into California. Regarding Huntington's shipment west of experimental coffee and date palm plants the railroad was giving to innovative California growers, E. R. Hewitt to Huntington, Los Angeles, May 29, 1880, *CPH;* and Huntington to Mills, November 12, 1894, *HEH.*

23. Norman E. Tutorow, *Leland Stanford: Man of Many Careers* (Menlo Park, CA: Pacific Coast Publishers, 1971), 160–99, and *The Governor: Life and Legacy of Leland Stanford,* 2 vols. (Spokane: Arthur H. Clark, 2004), chaps. 10–12; Joseph McConnell, "The Stanford Vina Ranch" (M.A. thesis, Stanford University, 1961); and Elizabeth Gregg, "History of Stanford Ranch," *Overland Monthly* 52 (October 1908).

24. Redding biography and bibliography, California Academy of Sciences, *In Memoriam: Benjamin B. Redding, Born January 17th, 1824, Died August 21st, 1882* (n.p., n.d.); obituaries in *Sacramento Record-Union,* August 22 and 25, 1882, and *Breeder and Sportsman,* September 2, 1882; Alonzo Phelps, *Contemporary Biography of California's Representative Men,* 2 vols. (San Francisco: A. L. Bancroft, 1882), 2: 77–83; Ella Sterling Mighels, *Story of the Files: A Review of California Writers and Literature* (San Francisco: Cooperative Printing Co., 1893), 253–55. In addition to those cited below, his agricultural writings include "Foothills of the Sierras," *Transactions of the California State Agricultural Society, 1878* (1879), 129–34, and *Resources of California,* January 6, 1878; "Sanitary Influence of Trees," *Resources of California,* February 1882; and "The Cost of Wheat

Production," *San Francisco Bulletin,* January 2, 1880. An authority on fish, Redding advised people on how to stock California waters with useful out-of-state species; Redding to R. W. Waterman, San Francisco, October 22, 1876, and January 3, April 28, November 17, and December 22, 1879, Waterman Family Papers, *BL.*

25. B. B. Redding, "Influence of Irrigation on Citrus Trees," *Pacific Rural Press,* August 16, 1879; *Pacific Rural Press,* February 7, 1880.

26. B. B. Redding, "Culture of the Olive in California," *San Francisco Bulletin,* March 6, 1878; "Oranges and Olives," *San Francisco Bulletin,* January 30, 1880; "The Olive in Tulare County," *Pacific Rural Press,* July 10, 1880, *Pacific Rural Press,* February 7, 1880; *San Francisco Bulletin,* March 3, 1880; Judith M. Taylor, *The Olive in California: History of an Immigrant Tree* (Berkeley, CA: Ten Speed Press, 2000), 80–82. Not all of his olive experiments were successful.

27. *Sacramento Record-Union,* September 26, 1890; Collis P. Huntington to William H. Mills, November 12, 1894, *HEH;* Mills to Norton P. Chipman (president, California State Board of Trade), November 20, 1906, and January 17 and 18, 1907, File 876, "California State Board of Trade—Miscellaneous Correspondence of William H. Mills," *SP-L;* Mills to W. D. Cornish, undated (ca. December 1906), enclosing unidentified clipping, December 8, 1906, Cornish Office Files, *SP-L.*

28. Barbara Richnak, *A River Flows: The Life of Robert Lardin Fulton* (Incline Village, NV: Comstock-Nevada Publishing Co., 1983), 83–84.

29. File 888, "Improved Winter Emmer for Dry Farming [1911–1913]," *SP-L,* esp. C. E. Wantland to Wyoming Plant and Seed Breeding Co., Denver, August 11, 1911; Wyoming Plant and Seed Breeding Co. to Wantland, Worland, Wyoming, July 29, 1911; B. C. Buffum (of the Wyoming Seed Co.) to B. A. McAllaster, Worland, August 16, 1911, and Buffum to Wantland, Worland, August 16, 1911; McAllaster to Buffum, San Francisco, August 24, 1911.

30. For rubber in California, File 763, "Guayule (A Rubber Plant)," *SP-L;* sugar beets in Arizona, "Resolution of the Arizona Eastern Railroad Company, Executive Committee, April 26, 1923" (typescript, 1923), File R195.72, *SP-PR;* rice in the Sacramento Valley, *Southern Pacific Bulletin* 3 (October 15, 1915): 6; alfalfa in Oregon, C. A. Malboeuf (district freight agent, Southern Pacific Company Oregon Lines) to J. R. Wyatt, Portland, September 23, 1907, John Knox Weatherford Papers, Southern Pacific Company Folder, Oregon Collection, University of Oregon, Eugene; milo maize and field peas in Oregon, *Portland Oregonian,* October 31, 1911, and *Livewire* (Pendleton, Oregon), October 31, 1911; for distributing new seed varieties of oats, barley, and wheat in Oregon, 1901, Scott, *Reluctant Farmer,* 175–76.

31. *Southern Pacific Bulletin* 10 (July 1921): 7, and 16 (July 1928): 15. Land agent William H. Mills arranged in 1890 for free transportation from New York for date palms being imported from Egypt by the U.S. Department of Agriculture for trial in California and Arizona; *Sacramento Record-Union,* September 26, 1890.

32. *Desert Barnacle* (Coachella), December 21, 1950; *Indio News,* May 15, 1980.

33. File 884, "Spineless Cactus," *SP-L;* esp. B. A. McAllaster to Luther Burbank, San Francisco, November 25, 1908, McAllaster to W. S. Sherlock, San Francisco, December 30, 1908, and McAllaster to Frederick S. Wythe, June 24, 1910, July 20, 1911, and

July 9 and 19 and October 8, 1912; Wythe to McAllaster, July 6, 1911, July 5 and 16, 1912; McAllaster to G. W. Luce, October 8, 1912; and Luce to McAllaster, September 26, 1912. See also Luther Burbank, *The New Agricultural Opuntias: Plant Creations for Arid Regions* (Santa Rosa, CA: Luther Burbank, June 1, 1907); Thornless Cactus Farming Company, *Burbank's Thornless Cactus, Fodder and Fruit* (Los Angeles: McBride Press, March 1909); *Pacific Rural Press,* December 26, 1908, p. 406.

34. Wooster, who had worked in modern orchards, described himself in his reminiscences as "a constant advocate of the planting of fruit trees." After taking his post in Auburn in the early 1870s, he helped farmers, particularly newly arrived settlers aboard Southern Pacific emigrant cars, to enter the orchard business. From his depot office, he advised about tree planting and care, the best fruit varieties for local climates, marketing potentials, and methods for shipping perishable fruit. In the 1870s, Wooster organized the first cooperative out-of-state marketing of fresh fruit; see chapter 12 and Wooster, "Railroading in the Seventies," *California Historical Society Quarterly* 38 (March 1939): 363–64.

35. Alban N. Towne to Collis P. Huntington, Sacramento, May 17, 1870; Huntington to Towne, New York, May 26, 1870; *CPH.*

36. *Sacramento Record-Union,* January 1, 1884, and *Tulare Register,* August 24, 1885; also chapters 8 and 14.

37. Robert LeRoy Santos, "The Eucalyptus of California," *Southern California Quarterly* 80 (Summer 1998): 125–26; also chapter 14.

38. *Southern Pacific Bulletin* 1 (December 10, 1913): 3.

39. *Los Angeles Times,* October 24, 1893; *San Francisco Bulletin,* June 15, 1887, and July 7, 1888; also chapter 8.

40. *Southern Pacific Bulletin* 3 (June 15, 1915): 5. One railroad demonstration was at Roseville, northeast of Sacramento, early 1900s. John Carson, in charge of a Southern Pacific water-pumping station at Roseville and impressed with increasing shipments of Imperial Valley cotton heading east along his line, experimented with cotton on company land around the Roseville water station, demonstrating that it could flourish in northern California. The railroad then distributed cotton seed to local growers; *Southern Pacific Bulletin* 1 (December 10, 1913): 2.

41. Frederick M. Maskew, *A Sketch of the Origin and Evolution of Quarantine Regulations* (Sacramento: California State Association of Horticultural Commissioners, 1925), 31ff.; California State Commission of Horticulture, *Horticultural Statutes with Court Decisions and Legal Opinions Relating Thereto . . . Corrected to February 1, 1912* (Sacramento: Superintendent of State Printing, 1912), passim; Nash, *State Government and Economic Development,* 147–51, 231–32. See *Sacramento Bee,* November 10, 1908, on how public opposition and low funds still paralyzed the state's quarantine system.

42. California Board of Horticulture, "Minutes" (ms., 1883–1902), 241ff., and "Minutes" (ms., 1912–1917), "Cabinet Meeting, May 15, 1915," California State Archives; Southern Pacific General Freight Department, *Circular No. G.D.F.97, Live Stock Quarantine* (San Francisco, October 11, 1898), Southern Pacific Collection, Oregon Historical Society, Portland; *Southern Pacific Bulletin* 2 (December 15, 1914): 6, and 10(January 1921): 29.

43. For Hilgard and scientific agriculture in California, Scheuring, *Science & Service,* chap. 2; Stadtman, *University of California,* 68–83 and 141–54; Ferrier, *Origin and Development of the University of California,* 369–72; Mayfield, "Agricultural Experiment Station," passim; Rosenberg, "Science, Technology, and Economic Growth," 11–12; Henry F. May, *Three Faces of Berkeley: Competing Ideologies in the Wheeler Era, 1899–1919* (Berkeley: Center for Studies in Higher Education and Institute of Governmental Studies, University of California, Berkeley, 1993), 38–40; Kent Watson and Peter S. Van Houten, *The University in the 1870s . . .* (Berkeley: Center for the Studies in Higher Education and Institute of Governmental Studies, University of California, Berkeley, 1996), 81–85.

44. For conflicts caused by the rise of large-scale businesses and other organizations, Robert Wiebe, *The Search for Order, 1877–1920* (New York: Hill and Wang, 1967); Samuel P. Hays, *The Response to Industrialism,* 2nd ed. (Chicago: University of Chicago Press, 1995).

45. Ward McAfee, *California's Railway Era, 1850–1911* (San Marino, CA: Golden West Books, 1973); Spencer C. Olin, Jr., *California Politics, 1846–1920: The Emerging Corporate State* (San Francisco: Boyd and Fraser Publishing Co., 1981) and *Prodigal Sons: Hiram Johnson and the Progressives, 1911–1917* (Berkeley: University of California Press, 1968); Richard Coke Lower, *A Bloc of One: The Political Career of Hiram W. Johnson* (Stanford: Stanford University Press, 1993). For more balanced treatments of anti-railroad politics, see R. Hal Williams, *The Democratic Party and California Politics, 1880–1996* (Stanford: Stanford University Press, 1973); William Deverell, *Railroad Crossings: Californians and the Railroad, 1850–1910* (Berkeley: University of California Press, 1994).

46. *Memorial of the California State Grange and Mechanics' Deliberative Assembly on the State University* (Sacramento: G. H. Springer, State Printer, 1874), 1–9; California Legislature, *Report of the Joint Committee . . . Appointed to Examine into Management of the University of California* (Sacramento: G. H. Springer, State Printer, 1874), 1–109; *Sacramento Record-Union,* May 12, 1875; *The California Patron* (Grange), July 20, 1878, January 18, 1879; *Orchard and Farm,* editorials, February and March 1909; *Town and Country Journal* (San Francisco), March 1, 1909, March 15, 1909, June 1, 1909; *California Cultivator* (Los Angeles), editorial, April 10, 1913; Scheuring, *Science & Service,* 11–19; Stadtman, *University of California,* 68–83; Ferrier, *Origin and Development of the University of California,* 355–64; Mayfield, "Agricultural Experiment Station," 12–22, 67–72; Veysey, *Emergence of the American University,* 14–15; Jane Apostol, "Jeanne Carr," *The American West* 15 (July/August 1978): 28–33, 62–63 (includes biographical information on husband Ezra); *Wisconsin Necrology* (State Historical Society of Wisconsin, Madison), 5:104 (Carr biography).

47. *California Cultivator,* April 10, 1913.

48. *Orchard and Farm,* editorial, February 1909. Also Wickson, "The University at Large in the State," 379 and 407, for a frank admission of popular opposition.

49. Mayfield, "Agricultural Experiment Station," 12–22; Wickson, "The University at Large in the State," 379, 407.

50. Ferrier, *Origin and Development of the University of California,* 519–21; Stadtman, *University of California,* 225, 252–53, 340; California Legislature, Special Legisla-

tive Commission on Agricultural Education, *Report* (Sacramento: State Printing Office, 1923), passim.

51. Close relationships between railways and agricultural colleges were common; see Chu Chang Liang, *Industrial and Agricultural Development Departments*, 96, 111, 128–90; Scott, *Reluctant Farmer*, 170–89.

52. University of California, College of Agriculture, Agricultural Experiment Station, *Report, 1895–1897* (Sacramento, 1898), 414.

53. Eugene W. Hilgard to B. B. Redding, November 3, 1879, Hilgard Papers, Letterpress Copy Books, vol. 1, and Hilgard to Redding, March 27, 1882, Letterpress Copy Books, vol. 7, *BL;* University of California, College of Agriculture, *Report, 1880* (1881), 71–72, and *Report, 1882* (1883), 120.

54. See Governor William Irwin's message to the legislature, *San Francisco Call,* December 7, 1877.

55. B. B. Redding to E. W. Hilgard, San Francisco, March 22, 1880, Hilgard Papers, *BL.*

56. Eugene W. Hilgard to B. B. Redding, Berkeley, January 26 and 29, 1880, Letterpress Copy Books, vol. 3, and March 20, 1880, Letterpress Copy Books, vol. 1; Hilgard to Francis A. Walker (superintendent of the census), Berkeley, February 21 and April 3, 1880, Letterpress Copy Books, vol. 3; Hilgard to N. J. Willson, Berkeley, February 27, 1880, Letterpress Copy Books, vol. 3; and Hilgard to Charles B. Turrill, September 12, 1882, Letterpress Copy Books, vol. 7, all in Hilgard Papers, *BL.* See also *San Francisco Call,* December 7, 1877; *San Francisco Bulletin,* February 23, 1880; *Kern County Gazette* (undated clipping, ca. March or April 1880), carton 6, "Soils File," Hilgard Papers, *BL.*

57. Hilgard, *Report on Physical and Agricultural Features of California,* passim, particularly vii–viii, 10–12, 87–125; University of California, College of Agriculture, *Report of the Professor in Charge to the Board of Regents . . . 1880* (Sacramento: Superintendent of State Printing, 1881), 5; Eugene W. Hilgard, *Report of the Experiment Station . . . 1888 and 1889* (1890), 38; Stadtman, *University of California,* 146.

58. Eugene W. Hilgard to Charles B. Turrill, September 12 and 25, 1882, Letterpress Copy Books, vol. 7, Hilgard Papers, *BL.*

59. B. B. Redding to E. W. Hilgard, San Francisco, March 22, 1880, Hilgard Papers, *BL.*

60. Eugene W. Hilgard to B. B. Redding, March 20, 1880, Letterpress Copy Books, vol. 1; June 1 and August 3, 1880, Letterpress Copy Books, vol. 5; Hilgard to R. E. C. Stearns, June 14, 1880, Letterpress Copy Books, vol. 5; and Hilgard to C. A. Wetmore, August 4 and 31, 1880, Letterpress Copy Books, vol. 5, all in Hilgard Papers, *BL.*

61. For Mills's sponsorship of date palm experiments by the universities of California and Arizona, *Sacramento Record-Union,* September 26, 1890. In 1913, B. A. McAllaster worked with Benjamin Ide Wheeler, university president, and Dean Thomas F. Hunt to further the College of Agriculture's experiments in dry-farming and irrigation in northeastern California; McAllaster to Wheeler, San Francisco, April 13, 1913; McAllaster to Hunt, San Francisco, May 7 and July 9, 1913; and Hunt to McAllaster, Berkeley, May 3, July 11, and August 8, 1913, College of Agriculture, Correspondence and Papers, box 12, University of California Archives, *BL.* Charles Frederick Crocker, vice president of the Southern Pacific and son of founder Charles Crocker, was a university regent and

patron of scientific research, particularly astronomy; "Charles Frederick Crocker," *Overland Monthly* 30 (August 1897): 184.

62. Benjamin Ide Wheeler to James Horsburgh, Berkeley, April 4 and 25 and July 12 and 26, 1905, Horsburgh to Wheeler, San Francisco, May 9, 13, and 27, 1902, April 27, 1904, April 25, May 2 and 3 and July 12 and 26, 1905, E. J. Wickson to Horsburgh, Berkeley, July 16, 1906, and November 12, 1907, Papers of the President of the University of California, University of California Archives, *BL;* H. A. Jones (freight traffic manager, Southern Pacific Company) to Ralph P. Merritt (secretary to the president, University of California), October 6, 1909, John Campbell Merriam Correspondence and Papers, *BL;* Thomas H. Hunt to W. M. Merz, Berkeley, January 18, 1916, College of Agriculture, Correspondence and Papers, University of California Archives; University of California, College of Agriculture, Agricultural Experiment Station, *Report, 1898–1901* (1902), 30, 181, and *Report, 1903–1904* (1904), 85; *The University of California Chronicle* 15 (April 1913): 307; *Southern Pacific Bulletin* 2 (March 1, 1914): 6 and (November 1, 1914): 2 and (December 1, 1914): 7; 3 (August 1, 1915): 6; 4 (July 15, 1916): 6; 5 (May 1, 1917): 5 and (September 15, 1917): 1.

63. William H. Mills to Collis P. Huntington, San Francisco, October 23, 1897, *CPH.*

64. See, in *Sunset:* Charles H. Shinn, "Experimental Agriculture in California: The University of California Stations, U.S. Department of Agriculture," 8 (November 1901): 15–19; Edward J. Wickson, "Luther Burbank: The Man, His Methods, and His Achievements," 8 (December 1901): 56–68, (February 1902): 145–56, (April 1902): 277–85, 9 (June 1902): 101–112; H. Morse Stephens, "University Extension in California and Elsewhere," 10 (March 1903): 439–46; Leroy Anderson, "What Modern Farming Means: Should the California Polytechnic School at San Luis Obispo Teach Agriculture," 10 (March 1903): 456–58; E. J. Wickson, "An Irrigation Pilgrimage," 15 (October 1905): 530–37; Edward Hughes, "Farming in the Schools," 16 (April 1906): 589–91.

65. University of California officials, including College of Agriculture leaders, in the university's tradition of opposing rival public colleges, at first resisted the idea of a state farm and school in the interior. For years after other groups had forced the creation of the University Farm and Farm School, university leaders remained ambivalent, if not hostile, toward the Davis institution. Although they recognized its public relations value, particularly among farmers, they refused to spend much money on the facility, and fought increased legislative appropriations for it. For a 1912 furor over the university's alleged neglect of the Davis facility, see *Davis Enterprise,* November 9, 12, and 30, 1912; Peter J. Shields, "Reminiscences" (typescript, 1953–54), 85 and 89, *BL;* Stadtman, *University of California,* 150–53, 198.

66. Peter J. Shields, *The Birth of an Institution: The Agricultural College at Davis* (Sacramento, 1954), 17.

67. William H. Mills to Benjamin Ide Wheeler, San Francisco, July 12, 1905 (including copy, Mills to Morris Brooke, San Francisco, July 12, 1905), Papers of the President, University of California Archives, *BL.*

68. James Horsburgh, Jr., to E. J. Wickson, San Francisco, August 8, 1905, E. J. Wickson Correspondence and Papers, *BL.*

69. The Davis University Farm and Farm School eventually developed into a sepa-

rate campus but within the University of California system and with the university's College of Agriculture managing agricultural research there and at Berkeley; Stadtman, *University of California,* 150–53.

70. Robert Glass Cleland and Osgood Hardy, *The March of Industry* (Los Angeles: Powell Publishing Co., 1929), 240–41; Mansel G. Blackford, *The Politics of Business in California, 1890–1920* (Columbus: Ohio State University Press, 1977), 4; California State Agricultural Society, *Biennial Report . . . 1909* (1910), 14–16; *Davis Enterprise,* January 30, 1909; *Sacramento Bee,* December 3 and 4, 1908; *Sacramento Union,* November 11–13, 1908; California State Board of Trade, *Biennial Report, 1904–1905* (San Francisco: California State Board of Trade, 1905), 5 and 19; Edwin S. Holmes, Jr., *Wheat Growing and General Agricultural Conditions in the Pacific Coast Region of the United States,* U.S. Department of Agriculture, Division of Statistics, Misc. Series, Bulletin No. 20 (Washington, DC: Government Printing Office, 1901), 33–37; Nash, *State Government and Economic Development,* 227–50.

71. Ellsworth, "Theodore Roosevelt's Country Life Commission," 155–72; William L. Bowers, "Country-life Reform, 1900–1920: A Neglected Aspect of Progressive Era History," *Agricultural History* 45 (July 1971): 211–21, and *The Country Life Movement in America,* esp. 7–14 and 62–85. For California, "Roosevelt on Technical Education and Farming," *Orchard and Farm,* December 1908, pp. 110–13; W. A. Beard, "Country Life," in California State Agricultural Society, *Biennial Report, 1910* (1911), 35–38; *Sacramento Union,* November 18, 21, 23, and 30, 1908; *Sacramento Bee,* November 30 and December 1, 1908; special issue, *The Great West* 8 (March 1909), ed. W. A. Beard, a California member of the Country Life Commission.

72. *Pacific Rural Press,* March 13, 1909, p. 120; Bremner, "Humors of the Demonstration Train," 127; *San Francisco Call,* February 5, 1909; *Sacramento Bee,* December 3 and 4, 1908; *Marysville Appeal,* November 15, 1908.

73. *Sacramento Bee,* November 13, 14, 17, 18, and 27, and December 9 and 21, 1908, and February 11, 1909; *San Francisco Call,* December 20, 1908, and February 21, 1909; *Berkeley Gazette,* February 3 and 11 and March 12, 16, and 19, 1909; Blackford, *Politics of Business in California,* 82–84; Nash, *State Government and Economic Development,* 251ff.

74. Deverell, *Railroad Crossings,* 123–71; Olin, *California Politics,* 54–71.

75. Wickson, "The University at Large in the State," 407, and "Agricultural Education in California," 391–92, 401; *Berkeley Gazette,* December 19, 1908, and February 12, 1909; *San Francisco Call,* February 12 and 13, 1909; *Sacramento Union,* February 11, 1909; *Sacramento Bee,* February 6 and 12, 1909; *Davis Enterprise,* January 23, February 13 and 27, and May 1, 1909; *Woodland Mail,* January 23 and February 8, 1909.

76. Scott, *Reluctant Farmer,* 10 and 136–40; John Hamilton, *Progress in Agricultural Education,* U.S. Department of Agriculture, Office of Experiment Stations, Circular 98 (Washington, DC: Government Printing Office, 1910), 11–12; for California's agricultural scientists' disillusionment with extension methods, see comments by E. J. Wickson in the *Riverside Press,* March 16, 1909; also *Gilroy Gazette,* October 23, 1908.

77. Maskew, *Quarantine Regulations,* 31ff.; California State Commission of Horticulture, *Horticultural Statutes* (1912), passim; *Sacramento Bee,* November 10, 1908.

78. Scott, "Railroads and Farmers: Educational Trains in Missouri," 3–15, *Reluctant Farmer,* 176–83, and *Railroad Development Programs,* 39–44; Swisher, "Corn Gospel Trains," 321–33.

79. University of California president Benjamin Ide Wheeler quoted in Clarke, "Agricultural and Horticultural Demonstration Train."

80. *San Francisco Call,* October 21 and 23, 1908; *Berkeley Gazette,* October 22, 1908; *Davis Enterprise,* October 24, 1908; *Gilroy Gazette,* October 23, 1908; *Biennial Report of the Horticultural Commissioner of the State of California, 1907–1908* (1909), 18; and Bremner, "Humors of the Demonstration Train," 126.

81. The railroad's announcement of the demonstration train, in *Pacific Rural Press,* October 24, 1908; *California Cultivator,* November 5, 1908; *Gilroy Gazette,* October 23, 1908. The *Gazette's* copy was followed by a cryptic disclaimer by the apparently anti–Southern Pacific newspaper: "The *Gazette* Prints Everything." For train's founders' intentions, see statements of dean of the College of Agriculture, E. J. Wickson, who attended the organizational meetings, in *Pacific Rural Press,* March 27, 1909, and *Riverside Press,* March 16, 1909; also the resume of the original ideas behind the demonstration train by Warren T. Clarke, professor and also a founder, in "Agricultural and Horticultural Demonstration Train" and "Sending the College to the Farmer."

82. For the train's personnel and program, *Sacramento Union,* November 17 and 18, 1908; Bremner, "Humors of the Demonstration Train," 127; *Sacramento Bee,* November 16, 1908; *Woodland Democrat,* November 6, 9, 1908; *Chico Enterprise,* November 13, 1908; *Davis Enterprise,* November 14, 21, 1908; *Rural Californian,* March 1909; *San Francisco Call,* February 9, 1909; *California Cultivator,* March 18, 1909; and "The Agricultural Demonstration Train," *University of California Chronicle* 11 (April 1909): 186–87.

83. For Jones's oratory, *San Francisco Call,* December 15–19, 1908; speeches by Horticultural Commission spokesmen, *Chico Enterprise,* November 13, 1908, *Sacramento Union,* November 18, 1908, and *Riverside Press,* March 16, 1909; of the university's, *Davis Enterprise,* November 21, 1908, and *Hanford Sentinel,* February 4, 1909.

84. *San Francisco Call,* February 5, 1909.

85. Bremner, "Humors of the Demonstration Train," 127.

86. For extensive, sometimes nearly verbatim, coverage of presentations, *Pacific Rural Press,* March 27, 1909; *Sacramento Union,* November 18, 1909; *California Cultivator,* March 18, 1909; *Sacramento Bee,* November 16, 1908; *Woodland Democrat,* November 9, 1908 (reporting on the train's first stop); *Chico Enterprise,* November 13, 1908; and *Davis Enterprise,* November 21, 1908.

87. Bremner, "Humors of the Demonstration Train," 127.

88. *Sacramento Union,* November 18, 1908.

89. See report by Minna E. Sherman, train lecturer on viticulture and later the second female University of California regent, *California Cultivator,* March 19, 1909.

90. *Marysville Appeal,* November 15 and 17, 1908; *Hanford Sentinel,* February 4, 1909; *California Cultivator,* June 9, 1910.

91. *Marysville Appeal,* November 13, 1908.

92. *Davis Enterprise,* December 12, 1908, and January 30, 1909; *Orchard and Farm,* March 1909; *California Cultivator,* December 3, 1908; *University of California Chron-*

icle 11 (April 1909): 186–87. Overcrowding persisted. At Selma and Hanford near Fresno, where virtually the entire towns turned out, local editors complained of the crowds and the visit's brevity, which prevented everyone from seeing exhibits and hearing presentations; *Hanford Sentinel,* February 4, 1909; *Fresno Republican,* February 6, 1909.

93. *Riverside Press,* March 10, 12, and 16, 1909; *Los Angeles Times,* March 13, 1909. For further refinements made to accommodate the train to the lemon-growing districts of the southern coastal plain, *Ventura Free Press,* April 16, 1908.

94. *Gilroy Gazette,* May 21 and 28, 1909.

95. *Santa Rosa Republican,* May 20, 1909.

96. *Sacramento Bee,* November 17 and December 11, 1908.

97. *Fresno Republican,* February 9, 1909.

98. *Riverside Press,* March 18 and 20, 1909.

99. *Pacific Rural Press,* March 27, 1909; Edward J. Wickson, "The Relation of the University to the Agriculture of the State," *University of California Chronicle* 12 (January 1910): 60.

100. *Berkeley Gazette,* December 19, 1908; also report by state horticultural commissioner J. W. Jeffrey, *Sacramento Union,* November 13, 1908; also description of the train personnel's bone-wearying routine, *Riverside Press,* March 12, 1909 (reprint from *San Francisco Chronicle*).

101. *Sacramento Bee,* November 15, 1908; also *Marysville Appeal,* December 12, 1908; *San Francisco Call,* February 2, 1909; *San Jose Herald,* May 22, 1909; *Riverside Press,* March 12, 1909; *Rural Californian,* March 1909, 90; Bremner, "Humors of the Demonstration Train," 129, for the "unanimous approval of the project" by the state's chambers of commerce and other commercial organizations; also *Sacramento Union,* November 17, 1908.

102. *Berkeley Gazette,* February 10, 1909; *San Francisco Call,* February 11, 1909.

103. E. J. Wickson, "Beginnings of Agricultural Education and Research in California," in University of California, College of Agriculture, *Report, 1917–1918* (1918), 58; U.S. Department of Agriculture, *Annual Report of the Office of Experiment Stations, United States Department of Agriculture, 1910* (1911), 394 and 418–21, and *Report, 1912* (1913), 360–75; *Oakland Tribune,* May 7, 1911; *San Francisco Call,* June 27, 1912. During the 1909–1910 season, for example, twenty-nine trains operated in eighteen states, for a total attendance of 189,645, nearly 75,000 of which was in California; see U.S. Department of Agriculture reports above. Peak year for California mileage, stops, and attendance (about 102,000) was 1911–1912. For the railroad's review of its involvement in California demonstration trains, see Charles S. Fee (passenger traffic manager) to Martin L. Hayes (professor of agricultural education, Texas A & M University), San Francisco, February 10, 1917, File R195, *SP-PR* (copy also in File 621A, *SP-L*); attendance, according to Fee: 1908–1909 (37,270); 1909–1910 (73,663); 1910–1911 (76,236); and 1911–1912 (101, 985). For the 1909–1910 train's program and personnel, see Southern Pacific Company, *Special Agricultural and Horticultural Demonstration Train, Operated Under the Auspices of the Southern Pacific Company and the University of California* (1910), for the San Joaquin Valley tour.

104. Roy V. Scott, "American Railroads and Agricultural Extension, 1900–1914: A

Study in Railway Developmental Techniques," *Business History Review* 34 (September 1965): 85, and *Reluctant Farmer,* 182.

105. Charles S. Fee to Martin L. Hayes, San Francisco, February 10, 1917, File R195, *SP-PR.*

106. Clarke, "Agricultural and Horticultural Demonstration Train," 19 and 31, and "Sending the College to the Farmer," passim. Clarke held that while the more than twenty eastern trains devoted all their attention to the two or three basic agricultural topics dominant in their states, the California train covered *seventeen* "divisions of agriculture," making it "the most pretentious and comprehensive effort of the kind ever attempted"; *Pacific Rural Press,* January 14, 1911.

107. See *California Cultivator,* January 19, 1911.

108. *California Cultivator,* January 27 and March 3, 1910. The College of Agriculture was expanding its curriculum to include what were seen as "female" subjects pertinent to farm life, including instituting new courses and programs, hiring more women professors and researchers, and sending them across the state to hold meetings and institutes in towns and rural areas; see University of California, College of Agriculture, Scrapbooks, for this period, University of California Archives, *BL.* Reflecting this, Warren T. Clarke believed that improving women's lot was essential to successful extension education and emphasized female-centered curriculum aboard the train. The work of farm women, he held, "is continuous and . . . of the confining and trying sort . . . frequently with no conveniences." The train's program freed women from some drudgery and helped them to "assume a more dignified, more rational, more human part of the household." Much might be done to improve the efficiency of production, "and yet that farm may be a failure because of the basic failure to recognize the all-important position occupied by the woman upon the farm. In her hands lies the success or failure of the farm as a producer of a contented citizenship"; Clarke, "Sending the College to the Farmer," 386–88.

109. *California Cultivator,* February 16, 1911.

110. *San Francisco Call,* December 12, 1911; *Sacramento Bee,* November 17 and 20, 1911.

111. Earnest B. Babcock, "Co-operation between the Schools and the College of Agriculture," *University of California Chronicle* 8 (July 1911): 341–42.

112. *Sacramento Bee,* November 17, 1911.

113. *Marysville Appeal,* December 12, 1908.

114. *Marysville Appeal,* November 17, 1908; *Riverside Press,* March 16, 1909.

115. *California Cultivator,* November 26, 1908; *Sacramento Bee,* November 14, 1908.

116. *Sacramento Bee,* November 11, 1908.

117. *Sacramento Bee,* November 18, 1909.

118. *Los Angeles Times,* March 19 and 21, 1909.

119. *Riverside Press,* March 16, 1909; *California Cultivator,* March 18, 1909.

120. *Los Angeles Times,* March 22, 1909; *Imperial Standard,* March 20, 1909.

121. *Ventura Free Press,* April 16 and 30, 1909.

122. Charles S. Fee to Professor Martin L. Hayes, San Francisco, February 10, 1917, File R195, *SP-PR.*

123. In 1911 in the northern Sacramento Valley, farmers reported excellent results

from earlier suggestions to convert to truck gardening, newer breeds of cattle, and different grain-cultivation methods, and also to shift livestock farms from meat-production to dairying; *Sacramento Bee,* November 21, 1911.

124. Scott, "American Railroads and Agricultural Extension," 98.

125. U.S. Department of Agriculture, *Annual Report of Experiment Stations* (1909), 333 and passim; for nation, Scott, *Reluctant Farmer,* 176–83, and "Railroads and Farmers: Educational Trains in Missouri," 5–15; Chu Chang Liang, *Industrial and Agricultural Development Departments,* 110–11.

126. *Merced Sun,* December 17 and 19, 1908; *Pacific Rural Press,* March 18 and 27, 1909; and *California Cultivator,* March 18, 1909.

127. *Fresno Republican,* February 8, 1909; for later years, *Washington Press* (Niles), April 9, 1910.

128. Bremner, "Humors of the Demonstration Train," 129.

129. Ferrier, *Origin and Development of the University of California,* 555–59; H. J. Webber, "New Buildings of the Citrus Experiment Stations," *University of California Journal of Agriculture* (May 1916): 319–22; *Davis Enterprise,* January 25, April 12, May 17 and 31, and June 21, 1913; *Berkeley Gazette,* April 16 and May 13, 1913; Clarke, "Sending the College to the Farmer," 388.

130. *California Cultivator,* February 17 and 24, 1910; also March 18 and June 3, 1909, and April 7, 1910. The anti-railroad *Sacramento Bee,* November 28, 1908, observed that the Southern Pacific's support of the first demonstration train proves its "willingness . . . to help in the development of the territory in which it operates"; also, the anti-railroad *Chico Enterprise,* November 13, 1908, and *Riverside Press,* March 16, 1909.

131. *Santa Paula Chronicle,* April 30, 1909.

132. *Chico Enterprise,* November 12, 13, 14, 16, 19, 20, and 23, 1908; *Sacramento Bee,* November 13, 1908.

133. *Fresno Republican,* February 5 and 8, 1909. The *Republican,* by the way, praised the demonstration train but, like other opponents of the railroad, gave the credit to the university.

134. Some newspapers, even while praising the university and railroad for bringing the train, in the same pages attacked the railroad for hypocrisy and ignoring the needs of farmers, as did letters to the editor; *Pacific Rural Press,* March 13, 1909; and esp. *California Cultivator,* September 23, 1909, p. 300, June 3, 1909, editorial, and March 18, 1909, in which the editor, who traveled with the train, reported that farmers, while appreciating the university and the Horticultural Commission for operating the train, "promiscuously condemn the Southern Pacific Company on general principles."

135. *Modesto News,* December 19, 1908; and February 6, 1909 (for the San Joaquin Eucalyptus Company). However unpopular his message, Shaw was correct. The tree was returning profits to virtually no one but dealers in land and nursery stock. Nevertheless, thirty-eight companies had leaped up overnight in the state by 1908 to sell eucalyptus land and tree-growing supplies. Although he remained sanguine about the long-term possibilities for the industry, state forester G. B. Lull warned potential investors that many projects were too isolated from transportation, lacked an appropriate climate, and were based on wildly exaggerated predicted markets and profits. Because of

environmental differences between California and Australia, the unsuitability of the wood for furniture and building construction, and the impossible economics of the business, the "eucalyptus crusade," as it was called, collapsed quickly, leaving behind ruined investors, huge tracts of worthless artificial forests prone to wildfires, and generations of newcomers who believe to this day that the ubiquitous eucalyptus is native to the state. See G. B. Lull, "The Eucalyptus Situation in California," in California State Agricultural Society, *Report, 1908* (1909), 26–28; *Riverside Press,* February 20, 1909. For the industry history in the context of other speculative, sometimes near-fraudulent, agricultural fads plaguing the state, see John E. Baur, "California Crops that Failed," *California Historical Society Quarterly* 45 (March 1966): 41–68; Viola L. Warren, "The Eucalyptus Crusade in California," *Historical Society of Southern California Quarterly* 44 (March 1962): 31–42; Santos, "Eucalyptus of California," 132–39. From its own failed experiments beginning in the 1870s, the Southern Pacific learned the hard way about the myth of a commercial eucalyptus industry; see above, this chapter, and Santos, "Eucalyptus of California," 125–26.

136. Rosenberg, "Science, Technology, and Economic Growth," 1–20, and "The Adams Act: Politics and the Cause of Scientific Research," *Agricultural History* 38 (January 1964): 3–12.

137. Scott, *Reluctant Farmer,* 136–37, 176–83, 195, 205, 279–88, and 288–313, "Railroads and Farmers: Educational Trains in Missouri," 15, and "American Railroads and Agricultural Extension," 86; Chu Chang Liang, *Industrial and Agricultural Development Departments,* 107–15; Ferrier, *Origin and Development of the University of California,* 615–21; and U.S. Department of Agriculture, *A Report on the Work and Expenditures of the Agricultural Experiment Stations . . . 1913* (Washington, DC: Government Printing Office, 1915), 14–15.

138. *California Cultivator,* July 18, 1912; *Davis Enterprise,* many issues, 1912–1913, on the redirection of the College of Agriculture; California State Legislature, Special Legislative Commission on Agricultural Education, *Report,* 50; Alfred C. True, *History of Agricultural Extension Work in the United States, 1785–1923,* U.S. Department of Agriculture, Misc. Publication 15 (Washington, DC: Government Printing Office, 1928), 28–30, 74–127, 200–201; University of California, Agricultural Extension Service, *Bertram Hanford Crocheron: Architect and Builder of the California Agricultural Extension Service* (Berkeley: Committee of Emeriti, University of California Agricultural Extension Service, 1967), passim; B. A. McAllaster to Thomas F. Hunt (recently appointed dean of the College of Agriculture), San Francisco, February 6, 1914, and Hunt to McAllaster, Berkeley, February 9, 1914, College of Agriculture Correspondence and Papers, box 12, University of California Archives, *BL;* College of Agriculture Scrapbooks for the period, University Archives, document the transition to the county agent system.

139. University of California College of Agriculture, *Report, 1912–1913* (1913), xli. For details of the freeze special train, *University of California Journal of Agriculture* 1 (December 1913): 19; *The University of California Chronicle* 15 (April 1913): 292; and College of Agriculture, "Scrapbooks" (1912–1914), 32; Thomas H. Hunt to Meyer-Wilson Company, Berkeley, March 4, 1913, College of Agriculture, Correspondence and Papers, box 12, University of California Archives, *BL; California Cultivator,* February

13 and 27, 1913, and June 26, 1913, issue on the freeze; *Orchard and Farm* (March 1913): 1; *Davis Enterprise,* February 15, 1913; *Los Angeles Times,* February 12, 14, 16, and 18, 1913.

140. *Los Angeles Times,* February 14, 1913; H. J. Webber, "New Buildings of the Citrus Experiment Stations," 319–22.

141. *California Cultivator,* April 3, 1913; *Davis Enterprise,* March 29, 1913, and *Berkeley Gazette,* March 25, 1913, for a "dairy demonstration train" of the university and the Santa Fe; College of Agriculture, "Scrapbooks" (1912–1914), 32, University of California Archives, *BL.* For a San Joaquin Valley hog demonstration train, *Stockton Record,* December 17, 1917. During World War I mobilization, an "Agricultural Preparedness Train" through California, Utah, and Nevada was visited by 55,000 persons; University of California, College of Agriculture, *Report, 1916–1917* (1917), 27.

142. Ferrier, *Origin and Development of the University of California,* 559; *Progress in Agricultural Extension* [University of California, College of Agriculture, periodical] (February 10, 1928): 8, (April 10, 1928): 2–3, and (May 9, 1928): 2; University of California, College of Agriculture, *The Agricultural Situation in California* (1928), passim; *California Countryman* 14 (February 1928): 16, and (March 1928): 12 and 19–20; *Pacific Rural Press* 115 (February 25, 1928): 250, (March 17, 1928): 349, (March 24, 1928): 372, (March 31, 1928): 1 and 408, (April 7, 1928): 450, and (April 21, 1928): 502; and "Special S.P. Train Lends Aid to Farmers," *Southern Pacific Bulletin* 16 (April 1928): 6. Nationally, demonstration trains revived briefly in the 1920s; Scott, *Reluctant Farmer,* 312.

143. *Southern Pacific Bulletin* 2 (November 1, 1914): 2.

144. *Southern Pacific Bulletin* 2 (December 1, 1914): 1.

145. James W. Hulse, *The University of Nevada: A Centennial History* (Reno: University of Nevada Press, 1974), 19–20.

146. *Reno Gazette,* December 14, 1877; for the Reno move, *Nevada State Journal* (Reno), June 3, 12, and 14, and July 21, 1885. For Stubbs's appointment and Fulton's role in it, Hulse, *University of Nevada,* 32ff., and Richnak, *A River Flows,* 136.

147. University of Nevada, Agricultural Experiment Station, *Annual Report for 1890* (Carson City: State Print Office, 1891), 37, *Annual Report, 1904* (1905), 14, and *Annual Report, 1905* (1906), 1; Hulse, *University of Nevada,* 148ff.

148. Biographical materials, John Knox Weatherford Papers, Oregon Collection, University of Oregon. On Herrin, biographical materials, including "William F. Herrin" (ms., n.d.), and valedictory address, Memorabilia Collection, William F. Herrin, Oregon State University Archives, Corvallis; *Portland Rural Spirit,* June 22, 1910, for his address at the college's twenty-fifth anniversary celebration; "Death Calls William F. Herrin, Chief Counsel," *Southern Pacific Bulletin* 16 (April 1927): 5–6.

149. Robert Mailtland Brereton, *Well Irrigation on Small Farms* (Portland: Passenger Departments, Oregon Railroad and Navigation Co. and Southern Pacific Co., ca. 1909); *Oregon: The Land of Opportunity* (Portland: Sunset Homeseekers' Bureau, 1909); John C. Burtner, untitled essay (originally published, ca. 1930, in *Portland Telegram*), Oregon State University Scrapbooks, D-45, Oregon State University Archives; *Bend Bulletin,* November 15, 1911; *Portland Oregonian,* April 30, 1910, August 27 and December 1, 1912, and March 13 and 16, 1930; *Klamath Falls Northwestern,* August 24, 1912; unidentified newspaper clipping, April 2, 1912, Oregon Agricultural College Newsclip-

pings, 1909–1932, box 1-A, Oregon State University Archives; *Southern Pacific Bulletin* 13 (November 1924): 33–34. On the long-term deep-well project, Ben C. Dey (general attorney, Southern Pacific Co.) to J. C. Ainsworth, Portland, October 2, 1929; J. A. Ormandy (Northwest passenger traffic manager, Southern Pacific Company) to W. J. Kerr (president, Oregon State College), Portland, November 8, 1929; Secretary to the President to Ormandy, Corvallis, November 9, 1929, and to E. B. McNaughton (First National Bank, Portland), Corvallis, December 13, 1929; and William A. Schoenfeld (dean and director, School of Agriculture, Experiment Station), "Brief History Deep Well Revolving Fund and Development (1929–1940)," in Schoenfeld to George W. Peavy (president, Oregon State Agricultural College), Corvallis, June 3, 1940; all in RG 13, reel 22, President's Office Files, Oregon State University Archives.

150. *Sacramento Record-Union,* September 26, 1890. Also, R. H. Forbes (director, Arizona Experiment Station) to O. F. Cook, Tucson, June 4, July 18, and August 5, 1899, and Cook to Forbes, Washington, DC, June 24 and August 1, 1899, box 10, folder 3, R. H. Forbes Collection, Arizona Historical Society, Tucson, and Walter T. Swingle to Forbes, April 11, 1900, folder 4. Also, Forbes to Epes Randolph, Tucson, September 12, 1904, Arizona Experiment Station Papers, box 14, folder 8, University of Arizona Library, Tucson.

151. Arizona Experiment Station, University of Arizona, *Annual Report* (Tucson, 1900–1910), passim; "University of Arizona Audit Funds Administered by Prof. R. H. Forbes, Fiscal Years 1913–14 and 1914–15" (typescript), box 13, folder 1, R. H. Forbes Collection, Arizona Historical Society, Tucson.

152. President, University of Arizona, to W. S. Tilton (agent, Southern Pacific Company, El Paso), Tucson, February 25, 1895; Memo from President, University of Arizona, May 20, 1895; William Stow Devol (director, Arizona Experiment Station), to Isaac Gates (Southern Pacific Company, New York), February 18, 1896; Gates to Devol, New York, February 26, 1896; R. H. Forbes to Epes Randolph, Tucson, September 15, 1899, and January 2, 1901; Randolph to Forbes, Tucson, September 23, 1899; all in box 14, folder 8, Arizona Experiment Station Papers, University of Arizona Library, Tucson; also *Arizona* 4 (December 1913): 11, for Southern Pacific support for University of Arizona's short courses for farmers.

153. R. H. Forbes to A. C. True (director, Office of Experiment Stations, U.S. Department of Agriculture), Tucson, December 22, 1906, and October 31, 1907; True to Forbes, January 2, 1907; all in box 9, folder 3, R. H. Forbes Collection, Arizona Historical Society, Tucson; see also, Forbes to True, Tucson, October 6, 1909, folder 5.

154. For extension courses, *Waco Tribune,* February 14, 1917, *Houston Post,* July 19, 1915 (segregated course for blacks), and *Houston Chronicle,* July 12, 1918, all clippings in E. J. Kyle Scrapbook; E. J. Kyle, "History of Farmers' Short Courses" (typescript, July 22, 1931), box 2–6; E. J. Kyle biographical materials; all in E. J. Kyle Papers, Texas A & M University Archives. Also, Texas A & M College, *Fifth Annual Farmers' Short Course . . . July 20–25, 1914* (College Station, 1914), passim; and *Extension Service Farm News* 10 (July 15, 1925): 1.

155. *Houston Post,* February 7, 1904; L. H. Shelfer, *Texas Tobacco and Diversified Farming on the Line of the Southern Pacific: What L. H. Shelfer, Former Tobacco Expert for the*

U.S. Department of Agriculture Has to Say of Agricultural Possibilities in East Texas (Houston: Passenger Department of the Southern Pacific, 1903); Southern Pacific Company, *Ten Texas Topics by Texas Tillers and Toilers* . . . (Houston: Passenger Department, Southern Pacific Sunset Route, ca. 1903), passim, esp. 9–15; Southern Pacific Company, *Timely Tips to Texas Truckers* (Houston: Passenger Department, Sunset Route, 1908); Southern Pacific Lines, *Agricultural Achievements and Possibilities along the Southern Pacific Lines in Texas* (Houston: Traffic Department, 1923), passim, esp. 10; Southern Pacific Company, Passenger-Industrial Department, *Dry Farming in West Texas* (Houston: Cumming and Sons, Printers, ca. 1909); Southern Pacific, Sunset Route, Passenger Department, *Growing Figs and Citrus Fruits in South Texas* (Houston: Cumming and Sons, Art Printers, 1910); Southern Pacific Company, *Central Texas is Calling You, Mr. Farmer* (Houston: Passenger Department, Sunset–Central Lines, ca. 1912); Southern Pacific Company, *Texas Rice Book* (Houston: Passenger Department, Sunset Route, ca. 1900); Southern Pacific Company, *Texas and Louisiana Rice: How It Is Grown and Cooked* . . . (Houston: Cumming and Sons, 1911); H. S. Kreedler, *The Coast Country of Texas: A General Study of the Region, Together with a Brief Outline of Its History, Agricultural and Industrial Possibilities, Its Social Conditions and Inducements to Homeseekers* (Cincinnati: A. H. Pugh Printing Co., 1896); Southern Pacific, *West Texas: Its Soil, Climate and Possibilities* (Houston: General Passenger Department, Southern Pacific–Sunset Route, ca. 1904); Southern Pacific Company, *Southwest Texas, An Agricultural Empire* (Houston: Sunset–Central Lines, ca. 1912); Southern Pacific Company, Passenger Department, *Facts and Figures for Farmers, Fruit Growers and Florists* (Houston: Cumming and Sons, Art Printers, 1909).

156. Henry C. Dethloff, *Centennial History of Texas A & M University, 1876–1976,* 2 vols. (College Station: Published for the Association of Former Students by Texas A & M University Press, 1976), 1:50–87, 71ff., 217ff., and 2:382–403; Clarence Ousley, *History of the Agricultural and Mechanical College of Texas,* Texas A & M College, *Bulletin,* 4th ser., vol. 6, no. 8 (December 1, 1935), passim, esp. 49–56, 131ff.

157. Edward B. Cushing Biographical File, Texas A & M University Archives; Dethloff, *Centennial History of Texas A & M,* 1:151, 170, 230, 408.

158. For conflicts between the university and the college through the 1920s, Dethloff, *Centennial History of Texas A & M,* 1:88–89, 123–30, 231–42, 254–60, 294–96, and 2:416–21. For Cushing's agitation against the 1913 amendment, *Houston Post,* July 21, 1913; unidentified Bryan, Texas, newspaper, July 15, 1913, clipping in R. T. Milner Scrapbook, Robert Teague Milner Papers, *UTA;* E. B. Cushing to Governor O. B. Colquitt, Houston, June 19 and 28 and July 3, 1913, Governors' Papers, 2–11/695, Texas State Archives, Austin; *Bryan Eagle,* July 4, 1913; E. B. Cushing Biographical File, Texas A & M University Archives.

159. E. B. Cushing to R. T. Milner, Houston, February 24, April 16, and May 2, 1914; Milner to Cushing, April 27, 1914; R. T. Milner, form letter sent under letterhead of the Executive Committee for the Promotion of Higher Education (headed by Milner and Cushing), Bryan, Texas, June 2, 1915; all in Robert Teague Milner Papers, *UTA.*

160. *Houston Chronicle,* February 18, 1924; *Houston Post,* February 19 and 20, 1924; *Dallas News,* February 19, 1924.

161. For the important 1904 boll-weevil campaign, resulting in the establishment of a nationwide farm-extension system, "Farmers' Cooperative Demonstration Work, Bureau of Plan Industry, U.S.D.A., 1904," box 5–22, and George W. Curtis to Prof. A. J. Pieters, February 24, 1904, box 23–54, Texas Agricultural Extension Service, Historical Files, Texas A & M University Archives; Neta B. Weaver, "History of Farmers' Cooperative Demonstration Work in Texas" (M.A. thesis, University of Texas, 1941), 41–78; Scott, *Railroad Development Programs,* passim, esp. 37ff.; Dethloff, *History of Texas A & M,* 1:189, 2:388.

162. *Houston Post,* January 29, February 19, 20, 21, 23, 24, 26, and 27, 1904.

163. Seaman A. Knapp, General Letter to Railroads, Lake Charles, Louisiana, December 26, 1906, box 1–11, Texas Agricultural Extension Service, Historical Files, Texas A & M University Archives.

164. See *Annual Report of the [Texas] Commissioner of Agriculture* (Austin: Austin Printing Co., 1910), 18ff.; "Teaching Agriculture by Train: Spectacular Colleges on Wheels Accomplish Wonderful Things for Advanced Agriculture," *Farm and Ranch* (Dallas) 30 (April 19, 1911), 1–2; "Annual Report, C. M. Evans, Extension Department, Texas A & M College, for the Year 1911" (typescript, 1912), and Texas Agricultural Extension Service, "Annual Report of Statewide Activity" (typescript, 1911), 2, Texas A & M University Archives; and *Southern Pacific Bulletin (Texas and Louisiana)* 9 (January 1923): 5.

165. "Demonstration Train: Agricultural Feature of Extension Work of the University of Arizona," *Arizona* 4 (November 1913): 7, and 3 (November 1912): 3; R. H. Forbes, "A Brief Report of Progress Made by the Experiment Station and Agricultural Instruction in the University, January 1, 1912, to June 30, 1913" (ms.), box 13, folder 1, R. H. Forbes Collection, Arizona Historical Society, Tucson; *Southwestern Stockman-Farmer and Feeder,* January 16, 1914; Charles C. Colley, *The Century of Robert Forbes: The Career of a Pioneer Agriculturalist, Agronomist, Environmentalist, Conservationist, and Water Specialist in Arizona and Abroad* (Tucson: Arizona Historical Society, 1977), 30–31.

166. *Portland Oregonian,* February 22 and December 17 and 25, 1911; *Cottage Grove Leader,* February 28, 1911; *Brownsville Times,* March 3, 1911; *Corvallis Gazette-Times,* May 24, 1911.

167. For description of the train and speeches praising the Agricultural College and railroad and college people aboard the train, *Portland Oregonian,* October 30 and 31 and November 2, 3, 4, 1911, and esp. November 12, 1911; *Redmond Spokesman,* October 26, 1911; *Aurora Observer,* October 26, 1911; *Condon Times,* October 28, 1911. In early September, Southern Pacific leaders addressed a state development convention in Portland with a plea for preservation, indeed expansion, of Oregon Agricultural College. Pacific Northwest Harriman Lines traffic manager Richard Miller called it "a matter of life and death of supreme moment," the college being essential to "obtain the changes in methods that will insure the development of this country to its proper and maximum production"; *Oregon Journal* (Portland), September 6, 1911. For other Southern Pacific Oregon farm demonstration trains, *Gresham Herald,* August 12, 1910, clipping in Oregon Agricultural College Newsclippings, 1909–1932, box 1-A, Oregon State University Archives; U.S.D.A., *Annual Report of Experiment Stations, 1912* (Washing-

ton, DC: Government Printing Office, 1913), 371; *Southern Pacific Bulletin* 2 (January 15, 1914): 6, and 5 (May 15, 1917): 2.

168. For the U.S. Department of Agriculture's prohibition on using its funds for demonstration trains, "Abstracts of Rulings by Dr. True on the Expenditure of Smith-Lever Funds" (April 1920), Texas Agricultural Extension Service, Historical Files, box 7–35; for a combined railway companies' train in which the Southern Pacific participated in the 1920s, see "Annual Report of T. B. Wood, District Agent, District #9 [West Texas], 1923," in Texas Agricultural Extension Service, "Report of Statewide Activity" (typescript, 1923), 728–35, both in Texas A&M University Archives. For Southern Pacific–Louisiana State University trains that operated for several years after 1910, "Southern Pacific Participation in Promoting Agriculture in Louisiana" (typescript, ca. 1952), 1–2, and passim, Public Relations Historical File, *SP-H*.

12　Marketing the Produce of Western Farms

The quotation in the chapter title is from refrigeration-car iceman Pete Holst's memoir, in Anthony W. Thompson, Robert J. Church, and Bruce H. Jones, *Pacific Fruit Express* (Wilton, CA: Central Valley Railroad Publications, 1992), 363.

1. H. E. Erdman, "The Development and Significance of California Cooperatives, 1900–1915," *Agricultural History* 32 (July 1958): 179–84, and *The California Fruit Growers' Exchange: An Example of Cooperation in the Segregation of Conflicting Interests* (New York: American Council, Institute of Pacific Relations, 1933); Lawrence J. Jelinek, *Harvest Empire: A History of California Agriculture,* 2nd ed. (San Francisco: Boyd and Fraser Publishing Co., 1982), 57ff.; Steven Stoll, *The Fruits of Natural Advantage: Making the Industrial Countryside in California* (Berkeley: University of California Press, 1998), chap. 3.

2. Jelinek, *Harvest Empire,* 58ff.; Richard Steven Street, "Marketing California Crops at the Turn of the Century," *Southern California Quarterly* 61 (1979): 239–53; articles in "Citriculture in Southern California," special issue of *California History* 74 (Spring 1995); Claude B. Hutchinson, *California Agriculture* (Berkeley: University of California Press, 1946), passim; Gerald D. Nash, *State Government and Economic Development: A History of Administrative Policies in California, 1849–1933* (Berkeley: Institute of Governmental Studies, University of California, Berkeley, 1964), 139ff. and 227ff.

3. Historians have generally overlooked the role of the railroads, including the Southern Pacific, in western agricultural marketing, assuming that it could be understood by studying growers, cooperatives, and government agencies. In his recent survey of the emergence of California fruit industries from the 1880s through the 1930s, for example, Steven Stoll pointedly excluded railroads and irrigation from his analysis. This was because, in his view, farmers during the period "rarely worried out loud" about irrigation or, with the exception of "an occasional resolution for lower rates and faster service," about railroads; Stoll, *Fruits of Natural Advantage,* xv. Abundant sources from the period, of course, demonstrate that there were few problems that California and other western farmers worried *more* about than irrigation and railroads. Also leaving

railroads out of the marketing story is Mansel G. Blackford, *The Politics of Business in California, 1890–1920* (Columbus: Ohio State University Press, 1977), chap. 2.

4. *Sacramento Record-Union,* February 22 and April 1, 1875.

5. See appreciation of the *Sacramento Record-Union's* support, in *The California Patron,* the Grange's statewide newspaper, July 19, 1876, and November 2, 1878. For Mills's speech, *Woodland Mail,* November 24, 1889, and *Record-Union,* November 26, 1889.

6. See many letters among Collis P. Huntington, William H. Mills, and Henry E. Huntington during the 1896 presidential campaign, discussing free coinage of silver and Bryan's other farmer-oriented campaign planks; esp. Collis P. Huntington to William H. Mills, New York, September 11, 1896, and October 4, 1897; Collis to Henry, New York, July 16, 1896, and telegram, New York, July 10, 1896; and Henry to Collis, San Francisco, July 11 and 17, 1896; *HEH.* Also *San Francisco Call,* August 24, 29, and 30, 1897, and *San Francisco Examiner,* August 24 and 30, 1897.

7. In the 1870s, Stanford and Colton supported the Grangers' Immigration Bureau. On Stanford's longtime advocacy of farm and worker cooperatives, Norman E. Tutorow, *Leland Stanford: Man of Many Careers* (Menlo Park, CA: Pacific Coast Publishers, 1971), 252–55 and 274–82; George T. Clark, *Leland Stanford: War Governor of California, Railroad Builder, and Founder of Stanford University* (Stanford: Stanford University Press, 1931), 459ff. As U.S. senator, Stanford introduced several unsuccessful bills to encourage cooperatives and institute other federal assistance to distressed farmers and workers; see also *San Francisco Argonaut,* June 11, 1887, and *New York Tribune,* May 4, 1887.

8. *San Francisco Bulletin,* September 24, 1885; *San Francisco Chronicle,* November 11 and December 3, 1885.

9. William H. Mills, "Annual Address Delivered before the State Agricultural Society of California . . . Sacramento, September 18, 1890," *Transactions of the California State Agricultural Society during the Year 1890* (Sacramento: State Printer, 1891), 184–208; Mills and Edwin K. Alsip, *Report on the Columbus, Ohio, Exhibit* (San Francisco: California State Board of Trade, 1888), 8–9; Mills, "Marketing of California Fruits," *Californian Illustrated Magazine* 2 (October 1892): 708–709; *Sacramento Record-Union,* September 12, 1881. Mills's papers on the advantages of cooperatives appeared also in San Francisco's *Examiner,* October 12, 1892, and *Chronicle,* November 23, 1893.

10. *Sacramento Record-Union,* August 30 and September 5, 1888.

11. *Sunset* 4 (April 1900): 246, and 14 (November 1904): 90, supported a meeting of the state's fruit growers in San Jose to create the organizations.

12. Clarence M. Wooster, "Railroading in the Seventies," *California Historical Society Quarterly* 18 (March 1939): 363–64.

13. Stanford reviewed Southern Pacific fruit-shipping practices at a convention of California fruit growers; *San Francisco Chronicle,* November 11, 1885.

14. *Sacramento Record-Union,* June 25, 1886; *Southern Pacific Bulletin* 11 (December 1922): 27; for the New Orleans expositions, later in this chapter.

15. In his address before the 1885 growers convention, Stanford explained how the absence of farmers' organizations also raised the tariffs the company had to charge for uncoordinated shipments in single- or partial-car lots, especially of perishables; *San Francisco Chronicle,* November 11, 1885.

16. *Sacramento Record-Union,* June 8, 1892, and March 9, 1895; *Sacramento Bee,* February 19, 21, and 27, and March 9, 1895; Blackford, *Politics of Business in California,* 18–19.

17. For a more detailed account of Southern Pacific support for California displays in the East and elsewhere, chapter 6.

18. A. Andrews, *Report of A. Andrews, United States Commissioner for California at the World's Industrial and Cotton Centennial Exposition, New Orleans, Louisiana, December 16, 1884, to June 1, 1885* (Sacramento: State Printer, 1886), passim; *California Spirit of the Times* (San Francisco), May 2, 1885; *Southern Pacific Company Circular Number 23, Office General Passenger Agent* (San Francisco, October 20, 1885); *North, Central, and South American Exposition Gazette,* September and November 1885; Southern Pacific Company, *Catalogue of the Products of California, Exhibited by the Southern Pacific Company, at the North, Central, and South American Exposition, New Orleans, November 10th, 1885, to April 1st, 1886* (New Orleans, 1886), 16–20; *San Francisco Chronicle,* April 4, 1886; *Daily States* (New Orleans), December 2, 1885, January 3 and 7, 1886; *New Orleans Times-Democrat,* March 27 and December 23, 1885; Los Angeles Board of Trade, *Annual Report* (Los Angeles, 1885), 30ff.; California Immigration Commission, Chicago, Illinois, *California: The Cornucopia of the World* (Chicago: Rand-McNally Co., 1886), 75.

19. See *New Orleans Picayune,* January 13 and December 31, 1885, and February 5, 1886; *New Orleans Times-Democrat,* March 5, 1885; *Buffalo Courier,* January 22, 1885; and *Evening Wisconsin* (Milwaukee), January 19, 1885.

20. *Alta California* (San Francisco), April 14, 1885; *San Francisco Chronicle,* April 13, 1885; *San Francisco Post,* April 6, 1885; Southern Pacific Company, *Catalogue,* passim; *New Orleans Picayune,* December 31, 1885, and February 5, 1886; *Evening Wisconsin* (Milwaukee), January 19, 1885; *Louisville Times,* October 16, 1885; *The Commercial* (Louisville), October 16, 1885; *Daily States* (New Orleans), January 4, 1885; *Buffalo Courier,* January 22, 1885; *New Orleans Times-Democrat,* February 25, 1888. See also Los Angeles Board of Trade, *Annual Report* (1885), 17ff.; Benjamin Truman, "The Fruits of California," *New York Times,* April 13, 1887; Charles Dwight Willard, *The Herald's History of Los Angeles* (Los Angeles: Kingsley-Barnes and Neuner Co., 1901), 326; Norton P. Chipman, *Report upon the Fruit Industry of California: Its Growth and Development and Present and Future Importance* (San Francisco: State Board of Trade of California, 1889), 15.

21. Mills and Alsip, *Report on the Columbus, Ohio, Exhibit,* 4ff. and 11–13; *Resources of California,* January, March, May, and December 1889, and April 1990; *San Francisco Examiner,* May 8, 1889; *San Francisco Bulletin,* January 4, 11, 23, and 31, 1890; *Alta California* (San Francisco), October 25 and 26, November 13 and 23, 1889, and January 8, 1890; *San Francisco Chronicle,* January 1, 1890; *Sacramento Record-Union,* December 5 and 7, 1889, and January 8, 1890; *Woodland Mail,* August 31, 1890; California State Board of Trade, *Two Grand Tours of the Unique Exhibit Train Known as California on Wheels Under the Auspices of the California State Board of Trade and the Southern Pacific Company* (San Francisco: California State Board of Trade, December 1889), and *Catalogue of the Natural Products of California Compiled by the State Board of Trade to Accompany Its Travelling Free Exhibit Known as "California on Wheels"* (San Francisco: California State Board of Trade, n.d.).

22. *Sacramento Record-Union,* June 8, 1892, for new fast-freight fruit service; Rufus

Steele, "What Pre-Cooling Means," *Sunset* 24 (March 1910): 339–43, for Sacramento cooling plant.

23. Reprints of the *New York Times* articles, *California Spirit of the Times* (San Francisco), February 5 and 19, March 5, 12, 19, and 26, and April 2, 16, and 23, 1887. *Spirit of the Times,* April 30, 1887, published an account of Truman's invitation in 1886 by the editor of the *New York Times* to write the series and how, with the support of vice president Charles F. Crocker and general manager Alban N. Towne, he traveled to the state's leading wine-producing districts and wrote the articles.

24. *Sunset* 2 (February 1899): 74–75, and (April 1899): 136, 6 (March 1901): 164–68, and (April 1901): 209–15, 7 (June–July 1901): 81, 15 (June 1905): 190–200, and 21 (July 1908): 280–81; Southern Pacific Company, *California Prune Primer* (San Francisco, 1901), *California Big Tree Primer* (San Francisco, 1901), *California for the Settler Primer* (San Francisco, 1903), and *Eat California Fruit* (San Francisco, 1904 and 1908).

25. For the Sunkist campaign, Josephine Kingsbury Jacobs, "Sunkist Advertising" (Ph.D. diss., University of California, Los Angeles, 1966), 18ff.; Rahno M. McCurdy, *History of California Fruit Growers' Exchange* (Los Angeles, 1925), 59–61; Street, "Marketing California Crops," 239–53; Erdman, "Development and Significance of California Cooperatives," 183–84; Frank L. Beach, "The Transformation of California, 1900–1920: The Effects of the Westward Movement on California's Growth and Development" (Ph.D. diss., University of California, Berkeley, 1963), 66–67; *California Citrograph* 5 (March 1920): 66–67; for the campaign in the larger history of advertising, E. J. Murphy, *The Movement West: Advertising's Impact on the Building of the West and the Years Ahead* (Denver: Sage Books, 1958), 30.

26. *Southern Pacific Bulletin* 9 (February 1920): 3–4.

27. William Robertson to E. J. Wickson, Fresno, April 5, 1909, E. J. Wickson Correspondence and Papers, *BL*.

28. For the initial campaign, *Los Angeles Times,* March 10 and 11, April 29 and 30, and May 1, 1909; *San Francisco Call,* March 11, 1909; *Pacific Rural Press,* March 20 and April 17 and 24, 1909; "California Raisins, Their Day," *Sunset* 22 (May 1909): 550. For subsequent development, *McFarland Tribune,* May 2, 1930; *Southern Pacific Bulletin* 2 (March 15, 1914): 3; also Fred K. Howard, *History of Raisin Marketing in California* (Fresno: Sun-Maid Raisin Growers, n.d.); Morris Wills, "California Raisin Day and the Raisin' of Fresno County" (Graduate course paper, Department of History, California State University, Hayward, 1998), this author's collection; Edith Meyer, "The Development of the Raisin Industry in Fresno County" (M.A. thesis, University of California, Berkeley, 1931).

29. *Southern Pacific Bulletin* 2 (March 1, 1914): 3, and 4 (February 17, 1917): 4.

30. For early history and problems of refrigerator cars, "Genesis of the Refrigerator Car," *Illinois Central Magazine* (October 1929), pp. 3–5; John H. White, *Great Yellow Fleet: A History of American Railroad Refrigerator Cars* (San Marino, CA: Golden West Books, 1986), chap. 1. For disappointing Southern Pacific experiments, *San Francisco Bulletin,* June 23, 1870; *Sacramento Record,* undated clipping, ca. early July 1870, "Southern Pacific Scraps," vol. 1, *HEH; Sacramento Record,* July 20 and 22, 1870; *San Francisco Chronicle,* March 28, 1894.

31. For problems with shipment of perishables, White, *Great Yellow Fleet,* passim; Thompson et al., *Pacific Fruit Express,* passim, esp. 4ff.

32. White, *Great Yellow Fleet,* 25ff.; Thompson et al., *Pacific Fruit Express,* 275–76. For Wells Fargo, "How Wells Fargo Handles Fruit in California," *Wells Fargo Messenger,* August 1913, pp. 191–93, 199; *Wells Fargo Messenger,* September 1912, pp. 5ff., March 1913, p. 110, April 1913, p. 132, and May 1914, p. 149; Robert Chandler, "Harvest Bounty" (unpublished typescript, November 16, 1983), Wells Fargo History Department, San Francisco. I am indebted to Dr. Chandler of the Wells Fargo History Department for information about Wells Fargo and other private companies.

33. Thompson et al., *Pacific Fruit Express,* 276.

34. For early history of Pacific Fruit Express, White, *Great Yellow Fleet,* 149–75; Thompson et al., *Pacific Fruit Express,* passim, esp. 3–54; Southern Pacific Company, "Historical Memoranda," I, chap. 19, *SP-E,* esp. for founding and financial history; Pacific Fruit Express Collection, *CRRM,* esp. for technology and rolling stock; C. M. Secrist, "P.F.E. Co. Takes Great Strides in 14 Years," *Southern Pacific Bulletin* 10 (July 1921): 13–14; J. W. McClymonds, "Proper Handling of Perishable Fruit Rests on Grower, Shipper, and Carrier," *Southern Pacific Bulletin* 2 (April 1, 1914): 1–2; *Southern Pacific Bulletin* 2 (July 1, 1914): 1–2; C. J. McDonald, "How Western Perishable Products Are Handled," *Southern Pacific Bulletin* (July 1924): 5–7; Don L. Hofsommer, *The Southern Pacific, 1901–1985* (College Station: Texas A & M University Press, 1985), passim, esp. 68–69.

35. Thompson et al., *Pacific Fruit Express,* 5ff.

36. Edna B. Patterson et al., *Nevada's Northeastern Frontier* (Sparks, NV: Western Printing and Publishing Co., 1969), 596–97.

37. On Roseville plant, Leonard M. Davis, *Roseville's Pacific Fruit Express, from 1909–1996* (Roseville, CA: Roseville Historical Society, n.d.), 1–35; John R. Signor, *Donner Pass: Southern Pacific's Sierra Crossing* (San Marino, CA: Golden West Books, 1985), passim; *Southern Pacific Bulletin* 2 (May 1, 1914): 3. On ice generally, Thompson et al., *Pacific Fruit Express,* chaps. 12–13 and pp. 293–95. Additional general Pacific Fruit Express sources: "The Story of a Half-Million Cakes of Ice," *Southern Pacific Bulletin* 16 (February 1927): 7; *Southern Pacific Bulletin* 5 (January 15, 1917): 2, for natural ice harvesting in Nevada and Truckee, California; David F. Myrick, *Railroads of Arizona, Vol. I: The Southern Roads* (Berkeley: Howell-North Books, 1975), 127–32. For Fresno ice plant and icing station, "New Terminal Speeds Fruit Movement," *Southern Pacific Bulletin* (December 13, 1930); at modern facilities like Fresno's, automation allowed as many as 150 reefers to be re-iced simultaneously in just a few minutes.

38. *Pacific Rural Press* (San Francisco), March 20, 1909, p. 226; Steele, "What Pre-Cooling Means," 339–43.

39. McDonald, "How Western Perishable Products Are Handled," 5–7.

40. *Southern Pacific Bulletin (Texas and Louisiana)* 11 (July 1926): 2.

41. Secrist, "P.F.E. Co. Takes Great Strides in 14 Years," 13–14; Davis, *Roseville's Pacific Fruit Express,* 15–16; White, *Great Yellow Fleet,* 151ff.

42. See McClymonds, "Proper Handling of Perishable Fruit," 1–2; *Southern Pacific Bulletin (Texas and Louisiana)* 9 (December 1923): 8; 11 (July 1926): 2; and 14 (December 1929): 7; Myrick, *Railroads of Arizona,* 1:127–32.

43. *Southern Pacific Bulletin* 13 (April 1924): 3–4; White, *Great Yellow Fleet,* 160–61.

44. Dividing the profits and credit from Pacific Fruit Express caused friction between the two, usually mutually hostile, railroad companies; W. A. Worthington to Julius Kruttschnitt, January 4, 1921, File: UP, box 35, *SP-E;* Southern Pacific Company, "Historical Memoranda," I, chap. 19; Thompson et al., *Pacific Fruit Express,* 5ff.; Secrist, "P.F.E. Co. Takes Great Strides in 14 Years," 13–14.

45. *Southern Pacific Bulletin* 2 (December 1, 1914): 1.

46. Pacific Fruit Express, Reports on Test Trips, Pacific Fruit Express Collection, *CRRM;* esp. "No. 27, Cantaloupes, Brawley, California, to New York, New York, June 1922."

47. For Pacific Fruit Express's organizational services, White, *Great Yellow Fleet,* 151ff.; Thompson et al., *Pacific Fruit Express,* passim.

48. See *Southern Pacific Bulletin* 3 (June 1, 1915): 5, for a Sacramento meeting. By the 1920s, such annual meetings were standard practice. Some were general and regional, some including only growers and handlers of one crop, such as cantaloupes in the Imperial Valley. For company leaders' views of perishables shipping and marketing and organizational services provided by the Southern Pacific and Pacific Fruit Express, McDonald, "How Western Perishable Products Are Handled," 5–7; McClymonds, "Proper Handling of Fruit," 1–2.

49. Secrist, "P.F.E. Co. Takes Great Strides in 14 Years," 13–14.

50. Early history of Imperial Valley cantaloupe industry, in Walter E. Packard, *Agriculture in the Imperial Valley: A Manual for Settlers* (Berkeley: University of California College of Agriculture Circular No. 159, January 1917), 55ff.; "The Start of the Cantaloupe Industry," *Western Grower and Shipper* (May 1979): 113–15; Thompson et al., *Pacific Fruit Express,* 360–61.

51. For the Southern Pacific, Pacific Fruit Express, and the development of the Imperial Valley cantaloupe industry, see Thompson et al., *Pacific Fruit Express,* 360–65. Articles on the railroad's cantaloupe shipment, including a photo survey of every stage, appeared in *Life Magazine,* July 15, 1940, abbreviated in *Southern Pacific Bulletin,* August 1940. See also, George R. McIntosh, "How Imperial's Cantaloupe Crop is Handled," *Southern Pacific Bulletin* 10 (October 1921): 21–22; *Southern Pacific Bulletin* 16 (September 1925): 5–6; "Fruits and Vegetables for Half the Nation," *Southern Pacific Bulletin* 17 (September 1929): 7–10; and "Perishables Require Specialized Handling: Southern Pacific Has Built Up Efficient Organization in the Imperial Valley," *Southern Pacific Bulletin* (November 30, 1929). The best source of primary documents, particularly from the 1920s, is in the San Diego and Arizona Railroad Collection, Operations File, box 5, folders 10 and 11, "Special Cargoes—Cantaloupes," San Diego Historical Society.

52. For the meetings, *Southern Pacific Bulletin* 12 (June 1923): 8, and 14 (June 1925): 10; and documents in the San Diego and Arizona Railroad Collection, Operations File, box 5, folders 10 and 11, San Diego Historical Society: esp. A. D. Hagaman to A. T. Mercier, San Diego, May 20, 1922, a report from a railroad agent who attended a shipment organizational meeting; Southern Pacific Company, "Annual Meeting of Representatives of the Cantaloupe Growers and Distributors of Imperial Valley . . . El Centro, May 12, 1924" (mimeo); Southern Pacific Company, "Minutes of Annual Meeting

to discuss and arrange handling of cantaloupe crop in Imperial Valley, Season of 1925" (mimeo); and other meeting reports; also, *San Diego Union,* June 25, 1922.

53. Thompson et al., *Pacific Fruit Express,* 360–63; and esp. folders 10 and 11, box 5, Operations File, San Diego and Arizona Railroad Collection, San Diego Historical Society: see esp. Southern Pacific Company, "Annual Meeting of Representatives of the Cantaloupe Growers and Distributors . . . Brawley . . . May 3rd, 1928" (mimeo); *Southern Pacific Bulletin* 16 (August 1927): 3–4.

54. Thompson et al., *Pacific Fruit Express,* 360; *Southern Pacific Bulletin* 2 (March 15, 1914): 8, 3 (July 15, 1919): 1, 5 (July 1, 1917): 6, and 16 (September 1925): 5–6; *Los Angeles Times,* July 13, 1927.

55. Thompson et al., *Pacific Fruit Express,* 360.

56. *Southern Pacific Bulletin* 16 (August 1927): 3–4.

57. "Recollections of Pete Holst," in Thompson et al., *Pacific Fruit Express,* 362–63; Holst's memoir covers the 1920s and 1930s.

58. Louis P. Hopkins, "A Lifetime of Railroading" (typescript autobiography), 28ff., Oregon Collection, University of Oregon.

59. McIntosh, "How Imperial's Cantaloupe Crop Is Handled," 21–22; Williams's statement, "Annual Meeting of Representatives of the Cantaloupe Growers and Distributors . . . Brawley . . . May 3rd, 1928" (mimeo), San Diego and Arizona Railroad Collection, Operations File, box 5, folders 10 and 11, San Diego Historical Society; "Recollections of Pete Holst," in Thompson et al., *Pacific Fruit Express,* 363.

60. San Diego and Arizona Railroad, "Freight Statistics—Fruits and Vegetables" (ms, 1928–1929), San Diego and Arizona Railroad Collection, Operations File, box 5, folder 10, San Diego Historical Society.

61. Reports and minutes of meetings, Operations File, San Diego and Arizona Railroad, box 5, folders 10 and 11, San Diego Historical Society, testify to the cooperation in the industry: see esp. "Summary of the 1922 Imperial Valley Cantaloupe Deal" (mimeo, Market News Service, U.S. Department of Agriculture, Bureau of Agricultural Economics), "Annual Meeting of Representatives of the Cantaloupe Growers and Distributors of Imperial Valley . . . El Centro, May 12, 1924" (mimeo), and "Annual Meeting of Cantaloupe Growers and Distributors [and railroad officials] . . . El Centro . . . May 12, 1925" (mimeo).

62. See *San Diego Union,* June 25, 1922; *Calexico Chronicle,* May 1, 1909, pp. 39, 48; *Los Angeles Times,* July 3, 1927; Associate Chambers of Commerce of Imperial Valley, *Brief Historical Sketch of Imperial Valley* (1946), 12, 15.

63. *Los Angeles Times,* July 3, 1927; *Southern Pacific Bulletin* (August 1927): 4.

64. For reefer crisis of 1920, see C. M. Secrist (vice president and general manager, Pacific Fruit Express), "The Refrigerator Car Supply," *Southern Pacific Bulletin* 9 (June 1920): 27; J. H. Dyer, "Moving the Perishable Freight Business," *Southern Pacific Bulletin* 9 (December 1920): 11; also *Southern Pacific Bulletin* 9 (July 1920): 10. Incredibly, on April 1, 1920, only 1,500 Pacific Fruit Express reefers were on Southern Pacific lines west of El Paso, a tiny fraction of what the region needed and only one-tenth the immediate requirement for Imperial cantaloupes.

65. For a brief review of other cantaloupe districts, Thompson et al., *Pacific Fruit Express*, 363. For cantaloupes and other products, also *Southern Pacific Bulletin* 11 (September 1922): 27, 12 (February 1923): 17, 16 (July 1927): 14, 16 (February 1928): 20, 9 (July 1920): 19 (for green fruit), and Leo C. Monahan (manager of grower and livestock relations, California Vineyardists' Association), "California Grapes Go to Market," *Southern Pacific Bulletin* 16 (September 1928): 9. For Texas, Arizona, and New Mexico, Clifford R. Morrill (superintendent of the Southern Pacific's El Paso Division, 1919–39), "Railroad History: El Paso Division, Southern Pacific" (typescript copy, Texas A & M University Library, 1971), *DG,* ms, A1994, 1954c. The cantaloupe system, only slightly modified, was used to ship Imperial Valley lettuce as recently as 1960; *Imperial Valley Press* (El Centro), December, 30, 1960.

66. "Fruits and Vegetables for Half the Nation," *Southern Pacific Bulletin* 17 (September 1929): 7–10; Morrill, "Railroad History: El Paso Division."

67. W. J. Smith, "The Value of the Crop Report," *Southern Pacific Bulletin* 9 (July 1920): 27.

68. William Sproule to Julius Kruttschnitt, San Francisco, August 24 and November 6, 1916; Kruttschnitt to Sproule, telegram, New York, November 16, 1916; G. W. Luce to Sproule, November 3, 1916; and other letters, telegrams, and documents (1916–18), some of which review the history of the practice, box 35, file 081, *SP-E.*

69. Southern Pacific Company, Pacific Lines, Accounting Department, "Statement of Money Loaned . . . to Outside Interests" (typescript, May 20, 1930), box 29, *SP-E; Southern Pacific Bulletin* 2 (August 15, 1914): 3. The practice was still used in the 1960s; Southern Pacific Company, "Historical Memoranda" (ca. 1960s), I, chap. 20, p. 15, *SP-E,* reporting many outstanding loans of nearly $1 million each to cooperatives and food processors.

70. For example of the Texas and Louisiana agricultural development department, *Southern Pacific Bulletin (Texas and Louisiana)* 9 (October 1923): 9; other issues of this regional company publication carried reviews. Also, *Houston Post,* July 20, 1913.

71. See Texas Farmers' Congress, *Proceedings of the Third Annual Session of Held at A & M College, College Station, Texas, July 3rd to 6th, 1900* (Houston: Sunset Central Lines, 1900), 5ff., 61–62, 251ff., and *Proceedings, 1911* (Austin: Texas Department of Agriculture, Bulletin 22, November–December 1911), 148–49; Sam H. Dixon, *Texas Fruits at World's Fair, 1904* (Houston: Southern Pacific, 1905), esp. 15–16; S. F. B. Morse (passenger traffic manager, Southern Pacific lines, Houston), *Railroads and Their Relation to Development and Immigration: Address at the Texas Real Estate and Industrial Convention, at San Antonio, Texas, June 27, 1900* (Houston: Cumming and Sons, Publishers, 1900).

72. See H. S. Kneedler (Southern Pacific Company), *The Coast Country of Texas: A General Study of the Region . . .* (Cincinnati: The A. H. Pugh Printing Co., 1896); L. H. Shelfer, *Texas Tobacco and Diversified Farming* (Houston: Southern Pacific, 1903); Southern Pacific, Sunset Route, Passenger Department, *Growing Figs and Citrus Fruits in South Texas . . .* (Houston: Cumming and Sons, Art Printers, 1910).

73. Pete Daniel, *Breaking the Land: The Transformation of Cotton, Tobacco, and Rice*

Cultures since 1880 (Urbana: University of Illinois Press, 1985), 40–42; Henry C. Dethloff, *A History of the American Rice Industry, 1685–1985* (College Station: Texas A & M University Press, 1988), 69–70.

74. *Texas Coast Country* (Houston: Southern Pacific, 1909), esp. 19–26; *Texas Rice Book* (Houston: Passenger Department, Southern Pacific, Sunset Route, ca. 1900); *Texas Rice Cookbook: Containing Two Hundred Recipes for Preparing Rice, Compiled by the Passenger Department of the Southern Pacific-Sunset Route* (Houston, 1901); Southern Pacific Company, *Texas and Louisiana Rice: How It Is Grown and Cooked . . . Compiled by the Sunset Route Passenger and Industrial Department, New Orleans, Louisiana, and Houston, Texas . . .* (Houston: Cumming and Sons, 1911).

75. Southern Pacific Company, *Texas Rice Cookbook*, 4–5.

76. Southern Pacific Company, *Texas and Louisiana Rice: How It Is Grown and Cooked*, 33.

77. *Fruit and Produce Distributor* (Portland), September 16, 1914; *Southern Pacific Bulletin* 2 (October 15, 1914): 8, and 3 (February 15, 1915): 1; Southern Pacific Company, *Apples—Apple Dish Recipes of the Southern Pacific Dining Car Department* (Southern Pacific Lines, 1927).

78. See documents in the Amos A. Morse Correspondence, Oregon Collection, University of Oregon Library, Eugene. Morse was much respected in the Northwest, and reviews of his career were published at his retirement in 1913; see *Portland Oregonian*, February 4, 1913; *The Tooter* (Portland; Harriman Lines employees' magazine) 1 (February 4, 1913): 2; also *Grays Harbor* (Oregon) *News*, February 8, 1911, for a summary of his development work.

79. Amos A. Morse to R. B. Miller, Portland, January 8, 1912, Morse Correspondence, Oregon Collection, University of Oregon, reporting on the Washington Horticultural Association meeting; Oswald Wish (governor of Oregon) to Morse, Salem, Oregon, September 19, 1919.

80. Amos A. Morse to R. B. Miller, November 10, 11, 15, and 26, 1907, July 20, 1908, and November 25 and 26, 1912; Miller to Morse, October 26, 1907; Miller, "Circular Letter No. 288, Oregon Railroad and Navigation Company . . . Freight Department" (Portland, February 1, 1908), Morse Correspondence, Oregon Collection, University of Oregon; *The Tooter* 1 (February 4, 1913): 2.

81. See discussion of cantaloupes in Nevada, above.

82. The Southern Pacific, particularly under William H. Mills's tenure as land agent, 1883–1907, had attempted to sell Central Pacific's land in the Great Basin, to little avail, except in small tracts in the Truckee-Carson Project, which got under way in 1902. For the persistence of the checkerboard pattern of railroad land over northern Nevada and Utah, see manuscript Central Pacific Land Company map books (ca. 1906 and following years), *CRRM*.

83. See documents in File 731, "Shearing Pens at Winnemucca," *SP-L; The Silver State* (Winnemucca), March 1, 1913; *Southern Pacific Bulletin* 11 (June 1922): 26.

84. The practice was used often through the early decades of the twentieth century; for the 1894 episode, *San Francisco Chronicle*, April 28, 1894. For emergency service that year, the company charged $25–60 per car, compared to its standard $90–125. In the

period, the Southern Pacific often moved ranchers' drought-ravaged herds and brought in emergency feed supplies at cost.

85. P. Bancroft, "Facilities for Shippers at Ogden," *Southern Pacific Bulletin* 11 (August 1922): 16–17.

86. For trails, File 444, "Trail Clauses," *SP-L;* and chapter 14.

13   Wilderness Preservation

The quotation in the chapter title comes from railroad land agent William H. Mills, who asked the question in his article attacking deforestation and pleading for forest preservation; "Are We Unwittingly Destroying a State?" *San Francisco Post,* June 21, 1899.

1. On railroads and national parks, see Alfred Runte, *Trains of Discovery: Western Railroads and the National Parks* (Flagstaff, AZ: Northland Press, 1984; rev. eds. 1990, 1998, published by Roberts Rinehart, Boulder, CO); Runte, "Pragmatic Alliance: Western Railroads and the National Parks," *National Parks and Conservation Magazine* 48 (April 1974): 14–21; Runte, *Burlington Northern and the Dedication of Mount St. Helens: New Legacy of a Proud Tradition* (Seattle: Burlington Northern, 1982); Kevin M. DeLuca, "Trains in the Wilderness: The Corporate Roots of Environmentalism," *Rhetoric and Public Affairs* 4:4 (2001): 633–52.

2. Part of this chapter, based on my " 'Wilderness Saint' and 'Robber Baron': The Anomalous Partnership of John Muir and the Southern Pacific Company for the Preservation of Yosemite National Park," *The Pacific Historian* 29 (Summer/Fall 1985): 136–56.

3. Arthur F. McEvoy, *The Fisherman's Problem: Ecology and Law in the California Fisheries, 1850–1980* (Cambridge: Cambridge University Press, 1986), 50.

4. *Southern Pacific Bulletin* 11 (January 1922): 13, (March 1922): 21, (November 1922): 31; *Salt Lake Tribune,* December 1, 1921. The causeway continues to cause occasional flood damage; see, for example, *Salt Lake Tribune,* June 10, July 7, and December 16 and 20, 1983; *Deseret News* (Salt Lake City), June 10 and December 20, 1983; *Ogden Standard-Examiner,* June 22, 1983; *Wall Street Journal (Western Edition),* March 29, 1983; *Time,* May 2, 1983.

5. See, for construction photographs, George Kraus, *High Road to Promontory: Building the Central Pacific across the High Sierra* (Palo Alto: American West Publishing Co., 1969), 93, 105, 108–109, 112–13, 117–18, 122, 132–33, 154–55, 164–66, 206–207, 234, and 239; also, for Alfred Hart's Central Pacific construction photographs illustrating destructiveness, Mead B. Kibbey, *The Railroad Photographs of Alfred A. Hart, Artist,* ed. Peter E. Palmquist (Sacramento: California State Library Foundation, 1995), esp. stereo nos. 1–25 (esp. of the Bloomer Cut, near Auburn, CA), 46–53, 70–73, 82, 85, 90–92, 202, 221–23, and 338. For disruption of wildlife, especially rattlesnakes, J. O. Wilder, "My Half Century of Railroad Service," *Southern Pacific Bulletin* 9 (October 1920): 22–23. For the Southern Pacific right-of-way and exotic organisms, Burton Gordon, *The Monterey Bay Area: Natural History and Cultural Imprints* (Pacific Grove, CA: Boxwood Press, 1977), 71; William L. Preston, *Vanishing Landscapes: Land and Life in the Tu-*

lare Lake Basin (Berkeley: University of California Press, 1981), 121–63; and for railroads in general, Joseph M. Petulla, *American Environmental History: The Exploitation and Conservation of Natural Resources* (San Francisco: Boyd & Fraser Publishing Co., 1977), passim. For a more complete review of railroads', particularly Southern Pacific's, impact on natural environments in California and the West, see Richard J. Orsi, "The Octopus in the Garden: The Dark Side of Railroading in the American West" (unpublished ms., 1991).

6. John R. Stilgoe, *The Metropolitan Corridor: Railroads and the American Scene* (New Haven: Yale University Press, 1983), 137ff.

7. John Muir, *Our National Parks* (Boston: Houghton Mifflin, 1901), 357–59.

8. *Sacramento Record-Union,* December 15, 1880.

9. Richard J. Orsi, *"The Octopus* Reconsidered: The Southern Pacific and Agricultural Modernization in California, 1865–1915," *California Historical Quarterly* 54 (Fall 1975): 197–220, and "Selling the Golden State: A Study of Boosterism in Nineteenth-Century California" (Ph.D. diss., University of Wisconsin, Madison, 1973), chaps. 4–6.

10. For example, the building of the Central Pacific in the late 1860s over Donner Pass to points east (along with the surging market of the Comstock Lode of western Nevada) caused a boom in logging and milling operations to provide fuel and building materials. Short, usually narrow-gauge railroads, connecting to the Central Pacific at Truckee and Reno and/or the Virginia and Truckee Railroad at Carson City, facilitated the virtual denuding of forests within reach of the lines and around the Lake Tahoe Basin by century's end; the man-induced second-growth forest that eventually developed was ecologically weaker, prone to devastation from drought, fire, and pests; Douglas H. Strong, *Tahoe: From Timber Barons to Ecologists* (Lincoln: University of Nebraska Press, 1999), 15–18; Dick Wilson, *Sawdust Trails in the Truckee Basin: A History of Lumbering Operations, 1856–1936* (Nevada City, CA: Nevada County Historical Society, 1992), passim, esp. xi–xiii, 25–29, 74–79, and 82–83. For railroad destruction of forests in Appalachia, Ronald L. Lewis, *Transforming the Appalachian Countryside: Railroads, Deforestation, and Social Change in West Virginia, 1880–1920* (Chapel Hill: University of North Carolina Press, 1998). For non–Southern Pacific railroads in the Pacific Northwest, Nancy Langston, *Forest Dreams, Forest Nightmares: The Paradox of Old Growth in the Inland West* (Seattle: University of Washington Press, 1995), 80ff.; Richard A. Rajala, *Clearcutting the Pacific Rain Forest* (Vancouver: University of British Columbia Press, 1998), xvii, 56–57, and passim. For the environmental devastation caused by mining and livestock ranching spreading along rail lines, especially the Southern Pacific's in southern Arizona, Conrad Joseph Bahre, *A Legacy of Change: Historic Human Impact on Vegetation in the Arizona Borderlands* (Tucson: University of Arizona Press, 1991), 36ff., 116ff. For altered land use the Southern Pacific's lines caused in the San Antonio and general south-central Texas area, Char Miller, "Where Buffalo Roamed: Ranching, Agriculture, and the Urban Marketplace," in *On the Border: An Environmental History of San Antonio,* ed. Char Miller (Pittsburgh: University of Pittsburgh Press, 2001), 70–78.

11. For environmental transformation of regions caused by railroad line construction and the resulting change in land use in California, see Preston, *Vanishing Land-*

scapes, 85–189; Gordon, *Monterey Bay Area,* 71; for lines radiating from Chicago, William Cronon, *Nature's Metropolis: Chicago and the Great West* (New York: W.W. Norton, 1991); for the larger United States, Stilgoe, *Metropolitan Corridor.*

12. Orsi, "*The Octopus* Reconsidered," 197–206.

13. Earl Pomeroy, *In Search of the Golden West: The Tourist in Western America* (New York: Alfred A. Knopf, 1957), passim, and for Hotel Del Monte, 19–20. Hal K. Rothman, *Devil's Bargains: Tourism in the Twentieth-Century American West* (Lawrence: University Press of Kansas, 1998), investigates how western railroads worked in conjunction with other social, economic, and technological changes to popularize a more positive, if culture-bound, appreciation of scenery and wilderness, 29–112; Rothman does not present much information on the Southern Pacific. Also, John Baur, *The Health Seekers of Southern California, 1870–1900* (San Marino: The Huntington Library, 1959); Peter Palmquist, *C. E. Watkins, Photographer of the American West* (Albuquerque: Published for the Amon Carter Museum by the University of New Mexico Press, 1983), and *C. E. Watkins: Photographs, 1861–1874* (San Francisco: Fraenkel Gallery in association with Bedford Arts, 1989); Jennifer Watts, "The Photographer [Watkins] and the Railroad Man [Collis P. Huntington]," *California History* 78 (Fall 1999): 154–59; Gary F. Kurutz, *Benjamin C. Truman: California Booster and Bon Vivant* (San Francisco: Book Club of California, 1984); Charles Nordhoff, *California: For Health, Pleasure, or Residence* (New York: Harper and Bros., 1872), and many other editions; and Kibbey, *The Railroad Photographs of Alfred A. Hart,* passim.

14. Thurman Wilkins, *John Muir: Apostle of Nature* (Norman: University of Oklahoma Press: 1995), xxvi. On the rise of nature cults in late-nineteenth-century America, Roderick Nash, *Wilderness and the American Mind* (New Haven: Yale University Press, 1967 and later eds.), which does not examine the railroads' role. For railroads' role in promoting tourism, national parks, and the celebration of wild and scenic western nature, often in league with conservationists and preservationists, see many writings of historian Alfred Runte, esp. *Trains of Discovery;* also, Richard West Sellars, *Preserving Nature in the National Parks: A History* (New Haven: Yale University Press, 1997), 8ff., 12–22, 32–35, 89.

15. Orsi, "*The Octopus* Reconsidered," 197–206; Samuel P. Hays, *Conservation and the Gospel of Efficiency: The Progressive Conservation Movement, 1890–1920* (Cambridge: Harvard University Press, 1959), 223; Petulla, *American Environmental History,* 230–31; Runte, "Pragmatic Alliance," 14–21, and *Trains of Discovery.*

16. Orsi, "*The Octopus* Reconsidered," 197–206. Redding was a researcher and writer on soils, climate, agriculture, zoology, and natural history and was an organizer and patron of the California Academy of Sciences and a member of the California State Fisheries Commission and the Board of Regents of the University of California; Alonzo Phelps, *Contemporary Biography of California's Representative Men,* 2 vols. (San Francisco: A. L. Bancroft and Co., 1882), 2:77–83; *Alta California* (San Francisco), August 22, 1882; California Academy of Sciences, *In Memoriam: Benjamin B. Redding* (n.p., n.d.). Even more deeply involved was William H. Mills. One of the first western conservationists, Mills and his newspaper, the *Sacramento Record-Union,* advocated scientific forestry, wilderness preservation, and comprehensive water management. He was a founder and/or officer of the American Forestry Association of California, the Inter-

national Irrigation Congress, California state's Yosemite Valley Commission, and the California Redwood Park Commission. He was also one of the originators of the 160-acre principle for limiting federally subsidized irrigation water to small farmers; Orsi, "*The Octopus* Reconsidered," 197–206; *San Francisco: Its Builders, Past and Present* (San Francisco: S. J. Clarke Publishing Co., 1913), 1:343; *San Francisco Chronicle*, May 25, 1907; and previous chapters. Although not as prolific a writer as Redding and Mills, McAllaster was an expert on irrigation, soil conservation, and forestry. He fostered scientific land management procedures on the Southern Pacific grant and participated in the organization or expansion of numerous local irrigation districts and national reclamation projects, most notably the Truckee-Carson Project, the first built under the 1902 National Reclamation Act; see esp. files 609, 610, 610A, 610B, 610C, and 610D on the Truckee-Carson Project, *SP-L*.

17. See esp. chapters 9 and 11.

18. Promoting conservation was a major theme in *Sunset* under Southern Pacific ownership: E. T. Perkins, "Redeeming the West," *Sunset* 16 (November 1905): 3–25; C. J. Blanchard, "Redeeming the West," 17 (September 1906): 207–214; the entire issue of 14 (February 1905); H. T. Payne, "Game Birds of the Pacific," 22 (January 1909): 65–73; Sumner W. Matteson, "Saving the Buffalo," 21 (October 1908): 498–503; George H. Maxwell, "Save the Forests and Store the Floods," 9 (May 1902): 42–43; E. A. Sterling, "The Use of Forest Preserves," 19 (May 1907): 10–17. Support by Crocker, Stanford, Huntington, and Stow for city parks is described (for Golden Gate Park) in Raymond H. Clary, *The Making of Golden Gate Park. The Early Years, 1865–1906* (San Francisco, 1980), 35–36, 51–52, 71–72, and 97–109. For Lake Merritt Park, *Southern Pacific Bulletin* (November 1930): 9; *Oakland Tribune*, May 1, 1952; Beth Bagwell, *Oakland: The Story of a City* (Novato, CA: Presidio Press, 1982), 123–28. For Fresno's city park, *Fresno Republican*, September 22, 1929. For Harriman's conservationism, George Kennan, *E. H. Harriman: A Biography*, 2 vols. (Boston: Houghton Mifflin Co., 1922), 1:30–41, 88–173, and 326–46; William H. Goetzmann and Kay Sloan, *Looking Far North: The Harriman Expedition to Alaska* (New York: Viking, 1982).

19. Kendrick A. Clements, "Politics and the Park: San Francisco's Fight for Hetch Hetchy, 1908–1913," *Pacific Historical Review* 47 (May 1979): 202; Clements maintained that, in contrast to the railroad's support for the creation of Yosemite National Park in the first place, the failure of the Southern Pacific to back Muir's fight to save the park from reservoir development was a major factor in San Francisco's victory. For Herrin's support of Muir's position on the Hetch Hetchy dam, William F. Herrin to John Muir, San Francisco, November 14, 1907, *JMP*. The environmental issues regarding Hetch Hetchy were far from clear for the Southern Pacific and other traditional protectors of Yosemite, however, and even many of Muir's friends, and the Sierra Club entirely, abandoned Muir on this issue. Building a reservoir in the valley, according to some project supporters, including a writer in the railroad's magazine, would enhance the beauty of the hitherto isolated and rarely visited region, as well its recreational opportunities, and "the transformation will convert it into a greater scenic wonder than it is at present [1909]"; John P. Young, "The Hetch-Hetchy Problem," *Sunset* (June 1909).

20. Clements, "Politics and the Park," passim; Elmo Richardson, "The Struggle for

the Valley: California's Hetch Hetchy Controversy, 1905–1913," *California Historical Society Quarterly* 38 (September 1959): 249–58; Roderick Nash, "John Muir, William Kent, and the Conservation Schism," *Pacific Historical Review* 36 (November 1967): 423–33, and *Wilderness and the American Mind*, rev. ed. (New Haven: Yale University Press, 1977), 161–81 and 222–23; and Hays, *Conservation and the Gospel of Efficiency*, 189–98.

21. Hays, *Conservation and the Gospel of Efficiency*, passim; Robert Wiebe, *Businessmen and Reform: A Study of the Progressive Movement* (Cambridge: Harvard University Press, 1962), passim, and *The Search for Order, 1877–1920* (New York: Hill and Wang, 1967), passim; Keith L. Bryant and Henry C. Dethloff, *History of American Business* (New York: Prentice-Hall, 1983), 258.

22. Holway R. Jones, *Muir and the Sierra Club: The Battle for Yosemite* (San Francisco: Sierra Club, 1965), 1–147; Hans Huth, *Yosemite: The Story of an Idea* (Yosemite National Park, 1975). For evidence that Yosemite was the first "national park," see esp. Alfred Runte, *Yosemite: The Embattled Wilderness* (Lincoln: University of Nebraska Press, 1990), passim.

23. *Sierra Club Bulletin* 1 (January 1896): 278–80; also *San Francisco Examiner*, November 11, 1888; Galen Clark, "To the Honorable Board of Governors of the Yosemite Valley and Mariposa Big Trees Grove" (typed copy, August 30, 1894), Yosemite Research Library, Yosemite National Park; *Biennial Report of The Commissioners to Manage Yosemite Valley and the Mariposa Big Tree Grove, 1880* (Sacramento: State Printer, 1880), 3ff.; Linnie Marsh Wolfe, *Son of the Wilderness: The Life of John Muir* (New York: Alfred A. Knopf, 1945), 157ff., 244–46, and 291–93; Emil F. Ernst, "Preliminary Report on the Study of the Meadows of Yosemite Valley" (typescript, May 15, 1943), file 880–01, Yosemite Research Library, Yosemite National Park; Robert P. Gibbens and Harold F. Heady, *The Influence of Modern Man on the Vegetation of Yosemite Valley* (Berkeley: University of California, Division of Agricultural Sciences, July 1964); Harold F. Heady and Paul J. Zinke, *Vegetational Changes in Yosemite Valley* (Washington, DC: U.S. Department of Interior, National Park Service Occasional Paper Number Five, 1978).

24. *Sierra Club Bulletin* 1 (January 1896): 271–84; Wolfe, *Son of the Wilderness*, 157ff., 244–46, and 291–93; Stephen Fox, *John Muir and His Legacy: The American Conservation Movement* (Boston: Little, Brown, 1981), 103–28; Hank Johnston, *The Yosemite Grant, 1864–1906* (Yosemite National Park: Yosemite Association, 1995); esp. chap. 6 and 164–68, 187ff.

25. Wolfe, *Son of the Wilderness*, 238–304; Fox, *Muir*, 103–107.

26. Central Pacific Railroad, *Popular Summer Resorts of California and Nevada via Central Pacific Railroad* (San Francisco, July 1872); Nordhoff, *California: For Health, Pleasure, and Residence*, 69–73. For *Sunset* magazine's first issue (May 1898), the editors chose the theme of "Yosemite and the High Sierra." In this and subsequent issues the magazine argued for preservation; see Carl E. Acherman, "President Roosevelt in the Sierra" (July 1903), and Galen Clark, "Yosemite—Past and Present" (April 1907).

27. Alban N. Towne (superintendent, Central Pacific Railroad) to A. W. Kaddie (superintendent, Cariboo Mining Company, Plumas County, California), San Francisco, July 5, 1876; Towne to Mr. Scott (superintendent, North Fork Mining Company, Dutch Hill, California), San Francisco, July 5, 1876; James Horsburgh, Jr., to John Muir, San

Francisco, March 9, 1907; Edward H. Harriman to Muir, Ogden, Utah, April 28, 1904; William F. Herrin to Muir, San Francisco, October 17, 1907, January 26, 1911, *JMP.*

28. For Mills's role in the hydraulic-mining controversy, chapter 9.

29. *Sacramento Record-Union,* February 5, 1876; Milton Goldstein, *The Magnificent West: Yosemite* (Garden City, NY: Doubleday, n.d.), 203–206; Michael P. Cohen, *The Pathless Way: John Muir and American Wilderness* (Madison: University of Wisconsin Press, 1984), 196–204. One letter illustrates the friendship, Mills to Carr, San Francisco, February 9, 1894, Carr Collection, *HL;* it is possible, even likely, that Carr introduced Mills to Muir, with whom he shared many interests. See also Jane Apostol, "Jeanne Carr," *The American West* 15 (July/August 1978): 30.

30. *Sacramento Record-Union,* August 26, 1882, January 1 and 15, 1883, July 3, 1886, March 20, April 27, August 17, and October 26, 1890; *San Francisco Call,* December 15, 1900, for Mills's address to the Water and Forest Association of California.

31. California Yosemite Valley Commission, "Record of Executive Committee," vol. 3145 (meetings of February 24, 1879, and February 5, 1880), and vol. 3018 (meetings of December 16 and 17, 1885); California Yosemite Valley Commission, "Minutes" (meetings of September 28, 1880, March 22, 1881, June 3, 1885, October 15, 1885, June 1 and 2, 1887, and June 7, 1888); William H. Mills to Governor Washington Bartlett, San Francisco, February 11 and March 16, 1887, all in California Yosemite Valley Commission Papers, California State Archives, Sacramento; Theodore A. Goppert, "The Yosemite Valley Commission: The Development of Park Management Policies, 1864–1905" (M.A. thesis, California State University, Hayward, 1972), 35, 41, and 67–68; Jones, *Muir and the Sierra Club,* 35; Johnston, *Yosemite Grant,* 165. On the 1880s commission's partially effective policies and Mills's role, Goppert, "Yosemite Valley Commission," 31–58; Ernst, "Preliminary Report on Yosemite Valley"; and *Biennial Report of the Commissioners to Manage Yosemite Valley and Mariposa Big Tree Grove* (Sacramento, 1880), 3ff., (1882), 1–13, (1883), 3–10, (1886), 8–31 (reprinting William Hammond Hall's report to the commission on how to return the valley to a more natural, open forest and meadow, titled "To Preserve from Defacement and Promote the Use of Yosemite Valley"), (1888), 9–19, and (1890), 7–15 (reviewing controversy over the commission's forest-opening practices); Johnston, *Yosemite Grant,* 187ff. For Mills's introduction of controlled burning and other forestry practices, see his testimony during the 1889 legislative probe of the commission, *In the Matter of the Investigation of the Yosemite Valley Commissioners,* California State Legislature, Assembly, Twenty-Eighth Session, 1889 (Sacramento: State Printer, 1889), 41ff. For the Muir group's condemnation of the Yosemite Valley Commission's practices as "deforestation," George C. Mackenzie to John W. Noble (secretary of the interior), November 1, 1890 (copy), box Y-1C, Yosemite Research Library, Yosemite National Park.

32. *Sacramento Record-Union,* April 6, 1890.

33. William H. Mills to Robert Underwood Johnson, San Francisco, June 30 and August 2, 1889, Johnson Correspondence, *BL;* Mills to Johnson, San Francisco, January 5, 1893, *JMP.*

34. *Sacramento Record-Union,* April 6, 1890; and William H. Mills to Robert Underwood Johnson, San Francisco, January 5, 1893, *JMP.* For Mills's views on the state's mismanagement of Yosemite and his conversion to federal takeover of the valley, see his

later pamphlet as chairman of a California State Board of Trade committee created to promote retrocession of Yosemite Valley back to the federal government for inclusion in the surrounding national park; California State Board of Trade, *Yosemite Valley: History, Description and Statement of Conditions Relative to the Proposed Recession to the National Government* (San Francisco: California State Board of Trade, ca. 1905), passim.

35. Wolfe, *Son of the Wilderness*, 244–51; Muir to Robert Underwood Johnson, Martinez, California, March 4, and April 19 and 20, 1890; Johnson to Muir, New York, June 27, 1889, February 20, March 24, April 14, 1890, *JMP.*

36. John Muir, "Treasures of the Yosemite and Features of the Proposed Yosemite National Park," *Century Magazine* 40 (August 1890): 483–500 and (September 1890): 656–67; Robert Underwood Johnson to Muir, New York, June 3, August 28, and September 20, 1890, *JMP.* For the legislative history of Yosemite National Park in 1890, Wolfe, *Son of the Wilderness*, 244–52; Fox, *Muir*, 103–107; Jones, *Muir and the Sierra Club*, 35ff.; Douglas H. Strong, "The History of Sequoia National Park, 1876–1926; Part I: The Movement to Establish a Park," *Southern California Quarterly* 48 (June 1966): 149–58. Most authors attribute passage of the Yosemite park bill to the efforts of Muir and Johnson, particularly Muir's *Century Magazine* articles on Yosemite in the summer of 1890. The actual origin of Vandever's Yosemite National Park bill, however, is obscure. There is no evidence that Muir and his friends had a direct part in it and much evidence that they played no role. Muir's articles appeared months *after* Vandever offered his bill. Vandever later pointedly disassociated himself from Johnson and Muir, who were publicly taking credit for Yosemite National Park. In September 1890, he wrote that "the 'Century Magazine' had nothing whatever to do with my introduction of the bill into Congress for the establishment of a National Yosemite Park"; William Vandever to John P. Irish, Washington, DC, September 9, 1890, in *Biennial Report of Commissioners to Manage Yosemite Valley* (1890), 7–8. Holway Jones concludes that, in the light of Vandever's connections to the railroad, it was probably the Southern Pacific that had Vandever introduce the bill; Jones, *Muir and the Sierra Club*, 46–47.

37. Robert Underwood Johnson to Muir, New York, June 27, 1889, and February 20, 1890, *JMP;* Fox, *Muir*, 105–106; for Muir's account of Stowe's aid, *Sierra Club Bulletin* 1 (January 1896): 275–76.

38. Robert Underwood Johnson to John Muir, New York, September 20, 1890, *JMP; Sacramento Record-Union*, September 1, 1890.

39. Strong, "Sequoia National Park, Part I," 149–58; Oscar Berland, "Giant Forest's Reservation: The Legend and the Mystery," *Sierra Club Bulletin* 47 (December 1962): 68–82; Kathleen E. Small, *History of Tulare County, California*, 2 vols. (Chicago, 1926), 2:463–65; Lary M. Dilsaver and William C. Tweed, *Challenge of the Big Trees: A Resource History of Sequoia and Kings Canyon National Parks* (Three Rivers, CA: Sequoia Natural History Association, 1990), 69–73. Following the lead of Berland and Strong and also lacking direct evidence, Dilsaver and Tweed, instead of placing the Southern Pacific's support for the Yosemite/Sequoia bill within the context of the company's long-term promotion of natural preserves, fell back on the time-worn "Octopus" myth and asserted the Southern Pacific's motivation was "presumably . . . nothing less than corporate greed—an irony seldom appreciated by modern students of

Sierran national parks" (73). Despite chronic tuberculosis, Zumwalt was an avid out-doorsman, a friend to California wilderness preservationists, and a guide on Sierra Club packing trips into the Sequoia and Kings River Canyon areas in the 1890s and early 1900s; J. N. LeConte to Daniel K. Zumwalt, Berkeley, May 13, 1902, *ZC-SP,* letter filed beginning of vol. 2, incoming correspondence; James M. Guinn, *History of State of California and Biographical Record of the San Joaquin Valley* (Chicago: Chapman Publishing Co., 1905), 632.

40. Robert Underwood Johnson to John Muir, New York, October 24, 1890, *JMP.*

41. *Sierra Club Bulletin* 1 (January 1896): 275–76.

42. Strong, "Sequoia National Park, Part I"; Dilsaver and Tweed, *Challenge of the Big Trees,* 66–73.

43. *Sierra Club Bulletin* 1 (January 1896): 272–85; *San Francisco Chronicle,* December 6, 1894.

44. Jones, *John Muir and the Sierra Club,* 57–58. The railroad also supported the Sierra Club by regularly taking out full-page ads for its passenger service and *Sunset* magazine in the *Sierra Club Bulletin,* issues 1890s–1910s, e.g., 6 (January 1908): 20.

45. Jones, *Muir and the Sierra Club,* 47ff.; Fox, *Muir,* 126–28; Wolfe, *Son of the Wilderness,* 301ff.; Michael Cohen, *The History of the Sierra Club, 1892–1970* (San Francisco: Sierra Club Books, 1988), 1–56; for the state commission's continuing problems administering the valley, Johnston, *Yosemite Grant,* 236ff.

46. John Muir to William Colby, Martinez, November 18, 1904; William E. Colby to Muir, San Francisco, December 19, 1904, *JMP;* Orsi, "Selling the Golden State," 634–55; California State Board of Trade, *Reclamation of Arid Lands by Irrigation* (San Francisco, 1889); "Memorial Ascription to the Late William H. Mills," in California State Board of Trade, *California: Resources and Possibilities* (San Francisco, 1907), 61–62.

47. William E. Colby to John Muir, December 18, 1904, *JMP;* California State Board of Trade, *Yosemite Valley,* reviews the board's views on Yosemite Valley and its work for retrocession.

48. Jones, *Muir and the Sierra Club,* 67–68.

49. William H. Mills to Governor George C. Pardee, San Francisco, December 14 and 15, 1904, Pardee Correspondence, *BL; San Francisco Call,* December 14, 1904, and January 20 and 23, 1905; Goppert, "Yosemite Valley Commission," 31–63 and 77–82; and California State Board of Trade, *Yosemite Valley,* 1–33.

50. William E. Colby to John Muir, San Francisco, January 7 and 13, 1905; Muir to Robert Underwood Johnson, Martinez, January 30, 1905, *JMP;* Wolfe, *Son of the Wilderness,* 301ff.; Jones, *Muir and the Sierra Club,* 67–71.

51. William E. Colby to John Muir, January 7 and 13, 1905; Colby to Senator George C. Perkins, San Francisco, January 7, 1905; Muir to Colby, Martinez, February 15, 1905, *JMP;* Jones, *Muir and the Sierra Club,* 67–71; Wolfe, *Son of the Wilderness,* 301ff.

52. Wolfe, *Son of the Wilderness,* 280–322; Fox, *Muir,* 126–28. Harriman supported Muir's conservationist projects from 1899, when he invited the naturalist on his Alaska expedition, until Harriman's death in 1909; Muir to Harriman, Martinez, January 1907, and Harriman to Muir, Arden, New York, July 31, 1908, *JMP;* Goetzmann and Sloan,

Looking Far North; Kennan, *Harriman,* 1:188, 193–95, 197–200, and 2:328–30, 352–53, 382–84.

53. John Muir to Edward H. Harriman, Martinez, January 1907, *JMP.*

54. Wolfe, *Son of the Wilderness,* 302.

55. John Muir, *Edward Henry Harriman* (New York: Doubleday, 1911), 3–5 and 37.

56. Kennan, *Harriman,* passim.

57. Robert Underwood Johnson also contacted Harriman in New York; John Muir to E. H. Harriman, Martinez, January 5, 1905; Johnson to Muir, New York, January 17, 1905, *JMP.*

58. E. H. Harriman to John Muir, New York, January 12, 1905, *JMP;* Jones, *Muir and the Sierra Club,* 71–72.

59. William E. Colby to John Muir, San Francisco, February 24, 1905; Muir to Robert Underwood Johnson, Martinez, 2 letters, February 24, 1905, *JMP;* Jones, *Muir and the Sierra Club,* 72–73; Fox, *Muir,* 126–28.

60. John Muir to Robert Underwood Johnson, Martinez, February 24, 1905, *JMP.*

61. John Muir to William F. Herrin, Martinez, February 26, 1905; Herrin to Muir, San Francisco, March 2, 1905; E. H. Harriman to Muir, March 13, 1905; and Muir to William Keith, March 13, 1905, *JMP.*

62. Herrin and Muir communicated often between 1905 and 1914. Especially after 1910, they spent weeks of each year traveling or retreating at Herrin's Mount Shasta lodge. Beset by illness, hurt by his losses in the Hetch Hetchy battle, and pressed by a grueling writing schedule, Muir was grateful for the release Herrin's companionship afforded; Herrin felt Muir brought him closer to nature; Muir to Herrin, Martinez, May 26, 1914, and Herrin to Muir, Shasta Springs, July 10, 1910, *JMP;* "Death Calls William F. Herrin, Chief Counsel," *Southern Pacific Bulletin* 16 (April 1927): 5–6. In 1907, although his company officially supported San Francisco's search for more water to revive the earthquake-ravaged city, Herrin personally wrote to Muir offering "anything I can do to help you as to Hetch-Hetchy"; Herrin to Muir, San Francisco, November 11, 1907, *JMP.*

63. William E. Colby to John Muir, San Francisco, March 5, April 12 and 16, 1906; Senator George C. Perkins to Muir, Washington, DC, April 17, 1906, *JMP;* Wolfe, *Son of the Wilderness,* 303–304; Jones, *Muir and the Sierra Club,* 73–78; and Fox, *Muir,* 128.

64. Edward H. Harriman to John Muir, New York, April 16, 1906, *JMP.*

65. Alexander Miller (secretary, Southern Pacific Company) to John Muir, New York, May 10, 1906; and L. W. Bushey (secretary to the Speaker of the House) to E. H. Harriman, Washington, DC, May 9, 1906, *JMP;* Wolfe, *Son of the Wilderness,* 303–304. Colby left recollections of the retrocession battle that acknowledged the importance of the Southern Pacific, "Yosemite and the Sierra Club," *Sierra Club Bulletin* 23 (April 1938): 11–19, and "The Recession of Yosemite Valley," *Sierra Club Bulletin* 47 (December 1962): 23–28.

66. All but a few historians, most notably Holway Jones and Alfred Runte in books and articles cited above, have overlooked or misconstrued the relationship of Muir and the Southern Pacific for the founding and improvement of Yosemite National Park. My 1985 article, "'Wilderness Saint' and 'Robber Baron,'" examined the reasons, gen-

erally most historians' failure to examine primary sources, to set the events in the larger context of Southern Pacific and western railroad history, and to free themselves from the "Octopus" myth, the assumption that the company's actions must have been anti-progressive and anti-conservationist.

67. Strong, "Sequoia National Park, Part I," 149–58; Berland, "Giant Forest's Reservation," 68–82; Small, *History of Tulare County,* 2:463–65; Dilsaver and Tweed, *Challenge of the Big Trees,* 69–73. James M. Guinn described Zumwalt's "indefatigable" efforts on behalf of Sequoia National Park as perhaps one of his "most far-reaching and memorable achievements"; Guinn, *History of the State of California and Biographical Record of the San Joaquin Valley,* 632.

68. Apparently, while traveling to Washington, unlike his usual procedure, he made no letterpress copies of outgoing letters, and likewise, his incoming correspondence was not saved, or was stored separately and not bound with his other incoming mail that survives. In the normal course of business, however, Zumwalt corresponded daily with Southern Pacific Railroad land agent Jerome Madden, the railroad's Washington land attorneys, and other company leaders. Presumably, at least some of this business must have continued during his extended stay in Washington, from late July through the end of September; see *ZC-SP;* for his trip to Washington and the nature of his land business there, Zumwalt to Madden, Visalia, May 28 and July 23, 1890, and Madden to Zumwalt, San Francisco, June 3 and 10 and September 26, 1890.

69. D. K. Zumwalt to Jerome Madden, Visalia, October 17, 1890; Madden to Zumwalt, October 18 and 20, 1890, *ZC-SP.*

70. Strong, "Sequoia National Park, Part I," 149–58; Berland, "Giant Forest's Reservation," 68–82; Small, *History of Tulare County,* 2:463–65; Dilsaver and Tweed, *Challenge of the Big Trees,* 69–73.

71. D. K. Zumwalt to Jerome Madden, Visalia, October 17, 1890, and Madden to Zumwalt, San Francisco, October 18 and 20, 1890, *ZC-SP.* The map was republished in Berland, "Giant Forest's Reservation," 79.

72. William B. May, Southern Pacific Passenger Department, to D. K. Zumwalt, Fresno, June 16, 1891 (telegram), *ZC-SP; San Francisco Bulletin,* October 11, 1890; *Visalia Delta,* October 16, 1890; Dilsaver and Tweed, *Challenge of the Big Trees,* 70–72; Strong, "History of Sequoia National Park, Part I," 157. For some promotional materials featuring the park, see Southern Pacific Company, *Big Trees of California* (San Francisco, 1904 and 1910), and *California Big Tree Primer* (San Francisco, 1901), and A. J. Wells, *Kings and Kern Canyons and the Giant Forest of California* (San Francisco: Southern Pacific Co., 1906). Regarding the Southern Pacific's long-term use of sequoia trees to promote tourism to California, see Lori Vermaas, *Sequoia: The Heralded Tree in American Art and Culture* (Washington, DC: Smithsonian Books, 2003), 110–11, 141–42, 146–49, 159–62.

73. Mark McLaughlin, "Sierra Stories: The Snowball Express," *Truckee-North Tahoe This Week* (March 14, 2001), 8.

74. Douglas H. Strong, *Tahoe: An Environmental History* (Lincoln: University of Nebraska Press, 1984), 19–33.

75. Quoted in Strong, *Tahoe: An Environmental History,* 31. Mills's newspaper had

condemned deforestation of the Tahoe region and the resultant destruction of water-sheds as early as 1878; *Sacramento Record-Union,* September 21, 1878.

76. Strong, *Tahoe: An Environmental History,* 56–94; Strong, "Preservation Efforts at Lake Tahoe, 1880–1980," *Journal of Forest History* 25 (April 1981): 78–97; Donald J. Pisani, "Lost Parkland: Lumbering and Park Proposals in the Tahoe-Truckee Basin," *Journal of Forest History* 21 (January 1977): 4–17.

77. William H. Mills to William M. Stewart, San Francisco, September 11, 1899, Stewart Papers, Nevada Historical Society, Reno; Mills, "Are We Unwittingly Destroying a State?" *San Francisco Post,* June 21, 1899.

78. William M. Stewart to William H. Mills, September 4 and December 19, 1899, and January 13, 1900, and Mills to Stewart, San Francisco, September 11, 1899, Stew-art Papers, Nevada Historical Society, Reno; for newspaper discussion of the park issue, see *San Francisco Call,* January 27, 1900; *San Francisco Examiner,* February 27 and March 24, 1900; *Reno Gazette,* January 22 and March 28, 1900. For Stewart's political life, es-pecially his longtime support of the Southern Pacific's political and business interests, see Russell R. Elliott, *Servant of Power: A Political Biography of William M. Stewart* (Reno: University of Nevada Press, 1983), passim, and 222–23, for Stewart and Mills's campaign for a Lake Tahoe national park. See also, Strong, *Tahoe: An Environmental History,* 68 and 71; Donald J. Pisani, *Water, Land, and Law in the West, 1850–1920* (Lawrence: University Press of Kansas, 1996), 136. Especially in forestry and water pol-icy, the California State Board of Trade, of which he was the principal founder and leader, was an instrument of Mills's conservationist ideas.

79. Strong, *Tahoe: An Environmental History,* 66–75.

80. Strong, *Tahoe: An Environmental History,* 75–79, and *Tahoe: From Timber Barons to Ecologists,* 36–43.

81. Carolyn deVries, *Grand and Ancient Forest: The Story of Andrew P. Hill and Big Basin Redwoods State Park* (Fresno: Valley Publishers, 1978), xv. Stanford thought the price was too high.

82. William H. Mills to George C. Pardee, San Francisco, December 29, 1902, March 2 and 7 and June 25 and 29, 1903, and January 6, 1906, Pardee Correspondence, *BL;* deVries, *Grand and Ancient Forest,* 1–38 and 41ff. Mills's service on the Redwood Com-mission was not without controversy. He at first maintained that the asking price for the land was too high for a deep basin that could not be harvested economically, and critics accused him of delaying the land purchase and perhaps jeopardizing the park. The bill creating the park was introduced and pushed through by Assemblyman Grove L. Johnson, notorious leader of the Southern Pacific's political faction in the legislature and father of future Progressive governor Hiram Johnson; important in the creation and enlargement of the park was also the California State Board of Trade, which had been founded by Mills, who continued until his death in 1907 to guide its water, forestry, and wilderness preservation activities; see also, for the creation of Big Basin Redwood Park and the role of Mills, Johnson, and the California State Board of Trade, Willie Yaryan, Densil Verardo, and Jennie Verardo, *The Sempervirens Story: A Century of Pre-serving California's Ancient Redwood Forest, 1900–2000* (Los Altos, CA: Sempervirens Fund, 2000), 3–17.

83. William R. Dudley, ed., "Forestry Notes," *Sierra Club Bulletin* 5 (January 1905): 265–66.

84. Douglas H. Strong, "The History of Sequoia National Park, 1876–1926: Part III: The Struggle to Enlarge the Park," *Southern California Quarterly* 48 (December 1966): 374; Melville Bell Grosvenor, "Today and Tomorrow in Our National Parks," *National Geographic* (July 1966): 4. McCormick biography, stressing his conservationism, *Southern Pacific Bulletin* (November 1929): 8–9.

85. Runte, "Pragmatic Alliance," 14–15. For the Santa Fe Railroad's work after 1890 promoting Grand Canyon National Park and opening it to mass tourism, see Rothman, *Devil's Bargains,* 50–80. Directly controlling access into the park and the major visitor facilities, the Santa Fe dominated Grand Canyon's image and most facets of the tourist experience there to the detriment of most local interests, a process that Rothman has characterized as the "tourism of hegemony." By contrast, the Southern Pacific was never able to monopolize Yosemite, since the railroad did not operate the branch line into the park and lacked facilities in the valley, and at all times rival interests retained power.

86. Sellars, *Preserving Nature in the National Parks,* 89; Runte has described the "pragmatic alliance" in many of his historical writings on the parks, esp. "Pragmatic Alliance."

87. *Los Angeles Times,* October 31, 1999; *Contra Costa Times* (Contra Costa County, California), November 17, 1999; *San Francisco Chronicle,* February 12, 2003. Characteristically, much land needed to expand the original Joshua Tree National Monument in the early 1950s had also been sold by the Southern Pacific to the Department of the Interior for just over one dollar per acre, far below market value; C. J. McDonald to L. Frandsen, August 11, 1949; Frandsen to L. B. Young, March 24, 1952, "Withdrawal of Grant Lands From Sale" (1948–1952), box 29, *SP-E.*

14   Resource Conservation

The quotation in the chapter title is a statement of the Southern Pacific's central resource policy in the early twentieth century, from Charles D. Eberlein (acting land agent) to E. E. Calvin (vice president, Southern Pacific Company), San Francisco, September 23, 1907, File 374, "National Forests," *SP-L.*

1. For the railroad's serious problems with resource theft, see chapter 3 above; see also land lease and purchase contracts on San Joaquin Valley land, 1860s–1890s, *ZC-SP.* Standard contract clauses prohibited lessees or time-payment buyers from harming soil, trees, water, and minerals.

2. D. K. Zumwalt to Jerome Madden, Visalia, January 25, 1878, and Madden to Zumwalt, San Francisco, January 26, 1878, *ZC-SP.* Increased squirrel population resulted from ground disturbance and the elimination of predators, both typical effects of new railroad construction and settlement.

3. For water development policies, chapter 9.

4. For black locust and other trees, Collis P. Huntington to Charles Crocker, New York, January 5, 1871; Crocker to Huntington, San Francisco, December 28, 1870; Al-

ban N. Towne to Huntington, Sacramento, May 17, 1870; *CPH.* For a review of the railroad's nurseries, *Sacramento Record-Union,* August 7, 1878.

5. The company's early San Joaquin Valley tree farms, specializing in eucalyptus, chapters 9 and 11; *Sacramento Record-Union,* January 1, 1884; *Tulare Register,* August 24, 1883; *San Francisco Post,* clipping, late June 1883, Southern Pacific Scrapbooks, vol. 13, *HEH;* California State Board of Forestry, *Biennial Report . . . 1885–1886* (Sacramento: J. J. Ayers, 1886), 228; "Tulare's First 100 Years," special centennial edition of the *Tulare Advance-Register* (Tulare: Tulare Advance-Register, 1972); Thomas H. Thompson, *Official Historical Atlas of Tulare County* (Tulare, 1892); and Robert LeRoy Santos, "The Eucalyptus of California," *Southern California Quarterly* 80 (Summer 1998): 125–26.

6. Jerome Madden to D. K. Zumwalt, San Francisco, September 26, 1885, *ZC-SP;* Southern Pacific Land Department, "Lands Granted to the Southern Pacific Railroad Company in California, Sheet 2" (ms. map, November 9, 1907), File 654, and J. M. Sharpe to B. A. McAllaster, November 1, 1909, File 400, *SP-L.*

7. *Chicago Railway Review,* February 27 and April 21, 1877.

8. *Riverside Enterprise,* August 12, 1966.

9. *Southern Pacific Bulletin* 2 (January 15, 1914): 6; Louis P. Hopkins, "A Lifetime of Railroading" (typescript autobiography), 14, Oregon Collection, University of Oregon Library. For Oregon dune reclamation, see Henry August Schoth (agronomist, Oregon State College) to E. L. King (superintendent, Oregon Division, Southern Pacific Company), Corvallis, November 26, 1928; King to Schoth, Portland, November 30, 1928; Schoth to Fred Duncan (Southern Pacific section foreman), Corvallis, November 15 and December 16, 1929; Duncan to Schoth, Hauser, OR, November 29, 1929; Henry August Schoth Collection, box 2, "Southern Pacific" folder, Oregon State University Archives, Corvallis.

10. Documents, File 851, *SP-L,* cover the renewed eucalyptus program, 1907–1916; for its inception, James B. Forbes to C. W. Eberlein, Los Angeles, April 16, 1908.

11. See Leslie W. Symmes to J. H. Wallace, assistant chief engineer, Southern Pacific Company, Berkeley, July 29 and August 9, 1907; Symmes, "Preliminary Report of Investigations Relating to Experimental Tree Planting for the Southern Pacific Company" (typescript, Berkeley, July 1907), and "Report of Investigation of Lands in the Tulare Lake Region for Adaptability to Eucalyptus Culture" (typescript, October 1909), File 851, *SP-L.*

12. Epes Randolph to W. R. Scott, Tucson, November 5, 1914, File 851, *SP-L.*

13. B. A. McAllaster to W. R. Scott, San Francisco, June 16, 1914; Scott to McAllaster, San Francisco, July 8, 1914, and October 13, 1916; Scott to President W. J. Sproule, San Francisco, November 9, 1914; Sproule to McAllaster, San Francisco, San Francisco, August 23, 1916, File 851, *SP-L.*

14. For program, 1890s–1900s, along the California & Oregon railroad line through the Sacramento River Canyon near the Oregon border, see William H. Mills to E. E. Calvin, San Francisco, November 17, 1906, and February 8, 1907; and Calvin to Mills, San Francisco, November 14, 1906, File 916, *SP-L.*

15. From the inception of national forests in 1890, the company supported the founding of such preserves in its territories, including regions in which it still possessed un-

sold granted lands; many documents, File 374, "National Forests," *SP-L*. For coopera-tion between national forester Gifford Pinchot and Southern Pacific land officials and higher executives to write and then secure congressional passage of a land exchange bill, see, in that file, esp. Gifford Pinchot to Charles W. Eberlein, Washington, DC, Sep-tember 10, 1904; W. D. Cornish to Eberlein, New York, December 13, 1906, and telegram, New York, December 21, 1906; Cornish to William H. Mills, New York, De-cember 13, 1906; Mills to Cornish, San Francisco, December 19, 1906; and Eberlein to Cornish, San Francisco, December 20 and 22, 1906; and Pinchot, "Proposed Agree-ment between Railroad Companies and the United States to Relinquish Lands in Na-tional Forests" (typescript), enclosed in Pinchot to Eberlein, December 10, 1904. As early as the 1880s, the Southern Pacific advocated trading land with state and federal governments to make its forests whole or to create uniform public wilderness preserves; C. Raymond Clar, *California Government and Forestry . . .* , 2 vols. (Sacramento: Divi-sion of Forestry, Department of Natural Resources, State of California, 1959 and 1969), 1:96. The Southern Pacific was the first of the land-grant railroads to attempt to ex-change land with the federal government, and thus in a sense was the catalyst for the eventual creation of an exchange system. Early 1898 overtures by the Southern Pacific to the General Land Office to exchange lands under general federal statutes foundered, however, because such complicated exchanges with railroads were not specifically men-tioned in an act passed in 1897, and because of widespread opposition to railroad land grants in principle among some congressional factions. A follow-up attempt later in 1898 by Southern Pacific lobbyists to get Congress to pass a law allowing exchanges of land with railroad companies also failed; Henry Beard to Jerome Madden, Washing-ton, April 4, 1898; D. A. Chambers to John Boyd, Washington, April 6 and 29, 1898, to Charles H. Tweed (Southern Pacific executive), Washington, April 12, 15, and 29, and October 31, 1898, to L. E. Payson, Washington, April 14, 1898, and to Madden, Washington, July 7, 1898; all in vol. 54, *SP-A*. For the history of Southern Pacific's at-tempts to start a land-exchange program, see, in vol. 54, *SP-A*, esp. Chambers to Mills, Washington, October 31, 1898, and to Tweed, December 13, 1898.

16. See File 995, "First National Conservation Congress [Seattle, 1909]," *SP-L*, esp. land agent Ben Irwin, "Why Do Tax Laws Necessitate the Destruction of the Timber Crop."

17. Gifford Pinchot to Charles W. Eberlein, Washington, DC, September 14 and December 10, 1904; Eberlein to Pinchot, San Francisco, October 1, 1904, File 374, "Na-tional Forests," *SP-L*.

18. For the railroad's forest management plan instituted in the early 1900s, see doc-uments, File 374, *SP-L*., esp. Charles W. Eberlein to E. E. Calvin, San Francisco, Sep-tember 7, 1907.

19. For the so-called "light-burning controversy," see Stephen J. Pyne, *Fire in Amer-ica: A Cultural History of Wildland and Rural Fire* (Princeton: Princeton University Press, 1982), 100–122. Southern Pacific land officials and foresters were among the leaders of the controlled-burning side; see esp. Pyne, 108; Clar, *California Government and Forestry,* 1:489–90, and 2:48. Pyne has characterized the behavior of the Forest Service in imposing fire-suppression as the prescribed method as being "often not merely hard-

nosed but hardheaded," motivated as much by politics and the agency's urge to save face as much as it was by science; p. 116.

20. For conflicts between federal and railroad foresters, see documents, 1890s–1920, File 374, "National Forests," *SP-L,* esp. R. L. Fulton to William H. Mills, Reno, December 1, 1906; Mills to W. D. Cornish, Oakland, December 19, 1906; Charles W. Eberlein to Cornish, San Francisco, December 20, 1906; Gifford Pinchot to Eberlein, Washington, February 25, 1907; A. A. Hoehling to B. A. McAllaster, Washington, March 12, 1909 (enclosing copy of "Inventory of Proclamations Creating Forest Reserves Which Affect the Various Grants of Constituent Companies of Southern Pacific Company" [typescript, 1909]), and October 18 and November 3, 1911, and to William F. Herrin, Washington, November 18, 1912; McAllaster to Hoehling, San Francisco, March 4 and 26, 1909, and September 21 and October 27, 1911, and to Herrin, San Francisco, April 9, 1909; and Charles W. Cobb (assistant U.S. attorney general) to Secretary of the Interior, Washington, November 12, 1912 (copy). In writing Herrin on July 11, 1913, land agent McAllaster critiqued Forest Service policies regarding grazing leases on railroad lands under rules adopted in 1911 and 1913, which according to McAllaster were reducing or even ending railroad revenues, while increasing Forest Service income from grazing fees. McAllaster described such practices as "inequitable and confiscatory" and recommended that the railroad protest.

21. See documents in dozens of files pertaining to various national forests, *SP-L,* for these cooperative programs. For the Trinity National Forest in northern California, see T. D. Woodbury (acting district forester, U.S. Forest Service, District 5, San Francisco) to B. A. McAllaster, San Francisco, August 15, 1917, and December 17, 1923, and to F. W. Houtz, San Francisco, March 30, 1918; and McAllaster to Woodbury, San Francisco, File 784. For the Cleveland National Forest southeast of Los Angeles, L. A. Barrett (assistant district forester, San Francisco) to McAllaster, San Francisco, May 7, 1924, File 796; and Barrett to McAllaster, San Francisco, February 15, 1930, File 801. Tahoe National Forest, C. F. Impey to Richard L.P. Bigelow (forest supervisor, Tahoe National Forest), San Francisco, December 24, 1929, and to J. W. Nelson (acting regional forester), San Francisco, March 22, 1932; Nelson to Impey, San Francisco, March 29, 1932; Bigelow to Impey, Nevada City, CA, January 4, 1930, and to R. C. Turrittin, December 20, 1927; C. E. Kelsey to Impey, Vista, CA, July 24, 1928, File 790. For the general cooperative program, see Woodbury to McAllaster, San Francisco, March 28, 1921, McAllaster to Woodbury, San Francisco, April 8, 1921, File 968.

22. For the account here and below of the pine-bark beetle and other forest pests, 1900–1930, see documents File 970, "Pine Beetle," and 970B, "Pine Beetle, 1918–1934," *SP-L.*

23. B. A. McAllaster to Dr. C. L. Marlatt (chairman, Federal Horticultural Board, U.S. Department of Agriculture), San Francisco, September 4, 1924, File 970B, *SP-L.*

24. See W. E. Glendenning (Southern Pacific fire warden) to B. A. McAllaster, Fort Jones, California, October 25 and 31 and December 26, 1910; John M. Miller (U.S. Forest Service, Department of Entomology, Berkeley) to Glendenning, ca. December 25, 1910; and other documents, 1910–1913; for overall Southern Pacific bark-beetle program, A. D. Hopkins (Bureau of Entomology, Department of Agriculture) to McAllaster,

Washington, DC, October 10, 1911, and esp. in McAllaster to William F. Herrin, April 29 and May 27, 1912; all in File 970. Also McAllaster to M. B. Pratt (California state forester) and Paul G. Reddington (U.S. district forester, San Francisco), San Francisco, May 21, 1923; McAllaster to S. B. Show (U.S. Forest Service, district forester, San Francisco) and M. B. Pratt, San Francisco, February 14, 1930; and J. M. Miller (senior entomologist, U.S. Department of Agriculture, Bureau of Entomology) to McAllaster, Stanford University, February 20, 1930; File 970B, *SP-L.*

25. See A. D. Hopkins (U.S. Bureau of Entomology) to B. A. McAllaster, Washington, DC, October 10, 1911, and April 5 and 13, 1912, File 970, *SP-L.*

26. B. A. McAllaster to William F. Herrin, San Francisco, August 20, 1920, File 970B, *SP-L.*

27. Donald Bruce (scientist at the University of California, Berkeley) to J. F. Kimball (Klamath Forest Protective Association, Klamath Falls), Berkeley, January 1, 1923; B. A. McAllaster to William F. Herrin, San Francisco, January 23, 1923; File 970B, *SP-L.*

28. California Senate Bill 119, Chapter 82, "An Act Declaring Insect Pests . . . To Be a Nuisance and Providing for the Control, Eradication and Destruction of Said Insect Pests" (Approved May 2, 1923).

29. B. A. McAllaster to W. F. Herrin, San Francisco, January 30, 1924; Herrin to U.S. Senator Samuel H. Shortridge, San Francisco, February 5, 1924; Herrin to U.S. Representative Julius Kahn, San Francisco, February 4, 1924; File 970B, *SP-L.*

30. U.S. Senator Samuel H. Shortridge to William F. Herrin, Washington, DC, February 11, 1924; and U.S. Representative Julius Kahn to Herrin, Washington, DC, February 12, 1924; File 970B, *SP-L.*

31. B. A. McAllaster to Dr. C. L. Marlatt (chair, Federal Horticultural Board, Washington, DC), San Francisco, September 4, 1924; and esp. McAllaster to William F. Herrin, San Francisco, September 4, 1924; File 970B, *SP-L.*

32. For the company's fire problem, see John R. Signor, *Donner Pass: Southern Pacific's Sierra Crossing* (San Marino, CA: Golden West Books, 1985), passim, esp. 48ff.; Gerald M. Best, *Snowplow: Clearing the Mountain Rails* (Berkeley: Howell-North Books, 1966), 29–37. Despite the railroad's efforts at fire prevention and control, the problem persisted well into the twentieth century, demanding constant vigilance. It was one of the reasons the company in the late 1890s converted first to oil as fuel and then in the 1930s to diesel-electric locomotives; T. Ahern, "Problems of Southern Pacific Line Over the High Sierra," *Southern Pacific Bulletin* 14 (July 1925): 5; *Southern Pacific Bulletin* 18 (June 1930): 3–5. How general railroad building and operation, esp. 1870–1920, aggravated the wildlands fire problem is analyzed in Pyne, *Fire in America,* 57, 60, 161, 199–201, 243, and 254; during the period of great fires in the northern Rocky Mountains, for example, Pyne estimated that railroad operation caused 56 percent of fires (p. 243).

33. For the *Grey Eagle,* see *Sacramento Bee,* June 25, 1930.

34. For the recollections of firefighting, 1870s, see Clarence M. Wooster, "More About Railroading in California in the Seventies: The Fire Train," *California Historical Society Quarterly* 22 (1943): 178–80; for the Dunsmuir water and firefighting facility, H. G.

Butler, "Report . . . on the Value of Water Rights of the Southern Pacific System as of June 30, 1916" (typescript), 126, Legal Files, San Diego & Arizona Railroad Collection, San Diego Historical Society.

35. For the Southern Pacific's fire service, see Best, *Snowplow*, 29–37; Joanne Meschery, *Truckee: An Illustrated History of the Town and Its Surroundings* (Truckee: Rocking Stone Press, 1978), 62; Paul A. Lord, Jr., *Fire and Ice: A Portrait of Truckee* (Truckee: Truckee Donner Historical Society, 1981), 12ff.

36. Drawings of firefighting equipment, *CRRM*, esp. "Tank and Fixtures, Lumber Details, 7200 Gallon Wooden Water Car for Fire Service," July 21, 1903; also Drawings Number 3839 and 7331.

37. Pyne, *Fire in America*, 428; Signor, *Donner Pass*, passim.

38. *Southern Pacific Bulletin* 18 (June 1930): 3–5.

39. *Reno Gazette*, September 1, 1877; Signor, *Donner Pass*, 48–49, 71, and 106–107; Best, *Snowplow*, 29–37; Pyne, *Fire in America*, 224; Clar, *California Government and Forestry*, 1:203n. Both Clar and Pyne err in dating the station to 1878; it opened two years earlier. The lookout could spy on nearly fifty miles of the Central Pacific. Two smaller supplemental railroad lookouts covered spots hidden from Red Mountain. At first a small wooden building with a high pitched roof, the Red Mountain station was rebuilt around 1900 in stone, roofed in iron; that structure was still standing when the author and his son climbed up Red Mountain in the early 1990s. In 1934, the last lookout agent was electrocuted by lightning striking the telephone wire he was talking on, and the facility never reopened; Signor, *Donner Pass*, 71. For the telegraph and patrol system, using advanced automatic telegraphic and recording equipment, above citations in Best and Signor; also, "Protecting a Line from Snow Troubles," *Southern Pacific Bulletin* 6 (March 23, 1917); also, 14 (July 1925): 5, and 18 (June 1930): 3–5.

40. *Southern Pacific Bulletin* 18 (June 1930): 3–5.

41. Pyne, *Fire in America*, 428. Railroads pioneered modern wildland firefighting throughout the United States; the Southern Pacific's accomplishments, then, were not unique in the industry, although its role was probably more significant in the company's territory, because much of it was extremely vulnerable to fire and lacked much population and institutional development other than the railroad; ibid., 60, 224, 226, 229–30, 428.

42. For railroad's local fire wardens, see documents, especially pertaining to W. E. Glendenning, a local rancher and the railroad fire warden in the northern California town of Montague, File 970, esp. Glendenning to B. A McAllaster, Fort Jones, October 25 and 31, 1910; Henry Conlin to William D. Cornish, San Francisco, June 4, 1908, Eberlein Correspondence; for fighting a fire, Conlin to Cornish, San Francisco, August 18, 1908, and telegram, Portland, August 12, 1908, Cornish Office Files; Southern Pacific's report on its forestry and firefighting program to the American Railway Engineering Association, in J. Q. Barlow (assistant chief engineer) to E. E. Calvin, San Francisco, December 27, 1911, and President William Sproule to Calvin and B. A. McAllaster, December 23, 1911, and McAllaster to Sproule, San Francisco, January 10, 1912, File 813; all in *SP-L*.

43. See J. O. Johnson (roadmaster, Southern Pacific Company) to John K. Weatherford, Salem, OR, May 27, 1894, Weatherford Papers, Oregon Collection, University of Oregon.

44. "State Forester Commends S.P. Fire Protection," *Southern Pacific Bulletin* 14 (September 1925): 13.

45. B. A. McAllaster to William F. Herrin, San Francisco, November 20, 1912, File 813; McAllaster to W. B. Rider (deputy state forester of California), San Francisco, November 30, 1925, File 763, *SP-L.* For cooperative fire-protection programs, Clar, *California Government and Forestry,* 2:20, 105.

46. For McAllaster's belief in centralized public firefighting, see letters and reports in File 813, *SP-L,* esp. McAllaster to the Conservation Commission of the State of California, San Francisco, March 4, 1912, and to A. W. Rees (Southern Pacific Oregon land office), San Francisco, May 25, 1912; and McAllaster, "Memorandum in Relation to the Proposed Act for the Prevention and Suppression of Forest Fires . . . " (typescript, San Francisco, July 22, 1912). That the State Forester's Office of California agreed that the current firefighting system was inadequate is clear in *Third Biennial Report of the State Forester of the State of California* (Sacramento: Superintendent of State Printing, 1910), 84–85. Also, Mansel G. Blackford, *The Politics of Business in California, 1890–1920* (Columbus: Ohio State University Press, 1977), 71–73, for the varied opinions of lumbermen and conservationists. Blackford errs in asserting that the Southern Pacific before 1912 "opposed forestry measures." Since the 1870s, the railroad had strongly supported scientific forestry generally on its lands and in state and federal policy. Specifically regarding an earlier proposal in 1904 to establish a state forest fire-protection program in California, the Southern Pacific opposed it not because it objected to forestry but because the bill had specific provisions the railroad thought ineffective, while placing an unfair tax burden on the railroad and allowing other landowners to escape payments. See also, Clar, *California Government and Forestry,* 1:344, also 295–428 on conflicts over firefighting, 1904–1919.

47. Louis R. Glavis (secretary, State Conservation Commission) to B. A McAllaster, San Francisco, February 29, 1912, File 813, *SP-L;* Blackford, *Politics of Business in California,* 71–73; Clar, *California Government and Forestry,* 1:344.

48. B. A McAllaster to the Conservation Commission of the State of California, San Francisco, March 4, 1912, File 813, *SP-L.* McAllaster found some modifications made by the Conservation Commission objectionable, not because the resulting fire-control system would be too drastic but because it would be too lax and made too few meaningful changes in current, ineffective practices. Particularly, he opposed a provision that would assess all costs for fighting fires to the owners of the property on which the fire happened to be fought, irrespective of where the fire had originated or which properties it had traversed. Such a finance system, he maintained, was inequitable and could bankrupt forest owners, particularly small-scale ones, who were unlucky enough to have their properties chosen for the stand against a fire. All property in a region is endangered by fire, he maintained, and all should pay a proportional share; McAllaster, "Memorandum in Relation to the Proposed Act for the Prevention and Suppression of Fire," passim, in above file.

49. Clar, *California Government and Forestry,* 1:295–428; Blackford, *The Politics of Government in California,* 71–73.

50. Clar, *California Government and Forestry,* 1: chap. 19, 429ff.; Blackford, *Politics of Business in California,* 73–74.

51. Clar, *California Government and Forestry,* 1:414, 462ff., 488–97, 2:46; Pyne, *Fire in America,* 108ff.

52. Clar, *California Government and Forestry,* 2:136ff.

53. See many examples in chapter 9.

54. Unless otherwise noted, the citations below on the smelter controversy are in File 853, "Smelter Smoke Damage," *SP-L.*

55. Chum Gibson to B. A. McAllaster, Redding, March 12, 1910; *San Francisco Examiner,* June 25 and July 6, 1910; *Courier-Free Press* (Redding), May 27, 1911.

56. B. A. McAllaster to H. H. Pooler, San Francisco, April 15, 1910; Pooler to McAllaster, Redding, June 5 and 19, 1910; McAllaster to Chum Gibson, San Francisco, June 13, 1910.

57. B. A. McAllaster to T. W. H. Shanahan, San Francisco, July 13, 1910; Shanahan to McAllaster, July 16 and 24 and October 18, 1910; McAllaster to William F. Herrin, September 29, 1910; Herrin to McAllaster, October 3, 1910.

58. Louis R. Glavis (secretary, State Conservation Commission) to the Southern Pacific Railroad Land Department, San Francisco, December 20, 1911, and B. A. McAllaster to Glavis, San Francisco, January 25, 1912.

59. B. A. McAllaster to William F. Herrin, November 9, 1910; President R. S. Lovett to Herrin, December 12, 1910.

60. R. T. White to E. E. Calvin, Coram, Shasta County, October 31, 1910; White to William F. Herrin, December 26, 1910; B. A. McAllaster to H. A. Jones, San Francisco, August 17, 1911; *Courier-Free Press* (Redding), October 31, 1910.

61. B. A. McAllaster to H. H. Pooler, January 25, 1912; Pooler to McAllaster, Redding, January 27, 1912.

62. L. E. Gibson to B. A. McAllaster, February 10, April 11, and May 18, 1914; McAllaster to Gibson, May 14, 1914; *Sacramento Bee,* December 14, 1912; *San Francisco Examiner,* December 17, 1913. In a long letter to chief counsel William F. Herrin on June 11, 1914, McAllaster, though he acknowledged favoring the agricultural side, dispassionately analyzed the conflicting corporate interests at stake in the controversy. Addressing the corporate interests in this and other environmental issues, and illustrating the careful weighing of interests that always went on, he wrote: "This company occupies the dual position of land owner and transportation company. As land owner its interests lie with the farmer, and it should become an active factor in compelling the smelters to comply with the injunction. As a transportation company its interests lie on the side of the development which will produce the greater and more continuous traffic, and in connection therewith consideration must be given to its position as land owner; that is, if the farming operations are supported, the value of its land holdings can be added to the traffic from farming, but, if the smelting operations are supported, the value of its land holdings must be deducted from such traffic." McAllaster kept pressing higher executives to support the farmers, but failing that, a decision as soon as possible.

63. William F. Herrin to B. A. McAllaster, San Francisco, July 20, 1914.

64. *Courier-Free Press* (Redding), March 12, 1915; *San Francisco Examiner,* July 1, 1915.

65. For Nevada situation, James W. Hulse, *The Silver State: Nevada's Heritage Reinterpreted* (Reno: University of Nevada Press, 1991), 133-48.

66. For Southern Pacific's support for federal regulation of grazing lands, the need for grazing fees on the public domain, and conservation of grasslands, see documents, 1890s–1930s, File 767, "Leasing Public Lands," *SP-L;* unless otherwise noted, references below to regulation and leasing are to that file. The quoted letter was Charles W. Eberlein to W. D. Cornish, San Francisco, February 13, 1907, in which Eberlein also outlined why the company supported federal regulation and leasing.

67. Land agent B. A. McAllaster reviewed two decades of company policy regarding grazing land regulation in a letter to President William Sproule, San Francisco, October 12, 1923.

68. B. A. McAllaster to William F. Herrin, San Francisco, March 4, 1914; also McAllaster to Herrin, San Francisco, January 8, 1914, and to Guy V. Shoup, San Francisco, December 12, 1915.

69. Harry H. McElroy to William F. Herrin, El Paso, June 29, 1925; on Southern Pacific's concerns about long-range conservation of grasslands, see also McElroy to Herrin, El Paso, September 1, 1925; and B. A. McAllaster to Herrin, July 16 and October 20, 1925, and to A. E. Kimball, San Francisco, September 4, 1925.

70. Copies of the 1921 articles, File 767; the series appeared over most of the year; also, William Sproule to George Winfield (president, Reno National Bank), September 29, 1923.

71. B. A. McAllaster to William F. Herrin, San Francisco, February 27, 1925; and to C. F. R. Ogilby (Southern Pacific attorney, Washington, DC), San Francisco, April 5, 1925.

72. William F. Herrin to J. P. Blair (general counsel, Southern Pacific Company, New York), San Francisco, March 5, 1925.

73. J. P. Blair to William F. Herrin, New York, March 11, 1925; Herrin to B. A. McAllaster, San Francisco, March 18, 1925; McAllaster to C. F. R. Ogilby, San Francisco, March 21, 1925; Ogilby to McAllaster, Washington, DC, March 31, 1925.

74. McAllaster to William F. Herrin, San Francisco, September 16, 1925.

75. See, for example, *Salt Lake Telegram,* August 22, 1925; *The Deseret News* (Salt Lake City), August 22, 1925; *Salt Lake Tribune,* August 25 and 26, 1925.

76. J. Russell Penny and Marion Clawson, "Administration of Grazing Districts," in Vernon Carstenson (ed.), *The Public Lands: Studies in the History of the Public Domain* (Madison: University of Wisconsin Press, 1968), 461ff.

77. Charles W. Eberlein to Julius Kruttschnitt, February 20, 1904, File 444, "Trail Clauses," *SP-L;* until otherwise noted, references below are to that file. The Southern Pacific, in planning and implementation of the trail system, was concerned not only about current needs, but was particularly looking to problems for the company and the region in the future, when farm, ranch, and town development along the Central Pacific lines had progressed further. In 1911, chief land agent B. A. McAllaster expressed a common worry among company officials: "You will realize that as long as a country of the

character of that in consideration [the Great Basin] remains open, or at least used solely by stockmen, it is not of material importance to designate particularly lands across which stock may be trailed in order to reach shipping points. On the other hand, when such a territory begins to be settled up by farmers, with the resultant fencing of lands, it reduces the area usable for driving purposes to established roads," which according to McAllaster, would be insufficient, narrow, and without grass and water, especially for sheepherders; McAllaster to Joseph Gutman (president, Pacific Reclamation Company, New York), San Francisco, November 9, 1911.

78. See documents in File 444.

79. The confused state of the company was cited as a reason for delaying the trail system; F. C. Radcliffe (acting land agent) to E. C. McClellan (field land agent), July 3, 1908.

80. E. C. McClellan to F. C. Radcliffe, Elko, NV, June 16 and 29, 1908.

81. On the building and operation of the trails, see esp. F. W. Houtz to Sam E. Andrews (field agent laying out a trail in Wells, NV), San Francisco, October 13, 1911, and Houtz to C. W. Skene (field agent, Brigham City, UT), October 26, 1911.

82. B. A. McAllaster to G. W. Luce, San Francisco, April 24, 1913; many maps bearing markings of trail locations, 1912–1913.

83. For livestock shipments, chapter 12; for Nevada and Utah, P. Bancroft, "Facilities for Shippers at Ogden," *Southern Pacific Bulletin* 11 (August 1922): 16–17.

84. Southern Pacific Land Company, "Trails" (typescript, November 25, 1912).

85. J. A. McBride (president, Eastern Nevada Wool Growers Association) to B. A. McAllaster, Elko, NV, March 30, 1912. See also McAllaster to McBride, April 4, 1912; Southern Pacific Land Company, "Trails"; McAllaster to G. W. Luce, March 21, 1913.

86. F. W. Houtz, "Memorandum" (typescript, December 3, 1915).

87. F. W. Houtz to C. W. Skene (Southern Pacific land agent, Reno), San Francisco, January 1, 1917.

88. Southern Pacific Land Company, "Land in Trails" (typescript, ca. July 1918); maps in File 444 suggest that Utah trails had perhaps one-quarter the Nevada acreage.

89. G. E. Hair to B. A. McAllaster, Elko, NV, December 16, 1917.

90. B. A. McAllaster to G. E. Hair, San Francisco, December 12, 1917, and January 18, 1918.

91. See F. W. Houtz, "Memo" (typescript, March 16, 1918); Southern Pacific Land Company, "Land in Trails" (typescript, ca. July 1918); G. E. Hair to B. A. McAllaster, San Francisco, April 30, October 26, 1918; McAllaster to Hair, June 24, 1918.

92. Southern Pacific Land Company, "Lands in Proposed Nevada Trails" (typescript, March 20, 1919), and "Lands in Trails" (typescript, ca. July 1918); Clay Tallman (General Land Office, Washington, DC) to J. H. Favorite (chief, Field Division, General Land Office, San Francisco), Washington, February 28, 1919. On the Southern Pacific's reserving the land for the long term, see B. A. McAllaster to Favorite, San Francisco, April 21, 1919, and February 14, 1920; T. E. Hunt to McAllaster, Salt Lake City, June 6, 1919; and McAllaster to Hunt, San Francisco, June 12, 1919.

93. F. W. Houtz to C. W. Skene, San Francisco, April 4, 1919; B. A. McAllaster to Ira Lantz (special agent, General Land Office), San Francisco, April 4, 1919; Southern

Pacific Land Company, "Lands in Proposed Nevada Trails" (typescript, March 20, 1919); Lantz to Commissioner, General Land Office, San Francisco, March 22, 1919.

94. See F. W. Houtz to C. W. Skene, San Francisco, April 4, 1919; James Dysart (Elko County Sheepmen's Association) to Southern Pacific Railroad, Elko, January 29, 1920; B. A. McAllaster to T. A. Graham, February 7, 1920, and to Dysart, February 7, 1920.

95. C. E. Rachford (assistant district forester, U.S. Department of Agriculture) to B. A. McAllaster, San Francisco, May 11, 1920.

96. See File 3866, "Sale of Traillands," esp. Louis Frandsen to E. R. Greenslet (Bureau of Land Management), San Francisco, December 22, 1949, March 3, 1950, and May 5, 1952; Frandsen to L. B. Young, San Francisco, April 11, 1952; Southern Pacific Land Company, "Memo" (typescript, February 2, 1952), and "Memo" (typescript, March 14, 1953); *SP-L*. A history of the livestock trails, in Louis Frandsen, "Resume . . . Land Department" (typescript, ca. 1968), appendix ("Trail Sections"), pp.1–2, *SP-E*.

Epilogue

1. James Deetz, *In Small Things Forgotten: An Archaeology of Early American Life* (New York: Anchor Press/Doubleday, 1977), passim; David E. Kyvig and Myron A. Marty, *Nearby History: Exploring the Past around You,* 2nd. ed. (Walnut Creek, CA: AltaMira Press, 2000), esp. chaps. 3, 7, 8, 9, and 10.

2. An excellent account of the Southern Pacific's demise in the 1980s and 1990s, its impact on employees and communities, and the obliteration of its name, identity, and history is in Larry Mullaly and Bruce Petty, *The Southern Pacific in Los Angeles* (San Marino, CA: Golden West Books and the Los Angeles Railroad Heritage Foundation, 2002), chaps. 9 and 10. Perhaps most symbolic of all, in the early 1990s the Denver & Rio Grande shut down the famous Summit Tunnel Central Pacific workers had dug so laboriously through the top of the Sierra Nevada in the late 1860s and ripped up much of the double-track E. H. Harriman had ordered installed to facilitate traffic on the line through the mountains. For the troubled period leading up to the mid-1980s, see Don L. Hofsommer, *The Southern Pacific, 1901–1985* (College Station: Texas A & M University Press, 1986), 276–323.

3. The incident is described in Mullaly and Petty, *The Southern Pacific in Los Angeles,* 262.

Index

Designer:	Sandy Drooker
Text:	Adobe Garamond
Display:	ITC Franklin Gothic, Davison Americana
Indexer:	Towery Indexing Services
Compositor:	Integrated Composition Systems
Printer and binder:	Thomson-Shore, Inc.